Public Service Operations Management

How do policy makers and managers square the circle of increasing demand and expectations for the delivery and quality of services against a backdrop of reduced public funding from government and philanthropists? Leaders, executives and managers are increasingly focusing on service operations improvement. In terms of research, public services are immature within the discipline of operations management, and existing knowledge is limited to government departments and large bureaucratic institutions.

Drawing on a range of theory and frameworks, this book develops the research agenda, and knowledge and understanding in public service operations management, addressing the most pressing dilemmas faced by leaders, executives and operations managers in the public services environment. It offers a new empirical analysis of the impact of contextual factors, including the migration of planning systems founded on MRP/ERP and the adoption of industrial based improvement practices such as TQM, lean thinking and Six Sigma.

This will be of interest to researchers, educators and advanced students in public management, service operations management, health service management and public policy studies.

Zoe J. Radnor is Professor of Service Operations Management at Loughborough University, UK.

Nicola Bateman is a Senior Lecturer in Operations Management at Loughborough University, UK.

Ann Esain is a Lecturer in Logistics and Operations Management at Cardiff University, UK.

Maneesh Kumar is a Senior Lecturer in Service Operations at Cardiff University, UK.

Sharon J. Williams is an Improvement Science Fellow with the Health Foundation and an Associate Professor at Swansea University, UK.

David M. Upton is American Standard Companies Professor of Operations Management at the Saïd Business School, University of Oxford, UK.

This book brings together a fantastic collection of articles around public service operations management. I am sure this book will become a core text for many studying service operations management and will influence researchers in the field of operations management and public sector management. But this book is not just for academics – I would urge anyone managing resources in the public sector to read this book.

Jill MacBryde,
Professor of Operations Management,
The York School of Management,
University of York, UK

This book brings together a range of authors to show how leading service operation management change initiatives have transformed public services. This gives direction to both practitioners and future researchers to continue to move the field of public service operations management forward.

Fiona Lettice,
Professor of Innovation Management,
University of East Anglia, UK

Public Service Operations Management

A research handbook

Edited by Zoe J. Radnor,
Nicola Bateman, Ann Esain,
Maneesh Kumar, Sharon J. Williams
and David M. Upton

LONDON AND NEW YORK

First published 2016 by Routledge

2 Park Square, Milton Park, Abingdon, Oxfordshire OX14 4RN
52 Vanderbilt Avenue, New York, NY 10017

Routledge is an imprint of the Taylor & Francis Group, an informa business

First issued in paperback 2019

British Library Cataloguing in Publication Data
A catalogue record for this book is available from the British Library

Library of Congress Cataloging in Publication Data
Public service operations management : a research handbook / edited by Zoe Radnor, Nicola Bateman, Ann Esain, Maneesh Kumar, Sharon Williams and David Upton.
pages cm
Includes bibliographical references and index.
1. Public administration. 2. Operations research. I. Radnor, Z. J. (Zoe J.)
JF1525.O6P83 2015
351—dc23
2015004492

ISBN: 978-1-138-81369-4 (hbk)
ISBN: 978-0-367-87056-0 (pbk)

Typeset in Bembo
by Fish Books Ltd.

Contents

Figures

Tables

Contributors

Simon Adderley, Research Fellow, University of Birmingham, UK.

James Aitken, Senior Lecturer in Operations Management and Head of Department for Business Transformation at the University of Surrey, UK.

Omar Al-Tabbaa, Senior Lecturer in Strategy, University of Huddersfield, UK.

David Bamford, Professor and Chair of Operations Management, University of Huddersfield, UK.

Nicola Bateman, Senior Lecturer in Operations Management, Loughborough University, UK.

Harry Barton, Professor and Head of Research at Nottingham Business School, University of Nottingham, UK.

Anthony Beresford, Professor, Cardiff University, UK.

Vikram Bhakoo, Senior Lecturer, University of Melbourne, Australia.

Mark Buckle, experienced change practitioner involved in the transfer of commercial marketing principles into change management best practice.

Nicola Jane Burgess, Assistant Professor, University of Warwick, UK.

Carolien de Blok, University of Groningen, The Netherlands.

Benjamin Dehe, Senior Lecturer, University of Huddersfield, UK.

Paul R. Drake, Professor and Head of the Marketing and Operations Department, University of Liverpool, UK.

Ann Esain, Lecturer in Logistics and Operations Management, Cardiff University, UK.

Joy Furnival, PhD candidate, University of Manchester, UK.

Mel Hudson Smith, Lecturer, Plymouth University, UK.

Katri Kauppi, Assistant Professor, Aalto University, Finland.

David William Knight, industry expert on logistics within the oil and gas industry.

Maneesh Kumar, Senior Lecturer of Service Operations, Cardiff University, UK.

Desmond Leach, Associate Professor, University of Leeds, UK.

Claire Lindsay, Lecturer, Edinburgh Napier University, UK.

Karen Maher, Researcher, University of Loughborough, UK.

John March, Senior Teaching Fellow, University of Leeds, UK.

Rupert L. Matthews, Lecturer, University of Nottingham, UK.

Olga Matthias, Head of the Operations and Information Management Group at Bradford's School of Management, University of Bradford, UK.

Joanne Meehan, Lecturer, University of Liverpool, UK.

Max Moullin, Director of the Public Sector Scorecard Research Centre, UK.

Claire Moxham, Senior Lecturer, University of Liverpool, UK.

Stephen P. Osborne, Professor and Chair, University of Edinburgh Business School, University of Edinburgh, UK.

Adam Parkhouse, Business Information Analyst, UK.

Sally Pastellas, Senior Commissioning Manager of Children and Maternity for the NHS, UK.

Stephen Pettit, Professor, Cardiff University, UK.

Zoe J. Radnor, Professor of Service Operations Management, Loughborough University, UK.

G. Ramesh, Associate Professor and Chairperson, Center for Public Policy, Indian Institute of Management Bangalore, India.

Ray Randall, Occupational Psychologist, Loughborough University, UK.

Ross Ritchie, Senior Teaching Fellow and Assistant Dean, Warwick Business School, University of Warwick, UK.

Inge Roukema, Legal Assistant to the public prosecutor at the fraud department of the Dutch National Public Prosecutor's Office for serious fraud and environmental crime.

Aline Seepma, PhD candidate, University of Groningen, The Netherlands.

Shahana Sheikh, Researcher, Centre for Policy Research, New Delhi, India.

Tammi J. Sinha, Lecturer, University of Winchester, UK.

Amrik Sohal, Professor, Monash University, Australia.

Minchul Sohn, PhD candidate, Hanken School of Economics and HUMLOG Institute in Helsinki, Finland.

Andrew Taylor, Professor, University of Bradford, UK.

Margaret Taylor, Professor, University of Bradford, UK.

David M. Upton, American Standard Companies Professor of Operations Management, Saïd Business School, University of Oxford, UK.

Dirk Pieter van Donk, Professor, University of Groningen, The Netherlands.

Kiera Vogel, industry professional with M&Y Maintenance, The Regenda Group.

Paul Walley, Senior Lecturer, Oxford Brookes University, UK.

Sharon J. Williams, Improvement Science Fellow with the Health Foundation and Associate Professor with the College of Health and Human Sciences, Swansea University, UK.

Acknowledgements

Many thanks to Rosamund Chester-Buxton and Russ Glennon for facilitating and note taking on our authors' days. It helped us wear two hats at once.

Also thanks to Kay Harris for her unflappable indefatigable help in administrating and organising the authors and compilation of the book. Our calm in the crazy-eyed hurricane.

Preface

In 2012, I was working on a case study at the Pentagon. I discovered that the cost of six key Defense Department Enterprise Resource Planning systems had ballooned from around $7 billion to $15 billion.[1]

The objective of these systems was to provide better service, integration and transparency in this critical part of public service. But just the overrun from this one set of projects *alone* cost every tax-paying American $50 – compared with about $2 for a B2 stealth bomber. What's more, some projects overran by 12 years, and were plagued with problems. When we examined the projects more carefully, it was clear that complexity and personal agendas had driven some of the overrun. The information technology itself didn't really fail. What was most important was that the basics of operations management – operations strategy, the subsequent improvement methodology, and the detail of how the systems would work on a day-to-day basis were sorely lacking. It was in operations that the roots of the failure lay.

More internationally, satisfaction with public services varies greatly from country to country across the Organisation for Economic Co-operation and Development (OECD),[2] but generally runs at about 70 per cent for education, the police and health care. We can compare this with the 2014 rates for commercial services such as credit unions (85 per cent), full-service restaurants (82 per cent) or life-insurance (80 per cent).[3] In public services, it seems, something is different. Operations (in spite of numerous case studies as exceptions) has been a backwater. Strategy is thought of differently than traditional operations people might view it – more a set of policies than a true operations strategy. So, the idea of constant, relentless improvement is hard to implement and sustain. Together with immediate and consequential policy pressure operations thinking is at danger of back-sliding almost ubiquitous. The essentials of the day-to-day running of operations are often sorely lacking. With some exceptions, there is an acceptance of errors as inevitable. Bureaucratic tangles rather than transparent processes characterise many operations. The diffusion of responsibility through committees is rife across the world.

After working in service operations in many countries while at the Harvard Business School it became clear that a very different approach to the management of operations in public services was needed. I had the great fortune of reconnecting with Professor Zoe J. Radnor, and discovered a kindred spirit in the operational opportunities that lay in public services. Operations – as a field – could have a big impact. But it needed to be different. It demanded a different approach.

Zoe has been the indefatigable engine behind this tremendous collection of articles. The highly regarded authors provide a wide variety of functional application and approaches to the topic. This eclecticism provides a wellspring of starting points for further work on the future of operations in public services. We hope that we have provided the kindling that will make a difference in the field. In operations, we know that it is implementation that makes the difference. This book will help make that difference and improve the experience of citizens around the world as they interact with their public services. In many cases, they deserve more. Attention to operations – at all its levels – can provide it.

Professor David M. Upton
American Standard Companies Chair of Operations Management
Saïd Business School, Oxford University

Notes

1 See www.dodig.mil/Audit/reports/fy12/DODIG-2012-111.pdf.
2 See www.oecd-ilibrary.org/governance/government-at-a-glance-2013_gov_glance-2013-en.
3 See www.theacsi.org/index.php?option=com_content&view=article&id=148&Itemid=213.

1 Introduction

The role and substance of public service operations management

Zoe J. Radnor and Nicola Bateman

This introductory chapter establishes the need for a book on public service operations management and then through unpacking the structure and content of the book explore what is meant by public service operations management. To begin let us reflect briefly on some of the concepts as a baseline for the focus of the book.

This book focused on operations management and public service. A public service can be considered to be a service or set of services provided to citizens directly through a public sector body or through financing of provision by private sector, third sector or voluntary organisations. The public sector is the economic body in which many public service organisations reside. At the most simplistic level operations management (OM) is concerned with managing inputs of processes, people and resources through a transformation process model to provide the required output of goods and services (Slack *et al.*, 2012). Service operations management is concerned with both the output or outcome of 'the service' in the sense of 'customer service' and also the service organisation itself – in the way it configures, manages and integrates its (hopefully value-adding) activities (Johnston and Clark, 2008). Operations tasks fall into three main areas; developing an operations strategy, improving the operation and, managing the day-to-day operations (Slack *et al.*, 2012). Within service operations two main components are evident: the front office and back office (Johnston and Clark, 2008). The front office is the interface between the organisation and user, while the back office is the activities, tasks and processes being carried out remotely from the user (Johnston and Clark, 2001). All these elements; transformation process, tasks and components are shown to be pertinent in the chapters within this book and support the development of operations management within the public sector and public service organisations.

So, why the need for presenting a body of knowledge focused on public service operations management? We argue that general operations management concepts, tasks and components are relevant to this sector but also, that public sector organisations should recognise that they are a service organisation so should engage with service operations management theory and frameworks. Authors, including the leading editor of this book (Radnor *et al.*, 2012), have noted that operations management methodologies are 'context specific' and this means that the discipline needs to adapt, rather than dismiss, the context (Radnor and Osborne, 2013). The chapters within this book aim to develop that adaption process through illustration and presentation of propositions culminating with a final chapter which gives some reflections on the implications and draws together future research agendas.

Operations management recognising public services

Periodically authors and editors of operations management journals state the need for more operations management research in not-for-profit and public sector organisations (Taylor and Taylor, 2009; Karwan and Markland, 2006; Verma *et al.*, 2005). In 2014 the Office of National Statistics quoted that 5.7 million people in the UK worked in the public sector, which equates to 19.1 per cent of the workforce (Office for National Statistics, 2013). In the US and UK in 2005 the total outlay on public services as a percentage of national gross domestic product (GDP) was 35.9 per cent and 44.5 per cent respectively (Pettigrew, 2005) rising from 12.7 per cent and 24.0 per cent in 2001 (Karwan and Markland, 2006). In 2011 the Index of Economic Freedom reported that government spending as a percentage of national GDP was 38.9 per cent for the USA and 47.3 per cent for the UK (Miller *et al.*, 2011: 331–2). During this same period (2005–11) both the UK and US, as well as other countries such as Greece and Portugal, have experienced financial crisis with debts in the billions and trillions leading to severe budget and spending cuts across the public sector. In the UK, the Operational Efficiency Report (HM Treasury, 2009) in April 2009 stipulated that potential savings of around £10 billion a year should be sought over three years across public services.

This growing pressure on public services across the western world has led to a focus on increased efficiency which, according to Berman (1998), traditionally receives less focus as an outcome measure than effectiveness and equity. However, although the focus on efficiency and productivity initially led many public organisations to consider information technology as a possible solution (Karwan and Markland, 2006) the pressure to reduce the cost base and reduction of budgets has meant many organisations have had to adopt private management concepts in order to improve their internal operations and processes. In particular, public services including health (Fillingham, 2008; Guthrie, 2006), central and federal government (Radnor and Bucci, 2007, 2010; Richard, 2008) and, local government (Seddon and Brand, 2008; Krings *et al.*, 2006; Office of the Deputy Prime Minister, 2005) have responded by implementing business process improvement methodologies. Business process improvement methodologies (BPIMs) include lean thinking, Six Sigma, Business Process Reengineering (BPR), Kaizen and total quality management, as well as blended approaches such as lean Six Sigma. In a recent literature review focusing on the use of business process improvement methodologies in the public sector 51 per cent of publications sourced focused on lean, 35 per cent of these were on health services (Radnor, 2010).

An analysis of the key operations management journals – *International Journal of Operations and Production Management* (IJOPM), *Journal of Operations Management* (JOM) and *Production and Operations Management* (POM) – from 1980 to 2014 shows how operations management thinking has evolved over the last thirty years and the role that public service operations has taken within this body of work. Of 3,607 papers published 114 were explicitly focused on the public sector with a further 140 as mixed public and private. The peak of publication for public sector (including mixed) was 2011, while during 1980–91 only a handful of papers were published and in some years none at all. In the past decade there has been consistent publication focusing on public service and mixed public and private; however, it may be that the 41 per cent of papers (1980–2014) where no sector is stated did have a public sector element that the authors chose not to explicitly state. The predominant types of papers published were surveys and case studies representing 30 per cent and 31 per cent of the 254 papers. Revealing that most research published is trying to establish the current state of public service OM. Whereas papers that set the agenda (i.e. positional and conceptual) only represent 1.2 per cent and 3.9 per cent of the public service OM papers. This may be a lack of research in this area, difficulty publishing this type of papers or, a reflection of the need for greater levels of field data and in-depth analysis to develop new concepts and theory in the area.

Of the 254 papers in public and mixed categorising by sector, healthcare was revealed as the biggest with 30 per cent of papers. The next largest single sector was education with 8 per cent, but papers that examined multiple sectors represented 24 per cent of the papers. In compiling this book the editors particularly sought to bring sectors other than healthcare to the fore and so we have drawn from a wider range of sectors than have been extensively documented in the past. These include:

- uniformed services (Ritchie and Walley, Chapter 7);
- fire services (Bateman, Maher and Randall, Chapter 8);
- police services (Barton and Matthews, (Chapter 15);
- ambulance services (Aitken, Esain and Williams, Chapter 21);
- social housing (Meehan, Drake, Vogel and Parkhouse, Chapter 9);
- local government (Ramesh and Sheikh, (Chapter 12);
- higher education (Adderley and Kirkbright, Chapter 10; Radnor and Osborne, Chapter 16); and
- third sector and voluntary organisations (Bamford, Moxham, Kauppi and Dehe, Chapter 2; Taylor and Taylor, Chapter 11; Moxham, Chapter 13).

The countries represented across the 254 papers in the journal analysis were dominated by the USA (37 per cent) and UK (17 per cent), China and India are surprisingly low, both with only 2 per cent of papers. Of the other BRICS countries only Brazil is represented with a single paper, Russia and South Africa are not specially mentioned at all. How public service is to be shaped for these large and growing countries has not been addressed in the literature.

Due to the GDP percentage spent on public services, the financial situation and, the response by public organisations in using operations management concepts and methodologies (particularly managing process improvement) there never has been a more important time for OM scholars to both research and publish on OM in the public sector. This has to go beyond merely reporting case study examples, giving survey results or focusing on healthcare and developed countries, but to use the opportunity to develop new OM thinking and theory which can be applied to public sector organisations and public services in general which we are defining as 'public service operations management'. This new discipline needs to adapt the traditional frameworks and concepts, developed through manufacturing and private service organisations, and develop on new frontiers taking into account the digital and information age.

However, the challenge is not just how the OM discipline should adapt to the context/sector but also how the context/sector adapts to the discipline. As the next section will explore and argue, public sector organisations have struggled to recognise that they are a service based organisation but instead considered themselves in terms of policy and product orientation.

Public sector organisations recognising public service operations

It has been argued that the increasingly fragmented and inter-organisational context of public services delivery (Haveri, 2006) necessitates asking new questions about public services delivery. It is now no longer possible to continue with a focus solely either upon administrative processes or upon intra-organisational management – the central pre-occupations of public administration and (new) public management, respectively. Rather these foci must be integrated with a broader paradigm that emphasises both the governance of inter-organisational (and cross-sectorial) relationships and the efficacy of public service delivery systems rather than discrete public service organisations. This broader framework has subsequently been termed the New Public Governance (Osborne, 2010). This framework does not replace the previous foci of course, but rather embeds them in a new context, an argument similarly made by Thomas (2012).

A second argument that has been presented is that much contemporary public management theory has been derived conceptually from prior 'generic' management research conducted in the manufacturing rather than the services sector. This has generated a 'fatal flaw' (Osborne and Brown, 2011) in public management theory that has viewed public services as manufacturing rather than as service processes – and that are created by professional design and input and then delivered to the user even though the business of government is, by and large, not about delivering pre-manufactured products but to deliver services. Nor are most relationships between public service users and public service organisations characterised by a transactional or discrete nature, as they are for such products (McLaughlin *et al.*, 2009). On the contrary, the majority of 'public goods' (whether provided by government, the non-profit and third sector or the private sector) are in fact not 'public products' but rather 'public services' that are integrated into people's lives. Social work, health care, education, economic and business support services, community development and regeneration, for example, are all services provided but service organisations rather than concrete products, in that they are intangible, process-driven and based upon a promise of what is to be delivered. Public services can of course include concrete elements (health care or communications technology, for example). But these are not 'public goods' in their own right – rather they are required to support and enable the delivery of intangible and process-driven public services.

We would suggest that the attitude of uncritically applying manufacturing ideas to public service is flawed although, many of the approaches and ways of thinking that helped evolve these original manufacturing ideas are useful. This approach of adapting operations management to the public service environment while learning from existing thinking is exemplified in a study of the UK's Royal Air Force by Bateman *et al.* (2014), and further developed in Chapters 4, 5, 9, 16 and 22 of this volume. We argue that public services should recognise themselves as services, with the distinctive service operations management logic and managerial challenges that this implies, and hence reject the potential flaw contained within current, product-dominant public management theory.

This product-dominant flaw, we argue, has persisted despite the growth of a substantive body of services management and service operations management theory that challenges many of its fundamental tenets for the management of services (Johnston and Clark, 2008; Gronroos, 2007; Normann, 1991). It is this latter body of service management theory, it is argued here and within the book, that should inform our theoretical and conceptual understanding and analysis of the management and delivery of public services.

Tasks of public service operations managers

Public service organisations are not homogeneous – they have different structures, governance, incentives, drivers and delivery modes. Even within a sector such as healthcare, policing, fire, social care or local government there can be high levels of variation between the local delivery of services. This challenge is acknowledged across the chapters within this book. It does then pose the problem of the degree to which 'best practice' (i.e. standardisation) should be imposed, implemented or utilised. The argument here would be to recognise the difference between standardising of the process with its benefits to quality and efficiency and standardising of the outcome, which can have a detrimental impersonalised outcome. Developing an operations strategy that allows for customisation through a standard offering of processes (such as in sandwich shops which only offer a limited choice of breads and fillings but the customer leaving with what they feel as their customisation sandwich) could be a means of developing both efficiency and effectiveness. Understanding how to develop appropriate operations strategy is considered in the first section of this book in Chapters 2–6. Chapter 2 is focused on sports OM, and highlights issues of scope from international to local groups; Chapter 3 considers strategy in non-profit organisations; Chapters 4 and 6 consider strategy in public health organisations; and Chapter 5 considers humanitarian supply chains and the associated responsiveness and flexibility required across organisations and countries.

Developing an operations strategy was the first task identified for an operations manager. The second, improving the operation has been identified as a key area of focus for public services. This has been due to the focus on efficiency, reduction in budgets and recognition of the importance of citizen or user involvement. Where process improvement methodologies have been implemented it has suggested they can offer significant impact related to quality, cost and time and even to the satisfaction of both staff and service users. The UK Ministry of Defence, for example, reported a fall in the cost of maintaining one aircraft from £711 to £328 together with a reduction in manpower required for this activity by 21 per cent; the Connecticut Department of Labour eliminated 33.5 staff hours in its work by the redesign of its processes, saving $500,000 in staff time over a year; and Solihull Borough Council produced £135,000 saving in the postal costs for its fostering service, through a lean review (Radnor, 2010). Other reported benefits have included the reduction of waiting time for public services and a reduction in service costs through a reduction in resource utilisation (Silvester *et al.*, 2004) as well as intangibles such as increased employee motivation and satisfaction and increased customer satisfaction (Radnor and Boaden, 2008). A number of chapters in this book reflect on the use of improvement methodologies. Moxham (Chapter 13) looks at how performance measurement and continuous improvement interact in public service and Moullin (Chapter 14) examines how the adaptation of the balanced score card can be used in two public sector cases. Burgess, Radnor and Furnival (Chapter 17), Kumar and Lindsay (Chapter 18), and Hudson Smith (Chapter 19) explore improvement in different healthcare settings, and Barton and Matthews (Chapter 15) examines improvement application and issues with professional norms in the police service.

In a recent article the lead author for this book noted that lean implementation in public services has led to a number of challenges (Radnor and Osborne, 2013). An over-reliance on workshops (rapid improvement events) with staff coming together to make quick changes; public service organisations although claiming to be carrying out integrated lean reforms, are in fact taking a toolkit-based approach leading to pockets of short-term impact rather than a systemic embedding of lean principles. So, although these tools can lead to short-term success in improving internal efficiency they rarely engage with core lean principles – the centrality of the service-user and external orientation to organisational effectiveness. Consequently these lean initiatives became inward facing (policy or finance) rather than outward facing to the benefit of service-users. This then led to the conclusion that the success of lean may be due to the fact that, as a process improvement methodology, it has been able to address the prior poor design of the public service (*ibid.*). So, once achieved, the larger issue remains of designing public services to meet the needs of end-users and adding value to their lives. This then raises the important point that the engagement of process improvement methodologies by operation managers in public services should not be ends in themselves, but consideration of the design of the processes (Chapters 6 and 16), and the final task of managing day-to-day operations (Chapters 8, 21 and 22).

The key challenge of managing the day-to-day operations of public services is that, as a number of the chapters in this book illustrate (e.g. Chapters 2 and 9), there is a lack of understanding of operations management concepts (even the notion of processes) and even the language used in the public and voluntary sector by organisations and individuals. This is particularly true for planning and control or capacity and demand management, as shown in Chapters 7 and 9.

The lack of understanding of service management is highlighted through how the citizen is cast as the co-producer of public services (Alford, 2009), which should be as a co-producer rather than as solely the client of public service agencies. Users should be able to manage their own journey (where possible) with providers, commissioners and regulators. There needs to be challenge of the line of interaction between the user and provider, between what is part of the front office and the back office. In re-designing the processes, increasing the user involvement and recognising how to manage the 'touchpoints', Chapters 4, 9 and 16 illustrate how user experience is increased, variety/variation (as from the provider) is reduced and, transparency (of the regulator) is apparent.

Another key aspect of the day-to-day management has been the use of performance measurement and management systems. At its peak most public sector organisations in the UK were reporting significant amounts of measures for audit, scrutiny, assessment and monitoring as a means to create 'market forces' (Radnor, 2008). The use of performance measures has spread around the globe along with debates and discussion on how measures can be used to manage more effectively the process and service delivery. More recently, the use of data gathered has changed with a reduction of top-down regulatory frameworks. This has an effect for us as researchers, as sets of data that could be collected and analysed over a period are no longer available, but it also has an effect on the autonomy of public service management. Without the pressure of the reporting the challenge becomes how managers and organisations utilise their data to support effective public service delivery. Performance measurement and management is considered within Chapters 11–14, but also in Chapter 8 with respect to the fire and rescue service.

Structure of the book

The book is divided into five parts, reflecting the components of service operations management and the tasks of operations managers:

- Part I: Strategy and service design.
- Part II: Responsiveness and resourcing.
- Part III: Performance management and measurement.
- Part IV: Improvement.
- Part V: Supply chain management.

In selecting these sections the editors reflect current active research and also address the agenda for new areas for research. Part I, on strategy and service design, looks beyond straightforward public sector and engages with other designs for public service delivery, including the third sector, such as charities and non-profitmaking organisations. Chapter 2 studies OM in sport and illustrates the diversity of the OM challenge in a sector that has an international profile but also engages with local grass sports clubs. Chapter 3 considers the non-profit sector and its implications for strategy including consideration of stakeholders. Chapter 4 contrasts the impact of piecemeal improvement in an NHS hospital and considers the impact strategy could make on this approach. Chapter 5 reflects on the extreme end of public service by looking at humanitarian supply chains examining cross-sectorial flexible response. Chapter 6 uses a rich picture approach to examine system design in a healthcare setting.

The responsiveness and resourcing section (Part II) deals with the challenging environment in which public services must be delivered particularly balancing issues between demand, resources and capacity. Chapter 7 examines demand and capacity in the police service, and Chapter 8 explores a similar theme in the fire service and its effect on wellbeing and working conditions for firefighters. Chapter 9 explores issues of demand management within a social housing environment and also considers the idea of social surplus. Chapter 10 looks at the operational impact of encouraging entrepreneurial activities in a university setting.

Performance management and measurement, the topic of Part III, is a widely researched area in the public sector and is perceived as a highly publishable and researchable subject. Although many chapters from other parts could have been included here, the editors chose to select papers that directly addressed issues in this area namely stakeholder theory in the context of UK Advocacy services (Chapter 11) and developing the idea of a public sector scorecard (Chapter 14). Chapter 13 explores what actually happens in voluntary organisations and the gap between the aspiration for performance measurement to support continuous improvement. Chapter 12 explores the use of performance measures placed on the public grievance redressal system in local government in India.

Part IV examines improvement, which is an active area, with much research and wider activity within public services focused around this topic. The papers selected for this section had a very 'lean' focus as this is the dominant paradigm for improvement in public service. Despite lean's predominance this section addresses health, policing, and education all taking different approaches. The wealth of research and relative maturity of healthcare in applying lean in public service is reflected in the three papers concerned with the health sector. The first of these is Chapter 17, which looks at whole-organisation transformation in an English healthcare setting, while Chapter 18 reflects on Scottish experience, particularly focusing on softer aspects of implementation. The final healthcare chapter in this section is Chapter 19, which particularly focuses on service quality using pre-existing patient survey data. Barton and Matthews (Chapter 15) explore policing concentrating on how knowledge creation ties into improvement and professional standards and, finally, Radnor and Osborne (Chapter 16) revisit the idea of service blueprinting and although their application of this is to university services their principle focus is on the need for maturity of operations management approaches in public service.

Part V looks at supply chain management (SCM); this reflects a growing area for public service research and has only been addressed in three of the 254 papers in previous public service papers from JOM, POM and IJOPM in the last thirty years. It has been included because there is a growing need to join up different elements of supply to the end customer and this section begins to address this under-researched area. Chapter 20 explores e-SCM in the health sector and explore the institutional drivers for adoption of such an approach. Chapter 21 considers the drivers of demand in the emergency services and its consequent chain of response. Chapter 22 applies well-established supply chain logic to the area of criminal law enforcement.

The book ends with a reflective summary addressing the future research agenda. It also summarises the difference between sectors of private, public and third sector (for-profit and not-for-profit). The implications for managers in the public sector are identified, highlighting tactical and operational effectiveness and integrated services and network capability.

The editors hope this book consolidates existing research in the area of public sector operations management, introduces some new areas of discovery and, most importantly, lays the foundation for future contributions, research agendas and allows the development of a discipline that can support and improve our public services.

Acknowledgements

Many thanks to Russ Glennon for the compilation and analysis of the academic papers for this chapter. His many hours spent reading and categorising the source material enabled us to benefit from his insights and complete the book within the time scale.

References

Alford, J. (2009) *Engaging Public Sector Clients: From Service-Delivery to Co-Production*. Basingstoke: Palgrave.

Bateman, N., Hines, P. and Davidson, P. (2014) 'Wider applications for Lean: An examination of the fundamental principles within public sector organisations'. *International Journal of Productivity and Performance Management*, 63(5): 550–68.

Berman, E.M. (1998) *Productivity in Public and Non-Profit Organisations*. Thousand Oaks, CA: Sage Publications.

Fillingham, D. (2008) *Lean Healthcare: Improving the Patient's Experience*. Chichester: Kingsham Press.

Gronroos, C. (2007) *Service Management and Marketing*. Chichester: John Wiley & Sons.

Guthrie, J. (2006) 'The joys of a health service driven by Toyota'. *Financial Times*, June 22.

Haveri, A. (2006) 'Complexity in local government change'. *Public Management Review*, 8(1): 31–46.

HM Treasury (2009) *Operational Efficiency Programme: Final Report*. London: HM Treasury.

Johnston, R. and Clark, G. (2001) *Services Operations Management*. Harlow: Pearson Education.

Johnston, R. and Clark, G. (2008) *Service Operations Management*. Harlow: FT/Prentice Hall.

Karwan, K.R. and Markland, R.E. (2006) 'Integrating service design principles and information technology to improve delivery and productivity in public sector operations: the case of South Carolina DMV'. *Journal of Operations Management*, 24(4): 347–62.

Krings, D., Levine, D. and Wall, T. (2006) 'The use of "Lean" in local government'. *Public Management*, 88(8): 12–17.

McLaughlin, K., Osborne, S.P. and Chew, C. (2009) 'Developing the marketing function in UK Public Service Organizations: the contribution of theory and practice'. *Public Money and Management*, 29(1): 35–42.

Miller, T., Holmes, K.R. and Feulner, E.J. (2011) *Index of Economic Freedom*. Washington, DC: The Heritage Foundation and Dow Jones & Company.

Normann, R. (1991) *Service Management: Strategy and Leadership in Service Business*. New York: Wiley.

Office for National Statistics (2013) 'At Q1 2013 around 19% of people in employment worked in the public sector'. Retrieved from www.ons.gov.uk/ons/rel/pse/public-sector-employment/q1-2013/sty-public-sector-employment.html (accessed 18 November 2014).

Office of the Deputy Prime Minister (2005) *A Systematic Approach to Service Improvement*. London: Office of the Deputy Prime Minister.

Osborne, S.P. (2010) *The New Public Governance?* London: Routledge.

Osborne, S.P. and Brown, L. (2011) 'Innovation, public policy and public services: the word that would be king?' *Public Administration*, 89(4): 1335–50.

Pettigrew, A. (2005) 'The character and significance of management research on the public services'. *Academy of Management Journal*, 48(6): 973–7.

Radnor, Z.J. (2008) 'Muddled, massaging, maneuvering or manipulated? A typology of organisational gaming'. *International Journal of Productivity and Performance Management*, 57(3): 316–28.

Radnor, Z.J. (2010) *Review of Business Process Improvement Methodologies in Public Services*. London: Advanced Institute of Management.

Radnor, Z.J. and Boaden, R. (2008) 'Lean in public services – panacea or paradox?' *Public Money and Management*, 28(1): 3–7.

Radnor, Z.J. and Bucci, G. (2007) *Evaluation of Pacesetter: Lean Senior Leadership and Operational Management, within HMRC Processing*. London: HM Revenue & Customs.

Radnor, Z.J. and Bucci, G. (2010) *Evaluation of the Lean Programme in HMCS: Final Report*. London: HM Court Services.

Radnor, Z.J. and Osborne, S.P. (2013) 'Lean: a failed theory for public services?' *Public Management Review*, 15(2): 265–87.

Radnor, Z.J., Holweg, M. and Waring, J. (2012) 'Lean in healthcare: the unfilled promise?' *Social Science and Medicine*, 74(3): 364–71.

Richard, G. (2008) *Performance is the Best Politics: How to Create High-Performance Government Using Lean Six Sigma*. Fort Wayne, IN: HPG Press.

Seddon, J. and Brand, C. (2008) 'Debate: systems thinking and public sector performance'. *Public Money and Management*, 28(1): 7–10.

Silvester, K., Lendon, R., Bevan, H., Steyn, R. and Walley, P. (2004) 'Reducing waiting times in the NHS: is lack of capacity the problem?' *Clinician in Management*, 12(3): 105–11.

Slack, N., Brandon-Jones, A., Johnston, R. and Betts, A. (2012) *Operations and Process Management: Principles and Practice for Strategic Impact*. Harlow: Pearson.

Taylor, A. and Taylor, M. (2009) 'Operations management research: contemporary themes, trends and potential future directions'. *International Journal of Operations and Production Management*, 29(12): 1316–40.

Thomas, J.C. (2012) *Citizen, Customer, Partner: Engaging the Public in Public Management*. New York: M.E. Sharpe.

Verma, R., McLaughlin, C., Johnston, R. and Youngdal, W. (2005) 'Operations Management in the not-for-profit, public and governement services: charting a new research frontier'. *Journal of Operations Management*, 23(2): 117–23.

Part I

Strategy and service design

2 Going the distance

Sport operations management in the public and third sectors

David Bamford, Claire Moxham, Katri Kauppi and Benjamin Dehe

Introduction

Sport is ubiquitous across the world. It is a ceremony, celebration, physical pursuit, leisure activity and a business (Chadwick, 2011). Sport can be amateur or professional, local or international and can be enjoyed as a participant or as a spectator. Sport is often funded by governments or from voluntary donations. It can therefore be classified as a public service, particularly in countries including the UK, Canada and Australia where there has been a steady increase in the allocation of public funds to sports activities (Houlihan, 2005). Sport is seen to have benefits at an individual level, which include fewer health care requirements and better quality of life, and at the collective social and economic level through lower crime rates and opportunities for urban renewal (Taylor and Godfrey, 2003). In addition, one of the fastest growing tourism segments is travel associated with sports or physical activities (Biddiscombe, 2004). It has been estimated that sport tourism accounts for 10 per cent (approximately $600 billion) of the international tourism market (Saltzman, 2011), mainly through sport mega-events such as the football World Cup, Olympic Games and other international tournaments. On an individual event basis, estimates of the total annual market size for sports and event tickets vary from $7 billion to $60 billion (Sainam *et al.*, 2010). These figures indicate how sport and sport tourism can make a significant economic contribution to national and local economies. They also highlight the importance of public access to sport facilities for the health and social wellbeing of citizens. This chapter examines the application of operations management (OM) strategies to off-field sporting operations in the context of public and third sector sporting organisations. It highlights a clear requirement for the further development of off-field Operations Management and performance measurement within this increasingly important area.

In considering sport, the big numbers are not limited to revenues: the Olympic Games is considered by experts to be the greatest, non-defence-related, world-wide logistics event (Minis *et al.*, 2006). For the 30th Olympic Games, in London in 2012, nearly 11,000 athletes participated during July and August, followed by 4,278 athletes taking part in the 14th Paralympics Games in August and September (Bamford and Dehe, 2013). Recent Games have typically attracted 20,000 members of the media, are supported by 150,000 staff members and volunteers, host over 5.5 million ticketed spectators and are watched by billions of television viewers (Minis *et al.*, 2006).

Sport is not confined to large scale events with millions of spectators. It is broad and varied; as are the off-field operations that are required to support sports clubs and events, be they professional or amateur, local or international. It is therefore interesting to note that OM scholars have thus far paid limited attention to the sports industry despite calls for more research on sport OM (Machuca *et al.*, 2007). The lack of interest from OM scholars is surprising as the consequences of operations failure have huge implications for the outcome of the on-field performance and are also visible to a range of stakeholders including fans, spectators and sponsors.

Examples of failure include the 2010 Commonwealth Games held in Delhi, India, which was criticised for empty stands, collapsing scoreboards, poor transportation arrangements and failing technology (Gilmour, 2010). These instances of failure were predictable to a certain extent and, from an OM perspective, could therefore have been prevented; particularly with regards to these Commonwealth Games which cost an estimated $7.5 billion (Madhavan, 2012). Sporting events often attract criticism for operations issues, which suggests clear potential for improved off-field performance. Drawing on OM concepts, tools and techniques the application of improved layout, queuing methods, process and job design may be used to increase customer throughput and sales during half-time breaks with capacity management principles improving facility utilisation and spectators' and athletes' satisfaction during events. This is not to suggest that sport OM does not exist in practice; many sporting organisations currently utilise a number of service OM strategies and practices. For example, operations events management, the scheduling of sporting events and stadium management are common OM 'good practices' that organisations deploy purposefully as outlined in textbooks, such as that by Schwarz *et al.* (2010). It is therefore equally important to identify areas of good and best practice for managing off-field operations in the sport industry so that this knowledge can be shared by managers and OM scholars to identify which OM approaches work best in a range of different sporting contexts.

To begin to understand the current application of OM strategies to off-field sporting operations, this chapter reports on the findings of interviews with international sporting practitioners. The chapter focuses on the OM strategies associated with planning, scheduling and control as these seemed the most appropriate for beginning an exploration of off-field sport OM. The sport industry value chain (Smith, 2008) suggests three defined categories of sport organisations:

- Category one is associated with government and public sectors, and includes institutions that are involved in the development of sport, determining sport policy, bolstering competitive performance and/or health promotion (e.g. Sport England).
- Category two comprises activities by the non-profit or voluntary sectors, and includes local clubs and international federations where the focus is on the development of sport through organised competition and participation, with a

heavy emphasis on the regulation and management of sport – for example, the Football Association (FA) and the Union of European Football Associations (UEFA).
- Category three comprises the professional sport sector and includes any club, league or major event in which the primary purpose is to make a profit (e.g. Manchester City and Manchester United).

Nine of our ten interviewees were classified as category one sports. The remaining interviewee was associated with a voluntary sports organisation and is therefore in category two. Interviewees from category three were not included in the study as the aim was to examine public and voluntary funded sporting organisations. Category three organisations are modelled on business paradigms, whereas we were interested to ascertain current practice in sporting organisations that were less focused on profit. The chapter also does not consider the potential application of OM to on-field sporting performance. This may be a fruitful area for further research, as tools including Statistical Process Control (SPC) and Six Sigma have potential to be used in improving athletic performance (Linderman *et al.*, 2003; Antony, 2000). The focus of this chapter is therefore on off-field operations in public and third sector sporting organisations.

The characteristics of the sport industry

Sport is a worldwide phenomenon and encompasses a spectrum of operating models from amateur sporting groups with low budgets and voluntary organisation to professional teams that command high ticket prices and multi-million dollar advertising deals (Sainam *et al.*, 2010). The management of sport is receiving increasing research attention and a variety of topics have been examined over the last decade. Areas of focus include sponsorship (Olson, 2010), ticket pricing and consumer options (Sainam *et al.*, 2010), financing of stadium construction (Baade and Matheson, 2006), gambling (Forrest and McHale, 2007; Sauer, 2005) and the effects of attitude on performance (Pritchard and Funk, 2010). Operations research (OR) practitioners have a long history of interest in sports management, which has been synthesised in an article examining 50 years of OR in sports (Wright, 2009). It is therefore clear that scholars in areas including marketing, organisational behaviour, accounting and finance, decision science, human resources management and operations research have a keen interest in examining the application of their particular theory base to sport. It is interesting that OM scholars have not yet shared this interest.

The sport industry is part of the service industry and shares many of the characteristics typical of services (i.e. perishability, intangibility, inseparability and heterogeneity; Prajogo, 2006; Karmarkar and Pitbladdo, 1995; Bitran and Logo, 1993). The need for further research has been highlighted by articles that call for more attention to be paid by OM journals to sport (Machuca *et al.*, 2007) and cite the distinctive characteristics of sport that make it a fertile area for research (Chadwick, 2011). Attention to off-field performance would be of interest to OM scholars, particularly as sport exhibits a number of characteristics that make it different from other industrial sectors. These characteristics create a compelling area for OM research; specifically:

- *Uncertainty of outcome* – not knowing who will win is captivating for consumers and sporting organisations alike (Stewart and Smith, 1999). It poses challenges for OM in that a poor outcome on-field may impact on the perceived quality of the off-field experience regardless of the level of quality that is actually delivered.
- *Product-led industry* – in contrast to many industries that are consumer-led, sport is predominantly product-led with new sporting formats (for example 20/20 cricket) and new sports (for example X-games) regularly introduced. As the value of the sport product is short lived (argued to be equal to the length of the competition), the delivery of new sporting products requires continued innovation from OM to deliver the new formats and sports as required (Szymanski, 2011).
- *Limited organisational control over the product* – as operating rules and regulations are often outside of the scope of sporting organisations, clubs or individuals, there is limited opportunity for the rules of engagement to be used to attain competitive advantage. Sport operations managers must therefore comply with externally imposed criteria and seek ways to work within the system to provide order winning products and services.
- *Co-ordination, co-operation and competition* – groups of individuals/ organisations need to work together to create competitions and to enact competitive contests. In contrast to many industrial sectors, sport operations managers must therefore collaborate to compete. The outcome of sporting events has been described as an inverted joint product as two 'production processes' by two organisations are needed to produce and supply one single product (Baloga and Lazar, 2011).
- *Performance measurement* – league tables, rankings and medal tallies add increased levels of scrutiny to sport operations. In addition, the contradiction between on-field and off-field measures of performance is often problematic for decision making and management (Stewart and Smith, 1999).
- *Fans are producers and consumers* – experience and perception are seen as essential to value determination (Vargo and Lusch, 2006) and one of the primary reasons that spectators attend sporting events is to be part of the atmosphere; which means that fans are co-producers of the sporting experience (Basole and Rouse, 2008; Vargo *et al.*, 2008). Co-production creates complexity for sport operations managers as fans not only purchase and consume the product, they also help to create the atmosphere which gives strength to the product. Fans are co-producers of the sporting experience but often have to pay for the experience and therefore have expectations in terms of both on-field and off-field performance. With respect to service quality, the concept of fans paying to attend *and* being part of the co-production of the event is extremely important to recognise. To maintain a high level of service quality the sport organisations must identify how to maintain interest, enjoyment and attendance at the events, even when games are not markedly exciting (Clemes *et al.*, 2011).

Building on direct calls for further research in sport OM (Kauppi *et al.*, 2013; Machuca *et al.*, 2007), this chapter identifies a number of interesting opportunities for OM research in the areas of planning, scheduling and controlling off-field sporting operations. Empirical data from in-depth semi-structured interviews with 10 sporting practitioners from seven countries is presented (see Table 2.1 for details of the participants of the study). The sports examined included cricket, skiing, tennis, basketball and netball. With the exception of karate, which was a volunteer run non-profit making organisation, all of the interviewees worked for sporting organisations that were funded by the government. The interviews were conducted either face to face or over the telephone.

As the research base for OM in sport is currently underdeveloped, a survey was considered inappropriate to gather rich data on the potential application areas and an exploratory research design was used (Eisenhardt, 1989; Hardy *et al.*, 2003). The interviewees were drawn from a 2011 postgraduate training programme delivered by the World Academy of Sport in the UK (www.worldacademysport.com). Part of this programme included a module examining OM in sport. Programme participants clearly had an interest in sport OM and were therefore considered as suitable for this study. All interviews were transcribed and coded using NVivo 8 software. Emergent coding was used and key nodes included: process design, strategy, project management and quality which were considered within the overarching themes of planning, scheduling and control.

Planning, scheduling and controlling sports operations

In analysing the interview transcripts, it became clear that the activities of planning, scheduling and controlling off-field operations posed challenges for the sporting practitioners interviewed as part of the study. This finding indicates a clear requirement for further work in this area. The following section highlights the emerging themes using the framework of planning, scheduling and control and is followed by a number of proposed directions for further research on this topic to encourage OM scholars to capitalise on the opportunities for theory and managerial development offered by the sporting operations context.

Planning

Off-field planning was perceived as critical to delivering on-field success by the majority of participants in the study. Activities including making travel arrangements, booking hotels and identifying support staff to work on a temporary basis were seen as paramount, 'otherwise the team isn't going to win any medals' (skiing, worldwide). Clear differences in the approaches used to plan off-field operations emerged from the data that was collected. These differences may be attributed to (i) the size of the sporting operation, (ii) the operating model of the sporting organisation (amateur versus professional or funded versus unfunded) and (iii) the budget of the operation. Smaller, amateur groups appeared to lack operations planning: 'there is no forward planning whatsoever. So if you ask me what our three, five, ten year plan for the

Table 2.1 Details of the participants of the study

Sport	*Location*	*Interviewee role*	*Sports experience (years)*	*Sport industry category*
Karate	Europe	Chair, karate club	5	Category 2: nonprofit
Cricket	Africa	Manager, cricket team	15	Category 1: government/public sector
Cricket	Caribbean	Senior project officer, cricket operations	20	Category 1: government/public sector
Paralympics	Europe	Manager, Paralympics	5	Category 1: government/public sector
Skiing	Worldwide	Director, sport academy	20	Category 1: government/public sector
Tennis	Worldwide	Account manager, major events team	4	Category 1: government/public sector
Triathlon	Europe	Founder and CEO, international sport group	20	Category 1: government/public sector
Skiing	North America	Coach/ski instructor/ manager, snowboard team	10	Category 1: government/public sector
Netball	Worldwide	Operations director, netball association	7	Category 1: government/public sector
Basketball	Asia	Director, media projects company	10+	Category 1: government/public sector

club was, I would laugh because we don't have one' (Karate, Europe). whereas larger, professional teams invested heavily in preparation. While interviewees confessed 'I don't think people actually understand what they are doing a lot of the time – I am talking both domestically working in the organisation and internationally when it is a world cup event' (cricket, Africa), some planning processes were in place to enable the sporting event to take place. Examples included:

- *Pre-tour planning for every away tour.* This planning activity involved a visit to every venue, every hotel and every practice facility, ensuring that telephone cards, internet facilities and 'all those kinds of things that would impact on performance' (cricket, Africa) were available. Meetings with stakeholders were arranged to discuss 'this is what is needed, this is what you have, these are the issues, how do we correct them?' (cricket, Caribbean). Stakeholder agreement was perceived as crucial; 'anyone can work to a system as long as that system is approved' (triathlon, Europe). The length of time between pre-tour planning and the actual event varied with examples given as two months in advance for cricket and eighteen months in advance for triathlon.

- *Pre-event planning for every match/tournament.* Examples from cricket included organising the number of bowlers, organising transportation, locating accommodation near to the cricket ground, arranging practice facilities and planning the amount of rehydration the cricketers would need. Cultural expectations were identified as a key challenge to pre-event planning as 'some people are not so tight on the delivery phase and not so specific on making sure they deliver to the specification' (cricket, Africa). In planning women's netball championships, the use of water and toilet paper increases by two or three times the norm for the venue; this often comes as somewhat of a surprise to the hosts.
- *Successive event planning* whereby a series of events take place in the same venue. European triathlon used this approach and cited events with a size and scale of £1 million budget and six to ten thousand spectators over the course of the successive events. As this event does not move, off-field operations may be less complex than those for touring events.

Emerging theme

The size, operating model and budget of a sporting operation impacts on its ability to plan its operations. Planning approaches are well defined in larger professional sporting operations.

Interestingly, business focused academic literature suggests that small and medium-sized enterprises (SMEs) may be differentiated from larger companies by a number of key characteristics, including severe resource limitations in terms of management and manpower, a reactive, fire-fighting mentality and informal, dynamic strategies (Hudson *et al.*, 2001). Research has also demonstrated that SMEs linking operations to their business strategies outperform the competition (*ibid.*), suggesting that better planning and a more strategic approach to operations is fruitful. This link between operations strategy and performance has been established both conceptually as well as empirically in previous OM research (Ward *et al.*, 1994; Vickery *et al.*, 1993; Hayes and Wheelwright, 1984; Skinner, 1969). For sport, it would thus seem plausible that linking competition, business and OM strategies would improve overall organisational effectiveness. For instance, applying formal strategic planning tools such as Hoshin strategy planning, the Balanced Scorecard (BSC) or Quality Function Deployment (QFD) within a sporting organisation may support the synchronisation and the alignment of strategy and operations and would be an interesting focus for further research. If we appreciate that the application of Hoshin, BSC or QFD may be difficult to implement in smaller volunteer sporting organisations, we also foresee their potential to address some of the complexity issues the industry is facing. For instance, the BSC may help to overcome some of the strategic dilemmas faced by the organisation as it supports a more balanced and integrated approach to on-pitch and off-pitch performance. Moreover, QFD would be a relevant mechanism to address the contradiction between the product led industry (as opposed to a customer led industry) and the fans being both producer and consumer. QFD would also support the co-ordination and co-operation required between the different partners in the planning phase of the sporting activity.

Scheduling

While approaches to planning sporting operations were defined and implemented by the interviewees, challenges relating specifically to scheduling were a key theme to emerge and were identified as:

- availability of resources;
- players not being named until the last minute; and
- inability to control weather conditions.

Availability of resources

Operationalising the sports strategy was perceived as a particular challenge. Examples were given from cricket, whereby the sports strategy included 'taking cricket to the masses' (cricket, Africa) which would require the scheduling of events throughout Africa; however a lack of financial resources had prevented this from happening. On the ground, the availability of resources such as hotels and places to practice were cited as challenges to scheduling. Examples were given from touring in the Caribbean whereby one hundred rooms were required yet the host venue had one hotel with only seventy rooms, leading the senior project officer to question 'how am I supposed to make that work?' (cricket, Caribbean).

Players not named until the last minute

For competitive reasons, many sports do not name their team until days or even hours before the event. Such practice supports the competitive strategy of the team, however it presents difficulties for operations scheduling. It is often unclear how many players will be participating in the event so it is difficult to book the requisite number of hotel rooms and arrange transportation. In addition, the host is often responsible for housing the television crew; the number of which may fluctuate and again not be confirmed until the last minute. Interviewees explained how they attempted to hold hotel rooms well in advance of an event, yet hotels were often unable to commit to the number of rooms available (due to renovations or prior bookings) so hosts often held rooms in a number of hotels which they were forced to cancel at a later date.

Key performance indicators generally focused on the ability to get the team(s) in a timely manner to the required location. Sports operations managers worked with airlines to book seats and charter planes, however the challenge of not knowing who would be travelling impacted on the ability to confirm passengers and obtain visas. 'Typically the day before the team travels you are still trying to get visas' (cricket, Caribbean). It was explained that teams like to travel together, and if this is not achieved 'it becomes an issue on my performance because I haven't been able to secure one of the necessaries to get the team to where they are going' (cricket, Caribbean). With so many passengers flying together, the amount of luggage can be significant. Typically a team of twenty-five players will have 120 pieces of luggage; such volume cannot be accommodated by the relatively small charter planes often used. Therefore luggage has to be transported separately and, as teams cannot play without kit, the waiting times involved can impinge on practice sessions. Some sporting operations have outsourced the transportation of kit to avoid such problems 'it is probably a little bit more expensive but it gives us far greater flexibility. We can also turn it on and turn it off at any one point and if we expand they [third party logistics provider] have the capacity to expand with us' (triathlon, Europe).

Inability to control the weather

For skiing in particular, weather conditions are paramount to a successful event. If conditions are not optimal, the operations must be moved to a more conducive environment. Decisions need to be taken based on weather forecasts. As forecasts generally deal with the short term, moving the event only days before it commences will significantly impact on operations scheduling. Natural disasters also impact on sporting operations, for example cricket matches scheduled to take place in Christchurch in 2011 had to be moved to Wellington and Napier in light of the New Zealand earthquake. The operations teams were not familiar with the new venues and had to schedule extra visits to assess the facilities.

Emerging theme

Sports operations scheduling presents significant challenges due to uncertainty. This uncertainty is focused on the availability of resources, the formation of the teams and expected weather conditions.

In terms of the issue of resource availability, possible future research themes might focus on reverse marketing (White and Hanmer-Lloyd, 1999). The concept focuses on the customer seeking the firm, rather than the firm seeking the customer (*ibid.*). Examples include universities being approached by conference organisers to hire out rooms and accommodation. Reverse marketing suggests not to use expedience as the primary means of selecting suppliers (it places too much emphasis on selecting a supplier because it already produces a semblance of what is required), but to locate capabilities (*ibid.*). In doing this, sporting organisations across different industries might create capacity-sharing alliances, to work around their sometimes counter-cyclical demands due to different competition seasons. Sport organisations that frequently visit certain areas to train or compete and experience resource scarcities could work together to develop capacity that could be shared. The concept of working in agreed collaboration with ones competitors is ripe for further formal research through an OM lens.

Furthermore, the challenges associated with team selection and player naming maybe be akin to those experienced by manufacturers in customising products. It may therefore be interesting to examine the application of techniques including process design, modularity and postponement to the processing of players in terms of flight and visa requirements (Brown and Bessant, 2003; Alford *et al.*, 2000), possibly working together with legislative bodies and airlines. Research exists which documents attempts at improving and speeding up visa application processes in general (Kuula *et al.*, 2013). A particular focus could be placed on developing visa processing for team travel in international competitions.

Control

The need to control and improve off-field operations was acknowledged. The impact of off-field operations on the sporting experience was made explicit:

> You go to a football match and it still staggers me. Even at a Premiership club, you know, the quality of catering, the length of queues for an industry like that. It's ridiculous and I think people are resistant to it, you know, and they accept that it should be better and I think clubs are having to change, and I think our event is the same. People, they expect to have a good service.
>
> (Triathlon, Europe)

Clubs expressed a desire to become more 'business-like' (karate, Europe) and acknowledged the importance of satisfying their customers; defined by many as the paying spectator, the players and the sponsor. A number of approaches to controlling off-field operations were discussed:

- adherence to standards;
- development and use of checklists;
- performance management; and
- benchmarking.

Adherence to standards

Interviewees discussed the various quality standards that governed their sport both nationally and competitively, controlled by organisations such as the International Federation of Netball Associations (IFNA) and the International Ski Federation (FIS). Standards detail venue requirements which are then 'taken as a given' (cricket, Africa). Hosts do not always conform to recognised standards and interviewees expressed frustration regarding an inability to control facilities on tour. Standards are also set for televised events; events starting one minute late impact on the entire programming schedule.

Development and use of checklists

Many of the sporting practitioners had developed checklists to aid off-field operations management. These checklists had been developed over time 'through planning, through comparing what has gone before and by developing new processes' (cricket, Africa). Transporting kit to the right place at the right time is paramount, so checklists were developed to ensure timely delivery of equipment. As one sporting practitioner stated: 'all of our deliverables are very public' (cricket, Caribbean).

Performance management

Performance measurement was alluded to, however much of the key performance indicators were based on financial measures only. Professional sporting operations were more focused on measuring competitive success than their amateur counterparts, and focused on measuring the success of each tour. For cricket, performance objectives were established at the beginning of the year and assessed at the end of the year through a written report. Managers and players were asked for improvement ideas through open-ended questions such as 'are you happy with how things are being run operationally?', 'are there any improvements on your side or any suggestions?'. Informal monthly meetings are held to examine off-field operations performance. 'The broad principle is that if everything is fine it is probably discussed once a year and I think a lot of that is just dependent on the fact that we are on the road so much' (cricket, Africa). 'Ultimately our players are the best judge of our [off-field operations] performance' (cricket, Caribbean). For triathlon, 10 per cent of spectators who attended an event were invited to complete a survey before they left which asked a range of questions including whether they were aware who the sponsor was and how they rated the quality of the catering. The responses guided the improvement strategy for the following year. For Paralympic athletes, 'the one thing we get measured on absolutely is the [Paralympic] Games which only happens once every four years and if we get there and something is not right, you can't do anything about it for another four years'.

Benchmarking

Some interviewees used benchmarking as a mechanism to control and improve off-field operations. 'We might be smaller than most of them but we still have the same deliverables' (cricket, Caribbean). Others expressed a desire to benchmark, but had found it difficult due to the secrecy associated with competitive strategies and did not want to be accused of 'sneaking or spying on anyone else' (skiing, North America). Examples from skiing explained how teams have informal agreements about training together and sharing each other's facilities, although nothing had been formally documented.

Emerging theme

Off-field sporting operations are controlled by standards, checklists, performance measurement and benchmarking. The approaches used are generally specific to the sporting operation or team and examples of good practice are rarely shared.

A well-established body of literature has examined the OM issues associated with measuring performance (Franco-Santos *et al.*, 2007; Neely and Austin, 2002; Bourne *et al.*, 2000). It has been suggested that the key characteristics of successful performance measures are as follows:

- derived from strategy;
- clearly defined with an explicit purpose;
- relevant and easy to maintain;
- simple to understand and use;
- able to provide fast and accurate feedback;
- able to link operations to strategic goals; and
- able to stimulate continuous improvement (Hudson *et al.*, 2001).

In examining the maturity of performance measurement and management systems Wettstein and Kueng (2002) propose four levels ranging from Ad-hoc (level 1) to Mature (level 4). In proceeding through the changes, several developments are expected:

1. The task of a performance measurement system changes from reporting to planning to people involvement.
2. The scope changes from internal business-oriented emphasis to customer-oriented needs and to stakeholder emphasis.
3. The structure changes from financial to integrated measurement.
4. Technology support increases.

The application of performance measurement systems to the off-field sporting context has received very little attention, but based on the interview comments it would appear that most organisations are only at level 2; stakeholders are involved in determining performance. The findings suggest that further work is required in the development of integrated measures and more systematic approach to the collection and storage of performance date – which would also allow for benchmarking.

Examining the characteristics of sport and the emerging themes identified

Through the interviews, three emerging themes were identified. These themes can be linked to the sport industry characteristics discussed earlier in the chapter. Specifically, the second emerging theme of scheduling challenges due to uncertainty is clearly linked to the limited control over the sport product. Teams and managers must be able to react within a very short time frame to operational aspects due to the inherent dynamics of sport and the environment in which it takes place. Contingency plans, postponement and forecasting are needed. The third emerging theme is tied both to performance measurement – the complexity of connections between on-field and off-field performance – and the aspects of simultaneous coordination and competition that complicate the joint development of standards. As to the first emerging theme related to planning; it appears here that the challenges do not so much relate to the characteristics of the sport industry operating environment but rather to the immaturity of sport OM as a discipline combined with typical career paths in the industry: people with a background on-field rather than off-field are often recruited. Nevertheless, in relation to this theme OM scholars can make a positive contribution through developing educational programmes targeted at the industry. Table 2.2 provides a summary of the characteristics of sport, the primary connection with the emerging themes and suggests potential tools and techniques for overcoming the challenges identified and discussed in the chapter.

Conclusions

Sport management is relatively immature as an academic discipline (Chalip, 2006); sport Operations Management even more so. This is reflected in the findings as the study highlights a clear requirement for the further development of off-field OM and

Table 2.2 Relationship between sport characteristics, emerging themes and operations management tools and techniques

Characteristics of sport	*Primary connection with emerging themes*	*Suggested application of tools and techniques*
Uncertainty of outcome	Theme 1: Planning off-field sports operations	Hoshin strategy planning, Balanced Scorecard, Quality Function Deployment
Product-led industry	Themes 1, 2 and 3: Planning, scheduling and controlling off-field sports operations	Balanced Scorecard, horizon scanning
Limited organisational control over the product	Theme 2: Scheduling off-field sports operations	Contingency planning, postponement, forecasting
Co-ordination, co-operation and competition	Theme 1: Planning off-field sports operations	Quality function deployment
Performance measurement	Theme 3: Controlling off-field sports operations	Standards, checklists, measurement systems, benchmarking
Fans are producers and consumers	Themes 1, 2 and 3: Planning, scheduling and controlling off-field sports operations	Expectations and perceptions mapping, satisfaction surveys, focus groups

performance measurement within public and third sector sport organisations. Within the context of on-going reductions in national budgets for sport (e.g.: local government closing down costly sport facilities) and with public health issues in the public sector such as obesity, recovery and rehabilitation, more effective and efficient solutions to training, competition travel and event organisation need to be found. This is important so as not to compromise public participation, engagement, and sporting success; which are all important performance measures for national sports teams and increasingly significant for 'national pride' during challenging economic times.

The findings of this study indicate a defined potential to add significant further value to sporting organisations through the use of proven and robust OM tools and techniques. The five main legitimations for sport are health, salubrious socialisation, economic and community development (through improving facilities and infrastructure), and national pride (Chalip, 2006). In achieving each of these, public and third sector organisations play a vital role, and OM can provide significant assistance. Whether it is in forecasting demand and ensuring adequate capacity for public sport facilities or in enabling economic and community development through forward looking multipurpose layout planning for facilities for major events, OM researchers would appear to have much to contribute to the continued development of sport operations management.

In terms of a wider perspective of the impact that sport has to society; sport can directly improve public health and acts as a realistic mechanism that ties in with strategic community cohesion objectives. Sport activities can act as a force for change and life style improvement; in this, there are many similarities with the S-curve developed around the context of humanitarian aid operations (Bloom and Betts, 2013) in helping to predict the rate at which innovations are adopted within society over time. While the traditional bell curve works through innovators, early adopters, early majority, late majority, and laggards, this can be translated into an S-curve when increased take up is achieved with the late majority and laggards. However, this potential will only be realised within sports if the existing sport operations management and event management theory is actually deployed and used appropriately. Through this the authors believe that the use of appropriate OM tools and techniques has the very real potential to increase the uptake and engagement of sport by communities. Making the arrangement of sport better organised has the potential to increase its availability and accessibility.

As mentioned at the start of this chapter, and as evidenced from the research reported, sport operations management and event management theory currently appears to be un/under-utilised. This creates a realistic opportunity for both strategic (long-term) and tactical (short-term) 'operational' improvement. Interestingly, this does fit with the mind-set of those involved in competitive sports – the athletes/performers often train and prepare throughout the year (long-term), yet the actual competitive element is frequently over a very short defined period (short-term). This issue of long-term and short-term focus in sports could work to the advantage of applying formal theory if part of a defined implementation strategy.

A final thought on the application of theory to practice in this context: in sports, winning is everything; in operations management, process is everything!

Acknowledgements

The authors would like to thank the World Academy of Sport (www.worldacademysport.com) and the participants of their Postgraduate Certificate in Sport Management programme for their kind cooperation.

References

Alford, D., Sackett, P. and Nelder, G. (2000) 'Mass customisation: an automotive perspective'. *International Journal of Production Economics*, 65(1): 99–110.

Antony, J. (2000) 'Ten key ingredients for making SPC successful in organisations'. *Measuring Business Excellence*, 4(4): 7–10.

Baade, R. and Matheson, V. (2006) 'Have public finance principles been shut out in financing new stadiums for the NFL?' *Public Finance and Management*, 6(3): 284–320.

Baloga, I. and Lazar, I. (2011) 'Management of sports organisations, components of sport structures'. *Managerial Challenges of the Contemporary Society*, 2: 12–15.

Bamford, D. and Dehe, B. (2013) *Paralympics Athletes Survey: Service Quality at the London 2012 Games*. 9–12 June. Dublin: International Annual European Operations Management Association (EurOMA).

Basole, R.C. and Rouse, W.B. (2008) 'Complexity of service value networks: conceptualization and empirical investigation'. *IBM Systems Journal*, 47(1): 53–70.

Biddiscombe, R. (2004) *Business of Sport Tourism*. London: Sport Business Group.

Bitran, G. and Logo, M. (1993) 'A framework for analyzing service operations'. *European Management Journal*, 11(3): 271–82.

Bloom, L. and Betts, A. (2013) *The Two Worlds of Humanitarian Innovation*. Working Paper series no. 94. Oxford: Refugee Studies Centre, University of Oxford.

Bourne, M., Mills, J., Wilcox, M., Neely, A. and Platts, K. (2000) 'Designing, implementing and updating performance measurement systems'. *International Journal of Operations and Production Management*, 20(7): 754–71.

Brown, S. and Bessant, J. (2003) 'The manufacturing strategy: capabilities links in mass customisation and agile manufacturing – an exploratory study'. *International Journal of Operations and Production Management*, 23(7): 707–30.

Chadwick, S. (2011) 'Editorial: The distinctiveness of sport: opportunities for research in the field'. *Sport, Business and Management: An International Journal*, 1(2): 120–23.

Chalip, P. (2006) 'Toward a distinctive sport management discipline'. *Journal of Sport Management*, 20(1): 1–21.

Clemes, M., Brush, G. and Collins, M. (2011) 'Analysing the professional sport experience: a hierarchical approach'. *Sport Management Review*, 14(4): 370–88.

Eisenhardt, K.M. (1989) 'Building theory from case research'. *Academy of Management Review*, 14(4): 532–50.

Forrest, D. and McHale, I. (2007) 'Anyone for tennis (betting)?' *The European Journal of Finance*, 13(8): 751–68.

Franco-Santos, M., Kennerley, M., Micheli, P., Martinez, V., Mason, S., Marr, B., Gray, D. and Neely, A. (2007) 'Towards a definition of a business performance measurement system'. *International Journal of Operations and Production Management*, 27(8): 784–801.

Gilmour, R. (2010) 'Commonwealth Games 2010: What's going wrong in Delhi today?' *The Telegraph*, 13 October.

Hardy, C., Phillips, N. and Lawrence, T. (2003) 'Resources, knowledge and influence: the organizational effects of interorganizational collaboration'. *Journal of Management Studies*, 40(2): 321–47.

Hayes, R.H. and Wheelwright, S.C. (1984) *Restoring our Competitive Edge: Competing through Manufacturing*. New York: Wiley.

Houlihan, B. (2005) 'Public sector sport policy: developing a framework for analysis'. *International Review for the Sociology of Sport*, 40(2): 163–85.

Hudson, M., Smart, A. and Bourne, M. (2001) 'Theory and practice in SME performance measurement systems'. *International Journal of Operations and Production Management*, 21(8): 1096–1115.

Karmarkar, U. and Pitbladdo, R. (1995) 'Service markets and competition'. *Journal of Operations Management*, 12(3–4): 397–411.

Kauppi, K., Moxham, C. and Bamford, D. (2013) 'Should we try out for the major leagues? A call for research in sport operations management'. *International Journal of Operations and Production Management*, 33(10): 1368–99.

Kuula, M., Putkiranta, A. and Tulokas, P. (2013) 'Parameters in a successful process outsourcing project: A case from the Ministry of Foreign Affairs'. *International Journal of Public Administration*, 36(12): 857–64.

Linderman, K., Schroeder, R.G., Zaheer, S. and Choo, A.S. (2003) 'Six sigma: a goal-theoretic perspective'. *Journal of Operations Management*, 21(2): 193–203.

Machuca, J., Gonzalez-Zamora, M. and Aguilar-Escobar, V. (2007) 'Service operations management research'. *Journal of Operations Management*, 25(3): 585–603.

Madhavan, N. (2012) 'Unlike Delhi CWG, London Olympics well within budget'. *Business Today*. Retrieved from http://businesstoday.intoday.in/story/unlike-delhi-cwg-london-olympics-well-within-budget/1/189362.html (accessed 21 August 2013).

Minis, I., Parashi, M. and Tzimourtas, A. (2006) 'The design of logistics operations for the Olympic Games'. *International Journal of Physical Distribution and Logistics Management*, 36(8): 621–42.

Neely, A. and Austin, R. (2002) 'Measuring performance: the operations perspective'. In Neely, A. (ed.), *Business Performance Measurement*. Cambridge: Cambridge University Press.

Olson, E. (2010) 'Does sponsorship work in the same way in different sponsorship contexts?' *European Journal of Marketing*, 44(1–2): 180–99.

Prajogo, D. (2006) 'The implementation of operations management techniques in service organizations'. *International Journal of Operations and Production Management*, 26(12): 1374–90.

Pritchard, M. and Funk, D. (2010) 'The formation and effect of attitude importance in professional sport'. *European Journal of Marketing*, 44(7–8): 1017–36.

Sainam, P., Balasubramanian, S. and Bayus, B. (2010) 'Consumer options: Theory and an empirical application to a sport market'. *Journal of Marketing Research*, 47(3): 401–14.

Saltzman, D. (2011) 'Agents can score big with fans and athletes'. Retrieved from www.travelmarketreport.com/content/publiccontent.aspx?pageID=1365&articleID=4887&LP=1 (accessed 21 August 2013).

Sauer, R. (2005) 'The state of research on markets for sports betting and suggested future directions'. *Journal of Economics and Finance*, 29(3): 416–26.

Schwarz, E.C., Hall, S.A. and Shibli, S. (2010) *Sport Facility Operations Management: A Global Perspective*. London: Butterworth-Heinemann.

Skinner, W. (1969) 'Manufacturing: missing link in corporate strategy'. *Harvard Business Review*, 47(3): 136–45.

Smith, A. (2008) 'Sport markets'. In Smith, A. (ed.), *Introduction to Sport Markets: A Practical Approach*, pp. 13–31. Oxford: Butterworth-Heinemann.

Stewart, B. and Smith, A. (1999) 'The special features of sport'. *Annals of Leisure Research*, 2(1): 87–99.

Szymanski, S. (2011) 'The assessment: the economics of sport'. *Oxford Review of Economic Policy*, 19(4): 467–77.

Taylor, P. and Godfrey, A. (2003) 'Performance measurement in English local authority sports facilities'. *Public Performance and Measurement Review*, 26(3): 251–62.

Vargo, S.L. and Lusch, R.F. (2006) 'Service-dominant logic: what it is, what it is not, what it might be'. In Lusch, R.F. and Vargo, S.L. (eds), *The Service-Dominant Logic of Marketing: Dialog, Debate and Directions*, pp. 43–56. Armonk, NY: M.E. Sharpe.

Vargo, S.L., Maglio, P.P. and Akaka, M.A. (2008) 'On value and value co-creation: a service systems and service logic perspective'. *European Management Journal*, 26: 145–52.

Vickery, S.K., Droge, C. and Markland, R.R. (1993) 'Production competence and business strategy: Do they affect business performance?' *Decision Sciences*, 24(2): 435–56.

Ward, P.T., Leong, G.K. and Boyer, K.K. (1994) 'Manufacturing proactiveness and performance'. *Decision Sciences*, 25(3): 337–58.

Wettstein, T. and Kueng, P. (2002) 'A maturity model for performance measurement systems'. Unpublished manuscript. Department of Informatics, Fribourg, Switzerland.

White, P. and Hanmer-Lloyd, S. (1999) 'Managing the input market: the strategic challenge'. *European Journal of Purchasing and Supply Management*, 5: 23–31.

Wright, M. (2009) '50 years of OR in sport'. *Journal of the Operations Research Society*, 60(S1): 161–8.

3 Nonprofit–business collaboration

Operationalising a strategy for nonprofit organisations

Omar Al-Tabbaa, Desmond Leach and John March

Nonprofit organisations (NPOs)[1] are a central part of the social fabric of modern economies, and have a growing role in the delivery of services that have been historically associated with the public sector, such as education and health care (Kelly, 2007; Kindred and Petrescu, 2014). The environment, however, in which NPOs operate has become increasingly challenging. Factors including an increase in uncertainty over government funding policy, an intensification in rivalry in the nonprofit sector (Al-Tabbaa *et al.*, 2013), and a lack of employee commitment (Kong, 2008) represent a threat to their sustainability. In response to such pressures, Osborne *et al.* (2012) have found that NPOs are, for instance, re-engineering their operations to reduce overhead costs (see Huatuco *et al.*, 2014), achieving economies of scale through merging with counterparts, emphasising the leadership role of trustees, and replacing government funding with new and non-traditional sources. This chapter concerns the latter, focusing on nonprofit–business collaboration (NBC) as an alternative source of tangible and intangible resources to support NPO sustainability. NBC is one of the three different forms of social partnership (Figure 3.1) that aim to create social value. We define NBC as a discretionary agreement between an NPO and a for-profit business, typically involving the exchange of specific organisational benefits between the partners, to address social and/or environmental issues.

In this chapter, we present and discuss NBC as a strategic option for NPOs; an important aspect of NBC inquiry that has been largely overlooked (Al-Tabbaa *et al.*, 2014; Harris, 2012). To begin with, we review various types of NBC and demonstrate their differences and similarities. We next discuss NBC as a tripartite value-creation mechanism (value to society, business, and NPOs). Following this section, we present a framework that we developed to help NPOs engage strategically in NBC. The framework is based on the 'three elements of strategy' concept (Pettigrew, 1985): context (the environment in which an organisation operates), content (the choices to achieve the strategy purpose), and process (the formulation and implementation of the chosen strategy). However, this concept assumes that production and consumption processes are separable (reflecting its manufacturing origin), whereas the public services that NPOs provide are typically produced and consumed concurrently. To resolve this apparent contradiction, we draw on the service management approach (Osborne *et al.*, 2013), which is a theory for managing

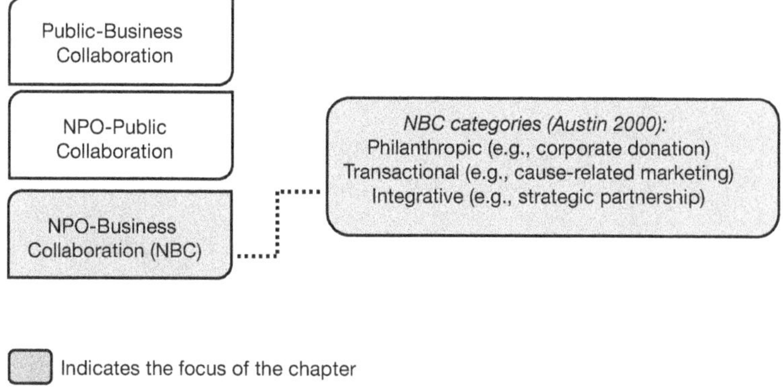

Figure 3.1 Forms of cross-sector social collaboration

public services providers (including NPOs). In the final section, we consider implications for cross-sector collaboration literature research and practice.

Nonprofit–business collaboration types

Several types of NBC are described in the literature, such as corporate philanthropy (Keys *et al.*, 2009; Smith, 1994), patronage (Sagawa, 2001), sponsorship and cause related marketing (Wymer and Samu, 2003), partnership (Waddock, 1991), alliances or strategic alliances (Berger *et al.*, 2004; Westley and Vredenburg, 1991). Austin (2000), however, conceptualised this variety of types as a continuum from philanthropic through transactional to integrative, as depicted in Table 3.1. The philanthropic level refers to a simple one-way relationship between the donor (business) and recipient (NPO), such as corporate giving. However, collaboration at this level is likely to be limited in delivering value to society (as well as to the partners) due to the narrow involvement of the business partner. At the transactional level, NBC involves a mutual exchange of resources between partners. Typically, the business partner would provide specific resources (mainly financial) to the NPO in return for publicity. Finally, the integrative level is the ultimate form of NBC. At this level, partners begin to merge their activities and missions toward more collective actions and organisational integration, forming a strategic partnership or alliance.

Nonprofit–business collaboration as a tripartite value creation mechanism

We argue that as a value creation mechanism, NBC can be viewed from three distinct perspectives. The first, or society perspective, relates to the formation and conditions under which NBC (and cross-sector collaboration in general) can deliver value to society (e.g. Austin, 2000; Berger *et al.*, 2004). This perspective draws on the assumption that collaboration between NPOs and businesses is the best approach to address social and environmental issues (Isett and Provan, 2005) which have been

Table 3.1 NBC types, examples and definitions

NBC level	*Example*	*Definition*	*Value to business*	*Value to NPOs*	*Value to society*
Philanthropic	Pet project	Small projects that reflect personal interest of senior management in participating in social activities	No direct/indirect benefits. Yet, some publicity may be attained as a result	Financial resources to implement unplanned activities	Minimal
	Corporate philanthropic	Monetary contributions made by a business to implement activities that are devoted to society and managed by NPOs	No direct economic benefits, but increased public awareness of its brand and a boost in staff morale can be attained	Tangible resources (including volunteering staff), mainly financial	Minimal to average
Transactional	Sponsorships	A business pays sponsorship fees to an NPO to advertise the business's brand as part of the NPO's activities	Promote brand	Schedule fund	Minimal to average
	Cause-related marketing	A business links its product with a specified NPO brand, where the business connects the amount of sales with the amount of contribution to the NPO	Direct increase in sales and promotion of the brand	Generate funding and increase visibility by reaching new audiences (i.e., business customers)	Average
Integrative	Strategic partnering/ Social alliances	Both partners put strategic objectives (both social and economic) as an outcome of their long relationship	Increase the effectiveness of CSR activities; enhance the company's strategy by improving their competitive context	Significant financial resources and transfer of business-knowledge (e.g. branding, IT, accounting, etc.)	Maximum: businesses and NPOs can implement strategic long term social/environmental projects and therefore, create more value for society

Sources: Al-Tabbaa (2012, 2013); Berger *et al.* (2004); Godfrey (2005); Porter and Kramer (2002); Selsky and Parker (2011); Wymer and Samu (2003)

referred to as 'complex' and exceed the capacity of a single sector to resolve (Selsky and Parker, 2011). Two theoretical approaches help to explain the value of this synergistic relationship. The resource-based theory perceives organisations as bundles of resources and capabilities (Barney, 1991). NBC enables the exchange of complementary resources and capabilities (e.g. expertise, capital, networking) that can be used to augment the partners' joint capacity to address societal issues. Similarly, knowledge-based theory suggests that through combining and exchanging knowledge, partners can accelerate their organisational learning (Hoffmann and Schlosser, 2001). Nonetheless, NBC (and social cross-sector collaboration more generally) has been criticised for being difficult to implement and, in turn, for failing to achieve its objectives (Koschmann *et al.*, 2012; Bessant and Tidd, 2007). Accordingly, researchers (e.g. Koschmann *et al.*, 2012; Wilson *et al.*, 2010; Bryson *et al.*, 2006) have focused on how partners can overcome the challenges and difficulties that limit NBC in delivering value to society.

The second perspective concerns the use of NBC as a vehicle for businesses to implement their social responsibility programs and create economic value (e.g. Holmes and Smart, 2009). A change in the institutional norms of society regarding NBC supports research in this area (Jansons, 2014). More specifically, society has started to accept the self-interest motives of businesses (i.e. the economic drivers of businesses), in addition to altruistic motives that underlie the response to social needs (Sud *et al.*, 2009). This institutional transformation has encouraged businesses to rethink their traditional philanthropic activities to extract economic value while doing 'good' to society (Austin, 2000; Vurro *et al.*, 2010). In particular, the assumption that there is no inherent contradiction between adding value to business and making a sincere commitment to helping society is proliferating (McDonald and Young, 2012). Reflecting this development, empirical findings suggest that NBC has become an important element of corporate social responsibility (CSR) strategy for the business sector (den Hond *et al.*, 2015).

Finally, the third perspective relates to how NBC can effectively deliver value to NPOs. It is evident, however, that this perspective has received substantially less academic scrutiny in comparison to the business and society perspectives (Harris, 2012). This is most likely because society and NPOs are often regarded as a single entity given that they typically follow a similar agenda (i.e. have the same problems to address). We contend, however, that distinguishing NPOs from society is important to enhance our understanding of NBC effectiveness, which requires a comprehensive appreciation of all partners in terms of their capabilities, demands, concerns, and expectations (Bryson *et al.*, 2006; Harris, 2012). Hence, we refer to NBC as a tripartite value creation process. However, understanding of how NPOs can benefit from NBC is still in its infancy. We next discuss a framework that can guide NPOs when engaging in NBC.

A framework to operationalise a strategy for nonprofit–business collaboration

The aim of this section is to present a framework that we developed to enhance the capability of NPOs to plan and implement a strategy for NBC. The framework is theoretically based on Pettigrew's (Pettigrew, 1985, 1987a) three elements of strategy (context, content, and process), but adapted to include factors within each element that relate specifically to NPOs.

The section is organised as follows. First, we discuss the three elements concept and state reasons for basing the framework on it. Second, because adopting this concept to study NPOs might be criticised due to its manufacturing origin (Beck *et al.*, 2008; Dart, 2004), we discuss the service management approach (Osborne *et al.*, 2013; Osborne, 2009) to demonstrate that, nonetheless, the framework relates to NPOs. Finally, we present the framework itself, including nine endogenous and exogenous factors.

The three elements concept

It has been asserted that the effect of three elements (i.e. context, content, and process) determines the realised shape of a strategy and predicts its effectiveness (Miller *et al.*, 1988; Pettigrew, 1987b). These elements, though, should not be perceived as independent but rather as reciprocally connected (Miller *et al.*, 1988). Context, the first element, concerns the environment in which an organisation operates and includes factors such as level of competition, stakeholder attitude, availability of resources, and trends that relate to change (Schmitt and Klarner, 2015; Wit and Meyer, 2010). Therefore, context functions as the background or setting for an organisation's strategy. Moreover, the role of context has been found to be critical in implementing the chosen strategy; that is, strategy effectiveness cannot be achieved unless there is a fit between an organisation and its operating context (Hambrick, 2003). In seeking a better understanding of this consistency, Pettigrew (1985) divided context into two levels: outer and inner. The former includes political, social, economic, and environmental conditions, whereas the latter covers aspects related to an organisation's internal features such as culture, structure, resources, and organisational politics. Johnson *et al.* (2011: 16), however, expanded this element to include four aspects: environment (political, economic, social, and technological factors), strategy capability (organisation resources and competences), strategic purpose (aims of the organisation that explain its actions), and organisational culture.

Content, the second element, relates to what an organisation needs to consider during a strategic change process (Pettigrew, 1987b). It includes the methods, plans, and practices that an organisation seeks to use in order to achieve predefined purposes (Johnson *et al.*, 2011; Moser, 2001). Furthermore, content addresses the issue of competitiveness in terms of creating and maintaining competitive advantage. Ketchen *et al.* (1996) propose that two types of fit should be considered when studying strategy content. The first, or inter-fit, concerns the relationship between the adopted methods and plans and the 'outer context' of the organisation. Alignment with the outer context is important to ensure that the selected options (e.g. methods, practices) are applicable within the external environment. The second fit, or intra-fit, relates to the alignment between the selected options and the organisation's internal components, such as its capabilities, internal policies, and culture (Wit and

Meyer, 2010). In other words, intra-fit is necessary to ensure that the selected options are feasible within the internal environment. Any fit misalignment would reduce the viability of the chosen strategy, and thus affect overall organisational performance (Zajac and Shortell, 1989).

The third element, process, incorporates different activities, procedures, and actions that enable the selected content (e.g. options) to achieve its objectives (Huff and Reger, 1987). Importantly, this element should not be considered in isolation from context (element 1) as Pettigrew (1992: 10) notes: 'context is not just a stimulus environment but a nested arrangement of structures and processes where the subjective interpretations of actors perceiving, learning, and remembering help shape process'. Extending this account, Wit and Meyer (2010) proposed a three-step systematic view of process: analysis (to identify external opportunities and threats, and to estimate the internal strengths and weaknesses of an organisation), formulation (to generate possible strategic options to pursue), and implementation (to specify activities to carry out the chosen strategy). This view emphasises the importance of realising organisational capabilities (i.e. in terms of strengths and weaknesses) and its external position (i.e. opportunities and threats) before developing a strategy and implementing its components.

Due to the conceptual strength of the context-content-process (CCP) concept, it is widely used in studies of organisations' performance. For example, Moser (2001) used the concept to examine the impact of sustainable business practices (SBPs) on the economic growth of less developed countries. This study shows the importance of the external context in which multinational corporations operate (e.g. government legislations, attributes of indigenous communities) and of the characteristics of the internal context (e.g. local staff, internal policies) to enacting and implementing SBPs. In the health sector, Raak *et al.* (2005) used the CCP concept to investigate the impact of contextual factors on decision making within partnerships. However, they adapted the concept to include an additional element 'subject', which refers to the substance of decision making. This element was used to address the complexity (e.g. involvement of staff from different organisational levels) and controversy (e.g. the extent to which a state of conflict exists) of the decision made. The CCP concept has been also used to improve evaluation of information systems (ISs). Traditionally, ISs have been evaluated solely from a technical perspective. Stockdale and Standing (2006) used the concept, in particular the process element which emphasises the importance of stakeholders, as a guide to assess socio-political aspects of ISs. Derived from the CCP concept, Pichault (2007) developed a framework to explain differences in the performance of three public organisations following reforms to human resources (HR). The lack of coherence between the organisational setting of each individual project (context), HR innovations (content), and the reform process, including power relationships among stakeholders, was found to reduce the effectiveness of the reforms in these organisations.

The examples above show the potential of the CCP concept to provide a comprehensive multi-element/level approach when studying NBC strategy. In regard to our framework, it helped us to identify factors that we contend are relevant to NPOs wishing to collaborate with businesses.

The service management approach

The service management approach (SMA) originates from service management theory, where calls have been made to incorporate SMA when studying organisations that provide public services (Osborne, 2009; Steane, 2008). The CCP concept, however, is rooted in research that has been conducted in the manufacturing rather than the public services sector (Osborne *et al.*, 2013; Beck *et al.*, 2008; Dart, 2004). As such, adopting this concept to enhance the delivery of public-service providers (such as NPOs) can be criticised. Theories from the manufacturing domain assume that production and consumption processes are separable (Osborne *et al.*, 2013). In contrast, SMA regards service production and consumption as inseparable because they are typically produced and delivered to end-users for consumption simultaneously, at the same time and place (e.g. educational and health services; Wheelen and Hunger, 1999). Theories from the manufacturing domain also view the consumer as a passive actor in any interaction process (Osborne and Strokosch, 2013). SMA, however, emphasises the importance of involving end-users in service provision (Powell *et al.*, 2010), and has been referred to as co-production (e.g. Osborne and Strokosch, 2013) or co-creation (e.g. Qian and Li, 2003) of services.

In addition to these points, Eikenberry and Kluver (2004) argue that the business and nonprofit sectors are inherently different due to the incompatibility between their values and cultures. NPOs are often characterised as socially driven, participative, and co-operative, whereas businesses are typically described as profit driven, hierarchical, and competitive (Berger *et al.*, 2004; Parker and Selsky, 2004). Relating to these issues, the current use of public-management theory to study and manage public service organisations is limited because it fundamentally regards public services as a product and it focuses on an organisation's internal processes rather than its wider service receivers (Osborne *et al.*, 2013; Coyte *et al.*, 2012).

In the next section, we present our NBC framework. Although it is based on the CCP concept, we draw on the principles of SMA to demonstrate that it is nevertheless relevant to NPOs as public services providers.

A framework to operationalise nonprofit–business collaboration strategy

Our framework to help NPOs develop an effective strategy for NBC is depicted in Figure 3.2. The framework comprises three elements and nine factors (four factors relate to context, two relate to content, and three relate to process). It is worth noting that the purpose of the framework is not prescription or to describe a specific strategy for NBC; rather, the aim is to emphasise factors that have potential to positively affect the development of a strategy.

Context (element 1)

Context reflects the external and internal settings that might facilitate or hinder the adoption of NBC. Furthermore, it involves the initial conditions that provoke the need for collaboration. The four factors that relate to this element are: NBC purpose, stakeholder pressure, nonprofit competition, and cultural barrier.

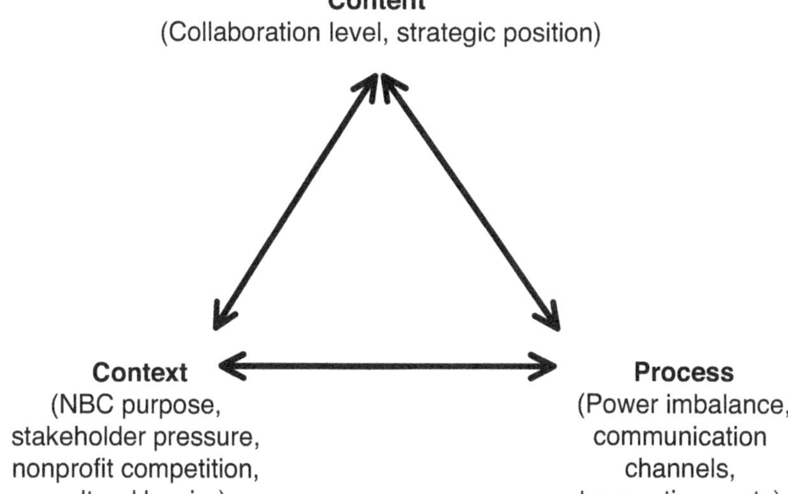

Figure 3.2 Factors that underpin the development of nonprofit–business collaboration strategy from the nonprofit organisation's perspective

NBC PURPOSE

Similar to any interorganisational relationship, the purposes or motives that drive NPO engagement in NBC are varied (van Fenema and Loebbecke, 2014). Such motives include the need to diversify and attain economic value, to enhance publicity and strengthen their brand, to expand supporters' networks, to influence business behaviour, and to acquire business-like knowledge, see Figure 3.3. With regard to the latter, this has become a vital requirement because NPOs are under continuous pressure from government and the general public to become more efficient and effective, and thus are encouraged to learn business-style cost-cutting techniques and to standardise operational procedures (Guo and Acar, 2005).

We contend that NBC purposes need to be highly focused because doing so should provide a clear direction for setting compatible activities to formulate a more robust strategy (Wit and Meyer, 2010). For instance, when NBC is sought only as a means to achieve financial gain (i.e. an economic purpose), NPOs are likely to focus on securing any type of collaboration (discussed later under collaboration level, element 2), as long as it does not conflict with their organisation's mission or values. In contrast, NPOs that endeavour to affect business behaviour would target a higher collaboration level (such as strategic partnership; see Table 3.1), rather than seeking a simple corporate philanthropic contribution (Austin, 2000). For instance, an environmental NPO might collaborate with a business that has a substantial impact on the environment (e.g. a high carbon dioxide footprint) to mitigate or change that impact (Yaziji and Doh, 2009). At a higher collaboration level, the likelihood of achieving a greater environmental impact would increase because staff interaction at

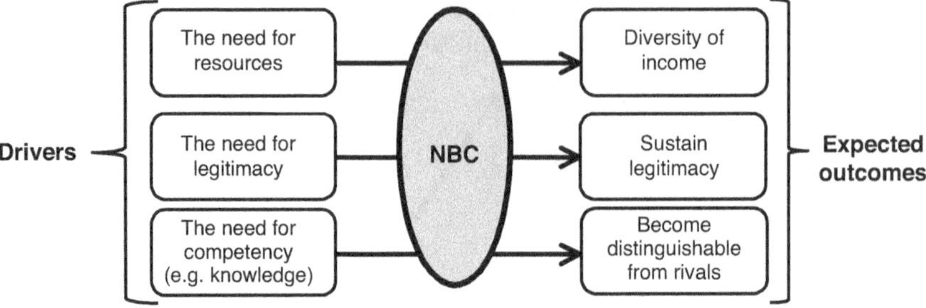

Figure 3.3 Nonprofit–business collaboration drivers and potential outcomes for nonprofit organisations

all levels across the organisations should eventually influence the overall behaviour of the business (Hendry, 2006). Also, such environmental NPOs might reject some types of collaboration, such as cause-related marketing (see element 2), that could put them in a position of promoting or being perceived as endorsing a particular business product (Berglind and Nakata, 2005).

In addition to the above point (see also element 3), a focused purpose should promote stakeholder support for NBC (Behn, 2003). In other words, a clear and focused purpose is likely to aid stakeholder appreciation of the requirements, timescales, and outcomes of any proposed collaboration, and thus enable them to gauge the collaboration's potential effectiveness.

STAKEHOLDER PRESSURE

Stakeholders are regarded as critical to the management of nonprofit and public organisations (Bryson, 2004). They are individuals or groups who can affect, or are affected by, the achievement of an organisation's objectives, and therefore should be taken into account when decisions are made (Bryson, 1988). Importantly, public service organisations should include stakeholder groups such as beneficiaries (i.e. service users) who might be perceived as powerless or unable to influence organisational strategy (Bryson, 2004). For NPOs in particular, stakeholders become even more important when planning for NBC. More specifically, research indicates that to address social and environmental problems NPOs need to consider all stakeholders' needs and concerns to design and implement an effective course of action (Berger *et al.*, 2004; Bryson *et al.*, 2006).

Some stakeholder groups (e.g. staff or volunteers), however, might perceive NBC as a dilemma. On the one hand, they might demand their NPO to demonstrate effective performance (Herman and Renz, 2008) and to seek opportunities to survive. On the other, they might be dubious about collaborating with a business because of potential 'mission creep' or when a gradual mission or goal deviation takes place due to, for instance, the interests of the business partner (Akingbola, 2012). Furthermore, some collaboration types (see content factor) might be more acceptable than others to stakeholders. For instance, should stakeholders voice concern about NBC (e.g. erosion of core values), the NPO might opt for an informal collaboration (e.g. corporate giving) to keep itself distant from the business partner (Simpson *et al.*, 2011).

The requirement for careful consideration of all stakeholders relates to a core aspect of SMA: strategic orientation (SO). In regard to NPOs and other public service organisations, SO refers to the capacity of these organisations to appreciate the current and future needs of their service users (Osborne *et al.*, 2013; Sofaer and Firminger, 2005).

In sum, the development of an NBC strategy should take into consideration stakeholders' needs and concerns. Consistent with SMA, NBC should be acceptable to all stakeholder groups including the powerless (e.g. service users) by ensuring that it is consistent with their expectations and with the NPO's philosophy and core values.

NONPROFIT COMPETITION

The nonprofit sector has been transformed during the last twenty years, largely due to an increase in competition between NPOs. Therefore, the sustainability or viability of NPOs has naturally become a critical issue as these organisations are competing for fixed or even deteriorating traditional funding sources (e.g. government funding). Similarly, we argue that NPOs are in competition for NBC opportunities. More specifically, the number of NPOs is increasing while the amount of resources that businesses are allocating for social responsibility activities, including NBC, is declining (Porter and Kramer, 2002). Businesses are also becoming more selective when choosing potential partners because they typically require a high return (both social and economic) from their investments (Godfrey, 2005). Accordingly, NPOs need to identify competitors in their operating context and recognise their strengths and weaknesses. In doing so, NPOs should become more distinctive and attractive to potential business partners, as discussed later (see strategic position factor).

NPOs, however, can reduce the intensity of competition by cooperating with each other when approaching businesses. This strategy relates to the term 'co-opetition', which is where a set of organisations engage in simultaneous cooperation and competition with each other (Gnyawali *et al.*, 2006). Interestingly, relationship marketing, a theoretical foundation of SMA, supports the co-opetition concept in arguing that inter-organisational relationships represent a valuable organisational resource (Narayanan, 2001). Through cooperation, NPOs can share ideas, best practices, and experiences, which can enhance their organisational learning and development. Moreover, NPOs can increase their attractiveness to businesses, or their potential to deliver greater value, by combining their resources and competencies (e.g. staff, networks, public-support base, geographical presence). Co-opetition can also strengthen their position in negotiations to reach a better collaboration agreement because their collective offer might appear more valuable to the business. However, co-opetition has its risks. First, the brand of individual NPOs might weaken when forming a group of similar NPOs, eroding their individual message (Guo and Acar, 2005). Second, the return from the cooperation for each individual NPO might be less than the initial investment (i.e. costs associated with establishing the cooperation and approaching the business) because the return, naturally, would be shared between the cooperating NPOs. An NPO, however, might receive a larger return if it were to invest the same amount into its own NBC rather than into a collective venture (cf. Arya and Lin, 2007).

Based on the discussion above, we claim that, despite increasing competition in the nonprofit sector, co-opetition (which is consistent with SMA principles) can become a possible option for reducing the intensity of competition between NPOs as part of their NBC strategy.

CULTURAL BARRIER

NPOs are increasingly called upon to adopt business-related approaches to optimise the use of their limited resources (Valeau, 2014). These approaches include operations management and positioning strategy to modernise the services they provide (Wicker and Breuer, 2012), and branding and marketing techniques to maintain and enhance income streams (Sargeant, 2005; Parsons, 2008). However, NPOs often develop an internal cultural barrier or resistance when adopting such approaches to improve performance, as Lindenberg (2001: 248) comments: '[NPOs] fear that too much attention to market dynamics and private and public sector techniques will destroy their value-based organizational culture'. As one of these new approaches, we contend that staff and volunteers might perceive NBC as a step change in values, which might create an internal cultural barrier (Mannell, 2010; Wilson *et al.*, 2010). Such resistance might result from the perceived incompatibility between NPO values, which are often characterised as socially driven and cooperative, and business values, which are widely described as profit driven and competitive (Berger *et al.*, 2004; Parker and Selsky, 2004). As part of strategy process (element 3), we discuss the means to address the issue of cultural barrier.

Content (element 2)

Content addresses the directions and choices that an organisation deliberately chooses to adopt/apply to achieve pre-determined objectives. Under this element, we identified two factors: collaboration level and strategic position.

COLLABORATION LEVEL

This factor is fundamental to the content of NBC strategy because it relates to the choice an NPO needs to make regarding the type of collaboration and to the degree to which each organisation is willing to engage in it. As discussed above (see also Table 3.1), NBC types can be categorised in terms of levels: philanthropic, transactional, and integrative. Importantly, each of these levels has different consequences for the internal and external context of the NPO. For example, a higher collaboration level would require greater staff and volunteer engagement and a better cultural fit between the two partnered organisations (internal context), and would incur higher public expectations and scrutiny (external context; Hudson, 2005). Similarly, different risks are associated with different NBC levels. For instance, cause-related marketing would put the NPO in a resource dependent position, which might weaken its ability to challenge business behaviour and therefore make it vulnerable to co-optation by its business partner (Baur and Schmitz, 2012). However, the level of collaboration should not be considered in isolation from the other factors. For example, stakeholder pressure (context, element 1) has a considerable influence on the selection of collaboration level, where some levels might be more acceptable to stakeholders than others. Simpson *et al.* (2011) found that the extent of compatibility between NBC and stakeholder expectations influenced the governance of the relationship. For example, stakeholders with high expectations (e.g. they have a strong ideology) preferred a low collaboration level (i.e. informal governance mechanism) to keep their NPO distant from the business partner. Moreover, an NPO might adjust the level of collaboration to satisfy its stakeholders. For instance, if high internal resistance is expected (see cultural barrier above), an NPO might seek a lower collaboration level to reduce NBC commitment and engagement, thereby mitigating the perceived risk of being associated with that prospective business partner (Baur and Schmitz, 2012).

In summary, we argue that a better NBC strategy can be reached when the chosen collaboration level aligns with the internal and external environment of the NPO, where a higher NBC level will be associated with higher organisational commitment, outcomes and risk, and vice versa.

STRATEGIC POSITION

Strategic position (SP) concerns a set of activities an organisation applies to create a unique identity for itself, thus making it distinguishable from its competitors (Porter, 1996). Such activities include the configuration of resources and competences, the determination of strengths and weakness, and the analysis of existing and future rivals, all of which can help to maintain the organisation's competitiveness in the marketplace. SP in the nonprofit context is built upon the NPO's values and capacity to fulfil its mission (Krug and Weinberg, 2004). SP contributes substantially to public perception of an NPO, which in turn can influence the extent of their support (Frumkin and Kim, 2001).

In relation to NBC, SP concerns the ability of an NPO to attract a prospective business partner, which is typically based on its potential to yield social and economic value for the partner (Porter and Kramer, 2002). For example, NPOs possess a deep understanding of problems in the social field (Kramer and Kania, 2006), which makes them attractive to businesses due to their potential to develop better solutions to such problems (Austin, 2000). In addition, NPOs are often more legitimate to society and possess links with communities that businesses might lack (Yaziji, 2004), such as networks of donors, regulators, and public lobbyists. Such features are also likely to attract business interest because they should help to generate economic value (e.g. scale up sales through sponsorship of an NPO) in addition to benefiting society. SP strongly relates to nonprofit competition (see context, element 1), which further emphasises the importance of a unique SP (Frumkin and Kim, 2001).

In addition to the above discussion, we contend that SP in regard to NBC strategy is consistent with SMA, which emphasises that organisations should genuinely seek mutual gains, rather than individual opportunistic benefit, from their interorganisational relationships (Gulati *et al.*, 2000; Osborne *et al.*, 2013). However, although the value to NPOs from NBC is relatively easy to determine in terms of tangible and intangible resources, the benefit to businesses is less clear (Berger *et al.*, 2004). The value of NPO characteristics, such as legitimacy, experience in addressing society's problems, and rich and diverse stakeholder networks, to businesses is typically difficult to quantify (Yaziji, 2004). Of practical importance, NPOs that develop their SP based on visualising and communicating such characteristics – to improve estimation of their value – are more likely to attract a business partner.

Process (element 3)

Process concerns the activities that support the emergence of the strategic choice (Huff and Reger, 1987). Two key issues relate to strategy process (Ketchen *et al.*, 1996). The first, political activity, concerns the actions of political actors (e.g. lobbying, dissemination of information) who seek to increase their power during the decision process and thus affect how the strategy is developed, agreed upon, and implemented (Narayanan and Fahey, 1982). The second issue, information usage, concerns the quantity and quality of available information with which to inform strategy formulation. Based on these issues, three factors relate to this element: power imbalance, feedback channels, and transaction costs.

POWER IMBALANCE

In regard to NBC, power imbalance refers to a situation where one party is perceived as stronger and holds more control over the relationship than the other (Mutch, 2011). Das and Teng (2001) note that power issues are more likely to emerge in situations where the self-interests of the partners and the collective goals of the collaboration are not congruent. Moreover, an imbalance can occur if the collaboration is more important to one partner than the other (e.g. the availability of alternatives to one organisation to achieve its objectives rather than through the collaboration) or one partner has more legitimacy than the other (Huxham and Vangen, 2005: 162).

Power imbalance can also affect the potential outcome of the collaboration because the resources and capabilities of the perceived weaker partner might not be fully recognised and hence poorly utilised (Berger *et al.*, 2004). By considering this issue early when planning for NBC, NPOs can anticipate the likelihood of such imbalance and consider how best to deal with it (Bryson *et al.*, 2006). Borrowing from relationship marketing literature (part of SMA), trust is essential in balancing power during an on-going relationship. Trust provides the basis for mutual commitment that can reduce uncertainties associated with opportunistic behaviour between the partners (Sheth *et al.*, 2000). However, building trust between an NPO and a business is often a gradual process because of the 'antagonistic' manner in which NPOs typically regard NBC (Arenas *et al.*, 2013). Therefore, there is a need for other means, in addition to trust, to address the imbalance issue. NPOs could, for instance, emphasise their strengths, such as strong brand and nested social networks (Berger *et al.*, 2004), to avoid being the weaker partner in prospective collaborations. Additionally, researchers argue that collaboration level might augment or attenuate an imbalance (e.g. Austin, 2000). For instance, the power of an NPO in a high-level collaboration (e.g. strategic alliance) might be stronger than in a lower level one (e.g. sponsoring) because the business is likely to appreciate the value of the nonprofit partner to a greater extent (Tracey *et al.*, 2005).

In summary, we contend that potential power imbalance should be discussed as part NBC strategy development. NPOs that proactively employ their capabilities to avoid power imbalance will become more successful in managing NBC.

FEEDBACK CHANNELS

Feedback channels relate to Ketchen *et al.*'s (1996) information-usage issue, which concerns how organisations gather and process information to support their strategic decision making (Arregle *et al.*, 2007). An investigation into the impact of feedback channels on the implementation of NBC found that such channels were important in allowing both partners to respond to the internal and external demands of stakeholders (Clarke and Fuller, 2011). In addition, the use of feedback channels can help NPOs to become innovative in their NBC strategy. By unlocking the 'tacit' knowledge that service users possess, NPOs can develop new service-related initiatives (Osborne *et al.*, 2013) that are likely to attract business interest.

Feedback channels are also vital to avoid potential conflict (Babiak and Thibault, 2009). For example, staff and volunteers at lower organisational levels might be aware of unforeseen risks, due to their understanding of what works on the ground and what does not, that contradict the positive view of decision-makers. Additionally, feedback can help to generate 'what if' scenarios to identify potential problems and to formulate remedial actions, such as how to respond to inappropriate or unethical business behaviour (Dunn, 2010). From a post-NBC perspective, feedback channels can also provide decision-makers with real-time information with which to determine whether or not activities and actions have been implemented smoothly and according to the NBC plan (Gates, 2010).

The use of feedback channels is also consistent with SMA, which emphasises the importance of listening to end-users. As mentioned previously, the overriding activity of the nonprofit sector is to provide public services. Value received from the business sector through collaboration (e.g. tangible and intangible resources) can support the delivery of such services (e.g. a literacy program carried out in partnership with a business). In contrast to the product-dominant approach that separates service production from consumption, SMA also emphasises the need to manage the service through coproduction (i.e. between NPOs and service users; Osborne *et al.*, 2013). In general, coproduction concerns 'regular, long-term relationships between professionalized service providers (in any sector) and service users or other members of the community, where all parties make substantial resource contributions' (Bovaird, 2007: 847). In essence, the value of coproduction stems from placing the experience and knowledge of services users at the heart of service design and delivery (Osborne *et al.*, 2013). Therefore, we contend that feedback channels are important in facilitating service co-production by enabling the collection of relevant information from service end-users.

TRANSACTION COSTS

We refer to transaction costs as the costs an NPO incurs when participating in NBC-related activities. Drawing upon Macher and Richman (2008), transaction costs can be divided into three broad categories. The first concerns costs associated with activities to find a suitable partner (e.g. time allocated for collecting information on a prospective business partner). This category also includes the cost of marketing the NPO's collaboration proposal to potential partners. The second category relates to negotiation costs that are typically required to develop the collaboration plan and refine its objectives to reach a mutually accepted agreement (e.g. staff time spent in meeting with the business partners to understand its needs). The third category concerns enforcement costs. These costs are necessary to implement the agreement and subsequent monitoring activity to ensure that partners comply with what had been agreed as part of NBC.

Typically, NPOs are under constant donor pressure to keep their costs at the lowest possible level (Andreoni and Payne, 2011). Moreover, they are expected to ensure that all expenditures are rationally allocated and carefully monitored, to guarantee that the public receive optimal value (Gils and Zwart, 2004). Although reducing transaction costs represents good practice, it should not be sought as an end in itself when planning for NBC. Research shows that minimising planning costs is not always associated with being viewed by society as efficient (Frumkin and Kim, 2001), but that value for money is becoming more important when assessing the effectiveness of NPO practice (Young and Steinberg, 1995). Therefore, we contend that NPOs should regard NBC transaction costs as an investment to create new opportunities, rather than as costs that should be blindly reduced. Through this mind-set, NPOs are expected to gain the trust of their stakeholders because the strategy that underlies NBC should be perceived as efficiently developed and based on informed decisions.

This section describes a framework that aims to operationalise the development and implementation of NBC strategy from the NPO perspective. The framework has unique value in that it identifies the factors that NPOs should consider when thinking proactively about NBC. It is based on the three elements concept and insights from stakeholder theory and the nonprofit and cross-sector collaboration literature. Importantly, we show that our framework is relevant to the nonprofit context in that the majority of the factors are consistent with SMA logic.

Implications for research and practice

This section begins with a discussion of potential areas for future research. First, despite its theoretical strength, it would be worthwhile to examine the generalisability of the framework. More specifically, it is important to examine the extent to which the framework (including its factors) is applicable to NPOs of various size (e.g. small, medium, and large) and scope (e.g. local, national, and international). Second, future research could examine the extent to which the factors are of equal importance for the development of NBC strategy. If some factors were found to be more important than others, then NPOs could use this information to prioritise their focus, helping them to make better use of their limited human and capital resources (Bryson, 2010). Third, it would be worthwhile to conduct a comparative study to investigate differences between successful and unsuccessful NPOs in NBC. This line of inquiry would help to identify any overlooked factors that might facilitate or hinder strategy implementation. Fourth, future longitudinal research could explore potential causal paths between the factors; do some factors predict others, which in turn predict the final outcome of NBC strategy? Finally, it would be worthwhile examining the extent to which the framework is relevant to collective NBC strategy development. The framework has been designed on the premise of how a single NPO might plan strategically to attract one or more business partners. Yet, we contend that the framework also has potential to assist a group of NPOs to develop a strategy for NBC. Therefore, it would be worthwhile to examine the extent to which the framework is relevant to intra-sector alliances or how multiple NPOs can work together to secure NBC. In particular, as highlighted under the strategic position factor, there is a need to understand how cooperation between NPOs might strengthen their strategic position and to investigate potential risks associated with this approach.

In addition to research, this inquiry has implications for practice. The framework can be used as a guide to help managers in the nonprofit sector to develop a strategy for NBC. In principle, it can be used as a checklist to help decision-makers pre-empt problems and risks associated with NBC. Such guidance should encourage a change in NPO practice from being opportunistic or reacting to business offers, to strategically targeting potential businesses partners. Although NPOs might be the weaker partner in NBC (typically due to the unequal flow of resources between the partners), we describe how they might be able to re-balance this status by advertising their distinctive capabilities, such as the possession of social and environmental expertise to address the concerns of society, when planning NBC. We contend that this form of power has potential not only to counter the economic strength of businesses, but to place NPOs in a stronger position vis-à-vis their business partner.

Conclusion

This chapter investigates cross-sector collaboration by focusing on one of its three forms, namely nonprofit–business collaboration (NBC; see Figure 3.1). Previous research has extensively studied NBC as a value creation approach for society and business; little attention has been focused on NBC from the NPO perspective. Our framework, we believe, helps to address this gap. Although the framework is theoretically based on the three elements of strategy, which is rooted in the manufacturing domain, we demonstrate how it is compatible with the basic principles of SMA. Given the relevance of SMA to public services providers such as NPOs (Osborne, 2009; Steane, 2008), we propose that such compatibility or fit enhances the conceptual validity of the framework. Accordingly, it is our belief that with the help of the framework, NPOs will be able to increase value for their beneficiaries and enhance their long-term sustainability.

References

Akingbola, K. (2012) 'A model of strategic nonprofit human resource management'. *Voluntas: International Journal of Voluntary and Nonprofit Organizations*, 24(1): 1–27.

Al-Tabbaa, O. (2012) 'Nonprofit–businesses collaboration: thematic review and new research agenda'. Retrieved from http://dx.doi.org/10.2139/ssrn.2191540 (accessed 15 December 2014).

Al-Tabbaa, O. (2013) 'From beggar to partner: nonprofit–business collaboration as a strategic option for nonprofit organizations'. PhD thesis, University of Leeds.

Al-Tabbaa, O., Gadd, K. and Ankrah, N. (2013) 'Excellence models in the nonprofit context: strategies for continuous improvement'. *International Journal of Quality and Reliability Management*, 30(5): 590–612.

Al-Tabbaa, O., Leach, D. and March, J. (2014) 'Collaboration between nonprofit and business sectors: a framework to guide strategy development for nonprofit organizations'. *Voluntas: International Journal of Voluntary and Nonprofit Organizations*, 25: 657–78.

Andreoni, J. and Payne, A.A. (2011) 'Is crowding out due entirely to fundraising? Evidence from a panel of charities'. *Journal of Public Economics*, 95: 334–43.

Arenas, D., Sanchez, P. and Murphy, M. (2013) 'Different paths to collaboration between businesses and civil society and the role of third parties'. *Journal of Business Ethics*, 115(4): 723–39.

Arregle, J., Hitt, M., Sirmon, D. and Very, P. (2007) 'The development of organizational social capital: attributes of family firms'. *Journal of Management Studies*, 44: 73–95.

Arya, B. and Lin, Z. (2007) 'Understanding collaboration outcomes from an extended resource-based view perspective: the roles of organizational characteristics, partner attributes, and network structures'. *Journal of Management*, 33: 697–723.

Austin, J. (2000) 'Strategic collaboration between nonprofits and business'. *Nonprofit and Voluntary Sector Quarterly*, 29: 69–97.

Babiak, K. and Thibault, L. (2009) 'Challenges in multiple cross-sector partnerships'. *Nonprofit and Voluntary Sector Quarterly*, 38: 117–43.

Barney, J. (1991) 'Firm resources and sustained competitive advantage'. *Journal of Management*, 17: 99–120.

Baur, D. and Schmitz, H. (2012) 'Corporations and NGOs: when accountability leads to co-optation'. *Journal of Business Ethics*: 1–13.

Beck, T.E., Lengnick-Hall, C.A. and Lengnick-Hall, M.L. (2008) 'Solutions out of context: examining the transfer of business concepts to nonprofit organizations'. *Nonprofit Management and Leadership*, 19: 153–71.

Behn, R.D. (2003) 'Why measure performance? Different purposes require different measures'. *Public Administration Review*, 63: 586–606.

Berger, I.E., Cunningham, P.H. and Drumwright, M.E. (2004) 'Social alliances: company/nonprofit collaboration'. *California Management Review*, 47: 58.

Berglind, M. and Nakata, C. (2005) 'Cause-related marketing: more buck than bang?' *Business Horizons*, 48: 443–53.

Bessant, J. and Tidd, J. (2007) *Innovation and Entrepreneurship*. Chichester: Wiley.

Bovaird, T. (2007) 'Beyond engagement and participation – user and community co-production of public services'. *Public Administration Review*, 67: 846–60.

Bryson, J.M. (1988) 'A strategic planning process for public and non-profit organizations'. *Long Range Planning*, 21: 73–81.

Bryson, J.M. (2004) 'What to do when stakeholders matter'. *Public Management Review*, 6: 21–53.

Bryson, J. (2010) 'The future of public and nonprofit strategic planning in the United States'. *Public Administration Review*, 70: s255–67.

Bryson, J.M., Crosby, B.C. and Stone, M.M. (2006) 'The design and implementation of cross-sector collaborations: propositions from the literature'. *Public Administration Review*, 66: 44–55.

Chew, C. and Osborne, S.P. (2009) 'Exploring strategic positioning in the UK charitable sector: Emerging Evidence from Charitable Organizations that Provide Public Services'. *British Journal of Management*, 20: 90–105.

Clarke, A. and Fuller, M. (2011) 'Collaborative Strategic Management: Strategy Formulation and implementation by multi-organizational cross-sector social partnerships'. *Journal of Business Ethics*, 94: 85–101.

Coyte, R., Ricceri, F. and Guthrie, J. (2012) 'The management of knowledge resources in SMEs: an Australian case study'. *Journal of Knowledge Management*, 16: 789–807.

Dart, R. (2004) 'Being "business-like" in a nonprofit organization: a grounded and inductive typology'. *Nonprofit and Voluntary Sector Quarterly*, 33: 290–310.

Das, T.K. and Teng, B.-S. (2001) 'Trust, control, and risk in strategic alliances: an integrated framework'. *Organization Studies*, 22: 251–83.

Den Hond, F., De Bakker, F.G.A. and Doh, J. (2015) 'What prompts companies to collaboration with NGOs? Recent evidence from the Netherlands'. *Business Society*, 54(2): 187–228.

Dunn, P. (2010) 'Strategic responses by a nonprofit when a donor becomes tainted'. *Nonprofit and Voluntary Sector Quarterly*, 39(1): 102–23.

Eikenberry, A.M. and Kluver, J.D. (2004) 'The marketization of the nonprofit sector: civil society at risk?' *Public Administration Review*, 64: 132–40.

Frumkin, P. and Kim, M.T. (2001) 'Strategic positioning and the financing of nonprofit organizations: is efficiency rewarded in the contributions marketplace?' *Public Administration Review*, 61: 266–75.

Gates, M.F. 2010. 'What nonprofits can learn from Coca-Cola'. Retrieved from www.ted.com/talks/melinda_french_gates_what_nonprofits_can_learn_from_coca_cola.html (accessed June 2014).

Gils, A.V. and Zwart, P. (2004) 'Knowledge acquisition and learning in Dutch and Belgian SMEs: the role of strategic alliances'. *European Management Journal*, 22: 685–92.

Gnyawali, D.R., He, J. and Madhavan, R. (2006) 'Impact of co-opetition on firm competitive behavior: an empirical examination'. *Journal of Management*, 32: 507–30.

Godfrey, P.C. (2005) 'The relationship between corporate philanthropy and shareholder wealth: a risk management perspective'. *Academy of Management Review*, 30: 777–98.

Gulati, R., Nohria, N. and Zaheer, A. (2000) 'Strategic networks'. *Strategic Management Journal*, 21: 203–15.

Guo, C. and Acar, M. (2005) 'Understanding collaboration among nonprofit organizations: combining resource dependency, institutional, and network perspectives'. *Nonprofit and Voluntary Sector Quarterly*, 34: 340–61.

Hambrick, D.C. (2003) 'On the staying power of defenders, analyzers, and prospectors'. *The Academy of Management Executive* (1993–2005), 17: 115–18.

Harris, M.E. (2012) 'Nonprofits and business: toward a subfield of nonprofit studies'. *Nonprofit and Voluntary Sector Quarterly*, 41(5): 892–902.

Hendry, J.R. (2006) 'Taking aim at business'. *Business and Society*, 45: 47–86.

Herman, R.D. and Renz, D.O. (2008) 'Advancing nonprofit organizational effectiveness research and theory: nine theses'. *Nonprofit Management and Leadership*, 18: 399–415.

Hoffmann, W.H. and Schlosser, R. (2001) 'Success factors of strategic alliances in small and medium-sized enterprises: an empirical survey'. *Long Range Planning*, 34: 357–81.

Holmes, S. and Smart, P. (2009) 'Exploring open innovation practice in firm-nonprofit engagements: a corporate social responsibility perspective'. *R&D Management*, 39: 394.

Huatuco, L., Moxham, C., Burt, E. and Al-Tabbaa, O. (2014) 'Third sector and performance'. *International Journal of Productivity and Performance Management*, 63(6): 1.

Hudson, M. (2005) *Managing at the Leading Edge: New Challenges in Managing Nonprofit Organizations*. San Francisco, CA: Jossey-Bass.

Huff, A.S. and Reger, R.K. (1987) 'A review of strategic process research'. *Journal of Management*, 13: 211–36.

Huxham, C. and Vangen, S. (2005) *Managing to Collaborate: The Theory and Practice of Collaborative Advantage*. New York: Routledge.

Isett, K. and Provan, K. (2005) 'The evolution of dyadic interorganizational relationships in a network of publicly funded nonprofit agencies'. *Journal of Public Administration Research and Theory*, 15(1): 149–65.

Jansons, E. (2014) 'The business leaders behind the foundations: understanding India's emerging philanthropists'. *Voluntas: International Journal of Voluntary and Nonprofit Organizations*, 1–23, doi:10.1007/s11266-014-9470-1.

Johnson, G., Whittington, R. and Scholes, K. (2011) *Exploring Strategy*. Upper Saddle River, NJ: Prentice Hall.

Kelly, J. (2007) 'Reforming public services in the UK: bringing in the third sector'. *Public Administration*, 85: 1003–22.

Ketchen, D., Thomas, J. and Mcdaniel, R. (1996) 'Process, content and context: synergistic effects on organizational performance'. *Journal of Management*, 22: 231–57.

Keys, T., Malnight, T. and Graaf, K. (2009) 'Making the most of corporate social responsibility'. *McKinsey Quarterly*, December.

Kindred, J. and Petrescu, C. (2014) 'Expectations versus reality in a university–community partnership: a case study'. *Voluntas: International Journal of Voluntary and Nonprofit Organizations*, doi:10.1007/s11266-014-9471-0.

Kong, E. (2008) 'The development of strategic management in the non-profit context: intellectual capital in social service non-profit organizations'. *International Journal of Management Reviews*, 10: 281–99.

Koschmann, M.A., Kuhn, T.R. and Pfarrer, M.D. (2012) 'A communicative framework of value in cross-sector partnerships'. *Academy of Management Review*, 37: 332–54.

Kramer, M. and Kania, J. (2006) 'A new role for non-profits'. *Stanford Social Innovation Review*, 4: 32–41.

Krug, K. and Weinberg, C.B. (2004) 'Mission, money, and merit: strategic decision making by nonprofit managers'. *Nonprofit Management and Leadership*, 14: 325–42.

Lindenberg, M. (2001) 'Are we at the cutting edge or the blunt edge? Improving NGO organizational performance with private and public sector strategic management frameworks'. *Nonprofit Management and Leadership*, 11: 247–70.

Macher, J. and Richman, B. (2008) 'Transaction cost economics: an assessment of empirical research in the social sciences'. *Business and Politics*, 10. Retrieved from www.bepress.com/bap/vol10/iss1/art1 (accessed July 2014).

Mannell, J. (2010) 'Are the sectors compatible? International development work and lessons for a business–nonprofit partnership framework'. *Journal of Applied Social Psychology*, 40: 1106–22.

Mcdonald, S. and Young, S. (2012) 'Cross-sector collaboration shaping corporate social responsibility best practice within the mining industry'. *Journal of Cleaner Production*, 37, December: 54–67.

Miller, D., Droge, C. and Toulouse, J.-M. (1988) 'Strategic process and content as mediators between organizational context and structure'. *Academy of Management Journal*, 31: 544–69.

Moser, T. (2001) 'MNCs and sustainable business practice: the case of the Colombian and Peruvian petroleum industries'. *World Development*, 29: 291–309.

Mutch, N. (2011) 'Does power imbalance matter in corporate–nonprofit partnerships?' PhD thesis, University of Otago.

Narayanan, V. (2001) *Managing Technology and Innovation for Competitive Advantage*. Upper Saddle River, NJ: Prentice Hall.

Narayanan, V.K. and Fahey, L. (1982) 'The micro-politics of strategy formulation'. *Academy of Management Review*, 7: 25–34.

Osborne, S.P. (2009) 'Delivering public services: time for a new theory?' *Public Management Review*, 12: 1–10.

Osborne, S.P. and Strokosch, K. (2013) 'It takes two to tango? Understanding the co-production of public services by integrating the services management and public administration perspectives'. *British Journal of Management*, 24, S31–47.

Osborne, S.P., Bond, S., Honore, E. and Dutton, M. (2012) *The Opportunities and Challenges of the Changing Public Services Landscape for the Third Sector in Scotland: Year Two Report*. Edinburgh: Scottish Government.

Osborne, S.P., Radnor, Z.J. and Nasi, G. (2013) 'A new theory for public service management? Toward a (public) service-dominant approach'. *American Review of Public Administration*, 43(2): 135–58.

Parker, B. and Selsky, J.W. (2004) 'Interface dynamics in cause-based partnerships: an exploration of emergent culture'. *Nonprofit and Voluntary Sector Quarterly*, 33: 458–88.

Parsons, L., Maclaran, P. and Tadajewski, M. (2008) *Nonprofit Marketing*. London: Sage.

Pettigrew, A.M. (1985) *The Awakening Giant: Continuity and Change in ICL*. Oxford: Blackwell.

Pettigrew, A.M. (1987a) *The Management of Strategic Change*. Oxford: Blackwell

Pettigrew, A.M. (1987b) 'Context and action in the transformation of the firm'. *Journal of Management Studies*, 24: 649–70.

Pettigrew, A.M. (1992) 'The character and significance of strategy process research'. *Strategic Management Journal*, 13: 5–16.

Pichault, F. (2007) 'HRM-based reforms in public organisations: problems and perspectives'. *Human Resource Management Journal*, 17: 265–82.

Porter, M.E. (1996) 'What is strategy?' *Harvard Business Review*, 74: 61–78.

Porter, M.E. and Kramer, M.R. (2002) 'The competitive advantage of corporate philanthropy'. *Harvard Business Review*, 80: 56–69.

Powell, M., Greener, I., Szmigin, I., Doheny, S. and Mills, N. (2010) 'Broadening the focus of public service consumerism'. *Public Management Review*, 12: 323–40.

Qian, G. and Li, L. (2003) 'Profitability of small- and medium-sized enterprises in high-tech industries: the case of the biotechnology industry'. *Strategic Management Journal*, 24: 881–7.

Raak, A.V., Meijer, E., Meijer, A. and Paulus, A. (2005) 'Sustainable partnerships for integrated care: the role of decision making and its environment'. *International Journal of Health Planning and Management*, 20: 159–80.

Sagawa, S. (2001) 'New value partnerships: the lessons of Denny's/Save the Children partnership for building high-yielding cross-sector alliances'. *International Journal of Nonprofit and Voluntary Sector Marketing*, 6: 199–214.

Sargeant, A. (2005) *Marketing Management for Nonprofit Organizations*. Oxford: Oxford University Press.

Schmitt, A. and Klarner, P. (2015) 'From snapshot to continuity: a dynamic model of organizational adaptation to environmental changes'. *Scandinavian Journal of Management*, 31(1): 3–13.

Selsky, J. and Parker, B. (2011) 'Platforms for cross-sector social partnerships: prospective sensemaking devices for social benefit'. *Journal of Business Ethics*, 94: 21.

Sheth, J., Sisodia, R. and Sharma, A. (2000) 'The antecedents and consequences of customer-centric marketing'. *Journal of the Academy of Marketing Science*, 28: 55–66.

Simpson, D., Lefroy, K. and Tsarenko, Y. (2011) 'Together and apart: exploring structure of the corporate–NPO relationship'. *Journal of Business Ethics*, 101(2): 297–311.

Smith, C. (1994) 'The new corporate philanthropy'. *Harvard Business Review*, May. Retrieved from https://hbr.org/1994/05/the-new-corporate-philanthropy (accessed 8 January 2015).

Sofaer, S. and Firminger, K. (2005) 'Patient perceptions of the quality of health services'. *Annual Review of Public Health*, 26: 513–59.

Steane, P. (2008) 'Public management reforms in Australia and New Zealand: a pot pourri overview of the past decade'. *Public Management Review*, 10: 453-465.

Stockdale, R. and Standing, C. (2006) 'An interpretive approach to evaluating information systems: a content, context, process framework'. *European Journal of Operational Research*, 173: 1090–1102.

Sud, M., Vansandt, C. and Baugous, A. (2009) 'Social entrepreneurship: the role of institutions'. *Journal of Business Ethics*, 85: 201–16.

Tracey, P., Phillips, N. and Haugh, H. (2005) 'Beyond philanthropy: community enterprise as a basis for corporate citizenship'. *Journal of Business Ethics*, 58: 327–44.

Valeau, P. (2014) 'Stages and pathways of development of nonprofit organizations: an integrative model'. *Voluntas: International Journal of Voluntary and Nonprofit Organizations*, doi:10.1007/s11266-014-9501-y.

Van Fenema, P. and Loebbecke, C. (2014) 'Towards a framework for managing strategic tensions in dyadic interorganizational relationships'. *Scandinavian Journal of Management*, 30(4): 516–24.

Vurro, C., Dacin, M. and Perrini, F. (2010) 'Institutional antecedents of partnering for social change: how institutional logics shape cross-sector social partnerships'. *Journal of Business Ethics*, 94: 39–53.

Waddock, S. A. (1991) 'A typology of social partnership organizations'. *Administration and Society*, 22: 480–515.

Westley, F. and Vredenburg, H. (1991) 'Strategic bridging: the collaboration between environmentalists and business in the marketing of green products'. *Journal of Applied Behavioral Science*, 27: 65–90.

Wheelen, T. and Hunger, J. (1999) *Strategic Management and Business Policy*. Reading: Addison-Wesley.

Wicker, P. and Breuer, C. (2012) 'Understanding the importance of organizational resources to explain organizational problems: evidence from nonprofit sport clubs in Germany'. *Voluntas: International Journal of Voluntary and Nonprofit Organizations*, 24(2): 461–84.

Wilson, E.J., Bunn, M.D. and Savage, G.T. (2010) 'Anatomy of a social partnership: a stakeholder perspective'. *Industrial Marketing Management*, 39: 76–90.

Wit, B.D. and Meyer, R. (2010) *Strategy : Process, Content, Context: An International Perspective*. London: Thomson Learning.

Wymer, W.W. and Samu, S. (2003) 'Dimensions of business and nonprofit collaborative relationships'. *Journal of Nonprofit and Public Sector Marketing*, 11: 3–22.

Yaziji, M. (2004) 'Turning gadflies into allies'. *Harvard Business Review*, 82: 110–15.

Yaziji, M. and Doh, J. (2009) *NGOs and Corporations: Conflict and Collaboration*. Cambridge: Cambridge University Press.

Young, D.R. and Steinberg, R. (1995) *Economics for Nonprofit Managers*. New York: Foundation Center.

Zajac, E.J. and Shortell, S.M. (1989) 'Changing generic strategies: likelihood, direction, and performance implications'. *Strategic Management Journal*, 10: 413–30.

Note

1 NPOs can be defined as organisations that are formally structured, operate exclusively for a not-for-profit purpose, are independent of the government and which utilise any financial surplus to improve the services they provide or to develop internally. Furthermore, the terms NPO and 'nongovernmental organisation' (NGO) are used interchangeably in this chapter.

4 Accidental lean

Performance improvement in an NHS hospital and reflections on the role of operations strategy

Olga Matthias and Mark Buckle

Introduction

This chapter reviews a management consultancy intervention at a wing of a hospital (referred to hereafter as 'Northern Hospital', or 'NH') where the consultants were engaged to execute a performance improvement project to train the general public how to behave more responsibly in a hospital with regard to hospital-acquired infections (HAI) such as MRSA.[i] The Northern Strategic Health Authority (NSHA) commissioned the work because NH had among the highest rates of infection in the region, falling far short of Department of Health (DoH) targets regarding HAI. The chapter's contribution to service operations management and the study of healthcare is to consider the implications of piecemeal improvement programmes and reflect on whether a more studied approach towards operational performance objectives, developing an operation strategy, might result in behavioural and performance step-change improvement.

The work belongs within an existing body of research on performance improvement in healthcare, much of which discusses the application of tools and techniques deriving from the Toyota Production System (TPS) collectively known as lean (Krafcik, 1988). A brief comparison is made between the case and other research before reflecting on service delivery and performance within the UK's National Health Service (NHS). Consideration is given as to whether the use of an operation strategy, another manufacturing-derived approach, could help the NHS have greater success in achieving its objective of using resources to best effect to deliver improved patient care (NHS Plan, 2000). Typically, an operations strategy provides the broader conceptualisation of service delivery and 'value' creating organisational knowledge and enabling planning to reconcile market requirements and resources (Slack and Lewis, 2011). The purpose of this chapter is to reflect on that reconciliation, or its absence, in the NHS in conjunction with the concept of 'patient value', a key priority area for health policy (Currie *et al.*, 2008) and a driver of the consulting intervention described.

Healthcare is perhaps the most personal and important service people experience. It is also a service people need but do not necessarily want (Berry and Bendapudi, 2007). Patient perceptions of safety and care are what make up the 'patient experience', something that transcends a purely medical perspective. Unlike other services where demand increases supply, in healthcare supply increases demand. More physicians or hospital beds in a given region translate into more medical services rendered on a per capita basis without necessarily improving the overall health status of that population group (*ibid.*).

Service quality is an approach to achieving better health outcomes, with both quality and value determined by the beneficiary, and has become an important corporate strategy for healthcare organisations. Groonroos (2007) suggests there are two distinct components to quality, the technical aspect, or what is provided, and the functional aspect, or how the service is provided. It is the functional aspect that patients perceive and receive. Patient satisfaction therefore demands consideration of both the service concept and the customer characteristic (Anderson *et al.*, 2008).

The NHS context leading to the consulting intervention

> Infections are the price we pay for advances in medicine which allow survival in patients who are unlikely to have survived their illness a few years ago.
>
> (Department of Health, 2006)

At its inception in 1948 it was assumed that quality would be inherent in the service offering of the newly formed NHS through the skills and ethos of the health professionals working within the system (Nicholls *et al.*, 2000). The culture of the organisation has been historically based upon clinical excellence and the assumed leadership of clinicians. Since the introduction of the 'internal market', numerous changes have occurred, including those of staff attitudes and perceptions, culture, patient expectations, and medical technology (Burgess and Radnor, 2012; Graban and Swartz, 2012).

In the NHS, quality is seen as a 'prevailing purpose', having become a statutory requirement in 1997, incorporating the principles of corporate governance and applying these for the first time to quality and clinical governance (Cullen *et al.*, 2000). The NHS Plan (2000) specified that funding was linked to modernisation. Implicit was an acknowledgement that in order to deliver the aims of the clinical governance agenda the culture of health care organisations needed to be changed (Waring and Bishop, 2010; Graban *et al.*, 2012). A 'patient-led' perspective does not challenge clinical excellence but suggests a better balance be struck between the perceived 'value' of clinical safety and care and the perceived 'value' of more general patient safety and care.

This has made healthcare a fast-mover in policy reform although change is beset with professional and policy constraints, burdened by a mosaic of professions, large-scale structural change and the presence of central targets (Currie and Lockett, 2011). Structural change in the NHS is framed by an increasingly prescriptive and centrally-driven set of performance measures (Currie and Suhomlinova, 2006) and makes radical change within a culture such as the NHS problematic (Radnor and Osborne, 2013; Esain *et al.*, 2008). Consequently most initiatives within Hospitals and within the NHS in general tend to follow the path of incremental change and improvement rather than breakthrough (Umble and Umble, 2006; Ritchie, 2002: 4). Choosing the tools and deciding the degree of emphasis in order to maximise the potential benefits and outputs of an action is difficult. It requires knowledge and planning. The former is not always easy to harness in a large organisation, and the latter, to be done properly, requires time, a sometimes rare commodity (Ritchie, 2002: 4).

A number of consulting projects have been carried out across UK hospitals, conforming in the main to Ritchie's contention, and increasingly choosing the 'business' tools of quality and continuous improvement such as Kaizen and lean (Boaden, 2009; Patwardhan and Patwardhan, 2008; Antony *et al.*, 2007), alongside the adoption of the models of performance management (Smith, 2002). Probably the most famous UK example is Gerry Robinson's televised improvement intervention at Rotherham General Hospital in 2006 (Towill, 2009). Burgess (2012) provides comprehensive coverage of such improvement projects. Given the already stated objective of operations strategy as the conceptualisation of service delivery and organisational knowledge so that market needs can be effectively met, consideration of the multiple lean interventions across the NHS raises a number of questions. The most obvious one is why are there so many interventions? Also, what lessons are learned from each one? How are, or indeed are, these lessons disseminated throughout the NHS? Are they used to encourage systematic learning, performance improvement and consistent service delivery, to leave quality deposits, as advocated by Dale *et al.* (2002)?

The operational context for the management consultants at Northern Hospital

While professionals and patients may define quality in different ways, HAIs, especially MRSA have become synonymous in the public eye with poor quality service. Centrally collated DoH statistics (Department of Health, 2006) show that MRSA occurs in the main outside hospitals, and in fact people come to hospitals to be cured of it. As a response, the DoH 'ring-fenced' funding in order to address specific hygiene issues within limited timescales. DoH targets surrounding infection control have a temporary impact and help to focus the minds of both clinical and non-clinical management for short periods of relatively intense self-examination, although Boaden (2009) suggests they are not always effectively embedded.

Arising from the obligation to comply with specific Department of Health demands regarding MRSA, and in an attempt to effectively embed improvement, the NSHA undertook to review the specific approaches to reducing MRSA infection rates at NH, which had among the highest rates of infection in the region. The NSHA saw patients and the public as implementers of change, and in looking for a practical, systematic, long-term sustainable solution, saw 'some form' of social marketing as the best way to proceed. Budget allocations were set aside to address service improvement objectives within NH, a Steering Group was set up, a broad engagement process scoped out, and an initial project plan developed. As such, the remit of this project differed from typical improvement projects in that although its orientation was primarily within patient care, the initial impetus was process improvement in the public through social marketing techniques. It was hoped performance improvement within the Wards would follow. Despite beginning with the public, at the project's core lay the idea of 'sustainable patient value', ensuring that the whole focus and energy of the Hospital was placed behind meeting the needs of the various audiences served – hospital staff, Health Management, patients and the wider public – so that the Hospital could be seen to have met its organisational quality and performance imperatives.

The approach taken by the management consultants at Northern Hospital

Against this backdrop the NSHA secured additional funding for social marketing support, intended to assist NH to meet its immediate objective of reducing MRSA infection rates. The NSHA believed that the best possible outcomes would be realised using a social marketing approach, whose purpose is to achieve specific behavioural goals for a social good. Its primary focus is on 'benefiting the target audience and general society', not the marketer (Andreasen and Kotler, 2003: 329). The NSHA believed if the behaviour and perceptions of external groups (patients and public) were understood, *internal* behaviours could be informed and developed accordingly. This is perhaps a counterintuitive view of how an organisation should plan its services.

To this end, a specialist change management consulting firm was hired to implement best practice approaches to social marketing to encourage patients and the public to behave differently. An initial review phase was the first step in the programme.

The review phase

The review was based on a preliminary assessment of the hospital's original proposed action plan. Its focus was to assess the extent of existing knowledge of MRSA and the actions required to control infection rates. A combination of data collection techniques was used. Partly this was to effect data triangulation, and partly because the target population varied in profile and accessibility. Survey and group discussions were employed for all the internal and external stakeholder groups. Internal stakeholder groups were hospital management, clinical management, nursing, clinical and support staff. External stakeholders were the patients and wider public. To strengthen generalisability the selection sample of individuals from a number of groupings was random: members of ward staff, four patient groups and seven employee groups:

- medical;
- theatre;
- matrons;
- porters;

- ward 29;
- phlebotomy; and
- renal.

Individual interviews were conducted face-to-face or over the telephone, lasting around 45 minutes. The questions asked were as follows:

1 What do you think is the current public perception of MRSA infections?
2 How do you think that means that patients feel when they enter hospital?
3 What actions do you and your colleagues take at present to address these feelings?
4 What could you do in the future to ensure patients feel more reassured about the real causes and likelihood of infections?
5 What could you do in the future to reduce the causes and likelihood of MRSA infections?
6 Where such initiatives have been tried/are in place, what stops them being adopted on an organisational-wide and sustainable basis?
7 How many of these initiatives have already been tried in the past and/or are currently in place in some areas?
8 How could these changes be made to work and to stick on a long-term basis?

For external stakeholders, four focus group sessions of 90 minutes each were held. The same questions were asked as in the staff sessions, re-worded for relevance. Participants were recruited against the following criteria:

- Mix of males and females in each group.
- MRSA involved group – definition:
  - have had a close friend or relative involved in an MRSA 'episode' within the past 24 months
  - have visited, *for any medical reason (self/other)*, NH within the past 24 months.
- Non-MRSA group – definition:
  - have visited, *for any medical reason (self/other)*, NH within the past 24 months
  - aware of MRSA.

All respondents within the consultation were broadly conversant with the challenges facing the NHS in its battle against HAI, and their profiles are shown in Table 4.1.

Findings from the review phase

Employees showed an underlying commitment to care and awareness of the wider cultural and organisational issues:

> We've all lost the focus of why we're here.
>
> (Nurse)

Table 4.1 Age and socio-economic profile of focus group respondents

Date	*MRSA involved groups*	*Non-MRSA groups*
Wednesday 28 November	25–44, C2D	25–44, C2D
Thursday 29 November	45+, C2D	45+, C2D

> The focus needs to shift to good practice rather than targets.
>
> (Matron)

> We don't work well as a team at an organisational level.
>
> (Nurse)

Staff focus was strongly on quality, performance improvement and cultural change. The recurring theme was the requirement for greater clarity and consistency of leadership across the organisation. Accountability and silo working were raised as issues, both identified by Klein (2010) as areas to be addressed across the NHS. Encouraging people to work together in multi-disciplinary teams toward a common patient-centred goal was identified as necessary – something already practised to good effect in the Mayo Clinic (Berry, 2004).

The public surveys highlighted inconsistency of service delivery, with puzzlement that an organisation could get things right and 'quite so wrong' at the same time. Some saw politicians as the root of all evil, but generally the buck came back to the Hospital's senior management. Doctors and nurses were largely exempt from being responsible for any professional shortcomings:

> It's a shame they can't they give proper support to the nurses and free them up to do what they do best, which is to care for the sick.
>
> (Member of the public)

> I wouldn't want to work in those conditions. How can they think it's OK to carry on like this in the 21st century?
>
> (Member of the public)

Patient and public focus was on service delivery and outcome (Groonroos's functional and technical quality; Groonroos, 2007). The assessment from the review phase indicated that internal issues were greater than the intended process improvements with the public. An internal change programme was recognised as vital to engender performance improvement and cultural change to create an improvement in overall service quality. Consequently, social marketing was removed from the project remit.

The internal change programme

Four phases – *engage*, *embed*, *energise* and *evaluate*, referred to as the '4Es' – were proposed, each with a specific thrust of activity, broadly based on 'capturing the hearts and minds' of staff (Figure 4.1).

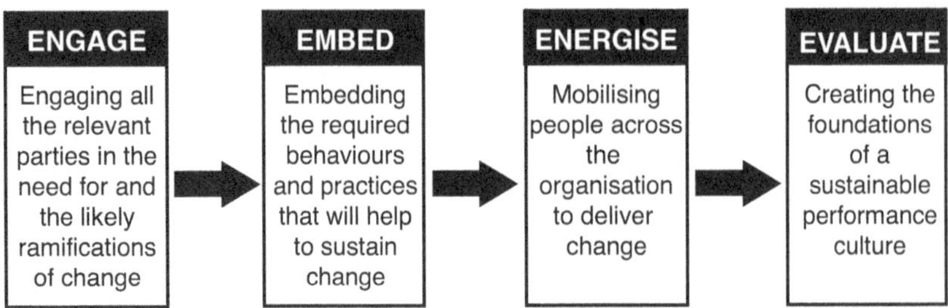

Figure 4.1 The generic change process

The engage phase

Key to engagement was a simple vision for change, emphasising that patients had to be prioritised as it was felt that being 'patient-led' would enable multifunctional teams to form, improving staff motivation as well as outcomes. The message was communicated visually throughout the ward (Figure 4.2).

Priorities were outlined as 'must do', 'should do' and 'could do', and an action plan developed, attempting to define the central organising principles for the hospital to shape and express 'the way things are done here'.

The engage phase centred on short-term initiatives with little or no reference to the cultural context for attempting to change internal behaviours, grouped around the headings of *people*, *process*, *practice* and *performance*, with the main orientation on process and performance. To become a patient-focused organisation, the hospital had to provide a consistent, organisation-wide response to public and patient concerns over healthcare associated infections.

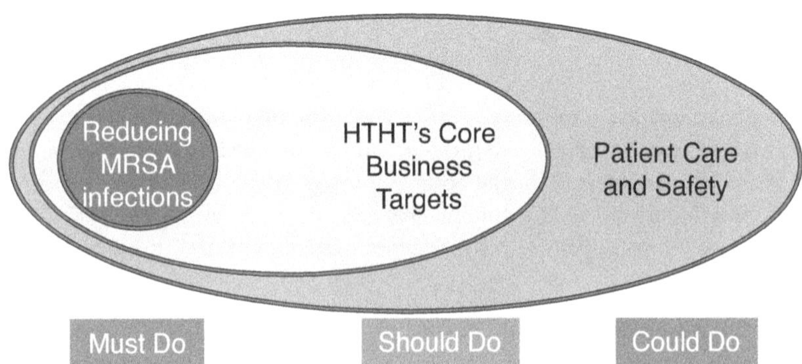

Figure 4.2 The vision to engage change

The 'patient-led' perspective was intended to suggest a balance between the perceived 'value' of clinical safety and care and the perceived 'value' of patient experience. Staff were encouraged to work towards a common goal, to consider addressing all issues that impact upon the total patient experience. The initiatives were developed under the overall umbrella of 'Safe Hands' rather than a specific change programme so that they could be embedded into everyday working practices. The chief executive of the hospital stated: 'This should not be seen as just another change initiative but core to the organisation's renewed focus on patient safety.'

The embed and energise phases

The embed phase used the tools of lean, process improvement and change management. The focus was for staff to understand if not create the 'need for change'. Toyota's '5 Whys' technique was used because it addresses single-problem events rather than broad organisational issues and gets to the root cause of the problem. This is necessary when dealing with the MRSA issue because it directs the receiver to the desire to create a 'positive and consistent hospital experience', which can only be done through the meaningful engagement of all staff with the same message and actions working towards this. Two parallel work streams were embarked upon, emanating from the core idea of 'creating a positive and consistent hospital experience' (Figure 4.3) for the energise phase:

- *Evolutionary change*: to embed sustainable, patient/customer-focused change across the organisation.

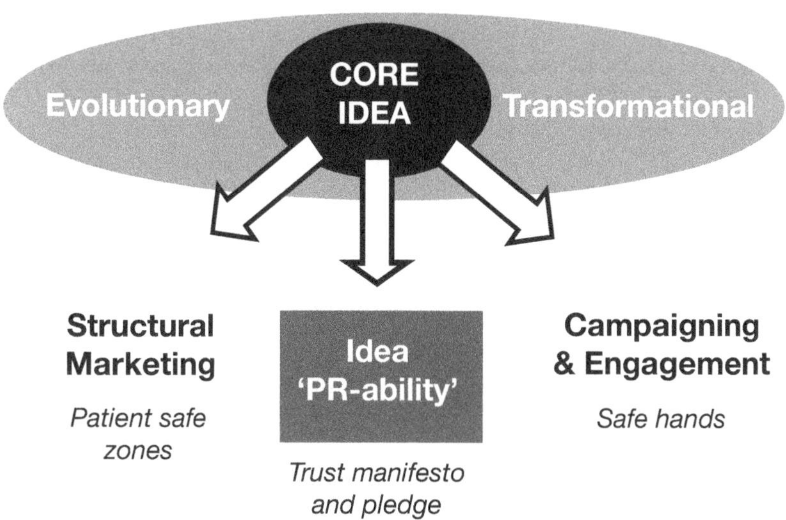

Figure 4.3 A balanced response to embedded improvement

- *Transformational change*: to make a quick and significant impact in the worst performing areas

'Patient safe zones' were created at ward level through Instant Impact Interventions initially focused on 'hot spot' areas. They were based on a combination of transformational change, lean and Kaizen principles. Cross-functional teams were formed, facilitated by transformational change experts. This phase followed the RIE format typical of lean change initiatives in the NHS which provides short bursts of improvement activity over 5 days with a cross-section of workers involved in a particular process (Burgess, 2012).

To promote the overall 'Safe Hands' principle of patient safety and care, internal and external communications campaigns were developed. Designed to focus on 'creating a positive and consistent hospital experience' through the four Ps – *public/patient*, *people*, *place* and *performance* – these interventions echo Glouberman and Mintzberg's (2001: 60) model in four quadrants where they discuss the four worlds of 'care, cure, community and control'. The intention of the four Ps approach was to demonstrate transparency and commitment of purpose, weakening the 'curtains' (*ibid.*) that inhibit communication and collaboration.

The 'Safe Hands' campaign (Figure 4.4) combined for NH the RIE approach, 5S and the consultants' proprietary phased approach shown in Figure 4.1. Of 124 ideas generated on the first ward alone, 85 were implemented. A total of five wards were involved.

The evaluate phase

The impact of 'Safe Hands' was measured with existing performance management data within the hospital. Hand hygiene audit, hand hygiene e-learning and MRSA e-learning scores improved by 24, 44 and 60 per cent, respectively. The performance of all five wards in the wing had converged at a significantly higher level. 'Soft' aspects of the work were also evaluated by means of a staff questionnaire. A summary of the key points is provided in Figures 4.5 and 4.6.

Figure 4.5 shows that staff in wards 33 and 34, the first two wards to complete the 'Safe Hands' process, were significantly more satisfied with their area of work. Overall, staff noticed change and the significant impacts achieved, demonstrated in terms of relative to control wing and over time, (compared to three months previous). Specifically, the improvements related to layout, cleanliness, availability of equipment and an emerging sense of teamwork.

However, Figure 4.6 shows there was less willingness to tackle longer-term issues around culture, leadership, engagement and evolutionary change. This may have been because of general resistance to change than to overall aims. This corresponds with the lack of accountability identified in the findings analysis as a significant issue at NH. It is also anecdotally representative of NHS culture as a whole, particularly in the hierarchies that exist within and between different professions, (consultants, doctors, nurses and managers), the evolution of which is detailed in Klein (2010).

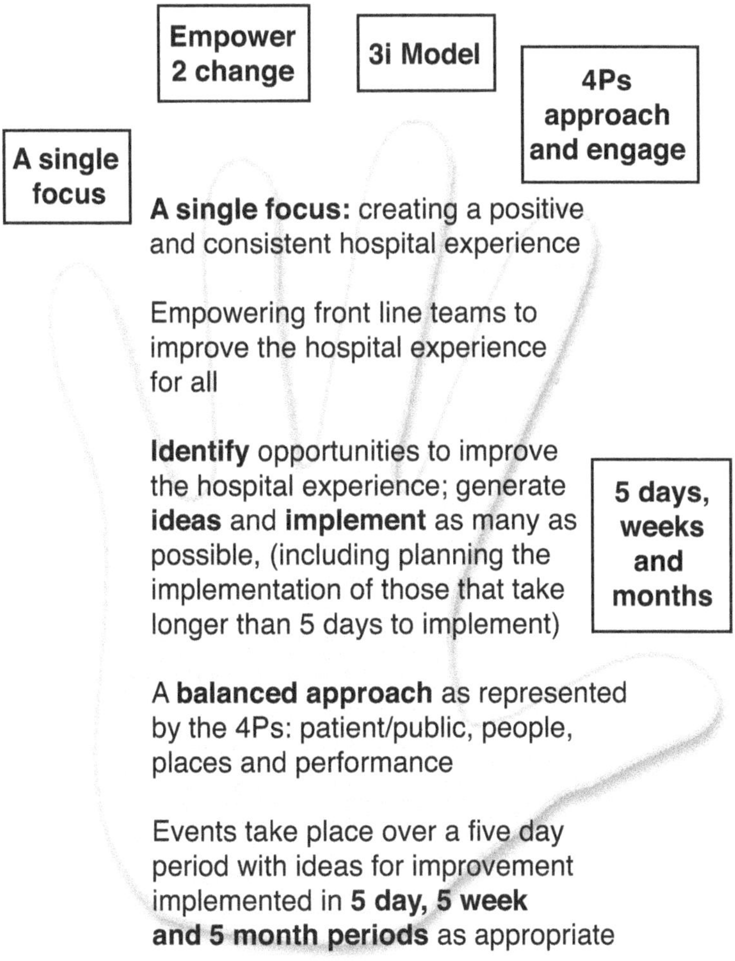

Empower 2 change
3i Model
4Ps approach and engage
A single focus
A single focus: creating a positive and consistent hospital experience
Empowering front line teams to improve the hospital experience for all
Identify opportunities to improve the hospital experience; generate **ideas** and **implement** as many as possible, (including planning the implementation of those that take longer than 5 days to implement)
5 days, weeks and months
A **balanced approach** as represented by the 4Ps: patient/public, people, places and performance
Events take place over a five day period with ideas for improvement implemented in **5 day, 5 week and 5 month periods** as appropriate

Figure 4.4 The safe hands concept

Greater cultural allegiance to the profession than the employer is typical of organisations aligned as professional bureaucracies (Mintzberg, 1983). Yet alignment with professional not patient-focused mores runs counter to the idea of 'creating a positive and consistent hospital experience' in terms of its impact on consistency of service delivery. Measuring culture to foster change for improved quality and performance is acknowledged as being important (Karp and Helgø, 2008), yet existing tools may be inadequate, given the paucity of information around understanding the culture measurements.

> This sounds fantastic – if we could have the same – but empowering staff needs to be backed up by both physical and financial resource.
>
> (Consultant from control wing)

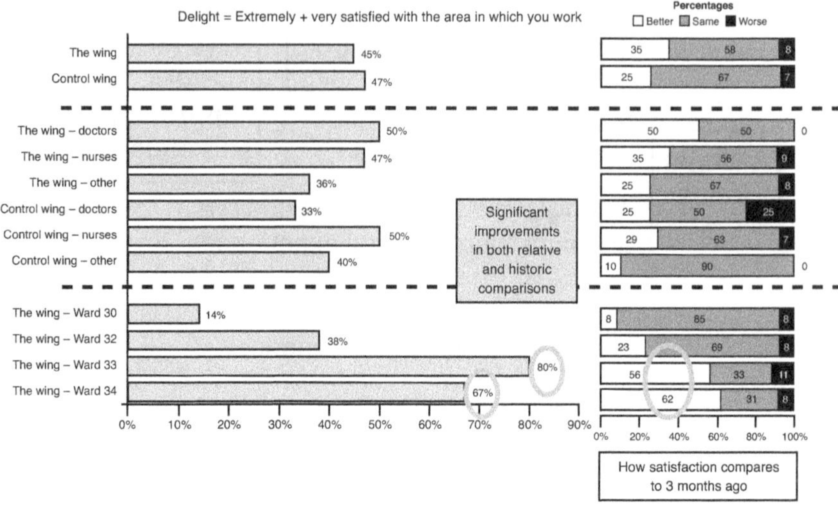

Figure 4.5 Staff delight with their work area (physical environment)

> Staff are happier at work – knock-on effects to other staff and to patients.
> (Consultant from the wing)

So what?

This project was a resounding success in the ward. MRSA infection rates had been reduced, which was the original objective. However, this had been achieved through an internal change programme and not a social marketing exercise, a consequence of which was that there were also a number of unintended staff-related improvements, highlighted in Figure 4.6. Morale had improved. Traditional silo working had reduced. The effects of greater co-operation were being felt by patients and shown in productivity figures the NH collated.

The smallest improvement area, 'Your overall working conditions', highlights in this hospital issues around systematic learning and consistent service delivery, identified earlier in the chapter. Given the evidence of this intervention, why did the hospital's management not use this project as a pilot and implement the same changes throughout NH? Why were the service outcome improvements not seen as important enough to be replicated hospital-wide? Further questions arise regarding the overview taken by both hospital management and the NSHA, such as why did neither body consider the wider results from the project and the potential implication for the hospital itself or the whole NSHA? Why did they simply accept that MRSA infection rates had fallen to 'acceptable' levels and therefore consider the project a success, and thereby completed?

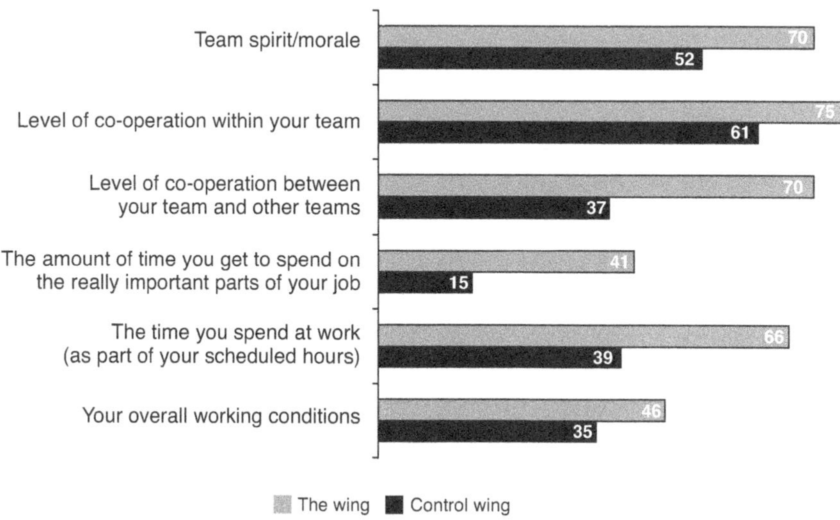

Figure 4.6 Staff satisfaction with their working lives

How does the Northern Hospital project compare with other NHS initiatives?

Research on NHS performance improvement projects using lean provides observations and commentary on specific situations. Service quality and effectiveness have become significant priorities and have led to the naïve application of external, business sector managerial policies, with the tools of lean and short-term activities as the primary focus, ignoring the over-arching cultural ethos and the centrality of the customer (Radnor and Osborne, 2013; Klein, 2010; Currie *et al.*, 2008). Operating processes and systems have internal indicators of success, focused on the reporting of centrally-set targets. Cannon (2013) assessed that as much as 90 per cent of work, and improvement projects, within the NHS are driven by failure demand, caused by a failure or an error. He argues systematic increase in demand is a function of the way the system has failure designed into it rather than inevitable. Cannon states the eradication of non-value-adding work is the only way to improve performance in the NHS. To do this, the NHS must only do what matters to the user. Cannon's exhortation epitomises the ethos of lean. As others have stated (Radnor *et al.*, 2012; Millard, 2011), success lies in patient-centred definitions of value and waste.

Burgess (2012) evaluated lean implementations in 143 NHS hospitals to explore the context, process and content of lean implementation by English hospitals. The findings from the case studies are shown in Table 4.2. NH has been added to this table for comparison purposes.

Typical of lean projects within the NHS, the NH project was also concerned with the organisation of work, and with the specific tasks and responsibilities therein. As explained, this is core to lean and could explain why the consultants gravitated towards using these tools having uncovered during the engage phase that problems

Table 4.2 Lean implementation – drivers and content

	Case study				
	UHCW	*ELHT*	*RBH*	*SHK*	*NH*
Drivers					
Performance targets and finance	✓	✓	✓		✓
Quality	✓		✓	✓	✓
Chief Executive			✓		
Impact					
Small simple changes	✓	✓	✓		✓
Focus on patient	✓		✓		✓
Learning to see	✓	✓	✓		✓
Implementing new standards	✓	✓	✓		
Challenging steps	✓	✓	✓		
Reduced 'did not attend'		✓	✓		
Improved morale			✓	✓	
Changing culture			✓		
Improved performance			✓		

Source: adapted from Burgess (2012: 261, 257)

were internal and not something the patients and public could change. While the stated focus for the consulting engagement was the end-user and the public the actual driver was a response to DoH targets with regard to HAI. Clearly, a reduction in infection rates improves quality. The 15 per cent year-on-year improvement resulting from the NH project is in keeping with other performance improvement projects where tangible outcomes are noted. However, less typically, the NH project also evaluated cultural change (Figure 4.5) and although it identified a reluctance to tackle longer-term issues, it did at least highlight the need for them to be considered.

In practice, lean was used at NH as a constellation of activities related to a pre-existing, target-led problem and not the wholesale organisational change ethos which true lean is (Radnor *et al.*, 2012). It used the most prominent tools encountered elsewhere, such as RIEs, looking at micro-level improvements to raise service quality and patient experience. However, as stated previously, this project differed from typical change programmes embarked upon within NHS hospitals in that the commissioning NSHA did not identify the problem correctly. It saw patients and the public as the implementers of change and for this reason wanted social marketing to be used to engender change in performance regarding MRSA in a wing of NH. It was the management consultants, who, once engaged and embarked on investigating the situation in the five wards in the wing, found through the Review phase that staff and the public saw internal issues to be more pertinent for resolution rather than external ones. Staff and the public showed a greater awareness of operational issues than management. Once again this highlights problems with the prevailing organisational culture and with accountability. This is interesting of itself, but does prompt questions about what service quality means to NHS management, and how they see their role in fulfilling this 'prevailing purpose'.

For this reason, this project was lean by accident. lean was not the primary purpose. Instead the tools of lean provided the most suitable mechanism for resolving the immediate issues, identified in the Review phase. In typical lean fashion, the root causes were found to lie elsewhere, and not in the stated identified problem. Yes, MRSA infection rates had exceeded the centrally set target and contravened centrally-driven performance measures. The review phase showed that working practices had led to this, and once they were changed, the corollary was that MRSA infection rates reduced. The CEO of NH announced on 17 January 2014 that they had achieved 135 consecutive days as an MRSA-free hospital, a sustainable performance improvement of note.

So why were the cultural changes not recognised and celebrated? Why was the link between the imperative of cultural change to the delivery of the clinical governance aims expressed in the NHS Plan first not acknowledged, and second not communicated throughout the organisations (locally, and the broader NHS)?

Papadopoulos *et al.* (2011) have noted, use of lean as a label for interventions in the NHS is widespread but the interpretation is varied. Lean should be a cultural transformation that changes how an organisation works. It requires new habits, new skills and a new attitude throughout the organisation in order to fulfil the underlying goal of improving value for the patient (Toussaint and Berry, 2013). Yet the reality appears to be that lean follows a line of service improvement that brings to the fore tensions between clinicians and service leaders around the organisation and the delivery of healthcare work (Mazzocato *et al.*, 2010). It seems lean principles have become entangled with other reforms and the competing voices of policy-makers, managers, clinical leaders and management consultants and illustrates the desire of policymakers to reorder clinical work thought the introduction of management philosophies and techniques (Waring and Bishop, 2010). This leads to question whether more could be achieved within NHS hospitals if government preoccupation with centralised control and micro-management through targets was replaced with a template intended to reduce boundaries within and across organisations and organisational members, synchronising policy aspirations with existing power arrangements (Klein, 2010; Currie and Suhomlinova, 2006).

Would an operation strategy approach make a difference?

Control is a necessary aspect of managing an organisation since it provides information and a starting premise for decision-making. However, at the micro-level that hospitals have to respond to, it becomes a static concept. The culture of continuous improvement, which emerges from a holistic lean implementation introduces a dynamic concept into an organisation. It requires choices to be made about the tools to use, in which order and in which emphasis (Garvin, 1992). These are surprisingly difficult decisions to make, and especially so without an over-arching framework within which to place thinking. operation strategy encourages an organisation to focus on a holistic understanding of needs in order to fully realise potential benefits. For a hospital, the primary need would be that of the patient, yet generally the policy-setter has been deemed the priority stakeholder, a situation which has resulted in value as specified by the public user at odds with the best use of resources against a backdrop of budget cuts and efficiency targets. The environment driven by policy and spending reviews means the requirement to engage with process improvements and other concepts is driven from management, making staff management-facing and not patient-facing, responsive to internal measures and targets and not patient requirements (Seddon and Caulkin, 2007). Indeed, the case outlined in this chapter illustrates that point exactly since the driver was a response to achieve DoH HAI targets, albeit the targets, being to reduce infection rates, in this case are patient-focused.

Currently, there are a number of issues which make an already complex situation more difficult to unravel. Patient value and patient needs can take on a variety of forms depending on who is expressing the need – the commissioners, the clinicians, the taxpayer or the patient (Radnor *et al.*, 2012). Costs in the healthcare sector are too high and growing too quickly, which places pressure on government budgets and threatens the availability of timely care and best treatments (Graban and Swartz, 2012). The strategies for patient care and meeting centrally-set performance targets appear to be pointing in different directions and removing an integrated care ethos (Currie and Suhomlinova, 2006).

Organisations in all industries develop strategies to respond to environmental factors and competitive challenges such as these. These strategies drive operational decisions. The idiosyncratic nature of the environment in hospital settings suggests the need to develop models that are specific to this industry and which align good overall system performance and minimise dysfunction effects between strategy deployment and operational practice (Esain *et al.*, 2008; Goldstein *et al.*, 2002). Good service operations management should lead to better or more appropriate services and experiences providing 'triple bottom line' benefits – better for patients, staff and the organisation (Johnston *et al.*, 2012).

To deliver better or more appropriate services, the NHS, like all service businesses needs to have over-arching strategies in place to try and prevent non-aligned and disjointed activities and decisions. A number of approaches exist, largely discussing similar principles but espousing different thinking or activities as a purpose and way of developing this strategy. Two of these approaches are now examined and their potential usefulness to the NHS reflected upon. First, the Slack and Lewis operation strategy framework is shown in Figure 4.7. According to Slack and Lewis (2011), the application of an operations strategy should be central to senior managers.

To understand how an organisation works, they say, the interaction between all resources needs to be examined. In the context of the NHS, this framework is useful because it brings together the four views which encompass an organisation – operational resources, market requirements, operational experience and corporate strategy. Examination of each view exposes the dilemmas inherent within an organisation, notably the tension between market requirements and the operational response possible according to resource capabilities. Part of the 'content' of operations strategy is concerned with the organisation structure and the responsibility relations within the operations function. For a hospital this encompasses the complexities of the power relations already discussed between commissioners, clinicians and managers.

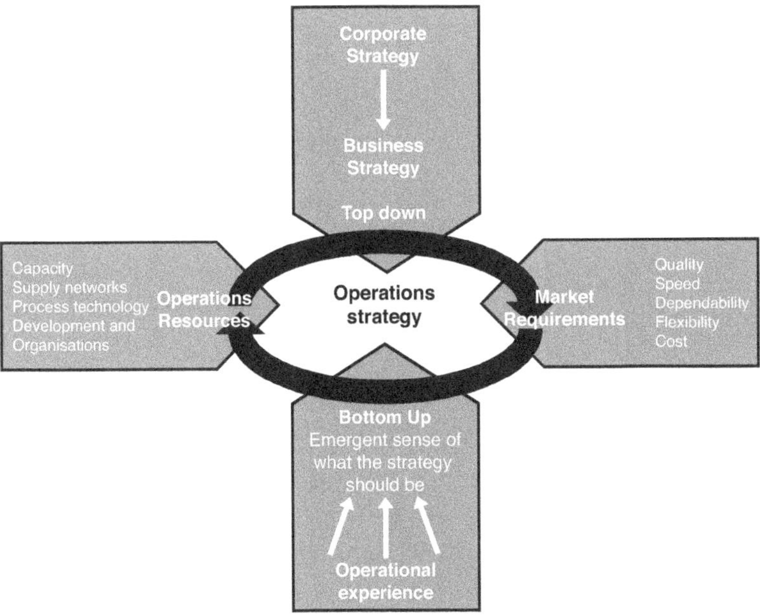

Figure 4.7 Operations strategy framework

Source: Slack and Lewis (2011: 2)

One of the problems with this framework for hospitals, or the NHS, is that it does not help identify what the priorities are and in what order they could be addressed. The diagram appears to show that everything should be treated equally at the same time. It is not clear whether it matters what we do, in what order and what the difference would be. Yet as Garvin (1992) and Ritchie (2002) have both stated, it is knowing the order of priority and the degree of emphasis to place on it that is critical if long-term success is to be achieved. The case presented confirms this, albeit through omission rather than commission. The potentially far-reaching development of new working-habits and the unlearning of some old working practices that could help deliver sustainable, accountable, patient-focused, quality healthcare was overlooked in favour of recognising an immediate performance indicator improvement.

The Sandcone model (Figure 4.8) is another way of developing an operation strategy. Unlike the Slack and Lewis approach, it provides an order for the journey of continuous improvement. Ferdows and de Meyer (1990) state that excellence is built on a common set of fundamental principles. The sand imagery is a stand-in for management effort and resources. The sequence represents building a stable foundation which as you continue to pour sand you move up the path towards the development of lasting organisational capabilities, needing exponentially more effort

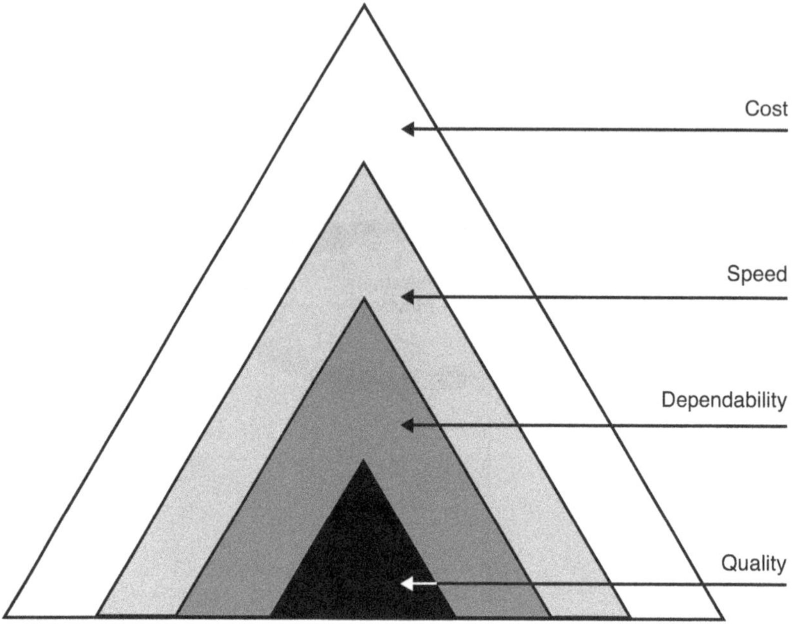

Figure 4.8 The sandcone model

Source: Ferdows and de Meyer (1990: 175)

and therefore a broader foundation as you move up through the steps. The sequence outlined helps organisations achieve substance and not just form. Cost is last not because cost improvements are an ultimate consequence of resources and management efforts invested in the improvement of quality, dependability and speed.

The NH case appears to conform to this view in that the Ward had shown service quality improvements, in patient-centric and target-compliance terms, due to its clear goal of MRSA infection-rate reduction. Where it falls is in the ensuing expansion and enrichment, since there is no evidence the gains were leveraged. This is an important point to emphasise, given the literature on lean in healthcare in the main seems to demonstrate that seeking 'low-hanging fruit' seems widespread while lasting cultural improvement is scant. The NH case appears also to confirm that in the NHS form seems to be a more significant driver than substance, with the short-term goal being given more emphasis than the potential benefit of exponential gain through cultural changes leading to the embedding of new working practices.

Speed refers to elapsed service provision time and responsiveness, which provides an organisation with flexibility – and thereby further enhanced performance. For patients, responsiveness and elapsed time are key features of the functional quality they perceive and receive. This is core to the idea of 'sustainable patient value', as espoused by NH management, yet the core pursuit was conformance to centrally set targets.

Improvements obtained in this way are more stable and likely to be more sustainable because they emerged as a result of the deeper penetration of good management practices. This is difficult at the best of times and tantamount to impossible if management effort and resources are focused on fulfilling a frequently-changing government agenda rather than on developing lasting organisational capabilities. If 'low hanging fruit' in the form of the meeting of centrally-set targets is the constant goal, then the more lasting operational successes achievable through holistic, organisational continuous improvement as advocated by the Sandcone concept will always remain a chimera.

The advantage of this model seems to be that it encourages the development and nurturing of organisational capabilities cumulatively, which appears to imply they will be more deeply ingrained and therefore longer lasting. Through its cumulative principles it takes into account the trade-off concept, suggesting the specific pattern of capability enhancement incorporates relevant trade-offs as the organisation moves up the pyramid.

Conclusion

The main contribution of this chapter is the consideration that an operation strategy developed specifically for Healthcare could lead to a holistic continuous improvement ethos. Lean addresses whole organisational issues, but its application in Healthcare precludes this. The tools of lean when used in isolation tend to address single-problem events and ignore the centrality of the customer. It was the centrality of the customer to a single-issue event which drove NH and NSHA management to engage consultants. The over-riding theme from staff was the requirement for greater clarity and consistency of leadership across the organisation. External stakeholder concerns were about inconsistency of service quality and delivery. This combination emphasises the 'patient-led' perspective, and the need for multi-functional teams, balancing patient experience with clinical safety and providing a common organisational goal. At NH, embedding changes into everyday working practices appears to have diluted organisation-wide action, resulting in keeping the changes isolated within one ward.

In line with an estimated 90 per cent of work within the NHS (Cannon, 2013), the NH consulting intervention was driven by failure-demand – the non-achievement of MRSA targets. This implies implying management emphasis on target-fulfilment, showing an internal, not customer, focus. As Radnor *et al.* (2012), Millard (2011) and Cannon (2013) state, success lies in patient-centred understanding of delivery and waste. Adopting an organisation strategy approach, like adopting lean, means changing how an organisation works. An operation strategy tries to prevent non-aligned, disjointed activities and decisions while allowing for local variations. It means developing new habits, skills and attitudes to reduce boundaries within and across organisations and organisational members, as happened in the ward at NH. Organising to deliver that is what an operations strategy can help achieve.

Service quality in a hospital is not just about reaching targets set by a central government department; it is about ensuring that the patient experience is consistent throughout a stay while nevertheless delivering a successful clinical outcome. This is probably achieved in the main throughout the NHS but the creation of an operation strategy would demonstrate a tangible audit trail from inception to implementation, showing patient value to all its stakeholders.

References

Anderson, S., Pearo, L.K. and Widener, S.,K. (2008) 'Drivers of service satisfaction'. *Journal of Service Research*, 10(4): 365–81.

Andreasen, A.R. and Kotler, P. (2003) *Strategic Marketing for Nonprofit Organizations.* Upper Saddle River, NJ: Prentice Hall.

Antony, J., Downey-Ennis, K., Antony, F. and Seow, C. (2007) 'Can Six Sigma be the "cure" for our "ailing" NHS?' *Leadership in Health Services*, 20(4): 242–53.

Berry, L.L. (2004) 'The collaborative organization: leadership lessons from Mayo Clinic'. *Organizational Dynamics*, 33(3): 228–42.

Berry, L.L. and Bendapudi, N. (2007) 'Health care: a fertile field for service research'. *Journal of Service Research*, 10(2): 111–22.

Boaden, R. (2009) 'Quality improvement: theory and practice'. *British Journal of Healthcare Management*, 15(1): 12–16.

Burgess, N. (2012). 'Evaluating Lean in healthcare'. Doctor of Philosophy in Business, University of Warwick.

Burgess, N. and Radnor, Z.J. (2012) 'Service improvement in the English National Health Service: complexities and tensions'. *Journal of Management and Organization*, 18(5): 594–607.

Cannon, M. (2013) '12 words to transform the NHS – part 3'. Retrieved from http://well being.vanguard-method.com/2012/12/20/12-words-to-transform-the-nhs-part-3 (accessed 23 June 2015).

Cullen, R., Nicholls, S. and Halligan, A. (2000) 'Reviewing a service – discovering the unwritten rules'. *British Journal of Clinical Governance*, 5(4): 233–39.

Currie, G. and Lockett, A. (2011) 'Distributing leadership in health and social care: concertive, conjoint or collective?' *International Journal of Management Reviews*, 13(3): 286–300.

Currie, G. and Suhomlinova, O. (2006) 'The impact of institutional forces upon knowledge sharing in the UK NHS: the triumph of professional power and the inconsistency of policy'. *Public Administration*, 84(1): 1–30.

Currie, G., Waring, J. and Finn, R. (2008) 'The limits of knowledge management for UK public services modernization: the case of patient safety and service quality'. *Public Administration*, 86(2): 363–85.

Dale, B.G., Williams, A.R.T., Van der Wiele, T. and Greatbanks, R. (2002) 'Organizational change through quality deposits'. *Quality Engineering*, 14(3): 381.

Department of Health (2006) *Mandatory Surveillance of Healthcare Associated Infections Report 2006.* London: Health Protection Agency.

Esain, A., Williams, S.J. and Massey, L. (2008) 'Combining planned and emergent change in a healthcare lean transformation'. *Public Money and Management*, 28(1): 21–6.

Ferdows, K. and De Meyer, A. (1990) 'Lasting improvements in manufacturing performance: in search of a new theory'. *Journal of Operations Management*, 9(2): 168–84.

Garvin, D.A. (1992) *Operation Strategy: Text and Cases.* London: Prentice Hall.

Glouberman, S. and Mintzberg, H. (2001) 'Managing the care of health and the cure of disease – part I: differentiation'. *Health Care Management Review*, 26(1): 56.

Goldstein, S.M., Ward, P.T., Leong, G.K. and Butler, T.W. (2002) 'The effect of location, strategy, and operations technology on hospital performance'. *Journal of Operations Management*, 20(1): 63–75.

Graban, M. and Swartz, J.E. (2012) 'Change for health'. *Management Services*, 56(2): 35–9.

Graban, M., Nexus, K. and Swartz, J. (2012) 'Feel human again'. *ASQ Six Sigma Forum Magazine*, 12(1): 16–20.

Groonroos, C. (2007) *Service Management and Marketing; Customer Management in Service Competition*. Chichester: John Wiley.

Johnston, R., Clark, G. and Shulver, M. (2012) *Service Operations Management: Improving Service Delivery*. Harlow: Pearson Education.

Karp, T. and Helgø, T. (2008) 'From change management to change leadership: embracing chaotic change in public service organizations'. *Journal of Change Management*, 8(1): 85–96.

Klein, R. (2010) *The New Politics of the NHS: From Creation to Reinvention*. Oxford: Radcliffe Publishing.

Krafcik, J.F. (1988) 'Triumph of the Lean production system'. *Sloan Management Review*, 30(1): 41–52.

Mazzocato, P., Savage, C., Brommels, M., Aronsson, H. and Thor, J. (2010) 'Lean thinking in healthcare: a realist review of the literature'. *Quality and Safety in Health Care*, 19(5): 376–82.

Millard, W.B. (2011) 'If Toyota ran the ED: what Lean management can and can't do'. *Annals of Emergency Medicine*, 57(6): A13–17.

Mintzberg, H. (1983) *Structure in Fives: Designing Effective Organisations*. Englewood Cliffs, NJ: Prentice-Hall.

NHS Plan (2000) *NHS Plan: A Plan for Investment, a Plan for Reform*. London: Department of Health.

Nicholls, S., Cullen, R., O'Neill, S. and Halligan, A. (2000) 'Clinical governance: its origins and its foundations'. *British Journal of Clinical Governance*, 5(3): 172–8.

Papadopoulos, T., Radnor, Z.J. and Merali, Y. (2011) 'The role of actor associations in understanding the implementation of Lean thinking in healthcare'. *International Journal of Operations and Production Management*, 31(2): 167–91.

Patwardhan, A. and Patwardhan, D. (2008) 'Business process re-engineering – saviour or just another fad?' *International Journal of Health Care Quality Assurance*, 21(3): 289–96.

Radnor, Z.J. and Osborne, S.P. (2013) 'Lean: a failed theory for public services?' *Public Management Review*, 15(2): 265–87.

Radnor, Z.J., Holweg, M. and Waring, J. (2012) 'Lean in healthcare: the unfilled promise?' *Social Science and Medicine*, 74(3): 364–71.

Ritchie, L. (2002) 'Driving quality – clinical governance in the National Health Service'. *Managing Service Quality*, 12(2): 117–28.

Seddon, J. and Caulkin, S. (2007) 'Systems thinking, Lean production and action learning'. *Action Learning: Research and Practice*, 4(1): 9–24.

Slack, N. and Lewis, M. (2011) *Operation Strategy*. Harlow: Pearson.

Smith, P.C. (2002) 'Performance management in British health care: will it deliver?' *Health Affairs*, 21(3): 103–15.

Toussaint, J.S. and Berry, L.L. (2013) 'The promise of Lean in health care'. *Mayo Clinic Proceedings*, 88(1): 74–82.

Towill, D.R. (2009) 'Gerry Robinson and the UK NHS: did he really make a difference?' *Leadership in Health Services*, 22(1): 76–85.

Umble, M. and Umble, E.J. (2006) 'Utilizing buffer management to improve performance in a healthcare environment'. *European Journal of Operational Research*, 174(2): 1060–75.

Waring, J.J. and Bishop, S. (2010) 'Lean healthcare: rhetoric, ritual and resistance'. *Social Science and Medicine*, 71(7): 1332–40.

Note

1 MRSA is methicillin-resistant *Staphylococcus aureus*, a bacterial infection resistant to many widely-used antibiotics. It spreads in crowded environments where there is frequent skin-to-skin contact, making it more common in people who are in hospital or nursing homes.

5 Humanitarian aid logistics

A new area for the public service research agenda?

Stephen Pettit, Anthony Beresford, David Knight and Minchul Sohn

Introduction

Context

There has been a considerable amount of research into how commercial organisations respond to fluctuations or uncertainty in their supply chains (Lin *et al.*, 2006). In the humanitarian context, research has been more limited; however, some authors have suggested that the application of lean or agile principles may help humanitarian inter-organisational networks to become more responsive to the disruptions and to imbalances in both supply and demand (Scholten *et al.*, 2010; Oloruntoba and Gray, 2006). Charles *et al.* (2010), for instance, also argue 'by constantly working in environments with high degrees of uncertainty, humanitarian organisations end up becoming specialists in the implementation of agile systems'. Similarly, as Tatham and Pettit (2010) explain 'the application of commercial supply network management theory and practice has received limited consideration within humanitarian logistics literature to date'. Therefore, a deeper investigation into the potential improvements in efficiency and effectiveness that commercial business concepts offer to humanitarian logistics is needed.

Problem

The problem in humanitarian aid (HA) distribution is that it is at an extreme end of 'public service' i.e. the recipients have few, if any financial or other resources and, crucially, they do not pay for the goods or services provided. When major physical events or political disturbances occur, a number of key questions arise: What type and form of human response is required? What level of resource commitment will be needed from the perspectives of both supra national agencies (UNHCR, WFP, etc.), governments and relevant non-governmental organisations (NGOs)? Lastly, how should the resource, either through practical help or material aid provision in some form, be delivered? Many of the issues surrounding the response of these various inter-organisational networks relate to the need to supply some form of aid to difficult, remote or unstable locations and to the processes required to deliver that aid to the beneficiaries. The response is likely to take place in an environment which is in some way volatile, whether that is an unsafe natural environment (risk of continuing flooding, volcanic activity etc.) or a man-made crisis such as war or civil strife. Such situations equate in some way to the commercial business environment. While many inter-organisational networks operate in relatively stable environments, like natural disasters, business can also face volatile and unpredictable environments.

Contribution

This chapter therefore discusses the shortcomings of HA logistics in response to natural disasters and provides an analysis of whether the concept of supply chain agility is appropriate in such turbulent or unstable environments. The overall objective of the chapter is to highlight the adjustments required in HA supply chains to suit need over very short timescales up to the point when activity moves from emergency response to rebuilding and, subsequently, to what is termed development aid. Further, it aims to highlight the logistics challenges involved in responses to natural disasters and to analyse the applicability of commercial logistics/supply chain management (SCM) concepts in humanitarian situations.

Background

Recent events suggest that natural disasters are increasing in frequency and that no major region is immune to this trend. While the majority of disasters have been in third world countries, Hurricane Katrina in the USA (2005), the Australian floods (2010–11), the T hoku earthquake/tsunami in Japan (2011) and Super-storm Sandy in the USA (2012) all highlight that even first world countries are susceptible. Natural disasters are uncertain by their nature, especially in terms of their timing, location and scale and it is therefore difficult for HA agencies to be completely ready for them (Holguin-Veras *et al.*, 2012a; Kovács and Spens, 2007). Severe problems can therefore occur in the provision of aid and its delivery, especially when the political environment is also unstable or authoritarian or where the physical environment is under stress. When a humanitarian crisis has its origins in civil unrest or war the logistics of aid provision becomes even more complex and solutions even more difficult and fragile. The 'Arab Spring' uprisings and, most recently, the instability in Syria and northern Iraq, have highlighted the need for appropriate and well-targeted HA logistical response.

Both governments and donor agencies continuously demand greater accountability, financial efficiency, and operational transparency from humanitarian organisations or from the partnerships within HA inter-organisational networks (Scholten *et al.*, 2010; Oloruntoba and Gray, 2009; Olsen *et al.*, 2003). Hofmann *et al.* (2004) indicate that such controls are required to an even greater extent for the humanitarian sector to assess their performance and impact, as a part of a broader results-based management culture. Hence HA organisations are keen to satisfy donors' interests and requirements to compete for the limited funding resources (Pettit and Beresford, 2009; Jahre and Heigh, 2008). Also, as Kovács and Spens (2009) have argued, some of the features which are interchangeable with commercial business practices, such as agility, responsiveness, risk management, and economic significance, might have stimulated the interest of business academics. However, the interest has been particularly centred on emergency, crisis and relief aid.

In order to gain up-to-date insights into emergency HA logistics response, a qualitative field study utilising semi-structured interviews (first stage) and questionnaires (second stage) targeted at emergency logisticians and directors in 10 HA organisations was conducted. The interviewees included NGO strategists as well as logisticians at an operational level. The second-stage questionnaire consisted of twenty one open-ended questions addressing general, operational and strategic activities within the organisation.

Humanitarian aid and development aid

In order to understand what HA is, three main humanitarian principles, need to be considered – humanity, neutrality and impartiality (OCHA, 2010):

- *Humanity*: Human suffering must be addressed wherever it is found, with particular attention to the most vulnerable in the population. This can be extended as the humanitarian imperative, which includes the right to receive and right to give humanitarian assistance.
- *Neutrality*: HA must not favour any side in an armed conflict or other dispute.
- *Impartiality*: HA must be provided solely on the basis of need, without discrimination between or within affected populations.

These principles provide an ethical framework that defines the 'humanitarian space'. The term 'humanitarian space' indicates 'a conducive humanitarian operating environment' within which humanitarian organisations are supposed to undertake the 'humanitarian action' (Volberg, 2006; OCHA, 2003; Mackintosh, 2000; IFRC, 1995). Then, what does 'humanitarian action' mean? The *Oxford English Dictionary* defines `'humanitarian' as 'concerned with reducing suffering and improving the conditions that people live in'. More precisely, a humanitarian crisis is described as 'an event or situation that causes or involves widespread human suffering, especially one which requires the large-scale provision of aid'.

From the above definition and principles, it can be taken that HA refers to logistical assistance of goods and services, or the provision of funds supporting the logistical assistance that is devoted to improvement of the people's circumstances. However, there is no single agreement internationally about what comprises HA (HPN, 2002). Thus, rather than trying to give a narrow definition, it is more useful to present some examples from various organisations. The HA department of the European Commission (ECHO) states in its Council Regulations that:

> Humanitarian aid, the sole aim of which is to prevent or relieve suffering, is accorded to victims without discrimination on the grounds of race, ethnic

> group, religion, sex, age, nationality or political affiliation and must not be guided by, or subject to, political considerations.
>
> (ECHO, 1996)

The UN High Commissioner for Refugees (UNHCR) defines HA as:

> Addressing the immediate needs of individuals affected by crises and is provided mainly by non-governmental and international organisations.
>
> (UNHCR, 2006)

While HA is traditionally seen as short-term (GHA, 2010), the report from the Development Assistance Committee (DAC) of the Organisation for Economic Co-operation and Development (OECD) explains HA as:

> A sector of Official Development Assistance (ODA) that includes disaster prevention and preparedness, reconstruction relief, relief coordination, protection and support service, emergency food aid and other emergency/distress relief.
>
> (OECD, 2011)

The perspective of DAC is broad, such that HA would not remain limited to disaster or emergency relief. Depending on the time-frame of aid provision, the characteristics of aid could be varied. Similarly some research has been described disaster relief management as a process with several stages (Kovács and Spens, 2007, 2009; Van Wassenhove, 2006; Nisha de Silva, 2001; Long, 1997). In their discussions, the activity phases that are subsequent to a particular disaster, either man-made or natural, can be denoted as reconstruction, rehabilitation, or even development (Pettit and Beresford, 2005; Ludema, 2000). In general, however, development aid differs from HA. Development aid is pre-planned and in the form of longer-term programmes that encompass both identified short/medium-term outcomes and targets relating to a long-term process of structural societal transformation (Sumner and Tribe, 2008). Development aid is aimed at achieving sustainable well-being for all, with capability enhancement and livelihood improvement based on the concept of partnership, at its core (Chambers, 2003). Such programmes mainly strive for poverty reduction, health improvement, and economic growth (Martinussen and Pedersen, 2003).

The transition from emergency HA delivery to development aid provision should be viewed in this context. The European Union has proposed that this transition period should be seen as 'linking relief, rehabilitation and development', or simply as a 'grey zone' (Europa, 2007). Figure 5.1 represents the spectrum of both humanitarian and development aid, while indicating the possible inclusion of two different aid periods as the 'grey zone'. Different disaster phases, such as disaster preparedness, response, recovery, rehabilitation and development, from the humanitarian logistics literature can also be identified on this horizontal time-line. From this perspective, it is possible to assume that HA provision is much wider in scope than merely an emergency relief operation alone. In fact a substantial body of humanitarian logistics literature has been focused on disaster-related issues from either a theoretical or practical standpoint (Holguin-Veras *et al.*, 2013; Chandes and Paché, 2010; McClintock, 2009; Kovács and Spens, 2007, 2009; Van Wassenhove, 2006; Pettit and Beresford, 2005). Specific papers on earthquakes (Beresford and Pettit, 2010; Gatignon *et al.*, 2010); tsunamis (Beresford and Pettit, 2009; Regnier *et al.*, 2008; Perry, 2007) and conflict and complex emergencies (Holguin-Veras *et al.*, 2012b; Beamon and Kotleba, 2006) also provide valuable insights gleaned from particular events. Some attempts to apply commercial business logistics and SCM concepts to humanitarian logistics have also been made (Scholten *et al.*, 2010; Blecken, 2010; Taylor and Pettit, 2009; Pettit and Beresford, 2009; Beamon and Balcik, 2008; Oloruntoba and Gray, 2006). An interesting case study was presented by Choi *et al.* (2010), which highlights the dilemma faced by logistics service providers (LSPs) operating in extreme, or very stressed, environments. The study shows that there is a complex interplay between not-for-profit organisations (e.g. the NGOs such as Médecins Sans Frontières and the World Food Programme) and the LSPs who provide much of the transport capability on the ground and charge on a 'cost-plus plus' basis for their services. The LSPs typically aim to cover their cost and the risk and uncertainty element by levying an above-market rate during crisis periods. This approach also enables the LSPs to absorb dramatic fluctuations in demand for capacity in transport provision, storage and other activities. The standard business model therefore temporarily breaks down in order to cope with the extreme operating environment. By implication the 'lean versus agile' paradigm is, in turn, tested by these extreme conditions.

The overlap between HA distribution and commercial logistics principles can be seen in the work of Thomas and Mizushima (2005) who have defined humanitarian logistics as 'the process of planning, implementing, and controlling the efficient, cost-effective flow and storage of goods and materials, as well as related information, from point of origin to point of consumption for the purpose of meeting the end beneficiary's requirements'. This definition can clearly be applied to logistics and

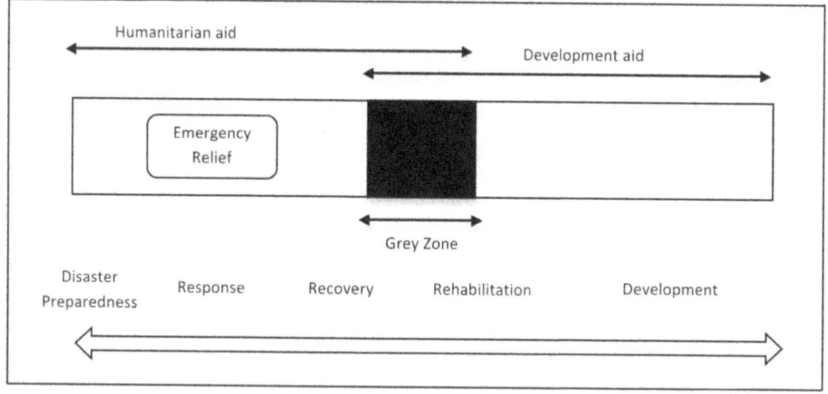

Figure 5.1 The spectrum of humanitarian and development aid and disaster phases

Source: adapted from Europa (2007)

SCM activities and processes in development aid provision as well as to commercial or business environments.

In this regard, research on HA logistics and SCM can possibly be extended towards the 'grey zone', where aspects and activities such as post-disaster rehabilitation and enhancement of warning systems are found. Furthermore, the current HA logistics discussion may be broadened to include logistics and SCM in long-term development aid provision. Ellis (2011) has also argued that supply chain discipline can be applied to 'everyday' disasters such as those involving simply impoverished and deprived people in developing countries. In any event, the supply chain, as configured, must satisfy certain key requirements, notably responsiveness and flexibility, aspects which have been addressed, especially in the lean and agile concepts.

Lean or agile?

In a commercial context. Naylor *et al.* (1999) define agility as 'using market knowledge and a virtual corporation to exploit profitable opportunities in a volatile market place'. Christopher and Towill (2001) argue it is 'a business-wide capability that embraces organisational structures, information systems, logistics processes and, in particular, mindsets'. Although there is clearly no single definition for supply chain agility, Charles *et al.* (2010) stress that 'from an academic point of view, supply chain agility is becoming a major field of research'. Power (2005) supports this and states that 'the requirement for organisations to become more responsive to the needs of customers, the changing conditions of competition and increasing levels of environmental turbulence is driving interest in the concept of "agility"'.

According to Power *et al.* (2001), agility evolved from flexible manufacturing systems, which captured the integration of the organisation's suppliers, business processes and customers as well as product use and disposal. Beresford *et al.* (2005) explain it is necessary to have excess capacity available within the supply chain in order to meet changing requirements while reducing inventory to a minimum. By having surplus capacity, HA inter-organisational networks are able to respond to changes in the market in the most responsive way. Christopher and Peck (2004) state that agility has many dimensions and a key to an agile response is to have agile partners along the supply chain. Power (2005) meanwhile asserts that 'the notion of agility is therefore recognised to be holistic rather than functional and of strategic rather than tactical importance'.

Christopher (2000) explains that, for a supply chain to be 'truly agile', it must have market sensitivity, as well as process and network integration. In order to achieve an agile supply chain, the key agencies must share information and knowledge with their suppliers and customers across common systems. Similarly, Power (2005) contends that this model assumes open relations between participants in the supply chain, the free sharing of information, and the use of technology to create connectivity. This allows organisations to share information in 'real time' which potentially optimises the overall performance of the supply chain.

An alternative supply chain strategy is based on 'lean thinking' which refers to creating a co-ordinated schedule with all chain segments operating at the same speed, thus minimising waste (Womack and Jones, 1996). Naylor *et al.* (1999) define leanness as 'developing a value stream to eliminate all waste, including time, and to ensure a level schedule'. It involves identifying what creates value and removing any activity that does not add value as perceived by the end customer. One potential problem with this approach is that, in emergency or humanitarian situations, the 'end customer' is unlikely to play a major role in feeding back value information. Beresford *et al.* (2005) contribute to this debate, suggesting that, although agility and lean are in some ways similar philosophies, 'there are nonetheless some differences between these two schools of thought'. Similarly, Mason-Jones *et al.* (2000) argue that lean works best when demand is known and stable; conversely, agility is suited to turbulent and fluctuating demand. However, in some circumstances it is prudent to employ both strategies on either side of a de-coupling point, thus facilitating the implementation of a total supply chain strategy.

While it may seem that lean and agile strategies fundamentally conflict, in reality many supply chains incorporate both lean and agile elements. Naylor *et al.* (1999) refer to this as 'leagility' and discusses a number of ways in which the two paradigms can be merged. The benefit of 'leagility' according to Beresford *et al.* (2005) is that 'this not only helps to minimise cost levels, but also enables the supply chain to be responsive to customer demands'. Childerhouse and Towill (2000) suggest that lean principles are best suited to stable and predictable demand; however, when a market is turbulent or uncertain, a hybrid strategy is necessary. Naylor *et al.* (1999) define leagile as:

> the combination of the lean and agile paradigms within a total supply chain strategy by positioning the decoupling point so as to best suit the need for responding to a volatile demand downstream yet providing level scheduling upstream from the marketplace.

Beresford *et al.* (2005) explain the decoupling point 'effectively separates the part of a supply chain driven by customer orders from the part based on forecast demand'. They propose that lean principles are decoupled at a point in the supply chain and combined with agility in order to increase responsiveness. In the case of HA supply chain structures, this could have important implications concerning, for example, warehouse locations for holding pre-positioned stock.

It has been suggested in previous research that HA inter-organisational networks are more suited to 'leagile' strategies. This is because of the increasing pressure on funding and the need to eliminate waste while providing rapid relief in response to natural disasters. Scholten *et al.* (2010) indeed argue that emergency relief supply chains can be cautiously described as 'leagile' as prepositioned stocks are decoupled in warehouses and once they leave these locations it operates in a responsive and agile way. The research indicates that a number of the organisations use prepositioned stock but keep this to a minimum and order goods that are not generic. As well as this, it is evident that stock is often customised after it leaves the warehouse in order to respond to individual needs; according to region, culture, religion, climate, etc. As suppliers do not have the capacity to respond rapidly to the demands associated with a quick-onset natural disaster, it is necessary to preposition long shelf life-stock, although it may not necessarily be cost effective to do so.

Leanness does not imply agility; however, an agile supply chain implies that many of the principles of lean have been adopted (*ibid.*). Mason-Jones *et al.* (2000) dictate that what constitutes 'waste' in a lean organisation maybe considered essential in an agile organisation, as eliminating too much slack can lead to decreased flexibility in operations. Christopher and Towill (2001) contend that 'lean methodologies can be a powerful contributor to the creation of agile enterprises'. Therefore it is important to consider 'leagile' strategies when implementing agility within an inter-organisational network (Mason-Jones *et al.*, 2000; Naylor *et al.*, 1999). Commercial SCM literature suggests that agility and the hybrid leagile strategies have allowed leading companies to handle demand uncertainty and volatility more effectively. On the one hand, it is suggested that HA inter-organisational networks are already agile and commercial business should take note of their capabilities. However, it is also argued that HA inter-organisational networks lack some of the fundamental characteristics that allow an agile supply chain to operate. It is therefore important to investigate the extent to which HA distribution structures are truly agile and to identify the most common barriers to the integration of agility within these organisations.

Key challenges in humanitarian aid logistics

Possible future research areas are suggested here under three headings:

- demand chain management;
- customer and market sensitivity; and
- information and communication technology.

Demand chain management

In distressed environments where humanitarian agencies operate there is a need for the most efficient and effective levels of response. Most consideration in the humanitarian literature has revolved around the application of SCM principles to the humanitarian space. While the phrase 'supply chain management' is widely used, Christopher (2011) suggests that the term 'demand chain management' could be used instead, in order to characterise the fact that the chain essentially begins from the market and customers, not from the suppliers. Holguin-Veras *et al.* (2012b) highlight the importance of 'knowledge of demand' in the decision making process. In the context of humanitarian environments, such an approach may provide a better understanding of how aid can be best provided to meet the requirements of the beneficiaries. In order to understand the demand chain approach, it is necessary to first examine how the concept was extended from the principles of SCM. For example, Holguin-Veras *et al.* (2013) resolve SCM into a series of objective functions which, combined with philosophical and behavioural considerations, enable cost and social cost estimations of a humanitarian crisis to be made.

It has been suggested that demand chain management does not deserve as much attention as SCM because the two approaches have no major differences between them. However, some authors argue that demand chain management is fundamentally different from SCM. Demand chain management embraces areas that were originally the domain of marketing. Customer value is derived from marketing activities enhancing value through their integration with SCM (Hilletofth and Ericsson, 2007; Jüttner *et al.*, 2007; Rainbird, 2004; Langabeer and Rose, 2001). While SCM focuses on efficient supply, marketing is concerned with identifying what customers value; in other words, marketing activities are centrally concerned with demand identification and creation (Hilletofth *et al.*, 2009). In humanitarian environments, the beneficiaries of aid (the customers) are arguably the more important consideration.

This approach is distinct from the traditional SCM concept and can be seen when the two different chains are presented side by side (Figure 5.2); the characteristics of each are clearly different. The supply-side approach is concerned with the efficient product configuration and cost-orientation while the demand-side

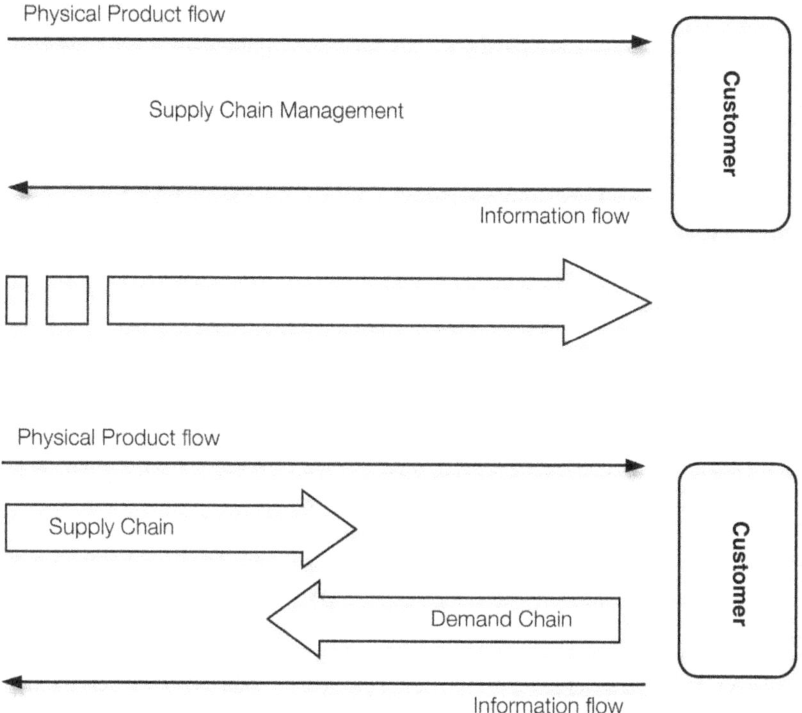

Figure 5.2 Traditional supply chain management versus demand chain and supply chain separation

Source: adapted from Jacobs (2006)

approach is comprised of all the activities necessary for creating and identifying demand (Hilletofth *et al.*, 2009; Walters, 2006). Langabeer and Rose (2001) provide a more detailed comparison of the characteristics of these two opposite flows (Table 5.1).

SCM is aimed at 'lowering the total amount of resources required to provide the necessary level of customer service' (Jones and Riley, 1985). Jüttner *et al.* (2007), however, argue that SCM focuses on the efficient matching of supply with demand while leaving behind the customer value and satisfaction. In demand chain management, customer requirements are a central issue as well as the starting point of system. Consideration of the needs of both the customer and the marketplace become the priority rather than pushing products and service forward from the supplier/-manufacturer (Heikkilä, 2002). Thus from demand chain management theory it can be deduced that it is important to recognise marketing activities such as market research and sales history analysis that identify and create customer value. Furthermore, it becomes possible, by focusing on demand chain management, for organisations to make the necessary synergies between marketing and SCM (Hilletofth *et al.*, 2009; Jüttner *et al.*, 2007; Walters, 2006). In the humanitarian context, although HA organisations or networks are not concerned with marketing in order to improve sales, they are clearly trying to achieve improved customer value through effective aid response. They are also very interested in concepts such as process review, continuous improvement and benchmarking, all of which have commercial origins. In some cases, this may involve complex cross-sectoral cooperation (Moan *et al.*, 2009). The importance of demand identification and creation can be found in the definitions of demand chain management that have been put forward in several ways (Table 5.2).

Table 5.1 A comparison of supply chain and demand chain objectives

Supply chain	*Demand chain*
Efficiency focus; cost per item	Effectiveness focus; customer-focused, product-market fit
Processes are focused on execution	Processes are focused more on planning and delivering value
Cost is the key driver	Cash flow and profitability are the key drivers
Short-term oriented, within the immediate and controllable future	Long-term oriented, within the next planning cycles
Typically the domain of tactical manufacturing and logistics personnel	Typically the domain of marketing, sales and strategic operations managers
Focuses on immediate resource and capacity constraints	Focuses on long term capabilities, not short term constraints
Historical focus on operations planning and controls	Historical focus on demand management and supply chain alignment

Source: adapted from Langabeer and Rose (2001)

Table 5.2 Demand chain management definitions

References	*Definition*
Hilletofth *et al.* (2009)	'The alignment of demand creation and demand fulfilment processes across functional, organisational, and inter-organisational boundaries'
Jacobs (2006)	'The chain of activities that communicates demand from market to suppliers'
Heikkilä (2002)	'Emphasis on the needs of the marketplace and designing the chain to satisfy these needs'
Hilletofth and Ericsson (2007)	'Not only with how to fulfil customer requirement, but also with how to identify and create consumer needs'
Selen and Soliman (2002)	'A set of practices aimed at managing and coordinating the whole demand chain, starting from the end customer and working backward to raw material supplier'
Langabeer and Rose (2001)	'Focus on creating demand strategy (what is optimal for each product-market?) and manage the entire organisation to meet this demand'

Many definitions of demand management presented in Table 5.2 have a resonance with the requirements of HA provision. When a crisis occurs, there is a need for an immediate understanding of the demand requirements and for the needs of those impacted to be quickly communicated to the aid agencies, a situation not dissimilar to that suggested by Jacobs (2006). Aid agencies have not generally considered logistics and SCM activities to be the highest priority, however their activities clearly relate to the approach outlined by Selen and Soliman (2002) where the customer is considered first and the demand chain is managed back to the supplier. Similarly, as Langabeer and Rose (2001) suggest, for commercial organisations a demand strategy focuses on the optimal situation for each product market and manages the organisation to meet this demand. From the point of view of aid agencies, the optimal situation is achieved by providing aid in the right form, at the right time and in the right place, essentially the same approach. The concept of agility is beneficial in situations where demand is not constant and could therefore create significant benefits both for HA organisations and those they seek to support them through aid provision.

Customer and market sensitivity

The research suggests that the supply chains of HA the inter-organisational networks observed meet the basic definitions of supply chain agility. This is evident as they are able to quickly establish their supply chains and mobilise staff, equipment and materials in response to natural disasters. However, when it comes to overarching supply chain strategies, there is considerable diversity among organisations; the extent to which they are employed and the general understanding of supply chain strategies available is also variable. The implication is that, in an HA logistics environment, demand chain management and SCM become blurred. Many of the organisations involved clearly face challenges and need to focus on their supply chain strategy, if indeed they have one. Some undoubtedly have no supply chain strategy and as a result they have thorough but cumbersome internal procurement policies and processes to deal with. These organisations are invariably reactive rather than proactive. In contrast, some organisations have several plans/strategies in place to deal with different scenarios (droughts, earthquakes, floods, cyclones, etc.). These cases highlight the importance of having the ability to approach a disaster with a broad degree of flexibility. They suggest that rather than a lean/agile strategy, a better description of their strategies would be a cost-effective and flexible approach. However, there was evidence of a leagile strategy in some responses: 'We now have a new global strategy for 2011–2016; it's all about being faster, cheaper and better' (regional logistics coordinator). This suggests that leagile tools and techniques could be involved as leagility 'not only helps to minimise cost levels as much as possible (cheaper) but enables the supply chain to be responsive to customer demands (faster and better)' (Beresford *et al.*, 2005). As Christopher and Tatham (2011) explain, there are a number of key prerequisites for an organisation to be agile. Agile organisations 'tend to exhibit certain characteristics; agility implies that they are demand or event driven, they are network based, they are process orientated and they are virtually integrated through shared information'.

'Agility implies that the supply chain is demand driven, reading and responding to real demand' (Scholten *et al.*, 2010). The research indicates that HA inter-organisational networks are primarily demand -driven. However, in most cases there is also a use of prepositioned stock. It is often argued that it has to be a mix due to the diverse nature of natural disasters and individuals' needs. Further, the interviewees explained that in emergencies prepositioned stock is not sufficient to supply all the items required and that it may not be appropriate to the needs of beneficiaries in a given emergency scenario. In terms of demonstrating sensitivity to cultural, religious and climate-related needs, some of the organisations show better awareness than others and hold prepositioned stock levels of items that are of equal importance to everyone. Other items held are basic necessities such as blankets, tents, jerry cans and so on, which do not need to be customised to individual needs. Many HA organisations have collected information on all major disasters for the last 20 years and use their previous experience to predict needs according to area/country, type of disaster and culture/religion of the locals. Organisations that display a leagile approach will use direct procurement as required for unusual items (e.g. fuel bowsers, boats, etc.), and the provision of goods, whether from stock or production, will be determined against need (or pull) rather than being forecast-based.

As mentioned previously, HA organisations and organisational networks follow a top-down approach and do not provide choice to consumers. The research also suggests that often not only are the products wrong, but the way in which they are distributed is incorrect, therefore, it is difficult to describe HA organisations as sensitive to their customers/markets. This opinion is shared by Scholten *et al.* (2010), who argue 'while the NGOs interviewed showed some sensitivity to the particular cultural, religious and climate-driven needs of aid recipients in different disaster areas, this falls short of the market sensitivity, required by agile supply chains'.

Information and communication technology: virtual, process and network integration

The improved flow of information through the effective use of information technology creates a strong probability for substantial improvement in demand chain effectiveness (Treville *et al.*, 2004; Langabeer and Rose, 2001). The use of information technology enables the direct capture of, and access to, the best data when demand arises (Christopher, 2011). It has been suggested that data capture is a key attribute for the transformation of the logistics function in cutting edge companies (Korhonen *et al.*, 1998). Through the use of information technology, data is shared and distributed between actors in the supply chain. Harrison *et al.* (1999) have articulated it as virtual supply chains that are information-based rather than inventory-based.

Power (2005) explains that in order for inter-organisational networks to be agile there needs to be significant use of technology to enable 'connectivity' (i.e. the ability for organisations to share information in 'real time'). This is supported by Oloruntoba and Gray (2006) who argue information technology is an essential enabler of agility. The research reveals that HA organisations support the role of ICT and technology but identify that in terms of logistics their systems are below the level they need to be at. However, the research also suggests that many of these organisations are currently assessing the best option due to the levels of investment required. Overall, the indications are that they not only realise the importance of better ICT, but that they are also actively seeking ways in which to improve. Gustavsson (2003) supports these findings and argues that due to the lack of investment in electronic infrastructure HA organisations suffer from increased time to handle information and process a shipment. It is argued that this leads to inefficiencies, duplication of functions, increased inaccuracies in reporting and increased costs. The lack of ICT and/or the constraints on ICT processes seem to be the biggest obstacle preventing them from meeting the definition of an agile supply chain. As stated by Scholten *et al.* (2010) 'this is expected to change over time as the development and implementation of the required technology and supporting systems drives the creation of virtual networks across global value chains, even in NGOs'. However, this can only occur when humanitarian donors fully appreciate the importance and value of providing resources for appropriate information systems and technologies.

The contention that successful emergency response hinges on information availability is supported by Christopher and Tatham (2011) who explain that there must be a corresponding level of connectivity for supply networks to achieve high levels of agility. Respondents highlighted the many layers of approval for the procurement of relief supplies and a lack of clear communication between procurement and logistics as a hindrance. When asked whether there was data sharing across the organisation and with suppliers the answers varied from: no data sharing to limited internal sharing to some sharing with suppliers, but more information than data. Many inter-organisational networks' ICT systems are not robust enough, with incompatibilities between partners within the network.

Many organisations still rely purely on paper and spreadsheet systems, virtual integration is, therefore, not an option. Further, some interviewees indicated that their organisations have not built the relationships necessary to achieve data sharing. Suppliers respond to their requests and are often treated to an adversarial style of contract management where failure to adhere to specification or quality requirements results in severe repercussions. Organisations that have worked on building relationships explain their supply chain is still some way off from being fully integrated but are optimistic. Christopher and Tatham (*ibid.*) make clear that the real challenge in becoming 'virtually integrated' is 'the reluctance that still exists within some inter-organisational networks to share information across boundaries – be these internal or external'. This is supported by the findings as some of the respondents suggest they would not want full information sharing as it would affect the transparency of vendor selection.

In order to achieve process integration there needs to be cooperation between all members of the supply chain as well as the elimination of any barriers obstructing the free flow of information/data. The clear pattern is that ICT systems are not advanced, or robust, enough to provide consistent, accurate real time information. Many find the idea of introducing vendor-managed inventory (VMI) an interesting one, but assert that suppliers and they themselves do not have the skills to introduce such systems. For a VMI system to work suppliers need to reliably provide goods and services, however 'often, due to cost or supply reasons, our vendors back out of their responsibilities and schedules' (head of logistics). Some HA organisations have introduced VMI into some aspects of their operations. They suggest the use of supplier stock in a response is common; however, the need to tailor packages and the economies of moving the combined goods needed rather than repeat sets of one good restrict the use of VMI. Christopher and Tatham (*ibid.*) argue it is critical that processes are aligned across organisational boundaries for a supply network to be effective across multiple units. They suggest that VMI is a good example of a concept that can enable this, therefore it is apparent that some of the inter-organisational networks are making significant inroads to achieving a higher level of process integration, however, it is also evident that suppliers are not always reliable enough.

Network integration assumes all members in the supply chain are involved and there is information sharing as well as transparency between them. Christopher and Tatham (*ibid.*) explain 'one way organisations can enhance their agility is by making use of the capacity, capabilities and resources of other entities within the network'. This revolves around the merging of individual supply chains into one holistic supply chain aligning all the echelons so as to maximise efficiency and also relies on them having a high degree of process integration. However, there is an apparent gap in the level to which HA organisations' and their suppliers cooperate. Indeed the majority of organisations argue that the biggest obstacle to achieving information sharing and transparency throughout their supply chains is 'the cluster system and the lack of desire to collaborate over supply chain practices and specification of goods' (logistics manager). Again this supports the findings of Scholten *et al.* (2010) that due to there being limited evidence of process integration, the foundation for network integration is absent among HA organisations.

Discussion

The challenge

In HA operations, the emphasis placed on logistics and SCM varies both between and within different organisations. The smaller organisations revealed they do not have a supply chain strategy in place, whereas larger organisations employ a number of strategies. These strategies are adapted and developed accordingly to best suit different scenarios. However, it is evident that none of them has taken a holistic view of their supply chain. Many have failed to recognise the importance of efficient collaboration among all members within their supply chains. It appears that logistics is seen from a functional perspective rather than a strategic one but, despite this, there is clear evidence of agility. Due to the characteristics of natural disasters, humanitarian organisations have, of necessity, developed some competencies in rapidly aligning their supply chains. Further, they are able to use market knowledge and logistical processes to be flexible in their responses to turbulent environments. However, their organisational structures and information systems are sometimes insufficiently developed to enable them to act as 'virtual corporations'.

While many of the organisations demonstrated agile capabilities, it is evident that it is common practice to hold prepositioned stock. It appears this is out of necessity as suppliers operating to commercial norms are ill-equipped to match surges in demand when natural disasters occur. It is evident also that humanitarian organisations and organisational networks lack the ICT capability to link together and that, in many cases, their suppliers often lack the capacity to meet such volatile demand requirements. As well as this, postponement principles are often used, as prepositioned stocks are customised according to, for example, region/climate/religion at the last minute before they are deployed. This suggests that a 'leagile' strategy is more useful, implementing lean principles upstream of the prepositioning point and agile principles downstream. This is becoming particularly important as donors are increasingly pressurising HA organisations to do more with less.

The research also revealed that there is comparatively little collaboration between HA organisations and suppliers (i.e. between participants within HA organisational networks). There was little evidence of strong relationships with suppliers (except in two organisations, and that was only for certain products with their most reliable suppliers). This, coupled with a lack of coordination with other HA organisations, acts as a significant barrier to process, virtual and network integration. Another barrier, and arguably the most significant, is a shortage of ICT and technology within HA operations. It is impossible for HA organisations to achieve the levels of integration required to be 'truly agile' without significant investment in their systems. A few of the bigger organisations have invested heavily and as a result have a better level of integration than the others. This has allowed them to introduce, for example, VMI in some form with success; however, they are far from being fully integrated. Without building relationships and an overall upgrade of the capability of all the supply chain members ICT systems, the benefit of one organisation in isolation investing is significantly reduced.

Nonetheless, it is clear that, although barriers still exist, some of the leading HA organisations and inter-organisational networks are becoming more agile, reconciling 'demand pull' with 'supply push' with some success. The biggest challenges currently being faced are a lack of investment in ICT, unreliable suppliers, and a lack of strong relationships with suppliers. The findings reveal that a significant problem area is a lack of coordination with other humanitarian bodies. It is evident that there is also a clear gap in the level of collaboration between supply chains members (suppliers, donors, etc.) which restricts the degree to which their supply chain is integrated. The majority of members (both large and small) exhibit many of the key characteristics of agile organisations. They are able to rapidly align their network and operations despite the volatile and turbulent environment in which they operate. Furthermore, there was frequent evidence of postponement, most commonly in the form of prepositioned stock. The popular practice is to hold generic stock and then customise 'last minute' to cater for individual needs. The organisations involved suggest their supply chains are predominately demand driven; however, prepositioned stock is used as suppliers can often be unreliable in crisis conditions and generally do not have the capacity to provide goods at very short notice on the 'just-in-time' principle. For unusual items that are very specific to certain disaster types, the organisations use direct procurement in order to rapidly respond.

The apparent increase in the frequency of at least natural disasters, and perhaps man-made emergencies, over recent years implies that intelligent structuring of supply chains, separating generic principles from customised elements, can only increase in importance. Better balancing 'supply push' with 'demand pull' activities, by maximum use of intelligence and appropriate business practices appears to be the way forward.

A new research agenda

Some of the specific areas where research could be fruitfully developed are highlighted below. The link between emergency or humanitarian logistics and lean thinking, for example, is under-explored and applying lean concepts to emergency or crisis events therefore offers several potential areas for future research. Specifically, strategic stock holding, quick response and needs assessment, just-in-time transport and emergency organisational structures all offer promising research opportunities. These areas have been identified both from the existing literature and the background research conducted for this chapter. This would suggest that there is scope for research in this area, which is, in effect the pursuit of a new service research agenda in the context of humanitarian or crisis environments. It is also in line with the thinking of Ostrom *et al.* (2010) who include the optimisation of service networks and value chains, and the improvement of well-being through transformative service in the list of research areas they propose. Both of these would appear to complement other future research fields such as HA delivery and emergency logistics.

A different approach is suggested by, for example, Schmenner (2012) who progresses the lean - agile debate by developing the concept of 'swift and even flow' in service delivery. The debate could be extended to examine the effectiveness of service provision in volatile circumstances and which could then feed back to inform commercial practitioners on strategy development. In this way commercial supply chain operations can potentially be improved by adopting relevant and appropriate HA service practices. Future research could also adopt a 'cross-sectoral' approach extending into other research areas where commonality exists, in order to best capture the full range of activities and processes involved. Examples of such areas could be: emergency health care, construction, information and communication technology and logistics and operations management. The above research propositions can be considered both as extensions of this study and within the wider context of public services operations. This latter field would enable, for example, case study based research to be tested against general principles of public service provision.

References

Beamon, B. and Balcik, B. (2008) 'Performance measurement in humanitarian relief chains'. *International Journal of Public Sector Management*, 21(1): 4–25.

Beamon, B. and Kotleba, S. (2006) 'Inventory management support systems for emergency humanitarian relief operations in South Sudan'. *International Journal of Logistics Management*, 17(2): 187–212.

Beresford, A. and Pettit, S. (2009) 'Emergency logistics and risk mitigation in Thailand following the Asian tsunami'. *International Journal of Risk Assessment and Management*, 13(1): 7–21.

Beresford, A. and Pettit, S. (2010) 'Humanitarian aid logistics: the Wenchuan and Haiti earthquakes compared'. In Kovács, G. and Spens, K.M. (eds), *Relief Supply Chain Management for Disasters: Humanitarian, Aid and Emergency Logistics.* Hershey, PA: IGI Global.

Beresford, A.K.C., Mason, R.J., Pettit, S.J. and Potter, A.T. (2005) *The Potential for Developing a London Gateway Logistics and Business Park.* Report for Baker Rose Consulting. Cardiff: Cardiff Business School, Cardiff University.

Blecken, A. (2010) 'Supply chain process modelling for humanitarian organizations'. *International Journal of Physical Distribution and Logistics Management*, 40(8–9): 675–92.

Chambers, R., (2003) *Whose Reality Counts? Putting the First Last.* London: ITDG.

Chandes, J. and Paché, G. (2010) 'Investigating humanitarian logistics issues: from operations management to strategic action'. *Journal of Manufacturing Technology Management*, 21(3): 320–40.

Charles, A., Lauras, M. and Wassenhove, L.V. (2010) 'A model to define and assess the agility of supply chains: building on humanitarian experience'. *International Journal of Physical Distribution and Logistics Management*, 40(8–9): 722–41.

Childerhouse, P. and Towill, D. (2000) 'Engineering supply chains to match customer requirements'. *Logistics Information Management*, 13(6): 337–45.

Choi, A. K-Y., Beresford, A.K.C., Pettit, S.J. and Bayusuf, F. (2010) 'Humanitarian Aid Distribution in East Africa, A study in supply chain volatility and fragility'. *Supply Chain Forum*, 11(3): 20–31.

Christopher, M. (2000) 'The agile supply chain – competing in volatile markets'. *Industrial Marketing Management*, 29(1): 37–44.

Christopher, M. (2011) *Logistics and Supply Chain Management* (4th edn). Harlow: Pearson.

Christopher, M. and Peck, H. (2004) 'Building the Resilient Supply Chain'. *International Journal of Logistics Management*, 15(2): 1–14.

Christopher, M. and Tatham, P. (2011) *Humanitarian Logistics: Meeting the Challenge of Preparing for and Responding to Disasters*. London: Kogan Page.

Christopher, M. and Towill, D. (2000) 'Supply chain migration from lean and functional to agile and customised'. *International Journal of Supply Chain Management*, 5(4): 206–13.

Christopher, M. and Towill, D. (2001) 'An integrated model for the design of agile supply chains'. *International Journal of Physical Distribution and Logistics Management*, 31(4): 235–46.

ECHO (1996) Council Regulation (EC) No 1257/96 of 20 June 1996 concerning humanitarian aid.

Ellis, D. (2011) 'The supply network's role as an enabler of development'. In Christopher, M. and Tatham, P. (eds), *Humanitarian Logistics*. London: Kogan Page.

Europa (2007) 'Linking relief, rehabilitation and development (LRRD)'. Retrieved from http://eur-lex.europa.eu/legal-content/EN/TXT/?qid=1412594055068&uri=CELEX:52001DC0153 (accessed 15 December 2014).

Gatignon, A., Van Wassenhove, L.N. and Charles, A. (2010) 'The Yogyakarta earthquake: humanitarian relief through IFRC's decentralized supply chain'. *International Journal of Production Economics*, 126: 102–10.

GHA (2010) *GHA Report 2010*. Wells: GHA.

Gustavsson, L. (2003) 'Humanitarian logistics: context and challenges'. *Forced Migration Review*, 18: 6–8.

Harrison, A., Christopher, M. and Van Hoek, R. (1999) *Creating the Agile Supply Chain*. Working Paper. Cranfield: School of Management, Cranfield University.

Heikkilä, J. (2002) 'From supply to demand chain management: efficiency and customer satisfaction'. *Journal of Operations Management*, 20: 747–67.

Hilletofth, P. and Ericsson, D. (2007) 'Demand chain management: next generation of logistics management?' *Conradi Research Review*, (2): 1–18.

Hilletofth, P., Ericsson, D. and Christopher, M. (2009) 'Demand chain management: a Swedish industrial case study'. *Industrial Management and Data Systems*, 109(9): 1179–96.

Hofmann, C.A., Roberts, L., Shoham, J. and Harvey, P. (2004) *Measuring the Impact of Humanitarian Aid: A Review of Current Practice*. HPG Research Report 17. London: ODI.

Holguin-Veras, J., Jaller, M. and Wachtendorf, T. (2012a) 'Comparative performance of alternative humanitarian logistics structures after the Port-au-Prince earthquake: ACEs, PIEs and CANs'. *Transportation Research Part A*, 46: 1623–40.

Holguin-Veras, J., Jaller, M., Van Wassenhove, L.N., Perez, N. and Wachtendorf, T. (2012b) 'On the unique features of post-disaster humanitarian logistics'. *Journal of Operations Management*, 30: 494–506.

Holguin-Veras, J., Perez, N., Jaller, M., Van Wassenhove, L.N. and Aros-Vera, F. (2013) 'On the appropriate objective function for post-disaster humanitarian logistics models'. *Journal of Operations Management*, 31: 262–80.

HPN (2002) *Legislating for Humanitarian Aid*. Retrieved from www.odihpn.org/report.asp?id=2462 (accessed 15 December 2014).

IFRC (1995) *The Code of Conduct for the International Red Cross and Red Crescent Movement and NGOs in Disaster Relief*. Annex VI to the resolutions of the 26th International Conference of the Red Cross and Red Crescent, Geneva.

Jacobs, D. (2006) 'The promise of demand chain management in fashion'. *Journal of Fashion Marketing and Management*, 10(1): 84–96.

Jahre, M. and Heigh, I. (2008) 'Does the current constraints in funding promote failure in humanitarian supply chains?' *Supply Chain Forum*, 9(2): 48–54.

Jones, T. and Riley, D. (1985) 'Using inventory for competitive advantage through supply chain management'. *International Journal of Physical Distribution and Materials Management*, 15(5): 16–26.

Jüttner, U., Christopher, M. and Baker, S. (2007) 'Demand chain management-integrating marketing and supply chain management'. *Industrial Marketing Management*, 36(3): 377–92.

Korhonen, P., Huttunen, K. and Eloranta, E. (1998) 'Demand chain management in a global enterprise – information management view'. *Production Planning and Control*, 9(6): 526–31.

Kovács, G. and Spens, K. (2007) 'Humanitarian logistics in disaster relief operations'. *International Journal of Physical Distribution and Logistics Management*, 37(2): 99–114.

Kovács, G. and Spens, K. (2009) 'Identifying challenges in humanitarian logistics'. *International Journal of Physical Distribution and Logistics Management*, 39(6): 506–28.

Langabeer, J. and Rose, J. (2001) *Creating Demand Driven Supply Chains*. Oxford: Chandos.

Lin, C.T., Chiu, H. and Chu, P.Y. (2006) 'Agility index in the supply chain'. *International Journal of Production Economics*. 100(2): 285–99.

Long, D. (1997) 'Logistics for disaster relief: engineering on the run'. *IIE Solutions*, 29(6): 26–9.

Ludema, M. (2000) 'Military and civil logistic support of humanitarian relief operations'. In Arnold, E. and Walden, D. (eds), *A Decade of Progress – A New Century of Opportunity, Proceedings of the 10th Annual International Symposium of the International Council on Systems Engineering*, pp. 143–50. Minneapolis, MN: INCOSA.

Mackintosh, K. (2000) *The Principles of Humanitarian Action in International Humanitarian Law*. HPG Report 5, March. London: Overseas Development Institute.

McClintock, A. (2009) 'The logistics of humanitarian emergencies: notes from the field'. *Journal of Contingencies and Crisis Management*, 17(4): 295–302.

Martinussen, J.D. and Pedersen, P.E. (2003) *Aid: Understanding International Development Cooperation*. London: Zed Books.

Mason-Jones, R., Naylor, B. and Towill, D. (2000) 'Lean, agile or leagile? Matching our supply chain to the marketplace'. *International Journal of Production Research*, 38(17): 4061–70.

Moan, F., Lindgreen, A. and Vanhamme, J. (2009) 'Developing supply chains in disaster relief operations through cross-sector socially oriented collaborations: a theoretical model'. *Supply Chain Management*, 14(2): 149–64.

Naylor, J.B., Naim, M.M. and Berry, D. (1999) 'Leagility: integrating the lean and agile manufacturing paradigms in the total supply chain'. *International Journal of Production Economics*, 62: 107–18.

Nisha de Silva, F. (2001) 'Providing spatial decision support for evacuation planning: a challenge in integrating technologies'. *Disaster Prevention and Management*, 10(1): 11–20.

OCHA (2003) *Glossary of Humanitarian Terms: In Relation to the Protection of Civilians in Armed Conflict*. New York: United Nations.

OCHA (2010) *OCHA on Message: Humanitarian Principles*. New York: United Nations. Retrieved from http://ochanet.unocha.org/p/Documents/OOM_HumPrinciple_English.pdf (accessed 15 December 2014)

OECD (2011) 'Glossary'. Retrieved from www.oecd.org/document/19/0,3746,en_2157 1361_39494699_39503763_1_1_1_1,00.html (accessed 15 December 2014).

Oloruntoba, R. and Gray, R. (2006) 'Humanitarian aid: an agile supply chain?' *Supply Chain Management*, 11(2): 115–20.

Oloruntoba, R. and Gray, R. (2009) 'Customer service in emergency relief chains'. *International Journal of Physical Distribution and Logistics Management*, 39(6): 486–505.

Olsen, G.R., Carstensen, N. and Høyen, K. (2003) 'Humanitarian crises: what determines the level of emergency assistance? Media coverage, donor interests and the aid business'. *Disasters*, 27: 109–26.

Ostrom, A.L., Bitner, M.J., Brown, S.W., Burkhard, K.A., Goul, M., Smith-Daniels, V., Demirkan, H. and Rabinovich, E. (2010) 'Moving forward and making a difference: research priorities for the science of service'. *Journal of Service Research*, 13(1): 4–36.

Perry, M. (2007) 'Natural disaster management planning: A study of logistics managers responding to the tsunami'. *International Journal of Physical Distribution and Logistics Management*, 37(5): 409–33.

Pettit, S. and Beresford, A. (2005) 'Emergency relief logistics: an evaluation of military, non-military, and composite response models'. *International Journal of Logistics: Research and Applications*, 8(4): 313–31.

Pettit, S. and Beresford, A.K.C. (2009) 'Critical success factors in the context of humanitarian aid supply chains'. *International Journal of Physical Distribution and Logistics Management*, 39(6): 450–68.

Power, D. (2005) 'Supply chain management integration and implementation: a literature review'. *International Journal of Supply Chain Management*, 10(4): 252–263.

Power, D., Sohal, A. and Rahman, S. (2001) 'Critical success factors in agile supply chain management'. *International Journal of Physical Distribution and Logistics Management*, 31(4): 247–65.

Rainbird, M. (2004) 'Demand and supply chains: the value catalyst'. *International Journal of Physical Distribution and Logistics Management*, 34(3): 230–50.

Régnier, P., Neri, B., Scuteri, S. and Miniati, S. (2008) 'From emergency relief to livelihood recovery: Lessons learned from post-tsunami experiences in Indonesia and India'. *Disaster Prevention and Management*, 17(3): 410–30.

Schmenner, R.W. (2012) *Getting and Staying Productive: Applying Swift, Even Flow to Practice.* Cambridge: Cambridge University Press.

Scholten, K., Scott, K.S. and Fynes, B. (2010) '(Le)agility in humanitarian aid (NGO) supply chains'. *International Journal of Physical Distribution and Logistics Management*, 40(8–9): 623–35.

Selen, W. and Soliman, F. (2002) 'Operations in today's demand chain management framework'. *Journal of Operations Management*, 20(6): 667–73.

Sumner, A. and Tribe, M. (2008) *International Development Studies: Theories and Methods in Research and Practice.* London: Sage.

Tatham, P.H. and Pettit, S.J. (2010) 'Transforming humanitarian aid logistics: the journey to supply network management'. *International Journal of Physical Distribution and Logistics Management*, 40(8–9): 609–22.

Taylor, D. and Pettit, S. (2009) 'A consideration of the relevance of lean supply chain concepts for humanitarian aid provision'. *International Journal of Services Technology and Management*, 12(4): 430–44.

Thomas, A. and Mizushima, M. (2005) 'Logistics training: necessity or luxury?' *Forced Migration Review*, 22: 60–61.

Treville, S., Shapiro, R. and Hameri, A. (2004) 'From supply chain to demand chain: the role of lead time reduction in improving demand chain performance'. *Journal of Operations Management*, 21: 613–27.

UNHCR (2006) *Master Glossary of Terms* (Revision 1). June. Geneva: UNHCR.

Van Wassenhove, L.N. (2006) 'Humanitarian Aid Logistics: supply chain management in high gear'. *Journal of the Operational Research Society*, 57(5): 475–589.

Volberg, T. (2006) 'The politicization of humanitarian aid and its effect on the principles of humanity, impartiality and neutrality'. European Master's Degree, Ruhr-University of Bochum. Retrieved from www.hapinternational.org/pool/files/politicizationofaid.pdf (accessed 27 August 2014).

Walters, D. (2006) 'Demand chain effectiveness, supply chain efficiencies'. *Journal of Enterprise Information Management*, 19(3): 246–61.

Womack, J. and Jones, D. (1996) *Lean Thinking*. New York: Simon & Schuster.

6 Service systems design and implementation

Tammi J. Sinha and Sally Pastellas

This chapter defines, explores and comments on service systems design, integration and implementation in a public sector context. Public sector service systems draw together many aspects of systems thinking, value co-creation, multiple stakeholders view of value, expectation management and scarcity of resources which is increasingly high on the agenda. The chapter expands these themes using the experiences of a team of Managers, clinicians, nurses and professional services in a case study, which documented the transition of separate contraception and sexual health (CASH) and genito-urinary medicine (GUM) into a newly commissioned 'one stop' service concept.

The experiences of this team, provides a rich picture of the challenges in the health and well-being sector, and explores implications for service operations in the redesign of service concepts, the integration of services and the needs of the professionals delivering that service. The work explored the views of health staff, when they were required to deliver a new model of service, which created a single specialist integrated sexual health service. This change had been initiated to transform services. The new service brought together staff from six organisations, and the disciplines of genitor-urinary medicine and contraception services.

The model required clinical staff to have training in the skills of a related specialism to their own, so that users have access to all sexual health services in one place, at one time and to be assessed by one clinician.

The chapter concludes with implications for service design practice, value co-creation and the management of stakeholders with multiple views.

Service systems and service concepts

Classic service systems design (Slack *et al.*, 2013; Brown *et al.*, 2013) has drawn on the development of design constructs from manufacturing and developed to incorporate services. The differences between products and services are predominantly tangibility. Products are tangible and services are less so. Products are created predominantly prior to consumption, whereas services are produced and consumed instantaneously. Services have an element of value co-creation, where the end user has an impact on the outcome of the service, as they are active in whether expectations are met or not.

When we apply this logic to the public sector, we face challenges of services, which are under massive budget constraints, with multiple stakeholders to satisfy. Many of these stakeholders have very different views as to what levels of service should be offered. However public services will also be produced and consumed instantaneously, be intangible and have a high degree of value co-creation with the end user. A conceptual model (Slack *et al.*, 2013) can be used to describe the elements of a service concept:

- The organising idea.
- The service experience.
- The service outcome.
- The service operation.
- The value of the service.

Outcomes are critical here, as taxpayers we have certain expectations of levels of public service, capacity and availability of those services. The recent austerity cuts have been deep, internationally, and in the UK (2010–14), cutting a swathe through public services. As service operations innovators and practitioners, how do we protect, develop and enhance public services when money is tight? Acknowledging that operational excellence and service design has a large part to play.

As taxpayers, end users 'buy' the service concepts, whether it is choosing the local school because it has an excellent history, because your child can walk to school, or because you have heard friends with children in the school indicate its excellence. In the healthcare context we may decide to go to a particular hospital because the consultant surgeon is the best at tackling aneurysmal bone cysts. We still 'buy' the service concept in public services. The service concept is built up from the 'idea' of the service, a consensus of what that service should be, the value proposition and offering, be clear and consistent with the operational strategy of the organisation (Johnston *et al.*, 2012). Many service designers use the Business Model Canvas (Osterwalder and Pigneur, 2010) to portray their service concept and to use visual management to convey their value propositions, delivery mechanisms and overall service concept.

As part of service system design, we can apply systems thinking principles and ensure the inputs to the system (people, information and materials) are transformed, with value added in some way to achieve positive outputs (again people, information and materials; Stowell and Welch, 2012). In public services, the transformation process becomes an experience and additional outputs as part of the human dimension include our values, our emotions, our judgements and our intentions. The transforming resources in a public service will also have their values, emotions, judgements and intentions affected in some way (Smith *et al.*, 2014).

This conceptual model is deconstructed using a health integration case study, and will be used as recurring themes in the chapter:

- The organising idea.
- The service experience.

- The service outcome.
- The service operation.
- The value of the service.

Background

In 2001, the UK government published its strategy for sexual heath and HIV (Department of Health, 2001), against a backdrop of rising teenage pregnancies and sexually transmitted infection. The strategy proposed a range of measures, which included the desire to integrate CASH and GUM services, to increase the user contact base to support people making the best choice in managing their fertility and preventing sexually transmitted infection.

The strategy embedded a notion proposed by the International Conference on Population and Development in Cairo in 1994 (Mayhew *et al.*, 2003). This notion explored the strategy of bringing together sexually transmitted infection and HIV services, with family planning services. This was in order to maximise the opportunities presented to women receiving reproductive health services and to widen the message regarding sexually transmitted infections. Although the issues relating to GUM and CASH service integration may not be the same in the UK as internationally, the 2001 strategy proposed 'The benefits of more integrated sexual health services, including pilots of one-stop clinics' (Department of Health, 2001: 3).

Although there had been some movement towards integration of sexual health services in the UK, this had been patchy (Kane and Wellings, 2003). Thankfully more than 10 years later some momentum is emerging. O'Reilly *et al.* (1999), comment that it is the accepted wisdom that sexual health service integration is a positive one, that there is a lot of attention on *how* to integrate and less evidence on *what* to integrate, with an overriding assumption that integration is more cost effective than separate service delivery.

Linking this to our model of service concept design:

- The organising idea: integration of GUM and CASH services will have many positive impacts on sexual health and positive outcomes for a large percentage of the population.
- The service experience: Depending on the level of integration, Patients access GUM and CASH services in one location, at one time, with a dedicated team of professionals.
- The service outcome: positive experience and relevant choices and treatments for patients.
- The service operation: location, layout, capacity planning, demand management, quality systems, performance measures and logistics. Respect for patients and staff.
- The value of the service: Positive outcomes and treatment for a large sector of the population.

Moving to an integrated service, with multiple stakeholders, it is important to consider what the implications are for the different stakeholder groups.

For the CASH staff (nurses and doctors) currently working in a predominately female focused service around fertility control. The clinicians and nurses would have additional training to deliver a service across a wider age group and a different gender mix as well as adding the skills to work in a different clinical discipline. The same but reverse will be the case for staff currently working in a GUM service. This was clearly not a small undertaking.

Local commissioners used a 'practice development approach' (Hampshire commissioner, personal communication, 12 February 2013) to work with a range of sexual health providers across their region. The team developed and proposed a model for the new integrated service, following a needs assessment across the geographical area. The commissioners were intent on bringing together level three providers of sexual health services in an integrated way. The national strategy for sexual health and HIV (2001) described three tiers of sexual health provision. The commissioners wished to procure a new provider for the level three specialist services and in so doing force the bringing together of GU and CASH provision, as well as other elements of a comprehensive specialist sexual health service. This was a bold and innovative progression in the design of CASH and GU provision.

In January 2012, the most qualified provider was chosen by the commissioners to be the single provider of sexual health services across the region. Staff from six NHS organisations, were brought together under the Transfer of Undertakings – Protection of Employment (TUPE) regulations.

The commissioners followed good procurement practice and engaged local stakeholders in the development of the model they wished to commission. This was to offer all users of sexual health services, an integrated one-stop shop model for

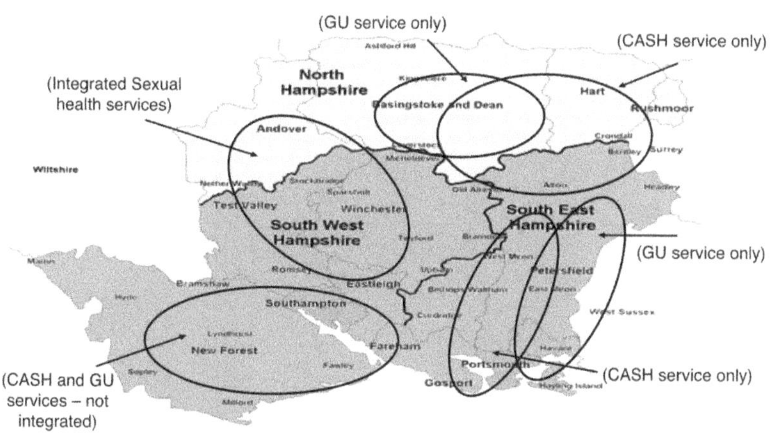

Figure 6.1 The sexual health providers before the recommissioning of sexual health services (December 2010)

access to both GUM and CASH services. This also included unplanned pregnancy, vasectomy, psychosexual counselling, outreach services, young people's specialist services, health promotion and management of the Chlamydia screening programme. The integrated service would have the same provider, in the same venues and for most users, ultimately from the same clinician.

Models of sexual health integration and the links to service design and concepts

Fleischman Foreit *et al.* (2002) provided the following definition of integration: 'any two services that are offered from the same place, for the same hours and that one provider actively encourages clients to use the other service during their visit'. This is similar to the 'one stop shop' model presented here.

In 2005 the Department of Health commissioned a study of three pilot 'one stop shop' sites which resulted in a comprehensive evaluation of three localised models. This model was reviewed as part of the national evaluation.

Linking this back to the service design model, this approach may not be innovative enough to provide optimum benefits. Although services are together in one place, they are not clinically integrated. Users walk into separate elements of sexual health provision although it is likely that staff working in such an environment have a more integrated mindset (French *et al.*, 2007). Staff may also be more likely to refer internally.

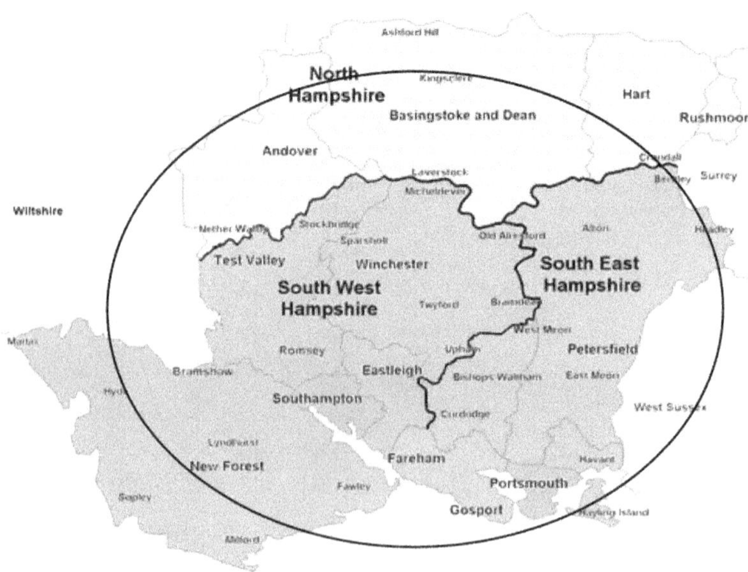

Figure 6.2 Single provider of integrated service post-tender (March 2012)

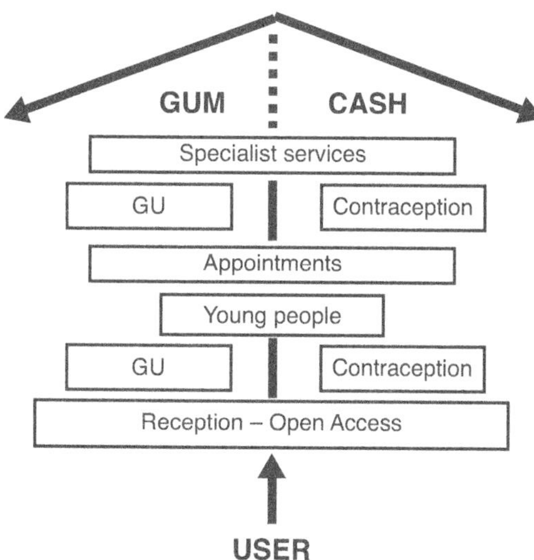

Figure 6.3 'One stop shop' model

Source: adapted from French *et al.* (2007)

It is possible to link the concept of one stop shop to the concept of cellular manufacturing, where each operator is expected to be multi-skilled and enabled to multi-task. Each unit of operation 'the cell' is dedicated to a specific type of product or service. Another example of which is the supermarket aisle next to the entrance, where you get all items for your lunch such as sandwiches, crisps, water, and your paper.

This model was not commissioned locally. This was due to a key performance indicator (which would be measured over the life of the new contract), the number and level of staff becoming dually trained and competent. A key driver for this service redesign was the vision for users of sexual health services to have both their GUM and CASH needs met from a single clinician if required, but who also have the skills to refer with-in the service to specialist elements of provision.

The newly commissioned service would radically change the way local services were delivered. Therefore as part of service redesign, it was important to consider the views and impact on the clinicians and nurses affected. The service design process has several stages and inputs. A SIPOC (suppliers, inputs, process, outputs and customers) is presented to show the service design process, and this particular case in context. The high level SIPOC shows the range of stakeholders involved in the service redesign and the importance of the engagement of staff in the models available and the integration model chosen.

In the service concept design process, the views of the clinicians, nurses and professional staff have been taken into consideration as to the levels of integration possible, and to which level of integration they would like to see. In any service concept design process, we draw on many disciplines. Our key focus here is on

Table 6.1 Suppliers, inputs, process, outputs and customers

Suppliers	*Inputs*	*Process*	*Outputs*	*Customer*
Department of Health General practitioners Patients Commissioners of the service **Qualified staff (clinicians and nurses)**	Medical info, skills and knowledge in CASH and GU Demand data from demographics Medical equipment **Qualified staff (clinicians and nurses)**	1 Service concept generation 2 Service concept screening 3 Preliminary service concepts 4 Evaluation and improvements of the service concept 5 Prototyping and final design	Fully integrated service Redesign service, meeting the service concept service concept Integrated GU and CASH service Improvement in GU and CASH outcomes for the local population **Dually trained staff (clinicians and nurses)**	Patients Clinical Commissioning Group General Practitioners **Qualified staff (clinicians and nurses)** Department of Health

service operations and service concept design, however we need to bring in aspects of insight management, demographics, marketing communications, visual leadership and change management into our service design process.

Operational excellence and service redesign

All organisations (whatever their size and goal) need to constantly adapt to both internal and external pressures. This is to ensure that they continue to be competitive in their field, or continue to deliver the service for which they are commissioned (Senior and Fleming, 2006). At any given time a range of factors, or indeed a single factor can alter the status quo and require an organisation, or part of it, to re-evaluate its direction and see if changes need to be made to hold and/or develop its position. The re-commissioning of sexual health services and the acquisition of six groups of staff from other organisations to deliver the new service has created a time of significant change.

Change in service concept and the individuals

All models of service delivery are clear that people are key to the delivery of that changed service. They can influence the outcome of a project by how much they wish to participate and how supportive they are of the process. Kubler-Ross's (1969) seminal work described the impact change can have on an individual by suggesting that there are five emotional phases through which colleagues move when a change is introduced to a service concept. These include denial, anger, bargaining, depression and acceptance. This model can be helpful when redesigning service concepts, as colleagues ability to deliver the improved service can vary according to where they sit on the Kubler-Ross curve.

Service concept design in the health and wellbeing change models

Iles and Sutherlands's (2001) review of leading service changes in the UK public health service (NHS) captures the most used of these models which offer opportunities for organisations to assess the drivers and impact of changes in service design. However, once agreement has been reached on what aspects of the service concept needs to change then tools/models of implementation are required. These are systems and processes that enable implementation through staff influence, and engagement to embed delivery.

Turner (2010) comments that change in public sector organisations particularly those that have within them influential professional groups can have issues of increased complexity in managing the change process. That this can be compounded by multiple stakeholder interests, from both within and outside the organisation. The new service model brings together very different specialist services, not only into one physical space but also into a single professional unit.

Integration

The evidence base for the effectiveness of integration in sexual health services is limited (Kane and Wellings, 1999), with most exploration undertaken in the 1990s and early 2000s. Curry and Ham (2010) explore what is understood and known about integration in their assessment of service and clinical integration in its widest context. They comment that integration is about the process of bringing professionals and organisations together, to improve outcomes for patients/users through the delivery of integrated care.

Curry and Ham (2010) suggest that integration may range from organisations linking together, or having more formal co-ordination between services, or that services become merged or acquired to become a single organisation to provide care. This final example of integration represents the outcome of the tender for local sexual health services.

Curry and Ham's (2010) review presents recognisable models of integration that happen in various ways across all NHS organisations. This is in order to improve service outcomes for patients. The proposed service concept of clinical integration however, by the potential merger of two clinical specialties into one, is not fully represented here. It is pertinent to conclude that the clinical integration of sexual health services is a service innovation in health service design.

Curry and Ham (2010) also suggest that integration of services will not bring benefits, if clinicians do not change the way they work. Therefore this is a key enabler of success for this service innovation, to bring the change in behaviours and skills needed to the forefront of service redesign.

Service concept redesign, integration and sexual health: the need for a redesign

Specialist sexual health services in the form of GUM services and family planning/contraception services (CASH) have historically been organised separately

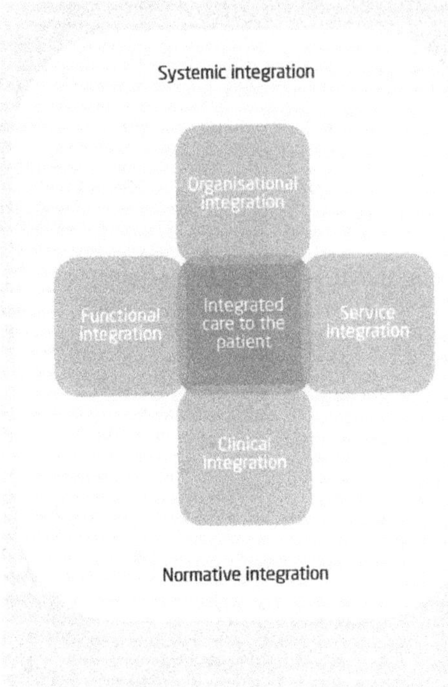
Systemic integration
Organisational integration
Functional integration
Integrated care to the patient
Service integration
Clinical integration
Normative integration
• Organisational integration, where organisations are brought together formally by mergers or through 'collectives' and/or virtually through co-ordinated provider networks or via contracts between separate organisations brokered by a purchaser.
• Functional integration, where non-clinical support and back-office functions are integrated, such as electronic patient records.
• Service integration, where different clinical services provided are integrated at an organisational level, such as through teams of multidisciplinary professionals.
• Clinical integration, where care by professionals and providers to patients is integrated into a single or coherent process within and/or across professions, such as through use of shared guidelines and protocols.
• Normative integration, where an ethos of shared values and commitment to co-ordinating work enables trust and collaboration in delivering health care.
• Systemic integration, where there is coherence of rules and policies at all organisational levels. This is sometimes termed an 'integrated delivery system'.

Figure 6.4 Curry and Ham's review

Source: Curry and Ham (2010)

in the UK (Kane and Wellings, 1999). The last 20 years have seen an increasing debate about bringing these services more closely together. This has resulted in the delivery of some 'integrated' services in the UK. The perception is that separate services offer fragmentation and poor access for users, that GUM clients have unmet contraception needs and that contraception clients have unmet sexually transmitted infection needs.

The following service model concept has been developed using multiple sources. The template shows the purpose of the service redesign and the expectations of improved outcomes. The work of the European Spider Project (www.thespider-project.eu) and Slack *et al.* (2013) is acknowledged in the development of the model. This is part 1 of the design process:

1 **Service concept generation.**
2 Service concept screening.
3 Preliminary service concepts.
4 Evaluation and improvements of the service concept.
5 Prototyping and final design.

Kane and Wellings (1999) conducted a study that asked 25 GUM and CASH consultants their views about integration. These staff were drawn from 6 different

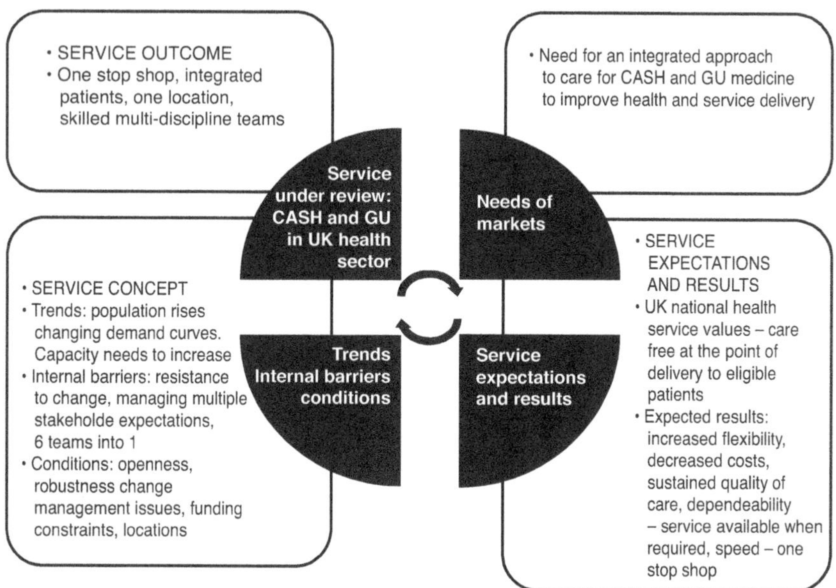

Figure 6.5 Service concept template

Sources: Pastellas and Sinha (2014), developed from European Spider Project (www.thespiderproject.eu) and Slack *et al.* (2013)

service types from stand-alone GUM/CASH services to integrated models. Their study consisted of in depth semi structured interviews with medical staff only. They found that for the most part the concept of integrated sexual health services was broadly welcomed. They found some distinct polarisation and concluded that staff views about integration must be anticipated, acknowledged and taken account of when planning services. Their study did not seek views from nursing staff working in these services. It is still not clear from their study what was meant by integration. There is an overall lack of clarity in the limited literature about what integration actually means for a sexual health service.

Church and Mayhew (2009) share that the rationale for integrating sexual health services, is that sexually transmitted infections and unwanted pregnancy share the same root cause – unprotected sexual intercourse or sexual activity, therefore it being a logical assumption that these services would work better together. In their review of the literature in 2009 they explored the integration of sexual health services and used 45 studies for comparison, however all these studies were undertaken in the developing world and it is unclear about how far their findings can be generalised to the UK. It is interesting to note that the recently published framework for sexual health services in England (Department of Health, 2013) use their developing countries work as the reference for integration in the UK. LaGanga (2011) has shown how lean service operations can provide opportunities for redirection and expansion of capacity in health outpatients services.

Service concept design and service integration

1 Service concept generation.
2 Service concept screening.
3 Preliminary service concepts.
4 Evaluation and improvements of the service concept.
5 Prototyping and final design.

Generating, defining and designing a service concept needs to take into account the expectations of key stakeholders. In this case the staff were engaged with the following questions to help with the design and implementation of the new service:

> What do staff understand by integration?
>
> At what level do they wish to see integration?

The responses to these questions offered an opportunity to understand staff wishes with the service redesign, their readiness for change and how far along the path of understanding and accepting clinical integration they are.

The following models were presented to colleagues to ensure all understood the service integration concept. These models, described below, have been designed by the service manager responsible for the delivery of the integrated service, in order to describe the implications of integration within a specialist service from the perspective of clinical members of staff, not users of the service (Pastellas, 2013).

Levels of service integration

1 Service concept generation.
2 Service concept screening.
3 Preliminary service concepts.
4 Evaluation and improvements of the service concept.
5 Prototyping and final design.

The models are described around:

- service concept;
- organisation;
- location;
- service users experience;
- manual systems and IT; and
- clinical skills.

The purpose of this work was to critically review staff views and beliefs about the benefits of an integrated sexual health service, and in so doing understand if the proposed service changes are ones staff feel positive or anxious about. This is an important step in service concept design.

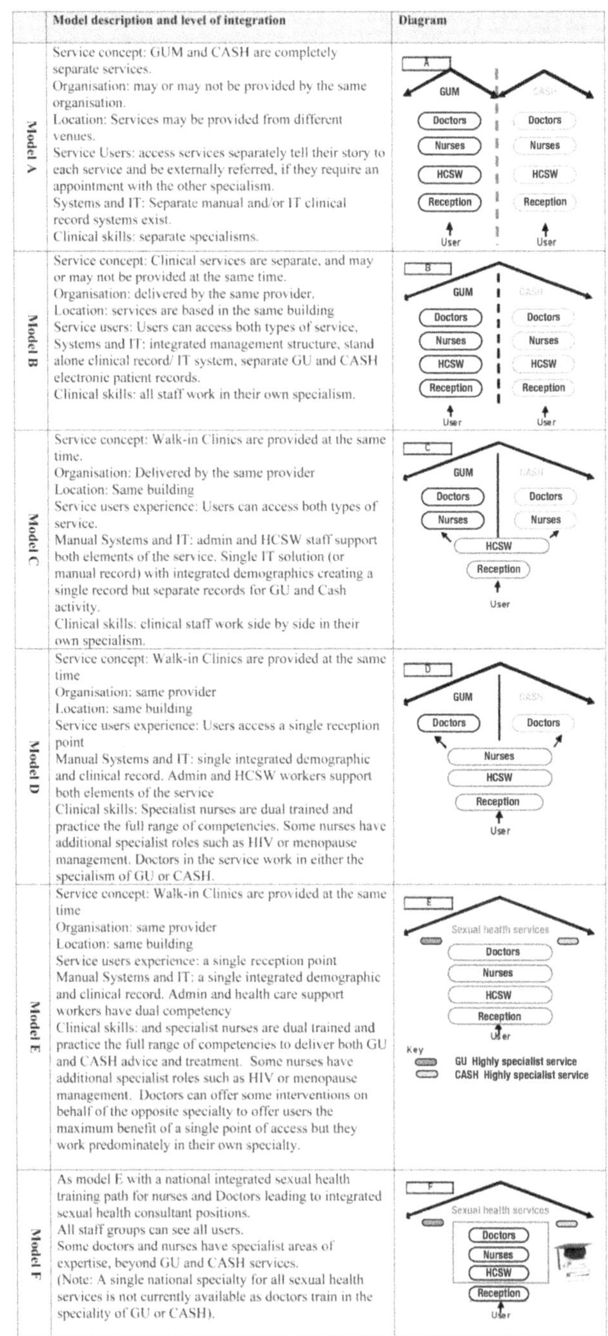

	Model description and level of integration	Diagram
Model A	Service concept: GUM and CASH are completely separate services. Organisation: may or may not be provided by the same organisation. Location: Services may be provided from different venues. Service Users: access services separately tell their story to each service and be externally referred, if they require an appointment with the other specialism. Systems and IT: Separate manual and/or IT clinical record systems exist. Clinical skills: separate specialisms.	A GUM / CASH Doctors / Doctors Nurses / Nurses HCSW / HCSW Reception / Reception User / User
Model B	Service concept: Clinical services are separate, and may or may not be provided at the same time. Organisation: delivered by the same provider. Location: services are based in the same building Service users: Users can access both types of service. Systems and IT: integrated management structure, stand alone clinical record/ IT system, separate GU and CASH electronic patient records. Clinical skills: all staff work in their own specialism.	B GUM / CASH Doctors / Doctors Nurses / Nurses HCSW / HCSW Reception / Reception User / User
Model C	Service concept: Walk-in Clinics are provided at the same time. Organisation: Delivered by the same provider Location: Same building Service users experience: Users can access both types of service. Manual Systems and IT: admin and HCSW staff support both elements of the service. Single IT solution (or manual record) with integrated demographics creating a single record but separate records for GU and Cash activity. Clinical skills: clinical staff work side by side in their own specialism.	C GUM / CASH Doctors / Doctors Nurses / Nurses HCSW Reception User
Model D	Service concept: Walk-in Clinics are provided at the same time Organisation: same provider Location: same building Service users experience: Users access a single reception point Manual Systems and IT: single integrated demographic and clinical record. Admin and HCSW workers support both elements of the service Clinical skills: Specialist nurses are dual trained and practice the full range of competencies. Some nurses have additional specialist roles such as HIV or menopause management. Doctors in the service work in either the specialism of GU or CASH.	D GUM / CASH Doctors / Doctors Nurses HCSW Reception User
Model E	Service concept: Walk-in Clinics are provided at the same time Organisation: same provider Location: same building Service users experience: a single reception point Manual Systems and IT: a single integrated demographic and clinical record. Admin and health care support workers have dual competency Clinical skills: and specialist nurses are dual trained and practice the full range of competencies to deliver both GU and CASH advice and treatment. Some nurses have additional specialist roles such as HIV or menopause management. Doctors can offer some interventions on behalf of the opposite specialty to offer users the maximum benefit of a single point of access but they work predominately in their own specialty.	E Sexual health services Doctors Nurses HCSW Reception User Key GU Highly specialist service CASH Highly specialist service
Model F	As model E with a national integrated sexual health training path for nurses and Doctors leading to integrated sexual health consultant positions. All staff groups can see all users. Some doctors and nurses have specialist areas of expertise, beyond GU and CASH services. (Note: A single national specialty for all sexual health services is not currently available as doctors train in the speciality of GU or CASH).	F Sexual health services Doctors Nurses HCSW Reception User

Figure 6.6 Service concepts with increasing levels of integration

Abbreviations: GUM, genito-urinary medicine; CASH, contraception and sexual health services; HCSW, health care support worker

Source: Pastellas (2013)

Research approach

1 Service concept generation.
2 Service concept screening.
3 Preliminary service concepts.
4 Evaluation and improvements of the service concept.
5 Prototyping and final design.

This case study sought to understand the views of as many staff as possible currently working in the sexual health service. This was in order to enable the most effective service concept to be implemented, taking into account key stakeholder views. It is acknowledged that the 'patient/client' is key here, however the expectations and experiences of patients are not the focus of this case and are covered in other studies. Data was collected from team members using a variety of methods. On-line questionnaires and staff interviews were used to get a balanced view. The data collected provided a snapshot of staff understanding of integration at a single point in time. The outcomes of the survey were shared with staff to validate the findings and facilitate debate around the service redesign. This was part of the service concept screening process and exploring preliminary service concepts. This study was approved by the appropriate stakeholders within the NHS and academic community.

Participant selection

This study explored the impact on staff in a new service which was one of the largest sexual health services in England. The consultation was part of the 'evaluation and improvements' element of the service concept design process. The medical and nursing teams were most affected by the impact of clinical integration as they are the groups of staff who will undertake additional training to add a further clinical specialism to their knowledge.

Admin/clerical teams and other specialist services such as health promotion and psychosexual counsellors continue to work in their own speciality within the services but they may also hold a view about the impact of integration. A decision was taken to include all staff working in the sexual health service in whatever capacity.

The questions were linked to the aims and objectives of the research project regarding service concepts and integration. In addition questions relating to age and staff group provided dependent variable information, so that analysis could include if age or staff group had an impact on the responses. In their review, Kane and Wellings (1999) found that older members of staff felt less comfortable about working in an integrated service. The questionnaire asked for commentary to add richness and to provide staff with an opportunity to share any other issues they may have.

Evaluation and improvement of the service concept of further integration

A total of 94 staff completed the survey via a web-based questionnaire. The following tables, graphs and commentary share the initial findings of the results. This

Table 6.2 Staff grouping and response rate

Staff group	*Head count*	*Respondents*	*Response rate (%)*
Doctors	38	22	57.9
Nurses	75	34	45.3
HCSW	21	7	33.3
Admin	68	23	33.8
Other	26	8	30.0
Total	228	94	41.2

information was subsequently shared with a small group of staff so that they could offer additional commentary and validity for the findings. Staff self-selected from a range of staff group types. The proportion of doctors and nurses who responded to the questionnaire was higher than the staff group as a whole. Therefore some themes and conclusions can be taken from all the responses but in particular from these two groups.

Integration: key findings

This explored the staff evaluation and understanding of integration and at what level they would wish to see integration in the sexual health service. The majority of staff understood that service integration was represented by service concepts D and above, meaning that all nursing staff are dual trained, but that doctors work in their own specialism.

However, it is also interesting to see that the service concept attracting the largest response rate (35 staff) is model E where both doctors and nurses are dual competent, with some additional specialist elements. Twenty-two staff understood integration to mean that all staff are dual trained and competent, and that both

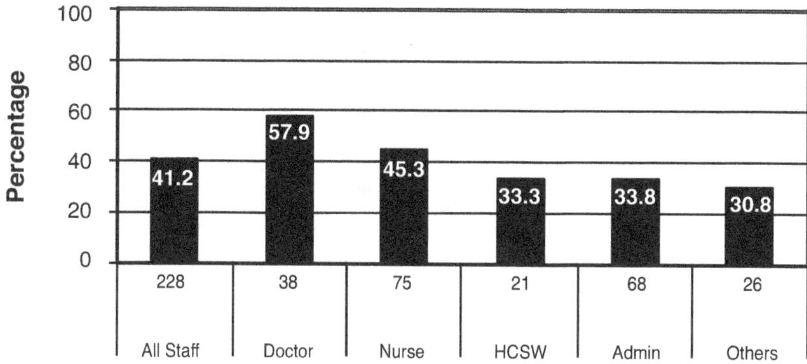

Figure 6.7 Percentage of staff by group who responded to the questionnaire

doctors and nurses have a single national training path in sexual health. In the words of one respondent:

> Model F would fit with a true integrated service but current training for doctors would mean that although doctors can provide basic services in GUM or CASH, they would still predominantly work in their speciality. I cannot see this changing for several years.

Consensus?

Although the results show that most staff appear to wish to see a clinically integrated service there were 9 staff (representing 9.6 per cent) that do not. If this was translated to the total staff cohort of 228, then 22 staff may feel that they do not wish to see a service with any clinical integration other than at health care support worker level. Depending on the grade and influence of this set of staff, the impact of their position may influence the progress that is made by a wider team.

1 Service concept generation.
2 Service concept screening.
3 Preliminary service concepts.
4 Evaluation and improvements of the service concept.
5 Prototyping and final design.

Further decomposition of the data has revealed the following insights, which should be taken into account when moving to stage 5: prototyping and final design. The

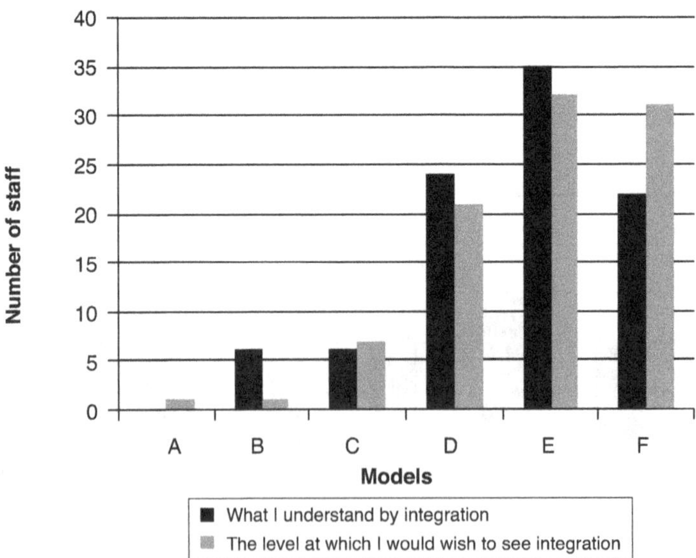

Figure 6.8 Number of staff by integrated model type

work for this service design is ongoing, the service has been integrated for over 12 months and further refinement and improvements will be made to the service concept and delivery. That is another story.

Caution should be attached to these responses as the number of staff in each group becomes smaller, therefore affecting the validity of the responses, and the ability to assume any representation of the wider group of staff views.

Exploring the service concept of dual competency within a health service

22.7 per cent of the doctor sample declared themselves to be using both GUM and CASH competencies in their daily work and 32.3 per cent of the sample of nurses. It is important to note that the doctor cohort had 22 doctors of whom 8 were GU doctors and 14 CASH Doctors. It is difficult to draw a conclusion from this information other than to see that there are staff that are already using dual skills. It may be that these staff are also those that have self-selected to answer the questionnaire. It may be the case that this level of dual competency would not be seen in the non-responder sample of service staff. One of the services was already working to an integrated model. It may be that nurses who said that they were using dual competencies were from this cohort although all services do have some nurses that use both competencies in their daily practice. What can be said is that as a minimum 14.1 per cent of doctors and nurses across the service are offering users an integrated service from one clinician. Understanding this baseline will be useful for assessment of staff dual competency in the future, as integration gets embedded with staff training.

Table 6.3 Staff views of service concepts leading to increased clinical integration

Topic	*View*
Staff position on understanding of integration and where they would wish to see integration	What was shown is that contraception doctors feel more comfortable about the level of integration they wish to see, with some GUM doctors wishing to see less integration than their understanding of integration. The numbers are, however, small.
Nurse's views by speciality type	Nurses indicated that they understood integration and wished to see to see integration at the higher level service concepts. A small number (3) of CASH nurses did not wish to work in an integrated way and in addition 3 nurses who have self selected as integrated nurses who do not wish to see integration for medical staff, choosing model D which is nurse integration only. *'Potentially for nurses, but I think the Doctor's being trained in their own specialities is vital to get the best expertise available' (Nurse).*
Admin, clerical and other members of the team	Views on integration are generally positive, most staff across all groups understood and wished to see a high level of clinical integration in the service, however there is a small group of both GUM doctors and some nurses who felt less positive about this approach.

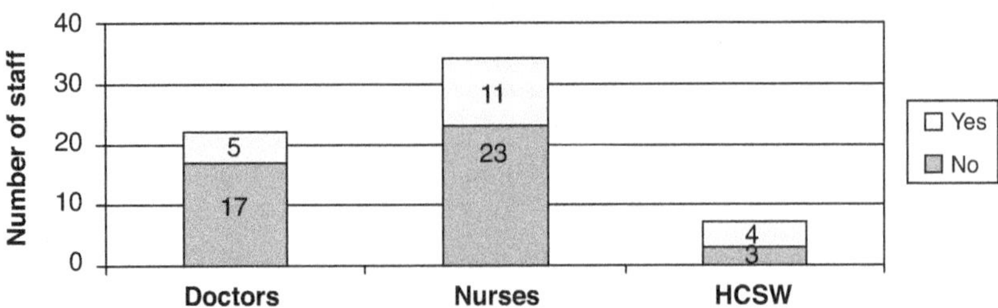

Figure 6.9 Use of dual competencies in daily practice: number of staff in each clinical group who say that they use dual competencies in their daily practice

Looking to the future of dual competency services in the health sector

As part of the service design process, views of colleagues are crucial to the success or failure of that service. Colleagues were asked to comment on whether full integration would be a positive experience, and whether they were looking forward to working in a clinically integrated service.

Most staff wished to see high levels of integration as 68 per cent of the sample agreed or strongly agreed with the statements. However, 20 staff responded with strongly disagreed, disagreed or didn't know if they felt positively about integration of if they were looking forward to it.

Combining these responses it can be inferred that most staff who responded to the questionnaire wish to see integration happen at level E and above, however that there are a large enough group of staff who may be expressing that they are not sure about the journey of getting there, or may feel fearful about what integration may mean for them even though they feel committed to the principle. It cannot be supposed that this level of positivity can be generalised across all the staff working in the service however it is possible to assume that it may be the case.

Feedback from staff

The findings of the questionnaire were shared with 3 doctors and 3 nurses in graph and commentary format for discussion.The purpose of these interviews was to share the findings to explore if when presented with the data, staff recognised them to be true and valid within the context of the piece of work undertaken.

All believed the overall positive response to see integration was in alignment with their experience of staffs' current perceptions about the way forward. They commented that even though the current working climate was very challenging, most staff wished to be in a position to provide a more holistic sexual health service and could see the benefits for patients from this approach.

They were aware of some staff that were finding the proposed changes difficult. They understood that drawing conclusions about the non-responders was not possible, however they believed from their experience that the 41 per cent sample was likely to be representative of those that did not respond. As the service is now one of the largest in the country having such a response rate will have assured a credible exposure to a range of clinicians in the service greater than in many other services.

> Although all staff should be able to offer the full service there will also be a need for some specialisms in the service.
>
> (Doctor)

> I see integration as freeing up doctors and nurses to do more specialist stuff.
>
> (Doctor)

> Working in this way will help staff to pick up on cues from patients that they might have missed before and will support a richer consultation which may include more health promotion and education.
>
> (Doctor)

> What the data shows is what nurses have been telling us in one-to-one supervision for some time, they want the training so that they can provide both elements of the service.
>
> (Nurse)

The results appear to show that the majority, but not all, staff across all staff groups indicated that they understood integration to be at level D and above with the highest number of staff understanding integration to be at level E. In addition the majority of staff wished to see integration at level E and above. This has positive outcomes for the redesign and implementation of the service.

Conclusion

The purpose of this chapter was to introduce and discuss service concept design within the context of a public sector organisation. Integration of services can have profound impacts for both the public and private sector. The contextualisation of the health and wellbeing sector and a focus on the providers view point of the integration of services provides a positive focus for service design and innovation.

It is acknowledged that patients/end users should also be part of this redesign. The issues of value co-creation, patient centred processes, and the scarcity of some services due to 'austerity' measures, can also be part of the service concept and service design conversation.

The development of the integrated GUM and CASH service is ongoing and in its second year. The engagement of staff at all levels in this process, should have a positive impact on the patient journey and experience. Their view of integration based on the models presented is crucial to the success of the service, and successful implementation of new designs of service are helped with staff engagement.

Most staff, described model D (nurse dual competent- doctors working in their own specialism) and above. The highest number of staff choose service concept E for their understanding of integration, this was represented across all staff groups. In addition the majority of staff shared that they not only understood integration to be at a high level but a few more of them wanted to see integration at the highest levels. This sexual health staff team have been together for a year and although the training to start the integrated model is only just starting at the time of the questionnaire, staff will have heard the integration message for some time during the recent restructuring process. Kotter (2012) is clear that a key step to achieve change is ensuring that staff repeatedly hear the message so that it becomes embedded.

Implications

The implications of these conversations relate to the end user (patient), the service organisation, the service itself, its managers, the staff as well as commissioners. Most staff were engaged in and committed to the service concept of integration. The service provider needs to ensure that the service has the resources to deliver staff and commissioner expectations, for leaders and managers to empower staff to action the new service design and to ensure that the benefits are sustained.

Clinical staff need to have the opportunities and adequate availability of training to support the service integration model, this must be ongoing, sustainable and properly resourced. If individual staff receive appropriate training, they will feel engaged with the integration and service excellence agenda and have a personal gain. Such staff are more likely to become service innovators to support embedding of the integration model in the service.

Recommendations

The findings, if representative of the service as a whole, would indicate that staff are engaged in the integration agenda and wish to see its development. This study indicates that there is a need for further research in this area to look at how integrated models have developed in other sexual health services and the outcomes these have had for staff and users. In addition it would be appropriate to suggest via sexual health networks the development of a framework for integration that describes models so that work can be undertaken to explore staff views and user outcomes, this would support future research and generalisability.

The outcome of this study was shared with all staff in an education day so that they had an opportunity to comment on the conclusions. The management team need to continue to share with all staff the vision for the future and work hard to have short term gains to maintain the motivation of staff for the project. Management team meetings could use the evidence based implementation models shared in this project to support success. It is recommended that the study is repeated in a year's time to understand if the by then completed dual training for all staff has had an impact on staff views of integration.

Summary

This chapter explored service system design. The theory was contextualised with the presentation of a service integration opportunity in the UK National Health Service. The commissioner in this case developed a proposal for an integrated GUM and CASH service, which was commissioned. The new service brought together staff from six organisations, and the disciplines of genito-urinary medicine and contraception services. As part of the service design process, staff stakeholders were engaged in order to enhance outcomes in implementation. This was achieved by consulting with health staff at the time of the change, when they were required to deliver a new model of service which created a single specialist integrated sexual health service. This service innovation was initiated to transform services, and improve patient outcomes.

The new service concept required clinical staff to have training in the skills of a related specialism to their own so that users can access all sexual health services from one place, at one time and be assessed by one clinician. The chapter presented the human side of service design in that it explored staff views about their understanding of integration and at what level they would wish to see integration in the sexual health service, and was particularly interested in the views of doctors and nurses in the service for whom integration had the greatest impact on their professional development and service provision.

Acknowledgement

The support of Solent NHS Trust is acknowledged and welcomed in this work.

References

Brown, S., Bessant, J.R. and Lamming, R. (2013) *Strategic Operations Management*. Abingdon: Routledge.

Church, K. and Mayhew, S. (2009) 'Integration of STI and HIV prevention, care and treatment into family planning services: a review of the literature'. *Studies in Family Planning*, 40(3): 171–86.

Curry, N. and Ham, C. (2010) *Clinical and Service Integration, the Route to Improved Outcomes*. London: The Kings Fund.

Department of Health (2001) *National Strategy for Sexual Health and HIV*. London: HMSO.

Department of Health (2005) *A Framework for Sexual Health Improvement in England*. London: HMSO.

Department of Health (2013) *A Framework for Sexual Health Improvement in England*. London: Department of Health.

Fleischman Foreit, K.G., Hardee, K. and Agarwal, K. (2002). 'When does it make sense to consider integrating STI and HIV services with family Planning Services?' *International Perspectives on Sexual and Reproductive Health*, 28(2): 105–7.

French, R.S., Gerressu, M., Griffiths, C., Mercer, C.H., Coope, C., Miles, K., Robinson, A., Stephenson, J., Graham, A., Gray, D., Coast, J., Hollinghurst, S., Salisbury, C. and Rogstad, K. (2007) *Evaluation of One-Stop Shop Models of Sexual Health Provision*. Bristol: University of Bristol.

Iles, V. and Sutherland, K. (2001) *Organisational Change. A Review for Health Care Managers, Professionals and Researchers*. London: NCCSDO.

Johnston, R., Clark, G. and Shulver, M. (2012) *Service Operations Management, Improving Service Delivery*. Harlow: Pearson Education.

Kane, R. and Wellings, K. (1999) 'Integrated sexual health services: the views of medical professionals'. *Culture Health and Sexuality,* 1(2): 131–45.

Kane, R. and Wellings, K. (2003) 'Staff training in integrated sexual health services'. *Sexually Transmitted Infections,* 79: 354–6.

Kotter, J. (2012) *Leading Change*. Boston, MA: Harvard Business Review Press.

Kubler-Ross, E. (1969) *On Death and Dying*. New York: Touchstone.

LaGanga, L. R. (2011) 'Lean service operations: reflections and new directions for capacity expansion in outpatient clinics'. *Journal of Operations Management*, 29(5): 422–33.

Mayhew, S., Lush, L., Cleland, J. and Walt, G. (2003) 'Implementing the component services for reproductive health'. *Studies in Family Planning*, 31(2): 151–62.

O'Reilly, K., Dehne, K. and Snow, R. (1999) 'Should management of sexually transmitted infections be integrated into family planning services: evidence and challenges'. *Reproductive Health Matters*, 7(14): 49–59.

Osterwalder, A. and Pigneur, Y. (2010) *Business Model Canvas*. Chichester: John Wiley & Sons.

Pastellas, S. (2013) 'A critical review of staff views and understanding of clinical integration in a sexual health service'. MSc dissertation, University of Portsmouth.

Pastellas, S. and Sinha, T.J. (2014) 'Change management in the NHS: clinical integration in a sexual health service'. Paper presented at the British Academy of Management Conference 2014 (BAM14), Belfast, 9–11 September.

Senior, B. and Fleming, J. (2006) *Organisational Change*. Harlow: Pearson Education.

Slack, N., Brandon-Jones, A. and Johnston, R. (2013) *Operations Management*. Harlow: Pearson Education.

Smith, L., Maull, R. and Ng, I.C. (2014) 'Servitization and operations management: a service dominant-logic approach'. *International Journal of Operations and Production Management*, 34(2): 242–69.

Stowell, F. and Welch, C. (2012) *The Manager's Guide to Systems Practice: Making Sense of Complex Problems*. Chichester: John Wiley.

Turner, S. (2010) *Leading Change Resource Pack 2010/11*. Portsmouth: University of Portsmouth.

Part II

Responsiveness and resourcing

7 The challenges of public sector demand and capacity management

An exploratory case study of police services

Ross Ritchie and Paul Walley

Introduction

Public sector organisations in all modern economies have found their budgets squeezed in the last few years following the Gershon report (Gershon, 2004) and the financial crisis from 2007. This has led to fewer resources available for the delivery of core and support services, with the Gershon report requiring approximately £2bn to be cut from Home Office budgets. The 2010 UK Government Comprehensive Spending Review (CSR) announced a real terms cut in central Government funding grants for the 43 police forces in England and Wales (HMIC, 2011; HM Treasury, 2010). The financial cuts mean that budgets in individual forces will have to be cut by between 9 and 14 per cent in real terms, but these cuts vary in magnitude across different forces. The HMIC estimated that between March 2010 and March 2015 the police workforce would be reduced by about 34,100 posts, half of which would be police officers. Other methods of achieving efficiency gains that are being tried include shared service centres, collaboration across forces, shift pattern reviews, neighbourhood remodelling and outsourcing. All services were reportedly looking at demand analysis as a means of becoming more efficient.

This chapter studies the management of demand and capacity in public services, looking initially at the relevant service management literature and its application to public sector operations. Following this review, we study demand and capacity management practices in the police services with a focused case study of the management of work flow in police custody suites in one region of England. We present data on demand patterns for these services and look at how this demand is met through the provision of both human and physical capacity in these custody suites. The workflow through the system has some similarity with the work flow through other complex service processes, such as emergency flows in healthcare. We will make these comparisons based on the data we have collected and determine whether or not there are lessons for the police in the ways that other sectors have tackled these issues. The main focus of attention concerns medium-term capacity planning, where resource profiles are normally developed to match seasonal changes in demand and make allowances for sudden spikes in demand. The case highlights the similarities between this application of theory and those previously studied in healthcare. In this case study there are issues of flow management of offenders through the system and gains in resource utilisation through the pooling of demand into more centralised facilities are partly countered by a loss of control of whole system flow through the compartmentalisation of responsibilities and oversight.

Capacity and demand theory

Capacity management is the process of reconciliation of resource requirements to meet demand over time. Existing theory of demand and capacity management largely comes from studies of mainly private sector operations. The problem of matching demand and capacity in services was initially highlighted by Sasser (1976) who showed that service demand seasonality and variability presented problems not normally seen in manufacturing operations. A number of factors make capacity management particular challenge, especially in services. First, services are often transient or perishable (Showalter and White, 1991) and so resources that are provided can be wasted if they are not utilised at the time of their provision. However, if demand occurs when resources are not currently available work backlogs can occur. Second, demand is rarely constant in most service processes. As well as long-term growth or decline patterns most operations see medium-term and short-term variations in demand caused by seasonal factors. These variations occur with a wide range of periodicities, over annual, monthly, weekly or daily cycles. It can become a considerable challenge to meet these fluctuations in demand without some mismatch between capacity and demand or without wasting resource. Third, capacity planning has to factor in the manager's ability to make adjustments to capacity. Fixed assets, such as facilities or buildings usually require a planning horizon of many years before new capacity can be introduced. Managers often find that the structural capacity cannot be flexed as readily as they would like. In the medium term, resources such as people or inventory can be flexed more easily as long as operations systems develop suitable methods.

Walley (2013) provided a synthesis of private sector theory showing how resource requirements could be determined. These elements can be summarised into three main stages of capacity management resource assessment provision, shown in Figure 7.1.

The three steps are:

- assessment of the volume and seasonality of demand;
- determination of capacity requirements; and
- resource requirements analysis.

Assessment of the volume and seasonality of demand

The first phase is to understand the market size and understand how the demand from this market appears as a pattern over time. Long-term capacity management adjustments primarily focus on growth or decline patterns. Managers must also be

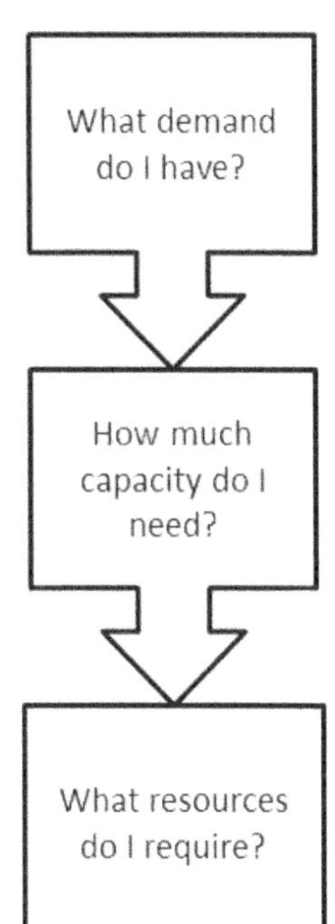

Understanding of:

- Market size
- Growth and decline patterns
- Seasonal adjustments (daily, yearly cycles)
- Alternative supply/substitution
- Mix variation
- Random variability

Analysis of:

- Market economics, e.g. profitability/utilisation trade-offs
- Service level attainment
- Market share
- Need to meet peaks
- Refusal to meet some demand?
- Erlang queue adjustments

Consideration of:

- Capacity management options (chase)
- Demand management options
- Variability of "takt time"
- Resource yield
- Impact of service variability
- Resource mix options

Figure 7.1 A framework for the assessment of service resource requirements

Source: Walley (2013)

aware of any significant seasonal patterns that would imply periods where demand is significantly greater than the mean level. This has implications for the availability of fixed resources and the need to build in capacity flexibility requirements. A particular challenge in the public sector is the understanding of what constitutes a market and how demand can be assessed. For example, in healthcare there are underlying causes of demand for healthcare that may change due to demographic adjustments and also lifestyle factors such as diet, exercise and obesity. These factors cannot easily be translated into useful numbers from an operations planning perspective. Historical analysis can provide details of *recorded* demand but this is often taken from databases of activity rather than demand (Walley *et al.*, 2006). This can result in inaccurate assessments of demand in the public sector. Historical analysis is useful in situations where the system is relatively stable and demand profiles can be interpreted (see Krueger and Schimmelpfeng, 2013).

Determination of capacity requirements

The amount of capacity needed is a complex function of a range of factors, usually based around market demand. In private organisations the market share expected provides a good indication of likely volumes in a competitive market. In the public sector it is more likely that the service provider is in a monopolistic situation but even here there will be a number of capacity adjustments that can be made. For example, in the provision of call centres there is a trade-off between system efficiency or utilisation and the service level, usually measured by the proportion of calls abandoned by the caller before the centre picks up the call. These additional capacity provisions to avoid excessive delays are often derived from queue theory (see Hall, 1990). Queue theory demonstrates that 100 per cent service availability is required is often expensive to provide. This has implications for public services where availability or access is an issue.

Resource requirements analysis

The level of resource needed to produce the appropriate output capacity requires another set of calculations to be made. Managers have to assess the yield of output they obtain for each resource. We have to consider the planned and unplanned losses of output due to factors such as planned working hours, maintenance losses and lost time due to errors or rework. There is also wastage of resource if a particular stage in a system is not the bottleneck, known as balancing losses (see Boysen *et al.*, 2007). Once the required quantity of a resource is known for a given level of output can be determined the nature of the timing and availability of that resource can be planned.

Lovelock (1992) identified the two main approaches to demand reconciliation. Services can either operate a 'level' capacity strategy whereby they try to load smooth demand to fit a simple capacity profile or they can 'chase' demand whereby they adjust capacity to meet the fluctuations in demand. In practice, most service organisations have a 'mixed' strategy which blends elements of level and chase. Other comparable approaches exist (e.g. Crandall and Marklund, 1996; Heskett *et al.*, 1990). Fitzsimmons and Fitzsimmons (2006) neatly summarise the practical ways in which level and chase strategies are implemented. They identify demand management practices such as price incentives, off peak adjustments, developing complementary services and reservations systems. Capacity management practices include sharing capacity across services, increasing customer involvement, work shift adjustments, cross training and part time working.

Weaknesses of the above approach

Two issues can be identified with the existing approaches:

- Demand management is a major element of the above approach and has been developed extensively (Pullman and Thompson, 2003; Klassen and Rohleder, 2001, 2002; Radas and Shugan, 1998; Rhyne, 1988; Zeithaml *et al.*, 1985) but this is limited in the public sector through the lack of pricing mechanisms at the point of consumption and the redistributive nature of the services (Spicker, 2009). Furthermore yield management, which improves resource efficiency, usually by adjusting pricing or incentive mechanisms to influence demand to fill existing available (perishable) resource (e.g. see Kimes, Chase and Wirtz, 2003; Kimes and Chase, 1998; Jones and Hamilton, 1992; Kimes, 1989), is also more limited for the same reason.

- The impact of stochastic demand and capacity variability is not factored into the above model. Queue theory can easily be used to demonstrate that random variation creates the need for excess capacity if queues and delays are to be eliminated. Seddon (2003) argues strongly that service variability must be understood and that conventional methods of both operations management and system design do not address these issues, leading to poorly delivered public services. The issues of variability and delay have been widely studied in public healthcare literature (e.g. Litvak *et al.*, 2005; Litvak, 2009; Silvester *et al.*, 2004) and we would suggest that the same issues may occur elsewhere in the public sector.

Public sector capacity management

In a critique of public sector capacity management, Walley (2013) suggested that many operations can still adopt private sector practices to a much greater extent to achieve some benefits. The issue is that public services are driven by the availability of resources rather than the levels of demand. In this respect public and private sectors sometimes adopt completely different planning mechanisms. This can lead to problems:

1. *Do public services lack market knowledge?* Public services often appear to provide resources based on the budgets they are allocated, rather than the demand for those services. In such cases there is less need to measure demand, especially if this indicates that funding cuts might be justified in particular departments. In practice resource decisions appear to often be based on historic allocations rather than actual need. The entire process of rationally allocating resources cannot start if there are no demand figures on which to base resource requirements.
2. *Can public services compute resource requirements?* The accurate allocation of resource also requires some measurement or knowledge of the work involved in the provision of a service. We suggest that there is often only rudimentary knowledge of resource requirements and this problem may be compounded by lack of standardisation of services or highly variable service standards.
3. *Is the impact of variation misunderstood?* There is already considerable evidence that public healthcare services in the UK and elsewhere have often based access initiatives on incorrectly judged decisions about the causes of waits and delays. Silvester *et al.* (2004) point out that many of the UK NHS access or waiting time initiatives have been founded on the belief that capacity shortages are the dominant cause of delays. In practice, many of these delays are actually caused by mismatches in the timing of demand and capacity rather than just a shortage of capacity. When looked at over the medium term we find that shift patterns do not necessarily match the demand arrival pattern. In the short term, variations in demand and capacity create unanticipated Erlang queues and

managers do not understand the resourcing implications if service availability is to be maintained.

4 *Complex services experience systems dynamics.* It has been known for a long time that manufacturing supply chains suffer from demand amplification effects such as the 'bullwhip effect' (Forrester, 1958). This is where the variability of demand increases as it is passed through the supply chain. It is only recently that the management literature has identified similar phenomena in service sectors (Akkermans and Voss, 2013). Similarly, where work flows through a complex system there are other sources of delay and poor flow caused by a lack of coordination or the batching of work. In healthcare the most commonly cited problems concern the lack of availability of beds in hospitals. These problems are often caused by the separate parts of the system not acting in coordination and, in particular, the timing of arrivals mismatching with the availability of resource due to the discharge processes out of hospital (see Allder *et al.*, 2010).

Flow management: more than capacity balancing?

The healthcare literature especially goes one step further than just looking at capacity management as a means to achieving adequate resource planning. The emphasis is more on achieving patient flow through the system (Litvak *et al.*, 2005; Litvak, 2009; Millard and McClean, 1996). Flow (i.e. the steady, uninterrupted movement of patients through the system) is now seen as a significant contributor to good service quality and may even influence clinical outcomes including mortality rates (see Silvester *et al.*, 2014). One of the principles that emerges from the Theory of Constraints (see Rahman, 1998) is that flow not capacity must be balances across a whole system. Flow is achieved by coordination and compatibility of adjacent processes as much as comparability of capacity levels. The failure to achieve this compatibility across supply chains or whole systems is widely reported in the public and private sectors (e.g. Silvester *et al.*, 2014; Womack and Jones, 1996).

Research methodology

The study site

The data from this study have been collected from a metropolitan police force in England. The force serves a population in excess of 2 million people in an area of over 300 square miles, with a workforce that includes over 7000 police officers and over 2000 support staff. The service is structured into ten smaller local units and neighbourhoods to allow for some local planning and detailed operational control.

Focus of the study

The choice of the work flow through custody suites is deliberate because these provide a good example of the changes being made in the delivery of services in an attempt to provide efficiency gains. Custody is also the pinch point between response and investigation processes. Historically, offenders arrested by officers would be taken to local police stations and kept in local police cells awaiting investigations or release. Many police stations have themselves been closed as asset rationalisation reflects the CSR, but, additionally, there has been much greater centralisation of the custody facilities so that each force now has fewer, larger custody sites in operation. Centralisation is a partial response to reducing inefficiency but also the co-location of specialist skills, for example embedded nurses. In theory this should achieve some efficiency savings as a consequence of the restructuring of management and also the pooling of demand. There is no standard size or design to a custody suite as advocated by the Home Office, but a typical 'new build' facility will have somewhere between 30 and 60 cells, with 2–4 custody sergeants and a team of civilian custody officers (where the service has not been outsourced).

The custody process

Figure 7.2 shows a representation of the custody process. The standard custody process follows three distinct phases:

- arrival and documentation;
- detention and investigation; and
- charge and disposal.

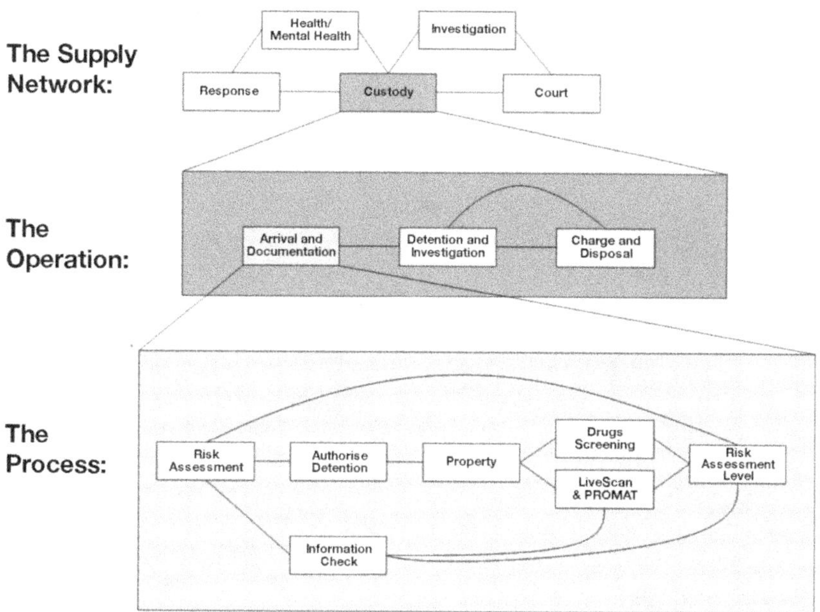

Figure 7.2 Overview of the custody process

Arrival and documentation

The arrival into the custody facility starts the custody process. The offender has to wait for a custody sergeant or civilian jailer to become available. During this wait phase the arresting officer completes all pre-assessment checks in preparation for the formal process of authorising detention. The offender is risk assessed, through a prescriptive series of questions, supported further by historical records from both the national and force level records. Having completed the risk assessment, the custody sergeant is then required to approve detention, and ensure that arrest has been appropriate. The vast majority of times detention is authorised. Documentation processes occur involving a range of sub-processes including finger-printing, drugs testing and documentation and removal of property, before the offender is moved into their cell. Although a highly standardised series of processes there are many different routes through this first phase of arrival and documentation, which may involve referral to the embedded health care and mental health staff.

Detention and investigation

The offender is then held in their cell, for an undefined period (as long as it does not exceed maximum detention times), for the primary purpose of investigation. However this detention period may also be used to ensure the offender has sobered up before interview (if intoxicated). For the custody process there is a continual overhead of welfare and domestic processes. This includes 'feeding and watering' and regular checks, dependent on their risk assessment. The minimum required standard is that physical checks are conducted once an hour. However some offenders may require much higher levels of supervision, including permanent close proximity watch where the person is very vulnerable and potentially self-harming. During this detention time, investigators managing the case will occasionally bring the offender out for interview. This again has multiple variants of a standardised process. It may involve appropriate adults (where a juvenile or vulnerable adult), interpreters and legal advisors ('briefs'). This iterative process will continue until the authorities decide on an outcome or run out of time as defined by law. This then leads to the disposal process, which may include a charge being put.

Charge and disposal

There are four outcomes to detention:

- no further action (NFA), where the offender is released with no impending action;
- bailed, where the offender is released (sometimes with conditions) with impending action, but their incarceration is stopped;
- remand to court, at this point they are charged, but released on a condition to attend court; and
- remanded in custody, where they are charged and kept in custody (police custody).

This final outcome is based on a number of factors including severity of crime, and the risk to them not attending court. The charging decision involves multiple sub-processes, including confirmation of evidence by an internal independent authorised officer and agreeing a charge with the Crown Prosecution Service (CPS). The charge may only be put to an offender by a custody sergeant. Where a person is remanded in custody, then the offender re-enters the detention process until they are transported to court. If this occurs on a Saturday afternoon this can be as long as 36 hours before a court reconvenes to hear the case.

So although the process is highly standardised, and follows a clearly defined path of activity, when documenting the sub-processes, there are high levels of customisation to each offender, and the routes through the process and complex.

Study methods

The authors have visited and worked with staff at a number of custody suites within the police force. The custody process was mapped as a whole system journey to understand the steps involved from arrest through the custody suite and then to follow-on stages, such as appearance of the offender at court. The resource constraints were assessed at each stage, in terms of both the structural and human resource requirements. The direct observation also allowed the researchers to obtain qualitative, explanatory data. Additionally a staff survey was distributed by Inspectors to all custody staff. Of the 278 staff available, 145 returned responses (52 per cent response rate). All facilities were represented in the responses. The survey was designed to test:

- The service delivery to internal and external operations.
- The contribution to the wider police system.
- Their understanding of priority.
- Their contact levels with external services.
- The perceptions of treatment and how they are valued.
- Their supervision and training support.

Further it provided the ability for the respondents to provide comment on the aspects in the system that are working well, and those aspects requiring improvement, and further identified these against the different interfaces to services existing in the custody operation. It was noted that in contrast to many data collection and survey processes run by the research team, across different sectors and sample frames, the detail and explanation provided was excellent, and far beyond expectation. The independent nature of the research meant that respondents were surprisingly candid in their assessment, highlighting issues which were not commonplace through the line of command.

It was not intended for the survey to be the primary source of research data, but it was to be used as a validation tool for the other quantitative analysis and to enrich the study with qualitative feedback. An inductively developed thematic analysis was completed to expose the common themes.

The primary analysis is the assessment of capacity and demand from empirical data. Demand was analysed using three years of custody data exported from the force's IT system using data taken between 20 March 2011 and 1 March 2014. The data contain records at an individual detainee level of the custody record number, arresting and investigating officers, timestamps for all the major checkpoints in the custody process and the disposal outcome. The data were cleaned to remove a small number of records where a discharge had not been recorded. There were also over 38,000 instances of bail returns, whereby an offender has been released on bail and reports to the custody suite as a bail condition. These events do not affect the availability of custody cells or make demands on custody sergeants' time, so these events were not assessed as part of this study. Similarly, some offenders with no fixed address were rarely kept in excess of 72 hours and these were treated as unusual cases. This analysis then provided 344,170 individual records of arrest and custody where the following measures could be accurately assessed:

- The arrival pattern in hourly time bands, day-of-week patterns and long-term trends.
- The disposal from custody in hourly time bands and day-of-week patterns.
- Occupancy statistics for individual custody suites by hour of day and day of week.
- The impact of special cause events such as the arrest rates on public holidays, etc.

Results

Figure 7.3 shows the demand pattern at the custody suites as a time series. There appears to be a downward trend in the demand figures, perhaps reflecting the changes in policy about dealing with minor offenders without detention. When studied by month the level of seasonal variation is low, July being the peak month and February the quietest month each year. There is an approximate 15 per cent difference in demand between these two months. There is also a seasonal pattern by day of week, with a slight trend towards fewer arrests in the earlier part of the week, shown in Figure 7.4.

On public holidays demand marginally reduces when compared to a normal working day. We can be fairly confident that this was a genuine reduction in demand and not a reduction in police activity because we discovered that historic planning activities had often encouraged more police officers to be on duty on these days, increasing the capacity.

When looked at as a daily arrival pattern, there is a trend showing that arrivals into custody peak at about 10am each day, with a second peak in the late afternoon (Figure 7.5). The arrival pattern mismatches to a great extent with the daily disposal pattern. Figure 7.6 shows a clear spike in disposals between 8 and 9 am each day. The primary reason for this spike is the transfer of many offenders to court by transportation services. Offenders who are released with no further action or are released with police bail are generally released later in the day after enquiries have been made.

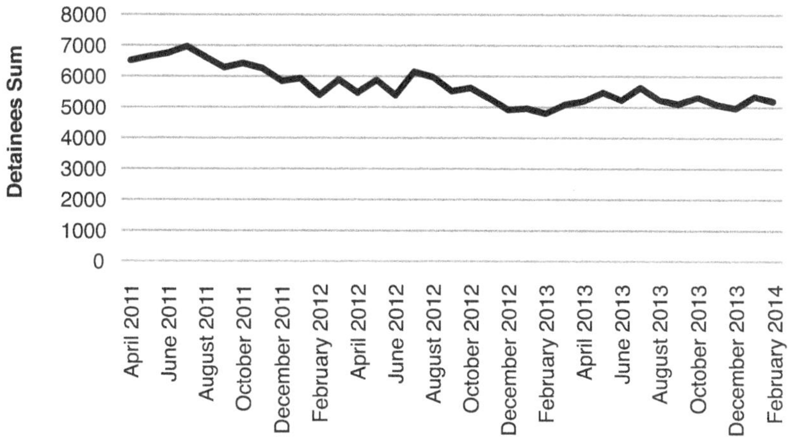

Figure 7.3 The total number of arrivals at custody suites in a police region by month

It was noticed that at many of the individual custody suites the average arrival pattern was less than one new arrival every hour. However, the arrival pattern was subject to highly significant levels of variability. Figure 7.7 shows the inter-arrival times for offenders. The average inter-arrival time is one arrival every 4.5 minutes but the data show that there are periods where the inter-arrival time is very low or zero. This variability suggests that the management of the peaks and troughs in

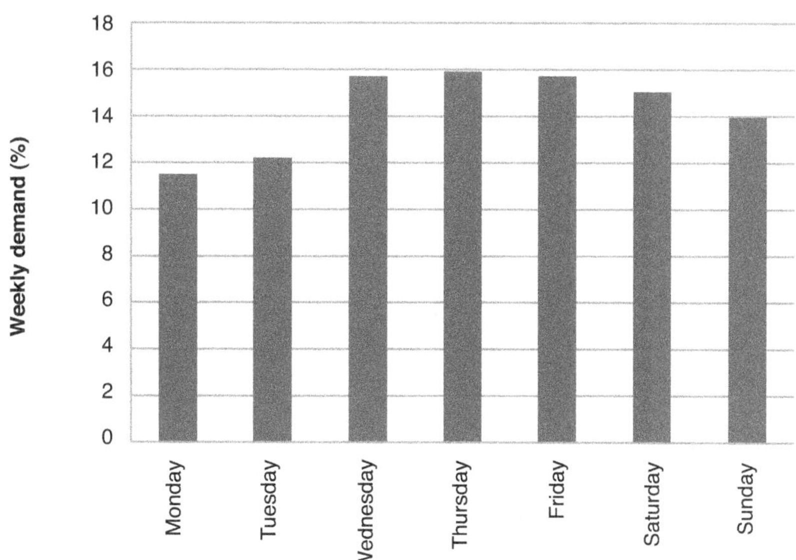

Figure 7.4 Custody suite demand by day of week

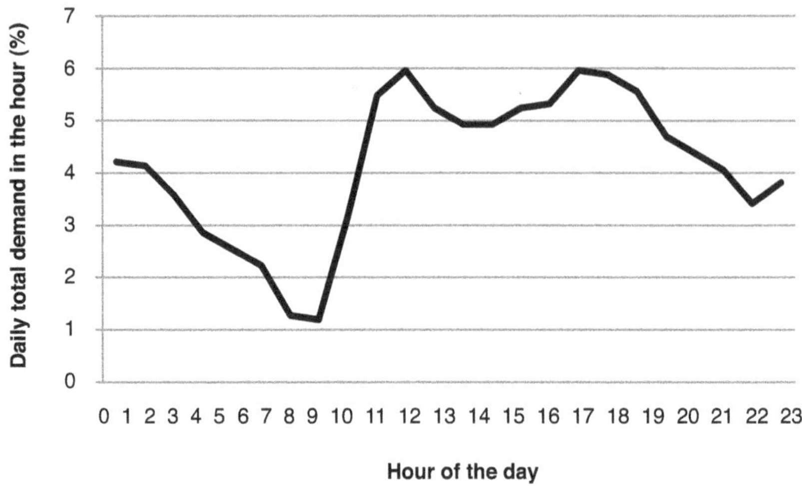

Figure 7.5 The daily arrival pattern

arrivals process is potentially much more difficult at peak times than the average figures would suggest by themselves.

Analysis of the data

Occupancy of custody suite facilities

A simple model of custody suite occupancy can be easily generated to establish the likely suite utilisation levels for predicted levels of demand. The analysis shows that,

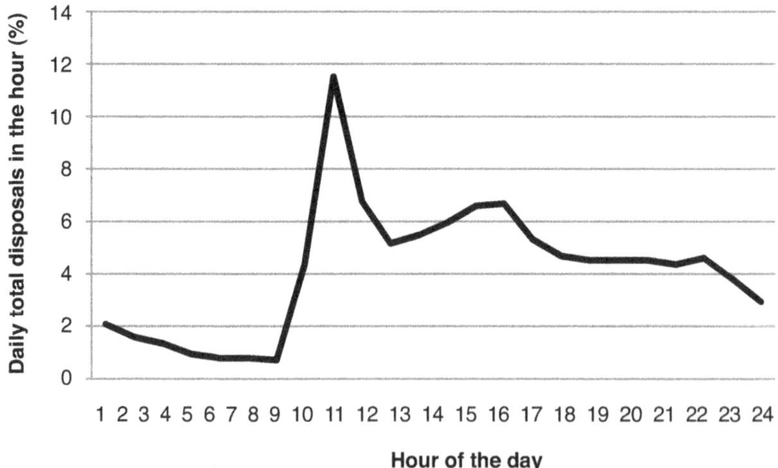

Figure 7.6 The daily disposal pattern from custody suites

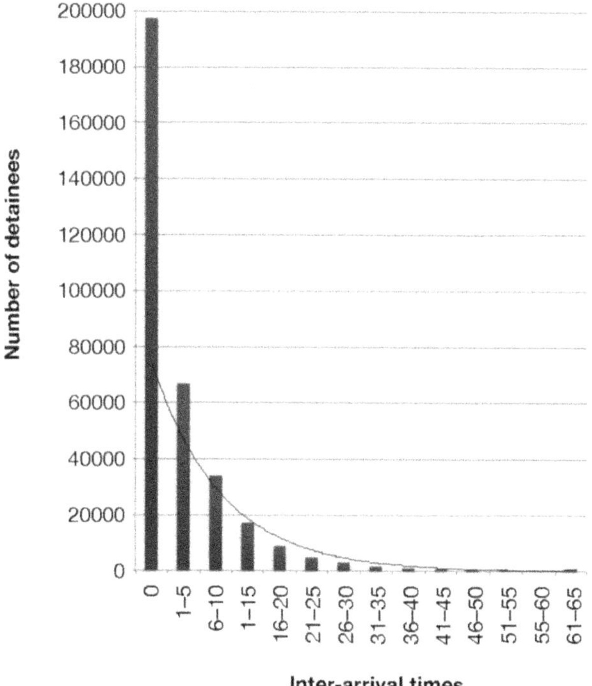

Figure 7.7 Statistical distribution of inter-arrival times

at average demand, suites are easily able to cope with the existing numbers of offenders arriving into the system and leaving in the usual disposal profile. This is because the peak in disposals occurs prior to the peak in new arrivals on each weekday. This provides a 2-hour time buffer where space is created for the day's new arrivals as existing offenders leave for court or are allowed to leave the facility. This contrasts with earlier modelling work in healthcare where the arrivals peak occurs several hours before the peak in discharges, leading to blocking of the facility. However, once we factor in the potential for an increase in demand above average, the occupancy levels of the suites increases significantly to the point where some facilities are running at levels of utilisation of 90 per cent or above and there will be problems on Sundays and Monday mornings because the lack of Sunday disposals to court and a peak in disposals to court and completion of investigation on Monday morning. Figure 7.8 shows how this model identifies the capacity issue.

Workload analysis for custody staff

Staff with appropriate skills can process on average 2 people per hour (including setup and completion time). The average time taken to process an arrival through to (and including) the risk assessment is 22 minutes but a comparative force study the

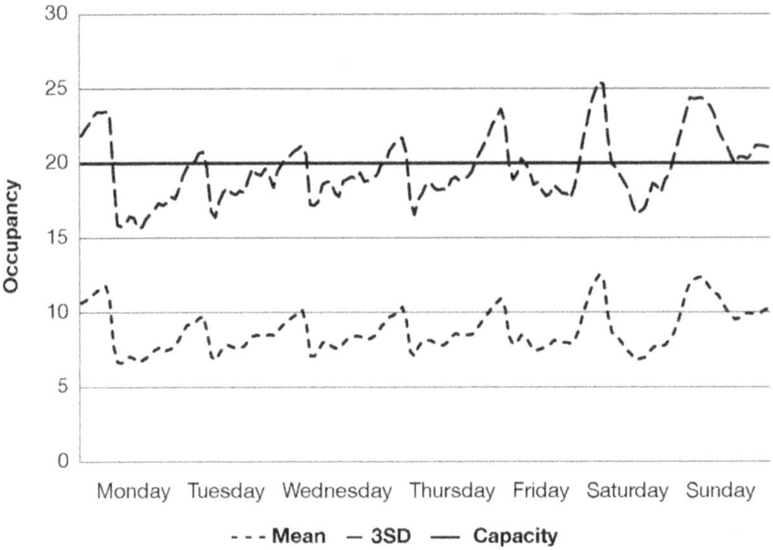

Figure 7.8 A model of predicted cell occupancy variation for a 20-cell custody suite

sites had some evidenced that attempts to deal plan for with more than two offenders per hour to be processed had caused issues in other custody suites of excess queuing, as setup time was not accounted for. Given that risk assessment needs to ensure that detainees are not likely to seriously self-harm the attitude is that the booking in process must not be rushed. Similarly, there are other risks associated with large backlogs of offenders waiting for the process to start, especially where their behaviour can be compromised by drug or alcohol intoxication. It should be noted that a disposal also takes a similar amount of time, so the workload pattern on custody sergeants becomes very complex throughout the day due to the pattern of arrivals and disposals. Further the requirement for a custody sergeant to multitask (essentially continuous swapping between parallel tasks), further reduces their effective capacity. Unlike cell capacity, staffing provision is flexed by altering shift patterns and the number of people on shift. There are additional constraints, such as the skill mix available within a custody suite.

Discussion

In this section we will tease out a number of issues that were raised by the analysis of the data and the feedback from staff within the system.

The nature of demand

The case study highlights that demand for this type of police service is partly self-generated. The timing of arrests and arrivals at the custody suite is dependent on the availability of beat officers. In this sense, the data still record activity in the system rather than some measure of true demand. There will be periods of time where crime is still occurring but is not being detected by patrols simply because no patrols are on duty in that location, or that the effect has yet to move through the system into custody. The daily arrival pattern of offenders mimics the shift pattern of the police and the site analysis showed that shift profiles in custody were a product of historical working practices and alignment to response officer shifts, rather than custody facility demand. A few local modifications of shift management had been implemented, for example 'super-lates' where the late shift stayed on shift for an additional 3 hours to cover night-time economy demand. However, this design was responsive to local understanding rather than as a deliberate capacity management strategy at force level. As a further example, there was evidence that additional staffing was being planned for public holiday periods even though the data show no increase in demand for these days in the year.

Demand can also be split into planned and unplanned categories in a similar manner to that of healthcare. While a small proportion of demand is both unplanned and urgent, the remainder of the unplanned work comes from the reactive patrol responses and the observation of crime as it happens to a great extent. Furthermore, the trend towards a reduction in the number of arrivals at custody suites is partly as a result of changes to police policy concerning who is arrested and who is released on the street (street disposal) and legislation has been developed to provide more opportunities for this to occur, based on officer discretion. It might be surprising to some that a large proportion of the work is planned and this occurs at a surprising range of seriousness of offence. For example, a raid on a property where there is a suspicion of drugs offences can be planned rather than being treated as an urgent 'soon-as-possible' type of response. Some of the most noticeable incidents of demand spikes were caused by 'proactive' policing, such as monthly initiatives to clear streets of homeless individuals – this often being undertaken without any coordination with the custody suites that were going to receive any individuals arrested as part of the initiative. Because these initiatives often result in multiple arrests over a short span of time there is a further analogy with healthcare in that the planned demand is more variable than the unplanned demand. Hence, many of the consequential issues associated with demand variability are caused by the system rather than imposed on the system.

Demand management approaches

Table 7.1 shows how the commonly applied methods of demand management have been applied in this case study. The main findings are that this service generally equates demand management with demand reduction. There is no incentive to deal with initial demand at a later date, although some investigation work might still continue after an offender has been released from the system.

Table 7.1 Demand management methods in the police service case study

Method	*Comments*
Demand reduction	There is increasing attention to challenge the necessity of bring offenders into custody. A 'street disposal' can be completed where the offender does not attend a custody suite. Some detainees require other services (i.e. mental health, before arriving in custody).
Complementary services	Different parts of the service share some resources and there is increasing awareness of the need to release capacity for the main value-adding tasks. Custody Suites now aim to release arresting officers back to their duties through better turnaround. 'Drunk tanks' (see below) or other field service alternatives to the arrest and detention of intoxicated individuals (e.g. 'pop-up' treatment units) have been used in some areas.
Reservations and booking systems	Overbooking is inappropriate in the custody system, however advance reservation can be completed through the contact centre when finding a custody to take the detainee. Further options are being explored to provide an on-line self-service booking facility for arresting officers.
Segmenting demand	Segmentation has not been explored by the force, as each custody is meant to provide an end-to-end service regardless of facility. However options are being considered as to whether certain facilities will have embedded partner agencies to speed up processing, therefore segmentation will make this allocation more effective.
Price incentives	Although price incentives seem totally inappropriate in custody. Nationally the idea has been communicated for providing drunk tanks – managed by 3rd parties who charge the detainees on departure for their stay. This cost incentive may then reduce demand on custody through reducing criminality (Barnes, 2013).
Off-peak working	Police forces have both response and planned activities. Planned operations may reflect the pressure on custody (i.e. arresting vagrants, when there is predicted low demand on custody).

The impact of demand pooling

The management literature consistently points to the benefits of the pooling of demand where variability is an issue. In the case of police services, this method of managing variation has been applied for both call centre responses and for custody suites. In the case of custody suites it can be seen that there are good theoretical principles for the pooling of demand. The centralisation of demand should create better availability of custody suite accommodation.

However, there are a number of caveats that must be applied to this issue. First, the data have revealed that the available space in custody suites is not the current bottleneck in the system. Instead, it is the availability of custody sergeants and civilian jailers that provide the clearest capacity constraint when the system becomes overloaded. Hence, many of the benefits of the demand pooling will not have been fully captured. We could also question the need for high utilisation of custody suites on the basis of cost. Unlike many healthcare resources, such as staffed beds or theatre suites we would expect the opportunity cost to be lower.

Second, the demand pooling has resulted in a change to the overall control of the processes. Non-pooled systems in local police stations generally had highly integrated and visible whole system flows. The officers in charge had good knowledge of and/or involvement in every activity in the process, including patrol capacity and activities, planned operations, detention and investigation activity, transport coordination and disposal planning. In the pooled system these stages in the process, and other related activities, are now separated out into a range of separately managed activities, where activities are even sometimes outsourced to third parties. Hence the gains made by pooling are partly offset by trade-offs with poorer coordination and flow.

Third, the logistics of pooled demand are very different. With fewer, larger sites the transport costs and journey times to custody suites can be higher, further reducing the financial benefits of the pooling. There is a principal difference in the cost of the transport between the ambulance service and response officers. Ambulance service respond to an incident, treat and transport; their value is in the rapid deployment of treatment, unutilised time offers availability to respond. The response officers (neighbourhood police/beat officers) have although deploy to incidents, and transport, the time in-between is preventative policing; they have a value in being out of the station, in their visible presence and ability to identify criminality. Therefore police tied up in transportation or in the custody system is direct waste to the wider police system. Some care has been taken to locate the centralised facilities in appropriate locations that reflect 'centres of gravity' for local demand. However, if systems do become overloaded, the system is less able to deflect demand to other locations as these locations are now further away.

Capacity management strategies

Historically, the capacity strategies seen in the custody operations have tended to not overtly match capacity with demand. Instead, the system has tended to 'cope' with demand in a relatively level capacity strategy. This is partly down to an historic lack of full understanding of the actual demands in the system where resources need to be applied. There is also considerable practical and cultural resistance to some attempts to chase demand. Police shift patterns have tended to be relatively fixed in nature and senior officers can find it a challenge to make the appropriate adjustments.

It is interesting to see some development of alternative services as complementary to those involving the arrest and transport of offenders. Pop-up facilities in city centres show a highly innovative way of providing alternative capacity.

Managing variation

One of the main challenges in this system is the variability of demand. The site investigations revealed that this manifested itself in two ways. First, the arrival pattern

Table 7.2 Capacity management strategies observed in the case study

Method	*Comments*
Chase demand	Assets (i.e. cells) are fixed, so in medium-term planning only adjustment of staff offers capacity change. There is limited focus on low utilization of cells, and to an extent staff. Therefore the attention to chasing demand is limited.
Increasing customer participation	In context of custody the arresting and investigating officers are the customer. The arresting officers have a specific influence on demand and throughput time. There has been awareness and engagement with arresting officers to complete all processing where possible in advance of entering the custody system.
Scheduling work shifts	A precedent has been set that although there are three shifts, these are consistent in their staffing. This is reflective of limited understanding of short term demand variability.
Creating adjustable capacity	Staff are paid both a shift and a rota allowance. However both through precedent and local affiliation the flexibility in staff assignment this is meant to provide the force is rarely used. Most of the flexibility is done through goodwill agreements.
Sharing capacity	The rollout of super-custodies is meant to deliver shared capacity in terms of physical assets and staff. Further the use of 'clusters' (geographically close facilities) also provides some short-term capacity sharing. Hence capacity is shared across similar facilities more than switching resource from one type of service to another.
Using part-time staff	Part time staff have been in use for many years, and are inseparable from the full-time staff in their roles.

shows extreme variation in inter-arrival time. This can mean long periods of very little activity followed by short periods where the system cannot easily cope with a rush of arrivals. This makes achieving efficiency very difficult. Second, and at least equally importantly, we also have to look at the impact of mix variation in the system. This has a particular impact on the detention part of the process and the necessary resources. In a facility with low risk detainees, one support officer will be able to monitor 10 cells simultaneously without placing the detainees in any danger. However, as soon as a custody suite receives one or more high risk individual, the resource requirements increase considerably as some offenders will need one-to-one direct, continuous observation. It is not possible to predict precisely when this is going to happen. Hence, one of the overlooked mechanisms for capacity shortage in this system is when the supervision capacity can become overloaded, even though a high proportion of the cells are empty and the arrival rate is low.

Impact on flow

One of the ironies of the greater focus on capacity and demand within this system is that the great local optimisation of processes has caused a loss of coordination across the system because of the loss of visibility and control by custody sergeants. This has resulted in some delays in the offender's journey, especially where responsibility is transferred from one organisation to another. Given that the existing focus of attention is on the efficiency (and utilisation) of resources, it could be quite difficult for a whole system approach to be adopted, whereby some parts of the system deliberately operate at with lower levels of utilisation to achieve better flow.

Conclusions

Within the literature review we highlighted some of the limitations of demand and capacity planning within the public sector. Four specific issues were identified and these have been tested against the case study of police custody suites.

1 IS PLANNING DEMAND-DRIVEN?

The case study suggests that the pressures for increased efficiency have resulted in an increasing look at the demand in the system, mainly because of the planning involved in the centralisation of the custody process and the development of custody suites where demand has been pooled.

2 CAN RESOURCES BE EFFECTIVELY PLANNED?

Our findings suggest that the police service still needs to develop its understanding of the nature of demand. The system still records activity, not true demand, and consequently there is still scope for errors in resource provision. Perhaps more importantly our findings indicate that the Police service can control its demand and, in the case of custody suites, much of the activity is driven by resource allocation decisions and short-run decisions concerning planned proactive policing or crime prevention work. The unexpected finding is that the focus on the pooling of demand has caused an unintentional loss of visibility of the flow in the system due to the increased dedication of resources to specific tasks. This does result in poorer decisions about the quantity and timing of resource allocation, especially when we look at the key role of bottleneck resources such as custody sergeants. We would also recommend further investigation of the relationship between the availability of capacity and demand. We suspect that the availability of capacity allows some demand to be recorded when it otherwise would not be.

3 THE CAUSES OF WAITS AND DELAYS

The application of queue theory to police service applications has already been made, in the planning context of both call centres and custody suites. A high proportion of front-line police work tends to be very short-term in its nature and there is far less of an issue for work backlogs when compared with healthcare, for example. Consequently the service is able to provide reactive resources in many situations to prevent queues from building. The key finding from this work is the impact of demand variability and mix variability on the system. Custody suites experience very high variability of inter-arrival times of new work. This places the early stages of the booking process under considerable strain at times and it makes efficient resource planning more difficult. Custody suites will inevitably experience periods of very low demand due to random variation and the underlying drivers of demand. Hence, we would highlight that performance measures such as utilisation could provide a very misleading impression of the efficiency and capability of custody suite to cope with demand.

4 SYSTEMS DYNAMICS

The journey time restrictions for work that moves through this system largely inhibit the likelihood of significant supply chain dynamics from occurring in the processes we observed. However, we did find evidence that the local optimisation of individual parts of the overall journey, such as transportation, have created poorer flow to some extent because of the batching of transport of offenders to court etc. This batching effect does have implications for service quality and the ability of the later stages of the processes to cope with demand and keep to schedules. Thus these are systems flow issues but not a systems dynamics problem of the type observed by Forrester (1958) or Akkermans and Voss (2013).

Finally, we have been able to compare the problems and issues in the police service with demand and capacity problems from within the public healthcare literature. The flow of work through this part of the police service mimics to a great extent the flow of emergency patients admitted into hospital. The problems of availability of police cells and hospital beds follow very similar principles. In this research we have found that the interaction between the police service, transport and courts allows the problems of physical capacity to be resolved more easily than that in healthcare. In this case the disposal earlier in the day, the regularity of discharge, the short and predictable length of stay provide an illustration of what could be achieved in healthcare systems if similar practices are observed.

The work has highlighted two areas for future research within the public sector. First we suggest that the nature of the relationship between demand and capacity is not fully understood within the public sector. In this case we found that the provision of capacity created some further opportunities to record crime. More research is needed to create a deeper understanding of whether and how extra capacity might generate additional demand in other service settings. Second, this case has provided an example of where the pressure for efficiency has encouraged local optimisation of processes rather than whole system improvement. More research is needed to see whether this is evident in the wider public system.

References

Akkermans, H. and Voss, C. (2013) 'The service bullwhip effect'. *International Journal of Operations and Production Management*, 33(6): 765–88.

Allder, S., Silvester, K. and Walley, P. (2010) 'Managing capacity and demand across the patient journey'. *Clinical Medicine*, 10(1): 13–15.

Barnes, L. (2013) 'Humberside PCC: drunk tanks could ease strain of alcohol policing'. Retrieved from www.policeprofessional.com/news.aspx?id=16679 (accessed 9 June 2014).

Boysen, N. Fliedner, M. and Scholl, A. (2007) 'A classification of assembly line balancing problems'. *European Journal of Operational Research*, 183(2): 674–93.

Crandall, R.E. and Markland, R.E. (1996) 'Demand management – today's challenge for service industries'. *Production and Operations Management*, 5(2): 106–22.

Fitzsimmons, J.A. and Fitzsimmons, M.J. (2006) *Service Management: Operations, Strategy, Information Technology*. New York: McGraw-Hill.

Forrester, J.W. (1958) 'Industrial Dynamics: a major breakthrough for decision makers'. *Harvard Business Review*, 36(4): 37–66.

Gershon, P. (2004) *Releasing Resources to the Front Line*. Norwich: HMSO.

Hall, R.W. (1990) *Queueing Methods for Service and Manufacturing*. Upper Saddle River, NJ: Prentice Hall.

Heskett, J.A., Sasser, W.E., and Hart, C.W. (1990) *Service Breakthroughs*. New York: Free Press.

HMIC (2011) *Adapting to Austerity*. London: HMIC.

HM Treasury (2010) *Spending Review 2010*. Norwich: HMSO.

Jones, P. and Hamilton, D. (1992) 'Yield management'. *Cornell HRA Quarterly*, 7(1): 89–95.

Kimes, S. E. (1989) 'Yield management, a tool for capacity constrained service firms'. *Journal of Operations Management*, 8(4): 348-363.

Kimes, S.E. and Chase, R.B. (1998) 'The strategic levels of yield management'. *Journal of Service Research*, 1(2): 156–66.

Kimes, S.E., Chase, R.B. and Wirtz, J. (2003) 'Has revenue management become acceptable? Findings from an international study on the perceived fairness of rate fences'. *Journal of Service Research*, 6(2): 125–35.

Klassen, K.J. and Rohleder, T.R. (2001) 'Combining operations and marketing to manage capacity and demand in services'. *Service Industries Journal*, 21(2): 1–30.

Klassen, K.J. and Rohleder, T.R. (2002) 'Demand and capacity management decisions in services; how they impact on one another'. *International Journal of Operations and Production Management*, 22 (5): 527–48.

Krueger, U. and Schimmelpfeng, K. (2013) 'Characteristics of service requests and service processes of fire and rescue service dispatch centers'. *Health Care Management Science*, 16: 1–13.

Litvak, E. (ed.) (2009) *Managing Patient Flow in Hospitals: Strategies and Solutions* (2nd edn.) Oakbrook Terrace, IL: Joint Commission Resources.

Litvak, E., Buerhaus. P.I., Davidoff, F., Long, M.C., McManus, M.L. and Berwick, D.M. (2005) 'Managing unnecessary variability in patient demand to reduce nursing stress and improve patient safety'. *Joint Commission Journal on Quality and Patient Safety*, 31(6): 330–38.

Lovelock, C.H. (1992) 'Strategies for managing capacity constrained service organisations' In Lovelock (ed.), *Managing Services: Marketing, Operations and Human Resources*. Upper Saddle River, NJ: Prentice Hall.

Millard, P.H. and McClean, S.I. (1996) *Go with the Flow: A Systems Approach to Healthcare Planning*. London: Royal Society of Medicine Press.

Pullman, M.E. and Thompson, G. (2003) 'Strategies for integrating capacity with demand in service networks'. *Journal of Service Research*, 5(3): 169–83.

Radas, S. and Shugan, S. (1998) 'Managing service demand: shifting and bundling'. *Journal of Service Research*, 1(1): 47–64.

Rahman, S. (1998) 'Theory of constraints: a review of the philosophy and its applications'. *International Journal of Operations and Production Management*, 18(4): 336–55.

Rhyne, D.M. (1988) 'The impact of demand management on service system performance'. *Service Industries Journal*, 8(4): 446–58.

Sasser, W.E. Jr. (1976) 'Match supply and demand in service industries'. *Harvard Business Review*, 54 (6): 133–40.

Seddon, J. (2005) *Freedom from Command and Control* (2nd edn). Buckingham: Vanguard Education.

Showalter, M.J. and White, J.D. (1991) 'An integrated model for demand-output management in service organisations: implications for future research'. *International Journal of Operations and Production Management*, 11(1): 51–67.

Silvester, K., Steyn, R., Bevan, H., and Walley, P. (2004) 'Reducing waiting times in the NHS: is lack of capacity the problem?' *Clinician in Management*, 12: 105–11.

Silvester, K., Harriman, P., Walley, P. and Burley, G. (2014) 'Does process flow make a difference to mortality and cost? An observational study'. *International Journal of Health Care Quality Assurance*, 27(7): 616–32.

Spicker, P. (2009) 'The nature of public service'. *International Journal of Public Administration*, 32: 970–91.

Walley, P. (2013) 'Does the public sector need a more demand-driven approach to capacity management?' *Production Planning and Control*, 24(10–11): 877–90.

Walley, P., Silvester, K. and Steyn, R. (2006) 'Managing variation in demand: lessons from the UK National Health Service'. *Journal of Healthcare Management*, 51(5): 309–22.

Womack, J. and Jones, D. (1996) *Lean Thinking: Banish Waste and Create Wealth in Your Organisation*. New York: Simon and Schuster.

Zeithaml, V.A, Parasuraman, A. and Berry, L.L. (1985) 'Problems and strategies in services marketing'. *Journal of Marketing*, 49(Spring): 33–46.

8 Drivers of change in the UK fire service

An operations management perspective

Nicola Bateman, Karen Maher and Ray Randall

Introduction

The UK fire and rescue service is subject to reform, along with other public sector services, resulting in later retirement age and budget limitations; the fire service is also subject to other societal changes such as shifts in fitness levels and a reduction in call outs. This chapter reviews these changes and considers them from an operations management perspective. A method for how to measure operational effectiveness is proposed and its use in informing changes to operating practice in the fire service is advocated.

Reform in the fire and rescue service in the UK is driven by multiple agendas including seeking continuous improvement, meeting cost reductions and a political desire to reform these established public services (Public Accounts Committee, 2011). Examples of these changes to working practices for the emergency services are documented for ambulance (*ibid.*), police (Windsor, 2012) and fire services (Connor, 2013). In addition to change driven by government, public services also need to respond to demographic and societal change. The average age of firefighters is likely to increase with the proposed implementation of later retirement and this could have implications for the typical levels of health, fitness and experience among firefighters. In addition, changes in geographic population density, road use and home safety affects both the nature and quantity of demand for fire and rescue services. This chapter explores how some of these changes are affecting the fire services. It includes reference to two cases where change is taking place and explores the role that operational effectiveness measurement can have in understanding and managing change.

This chapter initially explores the literature for the role of the fire and rescue service in the UK, changes to the demand and capacity for these services and how changes in fitness and average age of firefighters affects their wellbeing and effectiveness. The final part of the literature examines the type of operational data that is collected by different fire services. The chapter then goes on to explore two cases where operational effectiveness was measured (both cases use pseudonyms). The first case, 'the Shires', explores how fitness and age affect operational effectiveness; however the main outcome of this study was a better understanding of how to measure operational effectiveness. The second case, 'the Counties', develops the Shires approach for measuring operational effectiveness and applies it to a study examining a change in working practice and shift patterns. The chapter concludes with three propositions related to the evaluation of operational effectiveness and assessment of change in the fires service.

Literature

The government direction for fire and rescue services in England is set in the *Fire and Rescue National Framework for England* (Department for Communities and Local Government, 2012a) and follows an equivalent document for 2008–11. It states that it 'sets out high level expectations. It does not prescribe operational matters. These are best determined locally by fire and rescue authorities.' The priorities are:

> 1. identify and assess the full range of foreseeable fire and rescue related risks their areas face, make provision for prevention and protection activities and respond to incidents appropriately
> 2. work in partnership with their communities and a wide range of partners locally and nationally to deliver their service
> 3. be accountable to communities for the service they provide' (Department for Communities and Local Government, 2012a: 7)

Fire and rescue services are required to perform a wide range of services at an organisational level. These include risk registers, large scale incidence response planning and co-operating with other agencies. This chapter reviews the main changes and contemporary pressures on the UK fire service specifically changes to demand and capacity for fire and rescue services, and changes to the profile of firefighters and related HR policies with the fire service. Also reviewed are the operational data gathering activities for fire services.

Fire services are split up in to five family groups within England by the Department for Communities and Local Government for performance monitoring and are categorised as 'most similar services' (Department for Communities and Local Government, 2009). As an example, family group 1 is categorised as rural and family group 5 as metropolitan.

Changes to demand and capacity for the fire service

Over the last few decides the role of the fire service has changed. The demand from callouts has reduced and in terms of outcomes there has been a considerable reduction in deaths due to fires with over a 60 per cent reduction in deaths from domestic fires from the 1980s until the present day, with 168 in 2012/13 (Knight, 2013; Department for Communities and Local Government, 2013b). For 2012–13 fire services nationally attended 519,900 incidents of all kinds including fires, road traffic collisions (RTC) and false alarms, which has been a 14 per cent reduction on the previous year and a 46 per cent reduction from 2002–3 (Department for

Communities and Local Government, 2013b). The Counties, from the second case study, attended broadly 14,000 emergency calls in 2012–13 which showed a reduction in calls overall on the previous year. However there was an increase in RTC attendance and an increase in the number of special service incidents, which include such things as animal rescue and chemical spills, highlighting how the nature of the role of a firefighter is changing. This reduction in demand is due to a range of prevention activities by the fire service, societal change and various improvements in household safety.

Increasing community engagement activities to reduce the risk of fire appear to have had an effect as indicated by the reducing number of deaths in domestic fires. These types of activities include home safety visits, visits to schools and other community events and inspection of high risk premises. The time spent on fire safety activities in England (excluding London) changed from just over 500,000 hours (2002/03) to a peak in 2006–7 of 1,000,000 hours and then reducing to 700,000 hours in 2012–13 (Department for Communities and Local Government, 2013a). Thus the fire service has been fulfilling a societal desire to be more effective and in terms of 'stakeholder value' through the reduction of the causes of fire rather than literally just fire-fighting.

Other changes to the fire and rescue services activities include attending fewer road traffic accidents and other emergencies such as flooding. There were 156,000 of these non-fire incidents in 2008–9 and 134,700 in 2012–13 (Department for Communities and Local Government, 2010, 2013b). The fire service's prevention role in reducing road traffic accidents takes place in the form of many community and schools activities. Examples can be found on the Chief Fire Officers' Association web page (CFOA, 2014), which identifies activities undertaken for Road Safety Week (9 to 15 June 2014) by 28 fire and rescue services across the UK.

In conventional operations management this reduction in demand both for emergency fire and non-fire services would indicate that there was a case for lowering capacity. However, for each individual emergency there is a need to maintain and improve responsiveness. From the property holders' and firefighters' point of view the capacity to attend a fire quickly is critical. Therefore, response times need to be maintained and a geographic coverage of all areas still has to be upheld. This combination of a lower number of incidents to be dealt with and demands to maintain national coverage and response times represents a challenge to fire services.

In this context, one way of expressing capacity is the number of firefighters. In 2002–3 there were 31,699 'whole-time' (full-time) firefighters and this has reduced by approximately 11 per cent to 28,166 for 2010–11 (Knight, 2013). Over the same period the number of retained firefighters (FTE) has grown by approximately 9 per cent from 10,720 to 11,702. This may indicate that while overall numbers are similar, the working arrangements of staff are indicative of a drive to develop capacity in a way that reflects changes in demands.

The majority of whole-time firefighters are currently working the shift system laid out in '*The Grey Book*' (Fire Brigades Union, 2009), which outlines the conditions of service for firefighters. Although how this is managed can be agreed locally with each authority, in the most part this consists of two day shifts, two night shifts and four days off (2-2-4), requiring four watches (a watch also known as a crew is essentially a shift), to allow for full cover of the station. Alternate working systems are starting to appear within the UK FRS as a way of reducing costs by reducing the number of whole-time personnel required to offer the same level of cover, such as day crewing plus and day crewed/retained.

Fitness, age and wellbeing

Firefighters joining the service prior to 2006 are currently able to retire at age 50 and after 30 years of service. For those joining post 2006 the retirement age increased to age 60 and at the time of writing proposals are in place to change the pension rights and retirement age to 60 for all operational staff (Department for Communities and Local Government, 2012b; Firefighters' Pension Scheme, 2006; Williams *et al.*, 2013). The number of whole-time firefighters has been reducing in recent years and recruitment has been low (Department for Communities and Local Government, 2013a). These two factors have combined to make the average age of a firefighter increase over time (Bath Chronicle, 2014) as firefighters are retiring later and fewer, younger firefighters are recruited. It is well known that fitness reduces as we age (Health Survey for England, 2009; Allied Dunbar National Fitness Survey, 1992) and so an increasing mean age of firefighters would be likely to adversely affect overall fitness of the service. Fitness particularly affects firefighters as a role because of the physical requirements of the job.

Fitness and health have moved up the fire service agenda in recent years with a key document from the Firefit Steering group released in 2009 outlining best practice and key recommendations for fitness policy for the UK Fire and Rescue service (Firefit Steering Group, 2009). This suggests a minimum recommended aerobic fitness requirement for operational firefighters based on a review of the scientific literature on the physical demands of firefighting. Recent work has attempted to quantify the physical demands of various firefighting tasks within a UK cohort in order to rationalise any fitness requirement for the role (Siddall *et al.*, 2014). Findings of this work suggest that tasks related to firefighting can require an oxygen consumption of up to $47 ml \cdot kg^{-1} \cdot min^{-1}$ and up to 92 per cent of heart rate reserve, with running out hose and climbing stairs with firefighting equipment being the most demanding activities. This is equivalent to level 10.2 on the multi-stage shuttle run test (bleep test). Alongside this, it has been shown that risk profiles of firefighters for lifestyle diseases such as coronary heart disease, stroke, obesity and diabetes are in line with the general population (Munir *et al.*, 2012; Smith *et al.*, 2012; Plat *et al.*, 2012; Poston *et al.*, 2011). Therefore, as the average age of firefighters increases there is a risk that age-associated health problems will have a growing negative impact on firefighters' operational effectiveness. As a consequence, health promotion and wellbeing policies are becoming more common in many fire and rescue services. The majority of research on health and wellbeing within a firefighter population has been conducted outside of the UK, mainly in the US, but at the time of writing a major national study is being undertaken to assess lifestyle factors in UK firefighters (Turner, 2013). Preliminary results suggest similar findings to the previously mentioned studies showing trends in line with the general population for cardiovascular disease risk (Siddall *et al.*, 2014). The evidence of similar risk profile for firefighters is surprising considering the physical nature of the role and the requirement for applicants to achieve a high standard of fitness and health.

There are few data that directly relate firefighter fitness to its effect on operations, but one might expect fitter fighters to be more effective. However, little hard evidence exists to confirm this and to assess the relative sensitivity of firefighters' fitness to operational effectiveness. This was one of the purposes of the study conducted in the 'Shires' case study explored later in the chapter.

Operational data for fire and rescue services

Fire and rescue services publish annual reports on their performance (see individual fire service websites such Derbyshire Fire and Rescue, 2012–13; Greater Manchester Fire and Rescue, 2013) and these typically cover areas such as; number of primary fires, average response time – first appliance, home fire safety visits, commercial fire safety inspections and energy consumption by region. Much of this data is collected from response data that is collected by incident and details information such as incident types and time to attendance. There is some variation in how fire services define measures, for example for response times Essex measure the appliance leaving the station in under 2 min from the call coming through (this is also called turn out times by some services) whereas Leicestershire measure the appliance arriving at an incident in under 10 minutes and London is 12 minutes.

The reports published by different services do not follow a standard format, for example London Fire Brigade (2013) base data around their six key aims (prevention, protection, response, resources, people and principles) and cover key indicators such as those mentioned above. Essex Fire and Rescue Service's report tends to cover similar types of data but is less organised around aims and objectives (Essex Fire Authority, 2012). In these reports some fire services often compare their performance with performance for their 'family group'. Data in these reports are used by the Department for Communities and Local Government to compare performance of similar fire services within the family groups in key areas such as primary fires, road traffic incidents and fire safety. However, there appears to be limited measures that cover shorter term operational effectiveness that is likely to be important for highlighting changes to operating procedures. These reports are 'outward facing', written for public consumption, so it is likely that fire services are self-censoring and are less critical than they would be with internal data.

Two fire and rescue service cases

The following two cases explore the use of operational data for two different fire services in different parts of the country. The initial purpose of conducting the investigations into each of these fire services was not to examine the use of operational data but to use it as a yardstick for examining wider changes that affected operational practices in the service. As such the investigation into the use of operational data in these cases was not the primary function of the research, however, as part of the research in each case the use of operational data emerged as common theme, and hence its presentation here. To provide each case with a wider context the initial purpose of the case research is presented. This additionally demonstrates the importance of effective operational measures in monitoring change in public services, particularly in an environment where maintaining the service levels to the public is an overriding requirement.

The Shires fire and rescue service – age and operational effectiveness

The Shires Fire and Rescue Service (FRS) has a mix of rural and some larger non-metropolitan cities in its area and they were keen to put an emphasis on maintaining and improving fitness. They were also aware that the mean age of their firefighters was increasing and, conscious of the relationship between age and fitness, were interested in monitoring health and fitness levels (Munir *et al.*, 2012). The Shires mean age between 2008 and 2011 had increased from 38.5 to 40 years (data from Shires HR records). A review of the Shires health and fitness data revealed an increase in obesity in their firefighters with the number of firefighters in the obese category having risen from 10.9 to 12.9 per cent between 2008 and 2011. A change to on-station activities in 2005 had also removed allotted time to fitness training:

> In 2005 time allocated within the daily work routine for fulltime firefighters fitness training was removed, however, two hours a week (tour) is still provided on the night shifts. Firefighters who wish to exercise during the day shifts complete their training within their allocated lunch hour. Part-time firefighters have no regular time for exercise allocated. They have a requirement to be fit for role, but have to exercise in their own time. PT equipment is provided on their stations to facilitate this.
>
> (Shires FRS health and fitness adviser)

The important question for the Shires service was: did these changes to age and fitness have an effect at an operational level? To answer this question the Shires FRS wanted to use its existing operational data with the fire station as the unit of measurement. This was considered because change to working practices was likely to be taking place at the station level. There are also different types of fire stations such as full time and part time stations and the performance of these can be compared along with differences in fitness facilities and regimes and contrasting demographic profiles for firefighters from urban to rural.

In addition to the specific issues of fitness and demographic changes, the Shires also wanted to examine their performance measures to enable performance improvement at a local level 'giving greater emphasis to the operational readiness and competence of stations and watches' (Shires FRS area manager).

To address these issues the following research questions were posed:

- Using existing operational effectiveness measures is the effectiveness of fire stations influenced by fitness levels of their firefighters?
- Do the existing and proposed measures of operational effectiveness for fire stations allow managers within the Shires FRS to make informed decisions about management of fire stations?

Methodology

The research used existing data from two principle sources, health and fitness data for individual firefighters and existing operational performance data. Health and fitness data from 785 firefighters was sorted by fire station and those with more than thirty firefighters providing valid data were used. This resulted in nine fire stations being analysed (the smallest had 31 firefighters, the largest had 66). Using a series on one-way ANOVA analysis, fitness measures were compared between fire stations. There were several fitness measures available to us; BMI, waist size, VO_2 max and percentage fat.

Fire stations at each end of the fitness scales (i.e. the most fit and least fit) then had their operational effectiveness data interrogated to examine if there was any evidence of differences in operational performance. This operation effectiveness data was limited to turnout times.

This analysis served two purposes: first to initially explore if different levels of fitness affect operational effectiveness (RQ1), and second to explore if the existing performance measurement system was able to operate at this level of decision making (RQ2).

Results and conclusions

Of the nine fire stations (FS 1 and FS 2) two showed significant differences in fitness between their firefighters for VO_2 max and waist size, the rest of the fire stations were clustered with similar results, with a third fire station (FS 3) that had marginal significance also for VO_2 max and waist. There were also differences for percentage fat and BMI but these were not statistically significant. The causes of these differences are as yet unknown but could be due to different fitness regimes and age.

In terms of operational performance, the data that was provided related to turnout times and there were no significant differences either between FS 1, 2 or 3 or any of the other six fire stations. At first this might indicate that differences in fitness make no difference. However turnout times do not cover the range of activities performed by fire stations thus a more in depth analysis of effectiveness is required. Moreover, the urgency associated with firefighters' work may buffer the impact of fitness on the time taken to attend a fire (i.e. it may be more effortful for those with lower fitness levels to achieve a good response time but they are highly motivated to do so because of the importance of the task). It may have also been that local geography influenced responsiveness. Thus future work includes obtaining better measures for operational effectiveness that includes less urgent and / or more discretionary activities at fire station level to allow changes such as health and fitness levels to be tracked over time.

Exploration of operational effectiveness at the Shires

Following the inconclusive results from the fitness and operational effectiveness analysis it was decided to further explore how operational effectiveness could be measured using current data collected by the Shires and to this end a number of interviews were conducted with:

- A station manager – an operational manager of a station who runs four watches.
- Two group managers concerned with policy and response.
- Manager of HR information systems.
- Manager of HR Business Partners who look at performance issues, capability, discipline.

The interviews were semi-structured and reviewed the method for assessing operational effectiveness in the fitness study (i.e. in the response data and the unit of measure assessment – the fire station). The interviews went on to explore further ways of measuring effectiveness including how the current performance measurement system was used and ways to quantify other aspects such as preventative activities, for instance public engagement and assessing operational readiness and competence of fire crews. Interviewees were also given an opportunity to suggest any additional measures for effectiveness they would want to be included and how this data should be handled.

Results from interviews provided some fairly clear conclusions:

1 The appropriate unit of measurement is the watch not the fire station. This is because the watches are managed by watch managers who have different approaches and the operation of different watches at a single station can vary. So calculating effectiveness across watches to give an overall station measure will tend to mask variation and give a good measure.
2 Watches and stations in the Shires adhere to the targets set for response times set fairly consistently and so do not show up much variation of effectiveness.

Suggestions about what could be done to more adequately measure effectiveness were numerous and covered a wide range of areas. Reviewing these suggestions put the researchers in mind of the overall equipment effectiveness (OEE) measurement used primarily in lean context to assess the effectiveness of individual pieces of equipment. OEE was first proposed by Nakajima (1984) and then Rich (1999) and was promoted initially in the automotive sector and then adopted widely through endorsement by the Department of Trade and Industry (DTI, 2000). It consists of three areas; quality, availability and performance with the idea of assessing the important aspects of a particular piece of equipment. This idea can be translated into service application as quality, availability and performance are concepts that are highly relevant to service delivery. There is precedence for using OEE in non-manufacturing applications; for example, Simons *et al.* (2004) apply it to road freight transport. So an initial framework using OEE's three elements allowed the suggestions from the interviews at the Shires to be categorised as shown in Table 8.1.

The comments shown in the final column indicate some shortcomings in measures such as those associated with performance and for equipment maintenance the wider implications of this measure. The (neg.) notation indicates that as this measure increases it negatively impacts operational effectiveness.

Consideration of these suggestions, the comments and the role of the fire service as stated in the *Fire and Rescue National Framework for England* (Department for Communities and Local Government, 2012a) – to 'identify and assess the full range of foreseeable fire and rescue related risks their areas face, make provision for prevention and protection activities and respond to incidents appropriately' – would indicate that an assessment of 'responsiveness', 'availability' and 'preparedness' is appropriate. Hence the structure of performance measures from Table 8.1 has been altered to Table 8.2 to better fit this framework, with some of the quality related measures appearing in preparedness. So a further conclusion is that:

3 A measure of effectiveness should include some aspect of responsiveness, availability and preparedness.

Conclusions from the Shires study

From the study there is no indication that there are differences in operational effectiveness of stations but only if effectiveness is measured in response times at

Table 8.1 Summary of suggested operational effectiveness measures structured into overall equipment effectiveness categories

Conventional OEE	*Possible measures*	*Comments*
Performance	Turnout times Attendance times	Probably do not vary much Too incident specific and dependent on geography?
Availability	Sickness (neg) Stand down times (neg)	Is availability too narrow a measure for the fire service?
Quality	Commendations Training competency Breathing Apparatus tests Vehicle accidents (neg) Critical equipment fails (neg) Discipline cases (neg) Personal injuries (neg) Equipment maintenance	All pretty indirect and either look at preparedness or HR issues Maintenance is mainly performed by the firefighters and interviewees indicated that this measure seems to indicate a well-run station

Table 8.2 Operational effectiveness measure restructured

Conventional OEE	*Possible measures*	*Operational effectiveness for fire and rescue service*
Performance	Turnout times Attendance times	Responsiveness
Availability	Sickness (neg) Stand down times (neg)	Availability
Quality	Equipment maintenance Training competency Critical equipment fails (neg) Breathing Apparatus tests Commendations Vehicle accidents (neg) Discipline cases (neg) Personal injuries (neg)	Preparedness

the station level. Data used for effectiveness need to encompasses a wider range of firefighter activities and that a watch (shift) level operational unit of analysis is more likely to be appropriate. To this end the Shires fire service decided to develop its own way of assessing effectiveness that involved watch visits by senior managers, assessing condition of station, Q&A on incident command system policy, incident response feedback issues, operational drills, breathing apparatus checks and command point and equipment Q&A and this method of assessment is on-going at the Shires.

To allow future analysis fitness against operational effectiveness a better assessment of effectiveness data over considerable time periods and data across a large number of stations will need to be gathered.

The Counties – changing demand for fire and rescue services

The Counties FRS provides services to a largely rural area with a few medium sized cities and faces similar challenges in service delivery to the Shires, they are in the same 'family group'. Funding from central government for fire and rescue services has been cut in recent years and the Counties FRS was facing a deficit in their budget of £1 million in year 1 and up to £7 million in year 3. Fire and rescue services have a statutory requirement to present balanced books and therefore the Counties FRS was faced with looking for options to reduce the budget deficit. As part of public sector reform The Counties decided to change some fire stations over to Day Crewing Plus (DCP). DCP is a method of operating that still provides full time fire and rescue cover while requiring lower levels of manning. Traditional fire service systems use the '2-2-4' shift system mentioned earlier, whereby four crews (shifts) rotate over 12 hours shifts to provide 24 hour cover to a system. In contrast DCP operates by firefighters 'living-in' the fire station and working a number of 24 hour shifts, (usually between 1 to 5 days). During the 24 hours the firefighters are expected to sleep but are on-call in the case of emergency. If their rest time is interrupted by a call out, the rest time is extended to allow firefighters to catch-up with sleep. This change both to working conditions and corresponding home life clearly has potential implications – both positive and negative – for firefighter well-being (both physiological and psychological). There are also implications for the fire service and local community as they would want to ensure that the effectiveness of the service is maintained with the system of working hours. Within this context the Counties fire service commissioned research to investigate the effect of DCP on operational performance, and health and wellbeing of the firefighters on DCP with the following research questions.

RQ1 What are the implications of the change in shift pattern for the individuals working the new system?

RQ2 What impact has the change of shift pattern had on the performance of the stations highlighted for change, in terms of operational effectiveness?

Methodology

The method to investigate the health, wellbeing and operational performance of the firefighters was a longitudinal mixed methods study with data collection over three stages with the stations intended for DCP; pre-changeover, 6 months post-changeover, and 12 months post-changeover. Questionnaires assessing wellbeing, work demands, job satisfaction and job performance were triangulated with operational performance data and semi-structured interviews for a full and rich account of implementing DCP. 42 participants (out of 56 who are now working on the new system) over four fire stations have been interviewed at stage 1 and 22 participants interviewed over two stations at stage 2 with on-going interviews for stage 2 and future for stage 3. Inductive thematic analysis was used to analyse interviews as an iterative process. The operational performance data was derived from existing data that the Counties fire service already collected. Themes and issues emerging from either of the three collection methods were then triangulated against the other two data collection methods to see if the theme or issue was supported across the three types of data.

Assessing operational effectiveness has built upon the assessment framework from the Shires. The use of operational unit became a moot point for DCP because there are no separate watches just a single team on a station who deliver DCP so the unit of analysis is the station. Thus the following aspects shown in Table 8.3 were assessed. There are minor differences between the suggestions from Table 8.2 to that assessed in table 8.3 because the data collection was focused down to a fewer number of possible measure that were assessed by Counties Fire Service staff as the most useful.

The operational data at the stage of writing were collected from one fire station over a period of three months, not all of the data requested in Table 8.3 was available at fire station level.

Table 8.3 Assessment of operational effectiveness for the Counties

	Possible measures
Responsiveness	Turnout times Attendance times
Availability	Appliance availability Sickness (neg)
Team/personnel measures	Critical equipment failures Individual Training Equipment maintenance Commendations Vehicle accidents (neg) Discipline cases (neg) Personal injuries (neg)

Results and findings

Thematic analysis of the interviews allowed the richness of firefighters' expectations and early experiences of DCP to be fully explored. Interview questions focused on the impact of DCP on working conditions, work practices and on firefighters' work-life balance. Those yet to transfer were asked about their expectations of DCP while those already on DCP were asked to reflect upon their early experiences. They were also asked for their views about the implementation of change including the transition from the Watch system. Embedded in these questions were further probe questions designed to explore the links between DCP, individual health and well-being and operational effectiveness.

Those working in the DCP system indicated that the longer, unbroken periods of time at the station afforded them significant opportunities to shape how they organised and managed several work activities that contributed directly to operational effectiveness (for example the completion of their 'references'; individually-assigned tasks such as organising community fire safety events). A common theme was that work activities could be sequenced and prioritised more flexibly and carried out under less time pressure that was often the case in the 2-2-4 system with its 12-hour shifts. These job crafting activities were also reflected in the relatively high levels of job control reported in the questionnaire measure. There was also an enhanced sense of co-dependency as the new system meant that firefighters did not 'hand-over' tasks to a another watch at the end of their shift: many reported an increased sense of ownership over tasks and that they felt they had more opportunities and motivation to see tasks through to a conclusion within a batch of DCP working hours. Those interviewed also reported that working relationships were different within DCP as a result of firefighters spending longer unbroken periods of time together and with the changes to the team that occurred as firefighters finished their batch of hours and others took their place. Together these features of enhanced control, autonomy, influence over decisions and – at times – increased support from colleagues had fostered a strong team-working environment. Several managerial tasks were dealt with through effective collaboration between all the firefighters working at the station (e.g. managing work hours to ensure that there was sufficient cover at the station over every 24-hour period). Most indicated that overall workload was unchanged but that it felt more varied as extended periods within the station environment bought them into contact with a wider range of work activities. The majority view was that work time felt less pressurised as not all tasks needed to be completed within the 12-hour period attached to the 2-2-4 watch system.

Managers indicated that their role had changed with DCP with them needing to oversee a more diverse and larger group of firefighters drawn from several different watches. They indicated that this presented them with opportunities to shape the way that DCP was implemented in their station to ensure that it worked as well as it could. For example, they needed to be more aware of how long individual staff had been at the station since starting a batch of DCP so that their workload could be managed effectively. Managers felt that they had more flexibility over the setting of deadlines for work and the prioritisation of tasks as the end of a 12-hour shift no longer dictated the end-point for several tasked they allocated to firefighters. They also reported some additional demands associated with helping firefighters to adapt to the new ways of working and supporting them through the change process. Most reported that these activities could impact on organisational effectiveness, usually in a positive way, but that established measures might not be sensitive to the impact of these everyday managerial interventions. In some instances, different managers at the same station used their increased control to develop ways of working that differed from those implemented by another manager at the same station. However, in some stations managers chose to work closely together to develop consistent ways of working to ensure that DCP operated in the same way regardless of which manager happened to be on duty at any given time. Interestingly, awareness of a range of performance measures was generally limited to station managers with most firefighters focusing on day-to-day verbal feedback from their manager or colleagues to gain an insight into their own, and their crew's effectiveness. This suggested that published effectiveness data were not directly influencing firefighters' day-to-day work behaviour.

It was notable that different stations managed the transition to DCP in different ways. In some a very collaborative approach was taken with station managers collating and discussing suggestions from firefighters prior to the implementation of DCP. In other stations, managers collaborated with each other but there was less consultation before implementation with feedback being actively sought on new ways of working once they had been trialled. Discussions involving all stations staff that were seen to influence the implementation of DCP were viewed very favourably and cited as an important factor in successful transition.

There were some early indications of individual differences in firefighters' responses to DCP. Some indicated that working for longer un-broken periods of time suited their personal circumstances (as it was also accompanied by longer unbroken periods away from work). Others were still taking time to adapt to the longer periods of time away from home and the way that it influenced how they managed their commitments and relationships outside of work. There were also differences in the perceptions of DCP between those firefighters who had chosen to move for personal reasons such as pension boosting in the last few years of service, who had broadly positive perceptions, and those who felt they had to move in order to stay at a station they felt connected with, who were more negative in their perceptions.

An interesting point was made about the possibility of career stagnation because of DCP for two possible reasons; firstly due to the reduction of the number of personnel, fewer crew and watch manager posts are needed preventing those who are qualified from obtaining a promotion, and secondly, those firefighters who are working DCP are earning more with their enhancement than the standard salary for the next rank up reducing the incentive for those firefighters to attempt promotion.

The operational data collected from one fire station over a period of three months indicated that preventative measures included in preparedness marginally improved under DCP. The availability data was more complex to interpret because the change to DCP had affected manning for the part-time appliance and hence its availability. Responsiveness over the short term did indicate that it may be useful a measure of effectiveness for transfer to DCP, although analysis of the interviews did indicate that there was not a high awareness of this among the firefighters.

Conclusions from Counties study

The triangulation of wellbeing interviews and questionnaires with operational effectiveness data provides a valuable insight into changes to work practices in the public sector. In some cases the interview material supported operation data, for example around the area of references and preparedness data. Interview material about the use of performance measures indicated that they were not well used or known at an operational level, and they could be informative in managing the change to DCP.

The findings from the study are on-going and will be used to inform any possible further DCP implementation at the Shires.

Conclusions for measuring operation effectiveness in the UK fire services

This chapter highlights a tension in the public sector; in order to provide value for public service stakeholders prevention activities reduce demand, in this case prevention of fires and lowering the need for rescue. The reduction of demand creates an opportunity for lowering capacity and hence costs, but this causes two problems: first, in terms of geographical coverage for the individual who still needs FRS, and second, a reduction in staffing levels which can be met either by redundancy, shorter hours or recruitment freezes. A principal method of staff reduction used by the fires services has been recruitment freezes (Local Government Group, 2011) and this in turn then increases average age levels in the Fire Service. Increasing age levels combined with a reduction in general population fitness – a trend the fire service follows – tends to reduce overall fitness in the fire service, a service which is physically demanding. These drivers of change in the fire service lead us to propose three propositions:

- Proposition 1: A systematic and robust method of evaluating operational effectiveness would be helpful in assessing the current and future changes likely in the fire service. This would allow fire service to conduct the type of reform that is demanded of them, while still ensuring an effective service is available; a crucial tool in operational decision making.
- Proposition 2: The use of responsiveness, availability and preparedness measures seems to encompass appropriate aspects of effectiveness relevant at an operational level for fire stations and these should be at watch level for 2-2-4 fire stations.
- Proposition 3: The triangulation of wellbeing interviews and questionnaires with operational effectiveness data provides a valuable insight into changes to work practices in the public sector, particularly for the type of substantial change to DCP. The future findings from this research will be informative both to the Counties FRS in their own DCP deployment and other fire services undergoing similar change.

Future work includes completing the Counties study of DCP and fully realising the Operational Effectiveness measurement. To achieve this it would be useful to compare the more managerially hands-on approach to measurement in progress at the Shires as a cross validation of approach to operational effectiveness for the Counties.

In the longer term managing aging and societal change in the fire service represents a substantial challenge. Operations management has a role in this by providing insight to the operational effects and monitoring changes at an operational level.

References

Allied Dunbar National Fitness Survey (1992) *Allied Dunbar National Fitness Survey.* London: Sports Council and Health Education Authority.

Bath Chronicle (2014) 'Firefighter age time bomb for brigades across the region'. *Bath Chronicle*, 21 March. Retrieved from www.bathchronicle.co.uk/Firefighter-age-time-bomb-brigades-region/story-20846833-detail/story.html#ixzz3VOmWqU4R (accessed 19 June 2014).

CFOA (2014) 'UK road safety week 2014: fire and rescue service activities and initiatives'. Retrieved from www.cfoa.org.uk/17912 (accessed 17 July 2014).

Connor (2013) 'Firefighters' careers must change to cope with pension planning'. *Guardian*, 4 January.

Department for Communities and Local Government (2009) *A Review of Fire and Rescue Response Times.* February. London: Department for Communities and Local Government.

Department for Communities and Local Government (2010) 'Fire statistics monitor: April 2009 to March 2010'. 20 August. Retrieved from www.gov.uk/government/statistics/fire-statistics-monitor-april-2009-to-march-2010 (accessed 19 June 2014).

Department for Communities and Local Government (2012a) *Fire and Rescue National Framework for England.* July. London: Department for Communities and Local Government.

Department for Communities and Local Government (2012b) *Firefighters' Pension Scheme: Proposed Final Agreement.* May. London: Department for Communities and Local Government.

Department for Communities and Local Government (2013a) *Fire and Rescue Operational Statistics Bulletin for England 2012–13.* London: Department for Communities and Local Government. Retrieved from www.gov.uk/government/uploads/system/uploads/attachment_data/file/262002/Fire_and_rescue_service_operational_statistics_for_England_2012_to_2013.pdf (accessed 15 December 2014).

Department for Communities and Local Government (2013b) 'Fire statistics monitor: April 2012 to March 2013'. 26 June. Retrieved from www.gov.uk/government/statistics/fire-statistics-monitor-april-2012-to-march-2013 (accessed 19 June 2014).

Derbyshire Fire and Rescue (2013) *Annual Report 2012/13.* Retrieved from www.derbys-fire.gov.uk/files/2313/8986/2589/annual_report_2012-2013_print.pdf (accessed 4 July 2014).

DTI (2000) *Quality Cost Delivery: Seven Measures for Improved Competitiveness in Manufacturing Industry.* URN00/754. DTI/Pub4868/3k/9/00/NP. London: Department of Trade and Industry.

Essex Fire Authority (2012) *Annual Report 2011–2012.* Witham: Essex Fire Authority.

Fire Brigades Union (2009) *National Joint Council for Local Authority Fire and Rescue Services: Scheme of Conditions of Service 2004 – The Grey Book* (6th edn). Spelthorne: Fire Brigades Union.

Firefighters' Pension Scheme (2006) 'Firefighters' Pension Scheme (England) Order 2006'. Retrieved from www.legislation.gov.uk/uksi/2006/3432/made (accessed 3 July 2014).

Firefit Steering Group (2009) *Fitness for Fire and Rescue: Standards, Protocols and Policy.* Firefit Steering Group. Retrieved from www.firefitsteeringgroup.co.uk/firefitreport.pdf (accessed 25 June 2014).

Greater Manchester Fire and Rescue (2013) *Greater Manchester Fire and Rescue Service Annual Report 2012/13G.* Retrieved from www.manchesterfire.gov.uk/media/270573/annual%20report%202012.13.pdf (accessed 4 July 2014).

Health Survey for England (2009) *Health Survey for England 2008, Volume 1. Physical Activity and Fitness.* Leeds: NHS Information Centre for Health and Social Care.

Knight, K. (2013) *Facing the Future: Findings from the Review of Efficiencies and Operations in Fire and Rescue Authorities in England.* London: Department for Communities and Local Government.

Local Government Group (2011) *The Fire and Rescue Service: Going the Extra Mile.* London: Local Government Association.

London Fire Brigade (2013) *Our Performance 2012–2013.* London: Strategy and Performance Department, London Fire Brigade.

Munir, F., Clemes, S., Houdmont, J. and Randall, R. (2012) 'Overweight and obesity in UK firefighters'. *Occupational Medicine,* 62(5): 362–65.

Nakajima, S. (1984) *Introduction to TPM: Total Productive Maintenance.* Tokyo: Japan Institute for Plant Maintenance (English translation: Productivity Press, 1988).

Plat, M., Frings-Dressen, M. and Sluiter, J. (2012) 'Diminished health status in firefighters'. *Ergonomics,* 55(9): 1119–22.

Poston, W., Haddock, C., Jahnke, S., Jitnarin, N., Tuley, B. and Kales, S. (2011) 'The prevalence of overweight, obesity, and substandard fitness in a population-based firefighter cohort'. *Journal of Occupational and Environmental Medicine,* 53: 266–74.

Public Accounts Committee (2011) *Transforming NHS Ambulance Services.* 46th report, September. London: Public Accounts Committee.

Rich, N. (1999) *Total Productive Maintenance: The Lean Approach*. Bromborough: Tudor Business Publishing.

Siddall, A., Standage, M., Stokes, K. and Bilzon. J. (2014) *Enhancing the Health, Fitness and Performance of UK Firefighters: An Interim Report*. March. Bath: University of Bath.

Simons, D., Mason, R. and Gardner, B. (2004) 'Overall vehicle effectiveness'. *International Journal of Logistics Research and Applications*, 7(2): 119–35.

Smith, D., Fehling, P., Frisch, A., Haller, J., Winke, M. and Dailey, M. (2012) 'Prevalence of cardiovascular disease risk factors and obesity in firefighters'. *Journal of Obesity*, 2012, article 908267.

Turner, P. (2013) 'UK fire and rescue health and lifestyle survey'. Paper presented at the Firefit Steering Group Conference, Firefit Steering Group, Loughborough.

Williams, A.N., Wilkinson, D.M., Richmond, V.L. and Rayson, M.P. (2013) *Nominal Pension Age for Firefighters: A Review for the Firefighters' Pension Committee*. 12 January. Retrieved from www.fbu.org.uk/wp-content/uploads/2013/01/NPA-Review-12-Jan-2013.pdf (accessed 13 April 2015).

Windsor, T.P. (2012) *Independent Review of Police Officer and Staff Remuneration and Conditions: Final Report*. March. London: The Stationery Office.

9 Managing capacity and demand in a responsive repairs service

Lessons from social housing

Joanne Meehan, Paul R. Drake, Kiera Vogel and Adam Parkhouse

Overview

Responsive repairs of existing housing stock is the largest area of spend for most social landlords in the UK (Wickenden, 2012), and balancing their service capacity with unpredictable demand is challenging. The social housing context adds complexity, as service efficiencies need to be balanced against the sector's regulatory standards for service provision, tenant expectations and commercial considerations. This chapter reports the results of a two-year project with a UK social housing organisation that uncovered the underpinning challenges of managing capacity and demand in a responsive repairs building maintenance unit and suggests research propositions to enable the academic operations management community to increase the impact of future research for public services.

Introduction

This chapter provides a critical evaluation of the application of capacity and demand techniques in the social housing sector, and considers the challenges and adaptations required to deliver financial efficiencies while protecting the social dimension of service delivery. The empirical setting focuses on Cartrefi Conwy, a social housing provider in north Wales and reports on a two-year participative action research project designed to improve the efficiency and effectiveness of their in-house building and maintenance unit (BMU). The BMU provides responsive housing maintenance and repairs to Cartrefi Conwy's tenants in north Wales and has a longer-term goal of winning external contracts to secure additional revenue streams and deliver economies of scale. The BMU's strategic priorities are traditional in that they are; to reduce operational costs, increase performance efficiencies and improve service quality from the tenants' perspective. Throughout this chapter we highlight the service-orientation and regulatory context of social housing in the UK, which creates particular complexities to explore capacity and demand issues.

The current operations management (OM) literature suggests that philosophies like lean needs to be adapted for the public service environment to take account of thematic differences of people, process and sustainability (Radnor and Boaden,

2008). We argue that the existing body of knowledge can be augmented through the recognition of five underpinning and inter-related issues. The five thematic issues that need to be addressed in applying OM to the social housing sector are; language, lack of OM knowledge, motivation, measuring success, and tenant relationships.

The social housing context

Social housing refers to residential properties managed and let to tenants at affordable rents and represents a fifth of UK homes (Reeves *et al.*, 2010). The purpose of social housing is to provide affordable housing to people and families on low incomes and it is allocated on the basis of need. Under the 2011 Localism Act local authorities have the power to set their own qualification criteria and limits on who can apply for social housing within their areas, but are legally obliged to ensure that social homes go the most vulnerable, and those in greatest need. The government regulator limits rents to ensure they are kept at affordable levels and these are generally more affordable than private rental rates.

Local authorities traditionally managed the UK social housing sector through council housing provision. The sector has changed over the last decade as many councils sold municipal housing stock to newly formed Registered Providers who now provide the majority of UK social housing and who operate predominantly as not-for-profit organisations (Gibb and Nygaard, 2006). Strong links remain with local public bodies under the Localism Act and are a defining characteristic of social housing sector (Pittini and Laino, 2011). Registered Providers are technically outside of the public sector, but social housing is considered a 'quasi'-public sector as it is government-regulated, operates under central government's housing and welfare policy frameworks, and has to adhere to EU public procurement regulation. Moreover, two-thirds of providers' rental income is from government-controlled Housing Benefit (Laffin, 2013).

In 2013, the sector's turnover was circa £14.9 billion, an 8.1 per cent increase on the previous year, and is projected to grow steadily over the next 5 years to £19.6 billion by 2018 (Homes and Communities Agency, 2014). The social housing sector in England has seen the construction of approximately half a million new properties since the 1980s although the sector's recent growth is largely attributed to large-scale housing stock transfers from local councils to Registered Providers (Pawson and Wilcox, 2011). In Europe a range of national and regional federations are responsible for managing over 27million social homes – approximately 12 per cent of existing dwellings in EU member states. Similar provision, albeit often on smaller levels, exists in North America, Australasia and Africa/Middle East (Housing Europe, 2014).

Social housing and operations management

Social housing regulation has been used to promote growth and competition between Registered Providers through the implementation of strategic management principles and increasing efficiencies to decrease public spending (Rhodes and Mullins, 2009). Although it has helped to push a modernisation agenda, the regulatory framework sets performance targets that reduce the Registered Providers' level of control over the direction of OM and business growth strategies. It also creates cycles of uncertainty as the targets set are subject to political change, making longer-term planning difficult.

Registered providers have growing responsibilities beyond providing affordable housing stock, including growing local economies and achieving community integration. Cartrefi Conwy, the case organisation in this study, has to evidence social value in their operational outcomes under the Welsh government's regulatory framework. Social value can provide collective community benefit over-and-above the service delivered. Examples may include projects focused on health and well-being, training for the unemployed, back-to-work initiatives or environmental projects to reduce fuel poverty within a community. The Regulatory Framework for Housing Associations Registered in Wales publishes the standards of performance (delivery outcomes) that providers have to meet in relation to governance, financial management and landlord services (Welsh Government, 2014).

Public service organisations differ from those in the private sector in relation to their priorities, costs, capacity and output (Spicker, 2009). In the housing industry, private sector provision is predicated on economic motives; recipients must be able to afford payments (rent or mortgage), and investors require profits. In comparison, social housing is provided for those unable to be served by the private markets and considerations of providers' profits are secondary to recipients' need. Despite the lack of a profit motive, the increased squeeze on public funding of social housing and changes through welfare reform has created tight financial constraints on registered providers requiring efficiencies to be secured throughout their service delivery.

Background to the study

Cartrefi Conwy provides affordable housing within the county borough of Conwy, North Wales, with approximately one third being sheltered housing. Approximately 80 per cent of the homes are in urbanised coastal areas with the remainder dispersed inland in rural locations. Cartrefi Conwy was formed in 2008 when tenants voted for the stock transfer of local council housing to the new organisation that now owns and manages circa 4000 homes and employs approximately 150 staff. Cartrefi Conwy's Executive Leadership Team identified a need to improve the performance of their BMU and commissioned the University of Liverpool's Management School to assist in improving its efficiency and effectiveness. The BMU is responsible for managing repairs to the 4000 homes and was a resource heavy, but critical, tenant-facing service. Employing 38 trade operatives the unit had low productivity, high amounts of waste in sub-optimised processes, poor capacity-demand management and a high subcontractor spend. At the start of the project the turnover per operative was £26,000, which management deemed to be low. Through this project, the implementation of capacity and demand techniques saw this increase by 63 per cent to £42,000 for the 2012–13 period, and by 181 per cent to £73,000 per operative for 2013–14.

Maintenance in social housing is a core activity covering planned maintenance, responsive maintenance and void repairs and is a significant expense. Table 9.1 outlines the classifications of repairs in social housing and identifies how these services are delivered in Cartrefi Conwy's BMU.

Defining the operations management challenge

Planning and control was a major problem and the BMU struggled to meet the demand for repairs with their internal service capacity. Call centre staff classified repair requests logged by tenants as emergency, urgent or non-urgent, and when tenants moved out of a property (voids) all required repairs are completed before the property can be re-let. Void repairs are prioritised owing to waiting lists for social housing properties. BMU demand relates to the total number of repair works requested from tenants and the void repairs, and is reported in daily, weekly, monthly and annual units.

Demand uncertainty is at the heart of the challenge faced by responsive building maintenance activities, in comparison to planned maintenance works (Griffith, 2002). Demand uncertainty coupled with the urgency of emergency repairs makes responsive repairs challenging. To illustrate the challenge, the BMU's service level for

Table 9.1 Types of repair in Cartrefi Conwy's housing operations

Repair	*Demand characteristics*	*Examples of work*	*Managed by*	*Delivered by*
Planned	Predicted, cyclical, planned programmes of work	Preventative replacements, upgrades, adaptations and major projects. Upgrading heating systems, roof replacements, renewals of gutters, fascias and soffits, new fencing and installations of new kitchens and bathrooms.	Asset management team	External contractors
Voids	Regularly occurring but difficult to predict, takes place in between tenancies	Property inspections, full safety checks, removal of rubbish, cleaning and making safe utility supplies. All necessary major and minor repairs and any disability adaptations for new tenants.	Building and maintenance unit	Internal building and maintenance trades people
Responsive	Unpredictable, some repairs classed as emergency requiring response within four hours	Repairs to boilers, electrics, windows, doors, fencing, roofs, guttering and internal fixtures and fittings. Emergency repairs for gas, electrics or water bursts.	Building and maintenance unit	Internal building and maintenance trades people

emergency repairs is four hours for 'make safe' with the repair to be completed within a 24 hour period across a housing stock of 4000 properties with 2500 repair product lines, 250 of which are classed as core emergency lines.

Prior to the project Cartrefi Conwy employed unsophisticated approaches to balance capacity and demand and operated largely in a constant crisis mode. The BMU's capacity comprised of a permanent workforce of trade operatives (e.g. plumbers, roofers, gas-fitters, joiners, plasterers etc.) supplemented with short-term, temporary subcontractors during periods of high demand for repairs. The position confirms previous findings from a public healthcare setting where capacity is not demand-led; rather public services organisations meet as much demand as their resources will allow (Walley, 2013). Subcontractors were being used to cope with under-capacity and dynamic demand fluctuations and their use obscured underpinning internal issues of poor demand planning, suboptimal scheduling and the wrong trade mix of staff. Subcontracting was expensive and the BMU had concerns over losing control of a mission-critical, customer facing activity, which is a particular concern when dealing with vulnerable tenants.

The project sought to answer a number of broad research questions related to capacity and demand planning in social housing:

- Can standard capacity and demand management techniques be used effectively in non-profit service sectors?
- To what extent are capacity and demand approaches used in social housing organisations as a solution to issues of service efficiency?
- What adaptations, if any, are needed to enable capacity and demand techniques to deliver service efficiencies that are balanced against regulatory standards and tenant expectations?

This chapter addresses these questions through a case study of Cartrefi Conwy, a registered provider of social housing to shed new light on the role of capacity and demand planning and control in a public service context.

Methods

Cartrefi Conwy commissioned the research team through a two-year knowledge transfer partnership scheme partly funded by the UK's Technology Strategy Board. The project granted unique company access and allowed for a longitudinal action-based approach. A researcher was seconded to Cartrefi Conwy for the project's duration with open access to stakeholders and internal information, supported by the executive leadership team. Action research was adopted over a traditional case method to increase the potential for change (Ram *et al.*, 2007) through challenging the status quo, evaluating and adapting theories and working with stakeholders to implement recommendations (Eden and Huxham, 2005).

A multi-stakeholder approach involved over 30 tenants and 50 staff, spanning executives, operational staff, managers, heads of services and technicians. Context-rich data were gathered from stakeholder and tenant engagement activities, operational meetings, organisational documents, policy statements and internal communications. Quantitative internal data were assessed to identify improvement areas, including job performance data, demand and capacity planning data, numbers and skills of technicians, subcontractor spend analysis and financial information. Site visits and job shadowing allowed observations of operational constraints, working practices and tenant interfaces. Process maps were created of 'as is' repair procedures to identify waste, inefficiencies and opportunities to exploit capacity and demand planning techniques. Process maps were triangulated with system data and qualitative information from site visits to capture embedded knowledge (Tuggle and Goldfinger, 2004) and provide a baseline for the iterative cycles of intervention (Coughlan and Coghlan, 2002).

Balancing capacity and demand

The issues arising from the data collection confirmed capacity and demand problems. Cartrefi Conwy's geographical spread of their 4000 properties meant that operatives had to drive to each property to carry out repairs and waste was incurred in sub-optimal job routing as vehicles spent too much time driving back-and-forth between jobs and complaints from tenants over reliable start times were high.

Cartrefi Conwy's mixed housing stock increased the variability of the fixtures and fittings and reduced their ability to standardise services. To illustrate, one third of their housing stock comprises sheltered accommodation for the elderly or vulnerable, some with on-site warden services. The rest of the housing stock is classed as general needs, predominantly one, two or three bedroom houses and flats with a total of 2500 different repair product lines.

To balance capacity and demand, 'level' and 'chase' options are used for coping with demand fluctuation (Lovelock, 1984). Levelling strategies centre on keeping capacity constant through smoothing staff work with little regard for changing demand, largely achieved through make-in-advance approaches. The service element of responsive repairs makes levelling difficult, particularly as the vulnerabilities of some tenants and the nature of emergency repairs limit Cartrefi Conwy's tolerance to not meeting all demand in comparison to other service settings. Chase options involve the frequent adjusting of capacity to match demand using strategies including overtime, subcontracting and part-time staff.

Figure 9.1 provides an illustration of how the project addressed, and progressed a range of capacity and demand solutions in the three broad categories of variation, risk and functional flexibility.

Variation

Classifications of repair types

At a fundamental level demand data collection and analyses in the BMU was not robust and lacked integration with capacity information across a range of data points (repair line calls, staff levels, scheduling, etc.), a problem common across public sector

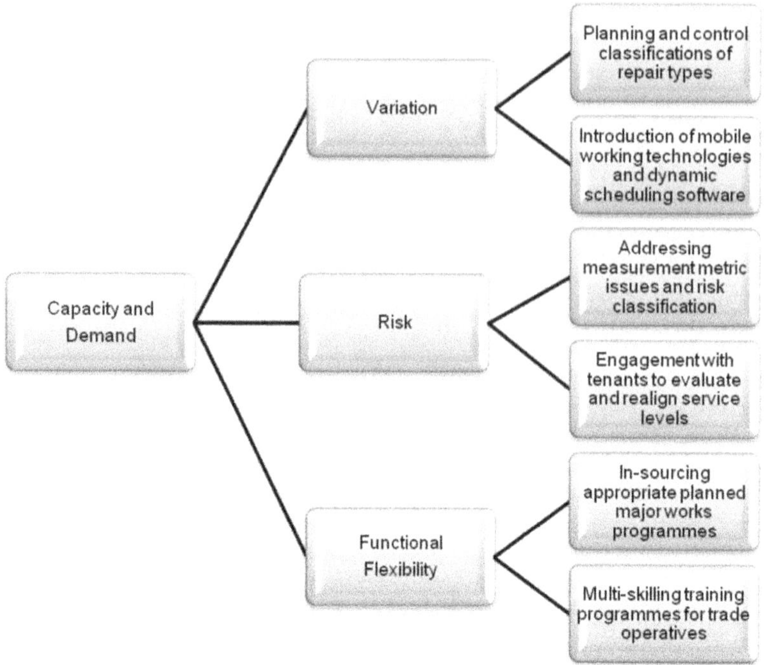

Figure 9.1 Capacity and demand solutions for Cartrefi Conwy

services operations (Walley, 2013). Failure to analyse and monitor demand meant that staff believed, often incorrectly, that demand was inherently variable and random. OM concepts were used to classify the different repair types (see Table 9.1) as runners, repeaters or strangers to provide a framework for breaking down different responses. Runners, repeaters and strangers are used in lean as a planning and control classification based on the demand frequency.

- Runners: Tasks performed regularly and have sufficient volume to justify dedicated resources and processes (planned maintenance).
- Repeaters: Regular tasks but with longer time intervals (void repairs).
- Strangers: Tasks occurring infrequently or ad-hoc with demand difficult to predict (responsive repairs).

Mobile-working technologies and dynamic scheduling software

Mobile-working technologies and systems were introduced to enable real-time job status and scheduling. As a schedule is only as good as the information on which it is based (Larsson, 2013), time was taken to consider the metrics required to enable analysis of job times, tenant need and prioritisation. The new technology moves the BMU operational system onto web-enabled, hand-held personal digital assistants (PDAs). Operatives and call centre staff communicate remotely logging repair requests and data on completed works, and the vehicle tracking system allows the dynamic scheduling of works based on technician availability and location. The system considers the type of repair (nature, priority and time), tenants (location, personal care circumstances), operatives (location, hours, skills) and the existing schedule. PDAs allow technicians to receive jobs remotely and in real-time without attending the office to collect paperwork reducing waste in travel time.

There were initial problems following the implementation of the mobile-working system, notably around persistent gaps in communication and understanding between the call centre that receive repair requests from tenants and the BMU team who scheduled the works. The two teams were in different physical locations and there were difficulties in seeing the wider implications of decisions made. To address the problems, the two teams were co-located into one office with visual displays on large screens of the mobile-working system showing real time vehicle locations, schedules and call centre volumes. An important finding from the research is that the visibility of the mobile-working system was a critical enabler to sustain the move towards more efficient operations. The visibility enabled better communication between staff and tenants, secured employee buy-in, and led to a greater appreciation and understanding of the positive impact of standard demand and capacity management techniques.

The mobile-working system and repair classifications enabled structured demand data collection, categorisation and analysis. For the first time this led to an acknowledgement that the demand, while still variable owing to the stochastic nature of breakdowns, did have some predictable trends. Seasonality emerged as a main source of variation, but importantly with a potentially predictable nature. Colder weather results in surges in demand for boilers and heating and the repairs tend to be required urgently. For example, in winter frozen water pipes burst causing collateral damage and heating failures result in dangerously low temperatures for the elderly. The corresponding trough to the winter peak is a fall in demand in the summer and some heating repairs can be less urgent. The longer daylight hours also allows for more outside work to be completed, for example repairs to gutters, fencing, and external painting providing an opportunity to plan and resource effectively for the peaks and move less urgent jobs to predicted troughs.

Risk

Metrics and risk classification

When tenants call to report a problem, call-centre operators must classify and set the job priorities depending on the risk. Frequently, cases were misclassified as 'emergency' or 'urgent' triggering an unnecessarily expensive fast response. Costs were incurred through responding to fast response times, hiring short-term contractors to manage peaks and/or pay overtime to staff, and the need to hold additional stocks of spares and equipment. Non-priority jobs were also affected as these were often rescheduled at the expense of emergency jobs that negatively impacted customer satisfaction. In more commercial situations demand can often be levelled through pricing, which is not applicable in public services which are free at the point of consumption (Walley, 2013). Analysis of job priority data revealed a high number of emergency classifications with 34 per cent of the annual 15000 repairs requiring a four-hour 'make safe' response. The remaining 66 per cent were non-urgent including repairs to minor fixtures and fittings such as taps, floorboards and toilet seats, but were not also scheduled more flexibly.

An emotive dimension to job classification became apparent given the importance of the need to provide services in a non-discriminatory manner (Spicker, 2009). Staff frequently erred on the side of caution as the consequences of 'missing' a vulnerable tenant's needs are prioritised over any negative downstream operational consequences of meeting these needs. At the heart of the prioritisation issue was a cultural orientation towards risk-averse rapid reaction rather than efficiency.

The over-inflation of the risk classification reflects the social orientation of the sector. Central government policies in the 1980s were designed to motivate the less dependent tenants to leave social housing, most notably through the right-to-buy legislation which has been described as 'one of the most significant transformations of the British social housing market' (van Ham *et al.*, 2012: 129). Coupled with the decline in new social housing, the legacy of government policy has led to long waiting lists of social housing (Department for Communities and Local Government, 2012) and a narrowing of the tenant base from a broad social base to one principally comprised of the least affluent in society (Fitzpatrick and Pawson, 2007). Social housing providers now disproportionately house the least advantaged (Hills, 2007); in 2003, 65 per cent of households in social housing had no earned income (Social Exclusion Unit, 2004), up from only 11 per cent in 1962 (Holmans, 2005). Consequently, prioritisation is challenging as the lack of diversity in the tenant mix leads to a perception of universal vulnerability and the conflation of tenant risk with repair job risk. A challenge for the project was the cultural barrier to move away from over-estimating the level of tenant risk and vulnerability and to correctly categorise some emergency jobs as urgent or routine.

The narrowing of the tenant mix raises issues for the adoption of OM techniques as social housing providers increasingly focus on delivering social value through wider community services. Social value had to be defined for a BMU context as informal discussions revealed that some operatives viewed the time spent with tenants as a proxy for social value, risk management and quality. Perversely, the longer the time spent on a repair (and therefore with a tenant), was culturally accepted in parts of the organisation as an important positive indicator; thus jobs overran, capacity was squeezed and costs grew.

The service level agreements for emergency repairs were amended to decouple 'make safe' and 'repair', creating two separate jobs. This allowed the immediate emergency need to be met and made safe within 4 hours, while allowing for a longer timescale for full repair. An example of this may be a broken window. Make safe as an emergency need might consist of fitting a temporary secure boarding, and repair may be the full replacement of the window, frame, hinges and handles as required. Redefining the metrics effectively reduces the need for emergency stock of a high number of products, enables less urgent fixes to be rescheduled to less busy and more convenient periods for tenants, and maintains tenant safety. Decoupling the metrics around make safe and repair saw the emergencies decrease from 34 per cent to 27 per cent that provided extra flexibility in job scheduling.

Tenant experience

Registered Providers do not have traditional customer trading relationships with their tenants, creating problems in applying OM philosophies developed from private sector contexts if the models assume a paying customer–provider relationship, and a 'market' with alternative competitors. In social housing, tenants lack the option to change their landlord if they are dissatisfied. Under the legal terms of the stock transfer from the council, tenants received guarantees on repair services (Whitehead, 1999), that constrain the changes to service levels offered and the risk-averse positions adopted by providers can become culturally entrenched.

Tenant experience was assessed through drawing on their existing feedback and the introduction of tenant focus groups. Focus groups were interactive to discuss BMU service experiences, listen to what was important to tenants in relation to responsive repairs, and identifying the reasons for their service priorities. The results revealed two important findings. Firstly, prior to the project, tenant engagement comprised of tenant surveys that lacked questions related to operational priorities, preferences and choice. Consequently, tenants' ability to influence future service provision was limited through the data collection method. Secondly, tenants revealed that their preference was for local, permanent BMU staff, rather than subcontracted labour; a convenient and reliable time slot rather than necessarily quick response time for non-urgent repairs; and repairs that are right-first-time. Tenant workshops were used to refine the repair service process and service levels were agreed to include specific appointment slots and a telephone call or text to confirm when the operatives are on their way to the property.

Another interesting issue from the tenant focus groups was their frustration at having to use the responsive repairs service for what they viewed as very minor issues. Non-urgent jobs were not prioritised and required tenants to be in the property when the job was scheduled, which was an inconvenience. Some tenants gave examples of small repairs including bleeding radiators, dripping taps, electrical trip switches and adjusting boiler pressure that they would like to be shown how to do themselves to reduce a reliance on the repairs service. Changing the tenant/provider relationship raises important opportunities for both parties to reduce demand, engage with tenants and increase tenant satisfaction. An issue for the organisation is ensuring there are sufficient reporting mechanisms and training of tenants to identify underpinning causes and problems, for example a potential water leak if a boiler is constantly losing pressure.

Functional flexibility

In-sourcing

Tenants discussed third party subcontractors in the focus groups and associated these with delays, poor communication, and lack of cleanliness in preparing work and tidying up after jobs. The internal reporting mechanisms did not allow for these perceptions to be verified with supporting data, and it was not clear whether these perceptions were reflective of a genuinely reduced service from subcontractors and/or the increased difficulties for the BMU in managing and coordinating this resource. Either way the finding was a critical marker that highlighted the need to reduce the reliance on subcontractors. Cartrefi Conwy's executive leadership team committed to recruit apprentices and new staff, in line with areas of high trade demand, and agreeing for the BMU to service some of the 'runners' category of planned maintenance. These categories were managed by the asset management team separate to the BMU, and were serviced by external contractors. Many of these programmes of work were too extensive and specialist for the current BMU operatives to service, but there were some minor planned works (fencing, guttering etc.) that were in-sourced to level demand troughs.

Multiskilling

Investment in longer-term training was made to multiskill the operatives across trades to allow a more flexible resource in line with analysis of the data and repair classifications. In total 30 operatives completed multiskilled training, moving them from having a sole primary trade to having multiple secondary skills. For example, a plumber is now able to carry out minor joinery and plastering tasks reducing the amount of specialist resource and enabling jobs to be completed in one fix. The multiskilling saw a 28 per cent increase in productivity across both responsive and void work streams, and the reduced reliance on external contractors resulted in a growth of £1.4 million in 2013–14.

Project impacts

In summary, radical change in the BMU performance was evidenced through the introduction of new working practices, increasing operational efficiency and effectiveness while reducing costs. There was greater visibility of performance as processes yielded accurate data (e.g. the date and time a job is logged and completed). Data were captured automatically allowing accurate analysis of performance. To demonstrate the impact of core capacity and demand management techniques in aligning the BMU's in-house capacity and demand, the subcontractor spend reduced from 39 per cent of turnover in 2010–11 to 26 per cent in 2013 and job costs reduced by over £1.35 million.

Table 9.1 highlights key performance metrics over the life of this study to illustrate the tangible commercial impacts achieved. A temporary dip in KPI performance of costs per urgent and non-urgent jobs, and in the percentage of routine repairs completed on time occurred during the transition to real-time scheduling (see indicators 3, 4 and 9 in Table 9.1). The overall improvements achieved are positive but are still not considered to have reached best practice in the sector and the journey to continuous improvement is a long one. It is difficult to accurately benchmark figures and performance in the sector as providers report data using different criteria, which can skew the figures, as can differences in providers' size, housing stock condition and type, locations and stability of the tenant base.

Conclusions and emerging propositions

A number of conclusions are drawn from this study. The regulatory context dictates the minimum service levels and can impact perceptions of provider-tenant relationships, often leading to overly cautious decisions that impact capacity and demand in responsive repairs. Social housing organisations hold a somewhat unique position in that they straddle the public and private sectors allowing them to offer revenue-generating services to external markets enabling profits to be reinvested into their communities and/or housing stock. External commercialisation of services demands that OM measures of success are externally calibrated to ensure they are competitive. The commercialisation agenda does create cultural challenges and tensions for the social housing sector and this is further hampered as the language of OM can create barriers to understanding its benefits in socially orientated organisations. Similarly, problems and issues of service capacity, tenant satisfaction, budget restrictions and service delivery are perceived to be housing issues rather than OM problems. Underpinning these issues is a lack of OM expertise in social housing organisations that can lead to sub-optimised, isomorphic solutions within the sector. A number of theoretical contributions and themes emerge from the study.

Emerging theme 1: language

The application of capacity and demand management techniques in the social housing sector provides a useful context for reflection. While cost minimisation is as critical as it is in the private sector, the financial efficiencies common in OM require

Table 9.2 Key performance metrics 2010–13

	Key indicator	*2010–11*	*2011–12*	*2012–13*
1	Actual job costs (total)	£4,147,058	£3,246,231	£2,792,760
2	Cost per void	£3809	£2670	£2701
3	Cost per emergency	£110	£128	£61
4	Cost per urgent	£99	£101	£65
5	Cost per non urgent	£281	£235	£117
6	Average cost per repair	£135	£129	£93
7	Emergency repairs completed on time	93.1%	89.6%	93.5%
8	Routine repairs completed on time	77.9%	78.4%	82.7%
9	Urgent repairs completed on time	79.3%	78.5%	85.2%

translation into social value gains rather than profit margin maximisation. Talk of efficiencies and waste minimisation are commonly understood in the OM community but in social housing, culturally these terms are emotive issues as they can infer cuts to tenant services and reductions in quality. Much of this is semantic and related to the cultural perceptions of the OM language that does not always sit comfortably with a socially orientated business. The term public service has a normative dimension that implies that organisations will act in a moral way and they lack the option to reduce costs through choosing to avoid expensive cases of need (Spicker, 2009). Public services have been criticised in the past for maintaining organisational slack, seen often as wasteful approaches (Peters and Pierre, 1998). In sectors insulated from direct private sector competition the costs of excess capacity may not be as keenly felt, particularly if demand is variable. The social housing sector has traditionally been well funded from central government through grants and financial incentive schemes such as Decent Homes in England and the Welsh Housing Quality Standard in Wales. The Housing Corporation, the regulatory body until 2008, also acted as the guarantor of over £27 billion of private sector investment (Laffin, 2013) saving Registered Providers an estimated annual £200–400 million in lower interest charges (Cave, 2007). This shielding from true commercial pressure has arguably led to a desensitisation to costs and a very high service level to tenants, although one that is not necessarily high in value given the sub-optimised operational processes. The role of language leads to our first proposition:

> Proposition 1: The language of OM can conflict with socially orientated public services as it brings connotations of privatisation and price-focused commercial exploitation.

Emerging theme 2: operations management knowledge

OM competence is limited in the sector evidenced through the lack of awareness of standard OM solutions available. The contemporary problems faced by providers – service delivery to tenants, managing staff levels, improving tenant satisfaction, dealing with reduced budgets – are positioned in the sector as 'housing' problems not OM problems. Where providers see a social housing crisis, OM scholars and professionals recognise these as core issues in the field and just another need for proficient OM. The difficulties arise when these two disciplines are seen as mutually exclusive owing to the different theoretical and philosophical roots.

Without sufficient OM knowledge organisations tend to imitate the approach of others in the sector leading to isomorphic solutions. Without OM knowledge, the other option is that organisations use valuable resource to try to solve each problem rather than turn to OM professionals and established OM techniques. The available options for common OM issues like balancing capacity and demand are typically limited, but without knowledge of these, providers run the risk of missing available options and sub-optimising decisions. A solution for the issues of language and gaps in OM knowledge is to adapt and align the language used to define OM's potential impact in public service delivery, which leads to our second proposition:

> Proposition 2: An adaptive approach to OM that is open to the subtleties of application to public service contexts can be mutually beneficial to both fields.

Emerging theme 3: motivations

The third contribution of the research is the recognition of the different motivations of using OM techniques in public services. This involves a challenge to the underpinning assumptions of OM theories and techniques. Although they address waste minimisation and efficiencies, OM theories were originally conceived and developed in private sector contexts particularly manufacturing and so their primary motivation is to make commercial organisations more cost-effective to enable them to grow. The motivation of OM adoption in public services differs in that it predominantly relates not to growth but contraction of services and resource. Registered Providers differ in this respect, as their unique quasi-public sector position and use of commercial trading arms does allow revenue-generating activity, perhaps providing a better opportunity to engage with the OM community. Our third proposition is:

> Proposition 3: OM scholars need to demonstrate how commercial impacts and efficiencies contribute to increased social surplus and employment stability in Registered Providers and the communities they serve.

Emerging theme 4: measuring success

The fourth key finding of this research demonstrates the impact potential of OM to social housing, and to the wider public services arena. However, there are important caveats to this apparent success. Firstly, and in support of previous public sector applications of OM techniques (Radnor and Walley, 2008), starting from such a low base of OM sophistication ensures that it is relatively easy to achieve efficiencies. The social housing sector is proactive in benchmarking activities and numerous benchmarking clubs exist and data is shared openly. The problem identified here is that this is rarely calibrated with service organisations outside of the sector creating a false reassurance and legitimising their 'innovations'. The danger is that people become seduced by the figures and assume they are 'best in class' and do not continue to strive for further improvements. This has important consequences for providers who are pursuing more commercial revenue streams and growth where will be in direct competition with private sector organisations.

To this end the BMU is driving its costs towards commercially competitive levels. However, the regulatory context demands that it must deliver social value in its services, which in some situations could add cost, for example through sourcing from small businesses, using local labour or investing in apprenticeships. A question facing Cartrefi Conwy is how to define social value in the context of responsive repairs in a way that creates commercial synergies, rather than adding cost. Winning external contracts can drive unit costs down by spreading overheads and achieving scale economies. However, to win these contracts it is essential that they are operating efficiently, not just measured against internal metrics, but also benchmarked against for-profit organisations that are not constrained by regulatory standards. For-profit competitors are able to drop non-commercially viable revenue streams and generally work on a demand led costs-to-income basis, not a resource led costs-to-budget approach as seen in public service organisations. The ability to deliver a commercially competitive service while maintaining social impact will be the true test for the success of OM for registered providers. The use of data and metrics to report forwards to improve predictive forecasting, as opposed to reporting historically, shifts the emphasis away from reporting 'what we did' to 'what we can do', that can be the first step in embedding the OM principles of continuous improvement. Our fourth proposition is:

> Proposition 4: To manage success rather than measuring success, measures of effectiveness and efficiency need to be more transparent, organisation-wide and acted upon

Emerging theme 5: tenant–provider relationships

The final contribution of this research is the recognition of the constraints of the tenant-provider relationships in social housing that must maintain the commitment to equity and moral priorities over purely economic considerations (Spicker, 2009). However, in social housing, the tendency for the assumption of vulnerability across all tenants blurs quality with social value and requires further challenge and investigation. The evidence from the tenant consultation identifies that tenants want quick, efficient and effective services. Although the tenant base is comprised of the least affluent, from a repairs service perspective at least, this does not necessarily correlate to being a vulnerable tenant. A number of tenants also requested appropriate training to be able to complete minor jobs themselves, highlighting a potential change in the relationship between provider and tenant. The evidence from this study reiterates calls that public service organisations need to be outwardly focused on external effectiveness for service users as opposed to focused on internal measures of success (Osborne, Radnor *et al.*, 2014). This change in focus has a range of consequences, including a reframing of existing relationships and user priorities as in this study, and can lead to coproduction opportunities. Coproduction and knowledge of the service users are central to effective public service design and delivery (Osborne *et al.*, 2013), which leads to our final proposition:

> Proposition 5: Public service providers need to embed knowledge of the service user's needs and priorities at the core of their service provision, and consider how to manage the implications of coproduction.

A future research agenda

The acute need to deliver economically and socially sustainable services within the social housing sector is seeing a current resurgence of interest in business models and techniques, predominantly through the new paradigm of New Public

Governance (NPG). NPG emphasises service processes and outcomes and is predicated on a pluralistic state with multiple organisations contributing to public service delivery (Osborne, 2006). Based on this study, and in line with similar calls (Osborne *et al.*, 2013) an agenda for future OM research in social housing is needed to assess how OM within social housing can lead to more externally effective, as opposed to just more internally efficient, tenant services. A future research agenda for OM in social housing needs to build on the propositions developed in this study, and may address a range of specific issues including, but not limited to:

- An exploration to further the application of OM techniques in other areas of social housing service operations, particularly waiting lists.
- An examination of the potential of lean to reconfigure service processes to enable registered providers to respond to financial pressures while maintaining more responsive services to tenants.
- Research that extends the timeframe of impact measurement to assess the extent to which registered providers implement demand/capacity techniques beyond the early wins, how a culture of continuous improvement is embedded.
- An examination of the benchmarking mechanisms with organisations outside of the social housing sector to assess how internal targets and performance related to demand/capacity are assessed and externally calibrated.

The nervous debates around whether socially oriented organisations can, or should, borrow from private sector techniques that in the OM arena are largely predicated on manufacturing, is to a large extent obscuring the opportunities. A central finding from our research reiterates that unless there is a shift in emphasis to outputs rather than merely monitoring processes (Hall *et al.*, 2003), the adoption is likely to be a difficult fit that risks damaging OM's reputation. The pace of change in the social housing sector has been great with an ever-increasing breadth of responsibilities such as reducing environmental impacts, growing local economies and leading community integration. Before the sector can respond fully to these it must first develop the highest levels of efficiency and effectiveness in its core operations to deliver fundamental best value to its stakeholders.

References

Cave, M. (2007) *Every Tenant Matters: A Review of Social Housing Regulation*. London: CLG.

Coughlan, P. and Coghlan, D. (2002) 'Action research for operations management'. *International Journal of Operations and Production Management*, 22(2): 220–40.

Department for Communities and Local Government (2012) *Housing Strategy Statistical Appendix (HSSA) Data Returns for 2010 to 2011*. London: Department for Communities and Local Government.

Eden, C. and Huxham, C. (2005) 'Action research for management research'. *British Journal of Management*, 7(1): 75–86.

Fitzpatrick, S. and Pawson, H. (2007) 'Welfare safety net or tenure of choice? The dilemma facing social housing policy in England'. *Housing Studies*, 22(2): 163–82.

Gibb, K. and Nygaard, C. (2006) 'Transfers, contracts and regulation: A new institutional perspective on the changing provision of social housing in Britain'. *Housing Studies*, 21(6): 825–50.

Griffith, A. (2002) 'Key considerations for developing corporate and operational approaches for managing the small building works portfolio of large client organizations'. *Construction Management and Economics*, 20(8): 679–87.

Hall, M., Holt, R., and Purchase, D. (2003) 'Project sponsors under New Public Management: lessons from the frontline'. *International Journal of Project Management*, 21(7): 495–502.

Hills, J. (2007) *Ends and Means: The Future Roles of Social Housing*. CASE Report 34. London: London School of Economics and Political Science.

Holmans, A. (2005) *Historical Statistics of Housing in Britain*. Cambridge: Centre for Housing and Planning Research.

Homes and Communities Agency (2014) *2013 Global Accounts of Housing Providers*. London: HCA.

Housing Europe (2014) 'Maintaining and managing social housing stock: the AFTER project conclusions'. 30 April. Retrieved from www.housingeurope.eu/resource259/maintaining-and-managing-social-housing-stock (accessed 15 December 2014).

Laffin, M. (2013) 'A new politics of governance or an old politics of central–local relations? Labour's reform of social housing tenancies in England'. *Public Administration*, 91(1): 195–210.

Larsson, A. (2013) 'The accuracy of surgery time estimations'. *Production Planning and Control*, 24(10–11): 891–902.

Lovelock, C.H. (1984) 'Strategies for managing demand in capacity-constrained service organisations'. *Service Industries Journal*, 4(3): 12–30.

Osborne, S.P. (2006) 'The new public governance?' *Public Management Review*, 8(3): 377–87.

Osborne, S.P., Radnor, Z.J. and Nasi, G. (2013) 'A new theory for public service management? Toward a (public) service-dominant approach'. *American Review of Public Administration*, 43(2): 135–58.

Osborne, S.P., Radnor, Z.J., Vidal, I. and Kinder, T. (2014) 'A sustainable business model for public service organizations?' *Public Management Review*, 16(2): 165–72.

Pawson, H. and Wilcox, S. (2011) *UK Housing Review 2010/11*. Coventry: Chartered Institute of Housing.

Peters, B.G. and Pierre, J. (1998) 'Governance without government? Rethinking public administration'. *Journal of Public Administration Research and Theory*, 8(2): 223–43.

Pittini, A. and Laino, E. (2011) *2012 Housing Europe Review: The Nuts and Bolts of European Social Housing Systems*. Brussels: CECODHAS Housing Europe's Observatory.

Radnor, Z.J. and Boaden, R. (2008) 'Editorial: Lean in public services—panacea or paradox?' *Public Money and Management*, 28(1): 3–7.

Radnor, Z.J. and Walley, P. (2008) 'Learning to walk before we try to run: adapting lean for the public sector'. *Public Money and Management*, 28(1): 13–20.

Ram, M., Theodorakopoulous, N. and Worthington, I. (2007) 'Policy transfer in practice: Implementing supplier diversity in the UK'. *Public Administration*, 85(3): 779–803.

Reeves, A., Taylor, S. and Fleming, P. (2010) 'Modelling the potential to achieve deep carbon emission cuts in existing UK social housing: The case of Peabody'. *Energy Policy*, 38(8): 4241–51.

Rhodes, M.L. and Mullins, D. (2009) 'Market concepts, coordination mechanisms and new actors in social housing'. *European Journal of Housing Policy*, 9(2): 107–19.

Social Exclusion Unit (2004) *Jobs and Enterprise in Deprived Areas*. London: SEU.

Spicker, P. (2009) 'The nature of a public service'. *International Journal of Public Administration*, 32(11): 970–91.

Tuggle, F.D. and Goldfinger, W.E. (2004) 'A methodology for mining embedded knowledge from process maps, *Human Systems Management*, 23: 1–13.

van Ham, M., Williamson, L., Feijten, P. and Boyle, P. (2012) 'Right to buy … time to move? Investigating the moving behaviour of right to buy owners in the UK'. *Journal of Housing and the Built Environment*, 28(1): 129–46.

Walley, P. (2013) 'Does the public sector need a more demand-driven approach to capacity management?' *Production Planning and Control*, 24(10–11): 877–90.

Welsh Government (2014) 'Housing regulation'. Retrieved from http://wales.gov.uk/topics/housing-and-regeneration/services-and-support/regulation/?lang=en (accessed 6 June 2014).

Whitehead, C.M.E. (1999) 'The provision of finance for social housing: The UK experience'. *Urban Studies*, 36(4): 657–72.

Wickenden, J. (2012) *Value for Money in Responsive and Voids Repairs: HouseMark's Repairs Value for Money Toolkit*. Coventry: HouseMark.

10 Enterprising citizens and the Big Society

The impact of the entrepreneurial university on public services

Simon Adderley and Paul Kirkbright

Introduction

As the various chapters within this book show the application of operational management theory to the public sector is not as some authors would attest oxymoronic. Neither does it necessarily support a neo-liberal stance whereby 'efficient' public services is a synonym for 'smaller' public services. Rather operational management theories can be utilised to explore mechanisms of *efficiency* which not only measure the *monetary value* of public services but also their *social value*. In this sense *efficiency* is based on the ability of the service to achieve a social aim with limited resources not simply on their ability to utilise less resources.

Since at least the 1970s and almost certainly before that there has been a widespread belief that the public sector would be improved by the implementation of private sector management techniques. To this end a host of new public management initiatives have been implemented each designed to meet perceived challenges to the public sector and each based on the concept that market orientated management of the public sector will lead to greater cost efficiency for governments (Ferlie *et al.*, 1996; Hood, 1991).

This has been done, mainly through introducing practices and programs, which have been developed within industrial organisations. As a result the practices taken on by the public sector have had almost as an *a priori* assumption the traditional 'goods logic' whereby an organisation's economic model can be seen as the monetisation of an exchange of goods.

Recently however academics have begun to view the creation of public services through a service dominant logic perspective. Service dominant logic is predominantly a marketing theory which challenges the 'goods logic' by stressing exchange of intangible resources such as relationships and service value (Vargo and Lusch, 2008). More recently this argument has been applied to the provision of public services. Authors here understand citizens not simply as end-users of services but also as the creators of value. In this sense the role of the public sector is to facilitate resources and/or through interaction to collaboratively co-create value (Radnor *et al.*, 2014; Virtanen and Stenvall, 2014; Osborne and Strokosch, 2013; Kaluza and Skålén, 2013).

One mechanism trumpeted by the UK coalition government formed in 2010 to achieve this social value was the development of the 'Big Society'. In the minds of its architects, key to the development of the Big Society was to be the emergence of social enterprises which would find 'new' and 'innovative' ways to deliver public services utilising less resources than the 'old' public sector dominated provision. Indeed, the Big Society's stated aim to 'support the creation and expansion of mutuals, co-operatives, charities and social enterprises, and support these groups to have much greater involvement in the running of public services' (Cabinet Office, 2010) was identified by the prime minister as

> a deep and serious reform agenda to take power away from politicians and to give it to people. That's because we know instinctively that the state is often too inhuman, monolithic and clumsy to tackle our deepest social problems. We know that the best ideas come from the ground up, not the top down. We know that when you give people and communities more power over their lives, more power to come together and work together to make life better – great things happen.
>
> (Cameron, 2010)

Simultaneously the coalition government sought to develop an 'enterprise' culture focussed upon innovation and the development of new products. Moreover it placed a large emphasis upon the role of universities in developing such a culture in a number of key strategies such as *The Plan for Growth* (HM Treasury, 2011) and the *Higher Education White Paper* (BIS, 2011), as well as by supporting the work of the National Centre for Entrepreneurship Education (NCEE) and its predecessor (NCGE) as well as the National Association of College and University Entrepreneurs (NACUE).

Nevertheless a 2012 report by Universities UK showed that while the government's focus upon enterprise skills being recognised as an important asset for graduates had found much traction with UK Universities, the potential for wider application of social enterprise across careers appears to not be so clearly recognised (Universities UK, 2012; HECSU, 2012).

This chapter explores the notions of 'enterprise' and 'innovation' inherent in the notion of the Big Society and the ways in which higher education institutions (HEIs) have understood and developed these concepts within their own provision and within the models they have established for future educational delivery.

The Big Society concept

Since 2010 the landscape of local public policy within the United Kingdom has been significantly altered, not only by the financial implications of the economic recession, but also by the introduction of the concept of the 'Big Society' and by a large scale government focus upon Entrepreneurship. In fact if ever two concepts could be said to underpin much of the coalition government's agenda it has been the focus on developing the economy through entrepreneurial activities but also using those same skill sets to develop notions of self and community reliance and service development.

The notion of the Big Society was first introduced to the British public within the Conservative Party draft manifesto for the 2010 election. Central to this was a sense that social progress would be achieved not through a top down, target led approach but through the interactions of individual citizens acting in an entrepreneurial way.

The manifesto itself, and subsequent policy statements have made clear the concept that the 're-introduction' of 'once-natural bonds that existed between people – of duty and responsibility' remains at the heart of much of the UK Government's attempts to promote civicism. However, rather than simply rely upon state withdrawal which would be naturally replaced by an emerging public duty a series of policies have been enacted which indicate a belief that the state is needed to sponsor and promote individual responsibility. To this end there has been a strong focus upon the development of co-produced services. Services specifically designed by service users as well as service providers and, policy makers assume, able therefore to find new and entrepreneurial social service 'products'. In this sense the enterprise lies not in the generation of profit but rather in the design of new and creative solutions to problems.

> To make these reforms work, we need to give new and existing social enterprises, charities and voluntary groups the long-term incentives they need to develop and deliver innovative and high quality public services … Our ambition for the UK is clear: we want every adult in the country to be an active member of an active neighbourhood group.
>
> (Conservative Party, 2010a; emphasis in original)

Despite being identified as central to the political philosophy of David Cameron's Conservative Party this concept has attracted a great deal of negative attention from political opponents of the coalition government, and has been met with either scorn or apathy by the general public. The traditional left have seen it as a cheap alternative to 'real' state led policies both relying too much on service users to find their own solutions and opening the door to large private sector providers (Ishkanian, 2014; Corbett and Walker, 2013; Morgan, 2013). The traditional right have seen the notion of 'society' as being too far removed from neo-liberal economics and its focus on the individual or families. Academics have often criticised the Big Society for its vague merging of different concepts: 'from a sociological point of view, it fails as a coherent political vision, and as a intellectual platform for "public sector reform", because it conflates critical differences between "society", "state", "government", "community", and "neighbourhood"' (Ransome, 2011).

The notion of the Big Society was first introduced to the British public within the Conservative Party draft manifesto for the 2010 election.

> If we are going to mend our broken society and make British poverty history, we need to address the causes of poverty and inequality, not just the symptoms.

> We need new answers to the social problems we face – and we believe that the truly effective answers will come from a big society, not big government; from social responsibility, not state control.
>
> (Conservative Party, 2010b: 2)

Central to this was a sense that social progress would be achieved not through a top-down, target-led approach, but through the interactions of individual citizens:

> Our reforms will rebuild the once-natural bonds that existed between people – of duty and responsibility – which are currently being replaced with the synthetic bonds of the state.
>
> (Conservative Party, 2010b: 4)

However, the draft manifesto accepted that the 're-introduction' of such bonds was not going to be an easy task. More would be needed than simply state withdrawal which would be naturally replaced by an emerging public duty. Rather state action was needed to sponsor and promote individual responsibility

> A Conservative government needs to go further than enabling people to take responsibility: it must actively help make it happen. We must use the state to help stimulate social action. We must use the state to help remake society, because the big society, not big government, is the way to make Britain safer and fairer, a country where opportunity is more equal.
>
> (Conservative Party, 2010b: 4)

These ideas, introduced within the draft manifesto, were a central element of not only the full manifesto but were also identified as lying behind many of the economic, social and environmental policies which the Conservative Party put before the public at the 2010 election.

> The Big Society runs consistently through our policy programme. Our plans to reform public services, mend our broken society, and rebuild trust in politics are all part of our Big Society agenda … But we recognise that it is not enough to create opportunities for people to get involved in building the Big Society; our reform plans require a social response in order to be successful. So building the Big Society is not just a question of the state stepping back and hoping for the best; it will require an active role for the state. The state must take action to agitate for, catalyse and galvanise social renewal. We must use the state to help remake society.
>
> (Conservative Party, 2010b: 37)

Such conceptions had been present within Conservative papers for a number of months prior to the publication of the manifestos. Stott (2011) has identified the 'genesis' of the policy within Conservative writings and speeches since 2009 through a series of policy ideas designed to 'revitalise democracy and strengthen community life'. While these papers have identified a series of developing ideas and conceptions an ever present theme was the notion that the state should support individuals to work together through a shared sense of duty and responsibility to help increase social equity and to address social problems.

Moreover such a notion has continued to be central to the policy proposals of the Coalition government following the election. The Coalition's *Programme for Government*, published only three weeks after the election went so far as to state in the foreword, co-authored by the prime minister and the deputy prime minister, that

> When you take Conservative plans to strengthen families and encourage social responsibility, and add to them the Liberal Democrat passion for protecting our civil liberties and stopping the relentless incursions of the state into the lives of individuals, you create a Big Society matched by big citizens. This offers the potential to completely recast the relationship between people and the state: citizens empowered; individual opportunity extended; communities coming together to make lives better.
>
> (HM Government, 2010: 8)

And this concept, one of citizens acting on their responsibilities as citizens to help, with state support, to build a better society continued to be present in speeches and announcements from the Government throughout the first years of the coalition. Typical of this were the Prime Minister's remarks from May 2011 that:

> The Big Society is not some fluffy add-on to more gritty and more important subjects. This is about as gritty and important as it gets … The problem today is that a culture of responsibility is too often absent in our country. And we need to restore it. Of course, this has to come from people. But government has a vital role to play … But responsibility extends beyond the family to the wider community. We are not just responsible for those we know and love. We have obligations to those beyond our front door, beyond our street … Its' about the things you don't do. But it's also about the things you do do.
>
> (Cameron, 2011)

However this notion of an active citizenship working collectively with state support to develop localised solutions to societal problems is not new to David Cameron's Conservative Party. The late Thatcher and Major Governments of the 1990s shared a similar conception and drew similar amounts of academic interest. At the time, many saw notions of community as representing a reaction against the rise of neoliberal governments in the 1980s. Lister (1990), for example, argued that:

> As we enter the 1990s, we can sense a shift away from the narrow, individualistic ethos of the 1980s. An important element in this shift has been the re-emergence of the language of citizenship as a potential challenge to the dominant language of consumerism and enterprise.
>
> (Lister, 1990: 1)

Paradoxically however, the ever increasing cost of welfare in Britain led many concerned with the future of welfare to place a new emphasis on the concepts of self-reliance and individualism which characterise the good citizen. This political debate consistently advocated the voluntary impulse, long associated with the good citizen, as necessary for Britain's future. For example during the late 1980s senior government figures felt able to put forward the idea that the voluntary sector created precisely the sort of 'active citizen' Britain (or at least England) needed.

> The English tradition of voluntary service ... Justices of the Peace from the fifteenth century to the present, the school and vestry boards of the Victorian age, councillors in modern local government represent a long outstanding tradition of public service. School governors are unpaid, so are jurors, so are residents; ratepayers and tenants leaders, so are neighbourhood watch co-ordinators, so are the thousands of people who give their time freely to the huge and thriving number of British charities ... Schemes based on this tradition are more flexible and more effective than bureaucratic plans drawn up by Fabian principles.
>
> (Hurd, 1988: 14)

The synergies between the discourse of active citizenship and the entrepreneurial citizen have been key to much policy. In April 2012 the Big Society Bank (later Big Society Capital) was established underpinned by £600 million of capital. With an initial management team chaired by Sir Ronald Cohen, former chair of Apax Partners and a well-known advocate of social entrepreneurship its CEO was Nick O'Donohue, ex-JP Morgan global head of research, while the chief financial officer was Keith Starling who had held similar roles at Gartmore Group and Credit Suisse. This was not a management team led by the third sector or traditional social policists. It was instead an attempt to provide financial incentives to enterprises and entrepreneurial action but with the promotion of 'self-government and responsibilisation' as its core aim rather than the development of financial return (Lister, 2014).

Enterprise education

Core to the narrative of a society of active citizens engaging in the designing new public services and finding entrepreneurial ways to deliver them is the notion of an educated population (Buser, 2013). Indeed if one explores the key messages that have emerged in recent years from the enterprise education literature the shared descriptors of 'entrepreneurial students' and 'engaged citizens' are obvious. Hannon (2007), in an extremely influential article, detailed thirteen 'primary enterprise learning outcomes' for enterprise students, virtually all of which are relevant to the development of social enterprises or entrepreneurial citizenship:

1 To raise awareness, knowledge and understanding about enterprise/entrepreneurship concept and practice

2. To develop individual enterprising/entrepreneurial skills, behaviours and attitudes
3. To develop personal self confidence and capability
4. To develop empathy with an entrepreneurial way of life
5. To embed entrepreneurial values and beliefs
6. To motivate and inspire students toward an enterprising or entrepreneurial career or life
7. To understand venture creation processes
8. To develop generic entrepreneurial competencies
9. To develop key business 'how-to's'
10. To develop personal relationship and networking skills
11. To prepare for becoming a freelancer or self-employed
12. To start a new business
13. To exploit institutionally owned Intellectual Property

(Hannon, 2007)

While some of these, particularly the latter three, are of course business dominated, the synergies between the skills sets of entrepreneurial students and citizens capable of engaging in the design and delivery of local public services is striking. Hannon's article spurred a host of authors to provide data on mechanisms for teaching entrepreneurial skills and engaging with university staff or students (see, among others, Jones and Iredale, 2014; Jones and Colwill, 2013; Moon *et al.*, 2013; Rae *et al.*, 2012; Rae, 2009). However more recently a new discourse has emerged which has instead of asking what enterprise education is and what it does asks what it should be and what it should do (Blenker *et al.*, 2011). From this discourse has emerged the concept of the 'New Entrepreneurial University'.

The 'new entrepreneurial university'

Initially this discourse sought to clarify the concepts of enterprise and entrepreneurship in a higher education (HE) context and begin to move the debate on the 'entrepreneurial' future of universities away from the narrow focus upon commercial exploitation of knowledge and the associated traditional business school corporate approach to entrepreneurship (Gibb and Hannon, 2006; Gibb, 2002, 2005).

Further work (Gibb, Haskins and Robertson, 2009) set out more broadly the nature of the challenges to leadership of universities arising from changes in the global environment and the implications for the entrepreneurial design of the HE sector. Gibb (2012) sought to provide a strong underpinning framework for reviewing the entrepreneurial development capacity of a university by exploration of existing and potential enterprising and entrepreneurial activity in five key areas:

- strategy, governance, organisation and leadership;
- knowledge exchange;
- stakeholder relationship development and partnership (local, regional, national and international);

- enterprise and entrepreneurship education; and
- internationalisation.

Gibb and Haskins (2013) examined turbulence within the UK HE sector and the immediate challenges facing HE institutions. They explored mechanisms whereby not only could HEIs develop their own academic standing and commercial success, but could also play a significant role in the development of local public services.

The imperative to develop entrepreneurial capacity in HE has stemmed from the sector's impact on the UK's ability to compete internationally and respond entrepreneurially (socially and economically) to the pressures of uncertainty and complexity induced by globalisation (Gibb and Hannon, 2006). To date the pressure has been for HE to serve the wider aims of society in this context in three ways, by:

- enhancing capacity to commercialise, and make more widely accessible, its intellectual property;
- contributing more substantially to processes of regional and local economic and social development; and
- seeking to equip students for a 'life world' of much greater uncertainty and complexity.

The vision behind the 'entrepreneurial university' is the creation of an institution that moves beyond merely responding to these pressures, and into being a significant force for transformation of the communities it resides within, and the wider communities its work affects. The foundation for this institution being a culture of 'academic enterprise' which is focused and relevant – to industry, business, public service, economic regeneration and one which would also be a force for social equality and widening access to knowledge, skills and opportunities for all. Engrained into the organisation's 'DNA' would be the development and effective translation of knowledge across all academic and research disciplines into effective action.

This concept perhaps found its apex in Hagen's proposal to the Welsh Government for *The Entrepreneurial University: A New University for South East Wales* (Hagen, 2012).

Hagen's paper was a specific proposal for the creation of a new, entrepreneurially focused university for southeast Wales. The proposal was a direct response to a Ministerial challenge to formulate a 'new type of University'. Hagan set out that such an 'entrepreneurial institution' would be characterised as being/having:

- one focused on providing clear, demonstrable benefit to students and employers;
- research performance at international standards of excellence based upon open innovation;
- sustainable research outputs, strongly linked to users and other beneficiaries;
- highly collaborative in thinking and operation – regionally, nationally and internationally;
- fully responsive to the skills needs of employers and their employees – present and future;

- one that works together with further education (FE) colleges in an integrated fashion;
- one which offers more coherently planned and organised provision based 'in region';
- locally accessible yet globally connected – providing opportunities beyond physical structures;
- stronger emphasis on more flexible, open and individually tailored programmes of learning;
- a focus/fulcrum for academic and business partnerships, innovation and investment; and
- as a force for economic regeneration and social renewal.

Gibb (2012) explored how such an 'entrepreneurial vision' could pervade the mission, aims and activities of the HEI and both inform and direct broader strategic goals of enhancing innovation, strengthening and building stakeholder relationships, enhancing student employability, improving teaching quality, diversifying income streams and enhancing the image of the institution in the competitive market (i.e. distinctiveness).

In fact Gibb and Hagen had not developed these ideas alone. Much of their work has been based upon the writing of Michael Crow, the President of Arizona State

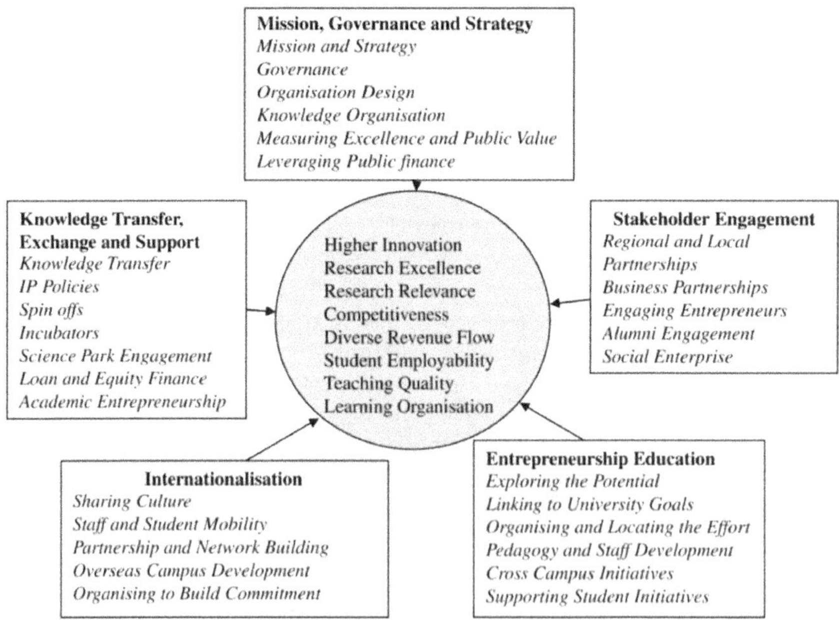

Figure 10.1 Exploring the synergistic potential in entrepreneurial university development

Source: Gibb (2012)

University. Crow has argued the case for the 'New American Research University' with 'academic enterprise' as the 'organising principle'. His vision for such an organisation was one built upon the foundations of:

- academic excellence focused upon and backed up by maximising social impact;
- competiveness;
- agility;
- adaptability;
- inclusivity;
- focusing globally yet also locally; and
- responsiveness to changing needs.

His view of such a university was one to be a 'force for societal transformation' with a culture of 'academic enterprise' focused upon 'user-inspired relevance' and transcending disciplinary based limitations. At the time Crow himself recognised that these concepts had major organisational and physical design, as well as intellectual, implications.

This vision had significant resonance for the development of the new approach to HE proposed by Hagan, particularly with its clear and demonstrable focus within its locality and an emphasis on developing the important sectors and public services within that locality.

> The guiding principle is the development of a knowledge-driven organisation where the organising feature is 'academic enterprise', where knowledge is created for use, as well as for disciplinary advance, and would be linked to, and measured by, social and economic advance. The new focus of knowledge and learning would be underpinned by a culture of entrepreneurialism.
>
> (Hagen, 2012: 8)

The institution would actively embrace innovation and embed enterprising behaviours/approaches across all academic and operational areas – including programme design, development, curriculum and pedagogy, stakeholder relationship and partnership development; research design and development; funding and resource acquisition; and internationalisation. This approach would encompass:

- formal factors: entrepreneurial organisational and governance structure, support measures for entrepreneurship, entrepreneurship education, support for the school/FE/HE 'pipeline';
- informal factors: academic community's attitudes towards entrepreneurship, entrepreneurial teaching methodologies, risk and reward systems;
- resources: human capital, recruitment, financial, investment, physical, and commercial activity;
- capabilities: status and prestige, visibility, networks and alliances, location.

In particular the institution would:

- have significant and proactive engagement between the university, industry, the public sector, 'mainstream' education – in particular extremely close alliances between HE and FE;
- regard external engagement not as a 'third stream', but as the driver of all activity with strong commercial operations including significant diversity of income streams (commercial contracts, research grants, consultancy, foundations, sponsorship etc.);
- be a catalyst/hub for innovation, empowering key players in industry, academia and local government to come together to develop networks between different organisations, agencies and institutions engaged in research activity, education and training, and commercialisation;
- have strong connections to local and regional science and technology parks/facilities, directly fed by staff and student accelerator and incubator facilities, providing opportunities for under and post graduate students;
- have trans-disciplinary approaches to research, teaching and learning with strong interdepartmental and cross boundary collaborations (including open modules and opportunities for teaching and learning within non-traditional environments);
- be underpinned by entrepreneurship (including social) including having entrepreneurs, business professionals and other 'professors of practice' working within the institution and, in return, academic staff working in companies and students learning from practice and placement;
- be committed to creating value with research centres focusing on applied research relevant to local industries and public services, and the translation of knowledge into commercial outputs, spin-outs and/or products for the 'public good';
- deploy optimal use of technology in all educational processes, including in the delivery of learning on campus and remotely via virtual learning environments, collaborative platforms and social media;
- be focused on maximising economic impact through targeted research and knowledge exchange activity (including prioritising digital/creative media/industries; land and environment; advanced materials and manufacturing; life sciences – health, bio, nursing, allied medical; and public service) and in using these sectors as a starting point, benchmark and renewal trigger for academic structures;
- have a management culture and processes based on an entrepreneurial ethos that encourages risk taking, empowers innovation and rewards successful engagement in knowledge exchange as strongly as success in teaching and research.

Of the previously listed 'characteristics' several are perhaps worthy of further exploration at this stage:

Trans-disciplinary approaches to research, teaching and learning

Academic programme design would focus on achieving greater multi-disciplinarity, inter-disciplinarity and trans-disciplinarity. The first implies a combination of disciplines, the second interaction between established disciplines and the last the creation of new structures to explore broader economic, societal and environmental challenges/issues. This new HEI model provides an opportunity to explore non-traditional academic structures and align the teaching and learning strategy closer to the demands and needs (present and future) socially, environmentally and economically.

Flexible academic structures would be established and focused in line with the requirements of the local economy and society, while research would be supported only where there was a clear association between activity and economic growth or public service innovation (i.e. industrial demand or policy imperative). With such a non-traditional structure it is possible that the new HEI would be extremely attractive to 'next generation' academics seeking to work more flexibly and innovatively across traditional academic divides. Attracting academic staff with the potential for high quality research and those with a track-record of producing nationally or internationally recognised work would be critical in terms of distinctiveness within the marketplace and the reputation/quality of programme design, delivery and renewal. These 'next generation' researchers would also be aligned to the post-graduate offering for teaching and supervisory duties. This would have the potential, over time, to lead to the development of doctoral programmes and other post-graduate research awards – critical in retaining graduate talent within the area or attracting it back to the area.

Underpinned by entrepreneurship

> The new University would plan to educate students for jobs that haven't yet been invented. This would require a series of underpinning skills modules, where 'skills' is a term to embrace the development of new knowledge, imagination, and analytical ability, and other enterprising skills, and develop the capacity to adapt and to learn new knowledge and skills in the years to come. The new University's focus would also be on developing young people with the ability to rapidly assimilate knowledge and develop competence on what would be an ever-changing work environment where they would also encounter a suite of technologies, and rapidly have to adapt to them on a week by week basis.
>
> (Hagen, 2012: 17)

Entrepreneurship education is not only aimed at stimulating entrepreneurship in the sense of business start-up and business ownership, but also at developing competence for increased entrepreneurial behaviour within existing organisations (now termed 'intrapreneurship') and within society itself. The purpose and aim of underpinning the teaching and learning experience with entrepreneurship would be to support the development of enterprising competences and behaviour (i.e. capability for autonomous action, initiative-taking, problem-solving, risk-taking, self-efficacy and resourcefulness) – 'enterprising behaviours' which are manifest in a multitude of different contexts including the active engagement in society as citizens as understood by the Big Society concept.

Across a range of activities, the new HEI would create widespread awareness among the student population and staff of the need to develop a range of personal enterprising competencies appropriate for a future personal and employment world of greater uncertainty and complexity. The 'distinctiveness' of the new HEI graduate would be not only a high degree of work-readiness but also a high degree of preparedness to engage within wider society. Key for Hagen was the notion that 'The New University will commit to creating *public value*: its research centres will focus on applied research relevant to Welsh industries and public services, and the translation of knowledge into commercial outputs, spin-outs and/ or products for the public good' (Hagen, 2012: 8, emphasis in original).

Significant and proactive engagement with further education

> The FE sector, working in closer collaboration with HE, can infuse its vocational traditions, such as BTEC HND/C, more firmly within HE, embedding the vocational/professional pathway at an earlier stage and offering students higher-grade qualifications through guaranteed access to a University. This 'lifelong' vocational learning process is particularly valued by employers. FE-derived routes are attractive to adults, many on low incomes, from families not traditionally involved in HE.
>
> (Hagen, 2012: 14)

A key element of the entrepreneurial university model is the creation of deeper and more locally relevant links between further education colleges (FECs) – as well as with other partner HEIs. While there have always been vocational elements in HE, the tradition has focused on full-time, three year, campus-based undergraduate programmes, mainly for the 18–24 year group. FECs have, in parallel, successfully developed strength in vocational, part-time programmes and flexible modes of access.

In his 2012 paper, Hagen commented on the opportunity for the creation of a new 'common purpose' between higher and further education which would seek to strengthen the recruitment of students from the community onto vocational and professional awards and ensuring fully articulated progression routes from FE into university higher programmes of study. This 'common purpose' would also encompass collaboration in areas such as marketing campaigns demonstrating the advantages of FE/HE education to those with no family tradition or awareness, assisted progression to self-employment for both FE and HE graduates through joint incubation services and work on attracting new investment and strengthening the skills base, particularly in key growth sectors.

Inherent within this model then is the creation of enterprising graduates capable of and encouraged to play an active role within their localities. Utilising skill sets traditionally associated with developing new businesses and services but now, within the framework of the Big Society, able to also use those same skill sets to fully engage in the design, development and delivery of new public services.

Conclusion

Education to promote citizens capable of fully engaging in society is not a new concept. In the early nineteenth century J. S. Mill was deliberately educated under a strict Utilitarian doctrine by his father, James Mill and Jeremy Bentham; a doctrine which influenced much Liberal thinking and hence social welfare for the remainder of the century. In the mid nineteenth century T. H. Green, influenced by Mill, led an immanentist movement which was to influence the future of philanthropic thought in Britain for three decades. Academics such as Bosanquet, Wallas, Urwick, Muirhead, Jones and Seth, many taught by Green himself, were to be highly influential in universities across the country. As Harris has stated, 'it was they who designed the curricula, wrote the texts books and gave the lectures by which the first generation of academically trained social workers and social scientists were taught' (Harris, 1992: 50).

Even in the twentieth century, Graham Wallas, socialist, educationalist and co-founder of the London School of Economics, wrote that:

> Since it is now necessary for us to co-operate on the scale of a modern industrial nation, and since that scale far surpasses the range of our senses, we should consciously aim at creating in our minds and in those minds whose training we influence, such an idea of our nation as will form the most reliable stimulus to large-scale co-operative emotion and co-operative action.
>
> (Wallas, 1920: 101)

However the HE sector has moved away from such aims in recent years. The focus firstly upon the extension of provision following a 'widening access' agenda increasingly meant that provision focussed upon retention and support rather than specific educational aims. In recent years the significant personal increase in cost to the student of attending education and the consequent shift from education as a right to education as a product to be purchased, coupled with the increased emphasis upon research outputs in the funding of HEIs has led to different targets being set for Universities.

Nevertheless much good work does take place within universities even if it isn't 'core business'. Volunteer schemes abound, work placements are common place, an increased emphasis on locally and regionally based projects is often supported through key UK and European funding streams. In the light of this activity and with the promotion of entrepreneurial mindsets growing in importance there is an opportunity, and indeed an obligation to ensure that our students and graduates are capable of engaging in the design, development and delivery of the public services which we need to develop in the twenty-first century.

References

BIS (2011) *Higher Education White Paper: Students at the Heart of the System*. London: BIS.

Blenker, P. Korsgaard, S. Neergaard, H. and Thrane, C. (2011) 'The questions we care about: paradigms and progression in entrepreneurship education'. *Industry and Higher Education*, 25(6): 417–27.

Buser, M. (2013) 'Tracing the democratic narrative: Big Society, localism and civic engagement'. *Local Government Studies*, 39(1): 3–21.

Cabinet Office (2010) *Building the Big Society*. London: Cabinet Office.

Cameron, D. (2010) 'Government launches Big Society programme'. Speech, London, 18 May. Retrieved from www.gov.uk/government/news/government-launches-big-society-programme--2 (accessed 7 April 2015).

Cameron, D. (2011) 'Speech on the Big Society'. Milton Keynes, 23 May. Retrieved from www.gov.uk/government/speeches/speech-on-the-big-society (accessed 7 April 2015).

Conservative Party (2010a) *Big Society Not Big Government: Building a Big Society*. London: Conservative Party.

Conservative Party (2010b) *Mending Our Broken Society: Conservative Manifesto 2010*. London: Conservative Party.

Corbett, S. and Walker, A. (2013) 'The Big Society: rediscovery of 'the social' or rhetorical fig-leaf for neo-liberalism?' *Critical Social Policy*, 33(3): 451–72.

Ferlie, E., Ashburner, L., Fitzgerald, L. and Pettigrew, A. (1996) *New Public Management in Action*. Oxford: Oxford University Press.

Gibb, A. (2002) 'In pursuit of a new "enterprise" and "entrepreneurship" paradigm for learning: creative destruction, new values, new ways of doing things and new combinations of knowledge'. *International Journal of Management Reviews*, 4: 233–69.

Gibb, A. (2005) *Towards the Entrepreneurial University: Entrepreneurship Education as a Lever for Change*. Policy paper 3. Birmingham: National Council for Graduate Entrepreneurship.

Gibb, A. (2012) 'Exploring the synergistic potential in entrepreneurial university development: towards the building of a strategic framework'. *Annals of Innovation and Entrepreneurship*, 3. Retrieved from http://journals.co-action.net/index.php/aie/article/view/16742 (accessed 9 June 2014).

Gibb, A. and Hannon, P. (2006) 'Towards the entrepreneurial university'. *International Journal of Entrepreneurship Education*, 4(1): 73–110.

Gibb, A. and Haskins, G. (2013) 'The university of the future: an entrepreneurial stakeholder learning organisation?' In Fayolle, A. and Redford, D. (eds), *Handbook of Research in Entrepreneurial Education*, volume 4: 25–50. London: Edward Elgar.

Gibb, A., Haskins, G. and Robertson, I. (2013) 'Leading the entrepreneurial university: Meeting the entrepreneurial development needs of higher education institutions'. In Altmann, A. and Ebersberger, B. (eds), *Universities in Change: Managing Higher Education Institutions in the Age of Globalization*, pp. 9–45. New York: Springer.

Hagen, S. (2012) *The Entrepreneurial University: A New University for South East Wales*. Newport: University of South Wales.

Hannon, P. (2007) 'Enterprise for all? The fragility of enterprise provision across England's HEIs'. *Journal of Small Business and Enterprise Development*, 14 (2): 183–210.

Harris, J. (1992) 'Victorian values and the founders of the Welfare State'. *Proceedings of the British Academy*, 78: 165–82.

HECSU (2012) *Work in Social Enterprises ... Satisfying Aspiration?* Manchester: HECSU.

HM Government (2010) *The Coalition: Our Programme for Government*. London: Cabinet Office.

HM Treasury (2011) *The Plan for Growth*. London: Treasury.

Hood, C. (1991) 'A public management for all seasons'. *Public Administration*, 69 (Spring): 3–19.

Hurd, D. (1988) 'Citizenship in the Tory democracy'. *New Statesman*, 29 April.

Ishkanian, A. (2014) 'Neoliberalism and violence: the Big Society and the changing politics of domestic violence in England'. *Critical Social Policy*, 34 (1): 1–22.

Jones, P. and Colwill, A. (2013) 'Entrepreneurship education: an evaluation of the Young Enterprise Wales initiative'. *Education + Training*, 55(8–9): 911–25.

Jones, B. and Iredale, N. (2014) 'Enterprise and entrepreneurship education: towards a comparative analysis'. *Journal of Enterprising Communities: People and Places in the Global Economy*, 8 (1): 34–50.

Kaluza, J. and Skålén, P (2013) *Addressing Public Sector Challenges from a Service Logic Perspective*. Paper presented at 22nd Nordic Academy of Management Conference.

Lister, R. (1990) *The Exclusive Society: Citizenship and the Poor*. London: Child Poverty Action Group.

Lister, M. (2014) 'Citizens, doing it for themselves? The Big Society and government through community'. *Parliamentary Affairs*, 6 January. Retrieved from http://pa.oxfordjournals.org/content/early/2014/01/03/pa.gst025.short (accessed 9 June 2014).

Moon, R., Curtis, V. and Dupernix, S. (2013) 'How enterprise education can promote deep learning to improve student employability'. *Industry and Higher Education*, 27(6): 433–48.

Morgan, H. (2013)'Sport volunteering, active citizenship and social capital enhancement: what role in the Big Society?' *International Journal of Sport Policy and Politics*, 5(3): 381–95.

Osborne, S.P. and Strokosch, K. (2013) 'It takes two to tango? Understanding the co-production of public services by integrating the services management and public administration perspectives'. *British Journal of Management*, 24(S1): S31–47.

Radnor, Z.J. Osborne, S.P., Kinder, T. and Mutton, J. (2014) 'Operationalizing co-production in public services delivery: the contribution of service blueprinting'. *Public Management Review*, 16(3): 402–23.

Rae, D. (2009) 'Connecting entrepreneurial and action learning in student-initiated new business ventures: the case of SPEED'. *Action Learning: Research and Practice*, 6(3): 289–303.

Rae, D., Martin, L., Antcliff, V. and Hannon, P. (2012) 'Enterprise and entrepreneurship in English higher education: 2010 and beyond'. *Journal of Small Business and Enterprise Development*, 19(3): 380–401.

Ransome, P. (2011) 'The Big Society fact or fiction? A sociological critique'. *Sociological Research*, 16(2). Retrieved from www.socresonline.org.uk/16/2/18.html. (accessed 9 June 2014).

Stott, M. (2011) 'The Big Society in context'. In M. Stott (ed.), *The Big Society Challenge*: 1–27. Cardiff, Keystone Development Trust.

Universities UK (2012) *Universities Enabling Social Enterprise: Delivering Benefits for All*. London: Universities UK.

Vargo, S. and Lusch, R. (2008) 'Service-dominant logic: continuing the evolution'. *Journal of the Academy of Marketing Science*, 36(1): 1–10.

Virtanen, P. and Stenvall, J.P. (2014) 'The evolution of public services from co-production to co-creation and beyond – new public management's unfinished trajectory?' *International Journal of Leadership in Public Services*, 10(2): 91–107.

Wallas, G. (1920) *Our Social Heritage*. London: George Allen & Unwin.

Part III

Performance management and measurement

11 The challenges of performance measurement in third sector organisations

The case of UK advocacy services

Margaret Taylor and Andrew Taylor

Introduction

The third sector (TS) is fast growing and increasingly important for the delivery of public services. Consequently, enhanced performance in TS organisations becomes more vital to their role. In this chapter we discuss the challenges of performance measurement (PM) in the sector and examine the relationship between performance and funding for organisations operating within it. We focus on UK-based advocacy services to provide the practical context for the chapter. These are services which seek to secure equality for vulnerable or marginalised groups of people; we articulate a taxonomy of advocacy services and use this to illustrate the discussion. The chapter draws on existing academic knowledge about performance measurement in order to investigate the particular needs of the TS. We argue that the characteristics of advocacy provision in particular, and of TS services in general, require the adoption of a multiple stakeholder perspective in the measurement of performance. We further argue that by understanding the varying stakeholder performance requirements, third sector organisations (TSOs) can maximise their chances of securing funding. To this end we draw on stakeholder theory to develop our arguments.

The chapter aims to raise awareness among the scholarly community of the issues surrounding performance measurement in TSOs and to simulate further research that will have both academic value and practitioner impact. It contributes to knowledge in a number of ways. First, we develop a picture of the research landscape which incorporates funding, stakeholders and performance measurement in the TS. Second, we provide a taxonomy of advocacy services accompanied by a discussion of performance measurement issues within this that highlights the need for appropriate measures to be developed. Finally, we propose a conceptual model which incorporates the relationships between stakeholders, performance and funding in this sector. In a research companion, such as this, this chapter represents a firm foundation on which future work may build.

After the introduction, the chapter is organised as follows. Drawing primarily on material from Taylor and Taylor (2013),[1] the second section describes the TS landscape in the UK before discussing the central issues of performance measurement, organisational stakeholders and funding within it. In order to illustrate this literature-based discussion, the third section provides an account of advocacy services in the UK and explores how the three central issues are linked in practice in this environment. The chapter concludes with presentation of the proposed conceptual model.

The third sector landscape in the UK

Globally, the characteristics of TS activity vary according to the political, social and economic environment in which they operate, leading to differences between, and even within, nations. This applies, not least, in the balance between state and private support and in terms of the influence of different stakeholders. However, as the core notions of public participation and service user involvement in welfare systems are reflected in continental Europe and elsewhere (Martin, 2011), many of the issues raised in this chapter apply beyond the UK. Thus, while the UK is used as the primary vehicle to illustrate our discussion, we suggest that the contribution of this work extends beyond the reach of national boundaries.

Although it is hard to precisely articulate the organisation types that comprise the TS (Dickinson *et al.*, 2012; Martin, 2011), it is generally regarded as comprising two distinct groups differentiated by whether or not they aim to make profit. Thus, social enterprises are profit-making businesses set up to tackle a social or environmental need, and include organisations such as development trusts, community enterprises, co-operatives, 'social firms' and leisure trusts. In the UK, in 2011, there were approximately 55,000 social enterprises with a combined turnover of £27 billion, contributing £8.4 billion per year to the UK economy (*ibid.*). By contrast, and accounting for around 765,000 paid employees in the UK in 2010 (Clark *et al.*, 2011), the second group – not-for-profit, voluntary and community organisations (VCOs) – do not aim to generate profit from their operations. Current trends suggest that TS growth is outpacing that of both the public and private sectors, with a 25 per cent increase in employment in the voluntary sector between 1996 and 2005, contrasting with just 13.7 and 10.9 per cent in the public and private sectors respectively (NCVO, 2007). In absolute terms, the proportion of the UK working population employed in the TS rose steadily from around 2 per cent in 2001 to 2.7 per cent of the workforce in 2010 (Clark *et al.*, 2011).

Reflecting their importance both for employment and in the provision of public services, for the most part, this chapter is based around VCOs (or non-profit organisations) rather than social enterprises. However, we follow the precedent set by Martin (2011) and sometimes use the more general terminology of 'third sector' 'inclusively and heuristically, to denote the various voluntary, non-profit and charitable organizations' (*ibid.*: 910) that constitute this segment of the sector. Rising employment in VCOs is partially accounted for by their growing use for the provision of services traditionally delivered by public sector bodies (Davies, 2011; Martin, 2011; Parry *et al.*, 2005; Little, 2005). In this context, they increasingly work alongside public and private bodies to deliver services across multiple policy areas in the UK (Bovaird *et al.*, 2012). Since 1999, UK government spending on the voluntary sector expanded significantly to reach £12.8bn by 2008 (Alcock, 2012) and continued government support for 'the expansion of the [voluntary] sector's role in the delivery of public services' (Davies, 2011: 644) means that this growth is likely to perpetuate.

Such is the importance of the TS in the UK that it is now represented by its own Cabinet Office[2] – the Office for Civil Society (OCS) (Alcock, 2012) – and by the establishment of a government-funded Third Sector Research Centre (see www.tsrc.ac.uk). Government support of the TS is premised on the notion of 'The Big Society', in which power is devolved from the state to its citizens (Alcock, 2012), and on the adoption of principles of New Public Management (NPM). This is characterised by decentralised authority and service delivery, the adoption of market or quasi-market mechanisms, customer-oriented services, and the establishment of targets against which performance is measured (Bovaird *et al.*, 2012; Dacombe, 2011; Martin, 2011).

Performance measurement in the third sector

Given the significance of the TS outlined above and the trend for its continued growth, it is important that research is undertaken which addresses knowledge gaps and which aims to help in the delivery of efficient and effective TS operations. Not least, is the need for work on performance measurement (PM) where views differ as to whether sectoral differences impact on the approaches taken. This leads to debate over whether or not PM methods developed for the private and public sectors can be applied effectively in the TS. On the one hand there is an argument that 'measuring the performance of non-profit organizations is not distinctly different from measuring the performance of private or public sector organizations' (Moxham, 2009: 745) and therefore similar approaches can be taken (e.g. Boyne, 2002). On the other hand, opponents of this view (e.g. Callen *et al.*, 2010; Dacombe, 2011), argue that TSOs operate in a unique context which requires them to 'develop different and more complex accountability systems to satisfy the competing claims of multiple stakeholders' (Costa *et al.*, 2011: 475).

The topic of performance measurement has, over the years, been a fairly constant focus of research activity in various contexts (e.g. Camarinha-Matos and Abreu, 2007; Walters, 2005; Franco-Santos and Bourne, 2005), and detailed accounts of its development exist (e.g. Bititci *et al.*, 2012; Franco-Santos *et al.*, 2007). Empirical studies have examined performance measurement both in private settings (e.g. Garengo and Sharma, 2014; Kumar Dey and Cheffi, 2013; Bourne, 2005) and in the public sector (e.g. Lega *et al.*, 2013; Tapinos *et al.*, 2005). However, there is relatively little equivalent work in the TS (Bititci *et al.*, 2012; Moxham, 2009; Moxham and Boaden, 2007; Micheli and Kennerley, 2005). One avenue of research that has been undertaken resulted in the proposal of a modified version of the balanced scorecard (BSC) being used for non-profit organisations (Kaplan and Norton, 2004), but the wide range and heterogeneous nature of TS activity is elsewhere argued to mean that this is not universally suitable (Kong, 2008, 2010). There has been very little empirical research carried out to study BSC implementation in non-profit organisations apart from a few descriptive single case studies (Greiling, 2010; LeRoux and Wright, 2010).

In comparative investigation, BSC implementation was seen to focus on measurement instead of strategy, and to place greater emphasis on financial indicators than non-financial and longer-term perspectives (i.e. it has been found to be largely unsatisfactory) (Greiling, 2010).

The Performance Prism (Neely *et al.*, 2002) is an example of another multidimensional PM model and is premised on the satisfaction of all stakeholders in order to achieve organisational success (i.e. it takes a stakeholder-centric view of performance measurement; Kennerley and Neely, 2002). Since (as we discuss later) TSOs have multiple stakeholders, often with conflicting views and requirements, this approach 'is considered by its authors to be particularly relevant to the public and non-profit sectors' (Micheli and Kennerley, 2005: 131). However, aside from one report of its successful adoption by a UK charity (Neely *et al.*, 2007), there is little empirical evidence of its use in TSOs. Overall, despite the Balanced Scorecard and the Performance Prism making 'explicit reference to their applicability to voluntary organizations ... There appears to be little systematic or independently evaluated evidence of the effectiveness of such models in the voluntary sector' (Moxham and Boaden, 2007: 830; see also Manville and Broad, 2013). This apparent lack of effectiveness may derive from the sheer multiplicity of stakeholders involved (Moxham and Boaden, 2007; Speckbacher, 2003) or from their focus on PM in a single organisation (Bititci *et al.*, 2012) rather than in circumstances – more typical of TS service delivery – where there is a high degree of inter-agency co-operation and collaboration. In such situations, a much stronger inter-organisational and network emphasis is required (Jones and Liddle, 2011; Osborne and Murray, 2000).

In summary, while it is clear that there is much interest in performance measurement in the TS, this is not yet matched by the adoption of effective models (Ritchie and Kolodinsky, 2003). Research in this area remains in its infancy (Rochette and Fenies, 2008; Schneider, 2006). In order to move forwards, we believe it is crucial to understand the characteristics of VCOs in more detail and to examine the implications of these for performance measurement. It is only when we have this knowledge, that effective PM systems can be developed and implemented successfully.

Voluntary and community organisations characteristics and implications for performance measurement

As indicated above, the features that distinguish VCOs from organisations in the for-profit and public sectors impact on their management and accountability systems (Figlio and Kenny, 2009) including those for performance measurement. Accordingly, in this section, we examine the need for, characteristics of, and challenges associated with PM in VCOs. We acknowledge that the debate over whether or not the TS is sufficiently distinct from other sectors to require different approaches is on-going (e.g. Macmillan, 2012; Alcock and Kendall, 2011) and remains unresolved. We take the stance that its unique features mandate a sector-specific approach and, in support of this, the distinctive characteristics of TSOs have been identified to include:

- their unique cultures, diffuse power structures, and special value systems (Blake *et al.*, 2006; Cairns *et al.*, 2005);
- their multiple and nebulous goals (Dacombe, 2011; Callen *et al.*, 2010; Cairns *et al.*, 2005);
- the existence of 'confounding ideological concerns' (Callen *et al.*, 2010: 103);
- the nature of voluntary work wherein the central role of volunteers is significant and 'whose involvement needs to be reflected in any approach to measurement' (Dacombe, 2011: 161);
- the multiplicity of stakeholders (Dacombe, 2011; Callen *et al.*, 2010; Carman, 2010; Packard, 2010; Cairns *et al.*, 2005);
- their distinctive ownership and governance structures, where 'the traditional division of stakeholders, such as owners, paid staff and consumers or users is replaced in voluntary agencies by a bewildering complexity of overlapping roles' (Billis and Glennerster, 1998: 81); and
- the distinctive funding arrangements and the lack of focus on profit maximisation in VCOs with the absence of a 'bottom line' against which to measure performance (Callen *et al.*, 2010; Micheli and Kennerley, 2005; Boland and Fowler, 2000).

The discussion that follows is based on these distinguishing characteristics and in particular we explore the nature of VCO funding and examine its implications for the measurement of performance before moving on to consider the challenges associated with the multiplicity and range of stakeholders that is typical in the sector.

Funding mechanisms

A major difference between public/private enterprise and the TS is the means by which income is generated. For VCOs, a variety of sources and mechanisms are used to access funding, with the primary routes being charitable donations, grants and contracts.

Of these, charitable donation represents a major and widespread income source, especially as more than 75 per cent of voluntary organisations do not receive any funding from statutory sources (Dawson, 2012). While donation tends to be less formal in nature than grant and contract funding (discussed below), there is evidence of increasing stricture in the terms under which donations are made. By way of example, it is becoming more common for individual donors not to rely solely on trust, but to seek assurances about performance before making donations (Iwaarden *et al.*, 2009; Cole and Cooper, 2005). Furthermore, although charitable donation by individuals is influenced by trust, it is argued that trust itself depends on the donor's views of organisational performance (Sargeant *et al.*, 2006). Thus, donors tend to withhold support from organisations that are perceived to be performing poorly and may increase support for those that perform well (Figlio and Kenny, 2009). In general, for funding by donation, it appears important for organisations to be able to achieve and demonstrate performance. As we discuss next, for the other income mechanisms, it is essential.

As indicated earlier, TS activity in the UK has expanded in recent years – in terms of both employment and the provision of services. Alongside these increases there has been a corresponding growth in the level of state funding such that, by 2008, the level of earned income exceeded half of charities' total income for the first time (NCVO, 2008). This rise reflected, in particular, increased government spending on public services: in 2008, 36 per cent of the total income for charities in England and Wales derived from state support (Alcock, 2012). Representing a pronounced shift away from grant funding, contracts are now the principal type of relationship between actors in UK public services (Dacombe, 2011). Since contract agreements are legally enforceable, with specified services being provided by one party in return for payment, this shift has knock-on effects for VCOs that deliver social care services (Davies, 2011). Where funding is awarded by contract, the services to be provided are articulated in full, and there is a legal requirement for effective service delivery that meets the contractual service specification. In such situations, the use of targets and key performance indicators (KPIs) is common. The growing contract culture can also introduce tensions between the defined purposes of many TSOs and the contractual requirements to provide services which are outside their stated mission or legal scope (Morris, 2012).

The commissioning process

Commissioning, which 'is the cycle of assessing the needs of people in an area, designing and then achieving appropriate outcomes' (Dawson, 2012: 6), is the most common means by which government funding is awarded. There is a degree of confusion over terminology related to commissioning and associated concepts (e.g. contracting, procurement and purchasing; see Bovaird *et al.*, 2012), but, in essence, commissioning is a process that defines the needs in a particular situation, decides on how the needs can be met and then considers how appropriate services can be acquired. Joint commissioning, whereby more than one public body is involved in this process, is increasingly common among government agencies in the UK (*ibid.*). It aims to deliver better outcomes for service users by adopting a holistic approach to solve complex problems.

The final stage of the commissioning cycle is the acquisition of services and here, too, there is complexity over the processes that can be used and the relationships between them. The direct purchase of services is an option which usually (but not always; *ibid.*) involves competitive tendering leading to the award of a legal contract specifying what is to be delivered. Alternatively, services can be acquired following the award of a grant. Confusingly, grant funding can also be awarded separately from commissioning where its role is seen as complementary to that of contract funding and is used where it will deliver better outcomes than would result from a commissioning approach (*ibid.*). Within commissioning, the activities of sourcing and monitoring both call for performance to be defined and measured. This requirement is further emphasised because of the focus within commissioning on outcomes rather than on the activities and processes by which services are delivered: 'successful outcome-based commissioning can lead to very different services being commissioned and using different methods to achieve the ultimate aim' (Dawson, 2012: 10).

Implications of funding mechanisms for performance measurement

Having described the key features of the VCO funding regime, in this section we explore how these impact on performance measurement in the sector. First, since grants are time-limited and contracts for VCOs are typically short-term (Dickinson *et al.*, 2012), providers tend to lack certitude and this leads to a disproportionate focus on short-term performance goals (Ellis and Gregory, 2008; Moxham and Boaden, 2007; Rapaport *et al.*, 2006). Regardless of the means by which funding is secured, financial cycles of 12 months or less are typical and frequent bids to secure new or repeat funding are characteristic of the sector. Such short-term funding arrangements encourage a focus on short term objectives associated with easily-measurable activities using straightforward performance indicators, rather than long-term objectives relating to less tangible aspects that are harder to measure (Costa *et al.*, 2011). As, for many services, it can take several years before outcomes become apparent, measurement against short-term contracts fails to capture evidence of effective performance for which longer time periods would be more appropriate. Furthermore, in an environment characterised by competitive bidding, there is an unfortunate tendency for organisations to target '2-year initiatives to promise 5-year outcomes (in 2 years), whereas agencies submitting to 5-year programs promise 10-year outcomes (in 5 years)' (Wing, 2004: 157). Making exaggerated promises clouds the contracting process and it has been suggested that TSOs would fare better in the award of public sector contracts if the commissioning bodies looked at 'performance rather than what people put in their tenders about what they will achieve' (Plummer, 2009: 2). Where contracts are awarded on the basis of false promises it is likely that demonstrable performance will be lower than promised, thereby harming the service provider's reputation and reducing their chances of future funding.

Second, the plethora of funding sources – each stipulating their own targets – leads to the specification of multiple and different performance indicators for providers (Ellis and Gregory, 2008; Bozzo, 2000). Not only does this result in an onerous amount of data collection, but also leads to a performance environment which is unduly complex and often ambiguous (Campbell, 2002; Leland, 1998). Since funders have their own criteria by which performance is assessed and impose their own reporting requirements, the workload on service-providers is inflated – often necessitating the use of parallel measurement systems (Dawson, 2010; Ellis and Gregory, 2008; Cairns *et al.*, 2005). It has also been found that funders frequently fail to understand what might be realistic for an organisation to achieve or measure; this too is problematic considering that monitoring and evaluation is frequently imposed by these parties (Dawson, 2010; Bhutta, 2005).

Finally, organisations in the sector are less able to develop balanced measurement systems because they are constrained by the requirements of those who provide funding. The needs of funders and other powerful stakeholders frequently take precedence over alternative groups, such as service users (Cairns *et al.*, 2005), who also have an interest in the performance of TSOs. The multiplicity of stakeholders that is characteristic of the sector differentiates organisations within it from those in other environments, and means that, in developing systems for PM and accountability, they have to deal with 'multiple and competitive stakeholder demands' (Costa *et al.*, 2011: 473). Consequently, in addition to the challenge of reporting performance to multiple funders (discussed above), there are wider pressures necessitating the re-orientation of PM approaches for different types of stakeholder (ibid). The implications for performance measurement that derive from the wider stakeholder base that is typical of VCOs, are considered in the following section.

Multiplicity of stakeholders

Key facets of the commissioning process, by which VCOs increasingly access income, include the definition/measurement of performance and engagement with stakeholders (Bovaird *et al.*, 2012). More specifically, a PM emphasis on the achievement of outputs and outcomes (rather than on inputs and processes) features alongside continuing dialogue with stakeholders in the contemporary TS environment (e.g. Baggaley, 2010). Recent increases in the extent of government funding for TS activity are mirrored by changes to its distribution and these have an impact on the stakeholder base. While in the past, support tended to focus on specific service areas, it is now increasingly common for a more 'horizontal' approach to be adopted whereby support is spread across the sector (Alcock, 2012). Alongside this there is a growing tendency for social care to be acquired and delivered through integrated initiatives including joint commissioning, inter-organisational collaboration and multi-agency service provision (Martin, 2011; Sowa, 2009; Babiak and Thibault, 2009; Paton *et al.*, 2007). These changes combine to broaden the range of stakeholders and complicate the measurement process. In effect, organisations face the twin challenges of reporting to multiple commissioning agencies and of measuring the separate contributions of each partner in the provision of the service. Since, in the contemporary commissioning process, the distributed delivery of social care requires individual organisations to co-operate with others for the achievement of performance goals, these partner institutions represent a further stakeholder group who – alongside the funding agencies – have their own priorities and perspectives on VCO performance.

In general terms, stakeholders are individuals and groups who have an effect on, or are affected by, an organisation (Waxenberger and Spence, 2003). Since the services provided by VCOs typically improve the wellbeing of citizens – especially those who are vulnerable and dependent – their stakeholder base is broad. In addition to the funders and partners (discussed above) various other parties, each having their own perspective on service delivery, hold an interest in defining and monitoring organisational performance. While, in summary form, service providers in the sector are accountable to patrons, clients and themselves (Costa *et al.*, 2011), more detailed scrutiny results in a much more extensive list of potential stakeholders and this demonstrates clearly the challenges the stakeholder base poses for the prioritisation and reconciliation of multiple accountabilities. The list of those with an interest in social care services can include, *inter alia*, central government, local government, government agencies, audit agencies and monitoring bodies, clients or service users, intermediaries such as the social services, health professionals, or other service providers who act as proxies for the users, carers, relatives, social workers, medical practitioners, funders, commissioners, primary care trusts (PCTs), the National Health Service (NHS), employees, and volunteers (Moxham and Boaden, 2007; Cairns *et al.*, 2005; Wisniewski and Stewart, 2004). To successfully balance the competing demands on them and manage operations, VCOs need to identify all stakeholders and to understand their different requirements. It is important also that they are able to recognise and differentiate between those stakeholders who have significant stakes in their organisation ('stockholders') and those who have legitimate claims upon it ('claimholders') (Waxenberger and Spence, 2003).

Implications of multiple stakeholders for performance measurement

For VCOs, efficiency (ratio of resources used to output achieved) and effectiveness (extent to which goals are achieved) are of strategic relevance in the assessment of performance (Costa *et al.*, 2011), and strong alignment between an organisation's strategic plan and its PM system is essential (Manville and Broad, 2013). Taking this further, it is generally the case that stakeholders such as funding bodies are primarily interested in resource efficiency and the output metrics that are associated with this. On the other hand, service users (and stakeholders who directly represent their interests) are chiefly concerned with service quality and how effectively the delivered service meets their individual needs. This means that for service users the key aspects of organisational performance relate to outcomes and impact (e.g. Greatbanks *et al.*, 2010; Dawson, 2010; McEwen *et al.*, 2010). As the business of VCOs is typically characterised by the customary service industry features of intangibility, heterogeneity, simultaneity in production and consumption, and perishability (Oakland, 2004), the measurement of performance using quantitative metrics is not always easy. Furthermore, traditional accounting-based performance metrics, such as return on investment, return on sales and productivity, are also not applicable (Herman and Renz, 1997).

It is clear, then, that for the TS, PM systems need to be put in place that measure both the outcomes of the service and the process of service delivery including assessment of how well service user needs are met. A twin-pronged approach which incorporates 'hard' measures such as productivity and efficiency alongside 'softer' measures such as adaptability and stakeholder satisfaction would therefore seem to be appropriate (Marchand and Raymond, 2008). Interestingly, these concepts resonate with those of technical and functional service quality (Grönroos, 1982) which underpin the long-established Service Quality model for assessing performance in service operations (Parasuraman *et al.*, 1985) – an approach that has nevertheless attracted some criticism (Asubonteng *et al.*, 1996). Tangible, quantifiable measures of outcome, which reflect what a customer receives from a service, can be used to assess technical quality. By contrast, functional quality, which refers to the manner of service delivery, is measured using more esoteric, less quantifiable metrics such as user perceptions of the appropriateness of the service and the process by which it is delivered. The need to measure dual aspects of service delivery supports the view that quality in non-profit organisations is 'multidimensional and costly to measure' (Figlio and Kenny, 2009: 1069).

Emerging from the discussion so far is recognition of the need for the user voice to be included in any VCO performance measurement regime. However, this runs contrary to much current practice in which the main drivers of PM criteria are government, funders, regulators, and (sometimes) the VCOs themselves (Moxham, 2009) rather than service users (Kong, 2010). Although measurement of service quality is part of performance assessment in other contexts (e.g. Poister, 2003), this absence of service user influence in the determination of performance criteria in the TS goes against its fundamental tenets of user-led service delivery, social inclusion and active citizenship (e.g. Jochum *et al.*, 2005; Yong and Wilkinson, 2002). It is suggestive of a situation in which performance systems have typically been implemented from the top-down rather than from the bottom-up (e.g. Flapper *et al.*, 1996; Ghalayini and Noble, 1996; Neely *et al.*, 2002), thereby under-emphasising stakeholder groups such as users and those who represent them. It is important to note that this lack of inclusion is not universal in the sector and there are examples of service users being given opportunities to influence decisions e.g. through Board and lower level committee membership (Manville and Broad, 2012).

Not only do users have a role to play in the specification of performance criteria but their central role as customers and clients means that they are also vital in assessing the service quality that is delivered. This is particularly the case for intangible functional quality elements that are usually more difficult to quantify than those which assess achievement against hard criteria in the generation of robust evidence to demonstrate performance. Although essentially anecdotal in nature, accounts of users' experiences of a service, its outcomes and the impact on them (either by the user or a proxy) can provide powerful testimony to performance. It is argued that such evidence is 'sympathetic to, and reflecting of, a voluntary organization's values, goals and achievements' (Greatbanks *et al.*, 2010: 581).

In the next section we consider the example of UK advocacy services and the part that stakeholder theory may play in linking performance measurement to funding but before we do that, we summarise the discussion so far. The increasing requirement for accountability within the TS (e.g. Christensen and Ebrahim, 2006; Kaplan, 2001; Morris, 2000) reflects an environment in which there are greater expectations of measurement (Paton, 2003). This in turn means that organisations are 'constantly striving to demonstrate efficiency and responsiveness to both beneficiaries and funders' (Cairns *et al.*, 2005: 144). Taken together, the short-term nature of funding arrangements, the wide range of funding sources and mechanisms, the nature of the services delivered, the multiplicity of stakeholders and the distributed, more inter-dependent nature of the delivery process render the development of improved PM approaches important and timely.

Advocacy in the UK

The following discussion which links performance measurement, stakeholder theory and funding is illustrated by the case of the provision of advocacy services, which aim to secure the rights and represent the interests of vulnerable members of society. We exclude the more general meaning of the term 'advocacy' where it refers to a political process in which an individual or group aims to influence public policy or actions taken within political, economic and social systems and institutions (e.g. as used in Silverman and Patterson, 2011). The empirical data used as evidence for the discussion derives from an ethnographic study undertaken in the UK over a 5-year period to 2012.

Advocacy organisations are increasingly funded by public sector bodies, and face the same challenges as other VCOs relating to evaluating performance and obtaining funding. Increasingly, it is necessary to provide performance monitoring information to funders and to be able to report on performance by a variety of metrics. Although a number of evaluation models have been proposed for the sector, they are limited in scope and all have drawbacks (Rapaport *et al.*, 2005). There are no widely agreed benchmarks to test performance, and there is a tendency for purchasers of advocacy (funders) to impose their own monitoring schemes (*ibid.*).

Like other VCOs, the performance of advocacy organisations is subject to the opinions of a wide-ranging set of stakeholders, which creates potential conflicts of interest. In broad terms, service providers need to meet the expectations of funders, partners and users, but this breaks down to include clients (service users), partners, carers, relatives, social workers, medical practitioners, funders, commissioners, local authorities, primary care trusts (PCTs), the NHS, government agencies, employees, volunteers, monitoring bodies and support agencies. Given these circumstances, it is essential to identify and categorise all stakeholders before developing understanding of their needs in relation to organisational performance. Stakeholder theory provides the vehicle by which this can be achieved and its application to the advocacy sector is discussed next.

Stakeholder theory and advocacy

As stated in section earlier, stakeholders are the individuals and groups who effect or are affected by an organisation. Stakeholder theory represents an approach by which the nature and influence of stakeholders may be examined (Donaldson and Preston, 1995). Its use for describing and managing the business environment is popular (Mitchell *et al.*, 1997) and necessary (Waxenberger and Spence, 2003). The range of organisation/stakeholder relationships that can occur, and the changing nature of these over time, point to the importance of distinguishing different stakeholders (Friedman and Miles, 2002). Just as stakeholders may select strategies to exert influence on a firm (Frooman and Murrell, 2005), so an organisation should identify, understand and manage its stakeholder base. Given the multiple relationships that exist within the advocacy sector, we suggest that stakeholder analysis represents an essential first step in the development of PM approaches for it, leading thereafter to the successful pursuit of funding. The work of Co and Barro (2009) in which stakeholder theory is used to examine stakeholder management strategies in supply chain collaboration, provides a recent example of the use of such an approach in the operations management field.

Taking guidance from Mitchell *et al.* (1997), the ensuing discussion shows how stakeholder theory can be used to utilise power, legitimacy, and urgency as attributes of the stakeholders of an organisation. While power refers to the ability of an entity to influence an organisation; legitimacy reflects the degree to which there is an expectation that a stakeholder has authority, right or mandate; and urgency reflects the criticality of a stakeholder intervention and is time-sensitive. Where managers perceive there to be only one of these attributes then the salience of the stakeholder will be low – so-called 'latent' stakeholders. Of these, 'dormant' stakeholders are those with the power to impose their will but no legitimate relationship or urgent claim; 'discretionary' stakeholders are those with legitimacy but no power or urgent claim; and 'demanding' stakeholders have an urgent claim without the power or legitimacy to influence the organisation. Although not necessarily an immediate concern to the managers of an organisation, its latent stakeholders are real and relevant. 'Expectant' stakeholders can be identified where two of the three attributes are perceived to be present. Thus, 'dominant' stakeholders have power and legitimacy; 'dangerous' stakeholders have power and urgency; and 'dependent' stakeholders have legitimate urgent claims on the organisation. Finally, to complete the classification framework proposed by Mitchell *et al.* (1997), 'definitive' stakeholders are those perceived to have all three attributes and 'non-stakeholders' are viewed as having none. Given the dynamic nature of stakeholder relationships (Friedman and Miles, 2002) it is important that all stakeholder categories (latent, expectant and definitive) be included in organisational stakeholder analysis.

This classification of stakeholders is relevant to the complex, multi-stakeholder situation in which advocacy organisations operate, and it provides a starting point by which the complexity of PM may be examined. In order to further illustrate the discussion we now present a taxonomy of advocacy types and discuss the PM issues associated with these.

A taxonomy of advocacy services

Mounting political will, shifting social attitudes and changes in the law have all contributed to recent consistent growth in the advocacy sector (Henderson and Pochin, 2001; Hussein *et al.*, 2006; Rapaport *et al.*, 2005, 2006). In the UK, council spending on generic advocacy services doubled from 2001 to 2004 (Valuing People Support Team, 2005), and there was an average funding increase of 30 per cent across learning disability advocacy services, from 2003–4 to 2006–7 (Department of Health, 2007). This increasing financial value evidences the importance of advocacy which seeks to benefit isolated, vulnerable or marginalised groups, including, but not limited to, those with learning disabilities, developmental disorders, physical disabilities, mental health problems, sensory or cognitive impairments and those who lack capacity (Department for Constitutional Affairs, 2007; Henderson and Pochin, 2001; Craig, 1998). Advocates work to secure people's rights, represent their interests and obtain the services they require (Action for Advocacy, 2009; Rapaport *et al.*, 2005).[3] They represent the needs of those who are at risk of social exclusion, marginalisation, abuse or mistreatment (Forbat and Atkinson, 2005). In general terms, advocacy is practiced in situations where people find themselves unable to exercise choice in decision-making processes, to redress power imbalances as a result of their vulnerability within society (Dunning, 1995).

Advocacy partners (also known as service users or clients) derive from broad backgrounds and have varying needs. As a result, although large national providers do exist, the majority tend to tailor their services towards specific markets. The process of service delivery also varies both within and between providers, ranging from short-term, issue-based support towards longer-term representation. The variety and range of advocacy services is summarised in Table 11.1 and discussed thereafter.

Performance measurement in advocacy

The complex nature of the advocacy sector and the variety of services offered pose operational challenges, not least in the development of PM systems. For measures to have practical application they must be appropriate to the specific environment in which each scheme is offered, and this precludes the use of universal approaches in the form of highly prescriptive models. In the light of this we provide a discussion of each form of advocacy which includes consideration of the associated PM issues, and which highlights the need for appropriate measures to be developed.

Citizen advocacy

Citizen advocates are volunteers who generally operate independently of service agencies. As 'valued' members of society, they typically connect to, and create a long term, sustained relationship with de-valued people who are at risk of social exclusion, in order to represent their interests and defend their rights (Bateman, 2000; Craig, 1998; O'Brien, 1987). Citizen advocates may act as a friend, counsellor, legal advisor and general supporter (Bateman, 2000). Clear outcomes are rarely articulated, implying that outcome-related performance measures would not capture the full benefits of the service. The process of service delivery is arguably more important than the end result: 'the process of citizen advocacy is important and valuable in itself, over and above outcomes' (Hanley and Davies, 1998: 17). In service quality terms, this suggests that functional quality is at least as important as technical quality (Grönroos, 1982), and implies the use of intangible and qualitative performance metrics such as how friendly the advocate was, if they were a good listener, if partners were made to feel empowered and so on.

Citizen advocates may be affiliated with a co-ordinated scheme, which is managed by a paid member of staff, or operate on an ad-hoc and informal basis whereby volunteers undertake the role of their own accord. In either case, formal regulatory mechanisms may not be in place, though where they are, evidence suggests that they have failed to determine impact, demonstrate outcomes or show what those in the advocacy relationship actually do together (Henderson and Pochin, 2001; O'Brien, 1987).

Table 11.1 A taxonomy of common UK advocacy types

Advocacy service	*Funding mechanism*	*Staff paid or unpaid*	*Advocates*	*Typical duration*	*Issues addressed*	*Instructed or n on-instructed**	*Level of regulation*	*Target audience*
Citizen advocacy	Non-statutory, multiple funding streams	Unpaid, but co-ordinator may be	Volunteers	Long term	Multiple, varied	Mixed	Low	Mixed
Crisis advocacy (aka case professional, and short-term)	Non-statutory, multiple funding streams	Paid	Trained Staff	Short term, issue based	Specific	Mixed	Variable	Specific
Self advocacy	Non-statutory	Service-users unpaid, co-ordinator may be	Service-users	Undefined	Multiple, varied	Instructed: Self-initiated/ user led	Low	Specific
Peer advocacy	–	Unpaid	Service-users	Undefined	Multiple, varied	Generally instructed	Low	Specific
Independent Mental Capacity Advocacy (IMCA)	Statutory funding through Primary Care Trusts	Paid	Trained staff	Short term, issue based	Very specific, accommodation/ medical treatment	Non-instructed	High	Very specific
Independent Mental Health Advocacy (IMHA)	Statutory funding through Primary Care Trusts	Paid	Trained staff	Short term, issue based	Very specific	Mixed	High	Very specific
Independent Complaints Advocacy Service (ICAS)	Statutory	Paid	Trained staff	Short term, issue based	Very specific, NHS complaints	Instructed	High	Very specific

* Instructed advocacy refers to a situation in which the service user has the capacity to direct the advocate's work; in non-instructed advocacy proxies direct the advocacy process on behalf of users who lack the necessary capacity to do this for themselves

Crisis advocacy (professional, case or short term advocacy)

Crisis advocacy is practiced by paid members of staff who provide representational, issue-based support to advocacy partners, usually for a short period of time. Examples include helping people to challenge their care providers, or supporting people to move house, gain more independence, or be allowed access to services which they are denied. In the UK, crisis advocacy is practised nationally through groups such as POhWER (2011), regionally through groups such as Cloverleaf (2011) and locally by a multitude of service providers (Action for Advocacy, 2009). In principle, crisis advocates only represent their partners with respect to a specific issue and therefore the relationship is based around clear outcomes and targets. The service tends to be more closely defined and narrower in scope than citizen advocacy and, since specific goals are articulated, the use of quantifiable performance metrics is more widespread. Indeed, these are often used by funders for monitoring and evaluation (Rapaport *et al.*, 2006).

Performance measures that are used in crisis advocacy include, for example, the number of hours worked per case (Henderson and Pochin, 2001), the average time spent per case (Rapaport *et al.*, 2005), the ratio of open to closed cases (Henderson and Pochin, 2001), demographic representativeness (Scottish Executive, 2001), and cost per case (Hussein *et al.*, 2006). These are consistent with a culture of upward accountability, wherein advocacy providers are required to monitor those characteristics of service provision which reflect the priorities of funders. However, quantifiable measures in themselves are inadequate in capturing all aspects of performance in an advocacy relationship (Henderson and Pochin, 2001), and a transition towards the measurement of (qualitative) outcomes is being encouraged (e.g. Action for Advocacy, 2009; Department of Health, 2007). The use of 'softer' measures, such as the extent to which users have been able to express their wishes or have increased their confidence, can provide a more comprehensive insight into performance from a user perspective.

Despite this encouragement, anecdotal evidence suggests that few attempts have been made to systematically engage with, and to involve, advocacy service users in the development of measures which are then fed back to funding bodies. This is an issue which is recognised with respect to disability services more generally (O'Reilly, 2007). Thus, although service user involvement has long being encouraged within the advocacy sector (Whittaker *et al.*, 1991), the evidence points to a failure of the practicing community effectively to link user-centric measures to those of upstream funding bodies.

Self-advocacy

Bateman (2000: 18) refers to self-advocacy as 'a process in which an individual, or group of people, speak or act on their own behalf in pursuit of their own needs and interests'. It is based on notions of self-determination, independence and control, whereby people are provided with the means to enact change in their own lives. Often this is practiced formally through collective organisations which consist predominantly of unpaid members. Examples of self-advocacy groups in the UK include People First, who operate at local, regional and national levels to uphold the collective rights of people with learning difficulties (*ibid.*), Speaking Up, who provide self-advocacy support to a range of groups (see www.voiceability.org), and the UK Advocacy Network (UKAN), a self-help group operating in the mental health field (see www.u-kan.co.uk). These organisations are premised on being user-led. The development of new life skills and confidence is a central tenet of many self-advocacy groups (Craig, 1998). Just as with citizen advocacy, an emphasis on functional quality and the use of qualitative metrics, is likely to be more appropriate in this context. The specific performance measures characteristic of crisis advocacy are arguably less informative in self advocacy, where an emphasis on user involvement and the service delivery process take precedence. Generic objectives, such as the establishment of patient councils, forums and particular advocacy projects (UKAN, 2009) reflect the over-arching philosophy of such schemes and provide insight into the kind of outcomes that may derive from self-advocacy. However, the extent to which these may be captured by specific indicators is unclear. Furthermore, outcomes in this context do not necessarily fit well with the kind of metrics most pertinent to funding bodies (Action for Advocacy, 2009).

Peer advocacy

A peer is someone who shares similar characteristics with the person they are advocating for (BILD, 2011). A peer advocate is likely to have had comparable experiences to the person they represent, and this helps to engender a shared sense of understanding, empathy and partnership. Peer advocates are unpaid. The service may consist of relatively informal one-to-one support or be organised using a case-based approach (Henderson and Pochin, 2001) such as reformed drug-users working with addicts, or people who have experience of mental health services supporting existing service users. The diversity which is inherent in this form of advocacy mitigates against the use of clearly defined measurement criteria, and although contingent on the extent to which such services are formally organised, one could question whether performance measurement is appropriate in peer advocacy at all. Attempts to 'control' the process or outcomes of service delivery are likely to be met with disapproval and resistance, particularly where peer advocacy is practiced through informal channels. Nevertheless in situations where the service is delivered in a professional capacity, and a co-ordinator is funded to organise delivery, there will generally be an expectation for providers to account for their actions.

Independent Mental Capacity Advocacy

The Independent Mental Capacity Advocacy (IMCA) service was launched in England and Wales in April 2007 following the Mental Capacity Act (MCA, 2005). It represents one of three statutorily provided advocacy services (alongside IMHA and ICAS, discussed below), which are funded by local authorities. The service is designed to

> help particularly vulnerable people who lack the capacity to make important decisions about serious medical treatment and changes of accommodation, and who have no family or friends that it would be appropriate to consult about those decisions ... The aim of the IMCA service is to provide independent safeguards for people who lack capacity to make certain important decisions and, at the time such decisions need to be made, have no-one else (other than paid staff) to support or represent them or be consulted.
>
> (Department for Constitutional Affairs, 2007: 178)

Since it is provided only to those who lack capacity to make the decision themselves, it is always non-instructed (i.e. directed by proxies on behalf of users). IMCA services have a very narrow remit, pertaining to a specific form of service provision, to satisfy clearly defined criteria. This has led to the use of funder-led, quantitative evaluatory systems, which incorporate a range of performance metrics such as monthly referral rates, number of eligible referrals, reasons for referral, hours spent per case and outcomes of the service encounter (Department of Health, 2008a). While these address predominantly technical aspects of service quality, arguably in situations where people are unable to exercise choice over decisions being made for them, additional forms of performance measurement that assess the functional quality are also desirable.

Independent Mental Health Advocacy

Typical users of Independent Mental Health Advocacy (IMHA), which works to protect, help and support patients with mental health problems (NIMH, 2008), are those who are liable to be detained under the Mental Health Act (MHA, 2007), are subject to guardianship, are on supervised control treatment (SCT) or have been conditionally discharged after being sectioned. Guidelines on how monitoring and evaluation should be conducted cover a wide range of performance measures (NIMH, 2008). These focus on both patient outcomes (receipt of information, support to understand their rights and involvement in the service), and service outcomes (referral characteristics, responsiveness of the IMHA service, operational requirements, working with other agencies, and response to comments of service users and professionals). The latter measures, which are primarily quantitative, more likely reflect the needs of the service commissioners and funders, and facilitate benchmarking between local authorities.

Independent Complaints Advocacy Service

Independent Complaints Advocacy Service (ICAS) supports patients and their carers in England and Wales who wish 'to pursue a complaint about their NHS treatment or care' (Department of Health, 2008b). To enact this, different advocacy providers cover different geographical regions (*ibid.*). As with IMHA, a number of 'hard' and 'soft' measures are used to assess performance (Department of Health, 2004), ranging from the number of complaints received each quarter (hard), to descriptive patient accounts providing feedback about their experiences of the service (soft).

Taking the specific example of ICAS, for which there are stated principles of empowerment, independence, confidentiality, inclusion, resolution and partnership (Department of Health, 2008b), we can begin to understand the underlying targets of organisations working in the advocacy sector. These customer focussed targets demonstrate the performance aims that govern generic advocacy services and which are also reflected in the Advocacy Charter produced by the sector-wide umbrella body, Action for Advocacy (2004). In spite of this there seems to be a split between measurement designed to assess the process of service delivery (i.e. functional quality) and that which demonstrates its outcomes (i.e. technical quality). The extent to which one is favoured over another seems to be driven by who measures performance and what type of scheme is offered.

Discussion

Conceptual framework

From the preceding discussion, it is clear that in the advocacy sector the measurement of performance is necessary, complex, resource intensive and under-developed. Organisations need to demonstrate their achievements in order to gain funding, but are faced with a plethora of different metrics and approaches depending on the service offered and the sources of finance. As discussed in the earlier section this situation is typical of many TSOs. The findings from the literature review point to the need for PM systems to be balanced (Neely, 2005; Moxham, 2009; Medori and Steeple, 2000), to link to organisational strategy (Johnston and Pongatichat, 2008; Medori and Steeple, 2000), and to cater for multiple stakeholders (Neely *et al.*, 2002). Within this context, the introduction of stakeholder theory facilitates the identification of the expectations and contributions of all stakeholders, thereby informing the development of PM approaches.

The conceptual model in Figure 11.1 captures the key arguments of the chapter, by relating stakeholder classification to performance measurement and to funding.

Every form of VCO service (e.g. each advocacy type in Table 11.1) will have its own unique set of stakeholders. Once identified, each one can be assessed against the attributes of power, urgency and legitimacy and thereby classified according to the types depicted in stakeholder theory. Thereafter, the within-type analysis in the model is completed by the identification of performance measurement issues relating to each stakeholder type. In situations and sectors where different models for service provision exist (e.g. in advocacy), the within-type analysis may be followed by cross-type examination in order to develop sector-wide understanding of performance measurement issues by distinguishing between those that are common to most types and those that are specific to a limited number. The resulting sector-wide knowledge will inform the development of performance measurement approaches that assess both efficiency and effectiveness, facilitate the demonstration of accountability and contribute to achieving future funding.

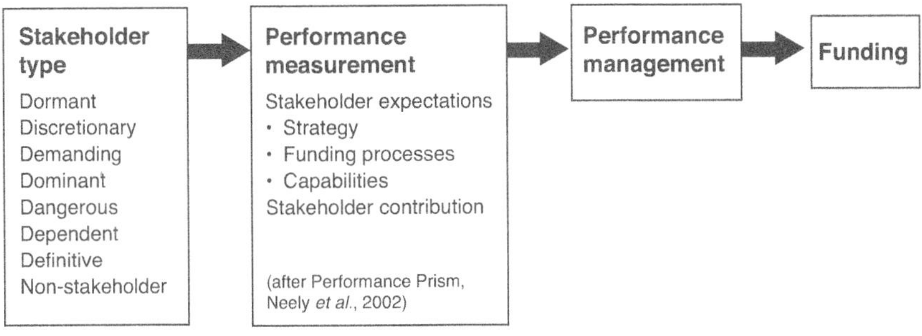

Figure 11.1 Proposed conceptual model

Conclusions

This chapter has contributed to knowledge by developing a detailed view of performance measurement, funding and stakeholders in the TS. The discussion has been illustrated using the case of advocacy service provision in the UK, for which the different types have been articulated. The performance measurement and funding issues for each type have been considered and the resulting discussion serves to highlight the need for appropriate measures to be developed. Finally, a conceptual framework, which draws on stakeholder theory, is used to point the way to future research by which the relationship between performance measurement and funding in the TS may be further investigated. The outcomes of such investigation should facilitate the development of systems and measures for assessing voluntary sector organisational performance in a transparent and unambiguous manner. This should then guide managers in the sector on how best to organise operations to improve performance and to secure future funding.

The chapter has argued that since many TS services share some or all the characteristics of advocacy provision (e.g. the nature of services offered, multiplicity of stakeholders, variety and complexity of funding mechanisms, requirement to demonstrate performance), while the specific findings relate to advocacy, there are lessons to be learned from this work throughout the TS.

On a final note, notwithstanding the arguments for greater accountability in the TS and the drivers for performance measurement, a wider debate on the desirability of such developments remains. The measurement of performance leads to changed behaviour; and, in an environment where payment is made by results, there is a danger that the most needy and difficult customers/clients/cases will be ignored at the expense of more straightforward cases for whom success is more likely and more easily achieved/demonstrated (Davies, 2011; Iwaarden *et al.*, 2009).

Acknowledgments

The authors gratefully acknowledge the contribution of Mark Heppinstall and Mei-Na Liao to background work that supports parts of this chapter.

References

Action for Advocacy (2004) *The Advocacy Charter*. Retrieved from www.aqvx59.dsl.pipex.com/Advocacy%20Charter2004.pdf (accessed 21 November 2011).

Action for Advocacy (2009) 'About advocacy'. Retrieved from www.actionforadvocacy.org.uk (accessed 10 March 2009).

Alcock, P. (2012) *The Big Society: A New Policy Environment for the Third Sector?* Working Paper 82. Birmingham: Third Sector Research Centre.

Alcock, P. and Kendall, J. (2011) 'Constituting the Third Sector: processes of de-contestation and contention under the UK labour governments in England'. *Voluntas*, 22(3): 450–69.

Asubonteng, P., McCleary, K. and Swan, J. (1996) 'SERVQUAL revisited: a critical review of service quality'. *Journal of Services Marketing*, 10(6): 62.

Babiak, K. and Thibault, L. (2009) 'Challenges in multiple cross-sector partnerships'. *Nonprofit and Voluntary Sector Quarterly*, 38: 117–43.

Baggaley, M. (2010) *Joint Commissioning Framework: Staffordshire Children's Trust*. Retrieved from www.staffordshirechildrenstrust.org.uk/NR/rdonlyres/C662B2AD-E61B-4508-B5D9-A0B9B883586D/136021/CTJointCommFramework.pdf (accessed 15 April 2013).

Bateman, N. (2000) *Advocacy Skills for Health and Social Care Professionals*. London: Jessica Kingsley Publishers.

Bhutta, M. (2005) *Shared Aspirations: The Role of the Voluntary and Community Sector in Improving the Funding Relationship with Government*. London: National Council for Voluntary Organizations.

BILD (2011) 'Types of advocacy'. Retrieved from www.bild.org.uk/about-bild/advocacy/advocacy-types (accessed 7 April 2015).

Billis, D. and Glennerster, H. (1998) 'Human services and the voluntary sector: towards a theory of comparative advantage'. *Journal of Social Policy*, 27(1): 79–98.

Bititci, U.S., Garengo, P., Dörfler, V. and Nudurupati, S. (2012) 'Performance measurement: challenges for tomorrow'. *International Journal of Management Reviews*, 14(3): 305–27.

Blake, G., Robinson, D., and Smerdon, M. (2006) *Living Values: A Report Encouraging Boldness in Third Sector Organisations*. London: Community Links.

Boland, T. and Fowler, A. (2000) 'A systems perspective of performance management in public sector organizations'. *International Journal of Public Sector Management*, 13(5): 417–46.

Bourne, M. (2005) 'Researching performance measurement system implementation: the dynamics of success and failure'. *Production Planning and Control*, 16(2): 101–13.

Bovaird, T., Dickinson, H. and Allen, K. (2012) *Commissioning Across Government: Review of Evidence*. Research Report 86. Birmingham: Third Sector Research Centre.

Boyne, G.A. (2002) 'Public and private management: what's the difference?' *Journal of Management Studies*, 39(1): 97–122.

Bozzo, S.L. (2000) 'Evaluation resources for nonprofit organizations'. *Nonprofit Management and Leadership*, 10(4): 463–72.

Cairns, B., Harris, M., Hutchison, R. and Tricker, M. (2005) 'Improving performance? The adoption and implementation of quality systems in UK nonprofits'. *Nonprofit Management and Leadership*, 16(2): 135–51.

Callen, J.L., Klein, A. and Tinkelman, D. (2010) 'The contextual impact of nonprofit board composition and structure on organizational performance: agency and resource dependence perspectives'. *Voluntas* 21: 101–25.

Camarinha-Matos, L.M. and Abreu, A. (2007) 'Performance indicators for collaborative networks based on collaboration benefits'. *Production Planning and Control*, 18(7): 592–609.

Campbell, D. (2002) 'Outcomes assessment and the paradox of nonprofit accountability'. *Nonprofit Management and Leadership*, 12(3): 243–59.

Carman, J.G. (2010) 'The accountability movement: what's wrong with this theory of change?' *Nonprofit and Voluntary Sector Quarterly*, 39(2): 256–74.

Christensen, R.A. and Ebrahim, A. (2006) 'How does accountability affect mission? The case of a nonprofit serving immigrants and refugees'. *Nonprofit Management and Leadership*, 17(2): 195–209.

Clark, J., McHugh, J. and McKay, S. (2011) *The UK Voluntary Sector Workforce Almanac 2011*. Retrieved from www.ncvo-vol.org.uk/sites/default/files/Workforce_Almanac_2011.pdf (accessed 15 April 2013).

Cloverleaf (2011) *Supporting People to Speak Up across Yorkshire and Humberside*. Retrieved from www.cloverleaf-advocacy.co.uk (accessed 18 November 2011).

Co, H.C. and Barro, F. (2009) 'Stakeholder theory and dynamics in supply chain collaboration'. *International Journal of Operations and Production Management*, 29(6): 591–661.

Cole, B. and Cooper, C. (2005) 'Making the trains run on time: the tyranny of performance indicators'. *Production Planning and Control*, 16(2): 199–207.

Costa, E., Ramus, T. and Andreaus, M. (2011) 'Accountability as a managerial tool in non-profit organizations: evidence from Italian CSVs'. *Voluntas*, 22: 470–93.

Craig, Y.J. (1998) *Advocacy, Counselling and Mediation in Casework*. London: Jessica Kingsley Publishers.

Dacombe, R. (2011) 'Can we argue against it? Performance management and state funding of voluntary organizations in the UK'. *Public Money and Management* 31(3): 159–66.

Davies, S (2011) 'Outsourcing, public sector reform and the changed character of the UK state-voluntary sector relationship'. *International Journal of Public Sector Management*, 24(70): 641–9.

Dawson, A. (2010) 'A case study of impact measurement in a Third Sector umbrella organization'. *International Journal of Productivity and Performance Management*, 59(6): 519–33.

Dawson, J. (2012) *A Beginner's Guide to Commissioning*. Retrieved from www.vawcvs.org/downloads/beginnersguidetocommissioningpdf (accessed 15 April 2013).

Department for Constitutional Affairs (2007) *Mental Capacity Act 2005 Code of Practice*. London: TSO. Retrieved from www.dca.gov.uk/legal-policy/mental-capacity/mca-cp.pdf, (accessed 18 November 2011).

Department of Health (2004) *Independent Complaints Advocacy Service (ICAS): The First Year of ICAS*. Department of Health. Retrieved from www.dh.gov.uk/prod_consum_dh/groups/dh_digitalassets/@dh/@en/documents/digitalasset/dh_4101844.pdf (accessed 18 November 2011).

Department of Health (2007) *World Class Commissioning: Vision*. Retrieved from www.dh.gov.uk/prod_consum_dh/groups/dh_digitalassets/documents/digitalasset/dh_080952.pdf (accessed 18 November 2011).

Department of Health (2008a) *The First Annual Report of the Independent Mental Capacity Advocacy Service*. Retrieved from www.dh.gov.uk/prod_consum_dh/groups/dh_digitalassets/@dh/@en/documents/digitalasset/dh_086477.pdf (accessed 18 November 2011).

Department of Health (2008b) *Independent Complaints Advocacy Service*. Retrieved from www.dh.gov.uk/en/Managingyourorganization/Legalandcontractual/Complaintspolicy/NHScomplaintsprocedure/DH_4087428 (accessed 24 July 2009).

Dickinson, H., Allen, K., Alcock, P., Macmillan, R. and Glasby, J. (2012) *The Role of the Third Sector in Delivering Social Care*. London: National Institute for Health Research.

Donaldson, T. and Preston, L.E. (1995) 'The stakeholder theory of the corporation: concepts, evidence, and implications'. *Academy of Management Review*, 20(1): 65–91.

Dunning, A. (1995) *Citizen Advocacy with Older People: A Code of Good Practice*. London: Centre for Policy on Ageing.

Ellis, J. and Gregory, T. (2008) *Accountability and Learning: Developing Monitoring and Evaluation in the Third Sector.* Retrieved from www.ces-vol.org.uk/downloads/cesresearchreport accountabilityandlearning-320-328.pdf (accessed 27 June 2011).

Figlio, D.N. and Kenny, L.W. (2009) 'Public sector performance measurement and stakeholder support'. *Journal of Public Economics*, 93: 1069–77.

Flapper, S.D.P., Fortuin, L. and Stoop, P.P.M. (1996) 'Towards consistent performance management systems'. *International Journal of Operations and Production Management*, 16(7): 27–37.

Forbat, L. and Atkinson, D. (2005) 'Advocacy in practice: the troubled position of advocates in adult services'. *British Journal of Social Work*, 35(3): 321–35.

Franco-Santos, M. and Bourne, M. (2005) 'An examination of the literature relating to issues affecting how companies manage though measures'. *Production Planning and Control*, 16(2): 114–24.

Franco-Santos, M., Kennerley, M., Micheli, P., Martinez, V., Mason, S., Marr, B., Gray, D. and Neely, A. (2007) 'Towards a definition of a business performance measurement system'. *International Journal of Operations and Production Management*, 27(8): 784–801.

Friedman, A.L. and Miles, S. (2002) 'Developing stakeholder theory'. *Journal of Management Studies*, 39(1): 1–21.

Frooman, J. and Murrell, A.J. (2005) 'Stakeholder influence strategies: the roles of structural and demographic determinants'. *Business and Society*, 44(1): 3–31.

Garengo, P. and Sharma, M.K. (2014) 'Performance measurement system contingency factors: a cross analysis of Italian and Indian SMEs'. *Production Planning and Control*, 25(3): 220–40.

Ghalayini, A.M. and Noble, J.S. (1996) 'The changing basis of performance measurement'. *International Journal of Operations and Production Management*, 16(8): 63–80.

Greatbanks, R., Elkin, G. and Manville, G. (2010) 'The use and efficacy of anecdotal performance reporting in the Third Sector'. *International Journal of Productivity and Performance Management*, 59(6): 571–85.

Greiling, D. (2010) 'Balanced scorecard implementation in German non-profit organizations'. *International Journal of Productivity and Performance Management*, 59(6): 534–54.

Grönroos, C. (1982) 'An applied service marketing theory'. *European Journal of Marketing*, 16(7): 30–41.

Hanley, B. and Davies, S. (1998) *CAIT: Citizen Advocacy Evaluation Pack.* London: CAIT.

Henderson, R. and Pochin, M. (2001) *A Right Result? Advocacy, Justice and Empowerment.* Bristol: Policy Press.

Herman, R. and Renz, D. (1997) 'Multiple constituencies and the social construction of nonprofit organization effectiveness'. *Nonprofit and Voluntary Sector Quarterly*, 26(2): 185–206.

Hussein, S., Rapaport, J., Manthorpe, J., Moriarty, J. and Collins, J. (2006) 'Paying the piper and calling the tune? Commissioners' evaluation of advocacy services for people with learning disabilities'. *Journal of Intellectual Disabilities*, 10(1): 75–91.

Iwaarden, J. van, Wiele, T. van der, Williams, F. and Moxham, C. (2009) 'Charities: how important is performance to donors?' *International Journal of Quality and Reliability Management*, 26(1): 5–22.

Jochum, V., Pratten, B. and Wilding, K. (2005) *Civil Renewal and Active Citizenship: A Guide to the Debate.* NCVO. Retrieved from www.ncvo-vol.org.uk/sites/default/files/UploadedFiles/NCVO/Publications/Publications_Catalogue/Sector_Research/civil_renewal_active_citizenship.pdf (accessed 29 November 2011).

Johnston, R. and Pongatichat, P. (2008) 'Managing the tension between performance measurement and strategy: coping strategies'. *International Journal of Operations and Production Management*, 28(10): 941–67.

Jones, M. and Liddle, J. (2011) 'Implementing the UK central government's policy agenda for improved Third Sector engagement'. *The International Journal of Public Sector Management*, 24(2): 157–71.

Kaplan, R.S. (2001) 'Strategic performance measurement and management in nonprofit organizations'. *Nonprofit Management and Leadership*, 11(3): 353–70.

Kaplan, R.S. and Norton, D.P. (2004) *Strategy Maps: Converting intangible assets into tangible outcomes*. Boston, MA: Harvard Business School Press.

Kennerley, M. and Neely, A. (2002) 'Performance measurement frameworks: a review'. In Neely, A. (ed.), *Business Performance Measurement: Theory and Practice*. Cambridge: Cambridge University Press.

Kong, E. (2008) 'The development of strategic management in the non-profit context: intellectual capital in social service non-profit organizations'. *International Journal of Management Reviews*, 10(3): 281–99.

Kong, E. (2010) 'Analysing BSC and IC's usefulness in nonprofit organizations'. *Journal of Intellectual Capital*, 11(3): 284–304.

Kumar Dey, P. and Cheffi, W. (2013) 'Green supply chain performance measurement using the analytical hierarchy process: a comparative analysis of manufacturing organisations'. *Production Planning and Control*, 24(8–9): 702–20.

Lega, F., Marsilio, M. and Villa, S. (2013) 'An evaluation framework for measuring supply chain performance in the public healthcare sector: evidence from the Italian NHS'. *Production Planning and Control*, 24(10–11): 931–47.

Leland, P. (1998) 'The call to greater accountability: implementing outcome-based evaluation systems into nonprofit organizations'. Paper presented at the Annual Conference of the Association for Research on Nonprofit Organizations and Voluntary Action, November.

LeRoux, K. and Wright, N.S. (2010) 'Does performance measurement improve strategic decision making? Findings from a national survey of nonprofit social service agencies'. *Nonprofit and Voluntary Sector Quarterly*, 39: 571–87.

Little, W. (2005) 'Charities ready to play with the big boys but say "let's be fair"'. *Health Service Journal*, 27, January: 14–15.

Macmillan, R. (2012) *Distinction in the Third Sector*. Working Paper 89. Birmingham: Third Sector Research Centre.

Manville, G. and Broad, M. (2012) *Servant Leadership and the Big Society: Performance Management in Third Sector Housing Associations*. Conference proceedings of PMA 2012, 11–13 July, Cambridge, UK.

Manville, G. and Broad, M. (2013), 'Changing time for charities: Performance management in a Third Sector housing association'. *Performance Management Review*, 15(7): 992–1010.

Marchand, M. and Raymond, L. (2008) 'Researching performance measurement systems: an information systems perspective'. *International Journal of Operations and Production Management*, 28(7): 663–86.

Martin, G.P. (2011) 'The Third Sector, user involvement and public service reform: a case study in the co-governance of health service provision'. *Public Administration*, 89(3): 909–32.

MCA (2005) 'Mental Capacity Act'. Retrieved from www.legislation.gov.uk/ukpga/2005/9/contents (accessed 21 November 2011).

McEwen, J., Shoesmith, M. and Allen, R. (2010) 'Embedding outcomes recording in Barnardo's performance management approach'. *International Journal of Productivity and Performance Management*, 59(6): 586–98.

Medori, D. and Steeple, D. (2000) 'A framework for auditing and enhancing performance measurement systems'. *International Journal of Operations and Production Management*, 20(5): 520–33.

MHA (2007) 'Mental Health Act'. Retrieved from www.dh.gov.uk/en/Healthcare/Mental-health/DH_078743 (accessed 21 November 2011).

Micheli, P. and Kennerley, M. (2005) 'Performance measurement frameworks in public and non-profit sectors'. *Production Planning and Control*, 42(3): 125–34.

Mitchell, R.K., Agle, B.R. and Wood, D.J. (1997) 'Toward a theory of stakeholder identification and salience: defining the principle of who and what really counts'. *Academy of Management Review*, 22(4): 853–86.

Morris, D. (2012) 'Charities and the Big Society: a doomed coalition?' *Legal Studies*, 32(1): 132–53.

Morris, S. (2000) 'Defining the nonprofit sector: some lessons from history'. *International Journal of Voluntary and Nonprofit Organizations*, 11(1): 25–43.

Moxham, C. (2009) 'Performance measurement: Examining the applicability of the existing body of knowledge to nonprofit organizations'. *International Journal of Operations and Production Management*, 29(7): 740–63.

Moxham, C. and Boaden, R. (2007) 'The impact of performance measurement in the voluntary sector: identification of contextual and processual factors'. *International Journal of Operations and Production Management*, 27(8): 826–45.

NCVO (2007) *The UK Voluntary Sector Workforce Almanac*. London: UK Workforce Hub.

NCVO (2008) *UK Civil Society Almanac*. London: NCVO.

Neely, A.D. (2005) 'The evolution of performance measurement research: developments in the last decade and a research agenda for the next'. *International Journal of Operations and Production Management*, 25(12): 1264–77.

Neely, A.D., Adams, C. and Kennerley, M. (2002) *The Performance Prism: The Scorecard for Measuring and Managing Business Success*. Harlow: Pearson.

Neely, A.D., Adams, C. and Crowe, P. (2007) 'The Performance Prism in practice'. *Measuring Business Excellence*, 5(2): 6–12.

NIMH (2008) *Independent Mental Health Advocacy: Guidance for Commissioners*. Retrieved from www.its-services.co.uk/silo/files/independent-mental-health-advocacy-guidance.pdf (accessed 21 November 2011).

Oakland, J. (2004) *Oakland on Quality Management*. Oxford: Elsevier Butterworth-Heinemann.

O'Brien, J. (1987) *Learning from Citizen Advocacy Programs*. Atlanta, GA.: Georgia Advocacy Office.

O'Reilly, P. (2007) 'Involving service users in defining and evaluating the service quality of a disability service'. *International Journal of Health Care Quality Assurance*, 20(2–3): 116–29.

Osborne, S.P. and Murray, V. (2000) 'Collaboration between non-profit organizations in the provision of social services in Canada: Working together or falling apart?' *International Journal of Public Sector Management*, 13(1): 9–18.

Packard, T. (2010) 'Staff perceptions of variables affecting performance in human service organizations'. *Nonprofit and Voluntary Sector Quarterly*, 39(6): 971–90.

Parasuraman, A., Zeithaml, V. and Berry, L. (1985) 'A conceptual model of service quality and Its implications for future research'. *Journal of Marketing*, 49(Fall): 41–50.

Parry, E., Kelliher, C., Mills, T. and Tyson, S. (2005) 'Comparing HRM in the voluntary and public sectors'. *Personnel Review*, 34(5): 589.

Paton, R. (2003) *Managing and Measuring Social Enterprises*. London: Sage.

Paton, R., Mordaunt, J. and Cornforth, C. (2007) 'Beyond nonprofit management education: Leadership development in a time of blurred boundaries and distributed learning'. *Nonprofit and Voluntary Sector Quarterly*, 36: 148S–62S.

Plummer, J. (2009) 'Sector might get some subcontracts'. *Third Sector*, 572: 2.

POhWER (2011) 'Annual reports and audited accounts'. Retrieved from www.pohwer.net/about_us/annual_reports.html (accessed 18 November 2011).

Poister, T.H. (2003) *Measuring Performance in Public and Nonprofit Organizations*. San Francisco, CA: Jossey-Bass.

Rapaport, J., Manthorpe, J., Moriarty, J., Hussein, S. and Collins, J. (2005) 'Advocacy and people with learning disabilities in the UK: how can local funders find value for money?' *Journal of Intellectual Disabilities*, 9(4): 299–319.

Rapaport, J., Manthorpe, J., Hussein, S., Moriarty, J. and Collins, J. (2006) 'Old issues and new directions: perceptions of advocacy, its extent and effectiveness from a qualitative study of stakeholder views'. *Journal of Intellectual Disabilities*, 10(2): 191–210.

Ritchie, W.J. and Kolodinsky, R.W. (2003) 'Nonprofit organization financial performance measurement: An evaluation of new and existing financial performance measures'. *Nonprofit Management and Leadership*, 13(4): 367–81.

Rochette, C. and Fenies, P. (2008) 'A framework to link patient satisfaction with customer satisfaction'. In *Tradition and Innovation in Operations Management: Proceedings of the 15th International Annual EurOMA Conference*. Groningen, Netherlands, 15–18 June.

Sargeant, A., Ford, J.B. and West, D.C. (2006) 'Perceptual determinants of nonprofit giving behaviour'. *Journal of Business Research*, 59: 155–65.

Schneider, J.A. (2006) 'An interdisciplinary conversation on research method best practices for nonprofit studies'. *Nonprofit Management and Leadership*, 16(4): 387–94.

Scottish Executive (2001) *Independent Advocacy: A Guide for Commissioners*. Edinburgh: Scottish Executive. Available at: www.scotland.gov.uk/library3/health/iagc-00.asp (accessed 20 April 2009).

Silverman, R.M. and Patterson, K.L. (2011) 'The effects of perceived funding trends on non-profit advocacy: a national survey of non-profit advocacy organizations in the United States'. *International Journal of Public Sector Management*, 24(5): 435–51.

Social Enterprise Coalition (2011) Retrieved from www.socialenterprise.org.uk (accessed 18 November 2011).

Sowa, J. (2009) 'The collaboration decision in nonprofit organizations: views from the front line'. *Nonprofit and Voluntary Sector Quarterly*, 38: 1003–25.

Speckbacher, G. (2003) 'The economics of performance measurement in non-profit organizations'. *Nonprofit Management and Leadership*, 13(3): 267–81.

Tapinos, E., Dyson, R.G. and Meadows, M. (2005) 'The impact of the performance measurement systems in setting the "direction" in the University of Warwick'. *Production Planning and Control*, 16(2): 189–98.

Taylor, A. and Taylor, M. (2013) 'Performance measurement in the Third Sector: the development of a stakeholder-focused research agenda'. *Production Planning and Control* 25(16), doi:10.1080/09537287.2013.839065.

UKAN (2009) 'About the UK Advocacy Network (UKAN)'. Retrieved from www.u-kan.co.uk/index.html (accessed 21 November 2011).

Valuing People Support Team (2005) *The Story So Far ... Valuing People: A New Strategy for Learning Disability for the 21st Century*. Retrieved from www.dh.gov.uk/prod_consum_dh/groups/dh_digitalassets/@dh/@en/documents/digitalasset/dh_4107059.pdf (accessed 18 November 2011).

Walters, D. (2005) 'Performance planning and control in virtual business structures'. *Production Planning and Control*, 16(2): 226–39.

Waxenberger, B. and Spence, L. (2003) 'Reinterpretation of a metaphor: from stakes to claims'. *Strategic Change*, 12: 239–49.

Whittaker, A., Gardner, S. and Kershaw, J. (1991) *Service Evaluation by People with Learning Difficulties Based on the People First Report*. London: King's Fund Centre.
Wing, K.T. (2004) 'Assessing the effectiveness of capacity-building initiatives: Seven issues for the field'. *Nonprofit and Voluntary Sector Quarterly*, 33(1): 153–60.
Wisniewski, M. and Stewart, D. (2004) 'Performance measurement for stakeholders'. *International Journal of Public Sector Management*, 17(3): 222–33.
Yong, J. and Wilkinson, A. (2002) 'The long and winding road: the evolution of quality management'. *Total Quality Management*, 13(1): 101–21.

Notes

1 Reprinted by permission of the publisher.
2 While the OCS is a UK government office, in reality it works only with the English third sector. The other three UK nations (Scotland, Wales and Northern Ireland) implement separate arrangements through their devolved administrations (Alcock, 2012)
3 For the purposes of this work we restrict our consideration to those advocacy arrangements in which the users do not pay for the services they receive. Therefore we omit services such as legal advocacy in which clients pay legal professionals typically to address short-term specific issues.

12 Extending operations management framework to public system

Public grievance redressal system in urban local bodies in Karnataka, India

G. Ramesh and Shahana Sheikh

Introduction

The decision making process in government is nothing but workflow management. A critical aspect of public service delivery is the grievance redressal management system. In terms of complexity, complaints management process in services sector, especially in the government system ranks the highest. On any indicator of services management like uncertainty, scale, variability, etc. complaints management in government ranks high. Besides, it involves significant involvement of clientele, in this case often the poor and illiterate. It will be interesting to study the influence of such complexities on the management of this part of the operational cycle. It was decided to study the grievances redressal system of the government of Karnataka, a state in India, to understand the complexity of this aspect of the operations management.

Implementation of e-governance reform is one of the mandatory reforms undertaken by urban local bodies (ULBs) as part of the Jawaharlal Nehru National Urban Renewal Mission (JNNURM), a national programme of the government of India. The services to be covered under the e-governance reform include the following: basic citizen services (such as birth and death registration and health programs), revenue earning services (such as property tax and licenses), development services (including water supply and other utilities, building plan approval), efficiency improvement services (such as procurement and monitoring of projects), back improvements (such as accounting and personnel management system) and monitoring (including citizen grievance redressal) (Government of India, 2011).

In Karnataka, the Municipal Reforms Cell (MRC) of the Directorate of Municipal Administration (DMA) was set up in 2005 with the primary objective of undertaking implementation of computerisation and other reforms. The MRC initiated the e-governance reforms in 213 ULBs of Karnataka (other than Bangalore, a state capital). The reforms were implemented in select 49 ULBs of Karnataka under the Asian Development Bank-funded project titled, 'Nirmala Nagar Project' and in the remaining 164 ULBs under the World Bank-funded project titled, 'Karnataka Municipal Reforms Project'. E-governance applications concerning the following were introduced by the MRC: birth and death registration and certification, fund-based double entry accrual accounting system (FBAS), public grievance redressal

(PGR), websites for ULBs, GIS-based property tax information, monthly information booklet, service level benchmarking (SLB) among others.

This study aims at assessing the performance of the e-governance application concerning the Public Grievance Redressal (PGR) System installed in these ULBs. The key areas of study of the PGR include the following: (i) performance of the e-governance application in terms of responsiveness to grievances; (ii) challenges faced during implementation; and (iii) the system gaps that continue to persist.

Literature review

In the public system sphere it emerges that appropriate process management itself can be an instrument of creating accountability for performance. Creating a proper process management structure itself can enable empowerment and accountability. Public service delivery systems are complex in nature and literature review was undertaken to explore relevant frameworks for evaluating service delivery. In this context, development administration literature in service delivery is also reviewed to understand its complexity in the broader canvass of governance and process management.

The central theme in public service delivery is accountability for delivery. The accountability framework of the 2004 *World Development Report* provides a useful framework (World Bank, 2003). As per this framework, there are two routes available to citizens (or clients) to engage with service providers. The first, is a long route wherein they are required to voice their concern to the state (which includes the politicians and specifically the elected representatives, i.e. the policy makers) and the state fixes accountability on the concerned service provider. The second, is a short route wherein the citizens exercise their 'client power' by directly engaging with the concerned service provider to fix accountability for the provisioning of a specific good or service. Hence, this framework helps in identifying the points for influencing quality, efficiency and responsiveness of service delivery (Ringold *et al.*, 2012: 4).

In the specific context of provisioning of urban services, a measure which is commonly suggested for improving urban governance is the establishment of grievance redressal mechanisms that allow citizens to demand more responsive, accountable, and transparent delivery of public goods and services (ADB, 2010:17). Hence, with regard to the accountability framework referred to earlier in this section, establishing grievance redressal mechanisms for urban services may be viewed as a step wherein 'citizens are encouraged to directly exert their 'client power' to directly demand accountability from public or private service providers rather than rely on the more traditional, long-winded chains of accountability through political actors' (Ranganathan, 2008: 3).

Accountability can be exerted for service delivery in various ways: top-down from higher-level officials; sideways (or horizontally) via internal competition or peer pressure; externally by international, multi-lateral organisations or other states; or bottom-up by citizens, civil society organisations, non-governmental organisations or the media (Griffin *et al.*, 2010, cited in Ringold *et al.*, 2012: 7).

Interventions undertaken as a part of 'bottom-up accountability', also called 'social accountability', are those wherein efforts are made towards information provisioning to citizens and creation of channels to enable citizens to use information to hold service providers accountable. Broadly, the two types of social accountability interventions are: information interventions and grievance redressal mechanisms. 'Information interventions' includes various project and policy measures ranging from simple information provisioning, such as right-to-information legislation, information campaigns, report cards, and social audits. 'Grievance redressal mechanisms' are formal channels for citizens to demand their rights, complain, and provide feedback to providers and policy makers about service delivery. Specifically, grievance redressal mechanisms are of three distinct types: (i) redressal mechanisms within government agencies; (ii) independent redressal institutions; and (iii) courts (Ringold *et al.*, 2012,: 8–9).

Grievance redressal mechanism corresponds to managing defects. Grievance redressal can be simple demand for service or often are complaints against non-performance or non-delivery of a service. If it is a complaint, it is already complicated and the client is frustrated by the delay. Grievance handling often requires escalation to higher hierarchy level requiring higher level of discretion unlike a routine service delivery. These make it difficult to programme the grievances handling system.

A report by TERI (2010) highlights the key benefits that a municipal body would reap from a grievance redressal system. These include the following:

- direct feedback from the consumers on the working of the ULB;
- identification of recurring systemic problems enabling effective resolution of complaints;
- building accountability and ensuring transparency in an organisation; and
- building confidence among citizens and encouraging public participation (*ibid.*: 4).

In terms of project management and service delivery, the study by Bajpai *et al.* (2010) based on a study of National Rural Health Mission observed that management of coordination among agencies as one of the key factors of effectiveness or lack of it. It also stressed that it is necessary to provide operational information for better service delivery and monitoring.

Over the last few years, increased use of information and communication technologies (ICT) to build systems for interactions between citizens and service providers in cities not only in India, but across Asia, has been observed. As Ranganathan points out:

> Several utilities in Asian cities now dedicate a telephone 'hotline' or call center for complaints regarding service disruptions. Sometimes hotlines are used in conjunction with helpdesks where citizens can file complaints in person. More recently, utilities have launched websites through which users can report problems online.
>
> (Ranganathan, 2008: 3)

A study by Paul on India's Citizen's Charter observed that:

> public agencies should develop norms or standards of service, and grievance redress mechanisms, and make them known to the public. This is clearly a more complex job, and may require more skills and experience to design them. The final stage is hen departments/agencies are able to put together all these elements in the form of a 'compact' between them and the citizens.
>
> (Paul, 2008: 72)

A study on right to education (RTE) in Karnataka by Bhattarcharjee, Mysoor, and Sivaramakrishnan observed that:

> The Karnataka RTE rules and other policy documents have contributed towards creating a web of 'local authorities' with unclear and overlapping jurisdictions. Though the system provides for multiple entry points for a compliant, it increases the chance of red tape and delays and does little to raise awareness or provide any space for social mobilization … With faltering administrative accountability, many complainants still find themselves with unresolved grievances and are tending to take recourse to political and even 'rude' forms of accountability.
>
> (Bhattarcharjee *et al.*, 2014: 40)

This shows that weak link or incomplete loop within the grievance handling system can create dissatisfactory situation.

The paper by Chander and Kush (2012) assessed the grievance redressing mechanism in India by studying its portals as a mode of communicating aspects like status updates, information richness and popularity, information related to services, impact, redressed rate, etc. These aspects indicate important characteristics of grievance management system.

The grievance handling system in Government can be fitted into the framework of Operations management (OM) easily. OM is characterised by flow and variation. The operating systems vary depending on the characteristics of the product line. Layouts performances are made complex by enormous criss-crossing of jobs, difficulty in production planning, very high throughput times, poor delegation of work and poor accountability, low motivation and low job satisfaction, and so on (Mahadevan, 2010: 119) which fits the grievance handling system. In services delivery in government client occupies the central stage. Important characteristics of client interface that impact service designing are 'The three parameters – contact, divergence, and complexity … determine service process and delivery system design' (*ibid.*: 157).

Silvestro *et al.* (1992: 63) mentions six service dimensions as dominating service operations management literature: equipment/people focus, length of customer contact time, extent of customisation, extent to which customer contact personnel exercise judgement in meeting individual needs, source of value added, front office or back office, and product/process focus. The study of 11 in-depth case studies of service organisations in UK showed that, as number of customers per unit increases per day: Focus moves from people to equipment orientation; length of contact time from high to low; degree of customisation from high to low; level of employee discretion from high to low; value added from front office to back office; and focus from a process to a product orientation (*ibid.*: 72). We observe similar trend in the current case under discussion.

Wemmerlov (1989) discusses contact based frameworks while describing taxonomy of service processes. He stresses customer perspective and distinguishes between direct and indirect customer contact. The descriptions which are relevant to public services are the fluid processes, which require 'low to relatively high level of technical skills' and 'a fairly large amount of information needed to be exchanged between the customer and the service worker', and 'the service worker (or the customer) often goes through unprogrammed search processes and makes judgemental decisions (i.e. the process is not well defined)' (*ibid.*: 31–2).

A paper by Kellog and Nie (1995: 323) introduces the conceptual framework of the service process/service package (SP/SP) matrix. The authors discuss service process structure in terms of expert service, service shop and service factory; and service package structure in terms of its uniqueness, selectivity, restrictedness (*ibid.*: 324). We will see later that in the case under study while the government tries to make service a generic package, the decision makers try to make it into a restricted service package. The customer is considered part of the service process and is called 'customer contact', 'customer interaction' and 'customer participation' (*ibid.*: 325). Schmenner classifies services as service factory, service shop, mass service and professional services based on the degree of interaction and customisation, and degree of labour intensity (Schmenner, 1986: 29).

David (2001) cites Landry *et al.*, who suggest that:

> The OR specialist should be prepared to modify or develop a new version of the model, or even a completely new model, if needed, that allows an adequate exploration of heretofore unforeseen problem formulation and solution alternatives … the OR specialist should make sure that the model developed provides a buffer or leaves room for the stakeholders to adjust and readjust themselves to the situation created by the use of the model.
>
> (David, 2001: 459)

The particular case under study requires such modifications to existing frameworks. David mentions that, 'It can be said that there are different models for each of the phases', especially 'models to assist in understanding the context and being aware of the problem' (*ibid.*: 464).

A paper by Chase and Tansik postulates that:

> control is difficult to effectuate in high-contact systems because of the customer being an uncertain input to the process being controlled … high contact subsystems should seek to maximize effectiveness goals; low contact subsystems

> seek to maximize efficiency gaols ... all high-contact subsystems tend to require some minimal capability to handle non-routine tasks even if they are imbedded in a mechanistic organization structure.
>
> (Chase and Tansik, 1983: 1044–5)

These are true of grievance handling in a bureaucratic system.

Public grievance redressal system in Karnataka

ULBs in Karnataka used to receive public grievances in paper form or via telephone, prior to the establishment of the PGR e-governance application across ULBs in Karnataka by the MRC. The process was not streamlined and there were difficulties in registering and more so in tracking complaints.

To resolve these problems, the MRC introduced the PGR application across ULBs in Karnataka. PGR Cells were established in each ULB and local non-governmental organisation (NGO) workers were involved as PGR operators. Many tools like auto-assignment of complaints, complaint-forwarding, etc. were introduced and a training manual was prepared. The application also allowed for regular generation of citizen-friendly GIS reports regarding complaints redressal. The expected outcomes of the usage of the PGR application were faster and systematic redressal of complaints, escalation of complaints to higher authorities and state-level monitoring of redressal of complaints.

A citizen can register a complaint using any of the three modes: by submitting an application to the PGR operator at the ULB office, through phone to the PGR operator, or by registering the complaint online on the website of the ULB.

The application asks for contacts of the persons and the specifics of the complaint. The person can select the nature of the complaint from a list which displays common complaints and if the complaint is 'uncommon', he can select the complaint from department-specific complaint lists (various functional departments of the ULB are listed including: engineering, community affairs, education, horticulture, veterinary, etc.). If the citizen is unable to find the complaint listed he/she can type in the details in a text box in the 'others' category.

The citizen gets a number and he can view the status of the compliant. The complaints are communicated through phone or wireless phone sets to the section officers who in turn communicates to the field offices. The section officer has the ownership for the complaints and he manages the whole process of registering, assigning, processing, and completing the task. The section officer keeps the PGR cell updated on the complaints.

On completion, the PGR Operator communicates with the concerned citizen to find out if he/she is satisfied with the redressal of the complaint. The complaint is closed if the citizen is satisfied. In case the grievance is not redressed in a timely manner (each service has a predefined 'expiry days'), it is escalated to the higher authorities. The processes are monitored by the project director of the District Urban Development Cell and the district commissioner.

Focus of this study

Previous studies on the PGR system at ULBs in Karnataka such as those by the City Managers' Association, Karnataka (CMAK) and Wallack and Nadhamuni have focused on the ULBs where the PGR e-governance application was introduced in the initial phase of implementation. The focus of the former study was on understanding the working of the system on the ground; and the latter was on an e-Governments Foundation, an Indian NGO engaged with ULB officials in developing and refining an e governance system for tracking public grievances and the performance of ULBs in redressing these (Wallack and Nadhamuni, 2009; CMAK, 2006).

This study analyses data concerning both, the citizen frontend and the ULB backend processes involved in the functioning of the PGR e-governance application. The citizen frontend includes the PGR operator and the PGR application (together, the PGR cell) and the ULB backend involves co-ordination between the PGR cell and the head of the section concerning the complaint and the action taken by the concerned operational staff of the section.

Methodology

A two stage methodology was adopted to study the completeness of the PGR application. The first included an analysis of data on redressal of public grievances across all ULBs in Karnataka, obtained from the website of the MRC. The reports from 11 April 2011 until 30 September 2012 were analysed. The reports included information on the registered complaints, on the un-attended complaints, the complaints processed, and the redressed complaints for each ULB ('completed complaints').

The second step entailed visits to ULBs in Karnataka to interview officials and staff of ULBs on various aspects of the PGR e-governance application. Field visits were undertaken to the following ULBs: Mangalore City Corporation, Channapatna City Municipal Council, Maddur Town Municipal Council, Chitradurga City Municipal Council and Davanagere City Corporation in Karnataka in consultation with the administration. These were undertaken to make it representative of the overall performance of the State.

Findings and analysis

Findings and analysis – based on public grievance redressal system data

Complaints redressal data is available for all ULBs in Karnataka for three periods: 1 April 2011 to 10 March 2012 (Period I), 1 April 2012 to 30 June 2012 (Period II) and 1 July 2012 to 30 September 2012 (Period III). The data for the first period is not directly comparable in absolute terms to the data in the second and third periods since the former is for duration of nearly a year and the other two are for durations of only 3 months each; however, certain observations regarding the performance of ULBs relative to each other can be made from this data.

For analysis purpose the data was classified based on the type of ULB – city corporation (ULBs with populations of more than 3 lakh), city municipal councils (ULBs with population in the range of 50,000 to 3 lakh), town municipal councils (population in the range of 20,000 to 50,000) and town panchayats (population below 20,000).

City corporations

The best and worst performers among the city corporations (CCs) are presented in the table below. Complaints data considered here is the percentage of complaints redressed within a day, a week (including those redressed within a day) and a month (including those redressed within a day and within a week). Bellary CC and Gulburga CC seem to be underperformers in terms of percentage of complaints completed during the three time periods.

Gulburga CC is an under performer during the first two time periods on the percentage of complaints completed. In Period I, 60 per cent of the complaints were completed and in II, only 58 per cent of the complaints were completed. However, Period 1, 41 per cent were completed within one day but in II, not a single complaint was completed in one day. In III, Further, the percentage of complaints completed was 99 per cent and hence, there appears to be a considerable improvement in terms of completed complaints.

Davanagere CC received the lowest number of complaints, less than 1000, during the first time period. However, 840 and 987 complaints were registered during the second and third time periods respectively. This could imply that in the first time

Table 12.1 Time periods for complaints redressed by city corporations

		Complaints redressed		
	Time period	*Within 1 day*	*Within 1 week (including within 1 day)*	*Within 1 month (including within 1 day and 1 week)*
Best performers	I	Hubli-Dharwad CC (49%)	Belgaum CC (95%)	Belgaum CC (99.5%)
	II*	Davanagere CC (53.5%)	Mysore CC (96%)	Mysore CC, Hubli-Dharwad CC (100%)
	III*	Hubli-Dharwad CC (42%)	Belgaum CC (95%)	Davanagere CC (100%)
Worst performers	I	Bellary CC (3%)	Davanagere CC (40%)	Davanagere CC (69%)
	II	Gulburga CC (0%)	Gulburga CC (38%)	Gulburga CC (54%)
	III*	Bellary CC (3%)	Bellary CC (59%)	Hubli-Dharwad CC (94%)

* Mangalore CC has been excluded from the analysis since its PGR data does not seem credible

period, the citizens were either not aware of the PGR mechanism or even if they were aware, they did not use it. During the field visit to Davanagere, officials expressed that most ward corporators go to their respective wards every morning and take rounds along with the health inspectors or supervisors. Citizens' complaints often come directly to the corporators, inspectors or supervisors during these rounds and they redress them then and there; hence, only some of the problems are registered by citizens using the PGR system.

While 98.2 per cent of the complaints had been completed at Davanagere CC during Period I, it ought to be noted that nearly 32 per cent of the completed complaints took more than 1 month to be completed. In Period II, a little over 28 per cent of the completed complaints took more than 1 month. However, in Period III, only 0.5 per cent of the complaints took more than a month to be completed. Further, it is also observed that whereas in the first period, only 13 per cent of the completed complaints were redressed within a day, during the second period a little over 53 per cent (highest among the city corporations) of the completed complaints were redressed within a day and for the third period, just under 2 per cent of the completed complaints were redressed within a day. This highly variable data for Davanagere CC suggests that the data may not be credible.

A peculiar observation is made with regard to the complaints statistics of Mangalore CC. During each of the time periods, when the percentages of complaints completed at different durations are added, the total is more than 100 per cent. For example, when the complaints completed within a day, week and a month are added, the total is 102 per cent.[1] This could imply that either incorrect calculations have been made or the date has been inflated or the complaints' data has been wrongly recorded.

City municipal councils

When the percentages of complaints completed are considered for the two time periods, there are some city municipal councils (CMCs) whose performance has improved considerably from the first period to Period II to Period III. The complaint statistics for these CMCs are presented in Table 12.2.

There are also CMCs whose performance seems to have worsened from Period I to Period II. However, for these CMCs when the data for the third period is considered, there is improvement in terms of percentage of complaints completed. The complaint statistics for these CMCs are presented in Table 12.3.

Table 12.2 Complaint statistics for city municipal councils (A)

Name of CMC	*Complaints completed in period 1 (%)*	*Complaints completed in period II (%)*	*Complaints completed in period III (%)*
Yadgiri	73.71	91.18	98.32
Chamarajanagara	81.98	96.30	99.31
Kolar	76.19	89.77	99.27

Table 12.3 Complaint statistics for city municipal councils (B)

Name of CMC	*Complaints completed in period I (%)*	*Complaints completed in period II (%)*	*Complaints completed in period III (%)*
Madikere	78.19	16.2	54.07
Robertsonpet	92.57	63.91	85.87
Bidar	80.89	54.05	99.08
Chintamani	99.58	73.90	100
Jamakhandi	97.69	80.37	100
Shahabad	93.53	76.33	98.59
Sindanoor	89.04	72.61	98.55
Shimoga	93.38	79.77	100
Nippani	98.55	85.10	100

Out of the total of 44 CMCs for Period I, there were eight CMCs where all completed complaints were redressed within a month's time, however, there were 12 CMCs for which more than 10 per cent of the completed complaints were redressed beyond 1 month. In Period II, in case of 20 CMCs, all the completed complaints were redressed within a month's time and there were only 4 CMCs for which more than 10 per cent of the completed complaints were redressed in time periods longer than 1 month. However, in Period III there were some improvements.

Further, during the first period, 33 CMCs had redressed more than 50 per cent of the completed complaints within a week's time and in Period II to Period III, the corresponding figure was 37 CMCs and 35 CMCs respectively. These observations imply that though there was a general increase in the responsiveness of CMCs to public grievances from the first to the second period, there has been a slight drop in responsiveness from the second to third period.

In case of a few CMCs, when the percentages of complaints completed at different durations are added, the total is more than 100 per cent. This could again indicate either some incorrect calculations or inflated figures.

Town municipal councils

When the percentages of complaints completed are considered, there are a few town municipal councils (TMCs) which had relatively poor performances in Period I but have shown a marked improvement in Period II. Ron and Malur TMCs have seen a further improvement from Period II to III, while the percentage of completed complaints decreased for the same period for Navalagund TMC. The complaint statistics are presented for these TMCs are presented in Table 12.4.

There are also TMCs whose performance seems to have worsened quite drastically from Period I to II in terms of the percentage of complaints completed. However, the performance of all these TMCs, except Manvi TMC, improved in Period III. The complaints statistics for these are presented in Table 12.5.

In TMCs also in some cases (like Holenarsipura, Bhatkal, Hiriyur, etc.), when the percentages of complaints completed at different durations are added, the total is more than 100 per cent.

Table 12.4 Complaint statistics for town municipal councils (A)

Name of TMC	*Complaints completed in period I (%)*	*Complaints completed in period II (%)*	*Complaints completed in period III (%)*
Ron	7.41	94.55	100
Malur	79.81	95.28	99.77
Navalagund	83.11	94.25	89.64

Table 12.5 Complaint statistics for town municipal councils (B)

Name of TMC	*Complaints completed in period I (%)*	*Complaints completed in period II (%)*	*Complaints completed in period III (%)*
Kustagi	96.46	62.26	100
Kumta	98.51	68.28	96.92
Gowribidanur	97.44	68.42	100
Muddebihal	85.4	58.21	86.67
Ramdurga	95.48	72.22	99.34
Nanjangud	99.77	77.9	99.2
Athani	97.61	79.45	100
Kadur	97.58	82.5	100
Gajendragad	94.59	79.9	100
Manvi	98.05	83.67	0

Town panchayats

Among the town panchayats (TPs), Virajpet TP appears to be a poor performer during both the time periods in percentage of completed complaints. However, its performance seems to have considerably improved in Period III wherein 98.7 per cent of the complaints were completed. Two TPs – Gurumitkal and Raibagh seem to have received no complaints in Period II and III; however these had 852 and 325 complaints respectively in the first period. It is possible that no complaints have been received by these TPs from April to June 2012; however, it could also be that either the PGR system cell has been discontinued for some reason at these TPs or the complaints have not been recorded into the computer systems.

When the percentages of complaints completed are considered for the three time periods, Hunagunda TP's performance has improved considerably from I to II and to the III as the performance progressed from 79.5 per cent to 96.15 per cent to 100 per cent. After excluding Gurumitkal TP and Raibagh TP, there are a few TPs where it is found that the performance in terms of the percentage of completed complaints decreased noticeably. The statistics for these are presented in table 12.6.

During Period I, 62 TPs had redressed more than 50 per cent of the completed complaints within a week's time; in Period II, the corresponding figure was 60 TPs; and during Period III, it was 58 TPs. These observations imply that though there was a general increase in the responsiveness of TMCs to public grievances from Period I to II, there has been a slight drop in responsiveness from Period II to III.

Table 12.6 Complaint statistics for town panchayats

Name of TMC	*Complaints completed in period I (%)*	*Complaints completed period II (%)*	*Complaints completed in period III (%)*
Jewargi	93.62	60.82	97.67
Kudalagi	93.65	68.65	98.78
Shirlakoppa	98.62	75.47	100
Alnavara	93.51	71.84	27.6
Virajpet	69.88	50	98.7
Shirahatti	98.32	81.82	80
Chincholi	94.61	78.57	100
Periyapatna	99.89	86.82	79.84

In the case of a few TPs like Aurad (104 per cent), Mudgal (103 per cent), Saligrama (116 per cent) when the percentages of complaints completed at different durations are added, the total is more than 100 per cent. This error seems to be prevalent across categories of ULBs.

Observations from the field visits

In this section is discussed certain critical findings based on field visits to the ULBs on the various aspects of the process management of grievance handling. Overall, it appears the responsiveness of the ULB staff to public grievances has improved since the PGR e-governance application was installed. There is also routine tracking of complaints by citizens, though most often this is undertaken by the mode of the telephone as citizens call the PGR cell to inquire about the status of their complaints. In case the complaints are not redressed within specified time limits, these are escalated to concerned senior officials (commissioner/joint commissioner/chief officer) of the ULB. However, one can make certain general findings which are of relevance to us.

It was observed that most complaints are of routine nature which means these are programmable activities in terms of process management. For example, in the case of Mangalore CC, during Period 1, 70 per cent of the registered complaints were for leaking water pipes, defective street lights, choked underground drain leaking, silting of storm water drains. Similar is the case with the CMCs of Channapatna and Chitradurga, and CC of Davanagere. In other words, most complaints are not related to major capital expenditure which would require approvals from the council and involving tendering process. It is observed that as long as the grievance redressal does not involve capital expenditure (or the tendering process), it is usually acted upon. The system has helped in completing the feedback loop in terms of alerting the officials.

PGR system has increased the interface between citizens and ULB staff. The smaller the Municipalities the more is the interaction. The PGR's cell number has helped in making citizen more proactive in registering complaints.

There is regular generation of reports but little analysis. The lacuna is that the reports are generated but hardly analysed. The PGR system has ushered in highly responsive system but there seems to be little or no intelligence in the system. This implies that there is no mining or analysis of the data regarding registered complaints. It was also observed that huge data is created but does not lend itself easily for analysis. The data is at aggregated level and could have been more granular.

It was observed that the senior officials hardly used the data for decision-making and planning allocation of resources such as staff and finances. For example, the GIS reports on public grievances could be used to analyse if the concerned operational staff in a particular ward is performing his duties adequately; these reports could also indicate a failure of systematic issue in a ward such as old water pipes which would need replacement. However, from our interaction with senior officials from ULBs, there is little indication that such analyses are undertaken.

It was observed that redressal of complaints handled by outsourced staff is usually faster than if handled by ULB staff. In case of permanent operational staff, if there is a complaint the concerned section officer has to inform the concerned supervisor of the specific ward and often needs to check personally if the complaint has been redressed. On the contrary, in case of outsourced staff, the concerned section officer just needs to inform the contractor who would ensure that the needful is done. If a contractor does not perform his tasks in a timely manner, the ULB could blacklist him and this possibility of getting blacklisted acts as a sufficient incentive for him/her to undertake the work tasks. This is a typical case of agency issue corrected through contracting and incentive system.

The administration seems to be satisfied with using the PGR e-governance application for problem fixing and specifically, for fire-fighting. The administration is still far from using it for planning, decision making and control. Rarely do ULB officials study the underlying trends in public grievances and lacuna in their resource management. One would have expected them to use the data on public grievances for planning and for rectifying imbalances and gaps on a long term basis. However, this was found to be lacking. In other words, we observed that the complaints are getting logged into the system and information is being gathered but the data is rarely analysed. The senior officials at ULBs tend to use the complaints' reports to look at the delivery time and conclusion of the problems rather than the information as a whole. One can conclude that valuable information is getting captured but rarely used for control or decision making.

The usage pattern of the system and information can be viewed like this. At the first stage the emphasis is on problem-fixing. At this stage, the whole machinery is geared towards attending to public grievances and the system including incentives and disincentives are built towards their resolution. Once the initial wave of complaints is addressed, the focus should ideally shift to planning and decision-making mode where the emphasis is on providing for resources and being proactive. Here, the administration is expected to engage with issues surrounding overall system efficiency and resource adequacy. It is in the second stage where analysis gains prominence that significant efficiencies can be seen. If the issues of resource adequacy is not fulfilled, redressal of grievances will remain at cosmetic level. In the third stage, the expectation of the citizens are likely to increase further and the ULB administrations would have to be even more diligent and proactive towards service delivery.

The PGR system itself can act as the trigger to ensure better performance, administration and citizen participation.

Proposed model

We observed in the public grievances handling system that there is constant stress between attempts to standardise the operations and keep it programmable, and to keep it flexible and non-programmed. This is a common battle found in the reforms of public systems. The administrators seek to maintain their importance and power by keeping the service non programmable, fluid and highly customised. The government on the other hand tries to make the process standardised and routine. The moment the processes are streamlined and automated the service deliverer loses his importance. They thrive in complexity.

We list below major characteristics of the operation of the services system that are usually alluded to in literature whether it is private sector or in public system. The two ends of the spectrum are also indicated for illustration. One can place the current system on the scale on these characteristics.

The commonly discussed characteristics of services sector that are relevant to our contexts are (Wemmerlov, 1989; Schmenner, 1985; Chase and Tansik, 1983):

1	Decision on hand:	Generic	→	Unique
2	Decision Rule:	Programmable	→	Non Programmable
3	Contact Time:	Low	→	High
4	Divergent services:	Minimal	→	Maximum
5	Customisation:	Low	→	High
6	Interface:	Technology driven	→	Employee driven
7	Process:	Rigid	→	Fluid
8	Discretion:	Low	→	High

The service delivery process in public system is basically managing the work flow. In the old system, each decision was treated as unique in terms of operating procedure. Each demand attracted its own set of documents, processes, and timeless. The demand for services was uneven and application of rules was non-standardised. The service levels were undefined and contact times were prolonged. The customers were required to make many visits and documents were collected sequentially. This added to the uncertainty of the process and to process flow. The client can rarely be sure of the service delivery time. The services were quite divergent and the treatment of each was highly customised. The processes were significantly employee centric and there was very less use of technology for even recording a complaint or tracking the progress. The impact of all these is the high level of discretion used by the service deliverer in processing the application, in sequencing the applications, in deciding on it, and in communicating it. These make them a very important actor. Shostack (1987: 37) stresses blueprinting to handle ambiguity and subjectivity which seeks to, 'educate consumers, focus their evaluative input on various aspects of the service system, elicit comparative or competitive assessments, and generate specific responses to contemplated changes or new service concepts'. Our analysis shows that the staff try to make the cases unique rather than proceed along the blueprint.

The new (PGR) system brought in some changes but there was still struggle in the system in adopting the system whole heartedly. The services were classified and the documentation was standardised. An application is accepted only if it is complete in all respect. This is important as the service level starts from the time the application gets accepted and a number is generated. This reduced multiple visits to the offices and reduced the contact time and intensity with the citizens. The services are still divergent but the services were definable. The processes were better defined in terms of receiving the application, movement of the application, and decision levels. The technology was utilised to the maximum. All complaints were registered and a number of given for tracking. Complaints can be given through phones also. The status gets communicated through the mobile numbers. Even the employees are informed of new complaints requiring service through mobiles. These steps reduced necessity for citizen–employee interface. The process got far more streamlined. Customisation was reduced as there was shared understanding of required documents, and the process flow was defined and tracked. There is less fluidity in the system and as a consequence of all these measures the service deliverer enjoys less discretion in the delivery of service. The contrasts between routine and fluid processes, and high contact and low contact have been brought out clearly in the operations management literature, but this chapter highlights the stress that happens when organisations try to standardise operations and take away power from the employee through minimal contact in public services (Wemmerlov, 1989; Kellog and Nie, 1995).

However, the stress in the system is quite evident. Sometimes the complaint numbers may not get generated, maybe due to power problem and consequent system shutdown. The complainant may have to make several visits to the office till his application gets accepted as the documents may not be complete. Earlier they would have started and the process might have started. So, there is still some uncertainty about the required documents. The staff can always find some uniqueness about the application to make it non-standardised. This again adds to the discretion. The service levels are defined with adequate surplus time. From the variation we find in the time taken to complete the applications, it is clear that queue system is not well defined and processes are not streamlined. There is also bunching of applications towards the end of application deadline. The usage of technology is limited to the admittance of the applications. Rest of the processes are manual. The same clerk could be attending to different services and so planning of services is still a far cry.

The cumulative effect of business as usual scenario of change in the context of service recovery can be that, 'failure to respond with proper levels of redress, responsiveness, and courtesy can be just as bad as when a problem occurs but is not recognised by the service provider' (Hocutt, Bowers, and Donavan, 2006: 205). The dissatisfaction with the system is still under control as probably they fall within the zone of tolerance. However, Johnston (1994: 59) cautions, 'while marketers have a key role in influencing pre–experience expectation threshold, operations managers have an important role in managing customers' perceptions during the service process'. It is quite possible that administrative reforms may increase clients' expectation and reduce the zone of tolerance; and operations managers have a clear role in ensuring that the clients expectations are met. Stodnick and Marley (2013: 37), measuring the 'voice of customer' in terms of 'specifications', and the 'voice of process' in terms of Six Sigma, mention that, ' As long as the voice of the customer allows for more variability than the voice of the process delivers, the process is considered "capable"'. So, while the high zone of tolerance give comfort level to the operations managers in public system, there is scope for and pressure on the managers to keep the processes efficient and effective.

Conclusion

This chapter looks at one part of the public service delivery of government (i.e. public grievance redressal system). It seeks to apply the operations management framework to this process and understand how the delivery of public service can be fitted into this. Operations management of public service delivery is quite complex. It tries to explore if there are any added complexities that arise from being service oriented. This chapter takes the public grievances redressal system in urban local bodies of a state in India as the case. It presents analysis of statistics of grievances redressed. In the final section the chapter lists out the characteristics of services sector as it emerges from literature review and discusses the findings from the field visits in this context. It concludes that while the government and the system seek to standardise and make the tasks programmable, the service deliverers seek to make it customised and non-programmable. This stress continues and it increases the importance of the actors. They have the comfort level that the zone of tolerance among the clients is high, and the system allows for more variability and non-standardisation.

The chapter points out that there is constant stress in public service organisations between attempts by the organisation to standardise operations and attempts by employees to make it unique to establish their relevance. This study needs to be repeated under several situations in different services to see its generalisability. The framework can also be extended to managing returns and repairs in manufacturing and services sectors. A typical case worker in medical reimbursement processing will try to make a case different from the template and try to make it unique. Similarly, a customer relationship person will try to explore how a particular return can be kept outside service guarantee. The operators will try to look for deviations from blueprint rather than trying to mapping to it. Also, in contrast to general trend in OM literature, we are suggesting through these findings to the researcher to extend the OM framework that is applied to public services, to general services and to manufacturing.

Acknowledgement

This study is funded out of the Grant provided by the Ministry of Urban Development of Government of India as part of the Centre of Excellence in Urban Governance project.

References

ADB (2010) *Access to Justice for the Urban Poor: Toward Inclusive Cities*. Mandaluyong City, Philippines: Asian Development Bank.

Bajpai, N., Sachs, J.D. and Dholakia, R.H. (2010) *Improving Access and Efficiency in Public Health Services: Mid-term Evaluation of India's National Rural Health Mission*. New Delhi: Sage.

Bhatacharjee, M., Mysoor, D. and Sivaramakrishnan, A. (2014) 'RTE grievance redress in Karnataka'. *Economic and Political Weekly*, 49(23): 37–41.

Chander, S. and Kush, A. (2012) 'Assessing grievances redressing mechanism in India'. *International Journal of Computer Applications*, 52(5): 12–19.

Chase, R.B and Tansik, D.A. (1983) 'The customer contact model for organization design'. *Management Science*, 29(9): 1037–50.

CMAK (2006) *Public Grievance Redressal System*. Draft report, Phase I Study Report. Karnataka: City Managers' Association Karnataka.

David, A. (2001) 'Models implementation: a state of art'. *European Journal of Operational Research*, 134(3): 459–80.

Government of India (2011)) *e-Governance: ULB Level Reform*. Retrieved from http://jnnurm.nic.in/wp-content/uploads/2011/01/Mandatory_Primer_1-e-governance.pdf (accessed 25 March 2015).

Hocutt, M.A., Bowers, M.R. and Donavan, D.T. (2006) 'The act of service recovery: factor or fiction?' *Journal of Services Marketing*, 20(3): 199–207.

Johnston, R. (1994) 'The zone of tolerance: exploring the relationship between service transactions and satisfaction with the overall service'. *International Journal of Service Industry Management*, 6(2): 46–61.

Kellog, D.L. and Nie, W. (1995) 'A framework for strategic service management'. *Journal of Operations Management*, 13(4), December: 323–37.

Landry, M., Banville, C. and Oral, M. (1996) 'Model legitimization in operational research'. *European Journal of Operational Research*, 92(3): 443–57.

Mahadevan, B. (2010) *Operations Management: Theory and Practice*. New Delhi: Pearson.

Paul, S. (2008). 'India's citizen's charters: in search of a champion'. *Economic and Political Weekly*, 43(7): 67–73.

Ranganathan, M. (2008). *Grievance Redressal Processes in Urban Service Delivery: How Effective Are They?* Governance brief. Manila: ADB.

Ringold, D., Holla, A., Koziol, M. and Srinivasan, S. (2012) *Citizens and Service Delivery: Assessing the Use of Social Accountability Approaches in the Human Development Sector.* Washington, DC: World Bank.

Schmenner, R.W. (1986) 'How can service businesses survive and prosper?' *Sloan Management Review*, 27(3), Spring: 21–32.

Shostack, G.L. (1987) 'Service positioning through structural change'. *Journal of Marketing*, 51 (January): 34–43.

Silvestro, R., Fitzgerald, L., Johnston, R. and Voss, C. (1992) 'Towards a classification of service processes'. *International Journal of Service Industry Management*, 3(3): 62–75.

Stodnick, M. and Marley, K.A. (2013) 'A longitudinal study of the zone of tolerance'. *Managing Service Quality*, 23(1): 25–42.

TERI (2010) *Framework for Effective Consumer Grievance Redressal System*. Draft final report prepared for Ministry of Urban Development, Government of India. April. New Delhi: The Energy and Resources Institute.

Wallack, J. and Nadhamuni, S. (2009) *User Innovation and E-governance Design*. Retrieved from http://cdf.ifmr.ac.in/wp-content/uploads/2011/03/User-Innovation-Egov.pdf (accessed 16 January 2013).

Wemmerlov, U. (1989) 'A taxonomy for service processes and its implications for system design'. *International Journal of Service Industry Management*, 1(3): 20–40.
World Bank (2003) *Making Services Work for Poor People: World Development Report 2004*. Oxford: Oxford University Press.

Note

1 For the third period, when the percentages of complaints redressed within a day and within a week are added, then the sum is a little over 104 per cent.

13 Are we closing the loop?

Examining the design of voluntary sector performance measurement systems

Claire Moxham

Purpose and structure of the chapter

By focusing on public services delivered by the voluntary sector, this chapter challenges the widely held assumption in operations management that the purpose of performance measurement activity is continuous improvement. The complexity of public service delivery creates measurement challenges that are very different to those experienced in a manufacturing context and a pervasive problem across public services is how to measure and manage service delivery. The chapter contributes to the topical debate on why and how we should measure public services by examining whether the continuous improvement loop of measurement and management is applicable to, and utilised by, public services that are delivered by the voluntary sector.

The chapter adopts a broadly UK policy focus and begins by examining the rationale for measuring the performance of voluntary organisations. Mechanisms for measuring such performance as documented in published international studies are then presented and a summary table is provided. Next the findings of a UK study in which empirical data exploring how the performance of voluntary organisations is measured in practice are discussed. These findings are considered in light of the literature and the shortcomings of the design of existing voluntary sector performance measurement systems are considered. The chapter concludes with a research agenda by offering propositions for interesting avenues for further work in this area.

Introduction

As in the private and public sectors, voluntary sector organisations are under pressure from stakeholders to measure performance in order to demonstrate achievement and improvement. The requirement to demonstrate the effectiveness of the services delivered by the voluntary sector has been thrown into sharp relief with the emergence of revised public sector funding structures; particularly outcomes-based performance measurement, payment by results and, more recently, the measurement of social value. Opportunities have arisen for voluntary organisations to engage in public service delivery through commissioning frameworks; an opportunity which comes with the caveat that performance reporting requirements must be adhered to.

Against this backdrop it is surprising that the design and development of voluntary sector performance measurement systems has received relatively limited attention. As voluntary organisations take the opportunity to move into mainstream public service delivery, it is timely to appraise how their performance can and should be measured.

Engaging voluntary organisations in public service delivery: implications for performance measurement

Performance measurement as a means of demonstrating improvement has been a key element of public sector reform and has become ubiquitous across the sector (Micheli and Neely, 2010; Pollitt and Bouckaert, 2000). It is argued that measuring performance permits service quality comparisons, engages stakeholders and improves the effectiveness of public services (Montesinos *et al.*, 2013). Emerging from new public management, public service performance measurement has taken a number of forms including measuring outputs, outcomes and impact (Hoque, 2008; Poister, 2003). Outputs are defined as countable units and are the direct products of a programme or of an organisation's activities (i.e. number of training sessions delivered) whereas outcomes are the benefits or changes experienced by the intended beneficiaries (Wainwright, 2003). Impact is a broader measure and is defined as all changes resulting from an activity, project or organisation. Impact includes intended as well as unintended, negative as well as positive, and long-term as well as short-term effects (*ibid.*). For healthcare services in particular, payment by results has been introduced whereby service providers are paid based on the achievement of specific performance objectives (Appleby *et al.*, 2012). Research points to a lack of clarity about the meaning or use of performance-based payment systems and consensus has not been reached as to how to measure the performance of public services (Eldridge and Palmer, 2009).

Opportunities for voluntary organisations to become involved at the margins of public service delivery have long existed, however in light of recent economic events and the emergence of public service commissioning, the voluntary sector is seen as well placed to provide innovative, flexible mainstream services that are responsive to needs (Davies, 2011; Cairns, 2009). Reaching agreement between stakeholders on a definition of 'the voluntary sector' is a challenge (Vincent and Harrow, 2005). The term is used to describe organisations that focus on wider public benefit as opposed to statutory service delivery or profit. The voluntary sector comprises independent agencies, campaigns, foundations, self-help federations, semi-detached public bodies and social enterprises (Paton, 2003). In the UK, voluntary organisations may be registered as charities if they meet the requisite criteria. The terminology around commissioning started to gain traction in 2004 and is predominantly part of the lexicon of UK government, although similar approaches to planning, designing, procuring and managing public services are in operation around the world (Bovaird *et al.*, 2012). Commissioning has been defined as 'the cycle of assessing the needs of people in an area, designing and then securing an appropriate service' (Cabinet Office, 2006: 4). Engaging voluntary organisations in the commissioning process offers advantages to the public sector in the form of increased capacity, greater choice of service providers, flexibility in service start-up and termination, user-centred service interventions and the ability to fulfil legislative mandates (Austin, 2003; Bovaird *et al.*, 2012). It is argued that voluntary organisations also benefit through increased financial resources and enhanced community reputation (Austin, 2003).

Voluntary organisations that choose to engage in the delivery of public services need to adhere to public sector performance measurement requirements. While the public sector may not be directly involved in delivering a particular service, it has a vested interest in ensuring that expected levels of service delivery performance are achieved. The commissioning of public services has been described as being more concerned with 'ends' rather than 'means' (Murray, 2009: 200). It is therefore unsurprising that one of the key drivers for voluntary sector performance measurement is accountability. This appears to be in contrast to the private sector literature in which measurement is often seen as a mechanism for continuous improvement (Franco-Santos *et al.*, 2007). Measurement practices in the voluntary sector are broad and varied, and have attracted criticism for the superficial nature in which they are used (Lynch-Cerullo and Cooney, 2011). While practice differs, the motivation for measurement is frequently cited as that of meeting the requirements of external funders. In a survey of South Carolina voluntary organisations, only 6 per cent of respondents reported on the use of performance measurement to improve services (Zimmermann and Stevens, 2006). In a similar study of voluntary organisations in Dallas, those respondents who had not evaluated their performance in the past two years stated that this was because it was not a requirement of their funder (Hoefer, 2000). Research points to voluntary organisations engaging in performance measurement to enhance the legitimacy of their activities (Dhanani and Connolly, 2012). It is argued that performance measurement is used in a 'ceremonial' fashion within the voluntary sector; resources are squandered and the process is purely symbolic (Hoefer, 2000; Thomson, 2010).

In parallel with the rather narrowly focused accountability rationale which pervades the voluntary sector literature, there are a number of operational challenges to measurement that appear particular pertinent to voluntary organisations. One that is frequently cited is the lack of standardisation of reporting requirements from public sector commissioners. Voluntary organisations can, in theory, deliver the same services to a range of commissioners and be required to adhere to different measurement requirements for each one. Research has found that such practice detracts from the capacity of the voluntary organisation to focus on service delivery and requires skills and experience that volunteers may not possess (Moxham and Boaden, 2007). Resources are spent on collecting performance data, however a paradox has been noted whereby funding ceases, yet there is an on-going requirement to measure the outcomes and impact of the services provided (Martikke and Moxham, 2010). In consequence, the instability of funding impacts on a voluntary organisation's ability to fulfil its reporting mandate. If data can be collected within time and financial constraints, it is often difficult to establish 'cause and effect'. This means that voluntary organisations are required to substantiate their contribution to an improved outcome, however this is often impossible as one organisation is rarely completely responsible for a change in an individual's circumstances (Lowe, 2013). Such operational challenges may be a result of public sector commissioners not fully understanding the consequences of the measurement criteria and processes they are asking voluntary sector organisations to use (Moxham, 2010).

In summary, studies point to a requirement for measuring the performance of voluntary organisations, yet the rationale for measurement appears to have a rather narrow focus. Scholars have commented on the myopic view of measurement in the sector due to its apparent disconnect with performance improvement (Ebrahim, 2005). In addition to these broader questions about why performance is being measured, voluntary organisations also appear to have sector-specific operational challenges to measurement. As the voluntary sector is seen as a key element of public service reform, it is suggested that these challenges warrant further research attention.

Studies examining the application of performance measurement approaches to the voluntary sector

When engaging voluntary organisations in service delivery many public sector commissioners stipulate the performance measurement approaches to be used. In addition, and possibly in parallel, voluntary organisations may choose to develop their own systems or to modify those already in existence. From the literature, documented approaches to measuring performance in the voluntary sector comprise:

- peer review;
- balanced scorecard;
- programme evaluation;
- outcome measurement;
- evaluation against social values; and
- participatory, empowerment and collaborative.

Peer review

The process of peer review requires an external actor who is familiar with the operational environment to conduct an assessment of the voluntary organisation. Organisations going through the process are required to self-assess and share this assessment with the reviewer who will validate the evaluation through data collection (often involving service users). The review report is shared with the voluntary organisation with the objective of providing constructive feedback to enable reflection and planning (Purcell and Hawtin, 2010; Fetterman, 2002). Examples of voluntary sector organisations in the UK that have used peer review to effect performance improvement include Action with Communities in Rural England, National Association for Voluntary and Community Action, Charities Evaluation Service and Relate (Purcell and Hawtin, 2010).

Balanced scorecard

Popular in the private, and to some extent, public sectors, the balanced scorecard has also been applied to voluntary sector organisations. The aim of the technique is to translate the mission and strategy of an organisation into objectives and measures which can be viewed through the four perspectives of financial, customer, internal business process and learning and growth (Kaplan and Norton, 1992). Its applicability to the not-for profit context has been emphasised (Kaplan, 2001). Studies detailing the implementation of the balanced scorecard usually take the form of a single case study (see Manville and Broad, 2013); therefore there is a dearth of comparative analysis. Mixed success has been reported, with some voluntary organisations finding that the framework is overtly business focused and overlooks value-based programmes, volunteer participation and compensation systems (Bozzo, 2000). In addition, the balanced scorecard model assumes full commitment from management staff to implement the evaluation; however it is argued that there is no clear role for frontline staff, clients or volunteers, which may impact on the results of the exercise (*ibid.*). Possibly as a consequence of its top-town implementation approach, findings suggest that the balanced scorecard is used primarily as a measurement tool rather than a management system in voluntary sector organisations (Greiling, 2010).

Programme evaluation

Anecdotally, programme evaluation appears to be a popular measurement tool in voluntary organisations. Yet, as with comparative empirical research on balanced scorecard usage, a similar lack of research on the use of programme evaluation approaches in the voluntary sector has been highlighted (Hoefer, 2000). A local study of Dallas-based voluntary organisations in the US identified three common approaches to evaluation and finds that these can be conducted simultaneously:

- *Implementation monitoring*: programme activities are checked to ensure that they are being delivered to the target population as designed.
- *Process evaluation*: programme activities are checked to assist in explaining why a programme did or did not achieve expected outcomes.
- *Outcome evaluation*: programme results are checked to see if programme goals are achieved.

These findings concur with a national study of US voluntary sector organisations in which the aim of programme evaluation was most commonly cited as measuring programme outcomes or impact (although subsequent analysis finds that the key driver was to enable reporting to a funding agency) (Fine *et al.*, 2000).

In terms of evaluation design, four types are generally employed:

- *Post-test-only*: client variables are measured only after the programme is completed. This approach is considered very weak terms of internal validity.

- *Single group pre- and post-test design*: clients' results are measured once before and once after the programme to determine if there is any change as a result of the programme.
- *Time series*: clients' results are measured several times before and after the programme.
- *Comparison group*: compares clients on the programme and compares their results to another group of similar people not on the programme.

Studies highlight the importance of the design of programme evaluation because a weak design can compromise the efficacy of the evaluation process and affect the credibility of the subsequent results (Fine *et al.*, 2000; Hoefer, 2000).

Outcome measurement

As discussed, the measurement of programme or service outcomes is often the main purpose of programme evaluation. Measuring outcomes appears to have superseded the measurement of outputs and is inherent in the vocabulary of public sector commissioning. A recent review of policy and practitioner commissioning literature found the 'securing' and improvement of outcomes for citizens to be a key element of many public service performance evaluation frameworks (Bovaird *et al.*, 2012). The review concludes, however, that 'the move to outcome-based commissioning has so far been aspirational rather than real' (*ibid.*:71). Defining appropriate measurement criteria and subsequently collecting relevant data appear to have stymied this initiative. Lowe (2013) questions if one can ever really know the impact that an intervention has had on an individual and challenges the entire notion of outcomes-based measurement.

Despite the challenges associated with measuring outcomes, it has been applied to voluntary organisations and frameworks have been developed. For example, the system used by the UK children's charity Barnardo's focuses on the changes that have taken place for the service user as a result of their involvement with the service provided (McEwen *et al.*, 2010). A hierarchical framework is employed that considers the aims of Barnardo's, the long-term outcomes for service users that contribute to these aims and the specific outcomes for service provision. Individual 'case files' are collated for each user and stored within a custom software programme where they can be accessed when necessary. In contrast to this individual organisational approach to measuring outcomes, Atkinson and Maxwell (2007) have developed a multi-agency framework for assessing outcomes in Children's Services Planning in Northern Ireland. The rationale for the framework was the realisation that agencies operating in isolation were collecting separate information that did not support the collaborative approach required to develop and deliver services. Like Barnardo's, an IT system was developed to facilitate the collation, analysis and dissemination of data. The process of outcome measurement is detailed as follows:

1. Identification of outcomes: expressed as statements of common purpose, of aspiration and of intent. Nine outcome statements were developed.

2. Definition of associated life factors and measurable indicators: hierarchy of life factors, indicators and measures are developed and associated with each of the nine outcome statements.
3. Data collection, analysis and reporting: data is collected across all agencies and analysed.
4. Review of achievements against outcomes, identification of areas for improvement and action planning: report used to critically review progress and to develop strategies for improvement (Atkinson and Maxwell, 2007).

A review of outcome measurement practices finds that many voluntary sector organisations may not have the internal capacity to undertake the sophisticated data collection methods that may be required (Bozzo, 2000). Similar findings are echoed in a study of US voluntary sector organisations; outcome measurement may be beneficial yet resource and technological constraints mitigate its effect (Thomson, 2011). It is worth noting that the studies by McEwen *et al* (2010) and Atkinson and Maxwell (2007) focus predominantly on the design of the outcome measurement system and there is limited detail as to how relevant data can or should be collected.

Evaluation against social values

There is some evidence to support the evaluation of voluntary sector performance against social values (Whitman, 2008). Such practice has gained importance in the UK with the passing of the Public Services (Social Value) Act in 2012. The Act requires all public bodies to consider how the services they commission might improve the economic, social and environmental well-being of the area in which the services are delivered. Voluntary sector umbrella organisations anticipate that the Act will open up opportunities for public service delivery by more voluntary organisations as many already demonstrate social value in their services. As the Act has only been law since March 2013 it is too early to review its impact.

Participatory, empowerment and collaborative

Participatory, empowerment and collaborative approaches to voluntary sector performance measurement involve programme staff, volunteers and other stakeholders in determining performance and setting goals (Bozzo, 2000). The overall aim of these approaches is broader than measuring outcomes and includes organisational development and programme improvement. Studies on this approach do not provide specific details as to how it can be implemented, however it is noted that the self-directed nature of the evaluation should be complemented by training, and with an experienced facilitator, in order to generate meaningful results.

From the literature that was examined, these six approaches to voluntary sector performance measurement are those that have received the most attention. Others may also be used, and bespoke systems developed, yet these did not emerge as part of the literature search. Table 13.1 provides a summary of the characteristics of the six approaches that have been discussed in this chapter.

Table 13.1 Summary of approaches to measuring voluntary sector performance

Measurement approach	*Procedure*	*Aim*
Peer review	Review of one or more elements of an organisation by others of equivalent status or standing	To improve the performance of any aspect of a third sector organisation's work
Balanced scorecard	Monitor programme activities by using a range of performance measures, many of which are non-financial	To improve the performance of an organisation through the use of a balanced set of performance measures
Programme evaluation	Monitor programme activities and results by using client files, organisational reports, surveys, tests, goal attainment scales and social indicators	To use the results of the evaluation(s) to make improvements in the programme's operations, verify programme outcomes and/or advocate for more resources
Outcome monitoring	Identify outcomes and collect relevant data pertinent to outcome indicators of performance	To enable organisations to assess the benefits or changes in participants as a result of programmes
Evaluation against social values	Use social values to develop organisational strategy	To align all organisational activities to the achievement of social values
Participatory, empowerment and collaborative	Discuss with participants, staff and clients to decide the course of an evaluation	Organisational development and/or programme improvement through stakeholder participation

Examining the design of voluntary sector performance measurement systems in practice

Studies suggest that the main driver for measuring the performance of voluntary sector organisations is accountability to funders. This emphasis on accountability appears to be at odds with the rationale for engaging flexible, grass-roots organisations to improve the provision of public services. As discussed, there is some empirical evidence to support the use of performance measurement frameworks by the voluntary sector; however the context in which these have been applied is unclear. To further our understanding, an examination of the types of performance measurement frameworks used by voluntary organisations was undertaken in an attempt to identify current practice in the sector.

The purpose of the study was to identify:

- The mechanisms by which the performance of voluntary sector public service providers is measured.
- Whether recognised performance measurement frameworks are utilised by voluntary organisations.

Data were collected from UK based voluntary organisations that were involved in delivering public services. A case study approach was used and six voluntary organisations and a sample of their funders were examined. Twenty-three managers from seventeen organisations were interviewed as part of the study. To try and examine a cross-section of the voluntary sector, different types of voluntary organisations were selected for examination. Two were small and regionally focused, delivering community services and projects. Two were larger, nationally focused organisations; one provided support to witnesses attending court and another offered learning disability, mental health and substance misuse services. The final two case studies were UK-based international development organisations, both of which focused on capacity building activities in developing countries. All of the organisations received public money to deliver their services and were required to report on their performance.

The qualitative data from the interviews were examined to ascertain how the performance of the six voluntary organisations in the study was measured. Unsurprisingly, financial accountability featured highly as the key focus of measurement practices. The majority of the funders required some evidence of expenditure, with many requesting copies of receipts. The funder generally checked whether the money had been spent as per the initial service specification and any unused funds had to be returned. Voluntary organisations that could account for expenditure and demonstrate the delivery of services as specified were allowed to apply for continued funding. In a similar approach to assessing service quality as per anticipated expenditure, a target-focused approach to measurement was adopted by the funders of the regional and national voluntary organisations. The design here was different to that of the payment by results framework in that the targets focused on quantitative measures such as how many people had used the service and the number of different types of services that were offered. Attention was not paid to the subsequent effects of any of the services provided on the user or the community.

Much has been written in the voluntary sector practitioner literature about the requirement to measure outcomes, however only one voluntary organisation in this study was required to do so by its funder. This organisation was regionally focused and during interviews the manager stated that they felt unsure as to how outcomes should be measured, and admitted that the process was only given some thought once the measurement forms arrived in the post. Invariably, the measurement forms arrived as the service or project was coming to an end, therefore little attention had been given to performance measurement system design at the outset. The other regionally focused voluntary organisation in the study was not required to measure outcomes; however it regularly collected stories and supporting photographs from volunteers and service users to demonstrate its services. These stories and photographs were displayed all over the building. The manager of this organisation perceived that it was important for all stakeholders to see the impact of the services provided regardless of whether this was a requirement of continued funding.

Some of the public sector funders conducted audit visits to the voluntary organisations that were commissioned to deliver services. During the audit visits, reports and internal documents were reviewed and feedback from service users was sometimes included. Interviews with voluntary organisations that had undergone audits revealed that they rarely received any feedback from the audit and assumed that 'no news was good news.' Follow-up interviews with funders pointed to the audit being primarily a process requirement which did not seem part of service improvement. Some public sector funders adopted a more unfocused approach to measurement and stressed their 'light touch' philosophy. These funders made informal visits to the voluntary organisation and initiated discussions with stakeholders, including trustees, to ascertain progress. The international voluntary organisations were the only ones in the study that were permitted by their funders to develop their own indicators of performance based on their mission. The regional and national organisations did have their own key performance indicators which were often different to those of their funders, however as they had to satisfy a range of stakeholders who stipulated different measures of performance, these organisations often had to operate parallel performance measurement systems. This was not the case for the larger internationally focused case study organisations. A summary of the measurement systems that were identified in the study is included as Table 13.2

Are we closing the loop on voluntary sector performance measurement? Implications for research and practice

In examining the design of voluntary sector performance measurement in practice, there is clear support for the findings of previous studies in that accountability

Table 13.2 Categorisation of design of performance measurement systems

Measurement system	*System developer*	*Performance information*	*Measurement process*
Expenditure	Public sector funder	Copies of receipts requested	Compliance checks against initial service specification
Target	Public sector funder	Quantitative details of users and beneficiaries, regularity of services provided	Compliance checks against original targets
Outcome	Public sector funder	Documented evidence of wider impact of services	Compliance checks against initial service specification
Audit	Public sector funder	Assessment of service provider documentation	Process not made clear to voluntary sector service provider
Unfocused	Public sector funder	No defined criteria or data collection process	Process not made clear to voluntary sector service provider
Mission	Voluntary sector service provider	Evidence of achievement of organisational goals	Evaluation of gaps in performance shared with stakeholders

Source: adapted from Moxham (2013)

appeared to be the key focus of measurement. Expenditure was often used as a proxy measure of service quality in that if money had been spent as per the initial service specification then commissioners seemed satisfied. This finding concurs with the assertion that commissioning is more concerned with 'ends' rather than 'means' (Murray, 2009). From the case studies there was a lack of clarity as to what constitutes 'ends' as some public sector funders required quantitative feedback about questions of how many and how often whereas others required more detailed feedback of any subsequent changes that had occurred. In consequence, there was no standard practice as to how performance was measured and a plurality of measures and processes in use. This created confusion for the case study organisations and, possibly, for their public sector funders.

From the categorisation of the design of performance measurement systems that were used in practice (see Table 13.2), few of those noted in previous studies were apparent. A version of informal peer review was evident but was rather unfocused and the mechanism for feeding back findings to the voluntary sector service provider was not determined. There was some support for the measurement of outcomes, however confusion and a lack of preparation in terms of measurement design appeared to detract from its efficacy. Those voluntary organisations that were able to develop and use their own mission-focused measures appeared to be operating a form of participatory, empowerment and collaborative measurement. It is interesting to note that only the internationally focused organisations which had longer-term funding relationships were permitted to adopt this practice.

From the literature and empirical findings there appears to be a real focus on accounting for the money used by the voluntary sector to deliver public services. If measurement is primarily used for compliance purposes, it is unclear how the commissioning of public services to voluntary organisations provides any scope for further improvement. If voluntary sector performance measurement is indeed used in a superficial, ceremonial fashion, it may be more cost effective to streamline the performance measures used and to explicitly focus on accountability for spend. Such an approach would appear to be in direct contrast with the move towards greater public sector engagement with the voluntary sector in order to provide flexible, responsive services that are designed and delivered by those with specialist skills and knowledge. Instead, a focus on how we can close the loop on voluntary sector performance measurement to support public service improvement seems apposite.

From an operations management perspective, there are a plethora of performance measurement and management frameworks that have been developed; many of which are directly linked to performance improvement. Further research could examine whether such frameworks are applicable to the voluntary sector context and work to overcome sector specific measurement challenges. Improving how we measure the performance of voluntary organisations has clear potential for a positive impact on the quality of public services delivered; a goal of governments across the globe. Moving from performance measurement to performance management will be a positive step towards closing the service improvement loop.

Propositions for developing a research agenda

To conclude the chapter it seems appropriate to offer propositions for further work in this area. The following propositions offer interesting avenues for further research:

- *Proposition 1: The funding structures of voluntary organisations impede the ability to measure the long term outcomes and impact of the public services they deliver.*
- Proposition 2: The collection of data for compliance purposes does not support the continuous improvement of public services.
- Proposition 3: Voluntary sector organisations need to be involved in the co-production of performance measurement systems as commissioners lack the skills and capabilities to develop appropriate systems.
- Proposition 4: The design of existing performance measurement frameworks does not reflect the value based focus of voluntary organisations and they are therefore unsuited to measuring voluntary sector service provision.
- Proposition 5: The co-production of performance measurement systems by public sector commissioners and voluntary organisations is required to enable the measurement of social value.

Finally, in considering the application of performance measurement to voluntary organisations, it should be noted that the 'voluntary sector' is not a collection of homogenous service providers. The voluntary sector is broad and varied. It encompasses, for example, micro organisations run solely on the goodwill of volunteers in addition to multi-national aid organisations employing hundreds of salaried professional staff. It is therefore impossible to generalise about organisations operating in the sector. The aim of this chapter was therefore not to make generalisations, but rather to highlight the difficulties in achieving improvement in public service delivery if measurement systems are designed to focus solely on accountability. There is an emerging body of evidence to support a link between voluntary sector engagement and improved public services. If, however, systems are designed to measure compliance rather than to support innovation and improvement it is doubtful whether the aims of public service commissioning will be achieved.

References

Appleby, J., Harrison, T., Hawkins, L. and Dixon, L. (2012) *Payment by Results: How Can Payment Systems Help to Deliver Better Care?* London: The King's Fund.

Atkinson, M. and Maxwell, V. (2007) 'Driving performance in a multi-agency partnership using outcome measures: a case study'. *Measuring Business Excellence*, 11(2): 12–22.

Austin, M.J. (2003) 'The changing relationship between nonprofit organizations and public social service agencies in the era of welfare reform'. *Nonprofit and Voluntary Sector Quarterly*, 32(1): 97–114.

Bovaird, T., Dickinson, H. and Allen, K. (2012) *Commissioning across Government: Review of Evidence*. Research Report 86. Birmingham: Third Sector Research Centre.

Bozzo, S. (2000) 'Evaluation resources for nonprofit organizations: usefulness and applicability'. *Nonprofit Management and Leadership*, 10(4): 463–72.

Cabinet Office (2006) *Partnership in Public Services: An Action Plan for the Third Sector Involvement*. London: Cabinet Office.

Cairns, B. (2009) 'The independence of the voluntary sector from government in England'. In Smerdon, M. (ed.), *The First Principle of Voluntary Action: Essays on the Independence of the Voluntary Sector from Government in Canada, England, Germany, Northern Ireland, Scotland, United States of America and Wales*, pp. 35–50. London: The Baring Foundation.

Davies, S. (2011) 'Outsourcing, public sector reform and the changed character of the UK state-voluntary sector relationship'. *International Journal of Public Sector Management*, 27(7): 641–49.

Dhanani, A. and Connolly, C. (2012) 'Discharging not-for-profit accountability: UK charities and public discourse'. *Accounting, Auditing and Accountability Journal*, 25(7): 1140–69.

Ebrahim, A. (2005) 'Accountability myopia: losing sight of organizational learning'. *Nonprofit and Voluntary Sector Quarterly*, 34(1): 56–87.

Eldridge, C. and Palmer, N. (2009) 'Performance-based payment: some reflections on the discourse, evidence and unanswered questions'. *Heath Policy and Planning*, 24: 160–66.

Fetterman, D. (2002) 'Empowerment evaluation: building communities of practice and a culture of learning'. *American Journal of Community Psychology*, 30(1): 89–102.

Fine, A., Thayer, C. and Coghlan, A. (2000) 'Program evaluation in practice in the nonprofit sector'. *Nonprofit Management and Leadership*, 10(3): 331–39.

Franco-Santos, M., Kennerley, M., Micheli, P., Martinez, V., Mason, S., Marr, B., Gray, D. and Neely, A. (2007) 'Towards a definition of a business performance measurement system'. *International Journal of Operations and Production Management*, 27(8): 784–801.

Greiling, D. (2010) 'Balanced scorecard implementation in German non-profit organizations'. *International Journal of Productivity and Performance Management*, 59(6): 534–54.

Hoefer, R. (2000) 'Accountability in action? Program evaluation in nonprofit human service agencies'. *Nonprofit Management and Leadership*, 10(2): 167–77.

Hoque, Z. (2008) 'Measuring and reporting public sector outputs/outcomes: exploratory evidence from Australia'. *International Journal of Public Sector Management*, 21(5): 468–93.

Kaplan, R.S. (2001) 'Strategic performance measurement and management in nonprofit organizations'. *Nonprofit Management and Leadership*, 11(3): 353–70.

Kaplan, R.S. and Norton, D.P. (1992) 'The balanced scorecard: measures that drive performance'. *Harvard Business Review*, January–February: 71–9.

Lowe, T. (2013) 'New Development: The paradox of outcomes: the more we measure the less we understand'. *Public Money and Management*, 33(3): 213–16.

Lynch-Cerullo, K. and Cooney, K. (2011) 'Moving from outputs to outcomes: a review of the evolution of performance measurement in the human service nonprofit sector'. *Administration and Society*, 35(4): 364–88.

Manville, G. and Broad, M. (2013) 'Changing times for charities'. *Public Management Review*, 15(7): 992–1010.

Martikke, S. and Moxham, C. (2010) 'Public sector commissioning: experiences of voluntary organizations delivering health and social services'. *International Journal of Public Administration*, 33(14): 790–99.

McEwen, J., Shoesmith, M. and Allen, R. (2010) 'Embedding outcomes recording in Barnardo's performance management approach'. *International Journal of Productivity and Performance Management*, 59(6): 586–98.

Micheli, P. and Neely, A. (2010) 'Performance measurement in the public sector in England: searching for the golden thread'. *Public Administration Review*, July–August: 591–600.

Montesinos, V., Brusca, I., Rossi, F. and Aversano, N. (2013) 'The usefulness of performance reporting in local government: comparing Italy and Spain'. *Public Money and Management*, 33(3): 171–76.

Moxham, C. (2010) 'Challenges and enablers to engaging voluntary organizations in public service delivery'. *Public Money and Management*, 30(5): 293–98.

Moxham, C. (2013) 'Measuring up: Examining the potential for voluntary sector performance measurement to improve public service delivery'. *Public Money and Management*, 33(3): 193–201.

Moxham, C. and Boaden, R. (2007) 'The impact of performance measurement in the voluntary sector: identification of contextual and processual factors'. *International Journal of Operations and Production Management*, 27(8): 826–45.

Murray, J.G. (2009) 'Towards a common understanding of the differences between purchasing, procurement and commissioning in the UK public sector'. *Journal of Purchasing and Supply Management*, 15: 198–202.

Paton, R. (2003) *Managing and Measuring Social Enterprises*. London: Sage.

Poister, T.H. (2003) *Measuring Performance in Public and Nonprofit Organizations*. San Francisco, CA: John Wiley & Sons.

Pollitt, C. and Bouckaert, G. (2000) *Public Management Reform: A Comparative Analysis*. Oxford: Oxford University Press.

Purcell, M. and Hawtin, M. (2010) 'Piloting external peer review as a model for performance improvement in third-sector organizations'. *Nonprofit Management and Leadership*, 20(3): 357–74.

Thomson, D. (2010) 'Exploring the role of funders' performance reporting madates in nonprofit performance measurement'. *Nonprofit and Voluntary Sector Quarterly*, 39(4): 611–29.

Thomson, D. (2011) 'The role of funders in driving nonprofit performance measurement and use in strategic management'. *Public Performance and Management Review*, 35(1): 54–78.

Vincent, J. and Harrow, J. (2005) 'Comparing thistles and roses: the application of governmental-voluntary sector relations theory to Scotland and England'. *Voluntas: International Journal of Voluntary and Nonprofit Organizations*, 16(4): 375–95.

Wainwright, S. (2003) *Measuring Impact: A Guide to Resources*. London: NCVO Publications.

Whitman, J. (2008) 'Evaluating philanthropic foundations according to their social values'. *Nonprofit Management and Leadership*, 18(4): 417–34.

Zimmermann, J. and Stevens, B. (2006) 'The use of performance measurement in South Carolina nonprofits'. *Nonprofit Management and Leadership*, 16(3): 315–27.

14 Improving quality and performance with the Public Sector Scorecard

Max Moullin

Introduction

Most public and third sector organisations – both within and beyond Europe – are struggling with two major problems: improving outcomes for service users and other key stakeholders without increasing overall cost; and developing measures of performance that help them improve and assure quality without motivating staff to achieve arbitrary targets at the expense of poor service to the public. Operations management has a key role to play in addressing both of these problems. This chapter describes with examples how the outcome-focussed Public Sector Scorecard, an integrated service improvement and performance management framework for the public and third sectors, can be used to improve both quality and performance, while keeping costs under control.

Many organisations in all sectors have impressive looking strategy documents. However the majority of these bear little relationship to what the organisation is actually doing. They are typically updated once or twice a year, few people in the organisation know what the strategy is or where it came from, and budgets and incentives are not linked to the strategy (Niven, 2003:11–13). In addition many public sector organisations have their strategy changed before the previous one has had a chance to be implemented!

Similarly there are many glossy brochures, dashboards and spreadsheets showing progress on a myriad of measures, which also look very impressive. However typically they will have been developed by brainstorming what measures might be useful or easy to measure with little consideration of what the organisation needs to achieve. Alternatively, they may simply reflect the information required by head office or central government.

What is needed is an integrated system to link strategy and performance measurement to address both of these issues. This is important for operations management, as an effective operations strategy needs to be consistent with the organisation's overall strategy and achieving that strategy requires appropriate performance measures to monitor progress effectively and understand cause and effect. This link between strategy and performance measures is an important feature of the two frameworks discussed in this chapter: the Balanced Scorecard and the Public Sector

Scorecard. The Balanced Scorecard (BSC) is an integrated strategy and performance measurement framework developed initially for the private sector, while the Public Sector Scorecard (PSS) extends and adapts the BSC to fit the culture and values of the public and third sectors. The PSS is even more relevant for operations managers, as it goes further than the BSC by linking strategy, service improvement, and performance measurement and not just the first and third of these.

This chapter describes both of these frameworks and their application to the public and third sectors. It also includes two case studies illustrating the use of the PSS across organisational boundaries – a central government task force and a project led jointly by the NHS and a city council to address child obesity.

Some key features of the PSS are then discussed – service user and stakeholder involvement, focussing on outcomes, emphasis on service improvement, integrating risk management, use of performance targets, and last but not least developing a culture of improvement, innovation and learning rather than a top-down blame culture. Each of these features is important to effective operations management in the public and third sectors and the chapter concludes that the PSS has much to offer in improving and monitoring quality and performance of public and third sector organisations.

The Balanced Scorecard

Originally introduced in 1992 by Kaplan and Norton to address the over-emphasis by accountants on financial measures, the BSC recommended that organisations measure performance on four perspectives: financial, customer, internal, and innovation and learning (Kaplan and Norton, 1992). While this was not particularly innovative – the European Excellence Model and the US Baldrige Award which pre-date the BSC already required a balanced set of measures – a major breakthrough came in 1996 with what has been called 'the second generation balanced scorecard' (Lawrie and Cobbold, 2004). This is a framework that helps organisations put strategy at the centre of the organisation by 'translating strategy into operational objectives that drive both behaviour and performance' (Balanced Scorecard Collaborative, 2004). The main addition was the development of a strategy map showing the link between different perspectives and the organisation's mission and vision (Kaplan and Norton, 2001a).

By basing performance measures on the strategy map, companies can ensure a clear link between the organisation's strategy and its performance measures. This gave the BSC a distinct advantage over self-assessment and awards frameworks such as the European Foundation for Quality Management Excellence Model (EFQM, 2013) and the Baldrige Performance Excellence Program (Link and Scott, 2011). The main reason for this is that once organisations completed their self-assessments, they tended to concentrate on improving their scores – which might involve tackling the easiest issues or the ones that they are performing worst on rather than those most crucial to the organisation and its stakeholders (Moullin, 2007b). This is backed up by Cairns *et al* (2005) in their in-depth study of UK voluntary and community organisations which found that the main benefits of such programmes were 'in the areas of organisational self-reflection, learning and development', while the 'benefits to service users and clients were mostly indirect' (*ibid.*).

However, the BSC does have its difficulties. In particular there is no explicit requirement to address organisational culture. Aspects like leadership, motivating and empowering staff, and better partnership working are generally ignored. It is frequently implemented top-down, with little involvement from employees or other stakeholders (Norreklit, 2000). Also many companies still effectively use the 1992 version, thinking up measures under each perspective and presenting them as a BSC. However it is the process of developing the scorecard – and in particular making sure that performance measures reflect the organisation's strategy – that is of prime importance, not just the measures themselves.

For the public and voluntary sectors, the BSC has additional shortcomings. In particular its language, architecture and methodology very much reflect its private sector origins. Indeed Gambles (1999: 24) says that 'in its usual form, [the BSC] is clearly not suitable for the vast majority of the public sector'. One of the main problems is that the most important perspective of the BSC is the financial perspective. Indeed most companies only measure non-financial factors because they recognise that they will at some point affect bottom-line financial performance (Pidd, 2012: 209; Moullin, 2009a). This is not the case in the public and voluntary sectors, where an organisation which has a large surplus at the end of the year, but has long waiting lists or poor outcomes is not a well-performing organisation.

Kaplan and Norton claim that all that needs to be done to adapt the BSC for use in public sector organisations is to 'rearrange the scorecard to place customers or constituents at the top of the hierarchy' (Kaplan and Norton, 2001b: 98). However, even though several attempts have been made to refine the BSC for the not-for-profit sectors (e.g. Irwin, 2002; Lawrie and Cobbold, 2004) evidence suggests that problems remain (e.g. Moore, 2003).

In local government Northcott and Taulapapa (2012) conclude from their research that although all eight New Zealand organisations in their sample which used the BSC 'had modified the BSC to fit their organisations, significant difficulties had been encountered in doing so'. One city council in their study felt that 'the breadth of the perspectives is limiting. For example, product and service outputs are addressed, but not leadership and governance, which are just as important to local government' (Northcott and Taulapapa, 2012).

Gurd and Gao (2008), reviewing the use of the BSC within healthcare, conclude that 'current applications do not tend to show the health of patients as being central to the development of the BSC; the balance is tilted towards the financial not the health outcomes'.

While the BSC has been used with varying degrees of success in many public sector organisations (e.g. Greatbanks and Tapp, 2007; Radnor and Lovell, 2003; Niven, 2003; Martin *et al*, 2002) the methodology is still private-sector-oriented, with little emphasis on service user involvement, risk management, or the need to work across organisational boundaries. However rather than adapt what is essentially a private sector model to fit all sectors, an alternative approach is to design a model specifically for the public and voluntary sectors – and this is the approach taken by the PSS.

The Public Sector Scorecard

The PSS is an integrated strategy development, service improvement and performance management framework for the public and third sectors (Penna, 2011: 243–45; Moullin, 2002: 199–200). It was originally developed in 2001 when the author was asked to develop an evaluation framework for an NHS Modernisation Task Force (Moullin, 2004). The aim was to incorporate the BSC's link between strategy and performance measurement via the strategy map and several of its other features into a model that fits the culture and values of the public and voluntary sectors. The changes required to overcome the BSC's shortcomings mentioned earlier required an outcome-focused approach with more emphasis on service user and stakeholder involvement. This was named the PSS in order to show its links to the BSC but to highlight that it was a performance management framework specifically designed for the public and voluntary sectors.

There are a number of important differences between the two frameworks. While the BSC focuses primarily on financial outcomes, the PSS looks at three types of outcomes: strategic outcomes, the raisin d'être of the organisation; outcomes affecting service users; and financial outcomes such as keeping within budget and value for money. Second, the BSC is generally implemented top-down with little or no customer or staff involvement. Indeed implementation of the BSC involves 'cascading the scorecard down the organisation' (Bourne and Bourne, 2007: 166–7). In contrast, a key element of the PSS is its emphasis on service user and stakeholder involvement. For example a project using the PSS for Sheffield's Stop Smoking Service began with three workshops with over 100 service users and was then steered by a reference group including managers and staff of the service, eight service users, a GP, a hospital consultant and representatives of the Strategic Health Authority (Moullin *et al.*, 2007).

Another major difference between the BSC and the PSS is that the latter has greater emphasis on operations management, with three phases: strategy mapping, service improvement, and measurement and evaluation, whereas the BSC concentrates on the first and third of these. The service improvement phase of the PSS can involve the use of tools such as lean, Six Sigma and systems thinking, where appropriate in an outcome-focused setting. It also aims to address the organisational, cultural and capability factors that can prevent processes from working effectively. Improving processes is not sufficient. Organisations need also to address the factors that lead to and result from poor processes (e.g. poor leadership, poor partnership working, poor policy and strategy, inadequate resources, and low staff morale).

At the heart of the PSS is the very simple, yet powerful, model on the left hand side of Figure 14.1. Processes lead to outcomes, while capability – defined as the organisational, cultural and resource-based factors that need to be addressed for processes to work effectively – leads to effective processes.

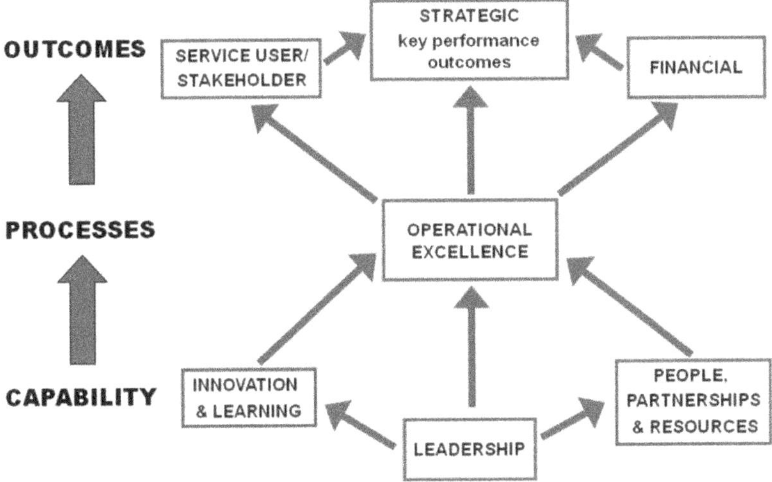

Figure 14.1 The Public Sector Scorecard

The right hand side of Figure 14.1 provides more detail on the different elements. Outcomes include the key performance outcomes that the organisation aims to achieve, those required by users and other key stakeholders, together with financial outcomes such as breaking-even, securing funding, and offering value for money. There will be a variety of processes within an organisation and the PSS aims to help organisations achieve operational excellence so that they can achieve the various outcomes. Capability comprises what needs to be done to support staff and processes in delivering the outcomes required. This might include trained and motivated people, good partnership working and sufficient resources, together with a culture based on innovation and learning rather than a blame culture – all underpinned by effective and supportive leadership.

An example illustrating what might go in the relevant boxes for a housing association is provided in Figure 14.2. This is based on information from Leeds Federated Housing Association (Elliot, 2012). As can be seen, in order to achieve the strategic objective of providing homes to the best affordable standard and an excellent customer experience, they need to ensure high quality timely repairs at the right cost. In order to do this, they need to have good knowledge of the housing stock, effective project management, motivated staff, and effective leadership.

The PSS is a flexible framework and the titles for the seven perspectives can be changed according to the needs of the organisations. For example a hospital might prefer the title 'patient and carer' perspective to 'service user and stakeholder'.

How the Public Sector Scorecard works

The PSS is a workshop-based approach working with managers, staff, service users and other key stakeholders. A variety of facilitation and problem structuring

Figure 14.2 Public Sector Scorecard housing association example

approaches will be used, depending on the group and the problems it is grappling with (Friend and Hickling, 2004; Rosenhead and Mingers, 2001). It has three phases – strategy mapping, service improvement and measurement and evaluation – see Figure 14.3.

Strategy mapping

As with the BSC, the strategy map is a key output of the PSS. According to Kaplan and Norton (2001a: 11) a strategy map 'describes how shareholder value is created from intangible assets'. However with the PSS it can be defined more simply as 'depicting the relationships between outcome, process, and capability elements' (Moullin, 2009a: 29).

The strategy map is developed following a series of interactive workshops with senior managers, staff, service users and other stakeholders. These workshops start by encouraging participants to identify the desired outcomes – strategic, service user, stakeholder and financial outcomes. As Pidd points out, 'there may well be some conflict between the strategic drivers (of the PSS) and any strategic thinking will need to balance differing claims and priorities' (Pidd, 2012: 211–12). This is important as most public and third sector organisations have a wide variety of objectives and stakeholders (Moriarty and Kennedy, 2012; McAdam, Hazlett and Casey, 2005).

Workshop participants then consider the outputs that the various processes need to achieve in order to deliver the various outcomes together with the *capability* outputs that are needed to ensure that staff and processes are able to achieve the outcomes and process outputs required. These capability outputs might include effective team and partnership working, sufficient resources, supportive leadership, together with an organisational culture which promotes innovation and learning rather than a target-obsessed blame culture.

The links between capabilities, processes and outcomes are then illustrated in a draft strategy map which is then brought to the next workshop to get feedback from participants. Risk factors will then be identified in a risk management workshop and added to the draft strategy map by considering the reduction of a key risk as a desired outcome. The processes by which risks are reduced, eliminated or mitigated are then reviewed, together with the risk management culture (a capability element) and added to the strategy map.

Service improvement

In this phase the strategy map will be used as a prompt to examine the effectiveness of different processes and how they can be improved. Feedback will have been gathered from participants and from data available from the organisation on the current problems with the processes and how to address them. This will be supplemented where appropriate with tools such as process maps, systems thinking and lean management – for example to highlight areas of duplication, processes that could be simplified or accelerated through better communication and eliminating non-productive activities such as talking to users who ring up because they have not received a service they were promised.

This or a subsequent workshop will then focus on what is required to achieve the capability outputs in the strategy map and in particular how management can

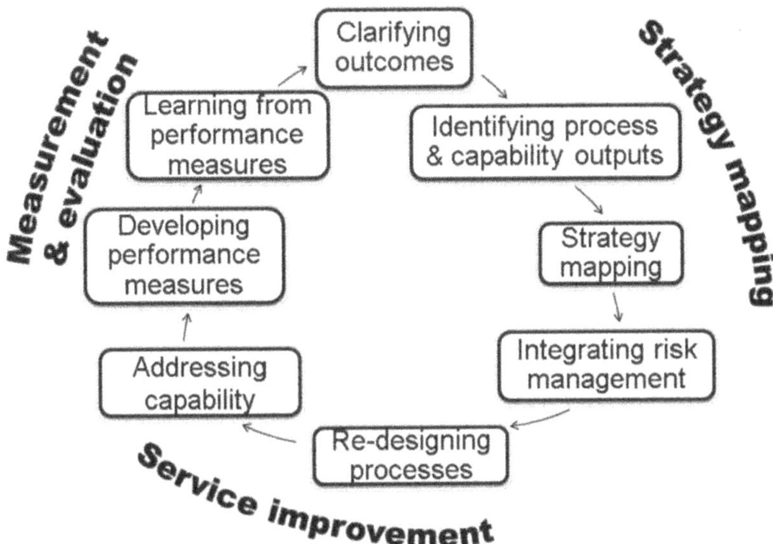

Figure 14.3 How the Public Sector Scorecard works

support staff and processes so that they can obtain the outcomes required. This could involve extra resources in a particular area, improving staff morale, and clear supportive leadership. It might also involve discussing how to develop a culture of improvement, innovation and learning rather than a blame culture.

Measurement and evaluation

This phase begins by identifying possible performance measures for each element of the strategy map. Discussion will take place with workshop participants, with information experts within the organisation, and with stakeholders and funders on their information requirements and the cost-effectiveness of different measures. It is important that the measures chosen are seen as reasonable by both staff and service users.

All potential measures identified will be reviewed by considering data quality issues, and aiming to minimise potential unwanted or perverse effects. A filtering process then takes place to ensure that the measures chosen are cost-effective and can provide value for money to the organisations concerned. Performance measurement has been defined as 'evaluating how well organisations are managed and the value they deliver for customers and other stakeholders' (Moullin, 2002: 188). This definition has a deliberate circularity – performance measurement is part of how an organisation is managed, so it too needs to deliver value to users and stakeholders (Moullin, 2007a).

Performance measures do not necessarily need to be quantitative. Indeed in many cases – particularly on some of the capability areas – more qualitative approaches are preferable. For example if improving partnership working is included in the strategy map, an assessment of progress and people's perception on what has been achieved will be better than recording the number of meetings with different organisations or other irrelevant measures.

Analysing and learning from performance measures provides insight into how well organisations are performing in the different areas of the strategy map. The use of statistical tools to determine cause and effect where possible is also useful here. Taking action to address areas needing attention is also needed!

Completing the cycle

Performance information is then used to revise the strategy map, identify further service improvements, and develop better performance measures – and so the cycle continues. Public and third sector organisations have frequent changes in strategy and it is important that the strategy map is a living document and that performance measures are aligned with a changing strategy (Johnston and Pongatichat, 2008).

Using the PSS across organisational boundaries

One of the many benefits of the PSS's outcome focus is that it facilitates working across organisational boundaries by enabling people from different organisations or departments to focus on the common outcomes required, rather than their narrower departmental objectives. This is more difficult with the BSC as this focusses on achieving greater profit or the mission of an individual organisation.

The importance of working across organisational boundaries can be seen by considering a third sector organisation whose aim is to reduce teenage pregnancy. In the UK research showed that 71 per cent of young women not in education, employment or training for over 6 months between the ages of 16 and 18 were parents by the age of 21 (DCSF, 2006). It follows that working together with schools, colleges and local employers to improve outcomes for this group is likely to be more effective than working in isolation.

The case studies below show how the outcome focus of the PSS can facilitate joint working.

Case study 1: the Ethnic Minority Employment Task Force

The UK Ethnic Minority Employment Task Force was unusual in that it included government ministers from five UK government departments, together with other stakeholders, mainly from the third sector. It was set up in 2003 to drive forward strategies designed to ensure ethnic minorities no longer faced disproportionate barriers to achievement in the labour market.

The Task Force began by recognising that to achieve the main desired outcome of increasing ethnic minority employment, they needed to address three subsidiary outcomes: building employability, connecting people to work, and equal opportunities.

The next stage was to identify the outputs needed to achieve these outcomes and which government departments should take the lead on each output. As can be seen from the strategy map (Figure 14.4), building employability was predominantly down to the Department for Education and Skills, while the other two outcomes were the joint responsibility of a number of different government departments. Also shown in Figure 14.4 are some of the capability aspects – specific activities that were identified as important to achieve the outcomes and outputs, together with effective partnership working between departments and leadership from the task force which were recognised as also vital to the achievement of these outcomes. The strategy map shows clearly how the contribution of each department related to the overall outcome, as well as helping in the evaluation.

A number of performance measures were developed for the different outcome and outputs in the strategy map. In addition each department was responsible for monitoring progress on the activities they were responsible for. One of the key performance criteria for the Task Force was to reduce the gap between the employment rate of ethnic minorities and that of Great Britain as a whole. This reduced from 18 to 12 percentage points from 2003 to 2010.

Case study 2: Sheffield Let's Change4Life

Sheffield Let's Change4Life (SLC4L) was a three-year £10 million programme set up to reduce obesity in children and families, part-funded by the Department of

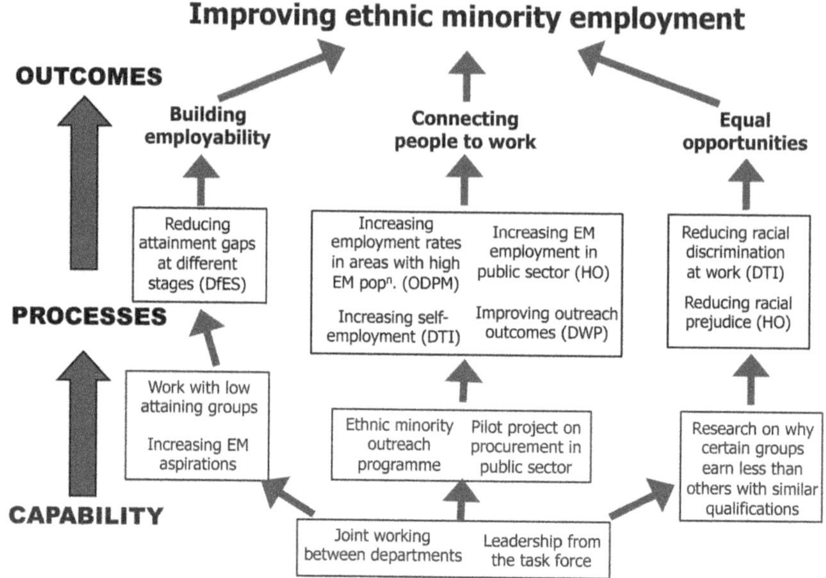

Figure 14.4 Strategy map for the Ethnic Minority Employment Task Force

Note: Abbreviations: DfES, Department for Education and Skills; OPDM, Office of Deputy Prime Minister; HO, Home Office; DTI, Department of Trade and Industry; DWP, Department of Work and Pensions

Health. The programme adopted a systems-based approach, aiming to tackle a number of the barriers to reducing obesity simultaneously. This was informed partly by the Foresight Report (Foresight, 2007) and partly by workshops using the PSS carried out as part of a government-sponsored Knowledge Exchange Programme between Sheffield Business School and NHS Sheffield. Once the bid was successful, it was decided to use the PSS to evaluate the programme.

The PSS approach to evaluation is to work with the programme team and relevant stakeholders to develop the evaluation strategy early on in the programme. This both enables the evaluation strategy to inform the project and avoids managers and staff later feeling aggrieved because the evaluation is based on factors they were unaware of.

A series of interactive workshops were therefore held early on with the programme board – which included the director of public health, the city council's executive director for children and families, a cabinet member (city councillor) and other stakeholders – with Sheffield Youth Council, and with the teams responsible for each of the eight programme strands to develop draft strategy maps both for the project as a whole and for each individual strand.

There was a problem though with all the initial strategy maps developed, as they were unable to pinpoint cause and effect between activities and outcomes. This is important – whether for the BSC (Kaplan and Norton, 2001a: 76) or the PSS.

None of the activities planned could actually get people to lose weight, eat more healthily or to be more active (three of the main desired outcomes) without people themselves changing their behaviour. So how could the project make sure that their strategies will actually change people's behaviour in the right direction? Also how will they know whether they have been successful or how any success was achieved?

The approach taken to resolve this problem was to incorporate the evidence-based theory of planned behaviour (Ajzen, 1991) into the PSS. The theory of planned behaviour (TPB) recognises that people's intention to change depends on their beliefs on how important it is to make the change, their attitude and those of others around them to the change, their perceived ability to make the change, and overcoming the barriers that they face. Given that actions taken to reduce obesity can only work by children and adults changing their behaviour, it is important to address – and monitor the progress of – the factors that influence such change.

The main relevance of the TPB for strategy mapping is that when developing a strategy which requires people to change their behaviour, it is important to recognise that the organisation needs to address a number of issues simultaneously: people's beliefs on how important it is to make the change, their attitude and those of others around them to the change, their perceived ability to make the change, and overcoming the barriers that they face.

The strategy map for the SLC4L programme as a whole is shown in Figure 14.5. This was developed following interactive workshops with the programme board, operational leads and stakeholders of the eight programme strands, and Sheffield Youth Council. Rows A and B show the main outcomes required for the project. The main desired outcome was to reduce obesity, while other key outcomes which will contribute towards this overall outcome include better diet and nutrition and increased physical activity. Satisfied stakeholders, sustainability and value for money were also key aims.

Row C contains the TPB outputs and outcomes – a greater desire to adopt a healthy lifestyle; favourable attitudes; confidence in their ability to change; and overcoming the barriers they face – while elements D1 to D8 refer to the desired outcomes and outputs of the eight strands of the programme.

The penultimate row, row E, shows the main elements that need to be in place to support individual strands including joint working and a shared vision between Sheffield City Council, the NHS, and the third and private sectors, community engagement, and effective project management, all of which need to be underpinned by effective leadership and support from the programme board (row F).

As can be seen, the outcome-focused approach of the PSS allowed it to incorporate the TPB relatively easily. Indeed, as with the BSC (Kaplan and Norton, 2001a: 76) identifying cause and effect between different elements is a key part of the PSS and the TPB provides a link between activities and outcomes. To be successful each of the eight strands needed to address the various elements in Row C, which in turn would lead to progress in achieving the outcomes in rows B and A. For example, for the breastfeeding-friendly city strand to achieve its main outcome of increased breastfeeding in the city, they needed to encourage more women to want to breastfeed, to see breastfeeding as a socially approved behaviour, to be more confident

Figure 14.5 Strategy map for Sheffield Let's Change4Life

that they can breastfeed successfully, and to help overcome the barriers that women face in trying to breastfeed.

Using the Public Sector Scorecard to evaluate Sheffield Let's Change4Life

The strategy map was used to help managers and strand leads focus on the desired outcomes, to understand and explore with them how change might be expected to happen, and to monitor and evaluate performance. The evaluation team assessed the impact of SLC4L on each of the elements of the strategy map in Figure 14.5, using a variety of measures and approaches (Moullin and Copeland, 2013). The TPB outcomes C1–C4 were assessed using questionnaires asking participants before and after a intervention on each of these aspects in turn. In some cases it proved difficult to get a high percentage of responses without burdening participants with questionnaires and/or affecting the relationship between client and provider.

Each of the eight strands was evaluated on its impact on the elements in rows A–C of the overall strategy map and also with respect to the desired outputs and outcomes on the relevant strand strategy map. In addition any insights from strand members in relation to the elements in rows E and F of the overall strategy map were also noted.

An example of the benefits of incorporating the TPB can be seen from the evaluation of a workshop on diet and exercise provided for workers at a Sheffield steel manufacturer. While feedback from participants was very positive, the evaluation also revealed that the company did not have space for a canteen on site – but there was a convenient mobile burger bar parked outside the factory gates every lunch-time! Clearly, unless that particular barrier is overcome, a single information-giving workshop was unlikely to lead to a significant change in obesity levels of workers or their families. Using the strategy map the evaluation team was able to capture increases in the desire of participants to gain a healthy weight and their confidence in their ability to do so – but also that a key barrier needed to be addressed before there was likely to be a significant change in obesity rates.

Feedback on the use of the PSS was very positive. Sheffield City Council's executive director of children, young people and families said that 'the strategy map is really useful as it simplifies a complex issue with a complex response into an orderly understandable approach', while the SLC4L programme director, commented:

> The SLC4L Strategy Map was a very useful tool in terms of explaining and evaluating the programme. The format of the map was easy to understand and was used to great success with deliverers of the programme, as well as other stakeholders, leadership across the City, and the public. It visually told the story of SLC4L, what we were trying to achieve and how. It also helped all those involved understand the outcome and process measures the programme was trying to achieve, and therefore being evaluated against. It provided an 'at a glance' understanding of SLC4L.

Key features of the Public Sector Scorecard

The PSS has a number of features which are critical to its success. These include the following.

Service user and stakeholder involvement

As mentioned previously, service user and stakeholder involvement is an important aspect of a PSS project. Service user involvement 'places the experiences and knowledge of the service user at the heart of effective public service design and delivery' (Osborne, Radnor and Nasi, 2013: 146). Similarly involvement of front-line staff was found to be crucial to the success of the BSC and other performance improvement initiatives (Barden, 2004). However managers – and facilitators – should also guard against tokenism – involving users and staff, but in practice ignoring what they have to offer (Buckley and Hutson, 2004).

By involving users, staff and other key stakeholders in an interactive workshop setting, the PSS enables the service to make use of participants' knowledge and understanding of service delivery and to address the needs of these stakeholders. It also leads to more successful implementation since participants feel they have contributed to the process of service improvement rather than feel that change is imposed on them.

Focus on outcomes

Identifying the outcomes required by the organisation, its service users and other stakeholders – including value for money – is the starting point of a PSS study and this outcome focus drives the entire PSS project, helping the organisation or group of organisations focus on achieving these outcomes.

Integrating service and process improvement

As mentioned earlier, the service improvement phase of the PSS provides considerably more emphasis on operations management than the BSC. The emphasis on outcomes in the PSS also ensures that work on process improvement is done in the context of improving outcomes, rather than activity-based measures. There are many process improvement methodologies originating from the manufacturing sector which have been used with varying success in the public sector, such as lean and Six Sigma (Womack and Jones, 2006; Antony, 2007). However care needs to be taken in adapting these methodologies to reflect differences between the two sectors. One of the differences between the sectors is that individual service users may have differing requirements and therefore a quality service for one person may not be the same as for another (Moullin, 2008). Another difference making the use of lean in the public and third sectors problematic is the conflict between different stakeholders and in particular service user and taxpayer requirements (Radnor, Holweg and Waring, 2012). Similarly because individual users – and different stakeholders – may have differing requirements, reducing variation – one of the main aims of Six Sigma – does not necessarily equate with improved quality. In addition, processes need to be robust, so that the system can cope under pressure (Moullin, 2008). Process improvement tools therefore need to be used with care to make sure that other aspects are not compromised. This is particularly important in services with unpredictable fluctuations in demand, for example a hospital or emergency service.

The PSS can overcome these issues by identifying all the outcomes required – strategic, user and stakeholder, and financial – before using a process improvement approach. Often improvement ideas come out of the workshop sessions, but further analysis is needed to make them work. For example workshops with the reference group on the Stop Smoking service project identified two problems with the processes. One was the telephone support service which was inadequate to meet demand. Given financial constraints, additional staff was not an option. So instead they worked with other health-related helplines (e.g. NHS Direct), who with the relevant information could answer calls in the evenings or weekends or when the Stop Smoking telephone support service was busy answering other calls. Another problem that came to light during the user workshops was that delays often occurred between a user making the momentous decision to quit smoking and being able to obtain prescriptions from the GP for nicotine patches or drugs to help them stop smoking. Through discussions with pharmacies and with GPs, innovative ways were found to bypass the GP and get the medicines direct from the pharmacy. Both these innovations resulted in better outcomes at lower overall cost (Moullin *et al.*, 2007).

Integrating risk management

Integrating risk management with strategy and performance management is another important feature of the PSS. As Moullin (2006) says, 'identifying and addressing key risks are essential for any high-performing organisation and therefore any evaluation of performance without considering risk is incomplete'. Arguably, lack of attention to this was the major cause of the banking crisis. Many people blame bonuses. However the real problem was not bonuses themselves but the fact that the performance measures on which bonuses were based did not take proper account of the risks to the banks, their customers, and society. If they had included risk factors, economic prospects in the world today would be very different!

While Kaplan (2009) recommends a separate risk management scorecard for use alongside the BSC, the PSS takes explicit account of risk by incorporating major risk factors into the strategy map. It does this by viewing the reduction of a key risk as a desired outcome, while the processes involved in reducing or mitigating the risk would appear under operational excellence. Ensuring that the organisation has a risk management capability – for example the absence of a blame culture and ensuring that the approach to risk does not stifle innovation – would appear in one or more of the capability perspectives.

Approach to targets

While the BSC typically recommends organisations to specify targets for each of the measures, this is optional in the PSS. The approach to targets is summed up in the sentence 'all targets are flawed, some are useful' (Moullin, 2009b). Targets should only be used if they relate to outcomes or evidence-based drivers of outcomes, the value of the measure exceeds its cost, the target is challenging but achievable, and potential unintended consequences identified and minimised (*ibid.*).

Nevertheless, targets can be useful too. Moullin (2010) cites the case of the UK National Health Service waiting time targets. These targets helped reduce the number of people waiting over nine months for admission to hospital from 175,000 to 223 from 1997 to 2004. It is important to note that this reduction could not have been achieved without the considerable investment in the NHS during this period. Otherwise there would have been what Deming calls 'goals without methods' which are always counter-productive (Deming, 1986: 19).

Culture of improvement, innovation and learning

Arguably the most important aspect of the PSS is its aim to assist in developing a culture of improvement, innovation and learning, rather than a top-down blame culture (Moullin, 2004). Several authors (e.g. Brooks, 2007; Smith, 1993) talk about the 'perverse' or 'unforeseen' effects of targets, but these are predictable consequences of a top-down performance management culture which encourages staff to prioritise an inevitably flawed target over service to the public (Moullin, 2009b).

Given that all targets are flawed, it does not make sense to blame managers for performance below target without a dialogue as to what might have caused the apparent level of performance. The Care Quality Commission did take note of this by allowing NHS Trusts to submit extenuating circumstances that might have affected their ability to meet a target (Care Quality Commission, 2009). Rewarding people for performance above target without further analysis is similarly premature – as the risk-ignoring bank bonuses scandal demonstrates.

The tone needs to be set early on in a PSS study with both a director of the service and the workshop facilitator emphasising the importance of openness and trust within a performance management culture based on improvement, innovation and change at the beginning of each workshop session.

Conclusion

Performance management in the public and third sectors is understandably controversial. When done well it can motivate staff to improve performance and can 'reveal the true performance of the system and the impact of any changes in real time' (NHS Modernisation Agency, 2004: 11). When done poorly, however, it can alienate employees and lead to a culture of blame where staff meet targets at the expense of service to the public (Moullin, 2009a).

The way performance is managed affects all areas of operations and therefore operations management has a key role here. The PSS is an effective framework for helping public and third sector organisations monitor and improve their services and focus on delivering desired outcomes including value for money. The incorporation of process mapping, systems thinking and lean management approaches ensures that service improvement is considered in relation to the outcomes required including value for money. Furthermore it does not stop at processes – it addresses risk management, organisation culture and capability to ensure that staff and processes are supported in delivering the required outcomes.

Finally, by measuring performance on outcome, process and capability elements, the PSS enables managers and others to identify where the organisation is making progress. Described as 'groundbreaking' by a former head of research at the New York Senate (Penna, 2011: 243–5), it is consistent with the recommendation in the Darzi report that 'NHS services … will need to develop their own quality frameworks combining relevant indicators defined nationally, with those appropriate to local circumstances' (Department of Health, 2008: 50). Applications include central and local government and health services, mainly in the UK, but also in North and South America, the Middle East and South Africa.

Three research questions would benefit from further investigation. The first of these is whether the outcomes and operations management focus of the PSS provides benefits for public and third sector organisations, compared with other performance management frameworks. A second area is examining whether the incorporation of service improvement within an outcome-focused framework like the PSS has advantages for public and third sector services, compared with using service improvement methods in isolation. A third research area would be examining different approaches to incorporating risk management within performance management frameworks such as the BSC and the PSS.

References

Ajzen, I. (1991) 'The theory of planned behavior'. *Organizational Behavior and Human Decision Processes*, 50(2): 179–211.

Antony, J. (2007) 'Six Sigma: a strategy for supporting innovation in pursuit of business excellence'. *International Journal of Technology Management*, 37(1–2): 8–12.

Balanced Scorecard Collaborative (2004) *Using the Balanced Scorecard to create value in the Electric Cooperative Community*. Lincoln, MA: Balanced Scorecard Collaborative.

Barden, P. (2004) 'A new prescription for NHS performance'. *Financial Management*, June.

Bourne, M. and Bourne, P. (2007) *Balanced Scorecard*. London: Chartered Management Institute.

Brooks, R. (ed.) (2007) *Public Services at the Crossroads*. London: Institute for Public Policy Research.

Buckley, J. and Hutson, T. (2004) 'User involvement in care: avoiding tokenism and achieving partnership'. *Professional Nurse*, 19(9): 499–501.

Cairns, B., Harris, M., Hutchison, R. and Tricker, M. (2005) 'Improving performance? The adoption and implementation of quality systems in UK nonprofits'. *Nonprofit Management and Leadership*, 16: 135–51.

Care Quality Commission (2009) *Annual Health Check 2008/9*. March. Newcastle upon Tyne: Care Quality Commission.

DCSF(2006) *Youth Matters*. London: HMSO.

Deming, W.E. (1986) *Out of the Crisis*. Cambridge, MA: MIT Press.

Department of Health (2008) *High Quality Care for All: NHS Next Stage Review Final Report*. London: Department of Health.

EFQM (2013) *The Excellence Model*. Brussels: European Foundation for Quality Management.

Elliott, C. (2012) 'Use of the balanced scorecard at Leeds Federated Housing Association'. *Customer Insight*, 2(2): 30–31.

Fältholm, Y. and Nilsson, K. (2010) 'Business process re-engineering and Balanced Scorecard in Swedish public sector organizations: solutions for problems or problems for solutions?' *International Journal of Public Administration*, 33(6): 302–10.

Foresight (2007) *Tackling Obesities*. Future Choices Report. London: Government Office for Science.

Friend, J. and Hickling, A. (2004) *Planning Under Pressure*. Abingdon: Routledge.

Gambles, I. (1999) 'A balanced future lies in the cards'. *Public Finance*, 16–22 April: 24–5.

Greatbanks, R. and Tapp, D. (2007) 'The impact of balanced scorecards in a public sector environment: empirical evidence from Dunedin City Council, New Zealand'. *International Journal of Operations and Production Management*, 27(8): 846–73.

Gurd, B. and Gao, T. (2008) 'Lives in the balance: an analysis of the balanced scorecard (BSC) in healthcare organisations'. *International Journal of Productivity and Performance Management*, 57(1): 6–21.

Irwin, D. (2002) 'Strategy mapping in the public sector'. *Long Range Planning*, 35(6): 637–47.

Johnston, R. and Pongatichat, P. (2008) 'Managing the tension between performance measurement and strategy: coping strategies'. *International Journal of Operations and Production Management*, 28(10): 941–67.

Kaplan, R.S. (2009) *Risk Management and the Strategy Execution System*. Balanced Scorecard Report, 11(6). Boston, MA: Harvard Business School Press.

Kaplan, R.S. and Norton, D.P. (1992) 'The balanced scorecard, measures that drive performance'. *Harvard Business Review*, 70(1): 71–9.

Kaplan, R.S. and Norton, D.P. (2001a) *The Strategy-Focused Organization*. Boston, MA: Harvard Business School Press.

Kaplan, R.S. and Norton, D.P. (2001b) 'Transforming the balanced scorecard from performance measurement to strategic management: part 1'. *Accounting Horizons*, 15(1): 87–104.

Lawrie, G. and Cobbold, I. (2004). *How a Public Sector Agency Re-invigorated its Balanced Scorecard*. Maidenhead: Active Management.

Link, A.N. and Scott, J.T. (2011) *Economic Evaluation of the Baldrige Performance Excellence Program*. Gaithersburg, MD: NIST.

Martin, J., Haines J., Bovaird, T. and Wisniewski, M. (2002). 'Developing a Balanced Scorecard in Somerset and social services community'. In Neely, A. and Walters, A. (ed.), *Proceedings of the Performance Measurement Association Annual Conference*, pp. 749–56. Boston, MA: Performance Measurement Association.

McAdam, R., Hazlett, S. and Casey, C. (2005) 'Performance management in the UK public sector: addressing multiple stakeholder complexity'. *International Journal of Public Sector Management*, 18(3): 256–73.

Moore, M.H. (2003) *The Public Value Scorecard: A Rejoinder and an Alternative to 'Strategic Performance Measurement and Management in Non-Profit Organisations' by Robert Kaplan*. Working Paper #18. Cambridge, MA: Kennedy School of Government, Harvard University.

Moriarty, P. and Kennedy, D. (2002) 'Performance measurement in public sector services: problems and potential'. In Neely, A. and Walters, A. (ed.), *Proceedings of the Performance Measurement Association Annual Conference*, pp. 395–402. Boston, MA: Performance Measurement Association.

Moullin, M. (2002) *Delivering Excellence in Health and Social Care*. Buckingham: Open University Press.

Moullin, M. (2004) 'Evaluating a health service taskforce'. *International Journal of Health Care Quality Assurance*, 17: 5.

Moullin, M. (2006) *The Design of an Alternative Balanced Scorecard Framework for Public and Voluntary Organizations*. Perspectives on Performance, 5(1). Boston, MA: Performance Measurement Association.

Moullin, M. (2007a) 'Performance measurement definitions: linking performance measurement and organisational excellence'. *International Journal of Health Care Quality Assurance*, 20(3): 181–83.

Moullin, M. (2007b) *The Public Sector Scorecard*. Excellence One. March. Brussels: EFQM.

Moullin, M. (2008) 'Lean and Six Sigma – Can they really be applied to healthcare?' *National Health Executive Magazine*, Lean and Six Sigma Supplement, September.

Moullin, M. (2009a) 'Using the Public Sector Scorecard to measure and improve healthcare services'. *Nursing Management*, September, 16(5): 26–31.

Moullin, M. (2009b) 'What's the score?' Feature Article, *Public Finance*, 21 (May).

Moullin, M. (2010) 'Careful targets can help to achieve goals'. *Local Government Chronicle*, 11 (February).

Moullin, M. and Copeland, R. (2013) 'Implementing and evaluating behaviour change programmes with the Public Sector Scorecard'. *National Health Executive*, July–August: 16–18.

Moullin, M., Soady, J, Skinner, J., Price, C., Cullen, J. and Gilligan, C. (2007) 'Using the Public Sector Scorecard in public health'. *International Journal of Health Care Quality Assurance,* 20(4): 281–89.

NHS Modernisation Agency (2004) *10 High Impact Changes for service improvement and delivery*. Leicester: NHS Modernisation Agency.

Niven, P.R. (2003) *Balanced Scorecard Step-by-Step for Government and Non-Profit Agencies*. Hoboken, NJ: John Wiley & Sons.

Norreklit, H. (2000) 'The balance of the balanced scorecard – a critical analysis of some of its assumptions'. *Management Accounting Research*, 11: 65–88.

Northcott, D. and Taulapapa, T.M. (2012) 'Using the balanced scorecard to manage performance in public sector organizations: issues and challenges'. *International Journal of Public Sector Management,* 25(3): 166–91.

Osborne, S.P., Radnor, Z.J. and Nasi, G. (2013) 'A new theory for public service management? Towards a (public) service dominant approach'. *The American Review of Public Administration,* 43(2): 135–58.

Penna, B. (2011) *The Nonprofit Outcomes Toolbox: A Complete Guide to Program Effectiveness, Performance Measurement, and Results.* Hoboken, NJ: John Wiley & Sons.

Pidd, M. (2012) *Measuring the Performance of Public Services*. Cambridge: Cambridge University Press.

Radnor, Z.J. and Lovell, B. (2003) 'Success factors for implementation of the Balanced Scorecard in a NHS multi-agency setting'. *International Journal of Health Care Quality Assurance*, 16(2): 99–108.

Radnor, Z.J., Holweg, H. and Waring, J. (2012) 'Lean in healthcare: the unfilled promise?' *Social Science and Medicine*, 74(3): 364–71.

Rosenhead, J. and Mingers, J. (2001) *Rational Analysis for a Problematic World Revisited*. Chichester: John Wiley.

Smith, P. (1993) 'Outcome-related performance indicators and organizational control in the public sector'. *British Journal of Management*, 4(3): 135–51.

Womack, J. and Jones, D. (2003) *Lean Thinking*. London: Simon & Schuster.

Part IV

Improvement

15 Deconstructing lean policing in England and Wales

A knowledge creation perspective

Harry Barton and Rupert L. Matthews

Introduction

Since the late 1970s successive UK governments have attempted to implement reforms across the English and Welsh police service (Seneviratne, 2004). From a financial standpoint, policing is expensive, with a budget approaching £13 billion and employing upwards of 230,000 operational and support personnel. Policing is also 'expensive' from a societal and political standpoint, with poor policing practice negatively impacting public trust. This creates a complex situation for police and crime commissioners (PCCs) and their respective chief constables, who are under pressure to reduce spending and to improve the effectiveness of the policing services they deliver. Notwithstanding such mutually exclusive drivers of improvement, further complexity has been introduced in recent decades. While public attitudes towards the police are generally positive, it is evident that the social context of policing is changing. As society has become increasingly divisive and fragmented, requirements of the police have changed. Consequently, the police services within England and Wales face an internal need and external pressure to undergo transformation.

The challenge for the police therefore is to introduce innovative ways of improving efficiency and productivity of existing services, while at the same time improving public opinion as to their effectiveness in their 'fight against crime'. This is likely to require significant reform, which will have a major impact on the form and structure of police organisations in England and Wales. To undergo such a dramatic transformation, it will also be necessary for those within the policing services to question their existing values and critically reflect on the role they see the service taking within society. As such, the pressure for 'reform' of established management practices as a proxy for improving performance within the police has led to tensions both internal and external stakeholders. While there is pressure from external stakeholders such as political leaders and the public for change, there is resistance from internal stakeholders who fear that significant changes will affect their ability to police effectively. For example, rank and file officers recognise that there is a need for some reform, although many reject calls for greater change (Garcia, 2005). Set against this resistance, successive governments have been frustrated in their many attempts at wide-scale reform.

Locating discussions with the backdrop of the 2008 global financial crisis, the coalition government's Comprehensive Spending Review (CSR) 2010 has been implemented. As a result significant budgetary cuts across the police service in England and Wales have been made that required significant structural change. Driven by the Police Reform and Social Responsibility Act, 2011, changes have included the direct election of PCCs in November 2012. The PCCs are responsible for the appointment of their chief constables, for the budget, staff, estate and other assets in their force area and to ensure that there are appropriate performance management systems in place. PPCs thus provide a new governance mechanism, able to critically review existing budgets and implement widespread reform.

Such radical reforms across the police service have been long overdue and it is the ability of organisations such as the police to resist reform that has often led to a situation of spiralling costs but little evidence of improvements in service performance. Contrast this situation to that of private sector organisations, who over the last decades have constantly been under pressure to reform working and operational practices.

For example western automotive manufacturers having experienced similar internal and external pressures during the 1980s and 1990s, employed methods that have transformed their industry. Such methods might now provide opportunities to support the transformation of policing. Work within the domain of operational improvement illustrates how selected improvement methods can deliver improvements in a range of organisational measures. Compared with traditional thinking, and consistent with the context of policing, the new approaches are able to perform well in terms of both cost and performance without experiencing traditional trade-offs in service levels (Ferdows and De Meyer, 1990; Womack *et al.*, 1990). From this perspective, the potential benefits of employing similar improvement frameworks make them highly appealing within the public sector context (Radnor and O'Mahoney, 2013). Of the improvement frameworks available, the 'lean' perspective is often favoured due to its emphasis on easily understood tools and techniques that can be quickly and relatively cheaply acquired (Hines, Holweg, and Rich, 2004).

Theoretical background

The origins of lean manufacturing are generally attributed to Japan in the 1950s, where resource limitations and the social climate necessitated and facilitated the development and acceptance of new manufacturing logics (Xu, 1999). However, key factors that supported a lean approach to operating can be traced further back to Henry Ford in the 1910s and even the American civil war (Womack *et al.*, 1990; Garvin, 1988). With the latest approaches to organisational improvement often being viewed as fads or fashions (Thawesaengskulthai and Tannock, 2008; Abrahamson, 1991), to differentiate lean from existing management approaches, attention has been given to how lean differs from existing improvement thinking. Hines *et al.* (2004) presented this as resulting in lean frequently being defined in terms of the use of tools and techniques developed within the automotive industry that help order work practices and reduce non-value adding activities (Bicheno and Holweg, 2009).

However, unless firms are able to appreciate the aims and underlying principles of lean, focusing upon the delivery of increased customer value rather than simply reducing waste, lean tools make a limited contribution to sustained improvement (Bateman, 2005).

Work attempting to unpack and untangle the critical components of lean have returned insightful results that support the transfer of practices across organisations and even domains. Survey based research has illustrated how good operations management, in terms of a formalised manufacturing strategy, combined with quality management practices facilitate lean techniques (Flynn and Flynn, 2004; Flynn, Schroeder and Flynn, 1999). Work has also illustrated how lean may provide the foundation on which to pursue other improvement frameworks that reflect the needs of specific operating environments, such as an agile orientation (Narasimhan, Swink and Kim, 2006). However, much of the work into lean appears to under estimate the role of process level changes, measurement and specific quality management practices, by instead emphasising what differentiates lean from existing management approaches.

While lean tools and techniques play an important role within Lean, they can be viewed as developments and refinements of existing quality management tools (Xu, 1999). Lean tools can be viewed as means of assisting in problem solving and focusing improvements upon the customers (by defining waste and activities the customer is not willing to pay for), rather than whole focusing upon controlling operational processes. A critical review by Womack *et al.* (1990), complemented by the insightful reflection by Holweg (2007), highlights the role quality management practices played in the development of lean manufacturing. This included the dissemination of quality management practices across the supply chain in Japan. By reducing the need for inspection of incoming goods, attention can instead be focused upon internal improvement. Without such practices in place, the implementation and maintenance of lean tools and techniques seems difficult at best. The implications of this insight create further problems when attempting to implement these techniques into the public sector and service context. Unless process inputs are consistent, lean techniques, developed within the high volume world of the automotive industry are unlikely to be appropriate (Towill and Christopher, 2005).

Although there appear to be inconsistencies between the contexts of manufacturing and public sector management, the need for public sector improvement have outweighed concerns for the limitations. The need for improvement has been driven by the poor health of public sector finances, balanced by the need to maintain or improvement standards (Barton, 2013). In response to this, recent years have seen a marked increase in the use of established improvement techniques within the public sector in order to achieve targets set by external stakeholders (Radnor and O'Mahoney, 2013). Waring and Bishop (2010) report on ethnographic research conducted in the healthcare sector, highlighting difficulties and resistance experienced during the introduction of lean management. Withstanding these inconsistencies in relation to the lean improvement framework, there is considerable literature associated with 'lean thinking' within public sector domains (Barton, 2013; Hines and Lethbridge, 2008; Bhatia and Drew, 2006; Radnor *et al.*, 2006).

The drive for improvement and limitations identified with lean is further emphasised by the implementation of more complex and structured improvement frameworks, such as Six Sigma in the public sector. Antony *et al.* (2007) presents Six Sigma as an alternate improvement methodology to overcome limitations of existing improvement frameworks within the public sector. While Six Sigma has greater investment requirements compared to lean, recent research illustrates how the greater emphasis given within Six Sigma to training and measurement supports its transfer to the public sector domain (Dedhia, 2005; O'Rourke, 2005; Revere *et al.* 2004; Revere and Black, 2003). While the current research is not exploring the Six Sigma framework, the differentiating characteristics of the framework provide additional practices of training and measurement to consider when analysing lean implementation within the police setting.

Combined with empirical evidence, logically argued cases for the relevance of these improvement frameworks for the public sector provide support for their potential utility within the police service. Various authors have presented arguments for their applicability, with substantial operational and organisational benefits realised from the adoption of lean thinking and management (Barton, 2013; Berry, 2009; Flanagan, 2008). To date, the most cited examples of lean application have been within the health services (Radnor and Walley, 2008), it appears logical to surmise that similar improvements can be made to other public service domains. While not defining their approach as explicitly lean, Greasley (2004) outlines aspects of a lean approach in order to make improvements to the human resource division of a UK police force. In fact, there is a growing body of evidence from the other public service environments of the relevance of an array of operational improvement frameworks (Radnor and Boaden, 2008). These illustrate that lean interventions can provide improvements in service performance, improved processing times, help achieve 'better value for money' and ultimately reduced costs (Barton, 2013; Hines and Lethbridge, 2008). However, at this point, there is insufficient evidence to begin drawing robust, cross-context, conclusions.

From research within the established domain of lean manufacturing, it is widely recognised that the engagement of staff is a critical success factor when implementing lean (Bateman, 2005). Lean transformations have been stated as requiring changes in both operational and organisational systems, within the police service, this means both operational police officers and administrative support staff need to be engaged in improvement activities. Further research in the police context will help extend the work of Greasley (2004), by relating improvements to a range of organisational stakeholder and long term aims of improvement initiatives outside human resource practices. Unfortunately, much literature focuses upon translating business process techniques into short term improvements in a limited range of performance measures realised in isolated interventions. Such work changes necessary for long term, strategic improvements, that include establishing changes in perceptions of those in the system (Vest and Gamm 2009; Eldridge *et al.*, 2006). Without considering how values and beliefs, that influence perception, have changed, research attention may focus upon behavioural changes in operational practices, that along will not result in organisational transformation (Vest and Gamm, 2009).

Appreciating the need to engage with those in the system and structuring an intervention accordingly is likely to have a major impact on the success of an improvement intervention. Evidence suggests that effective 'lean' implementation is predicated on the construct of people, notably 'front line staff' to make it happen and deliver improvements to the customer (Berry, 2009; Hines, Holweg and Rich, 2004; Womack *et al.*, 1990). However, appreciation of lean concepts also illustrates that frontline staff do not operating in isolation, with their success being equally reliant on other organisational members contributing to the value stream that they operate within (Hines, Holweg and Rich, 2004). While this re-emphasises the role of suppliers within lean thinking mentioned earlier, this highlights potential concerns with how lean is implemented within the public sector. Berry effectively illustrates issues with this situation, where focusing attention on frontline staff in isolation in terms of training rather than educating them and their managers in lean: '[there is a] danger that forces will seek to apply a few 'lean' tools and techniques to produce impressive short-term results, instead of seeking sustainable, continuous improvement and a true cultural shift' (Berry, 2009: 11).

While short-term cost savings may be impressive, without embedding new, and revised values and beliefs within those affected, improvements are likely to be short lived until behaviours revert to pre-intervention levels (Vest and Gamm, 2009; Bateman, 2005). In order to address this issue, 'developing a culture that creates the involvement of everyone in the organization is critical for the implementation of the lean philosophy' (Radnor and Walley, 2008: 14). However, Bititci *et al.* (2006) illustrate in their longitudinal study of performance measurement that perceptions of those in an organisation change as a result of performance measurement. De Leeuw and van der Berg (2011) provide further insight, in terms of managerial support developing operator understanding, promoting motivation and ultimately improving performance. However, such processes requires the sustained support of management to both maintain measurement systems and support operators in using them, which short-term lean interventions do not account for, reiterating the critical role of measurement systems in improvement approaches.

Such a focus on key behavioural characteristics recognises a paradox among, and a cross-over between both public and private sector organisations. Understanding of these key elements of an organisation's occupational sub–culture are likely, to an extent, to predict the (un)successful outcome of significant change programmes or any attempts at whole scale organisational reform. To address such issues, systematically developed, strategically oriented performance measurement systems may play a key role in aligning perceptions of those in the organisation toward improvement.

A further issue for consideration within the public sector, is that roles are considerably more defined, with established professional identities that may have been developed through extensive practice based training (Drucker, 1955: 292). McNulty (2003) illustrates how professionals may deliberately subvert managerial improvement programmes that attempt to reorganise their complex work practices. Consequently, automotive workers may be more willing to accept and implement new manufacturing techniques, when compared to doctors, nurses or police constables, who may resist changes to a much greater extent, as illustrated by Waring and Bishop (2010) and Radnor *et al.* (2012). Without characterising and understanding these behavioural elements, organisations will have little chance in innovatively and proactively changing as well as sustaining that change.

In addition to the difficult in embedded change into public sector staff, a key difference is also related to defining the form of changes required by improvement initiatives. The need to reduce non-value adding activities and improvement reliability as defined by the customer is an accepted pressure within the manufacturing sector resulting from global competition and has been researched in depth (Barton and Delbridge, 2006). In comparison, the multiple stakeholders in the public sector and the complexity of the process make it difficult to define where improvements need to be made and when they have been made. In addition, the protected nature of public sector organisations has resulted in institutionalised processes being protected from the changes in the organisational environment. As a result, those working in the public sector may not appreciate there is a pressing need for change and even if they did realise there was a need for change, they may not know what needs to be changed.

Conceptual framework development

Browning and Eppinger (2002: 428) stated that 'process improvement requires process understanding', where it is necessary for practitioners to explore operational processes in order to make appropriate changes that will deliver the desired improvements. To integrate the above discussions in terms of balancing the use of tools, changes in values and beliefs and improvements in performance, research into lean implementation can benefit from drawing from a knowledge based perspective (Grant 1996). Previous research into operations improvement initiatives has illustrated the critical role of knowledge creation in terms of the outcomes of quality improvement projects (Anand *et al.*, 2010; Choo *et al.*, 2007; Linderman *et al.*, 2003; Mukherjee *et al.*, 1998). This perspective accounts for the changes in practices that realise immediately from process changes, but also how conceptual learning can be applied within subsequent operational and improvement behaviours. Hines *et al.* (2004) applied this perspective specifically within the context of lean, conceptualising lean as an organisational learning process, drawing from work by Fiol and Lyles (1985: 803), as 'a process of improving action through better knowledge and understanding'.

From this theoretical perspective, lean tools can be conceptualised in as means of knowledge creation, with tacit knowledge representing changes in values and beliefs that individuals may not be able to articulate, but may affect their perceptions and behaviour (Nonaka and Takeuchi, 1995). More traditional operations management practices of performance measurement then represent means of maintaining changes in behaviours. Performance measurement practices also allow the gradual accumulation of tacit knowledge, that is then internalised and embedded as revised values and beliefs (Bititci *et al.*, 2006). To enable these concepts to be explored within the police service, the analytical framework proposed by Mukherjee *et al.* (1998) and developed by Anand *et al.* (2010) will be applied to the context of lean implementation in the context of police. The framework relates quality management tools to different points of Nonaka's (1994) knowledge creation cycle. The framework will be adapted for the use of lean by drawing from Kumar *et al.* (2006) who presented how a selection of quality management tools were related to lean and Six Sigma (Table 15.1).

This perspective on lean may begin to explain why so many lean implementation initiatives, particularly within the public sector, have failed. Consistent with Waring and Bishop (2010), but within a manufacturing environment, Browning and Heath (2009) argue that key limitations lie in the impact environmental contexts or organisational contingencies can have on lean initiatives. Such contingencies can significantly affect the relationship between lean practices and cost reduction. This suggests that regardless of establishing *what* lean is, it remains important to establish, that 'to operate in an efficient and effective manner, this is defined as a firm becoming "lean"' (*ibid.*: 23). A knowledge creation perspective on lean implementation emphasises the need for practitioners to create new knowledge relevant for a changing operating environment, with the tools simply providing a means rather than an end of the initiative. This perspective is consistent with Pil and Fujimoto (2007) and Lee and Jo (2007), who illustrated the need to adapt the implementation of lean within the automotive sector, to account for organisational contingencies.

As a consequence, the reality may be that in the policing context, the adoption of some of the principles of 'lean' may prove more useful within a broader framework of progressive operational management. This may leave broader performance improvements to be advanced through police force benchmarking in order to develop context specific best practice approaches that are adapted to individual contexts. This perspective on operational practices is consistent with scholarly observations, where the best firms need not necessarily have implemented a particular improvement framework to perform well (Powell, 1995; Womack *et al.*, 1990). Such a perspective provides organisations support for using process improvement frameworks provided by operations management to develop best practices of their own (Greasley, 2004).

Table 15.1 Lean tools

	To tacit	*To explicit*
From tacit	Brainstorming, 5 why, team problem solving	Value stream mapping, cause effect (fishbone diagram)
From explicit	Error (mistake) proofing, control charts, training for frontline operators, training for senior managers, job rotation, visual management	Scatter diagram, histograms, Pareto analysis

Source: adapted from Anand *et al.* (2010)

Research approach

To explore how individual police forces implemented these business improvement initiatives and the long-term impact of these initiatives, in July 2011 funding was secured to conduct a pilot study of five police forces within England and Wales. The intention was to observe the reality of lean implementation, rather than believe the reported rhetoric (Waring and Bishop, 2010) surrounding the nature, variety and scope of Lean initiatives being pursued across the police service in England and Wales. The research took the form of a theory building case study approach (Meredith, 1998; Eisenhardt, 1989), related to operations management techniques within the context of policing, drawing from established theoretical frameworks. By taking an abductive (Järvensivu and Törnroos, 2010) approach, while a theoretical framework is employed deductively, analysis remained inductive to facilitate the emergence of key themes.

This process was achieved by pursuing an interpretivist perspective on research interviews (Kvale and Brinkman, 2009; Radnor 2001), rather than adhering to tightly defined interview protocols. The interview technique emphasised eliciting rich stories from the interviewees, allowing them to emphasis aspects they considered relevant, reducing potential bias that can be caused by leading questions (Kvale and Brinkman, 2009; Radnor, 2001). The personal experience of the context of the lead author assisted the data collection process, providing creditability and building trust with interviewees that assisted in developing an appropriate interview context to promote open discussions (Miller and Glassner, 2004). The approach led to an active interviewing approach, that took the form of a two way conversation, that facilitated the mutual development on understanding between the interview participants about the topic of discussion (Matthews *et al.*, in press; Holstein and Gubrium, 2004). This not only reduced bias of the data collected, but through a two way dialogue, the interpretations could be continually confirmed by the author, ensuring the correct interpretation were taken from the interview, thus improving internal validity (Yin, 2009).

In the first instance, 14 chief officers and borough commanders (London) were contacted by mail. They were identified as having been engaged in an improvement initiative. Of these 14, five agreed to participate in the study, which represents an accepted response rate.

The following section reports on the analysis, initially discussing findings in terms defined by the topics of the interviews (characteristics of the lean initiative). Following an outline of the diversity of the characteristics of the lean initiatives, the framework presented in Table 15.1 is used to interpret the relevance of the findings in terms of how lean tools facilitated organisational transformation.

Case evidence and analysis

The implementation of lean is a complex process, likely to be caused by the organic process through which it developed within the automotive sector. The result is that lean is the complex collection of routines and processes that have been identified as difficult to define and replicate, providing firms that have become lean to command a sustainable competitive advantage. This introduces issues for implementing lean within police forces, where the underlying processes are qualitatively different to those present in the automotive sector. Consequently, there was great variety in how lean was conceptualised and implemented across the five police forces. Table 15.2 provides an overview of the data collected from the five police forces in relation to the types of lean practices they engaged in and characteristics of the lean interventions at each police force. While differences may have been the result of, or influenced by, a range of context specific issues, the process of selection of the lean approach is outside the scope of the current research. As a result, the activities that constitute lean and their impact on outputs will be the focus of discussions.

With each of the police forces operating within the wider context of police reform and financial constraints, there was a degree of homogeneity among the police forces in terms of the aims of their lean initiatives. Even with this consistency, each forces selected particular externally facing measures of improvement to focus their lean initiative. These included demonstrating funding delivered value for money for tax payers (Central and Swest), support investment decisions for senior officers (South), resolve operational issues (Welsh) and even as a means of improving staff morale (Metro). Importantly, with this range of objectives, it can be appreciated that a standard improvement framework is unlikely to deliver improvements on all the criteria defined by the police forces. However, it was not apparent whether the approaches of the different police forces were selected deliberately to achieve their selected aims, but the level of success does reflect some inconsistencies between approaches employed and outcomes realised.

While the specific targets had variety, the high level aims were to reduce costs and improving efficiency, unfortunately, while what needed to be achieved was largely accepted, how improvements were to be realised was less so. By viewing lean as a defined set of practices and approaches, three of the forces engaged in lean training, to acquire knowledge of what lean was and develop understanding of the tools that constituted lean. In two of the cases (South and Central), a third party consultant was employed to work with the force to implement improvements. These consisted primarily of developing improvement plans to help demonstrate to external stakeholders improvements that had been made. However, within these two cases, limited attention appeared to be given to the dissemination of lean practices throughout the organisation, with only one of the chief constables having engaged in training (South). While providing some financial benefits, the approach had no notable impact on the forces as a whole. While one of these interventions was viewed as a success by a chief constable (Central), the intervention only resulted in short-term benefits and did not promote continual improvement.

The third force that engaged in training (Swest) gave emphasis to the development of understanding of lean from within the organisation by training 'lean champions'. Following training, the 'champions' was tasked within initiating improving activities and delivering productivity and performance improvements. While champions were engaged in small group activities, that completed a number of projects that delivered 'value for money' improvements, lean initiatives were later disbanded. This was cited as a decision made by senior officers not only as a cost

Table 15.2 Case database summary

Police force	*Driver*	*Nature*	*Aims*	*Tools*	*Direct outcomes*	*Indirect outcomes*
Welsh	Following critical external audit by CPS, sponsored by Local Criminal Justice Board	Lean review of criminal justice services	Develop understanding of the process from arrest to summary trials	Brainstorming, 5 why, Value stream mapping, cause effect, cross functional workshops, visual management	Process changes, cost savings, daily team briefings	Good evidence of cultural change leading to a multi agency approach
Metro	Imposed cost cutting, Borough commander not wedded to idea that lean was the answer	Strategic objectives measured against performance indicators	Maintain staff morale during cuts	Visual management	No evidence of any adoption of lean methodologies	–
South	Chief constable	Externally supported performance improvement programme	Deliver benefits, support senior officers with investment decisions and build continuous improvement capabilities	Training for senior management, visual management, process mapping	Reduce process times of arrests	Doubts about sustainability of initiative, following removal of low hanging fruit
Central	Annual Policing Plan	Adopted Home Office QUEST (lean) programme for productivity and performance improvement	Ensure people see staff, budgets and all other resources being used wisely to deliver value for money	(Cross functional workshops, value stream mapping, cause effect, 5 why) from QUEST	Chief constable viewed initiative as a success	Chief constable to review way services are structured, planned savings to be redirected
Southwest	Funding secured to pursue productivity and performance improvements	Champions trained in lean implementation with previously secured funding	Initiate improvement activities to improve productivity and performance	Small teams, value stream mapping? Job rotation (team disbanded)	Small savings	Lean initiative disbanded

cutting measure, but also a means of disseminating lean thinking and lean practices through the organisation. Unfortunately, without subsequent resourcing or monitoring, the impact of the dissemination of lean on the organisation as a whole could not be validated.

The remaining two police forces (Metro and Welsh) engaged in less formal lean practices of measuring and sharing performance data among those affected by the need to improvement. Welsh had received a critical external audit from the Crown Prosecution Service that highlighted the need for improvement, and resulted in the improvement intervention being sponsored by the local criminal justice board. Through the application of process mapping techniques for a key activity (arrest to summary trial readiness) and multi-agency workshops, changes were made to operational processes. These activities led to the continual review of process performance within daily team briefings using team information boards. The intervention was described a resulting in a change in culture, with a greater willingness and readiness to work across agencies to develop new processes in order to benefit users.

The final police force (Metro) took a similar approach to Welsh, although improvements were not initiated by an unfavourable external audit. With significant external pressures on improving internal processes and making cost savings, emphasis had been given to maintaining staff morale by measuring strategic objectives against key performance indicators and setting clear objectives. While this information was presented at daily and weekly meetings, which helped engage staff in the improvement process, there was limited evidence of other lean behaviours. Acceptance of a performance measurement reflects the reality of progressive improvement within the police force, the lack of improvements to operational processes and use of improvement tools reflected a Borough Commander not wedded to the utility of lean within the policing context.

The evidence from the police forces highlights a number of issues that appeared to impact the effectiveness of each intervention. Of particular note was the role of external support, to assist in the transfer of knowledge to the policing context. Where consultants were employed, there was notably less involvement of staff, and the approaches closely matched frameworks and tools that had been developed by the consultant. While the consultants and external training provided necessary resources for initiating change activities, the improvement frameworks did not give sufficient emphasis to engaging staff or to support them in understanding why they should engage with lean improvement techniques. The role of senior personnel also appeared to play a key role in terms of acquiring resources, supporting improvements and at times involvement in improvement activities. However, with responsibilities other than lean implementation and external pressures, engagement in an initiative for the most part waned over time.

Of particular note in the Welsh force were two key points that appeared to compliment the use of a range of lean practices. While measurement systems were employed, in a similar manner to South and Central, as a result of the external audit, measures were focused upon what was deemed unsatisfactory. Consequently, rather than attempting to make the whole organisation lean, attention was focused upon a key process and explicit targets set for the level of improvement required.

Improvement behaviours further enhanced by multi-agency workshops, acknowledging the range of different parties able to contribute to a lean initiative. By having explicit metrics to improve and lean practices to apply, on completion of the project, it was possible to illustrate to external stakeholders the success of the initiative. The process thus helped to demonstrate the utility of a lean approach within the police force and to external stakeholders, so providing a necessary foundation on which to engage in further improvement behaviours.

In summary, the five police forces provide a range of perspectives on lean implementation, ranging from relatively successful initiatives resulting from negative feedback to others that had negligible long-term impact. The data also provides evidence on the role of consultants and management figures in initiating, facilitating and developing long-term changes in behaviour. The next section employs the theoretical framework presented in the theory develop section to interpret findings and build greater understanding of the lean implementation processes in the five police forces.

Discussion

This exploration of the implementation of lean within the police services illustrates a diversity of approaches to implementation, aims and outcomes, reflecting the complexity of the public sector environment (Waring and Bishop, 2010). While the case data reports on implementing the same underlying philosophy and concept within largely the same context, different constabularies approached lean in very different ways. To overcome, or at least mitigate this complexity, Osborne *et al.* (2013) identify the need to develop a body of theory rooted in a 'public service dominant-logic'. Rather than picking and choosing individual elements of standard lean tools, they suggest that lean needs to be comprehensively re-imagined in order the embrace public services and the requirements of the context. Such a view is remarkably consistent with the transfer of lean knowledge even within the automotive sectors. Manufacturers new to the concept have become lean by developing their own, 'mutated emulation' of lean, appropriate for their particular context (Lee and Jo, 2007: 3665). This further justifies why Nonaka's (1994) highly influential knowledge creation cycle has been applied within the current research, to focus on the creation of context specific knowledge compared to the transplantation of knowledge.

Osborne *et al.* (2013) identify that such a 'public service dominant-logic' perspective on lean implementation may provide a fertile direction for the evolution of public services, in order for them to be both internally efficient and externally effective. Critically, the current research highlights a direct contradiction to this insight. Central government support the use of consultancies to facilitate change, who apply improvement frameworks developed through involvement with private sector companies (e.g. Lean Quest, www.lean-quest.com; see also Radnor and O'Mahoney, 2013). Without adapting their lean implementation approaches to the requirements of the context, or allowing their clients to develop their own tools, there is an increased likelihood of failure. Such an observation is consistent with Bateman

(2005), where improvement interventions did not help participating firms develop their own solutions, so resulting in limited long term changes to practice. In order to address this gap between lean approaches and context requirements, Osborne *et al.* (2013) suggests that there is a need for greater 'fit for purpose' of interventions, and provide a new direction for public management theory. This consists of giving greater emphasis to the 'service dominant logic' (Vargo and Lusch, 2004) to differentiate between technologies developed for manufacturing goods and the need to adapt them in order to be relevant for the delivery of services.

Viewing the implementation of operational improvement techniques from a service dominant perspective can provide illuminating insight. This perspective moves away from viewing the product as a primary output of a process, instead viewing the product as a means of delivering a service to the customer (*ibid.*). Viewing a lean approach from this perspective gives greater emphasis to the end user, by ensuring the customer receives the services they require. While Kaynak (2003: 420) stated the line between products and services was often blurred, key differences are present that are likely to impact how improvement initiatives developing within manufacturing are implemented within the public service context.

Improvements made to manufacturing processes to reduce waste or improve process consistency can have direct and indirect outcomes for customers in terms of reduced costs and improved reliability (Harry and Schroeder, 2000; Ferdows and De Meyer, 1990). However, within the service context, production and consumption often occur at the same point, meaning efficiency and effectiveness of systems are intimately related. An additional characteristic of many service contexts is that unless the process is automated, the service received by the customer is affected by the personnel delivering the service. Roth and Menor (2003) highlight this as the key role of people in the delivery of services, in terms of how they perceived and were supported by management in delivering and developing the services they provided. For this reason, a more contemporary perspective on lean implementation was employed within the current research.

With the need to reconstruct lean theory within public services in the context of policing, the knowledge creation perspective was taken to analysing lean initiatives. Rather than viewing lean implementation as the transfer and implementation of commodified knowledge (Radnor and O'Mahoney, 2013), lean is viewed as a process for exploring existing practices and using tools to develop new knowledge and approaches to working. Such a perspective is consistent with Barton (2013: 222) who stated there was 'a requirement to fundamentally review how police services are delivered'. To achieve this, fundamental or transformation change is necessary, which requires changes in both behaviours and values and beliefs (Vest and Gamm, 2009). By viewing lean implementation in terms of the knowledge creation process, it is possible to identify whether tacit and well as explicit knowledge was created, that are necessary for changing individuals values and beliefs (Nonaka and Takeuchi, 1995).

By employing lean tools as a means of unearthing assumptions, individually held values and beliefs can be made explicit, questioned within group discussions and then consciously changed (*ibid.*). These processes can allow institutionalised processes and procedures to be effectively re-engineered in order to reduce complexity, waste, cost and ultimately improve the service received by the end user. However, where the knowledge creation perspective extends from more traditional conceptualisations of operations management it that conceptual learning from on project can indirectly contribute to subsequent improvements (Mukherjee, Lapre and Van Wassenhove, 1998). Within the context of the police service, the output of a lean initiative is not only the tangible deliverables in terms of changes processes and cost savings, but also changes to individual perceptions that are able to drive subsequent improvement behaviours.

While limited and to a degree, too diverse to draw definitive conclusions, the evidence does however provide insight to raise questions related to existing approaches to lean implementation within the policing context. The tools employed within the case organisations are those most consistently associated with lean, such as value stream mapping, group problem solving and visual management. Interestingly, emphasis tended to be given to those tools that promote the creation of tacit knowledge, which appears logical in terms of the need to change values and belief to promote transformation. However, without building such activities upon understanding of the philosophies of lean or progressing through the whole knowledge creation cycles, limitations can be identified with the approaches employed.

While two of the forces employed an external consultant to provide the foundational understanding of lean to drive the knowledge creation process, within the other cases, there was less evidence of a base understanding of the concept. The result was that existing knowledge (both tacit and explicit) of processes was shared between individuals involved in the process, but not necessarily critically reviewed to allow the creation of new knowledge. Counter intuitively, a similar situation was also present within the firms engaged with the external consultancy. Without engaging a range of practitioners and delivery standardised lean products, the understanding of lean, including the associated tools and techniques, remained within the consultancy. The result of this was that after initial lean activities, there was limited evidence of changes in values and beliefs or engagement in follow-up improvement activities.

Three interconnected observations can be taken from the case data that provide insight to why the initiatives were not sustained. First, while the overarching aims and drivers for each lean initiative were for cost reduction and effectiveness improvement, the specific aims of a number of individual activities were not clearly defined. This has been identified as important for motivating those within the project (Linderman *et al.*, 2003; Revere and Black, 2003). Second, an identified performance gap can provide a foundation for developing improvement targets that may stretch those in the team to develop new knowledge to make the required improvements. Third, not all the initiatives had appropriate infrastructure in terms of lean champions, with particular initiatives appearing only to involve external parties. This appeared to reduce the need for management to support improvement behaviours by providing staff to engage in activities. Table 15.3 presents the analysis of the case data to identify the form of knowledge created based on the types of tools used by each police force.

Table 15.3 Analysis of case data

Police force	*Tools*	*Tacit*	*Explicit*
Welsh	brainstorming, 5 why, value stream mapping, cause effect, cross functional workshops, visual management	3 Socialisation, 1 internalisation	2 externalisation
Metro	Visual management	1 Internalisation	–
South	Training for senior management (QUEST), visual management, process mapping	2 internalisation	1 externalisation
Central	(Cross functional workshops, value stream mapping, cause effect, 5 why) from QUEST	3 socialisation	1 externalisation
Southwest	Small teams, value stream mapping? Job rotation (team disbanded)	1 socialisation, 1 internalisation	1 externalisation

A key observation of the analysis is that tools from the 'combination' quadrant of the knowledge creation cycle (Table 15.1) were notably missing. The combination quadrant relates to those activities that analyse performance data to identify relations to ensure improvements focus on particular variables that are correlated with the requirements of the end user (Harry and Schroeder, 2000). Such tools can be important in order to translate, complex, socially embedded practices, into objective business results that can be communicated with external stakeholders (Radnor and O'Mahoney, 2013). However, before such tools can be employed, there is a need for robust and appropriate measurement systems that explicitly acknowledge the presence and relationships between the various external stakeholders. While some of the case companies have begun to measure key performance indicators, analysis of this data could provide targets to key operational processes that were related to performance indicators.

For Swest and Metro in particular, such practices could have garnered the necessary commitment of management to continue investment in improvement activities. The focus given to the improvement initiative within Welsh by the external audit addressed this issue ensuring support was maintained until new practices had become embedded. To date, focus on key variables related to the external end-users and external effectiveness has been overlooked in favour of internal customers and efficiency (Radnor *et al.*, 2012).

Radnor *et al.* (*ibid.*) would identify such case evidence as 'unsurprising' in the context of their own recent research. Indeed, they argue:

> [T]he model and implementation of Lean to date has been defective. The current implementation of Lean in public services has focused on the technical tools without an understanding of the principles and assumptions of Lean or, the context in which it is being implemented.
>
> (Radnor *et al.*, 2012: 324)

The knowledge creation perspective taken within the current research highlights a revised theory for investigating lean implementation within the service sector specifically the public service sector. Knowledge is widely accepted as the foundation of competitive advantage within modern business, with the knowledge based view of the firm (Grant, 1996) gaining wide acceptance. Taking this perspective highlights why lean is of relevance within the service sector to help organisations continually create and recreate their knowledge based resources (Nonaka and Takeuchi, 1995). This perspective will help public service organisations account for a changing environment and develop new services in the same way as manufacturing has done in the last 30 years.

Contribution

'Lean' has been applied very effectively within manufacturing organisations to the point where manufacturing is considered to have moved into a 'post-lean age' (MacCarthy *et al.*, 2013). Consequently, it has not been an unreasonable assumption that the principles of 'lean' could be adapted for utilisation within public service organisations. However, what has tended to result, is the over transfer of the easily codified tools and techniques that often define lean, while overlooking the underlying philosophies and principles, that are more embedded within exemplar organisations (Hines *et.al.*, 2004; Womack *et al.*, 1990). The current research has thus attempts to analyse a lean implementation within the public service sector, in order to identify key practices to facilitate the development of a lean philosophy that promote knowledge creation within the public service context.

The police service, under extreme pressure from successive governments to reform, has adopted new business methodologies including 'lean', in the anticipation of a quick and significant improvements in performance. The findings of the research are broadly consistent with wider literature on both manufacturing and service contexts, that the initial adoption of a few 'lean' tools and techniques can provide a starting point for the elimination of certain types of waste. However, this evidence is diffuse and the current research illustrated that within the police, improvements have been varied in terms of commitment of the police to adopt the deeper, more philosophical and cultural underpinning of 'lean' principles. This is consistent with tensions between professional and managerial targets, with practitioners deliberately undermining improvement efforts that are not in line with accepted professional norms (Waring and Bishop, 2010; McNulty, 2003). This highlights the need for a more holistic conceptualisation and implementation of lean, in order for the underpinnings of lean to become embedded in an organisation in order to drive continuous, rather than isolated, short term improvement.

The knowledge creation perspective taken in the current chapter provides a key insight on this issue. The professionalised nature of many of those working within the public sector represents an important variable to consider. Values and beliefs of practice established over many years are unlikely to be replaced by a short-term engagement with an external consultancy. Professionalised workers may actively resist the acceptance of new ideas and techniques that devalue their existing knowledge. Such resistance may result in limited contributions and openness within group problem solving activities, reducing the extent of knowledge creation. Choo *et al.* (2007) demonstrated that the psychological safety, where individuals felt comfortable in questioning their own beliefs in project teams, significantly affected the level of knowledge creation. In addition to providing resources and performance measurement system, management may play a key role in developing an appropriate organisational context to promote knowledge creation.

Conclusion

In this chapter, we have highlighted the work of Radnor *et al.* (2012) and Osborne *et al.* (2013) as offering some explanation to this apparent failing of lean within the public sector, who proposed a revised theory of 'lean' within the public services. Building upon these, we have proposed a knowledge based and knowledge creation perspective as one potentially fruitful angle to explore public service management from. This provides new insight to develop public service-dominant theory of lean.

Radnor *et al* (2012) and Osborne *et al.*'s (2013) conceptual argument draws upon a logical differentiation between public governance theory, which has been traditionally grounded through reference to manufacturing and public service theory. The current research instead draws from accepted management theories to inform interpretations of lean practices within the public service context. This provides fresh insight into the aims of lean implementation within the public service context, and potentially more broadly within the service sector. Instead of emphasising the transfer of easily learnt tools and techniques to new and potentially inappropriate contexts, the current approach focuses on using the tools and techniques to create new and relevant knowledge for the context of public service. The perspective also gives emphasis to the need for individuals to apply the tools in order to critical reflect on their existing values and beliefs, to support them in refining them to ensure they are appropriate for their current environment.

Moving away from isolated improvement initiatives with limited success, the research provides the first steps towards a framework to facilitate continuous improvement within the public service sector. By emphasising how lean practices can embed changes in values and beliefs, emphasis is given to the factors that embed lean practices and can facilitate subsequent improvements. Compared with tools and techniques, lean is defined as a system to promote continual knowledge creation, which in turn may lead to waste elimination activities and organisational change.

Continually improving and continually creating new knowledge will provide public service organisations with mechanisms to reduce external pressure and deliver services required by their external stakeholders. This view is wholly consistent with Womack *et al.* (1990: 249), who stated 'When the system [lean] works properly, it generates a willingness to participate actively and to initiate the continuous improvements that are at the very heart of leanness'. To further develop this insight, further research will be required, with the police service presenting an interesting organisation in which to further explore and test the theoretical possibilities put forward in this chapter.

References

Abrahamson, E. (1991) 'Managerial fads and fashions: the diffusion and rejection of innovations'. *Academy of Management Review*, 16(3): 586–612.

Anand, G., Peter, T.W. and Mohan, V.T. (2010) 'Role of explicit and tacit knowledge in Six Sigma projects: an empirical examination of differential project success'. *Journal of Operations Management*, 28(4): 303–15.

Antony, J., Kay, D., Frenie, A. and Seow, C. (2007) 'Can Six Sigma be the "cure" for our "ailing" NHS?' *Leadership in Health Services*, 20(4): 242–53.

Barton, H. (2013) 'Lean Policing? New approaches to business process improvement across the UK police service'. *Public Money and Management*, 33(3): 543–53.

Barton, H. and Beynon, M. (2012) 'Policing for the people: a cluster based investigation of the relationship between police force operational performance and public opinion'. *International Journal of Emergency Services*, 1(1): 1–12.

Barton, H. and Delbridge, R. (2006) 'Delivering the learning factory? Evidence from the US and UK automotive components industries'. *International Journal of Human Resource Management*, 15(2): 331–45.

Bateman, N. (2005) 'Sustainability: the elusive element of process improvement'. *International Journal of Operations and Production Management*, 25(3): 261–76.

Berry, J. (2009) *Reducing Bureaucracy in Policing: Full Report*. London: Home Office.

Bhatia, N. and Drew, J. (2006) 'Applying Lean production to the public sector'. *McKinsey Quarterly*, (June): 1–5.

Bicheno, J. and Holweg, M. (2009) *The Lean Toolbox: The Essential Guide to Lean Transformation* (4th edn). Buckingham: Picsie Books.

Bititci, U.S., Kepa, M., Sai, N., Patrizia, G. and Turner, T. (2006) 'Dynamics of performance measurement and organisational culture'. *International Journal of Operations and Production Management*, 26(12): 1325–50.

Black, K. and Lee, R. (2006) 'Six Sigma arises from the ashes of TQM with a twist'. *International Journal of Health Care Quality Assurance*, 19(3): 259–66.

Browning, T.R. and Eppinger, S.D. (2002) 'Modeling impacts of process architecture on cost and schedule risk in product development'. *Engineering Management, IEEE Transactions*, 49(4): 428–42.

Browning, T.R. and Heath, R.D. (2009) 'Reconceptualising the effects of lean on production costs with evidence from F-22 program'. *Journal of Operations Management*, 27: 23–44.

Choo, A.S., Linderman, K.W. and Schroeder, R.G. (2007) 'Method and psychological effects on learning behaviors and knowledge creation in quality improvement projects'. *Management Science*, 53(3): 437–50.

Dedhia, N.S. (2005) 'Six Sigma basics'. *Total Quality Management*, 16(5): 567–74.

de Leeuw, S. and van der Berg, J.P. (2011) 'Improving operational performance by influencing shopfloor behaviour via performance management practices'. *Journal of Operations Management*, 29: 224–35.

Drucker, P.F. (1955) *The Practice of Management*, M. Belbin (ed.) Oxford: Butterworth-Heinemann.

Eisenhardt, K.M. (1989) 'Building theory from case study research'. *Academy of Management Review*, 14(4): 532–50.

Eldridge, N.E., Woods, S.S., Bonello, R.S., Clutter, K., Ellingson, L., Harris, M.A., Livingston, B.K., Bagian, J.P., Danko, L.H. and Dunn, E.J. 2006. 'Using the six sigma process to implement the Centers for Disease Control and Prevention Guideline for Hand Hygiene in 4 intensive care units'. *Journal of General Internal Medicine*, 21(S2): S35–42.

Ferdows, K. and De Meyer, A. (1990) 'Lasting improvements in manufacturing performance: in search of a new theory'. *Journal of Operations Management*, 9(2): 168–84.

Fiol, C.M. and Lyles, M.A. (1985) 'Organizational learning'. *Academy of Management Review*, 10(4): 803–13.

Flanagan, R. (2008) *The Review of Policing – Final Report*. London: Home Office.

Flynn, B.B., and Flynn, E.J. (2004) 'An exploratory study of the nature of cumulative capabilities'. *Journal of Operations Management*, 22(5): 439–57.

Flynn, B.B., Schroeder, R.G. and Flynn, E.J. (1999) 'World class manufacturing: an investigation of Hayes and Wheelwright's foundation'. *Journal of Operations Management*, 17(3): 249–69.

Garcia, V. (2005) 'Constructing the 'other'within police culture: an analysis of a deviant unit within the police organization'. *Police Practice and Research*, 6(1): 65–80.

Garvin, D. (1988) *Managing Quality*. New York, NY: Free Press.

Grant, R.M. (1996) 'Towards a knowledge-based theory of the firm'. *Strategic Management Journal*, 17 (Winter Special Issue): 109–22.

Greasley, A. (2004) 'Process improvement within a HR division at a UK police force'. *International Journal of Operations and Production Management*, 24(3): 230–40.

Harry, M. and Schroeder, R. (2000) *Six SIGMA: The Breakthrough Strategy Revolutionizing the World's Top Corporations* (1st edn). New York: Doubleday.

Hines, P. and Lethbridge, S. (2008) 'New development: creating a lean university'. *Public Money and Management*, 28(1): 24–86.

Hines, P., Holweg, M. and Rich, N. (2004) 'Learning to evolve: a review of contemporary lean thinking'. *International Journal of Operations and Production Management*, 24(10): 994–1011.

Holstein, J.A. and Gubrium, J.F. (2004) 'The active interview'. In Silverman, D. (ed.), *Qualitative Research*, pp. 140–61. London: Sage.

Holweg, M. (2007) 'The genealogy of lean production'. *Journal of Operations Management*, 25(2): 420–37.

Järvensivu, T. and Törnroos, J.-A. (2010) 'Case study research with moderate constructionism: conceptualization and practical illustration'. *Industrial Marketing Management*, 39(1): 100–108.

Kaynak, H. (2003) 'The relationship between total quality management practices and their effects on firm performance'. *Journal of Operations Management*, 21(4): 405–35.

Kumar, M., Antony, J., Singh, R.K., Tiwari, M.K. and Perry, D. (2006) 'Implementing the Lean Sigma framework in an Indian SME: a case study'. *Production Planning and Control*, 17(4): 407–23.

Kvale, S. and Brinkman, S. (2009) *Interviews: Learning the Craft of Qualitative Research Interviewing* (2nd edn). Thousand Oaks, CA: Sage.

Lee, B.-H, and Jo, H.-J. (2007) 'The mutation of the Toyota production system: adapting the TPS at Hyundai Motor Company'. *International Journal of Production Research*, 45(16): 3665–79.

Linderman, K., Schroeder, R.G., Zaheer, S. and Choo, A.S. (2003) 'Six Sigma: a goal-theoretic perspective'. *Journal of Operations Management*, 21(2): 193–203.

MacCarthy, B.L., Lewis, M., Voss, C. and Narasimhan, R. (2013) 'The same old methodologies? Perspective on OM research in the post-lean age'. *International Journal of Operations and Production Management*, 33(7): 934–95.

Matthews, R.L., Tan, K.H. and Marzec, P.E. (In press) 'Organisational ambidexterity within process improvement: an exploratory study of 4 project-oriented firms'. *Journal of Manufacturing Technology Management*, (26)5.

McNulty, T. (2003) 'Redesigning public services: challenges of practice for policy'. *British Journal of Management*, 14(s1): S31–45.

Meredith, J. (1998) 'Building operations management theories through case and field research'. *Journal of Operations Management*, 16(4): 441–54.

Miller, J. and Glassner, B. (2004) 'The "inside" and the "outside" Finding realities in interviews'. In *Qualitative Research*, Silverman, D. (ed.). 125–39. London: Sage.

Mukherjee, A.S., Lapre, M.A. and Van Wassenhove, L.N. (1998) 'Knowledge driven quality improvement'. *Management Science*, 44: S35–49.

Narasimhan, R., Swink, M. and Kim, S.W. (2006) 'Disentangling leanness and agility: an empirical investigation'. *Journal of Operations Management*, 24: 440–57.

Nonaka, I. (1994) 'A dynamic theory of organizational knowledge creation'. *Organization Science*, 5(1): 14–37.

Nonaka, I. and Takeuchi, H. (1995) *The Knowledge-Creating Company*. New York: Oxford University Press.

O'Rourke, P. (2005) 'A multi case comparison of Lean Six Sigma deployment and implementation strategies'. *ASQ Conference on Quality and Improvement Proceedings*: 581–91.

Osborne, S.P. and Strokosch, K. (2013) 'It takes two to tango? Understanding the co-production of public services by integrating the services management and public administration perspectives'. *British Journal of Management*, 24(supplement S1), doi:10.1111/1467-8551.12010.

Osborne, S.P., Radnor, Z.J. and Nasi, G. (2013) 'A new theory for public service management? Towards a service-dominant approach'. *American Review of Public Administration*, 43(2): 135–58.

Papadopolus, T. and Merli, Y. (2008) 'Stakeholder network dynamics and emergent trajectories of Lean implementation projects: a study in the UK National Health Service'. *Public Money and Management*, 28(1): 41–8.

Pil, F.K. and Fujimoto, T. (2007) 'Lean and reflective production: the dynamic nature of production models'. *International Journal of Production Research*, 45(16): 3741–61.

Powell, T.C. (1995) 'Total quality management as competitive advantage: a review and empirical study'. *Strategic Management Journal*, 16(1): 15–37.

Radnor, H.A. (2001) *Researching your Professional Practice: Doing Interpretive Research, Doing Qualitative Research in Educational Settings*. Buckingham: Open University Press.

Radnor, Z.J. and Barnes, D. (2007) 'Historical analysis of performance measurement and management in operations management'. *International Journal of Productivity and Performance Management*, 56: 384–96.

Radnor, Z.J. and Boaden, R. (2008) 'Editorial: Lean in public services – panacea or paradox?' *Public Money and Management*, 28(1): 3–7.

Radnor, Z.J. and O'Mahoney, J. (2013) 'The role of management consultancy in implementing operations management in the public sector'. *International Journal of Operations and Production Management*, 33(11/12): 1555–78.

Radnor, Z.J. and Walley, P. (2008) 'Learning to walk before we try to run: adapting lean for the public sector'. *Public Money and Management*, 28(1): 13–20.

Radnor, Z.J., Walley, P., Stephens, A. and Bucci, G. (2006) *Evaluation of the Lean Approach to Business Management and Its Use in the Public Sector*. Full Report. Edinburgh: Scottish Executive.

Radnor, Z.J., Holweg, M. and Waring, J. (2012) 'Lean in healthcare: the unfilled promise?' *Social Science and Medicine*, 74(3): 364–71.

Revere, L. and Black, K. (2003) 'Integrating Six Sigma with total quality management: a case example for measuring medication errors'. *Journal of Healthcare Management*, 48(6): 377–91.

Revere, L., Black, K. and Huq, A. (2004) 'Integrating Six Sigma and CQI for improving patient care'. *The TQM Magazine*, 16(2): 105–13.

Roth, A.V. and Menor, L.J. (2003) 'Insights into service operations management: a research agenda'. *Production and Operations Management*, 12(2): 145–64.

Seneviratne, M. (2004) 'Policing the police in the United Kingdom'. *Policing and Society*, 14(4): 329–47.

Thawesaengskulthai, N. and Tannock, J. (2008) 'Fashion setting in quality management and continuous improvement'. *International Studies of Management and Organization*, 38: 5–24.

Towill, D.R. and Christopher, M. (2005) 'An evolutionary approach to the architecture of effective healthcare delivery systems'. *Journal of Health, Organisation and Management*, 19(2): 130–47.

Vargo, S.L. and Lusch, R.F. (2004) 'Evolving to a new dominant logic for marketing'. *Journal of Marketing*, 68(1): 1–17.

Vest, J.R. and Gamm, L.D.(2009) 'A critical review of the research literature on Six Sigma, Lean and studergroup's hardwiring excellence in the United States: the need to demonstrate and communicate the effectiveness of transformation strategies in healthcare'. *Implement Science*, 4(1): 35.

Waring, J.J. and Bishop, S. (2010) 'Lean healthcare: rhetoric, ritual and resistance'. *Social Science and Medicine*, 71(7): 1332–40.

Womack, J.P., Jones, D.T. and Roos, D. (1990) *The Machine that Changed the World*. New York: Rawson Associates.

Xu, Q. (1999) 'TQM as an arbitrary sign for play: discourse and transformation'. *Organization Studies.* 20(4): 659–81.

Yin, R.K. (2009) *Case Study Research: Design and Methodology (Applied Social Research Methods)* (4th edn). Thousand Oaks, CA: Sage.

16 Operationalising lean in services

Rediscovering service blueprinting

Zoe J. Radnor and Stephen P. Osborne

Introduction

'Lean thinking' has become a recent prominent and popular approach to public service reform. In the current era of constrained and reduced public spending it has promised to maintain service productivity, improve resource utilisation and maintain service quality. In short, it has been promoted as enabling public service providers to 'do more, with less' (Radnor *et al.*, 2012). Recently, Radnor and Osborne (2013) have argued that the implementation of lean within public services has been defective due to a lack of understanding of the principles and assumptions of lean or, the context in which it is being implemented. Most critically their paper concludes that there has been a lack of consideration of the underlying logic and theories of service management within the public sector and, without utilisation of a service-dominant logic the lean approach will be doomed to failure as an approach to public services reform – both as a set of managerial practices and as a theory (*ibid.*). If the current mode of implementation of lean continues in public services based around workshops and tools with little regard to the user or citizen it will only serve in ensuring that public sector organisations become internally efficiency but permanently failing in delivering the required services (*ibid.*). This chapter will argue and illustrate through a secondary data case study how the adaptation of the lean as a theory through using service blueprinting can ensure that effectiveness as well as efficiency is achieved in practice.

Services need to be designed and that design needs to take into account the relationship between the service provider and service user. Within a service this relationship is not the same as having a physical object. As Shostack (1984) states when we buy the use of a hotel room we take nothing away with us. In delivering an appropriate service we need to codify the processes – this could be done through procedures and policies but another way is to visualise it in a way which considers the consumer's (or participant's) relationship to, and interaction with, the service (*ibid.*). Designing a service this way can lead to the production of service blueprint which consists of key components of; customer actions, visible contact employer actions, invisible employee actions as well the support processes (Bitner *et al.*, 2008). Critical aspects of the blueprint are the 'line of visibility' and 'line of interaction' which consider the points of interaction or 'moments of truth' between the invisible, visible employee actions and the customer/ participant in the service (Shostack, 1984).

Radnor *et al* (2012) argued lean in the public sector is context dependent. Radnor and Johnston (2012) presented evidence that to date lean implementation in the public sector focused around large government departments was focused around internal efficiency and not customer service. This conceptual chapter will start to operationalise that context dependency by unpacking how a services approach can be developed in public sector organisations (PSOs) by the application of service blueprinting as a tool within lean implementation to allow value and customer (user) service. In particular, the chapter will present an empirical example within higher education where the creation of a blueprint brought together staff and students to focus on improving the service design of student enrolment. It compliments a related paper which considers how service blueprinting supports co-production (Radnor *et al*, 2014). The case study is used an illustration to draw wider contributions to the use of lean, and service management, in PSOs and was not carried out as primary research.

Service management, lean and service blueprinting

Service management

Previously Osborne (2010) has argued that much public management theory is currently not fit for purpose. It derives from a larger body of generic management theory that has its roots in the experience of the manufacturing sector and which has invariably treated services simply as an anomalous or fragmented industry (Nankervis, 2005). This latter body of theory assumes a product-dominant logic where the production process is dominated by discrete transactions and where the production and consumption processes are entirely separate. This is not the case for services, however, where the production process is iterative, relational and where production and consumption occur contemporaneously (Gronoos, 2007).

This grounding of public management theory in an aberrant logic not suited to their service context has had profound and damaging consequences for the delivery of public services, as successive public management reform initiatives has attempted to find the 'missing product' (Grönroos, 1998) of public services delivery rather than embracing and working with their service-dominant logic. Most relationships between public service users and PSOs are not characterised by a transactional or discrete nature, as they are for such products, but by on-going, iterative, processes (McLaughlin *et al.*, 2009). The majority of 'public goods' (whether provided by the public, third or private sector) are in fact not 'public products' but rather 'public services'. For example, social work, health care, education, economic and business support services, community development and regeneration are all services rather than concrete products, in that they are intangible, process driven and based upon a promise of what is to be delivered. The fatal flaw of public management theory over the last decade and beyond has been to consistently draw upon generic management theory derived from manufacturing and product-dominant experience. This has tried to understand public services as if they were discrete tangible products rather than service processes. This product-dominant flaw has persisted despite the growth of a substantive body of services management and service-dominant theory that challenges this product-dominant approach to public services delivery (Johnston, 2008; Lusch *et al.*, 2007; Grönroos, 2007; Lovelock and Wirtz, 2004; Normann, 1991).

What is required therefore is that we ask new questions of public management reform (Osborne, 2008) and develop a body of theory rooted in a 'public service dominant-logic' that is context-specific to public services, embraces their true nature a services rather than products and provides fertile rather than sterile directions for the evolution of public services that are both internally efficient and externally effective (Osborne *et al.*, 2013). Lean can be both a useful and relevant concept to drive the developmental of public services dominant logic if, as will be argued below, it is not perceived to be an 'add on' but an inherent part of the service design and delivery process.

Lean in public services

Public service reform has been on the political agenda since the late 1970s and has included such approaches as the 3Es (economy, efficiency and effectiveness) through to best value and new public management (NPM) (Rashman and Radnor, 2005). However, recently the growing pressure on public services across the western world has led to a focus on increased efficiency over and above the outcome measures of effectiveness and equity. Both public services, including health (Fillingham, 2008; Guthrie, 2006) and local government (Krings *et al.*, 2006; Office of the Deputy Prime Minister, 2005), and central and federal government (Radnor and Bucci, 2010; Richard, 2008) have responded by implementing a range of business process improvement methodologies including lean thinking, Six Sigma, business process reengineering (BPR), Kaizen and total quality management.

Lean seeks to 'design out' overburden, inconsistency, and waste in the operational processes of service delivery. It is predicated upon the need to design service processes to produce maximum value for their end users and to lead to sustainable service businesses by shifting the organisational culture towards one of continuous improvement focused upon (external) customer value (Womack and Jones, 1996). Research on lean has suggested it can offer significant impact related to quality, cost and time and even to the satisfaction of both staff and service users. The UK Ministry of Defence, for example, reported a fall in the cost of maintaining one aircraft from £711 to £328 together with a reduction in manpower required for this activity by 21 per cent; the, Connecticut Department of Labour eliminated 33.5 staff hours in its work by the redesign of its processes, saving $500,000 in staff time over a year; and Solihull Borough Council produced £135,000 saving in the postal costs for its fostering service, through a lean review (Radnor, 2010a). Other reported benefits have included the reduction of waiting time for public services and a reduction in service costs through a reduction in resource utilisation (Silvester *et al.*, 2004) as well as intangibles such as increased employee motivation and satisfaction and increased customer satisfaction (Radnor and Boaden, 2008).

However, as recently stated by Radnor and Osborne (2013) although lean appears to have had a successful impact within public services, the actuality has been one of easy successes and a lack of sustainability and resilience in the benefits achieved. They argue that lean does have the potential to have a substantial impact upon public services reform. However, to achieve this it cannot be treated as a theory in its own right. It is only a set of tools. Rather it needs to be situated in a 'public service-dominant business logic' (Osborne *et al.*, 2013) to achieve enduring benefits for public services and their users (Radnor and Osborne, 2013).

In reality lean over the last decade has been seen in both the US and the UK as a panacea for poor public service performance. Indeed, their early implementation did lead to significant improvements in the efficiency of public services delivery in a range of areas including local government, the health service and national government functions (Radnor *et al.*, 2012; Waring and Bishop, 2010; Radnor, 2010b; Silvester *et al.*, 2004). However, such efficiency gains did not prove to be sustainable in the longer term. There were two reasons for this (Radnor and Osborne, 2013). First these savings came primarily from lean addressing prior design faults in PSOs rather than addressing longer term sustainability issues. Second, and most relevant here, the application of lean within PSOs mistook the nature of customer value. It has been universally inward-focused upon internal customers and customer value, rather than externally focused. Put simply, such an approach is able to create more efficient PSOs (by improving internal efficiency) but fails to address public service effectiveness because it does not orient itself to customer value as expressed by its external customers – the users of public services (Radnor and Johnston, 2012). Bluntly, it is a recipe for creating very efficient but permanently failing PSOs.

Therefore, if we accept that lean can be used to improve the public service effectiveness beyond internal efficiency and that public services should take a service-dominant approach a question is how to 'operationalise' lean especially to improve and innovate service? This paper will argue that to truly engage with lean within public services a range of approaches need to be embraced which support developing a service mindset and truly understanding the nature of customer value. One particular approach to do this, we argue, is 'service blueprinting'.

Service blueprinting

Service design is an approach where the end-users are the main focus and their experience is viewed holistically rather than concentrating on the individual processes which support service delivery. The concept of a service blueprint was presented by Shostack in an article in *Harvard Business Review* in 1982. In the paper she argues that 'a service blueprint allows a company to explore all the issues inherent in creating or managing a service' (Shostack, 1982: 135). Service blueprinting is a graphical representation of the service process and shares similarities with other process modelling approaches - it is a visual representation of the key activities in the service process and the detailed sub-processes and sub-systems, which reflect the service delivery. As Shostack (*ibid.*) explains the service blueprint is more precise that verbal definitions, gives a focus on processes (support by the works of Deming), and, encourages creativity and problem solving. Bitner *et al.* (2008) outline the evolution of service blueprinting stating that it has moved to include physical evidence and other techniques including critical incident and other process modelling approaches. However, they state that the benefit of the service blueprinting is the creation of the service blueprint which should be kept simple and as a graphical representation for all stakeholders – service designer, managers and staff of the service and, service users – at the organisation boundaries to learn, use, and modify the service in order to improve and innovate the connection between the user actions and processes (Bitner *et al.*, 2008).

The blueprint is a living document and should be used to continue to refine the systems and processes it describes. It consists of identifying processes, fail points (where the service can go wrong – identifying these and fail-safe processes can increase the quality of the service execution (Shostack, 1982), establishing the time frame and efficiency of the service. The identification of the key fail and wait points, drawn from the end-user feedback, enables the project team to drill down into these aspects of the service delivery and make recommendations to managers to focus resources to best effect. There are five main components in a typical blueprint:

- customer actions (stages of the service process including timing and relationships);
- frontstage participants and contact employee actions;
- evidence (tangible and intangible);
- backstage participants and principle actions; and
- support systems (Bitner *et al.*, 2008).

The complete service blueprint needs to include all the steps that the user encounters as part of the service delivery process. These 'touchpoints' are plotted in a sequential order from left to right at the top of the blueprint. When developing a blueprint it is advisable to start at the 'big picture level' and then drill down to obtain a greater level of detail. The blueprint is further divided into two zones: frontstage and backstage, separated by the line of visibility. Everything that appears above the line of visibility is what the user is exposed to and comes in direct contact with. Below the line of visibility, so-called backstage elements of the blueprint are drafted. These include participants (actors) and the actions which need to be performed in order to support the frontstage activities. Conventional understanding of the backstage operations as being secondary to the frontstage activities is challenged by the service blueprinting approach. Both are shown to be equally important for the success of the service process, both need to be properly resourced and managed, both need to be made aware of the importance of the other for the delivery of quality services (Lovelock *et al.*, 2008).

The blueprint can also display the 'areas of excessive wait' (AEW) in the service system and which often contribute to significant 'fail-points' within a service. This is because flow is interrupted either by 'batch and queue' service design or failure of information flows to reach decision points. The 'fail points' are the critical incidents on which users base their perception of their quality of experience (Palmer, 2008). The task of service redesign then subsequently becomes one of how to eliminate these AEWs and 'fail-points' from the service system if possible, or to minimise their negative impact on user perceptions of service quality and performance. This redesign might include setting standards for task completion within the service system, clarifying the maximum 'wait time' that service users should expect at different stages of the service system and the maximum wait times between different elements of the service system. A coherent approach to addressing risk within the system is also needed. This has to be based upon an understanding of risk as an inevitable part of service delivery, and especially for public services, and which seeks to govern this risk by negotiation between the key actors involved, rather than to imagine it can be 'managed' out of existence (see Brown and Osborne, 2013 for the application of such a risk governance approach to innovation in public services).

Inevitably, such targets can always be subject to 'game playing' and manipulation by staff if used in isolation (Radnor and McGuire, 2004). They therefore need to be implemented as part of a broader package of service improvement that includes training for staff to inculcate an understanding of the significance of these targets for effective service delivery and that addresses how to undertake service recovery when failure does occur. No service system and its processes can ever be perfect. Consequently, successful service recovery is a core feature of effective service delivery (Hart *et al.*, 1990) – and is often neglected within the public service arena.

Even though service blueprinting is over 25 years old and some may argue beyond its usefulness we would like to argue that due to the main objective of service blueprinting to create a solid foundation for service improvement across the service system as a whole – through improvement, redesign or re-engineering – it is very relevant in the implementation of lean in a service context as it moves the traditional process mapping (usually very focused on the activities and tasks within the organisation) to one where the interaction or 'touchpoints' with the customer are clearly identified. Therefore, because of its prime focus upon the service user as being at the heart of the service delivery system, we argue in this paper that it can be a powerful tool for embedding the first principle of lean – value. By allowing for a clearer understanding of the touchpoints of public service delivery, it can offer two things previously missing from the theory and practice of lean. First, it can open these touchpoints up to a sharper analysis and evaluation of service operations management than has previously been the case by clarifying the public service delivery and its impact upon the quality and performance of these services. Second, it can become a tool through which service users, staff and managers can operationalise lean in service based practice. This can then point the way towards both improving the, quality and performance of the delivery process of public services. This is a novel and important contribution to operations management theory and practice as it moves away from pure manufacturing application and context. The case study below offers one discrete example of how this might be enacted for public services, in the context of the process improvement in a higher education institution in the UK.

Operationalising lean: service blueprinting at the University of Derby[1]

The University of Derby ran a project titled the Development and Enhancement Review of Business Interfaces (DERBI). From 29 June 2009 to 30 April 2010 they focused on an Enrolment Project under their Student Lifecycle Relationship Management umbrella. In these 10 months they reviewed the student experience of the enrolment process at the University of Derby with a specific focus on the University enrolment and registration processes (Baranova *et al.*, 2011). The remit of the project was clearly focused on establishing the perceptions and expectations of students about their experience of the university:

> modes of study at Derby run into double figures attracting a very diverse student body. Given that processes which could affect the efficiency and effectiveness of enrolment begin months before any students even enrol on a programme, there were a lot of potential potholes. However, we started from the perspective that relationships are all about the student, not the system.
>
> (Baranova *et al.*, 2010)

As a result of this perspective, the Derby project aimed to improve the quality of the student experience from pre-entry preparing students to engage in learning and teaching. Enrolment was defined as the point at which an individual's status changes from an applicant to a student. It was argued to be a significant point at which to commence a review of service design and student relationship management for the university – because of its significance in establishing the expectations of students about their future university experience as a whole. The aim of the project as outlined in the documentation was to:

- Use service improvement strategies (and specifically service blueprinting) to map the student lifecycle from pre-entry to readiness for learning and teaching and scrutinise these with stakeholders.
- Develop a blueprint of the enrolment process from the student's point of view considering main stages of the process, timing, and participants, tangible and intangible aspects of student's experience. This analysis would form the basis of the service improvement plan (Baranova *et al.*, 2011).

The five key stages of the service design/redesign and improvement process that the University of Derby used for the enrolment project are described below and illustrated in Figure 16.1. However, at the heart of the process and illustrated in Figure 16.1 is the consultation with service design and improvement participants (students, staff and experts).

Service design requires a wide range of research methods to inform the development of the blueprint and enhancement approaches. Creating the blueprint was therefore undertaken with both students and university personnel (backstage and frontstage to the enrolment process). As enrolment touched many aspects of university business processes: finance (fees and invoicing), quality (validation and programme audit and review), registry (the Student Finance Company, student records, etc.), and faculties (academic and administrative support) personnel from all these departments were involved as well as students with the support from the Students' Union. The approach adopted was one of inclusivity and research was

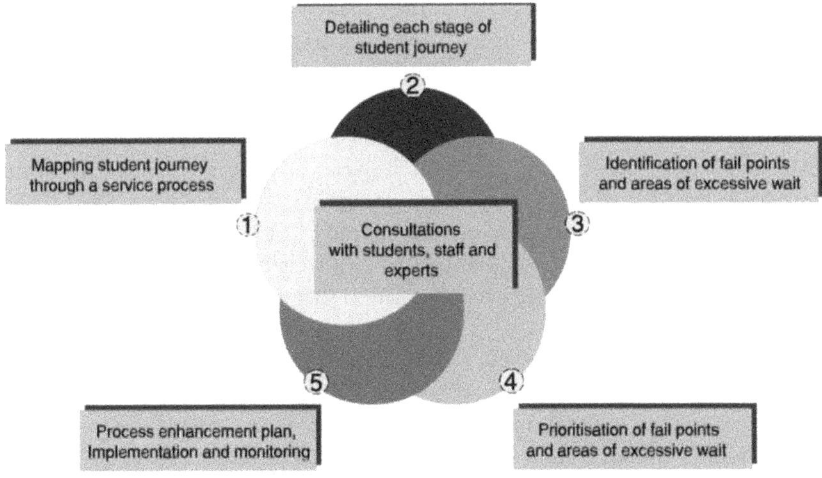

Figure 16.1 Enrolment service design project stages

Source: Baranova *et al.* (2010)

conducted with the key stakeholders using primary and secondary data sources and of qualitative and quantitative data provided multiple insights through which to triangulate student perceptions and expectations of service quality in the enrolment process. Primary data included: Staff and student focus groups; one - to - one interviews; pilot/trialling; video feedback; mystery shoppers; timing techniques (queuing, time-cards, etc.) and observation. Secondary research involved considering the outcomes from previous staff and student questionnaires, evaluating a selection of programme and subject area annual monitoring reports and, external examiners' reports and, reviewing enrolment planning group minutes and action plans.

The project was successful because of the experience of the core project team, the fit with the established strategic focus of the student experience strategy the governance established through the Project Management Committee and the steps taken to ensure students were fully engaged with the project. Student engagement was achieved through having a placement student as part of the project team, focus groups, surveys and mystery shoppers. This rich collaboration ensured students co-produced the project and went on to co-produce the induction and enrolment service.

In order to begin to define the process steps and student touchpoints which make up the journey from applicant to enrolled student, two training sessions were held on the theory of service design and techniques for blueprinting. Using local knowledge, key staff from each of the critical areas were personally invited to attend one of these sessions. Following each session, these staff then worked with the project manager to map out the roles which they and their departments had in the student transition process. The interoperability of the processes began to emerge and the actors and actions, both above and below the line of end-user visibility, were mapped out and connections made. In the end three such workshops were held, to ensure that all relevant aspects of the service were captured.

Not only did this process deliver data to inform the blueprinting process, in its own right was felt to have heightened employee awareness of the service delivery process, capabilities for service recovery and perceptions of student needs, wants and satisfaction levels. Wide-ranging consultations were carried out with input from staff that managed and carried out the various processes to capture the frontstage and backstage operations that lay beneath the identified student touchpoints (Figure 16.2). In the Derby project, over 100 participants were involved in drawing up the student transition. As the project documentation stated:

> it is important that, throughout the development of the blueprint, the end-user remained the focus. Blueprinting participants should not be too engrossed with the steps in the process, operational issues and 'blame' talk. They need to be constantly reminded of the student being at the centre of service improvements, experience design and quality.
>
> (Baranova *et al.*, 2010)

Stage 1: mapping the student experience

The first stage was to map the student experience of enrolment. However, as the project progressed, it became clear that the original scope of the project was too generic and ambitious in seeking to map out the experience of the totality of students in the enrolment process. It was calculated that there were actually more than fifteen different student profiles with differentiated experience through the enrolment process, such as international, undergraduate and postgraduate, mature, part-time, collaborative, and e-learning students. All these student profiles had different routes through enrolment, and consequently expectations and experiences of the process. Therefore, when it came to drawing up the blueprint it became apparent that the level of detail required in the blueprint would necessitate refining the initial focus to one particular cohort of students in the enrolment process. In this case the eventual decision was to focus in the initial project upon undergraduate students on a Joint Honours programme. Despite this refined focus, though, the service blueprint that emerged was still immensely complicated, demonstrating the interoperability and interaction of the range of discrete service sub-processes within the overall enrolment process. Figure 16.2 is an example of just a small part of the service blueprint that emerged out of this service blueprinting exercise.

Stage 2: detailing the stages of the student journey

The service blueprint (Figure 16.2) explored the linkages between staff and activities on both sides of the line of visibility and illustrated the following components of 'the student journey' through enrolment:

- *Touchpoints*: the stages of transition from applicant to student were plotted from their initial attendance at a university Open Day to the point where a student received an enrolment completion e-mail. Target and actual service delivery times were identified for each of the stages.
- *Frontstage participants and their principal actions:* all frontstage university staff (such as academic staff, administrative and support staff, reception staff and university porters) with whom students came into direct contact (through face-to-face, telephone or virtual means of communication) were identified and listed, together with the activities that they undertook. Crucially students were identified at the outset as a core frontstage participant and their role as co-producers was essential to the performance of the enrolment system.
- *Evidence (tangible and intangible):* two differing locations for enrolment on the main campus were considered to provide evidence of two quite distinctive enrolment experiences – the library (a modern air-conditioned building) and a nondescript university corridor (with no natural light and which could get very stuffy, especially when the queues of students waiting to enrol grew).
- *Backstage participants and their principal actions:* all support staff (such as ICT, registry, disability services, university finance staff) were identified together with the activities that they undertook to support the frontstage staff and activities.
- *Support systems:* the ICT systems supporting the enrolment process were displayed at the bottom of the blueprint, and in some instances connected by vertical lines with other areas of the blueprint to show interoperability links.

Stage 3: identification of the fail-points in the enrolment process

The focus of any blueprinting project is upon the experience of the service system and process by the service user. In the University of Derby project, therefore, the focus was consistently upon the experiences of applicants/students in the processes of enrolment. In Stage 3, the project sought to identify the fail-points experienced by students, where the system failed to meet expectations or to address needs. These were captured by a range of approaches, including 'mystery shoppers', real-time student video diaries, focus groups and surveys. Those stages of the enrolment process identified by academic and administrative staff as posing the highest risk of service failure were also examined in greater detail - these were identified as a red 'F' in the blueprint (Figure 16.2).

Stage 4: prioritisation of the failpoints

Through focus groups with students and staff fail-points were highlighted that needed the most immediate action in order to enhance the enrolment process. One of the key fail-points identified, for example, was the non-completion of the on-line enrolment process by students, and which forms a vital part of the success of the overall enrolment process. The focus upon this fail-point generated a number of suggestions to minimise its risk in future. These included the redesign of the web-layout for the on-line enrolment interface, rephrasing the instructions on the screen

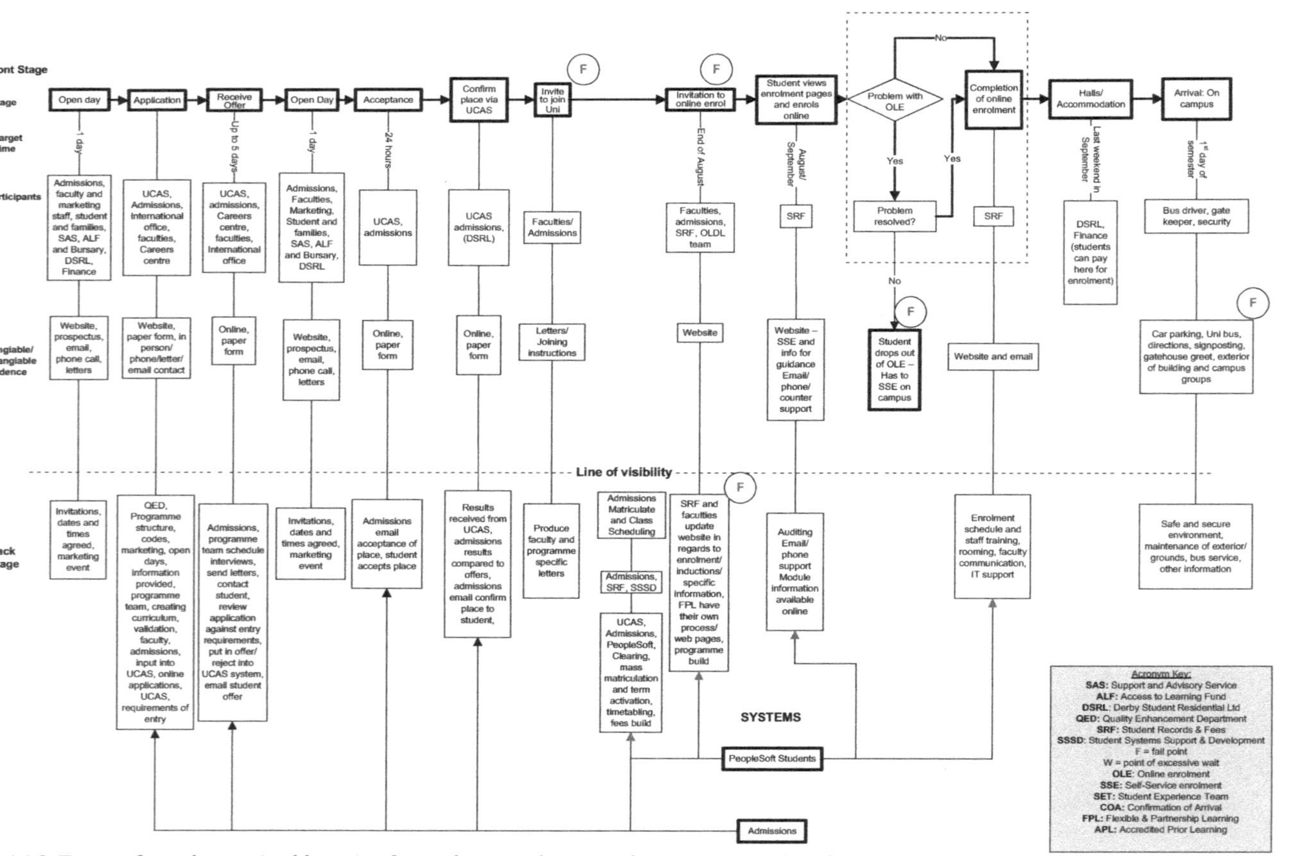

Figure 16.2 Extract from the service blueprint for student enrolment at the University of Derby

to avoid future misunderstandings, and the use of a progress bar as a tracking tool in the process. All of these suggestions sought to improve the experience of the on-line process by the student and hence its successful performance by them as part of the overall enrolment process.

Stage 5: process enhancement plan

The final stage of the blueprinting project at the University of Derby was the creation of an integrated process enhancement plan for enrolment at the university. This addressed activity by both frontstage and backstage staff on both sides of the line of visibility.

Discussion

For the University of Derby, considering the student enrolment process, service blueprinting was a powerful tool for appreciating the centrality of the student (service user) to improving the process and performance of university systems. In this regard it also supported the principles of lean in focusing on value from the customer (user) perspective, allowing flow (or reduction in waiting times) and reducing unnecessary tasks or waste (addressing the 'fail points') (Radnor *et al*,. 2012). It allowed process and system improvement in a service context to be achieved by moving the focus away from internal efficiency to external effectiveness placing the user (student) at the heart of improvement. This complexity of the system could also be presented in a diagrammatic form, highlighting and identifying fail-points and wait-points to provide a very powerful approach to focusing effort on enhancements where the biggest impact will be made to the felt student experience and the performance of the university system.

The use of the service blueprint rather than the traditional process mapping tool we argue would allow lean to be implemented in a service context which supports its utilisation beyond a set of tools and workshops as it lays bare the 'unavoidability' of the interaction between the front- and backstage and so, the service provider and service user (Radnor and Osborne, 2013). It was felt that the blueprint fostered empathy, and helped staff to understand the role others have to play in delivering the service. In developing a new, holistic, service enhancement plan they were able to say that they had planned and mapped out improvements and interventions with the key stakeholders. As stated by one of the university staff involved in the project, 'the fundamental change has been in rather than assuming that what we knew, or thought we knew, would be best for the students, we have actively sought their input as end-user designers and co-producers of their own student experience' (Baranova *et al.*, 2010).

It has been argued earlier in the paper that lean has been considered as an 'add on' in public services used to drive internal efficiency not to consider customer service (Osborne *et al.*, 2013). However, in this paper through the illustration of service blueprinting we argue that in order to offer a quality student (user) experience, universities and colleges as indeed all public services need to ensure that the service experience does not feel like a burden for the end user, but as an experience that adds value, or one that is so simple and straightforward that it appears effortless. For the case of the University of Derby this meant that the experiences and expectations of students needed to be clearly understood and managed. The evidence both quantitatively and qualitatively of the impact of engaging with service blueprinting and truly understanding customer (user) value so improving the process could be argued to support the further development of lean in public services. With regard to the measures taken to assess the student experience of the enrolment process 2009's figures were compared with 2010's, which indicated many positive outcomes from the interventions identified during the project, such as a reduction in queuing (i.e. the mean wait times for all stages of enrolment was reduced to half the time of 2009, for both self-service and confirmation of enrolment, and, for the ID card collection part of the process, there were no queues recorded on any of the sampling occasions in 2010). Most notably, there was a 32 per cent increase in student satisfaction – in 2009, 36 per cent of returning students rated their whole enrolment experience as 'better than last year' (Baranova *et al.*, 2011). In 2010 this figure increased by 32 per cent to 68 per cent. Also wait times for all stages of enrolment had reduced to half the time in 2009, with no queues in 2010 (*ibid.*). Qualitatively many positive quotes were collected during the project including:

> I attended one of the Service Design workshops, and worked on the initial Blueprint for our enrolment process. It was really enlightening to place myself as the student and imagine the experience from their standpoint, rather than putting process first, which we do too often. After seeing the outcomes broken down into a service design plan with such tangible elements I can really see where I can apply this to other processes that my team work on.
>
> (University of Derby programme advisory service co-ordinator, quoted in Baranova *et al.*, 2010)

The university is now working upon how this increased engagement of students and increased level of satisfaction at an early stage of their career can form the basis for enhancing their engagement and satisfaction throughout their university careers (Baranova *et al.*, 2011).

On one hand theory and current rhetoric is stating that lean is important – not just as an added on but as an integrated element of supporting public service reform. On the other hand the example presented in this paper indicates the application of service design techniques, particularly blueprinting, challenges the extent to which organisations truly place the citizen, in this case the student and so customer value at the heart of what they do. This is all within a context that public sector organisations should be doing more to engage with service management logic (Osborne *et al.*, 2013). Therefore, we argue that techniques and methods such as service blueprinting allow lean to be operationalised and, services to be designed as services not products. The student enrolment project at the University of Derby through the use of service blueprinting allowed for improvement and innovation. It moved beyond improving the quality and impact of existing services (internal efficiency) to bringing consumer experience together with participative planning to generate new approaches to public services. The project team strongly believe that the results regarding the design and delivery for student enrolment were only achieved due to engaging and bringing in the student to the heart of service process redesign (externally effective). This supports the continuing need and development for lean beyond a tool to drive internal efficiency. It also supports the use of approaches such as service blueprinting to operationalise concepts such as lean and co-production to design services with user experience and customer value at the heart (Radnor *et al.*, 2014).

Conclusions

Over the past few years there has been considerable focus on public sector organisations to become more efficient and effective. The implementation of approaches such as lean, have risen together with greater awareness of operations management within public service in general. This chapter has aimed to take a multi-disciplinary approach drawing in public management, operations management and service management in order to understand how lean can be operationalised and to support the need for service logic in the public sector. Public sector bodies are by and large 'services' and so need to engage with the theory and discipline of service (operations) management. It has achieved this by presenting an illustration of service blueprinting in a university project. The chapter suggests that service blueprinting supports the lean (continuous improvement) agenda while also promoting a services approach.

The research and findings within the chapter also allows us to raise some broader reflections related to public service operations management. The use of the service blueprinting tool allowed opportunity to create some language and understanding about processes and services. The tool allowed, but did not bring about, and supported a maturity to be developed in the concepts of public service operations management. In the main this was to support incremental change rather than disruptive, large scale change but still facilitated a multi-stakeholder group to focus on the process and delivery of service rather than the discreet elements or tasks. With a maturity of the language and concepts then issues of how to create capacity to support and sustain the improvements will grow. Giving public service organisations tools such as service blueprinting to help in conceptualising service operations management is not only important but critical as traditionally such ideas and concepts have been void. The service blueprint at the University of Derby gave the opportunity to understand the complexities of multi-stakeholders i.e. students, departments, university administration and their role in the process but with a focus on the user delivery end rather than individual activities. This can help in managing user expectations and recognising how to deliver in 'difficult to reach' situations where the user is more challenging to engage (i.e. the elderly or criminal offenders) without making assumptions or lack of understanding of the service process.

This chapter presented only one example of a service blueprint so future research should aim at seeking and developing other examples. But what it has illustrated is that tools such as service blueprinting can allow the language, concepts and theories of process, user, capacity, demand etc. to be developed which is critical if public service organisations are to generate a greater understanding of service operations management for the public sector.

References

Baranova, P., Morrison, S. and Mutton, J. (2010) *Service Design in Higher and Further Education: A Briefing Paper.* JISC CETIS. Derby: University of Derby.

Baranova, P., Morrison, S. and Mutton, J. (2011) 'Enhancing the student experience through service design'. *Perspectives*, 15(4): 122–8.

Bitner, M.J., Ostrom, A.L. and Morgan, F.N. (2008) 'Service blueprinting: a practical technique for service innovation'. California Management Review, 50(3): 66–94.

Brown, L. and Osborne, S.P. (2013) 'Innovation and risk in public services: towards a new theoretical framework'. *Public Management Review*, 15(3): 186–208.

Fillingham, D. (2008) *Lean Healthcare: Improving the Patient's Experience.* Chichester: Kingsham Press.

Grönroos, C. (1998) 'Marketing services: the case of a missing product'. *Journal of Business and Industrial Marketing*, 13(4–5): 322–38.

Grönroos, C. (2007) *Service Management and Marketing.* Chichester: John Wiley & Sons.

Guthrie, J. (2006) 'The joys of a health service driven by Toyota'. *Financial Times*, 22 June.

Hart, C.W.L., Heskett, J.L. and Sasser, Jr, W.E. (1990) 'The profitable art of service recovery'. *Harvard Business Review*, July–August: 148–56.

Johnston, R. (2008) 'Internal service – barriers, flows and assessment'. *International Journal of Service Industry Management*, 19(2): 210–31.

Krings, D., Levine, D. and Wall, T. (2006) 'The use of "lean" in local government'. *Public Management*, 88(8): 12–17.

Lovelock, C. and Wirtz, J. (2004) *Services Marketing: People, Technology, Strategy.* London: Pearson Educational.

Lovelock, C., Wirtz, J. and Chew, P. (2008) *Essentials of Services Marketing.* New York: Pearson Education.

Lusch, R.F., Vargo, S.L. and O'Brien, M. (2007) 'Competing through service: insights from service dominant logic'. *Journal of Retailing*, 83(1): 2–18.

McLaughlin, K., Osborne, S.P. and Chew, C. (2009) 'Developing the marketing function in UK public service organizations: the contribution of theory and practice'. *Public Money and Management*, 29(1): 35–42.

Nankervis, A. (2005) *Managing Services.* Melbourne: Cambridge University Press.

Normann, R. (1991) *Service Management: Strategy and Leadership in Service Business.* New York: John Wiley & Sons.

Office of the Deputy Prime Minister (2005) *A Systematic Approach to Service Improvement.* London: Office of the Deputy Prime Minister.

Osborne, S.P. (2008) 'Delivering public services: time for a new theory?' *Public Management Review*, 12(1): 1–10.

Osborne, S.P. (2010) *The New Public Governance?* Abingdon: Routledge.

Osborne, S.P., Radnor, Z.J. and Nasi, G. (2013) 'A new theory for public service management? Towards a service-dominant approach'. *American Review of Public Administration*, 43(2): 135–58.

Palmer, A. (2008) *Principles of Services Marketing.* London: McGraw-Hill Education.

Radnor, Z.J. (2010a) *Review of Business Process Improvement Methodologies in Public Services.* London: Advanced Institute of Management.

Radnor, Z.J. (2010b) 'Transferring Lean into Government'. *Journal of Manufacturing Technology Management*, 21(3): 411–28.

Radnor, Z.J. and Boaden, R. (2008) 'Lean in Public Services – Panacea or Paradox?' *Public Money and Management*, 28(1): 3–7.

Radnor, Z.J. and Bucci, G. (2010) *Evaluation of the Lean Programme in HMCS: Final Report*. London: HM Court Services.

Radnor, Z.J. and Johnston, R. (2012) 'Lean in UK government: internal efficiency or customer service'. *Production Planning and Control*, 24(10–11): 903–15.

Radnor, Z.J. and McGuire, M. (2004) 'Performance management in the public sector: fact or fiction?' *International Journal of Productivity and Performance Management*, 53(3): 245–60.

Radnor, Z.J. and Osborne, S.P. (2013) 'Lean: a failed theory for public services?' *Public Management Review*, 15(2): 265–87.

Radnor, Z.J., Holweg, M.and Waring, J. (2012) 'Lean in healthcare: the unfilled promise?' *Social Science and Medicine*, 74(3): 364–71.

Radnor, Z.J., Osborne, S.P. and Mutton, J. (2014) 'Operationalizing co-production in public services delivery: the contribution of service blueprinting'. *Public Management Review*, 16(3): 402–23.

Rashman, L. and Radnor, Z.J. (2005) 'Learning to improve: approaches to improving local government services'. *Public Money and Management*, 25(1): 19–26.

Richard, G. (2008) *Performance is the Best Politics: How to Create High-Performance Government Using Lean Six Sigma*. Fort Wayne, IN: HPG Press.

Shostack, G.L. (1982) 'How to design a service'. *European Journal of Marketing*, 16(1): 49–63.

Shostack, G.L. (1984) 'Designing services that deliver'. *Harvard Business Review*, January–February: 133–9.

Silvester, K., Lendon, R., Bevan, H., Steyn, R. and Walley, P. (2004) 'Reducing waiting times in the NHS: is lack of capacity the problem?' *Clinician in Management*, 12(3): 105–11.

Waring, J.J., and Bishop, S. (2010) 'Lean healthcare: Rhetoric, ritual and resistance'. *Social Science and Medicine*, 71: 1332–40.

Womack, J. and Jones, D. (1996) *Lean Thinking: Banish the Waste and Create Wealth in your Organisation*. New York: Simon & Schuster.

Note

1 See www.jisc.ac.uk/media/documents/programmes/bce/derbicasestudy.pdf for original case study.

17 Delivery not departments

A case study of a whole organisation approach to lean implementation across an English hospital

Nicola Burgess, Zoe J. Radnor and Joy Furnival

Introduction

The English National Health Service (NHS) represents an exemplary context within which to examine the implementation of lean. Austere economic conditions, coupled with rising demand for services, means that healthcare organisations must do more with less. But doing more with less should never come at the expense of quality. Quality, defined broadly as encompassing the three dimensions of effectiveness of care, safety of care and patient experience (as in the Health and Social Care Act of 2012), is a critical aspect of healthcare that (should) share centre stage with efficiency. Efficiencies must therefore arise from improvements, and improvement requires change. But how do you effect change across a whole organisation? How do you overcome resistance to change in an organisation characterised by a dominant professional core (i.e. elite professionals seeking to maintain their professional jurisdiction)? And how do you mediate between the regulatory environment and corresponding managerial requirements for efficiency through financially incentivised performance based targets and the mandate for patient-centred care?

In this chapter, we chronicle one hospital's attempt to effect strategic change across a whole organisation, to produce patient centred services that are effective, safe and efficient, through the implementation of an improvement system underpinned by lean. The case study highlights the importance of a whole system approach to lean implementation, and perhaps most importantly, the role of senior management in sustaining a whole system approach.

This chapter proceeds as follows. First we outline the concept of lean and its application to healthcare, following which, we provide details of the case study organisation and describe our research design. The case study showcases the evolution of lean in one hospital from a 'few projects' approach (Burgess and Radnor, 2013), to a 'whole system approach' led by the chief executive. Our findings highlight the influence of the chief executive in engaging the organisation in lean at multiple levels, proactively sustaining lean implementation across his six-year tenure. Given the significant influence of the chief executive in leading lean across the organisation, many regarded his departure as a 'litmus test' to the success of lean implementation – would it thrive and continue, or wither and fade? Thus, when the pioneering chief executive did leave the organisation in

2010, the lead author undertook further interviews with the incumbent chief executive to get views on the future of lean in the organisation.

Our case study also highlights some impressive examples of service improvement that has seen the organisation collect a host of prestigious awards for exemplary patient care including numerous *Health Service Journal* awards, one *British Medical Journal* (BMJ) award, one *Nursing Times* award, two Process Excellence Awards and several others. Finally, the authors conclude this chapter by bringing the story to present day where performance and financial crises in the year of 2012 led to regulatory intervention and the departure of many senior members of staff. We highlight the need for further research into the sustainability of improvement approaches when financial and performance crises hit.

A brief outline of lean

Lean is best described as a philosophy of continuous improvement that adheres to a set of principles designed to 'make value flow at every step' (see Womack and Jones, 2000). The goal: a total elimination of non-value adding activities (collectively referred to as 'waste'). Lean implementation typically involves the application of various quality improvement tools. For example, in order to make value flow, we first need to understand what value is from the perspective of the customer. If we assume the customer to be the patient, then the organisation needs to understand what activity the patient values (e.g. friendly staff, effective treatment, safe procedures), and what activity the patient does not value (e.g. waiting for a bed, duplicate paperwork, stressed and overworked staff, healthcare acquired infections), before we can begin to assess how we might seek to eliminate non-value adding activity. Value stream mapping and process mapping techniques are then commonly employed by cross-functional teams as part of a 'rapid improvement event' (RIE) to understand the sequence of activities that make up the process. This process mapping activity allows RIE participants to identify activities that do not provide value to the customer. At this point, improvement tools such as Ishikawa's fish-bone diagram are employed to determine the root cause of why something happens and to help the team to eliminate non-value adding steps, improving the flow of value-adding activity to the patient. During the RIE it is common for some 'quick wins' to be identified for example using 5S and visual management to improve ward organisation and communication, alongside some medium and long term projects to redesign processes and improve services from the value perspective of the patient.

The above example is a very brief outline of lean implementation using an RIE as a vehicle for improvement and change. However, an RIE, or even several RIEs across a whole organisation, does not constitute a whole system approach. 'Real Lean' (Emiliani, 2007), is defined as: 'a true systems approach that effectively integrates people, processes, and technology - one that must be adopted as a continual, comprehensive and coordinated effort for change and learning across the whole organisation' (Liker and Morgan, 2006: 5).

The case for lean in healthcare

The need for efficiency savings in the NHS alongside other public services is now greater than ever (Department of Health, 2009). Reports highlighting the need for efficiency savings in the public sector such as the Government's Independent Review of Public Sector Efficiency (Gershon, 2004) have been identified as key drivers of lean implementation in the public sector as a whole (Radnor, 2010). The Operational Efficiency Programme report (HM Treasury, 2009) highlights the success of the efficiency agenda in delivering £26.5 billion pounds of efficiencies against a target of £21.5 billion set by the Gershon Review (2004). Aligned to this, the Operational Efficiency Programme is explicit in its recommendation for the use of continuous improvement tools such as lean, systematically throughout the public sector, commending the approach as 'effective, sustainable and comparably inexpensive' (HM Treasury, 2009: 83).

Service improvement methodologies such as lean have become progressively widespread in healthcare in the UK, Europe and worldwide (Brandao de Souza, 2009). Burgess and Radnor (2013) present empirical data suggesting that 78 per cent of English hospitals purport to be implementing lean in their Annual Reports during the operating year 2009–10; the authors report this figure as an increase from 53 per cent during 2008–9. However, despite this ostensibly high rate of lean implementation in English hospitals, the success rate of 'transformation' through service improvement methodologies per se is historically poor (Kotter, 1995; Lucey *et al.*, 2005).

Many authors deride attempts to implement lean that are focused on the use of tools to deliver localised pragmatic changes that at best deliver pockets of best practice, but fail to harness the value of lean as a management system (Proudlove *et al.*, 2008; Young and McClean, 2009; Radnor and Walley, 2008; Emiliani, 2007; Liker and Morgan, 2006; Roth, 2006). Organisations adopting a whole system approach to improvement are differentiated from other, more partial and fragmented approaches to service improvement; these hospitals clearly state the organisations commitment as 'this is the way we do things around here' (Burgess and Radnor, 2013).

A whole system approach to improvement requires engagement at all levels of the organisation from the very top to the very bottom, and every level in between. In healthcare, professional bureaucracy incorporating both inter and intra-professional stratification, gives rise to behaviours that resist service change where the service change is perceived as directed from management (see for example Currie *et al.*, 2008). On the other hand, there is a wealth of literature that highlights the critical importance of managerial and leadership commitment to the use of lean in order for implementation to be a success (see for example Mann, 2009). In order to mediate between these two extremes, a whole system approach to improvement needs to build legitimacy for the use of lean as an improvement methodology.

Research design

The case study organisation, referred to here as 'Gossamer Hospital', is a medium-sized hospital based in northwest England. Since Gossamer Hospital began their lean endeavour in 2004, they gained substantial worldwide attention for their work, with healthcare organisations from all over the world visiting the hospital to observe lean in practice, hear about the implementation of lean, and learn from their story. Through the use of semi-structured interviews we document the evolution of lean in our case study from a 'few projects' approach during the early years, to a whole system approach during the latter. Fifteen interviews took place with a cross section of the organisation during 2009, representing a cross section of the trust from the chief executive (one respondent) and other directors (three respondents), to senior clinicians (four respondents), more junior clinicians (four respondents) and improvement facilitators (three respondents). Following the chief executive's departure in 2010, the lead author undertook a further interview with the incumbent chief executive in April 2011 to discuss her views on the continued use of lean as a whole system approach to continuous improvement in the hospital. The authors also observed the implementation of lean via rapid improvement events (RIEs) totalling approximately 100 hours of observation, from which a journal of observations was maintained by two of the authors (NB and ZR). All interviews were recorded and transcribed verbatim, coded inductively by the lead author using NVivo software. The findings were validated by the case study organisation.

This case study portrays the development of a whole organisation approach to lean implementation in a healthcare organisation through the example of Gossamer Hospital. The case study begins with an overview of the key facets of the early years when the hospital was only concerned with delivery of acute services, before the organisation began to focus on more complex activities, which meant rejuvenating and developing the concept across patient pathways in primary, community and some tertiary services as the remit of the Hospital expanded. We provide a narrative based on interviews with senior directors in Gossamer Hospital to reflect on the challenges of a whole organisation approach to lean implementation in a healthcare context.

Implementing lean – a change imperative

The story of lean implementation at Gossamer Hospital begins in 2004–5, when the hospital was in formal financial turnaround with considerable deficit. The hospital had long waiting times for both elective and emergency services, unacceptably high mortality rates and poor staff morale. In common with other exemplar lean implementations in healthcare, such as the Virginia Mason Medical Center in Seattle (see Bohmer and Ferlins, 2006), Gossamer Hospital urgently needed to adapt and change in order to survive.

> In 2004/5 [the] Hospital was in difficult circumstances and in many ways it was (and still is) facing a fight for its survival as a local service and institution. It was this specific challenge that [Gossamer Hospital's improvement system] in essence was (and still is) trying to address. How can an organisation skill itself up to be both resilient and adaptable in a healthcare environment that is frequently changing and increasingly competitive?
>
> (Senior director)

It was at this point that Gossamer Hospital appointed a new chief executive. This new chief executive had previously been employed as director of the NHS Modernisation Agency, a body responsible for implementing much of the reform agenda across the UK's National Health Service (NHS) and building skills and capability for improvement. Based on this experience the chief executive was keen to find out whether lean could work across a whole healthcare organisation.

Analysis of interview data reveals the early process of developing lean at Gossamer Hospital as a period made up of two essential phases, the first consisting of a period of intense learning, and a second phase which was about the development of a framework for a systematic approach to whole system improvement.

Intensive learning

Gossamer Hospital's lean endeavour was launched with the help of external management consultants. Two initial projects took place: one based on a critical need to improve, namely the fracture neck of femur pathway where mortality rates were said to be 'inexplicably high'; a second 'simple' day-care pathway was chosen for contrast. A senior director describes the immediate impact of the project:

> No-one expected to be drawn in as quickly as we were, no-one expected to see the potential quite so quickly, so when we started it really was a proof of concept ... within a matter of months, mortality rates were falling.
>
> (Senior director)

The 'simple' day-care project turned out to be far more complicated than anticipated, but still provided important learning, particularly around the importance of preparation for the improvement activities and making sure that the right people are in attendance.

> It was an interesting contrast in two ways really, not only were they completely different processes but we completely got it wrong on day care, it was really instructive: we didn't prepare well enough, we didn't deal with the human relations issues as well as we should have done because you know, the day care unit gets occupied by different surgeons on different days so every debate we did have, we had to have the next day!
>
> (Senior director)

Despite the difficulties of the day-care project, improvements were being evidenced and thus lean was increasingly seen as something that could work, building legitimacy for the method and stimulating further small projects across the next 12–18 months. The chief executive, senior directors, clinicians and improvement facilitators interviewed during 2009 all reflected upon this time as an intense learning period: 'learning by doing' and, 'learning from others'.

Learning from other companies who were implementing lean across their organisation both in the public and private sector was considered an important source of inspiration, knowledge and confidence building in the concept of lean. A senior director emphasised the necessity of double loop learning to 'raise the bar of service improvement in healthcare' and acknowledged the continuing importance of onsite learning from others, citing visits to: Toyota, Thedacare in Wisconsin USA, Warburtons Bread, the Royal Air Force and Unipart in the UK as central to developing their own path towards becoming a lean organisation. The chief executive of Gossamer Hospital claimed that it was the chief executive at Thedacare in the US who convinced him that lean really does work in healthcare. The following excerpt highlights networking among the communities of chief executives at healthcare organisations where a similar endeavour towards organisation wide lean is taking place as an important source of inspiration and confidence in the approach.

> I suppose what finally convinced me to use lean was hearing John Toussaint who is the CEO at Thedacare speak about their journey and they're about 3-4 years ahead of us so I was looking at their work and one of the early things we did was send a couple of teams of people out to Wisconsin, a week each to participate in their event. I haven't visited Virginia Mason but we've met with a number of their people on a number of occasions, I know the chief exec Gary Kaplan very well as well and we have links to Flinders hospital in Adelaide.
>
> (Chief executive)

Following 12–18 months of learning by doing and learning from others, the executive board took stock and began to make decisions about corporate goals and how to align improvement work to these goals: '[We] began to coalesce into an agreement that you can't do a bit of everything everywhere, you've got to harness it to your big corporate goals' (senior director).

The 'how' of moving from a 'few projects' approach to taking a 'systemic' approach to lean created what the chief executive describes as 'a real tension' and culminated in the establishment of 'Gossamer Hospital's improvement system' as a vehicle for communicating the approach to service improvement in the Trust.

> it is a balance of the narrow and deep, so how do you go from the model line when you want to keep making improvements through a cycle and yet you want to change the whole organisation? You know you're only ever going to touch a small cross section of people by that experience. But we need to take the whole organisation's understanding with us and that's a real tension.
>
> (Senior director)

In summary, the evolution of Gossamer Hospital's improvement system during the early years emerged from the interplay of three key factors: a chief executive with an interest in lean and healthcare innovation; a burning platform in terms of performance; and the capacity to learn from the experiences of others.

Developing a framework for whole system change – the formative years

Gossamer Hospital formalised their commitment to the implementation of lean across the whole organisation through the development of a framework for system wide change. The framework was based upon two core pillars of lean: continuous removal of waste, and respect for people and society. During the early formative years the initial struggle was to build legitimacy for lean in healthcare. For example, the chief executive highlighted some of the difficulties faced when introducing lean to the NHS, such as 'we're not Japanese, and we don't make cars' accompanied by negative perceptions of lean as 'mean' with the result being: 'a lot of challenging conversations with unions regarding job security' (senior director).

Reflecting on this period, a senior director described the initial introduction of lean as 'a tough sell, to a lot of sceptics', however, the chief executive sought to overcome these barriers from the onset through engaging staff in master classes and workshops. The workshops were led by the chief executive and other senior directors to facilitate an exchange of views and ideas with middle managers and clinicians. It was from these early sessions that Gossamer Hospital formalised their organisational 'True North' goals (organisational purpose and values), (see Figure 17.1). During 2009, the authors observed the True North goals to be visible throughout the whole organisation, with brightly coloured posters placed on the walls of virtually every corridor, every department and ward in the hospital. The posters were designed to unite the organisation towards a distinct and clear strategic purpose, providing a critical link between organisational strategy and operational activity at all levels of the organisation. This clarity of organisational purpose is considered critical for facilitating a 'receptive context' for strategic change (Pettigrew *et al.*, 1992), ensuring that all operational activity can be clearly aligned to strategic goals (Hines *et al.*, 2004).

As a framework for a whole organisation approach to lean implementation, a number of key facets emerged during the early years, specifically: the use of policy deployment; a team of internal facilitators and a rolling cycle of RIEs; senior leadership commitment and engagement; and organisational learning through the development of an externally accredited lean academy. Each of these components is described in the following section.

Policy deployment: aligning organisational strategy to operational activities

Gossamer Hospital sought to link the organisational strategy with operational objectives using a process known as 'policy deployment' (also known as strategy deployment), a conceptualisation of the Japanese method known as '*hoshin kanri*'. Policy deployment is Gossamer Hospital's approach to aligning and communicating strategic intent with operational goals throughout the organisation. The process involves a way of setting objectives across all aspects of an organisation but in a way that involves as many people as possible through several conversations (termed 'catchball'), where priorities and details of 'what' is needed to be done, and 'how' the directorate or division will meet these priorities can be debated and agreed in a consensual way. In this sense this allows more involvement and engagement of staff in the process, rather than just 'top down' management.

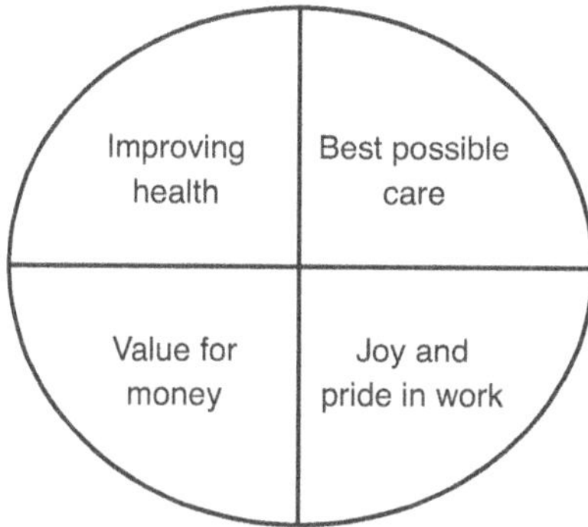

Figure 17.1 Original 'True North' goals

A team of internal facilitators and a rolling cycle of rapid improvement events

In 2007 an internal team of facilitators was created with a formal remit of facilitating lean across the whole organisation via a systematic rolling cycle of rapid improvement events (RIEs). In the beginning, RIE facilitation was jointly delivered by the internal improvement team and external management consultants specialising in lean, with the use of external consultants being gradually phased out as experience and capability grew. An improvement facilitator described the role of the internal improvement team:

> I'm always very clear that [Gossamer Hospital's improvement system] isn't just a team that sits in an office … [Gossamer Hospital's improvement system] is the whole hospital; it's the way we do improvement. At the moment, while we try and embed the principles, it's about teaching the tools, about facilitating people through events [RIEs] (as people still aren't clear what a rapid improvement event is, what it should look like); it's about supporting the team members so that after the event they have got help with sustainment and each week it is about making sure the team uses the tools correctly because if you use the tools correctly, you will get further than before.
>
> (Improvement facilitator)

In the above excerpt the facilitator emphasises the importance of teaching the tools however, she is also clear that on-going support from the organisation is critical to sustain and grow Gossamer Hospital's improvement system via developing people with the skills to lead change in the organisation every day. As a senior manager explains: 'it's about how do we get teams to do [Gossamer Hospital's improvement system] as daily work and how we embed problem solving locally … it's about removing fear and building confidence'.

Senior leadership commitment and engagement

Commitment of senior leadership and board level buy-in was instrumental in the early years of Gossamer Hospital's improvement system. A whole organisation approach to improvement ultimately requires everyone to become engaged in daily problem solving so that it becomes 'the way we do things around here', however, such cultural change takes considerable time, particularly when faced with a changing political environment and a challenging organisational context wherein professional power can sometimes be at odds with managerial goals.

> There's evidence now that the first ten years in an organisation this size is just going to be infrastructure building. If you look at other companies that have done big change they have put a lot of resources in, more proportionally than we've done and they've done it in 5–10 years and we don't have the luxury of having lots of money to play with or to reinvest, we're not able to reinvest the same proportions so I think the political environment affects us.
>
> (Senior manager)

The impact of good board-level commitment in the early development of Gossamer Hospital's improvement system is evident at two levels. First it was vital in building the infrastructure for system wide improvement, commissioning the internal Improvement Team, funding associated posts and developing mechanisms to align organisational goals to operational activities; second, board level commitment provided legitimacy for change. For example, the visibility of board members actively supporting and engaging with the work stimulated change by helping to overcome the resistance of others. One respondent described the impact the chief executive had on a rapid improvement event she was involved in during 2008:

> We were really lucky to have him [the chief executive] on the team. At first it was a bit intimidating because he's like the pioneer in our hospital but he had some really good views on what we could do which was great, and he was very passionate. At first it was hard trying to get the senior managers to actually understand where we were coming from … so having the Chief executive on the team really helped … It's just getting people to listen and to open their mind.
>
> (Junior clinician)

Further board support was evidenced through the presence of directors at monthly workshops. The monthly workshops (called 'out-brief'), were where participants of RIEs that had taken place that month were given the opportunity to showcase their work, share results and generally celebrate their achievements with others across the organisation. Board-level buy-in reduced the level of bureaucracy that frequently inhibits change at an operational level. Simple changes such as the relocation of plug sockets so that equipment can be moved to an area in order to reduce non-value adding activity (such as excess movement), can sometimes take several weeks or months to initiate, however a mid-week meeting of the board took place during

RIE weeks in order to highlight such activities, remove the need for paper work and official procedures and simply expedite the required actions.

The improvement team and improvement academy

Training in lean principles for all employees through Gossamer Hospital's improvement academy lay at the heart of Gossamer Hospital's whole system approach to lean implementation. Training was available to all staff comprising a graduated curriculum of lean learning and leading to staff certification at green, bronze, silver, gold and platinum levels. Fillingham (2008) describes platinum as close to sensei (great master). All new staff at Gossamer Hospital were required to undertake green training, which taught the basic principles of lean and conveyed why the organisation was using lean. Staff wishing to progress their roles to managerial positions were required to attain more advanced levels of accreditation. This process ensures that all new staff have experience of Gossamer Hospital's improvement system, are able to engage in Gossamer Hospital's improvement system as 'the way we do things around here', and contributes towards a gradual cultural shift at all levels of the organisation, with those attaining higher levels of certification moving into more senior and managerial roles.

A new leader and a new era for Gossamer Hospital

At the end of 2010, the former chief operating officer and chief nurse of Gossamer Hospital took over as chief executive. It was during this changeover that Gossamer Hospital was experiencing difficulties in sustaining some of the improvement work. Staff attendance at 'out-brief' meetings where lean activity was shared and celebrated had dropped off considerably. This drop in attendance was significant as it is signalled that interest in Gossamer Hospital's improvement system was declining and thus the culture of continuous improvement had yet to embed across the organisation. In other words, knowledge and experience of lean implementation was not yet a core capability for a sustainable performance advantage.

Hailed as a pioneer of lean in the English NHS, the loss of the previous chief executive heralded a compelling phase in the development of Gossamer Hospital's approach to whole system improvement. In addition, during 2011, under the UK government's *Transforming Community Services* white paper, the former hospital integrated with community services, and also became a tertiary centre for specialist women's and children's centre in the northwest of England. This 'integration' had the effect of considerably changing the focus of the organisation to one not only focussed on hospital services, but also focussed on the whole value stream from the GP right through to post hospital rehabilitation and preventative care.

The incumbent chief executive recalled a period of dramatic change, which called for a re-examination of organisational purpose through the 'fresh eyes' of a new leader; the first thing she did was conduct a systematic strategic review right across the organisation led by Gossamer Hospital's improvement team. She explained her rationale:

> If you take on a legacy you have to review it. What we hadn't done before was find out what the staff felt. This process exposed a lot of medical staff to Gossamer Hospital's processes for quality improvement and analysing information. I wanted to get clinical engagement.

A good start…

The findings of the strategic review allowed the incumbent chief executive to look objectively at whether Gossamer Hospital's improvement system had clinical engagement. The review found that doctors liked the processes for data analysis and improvement and in view of coming together as an integrated organisation, some specialities indicated that they wanted the improvement team to help them to adapt to the new integrated organisational context. The organisation was changing and while Gossamer Hospital's system for improvement had clinical engagement, the executive team knew that they could soon lose this engagement if they didn't follow through with the system, so the question from the top of the organisation became: 'how do we do the strategic aspects of the work from lean?' Policy deployment had been used in the past and the chief executive sought to develop and adapt this approach further in line with the changing priorities of a new integrated organisation. An organisation wide value stream analysis (VSA) took place to ascertain the fundamental purpose of the new organisation: 'what would it do and what would it be about?' This work led to a refinement of the original True North goals. Developed jointly by staff, governors and patients the focus was on establishing new organisational values at the same time as maintaining a constancy of purpose. These new organisational goals have evolved to become 'Best care for better health; valued, respected and proud; and responsible use of resources' (see Figure 17.2).

No more heroes

Despite the organisation's decision to move onto the next iteration of Gossamer Hospital's improvement system, it wasn't until the incumbent chief executive attended a conference in Australia that she finally took a 'leap of faith' in the system. Like the chief executive before her, it was through discussions with others, sharing and learning about their experiences with lean that finally convinced her that this was something that could really work. In her own words, the incumbent chief executive recalls an 'aha moment': 'I suddenly realised I was talking about [Gossamer Hospital's improvement system] and it was like heroic leadership – I asked myself: did I really live and breathe it?' Aligned to this, a critical reflection of the hospital's approach to improvement led to a realisation that there were some important layers of the organisation that the improvement system had failed to penetrate. Specific tensions identified by the new chief executive included:

- a lack of active board commitment: the improvement system was considered the domain of the director of strategy and improvement, other members of the board were not actively engaged;

Figure 17.2 New 'True North' goals

- tensions with the finance director relating to benefits realisation; and
- tensions with the operations director around how much an organisation can really be redesigned.

The outcome of this frank reflection was the recognition that the organisation needed to move away from a heroic leadership style towards distributed leadership: 'If you say we are going to be ABC, your board must be able to sell it; push the pride.'

In response to this recognition, the incumbent chief executive resolved that all directors must take part in RIEs and all middle managers must attain at least bronze training through the Gossamer Hospital's improvement academy. This was a brave move since, historically, it is the middle managers who are the most resistant to change, and this is the layer that can be most threatened through implementing lean. As one respondent stated, middle managers 'have the most to lose', in other words, lean implementation signals a move away from a command and control approach to one that empowers staff to identify and improve their work directly. This presents a disconcerting shift in management style, and one that does little to assert the value of the middle manager, a subject of recurrent debate in healthcare and across the public sector (Burgess and Currie, 2013). However, middle managers, and particularly hybrid middle managers (those with clinical and managerial roles) are the people who can have the most impact on the environment in which change happens (Burgess and Currie, 2013; Balogun, 2003; Nonaka and Takeuchi, 1995).

From 'the a-ha moment' to 'the memo moment'

While speaking at a lean conference in Australia, the incumbent chief executive sent a 'memo' via email to two senior directors outlining her thoughts on

Gossamer Hospital's improvement system and cementing her commitment to lean stating:

> We need a LEAN mission statement and that is to truly deserve the title of one of the best LEAN organisations in the world … [Following which,] 'they' [the directors,] told me they sat down with pure relief – their chief exec had finally got it!

Upon her return to Gossamer Hospital from the conference, the chief executive resolved to ensure that the whole organisation, including the board, were clear that Gossamer Hospital's improvement system was the vehicle to make Gossamer Hospital an independent organisation capable of adapting to change and building the capacity to adapt and thrive in an austere environment. It was this memo that also outlined the chief executive's explicit intention to break the current culture of mere compliance with externally derived performance targets, to a culture where Gossamer Hospital aims to be 'best in class'. Thus, she emphasised the organisation should not work towards targets and then stop when they get there but keep going in pursuit of perfection.

This leap of faith was a catalyst for a renewed organisational commitment to Gossamer Hospital's improvement system as a framework for implementing lean. The chief executive's renewed stance to the organisation was that lean was, 'non-negotiable'. In the following months, the new chief executive dramatically improved attendance at the out-brief meetings, ensuring that improvement activity was shared among employees and helping to build a culture where values and behaviours were driven by a shared belief in the hospital's improvement system as a vehicle improvement linked to Gossamer Hospital's values (see Figure 17.2), while building the skill base (through the improvement academy and through participation in RIEs). The stated mission was to develop an organisation of '6000 daily problem solvers'. With regard to the changing structure of the organisation, this was viewed as an opportunity for Gossamer Hospital to improve service delivery right across the patient pathway in a manner that was previously inhibited by fragmentation across separate organisations with sometimes conflicting priorities.

Impact of system wide lean implementation upon performance

During the lifetime of lean implementation via Gossamer Hospital's improvement system, significant improvements occurred within departments and across pathways right across the organisation. Improvements to the respiratory pathway underpinned by lean principles led to impressive reductions in length of stay (reduced by 23 per cent), mortality (reduced by 23 per cent), and patient escalation to the intensive care unit (reduced by 34 per cent). Alongside this, the amount of time spent with patients by specialist respiratory nurses was increased by 50 per cent, and patients now see a consultant every day as opposed to the traditional ward round rotation which can leave patients without consultant care for up to four days at a time (see Bradley *et al.*, October 2011 for a detailed account). Improvement activity such as this is testament to the practice of the improvement team leaders in promoting honest and at times, difficult discussions among key members of staff, while at the same time always ensuring focus is maintained on the prime purpose – the patient. The improvements were facilitated by a combination of significantly increased multi-disciplinary working and a move away from traditional structuring of ward rounds to facilitate 'one decision flow' where the right team members and the right information is present at the right time to add value to every step of the patient's journey. Such improvements are testament to the joint approach of staff to acknowledging and addressing the problem and a willingness to change traditional ways of working and engage with new ones in view of making things better for the patient. A similar story, but related to the gastroenterology pathway, is recounted in the *Frontline Gastroenterology* journal (see Singh *et al.*, 2011). Again the results are equally impressive with length of stay reduced from 11.5 days in 2009 to 8.9 days in 2010, and 30-day mortality reduced from 121 (15 per cent) in 2009 to 87 (8 per cent) in 2010. Overall, hospital mortality for the trust has significantly fallen from HSMR 122 (2008–9, Dr Foster), which means 22 more deaths than are expected, to 103 in 2010–11, meaning the hospital was one of the fastest-improving hospitals in England.

Challenges of an organisational approach to lean implementation in the NHS

In practice, like all change, there was inherent 'mess' in implementing a whole system approach to improvement, and while the early years provided the infrastructure for cultural change in the organisation, without skilling the whole organisation and distributing leadership, then Gossamer Hospital will remain a telling organisation as opposed to an organisation with '6000 problem solvers'. In outlining the story of lean implementation at Gossamer Hospital we highlight that a whole organisation approach is a journey beset by many trials and tribulations along the way - it is not for the faint at heart and requires a tenacious commitment to leading lean fully to include the whole organisation, not just the 'happy few' or early adopters. Committed leadership plays a central role throughout the journey, but heroic leaders by themselves are not sufficient to facilitate whole system change. This finding aligns with work by the King's Fund Commission on Leadership and Management in the NHS (2011), citing the work of Turnbull James (2011). The report argues that we need to:

> move beyond the superhero model of leaders to a post-heroic model where the ability to work across boundaries and to persuade others over the right course of action has become more important than the cavalry charge on behalf of a single institution or organisation.
>
> (King's Fund Commission on Leadership and Management in the NHS, 2011: 18)

In the UK, healthcare providers operate in a complex, challenging and uncertain external environment. This level of complexity might suggest that a robust methodology such as lean is incommensurate with change of this degree, and that innovation is best created in a more emergent environment. Stacey (2003) and Shaw (2002) argue that institutions and organisations are made up of multiple daily interactions that are continuously changing the culture and the environment in which work is done and so the challenge is to continuously create an environment for change and innovation within an atmosphere in which there are receptive conditions such as having the right skills and the available time and space for experimentation. This is counter to the metaphor of the organisation as a 'machine' where levers can be 'pulled' to ensure specific outcomes (Morgan, 2006). Hartley and Bennington (2011) argue that organisations need to view themselves as organic living systems that continuously evolve and adapt as they interact with a changing external environment. Thus, the challenge for Gossamer Hospital is in creating a dynamic responsive organisation, when there are thousands of employees, millions of 'customers' and in reality, very little by way of control and levers.

The National Health Service is the biggest area of expenditure proportionally for the British Government and inevitably this means that there is considerable debate and reform on how well British taxes are spent on healthcare. This in England has led to considerable restructuring over the last few years, with new legislation and regulation imposed, creating a peculiar operating environment for organisations such as Gossamer Hospital where a fragile eco-system is emerging. Staff and clinicians are increasingly feeling encouraged and empowered, beginning to experience autonomy and with it the capacity to work together and to be held accountable; yet the organisation operates within a macro-system that is trying to define and manage at micro-level with thousands of national standards, guidance, and regulator and commissioner requirements. This need for control and certainty from regulators trickles through via governance arrangements within the organisation and needs deft manoeuvring to keep to the principles of 'those who are doing the work are best to make decisions about change'. The external environment thus presents an on-going challenge in sustaining a whole system approach to improvement – how can the organisation maintain adequate internal control to deliver safe services and comply with the terms of its registration, which is absolutely needed, while at the same time devolve power to frontline teams and increase innovation. In committing to a whole system approach to improvement, Gossamer Hospital believed that everyone in the organisation had the capacity to add value to patient care and, if given the freedom, support and environment to work in, patient care will continuously improve. The challenge for Gossamer Hospital in the years ahead is in continuing to nurture these conditions for sustainable change within this external context.

This chapter chronicles one organisation's approach to the implementation of lean across a whole organisational system, of which there are very few examples. Further work is needed to examine how organisations adopting a whole system approach to improvement can sustain focus on improvement beyond that required by external regulators, particularly during an era of large scale budget cuts and a plethora of performance targets. This applies as much to the health system within which Gossamer hospital operates as it does to other public sector organisations and health systems in other parts of the world.

Post-case addendum

Since this case was written, Gossamer Hospital encountered severe financial difficulty when the organisation was found to be in breach of its authorisation by the NHS Foundation Trust regulator monitor. The breach was based on serious concerns regarding the hospitals governance and was triggered by failure to meet specific targets at the time. As a result, the chief executive took early retirement and a team of interim directors were drafted into the organisation creating a time of considerable change and uncertainty. Presently, all of Gossamer Hospital's previously available material regarding improvement activity using lean methodology has been removed from their website indicating that the era for whole system change has been destabilised, although the new Quality Improvement Strategy 2014–17, describes building on strong foundations of existing improvement methodology and indicated that lean tools such as value stream analysis will continue to be used. To conclude, even the most ostensibly successful of lean implementations is not without challenge, the imperative to pursue perfection will be continually tested and the resolve to continue requires a very strong leader with a very committed team. Hopefully, the story of the lean implementation as a 'whole systems' approach in Gossamer Hospital has not ended with the foundation and previous work and achievements allowing the development of the culture to continue. Only time will tell …

References

Balogun, J. (2003) 'From blaming the middle to harnessing its potential: creating change intermediaries'. *British Journal of Management*, 14(1): 69–83.

Bohmer, R.M.J. and Ferlins, E.M. (2006) *Virginia Mason Medical Center*. HBS Case 9-606-044. Boston, MA: Harvard Business School.

Bradley, B., Bowden, M., Furnival, J. and Walton, C. (2011) 'Service redesign: a change is in the air'. *Health Service Journal*, 13 October: 29–31.

Brandao de Souza., L. (2009) 'Trends and approaches in Lean healthcare.' *Leadership in Health Services*, 22(2): 121–39.

Burgess, N. and Currie, G. (2013) 'The knowledge brokering role of the hybrid middle level manager: the case of healthcare'; *British Journal of Management*, 24: S132–42.

Burgess, N. and Radnor, Z.J. (2013) 'Evaluating Lean in healthcare'. *International Journal of Health Care Quality Assurance*, 26(3): 220–35.

Currie, G., Waring, J. and Finn, R. (2008) 'The limits of knowledge management for public services modernisation: the case of patient safety and service quality'. *Public Administration*, 86: 365–85.

Department of Health (2009) *Operating Framework for the NHS 2010/11*. London: Department of Health.

Emiliani, B. (2007) *Real Lean: Understanding the Lean Management System*, volume 1. Wethersfield, CT: Center for Lean Business Management.

Fillingham, D. (2008) *Lean Healthcare: Improving the Patient's Experience*. Chichester: Kingsham Press.

Gershon, P. (2004) *Releasing Resources to the Front Line: Independent Review of Public Sector Efficiency*. London: HM Treasury.

Grove, A.L., Meredith, J.O., MacIntyre, M., Angelis, J. and Neailey, K. (2010) 'UK health visiting: challenges faced during Lean implementation'. *Leadership in Health Services*, 23(3): 204–18.

Hartley, J. and Benington, J. (2011) *Recent Trends in Leadership Thinking and Action in the Public and Voluntary Service Sector.* A review for The King's Fund. Retrieved from www.kingsfund.org.uk/sites/files/kf/recent-trends-in-leadership-thinking-action-in-public-voluntary-service-sectors-jean-hartley-john-benington-kings-fund-may-2011.pdf (accessed 26 March 2015).

Hines, P., Holweg, M. and Rich, N., (2004) 'Learning to evolve: a review of contemporary Lean thinking'. *International Journal of Operations and Production Management*, 24(10): 994–1011.

HM Treasury (2009) *Operational Efficiency Programme: Final Report.* London: HM Treasury.

King's Fund Commission on Leadership and Management in the NHS (2011) *The Future of Leadership and Management in the NHS: No More Heroes.* Retrieved from www.kingsfund.org.uk/blog/2011/05/no-more-heroes-lesson-our-future-leaders (accessed 26 March 2015).

Kotter, J.P. (1995) 'Leading change: why transformation efforts fail'. *Harvard Business Review*, March–April: 1–10.

Liker, J.K and Morgan, J.M. (2006) 'The Toyota Way in services: the case of Lean product development,' *Academy of Management Perspectives*, 20(2): 5–20.

Lodge, A. and Bamford, D. (2008) 'New development: using lean techniques to reduce radiology waiting times'. *Public Money and Management*, 28(1): 49–52.

Lucey, J., Bateman, N. and Hines, P. (2005) 'Why major Lean transitions have not been sustained'. *Management Services*, Summer: 9–13.

Mann, D. (2009) 'The missing link: lean leadership'. *Frontiers of Health Services Management*, 26(1): 15–26.

Morgan, G. (2006) *Images of Organizations.* London: Sage.

Nonaka, I. and Takeuchi, H. (1995) *The Knowledge Creating Company.* Oxford: Oxford University Press.

Pettigrew, A., Ferlie, E. and McKee, L. (1992) 'Shaping strategic change: the case of the NHS in the 1980s.' *Public Money and Management*, 12(3): 27–31.

Proudlove, N., Moxham, C. and Boaden, R. (2008) 'Lessons for Lean in healthcare from using Six Sigma in the NHS'. *Public Money and Management*, 28(1): 27–34.

Radnor, Z.J. (2010) *Literature Review of Business Process Improvement Methodologies.* London: Advanced Institute of Management Research.

Radnor, Z. and Walley, P. (2008) 'Learning to walk before we try to run: adapting Lean for the public sector'. *Public Money and Management*, 28(1): 13–20.

Roth, G. (2006) 'Distributing leadership practices for Lean transformation'. *Reflections*, 7(2): 15–29.

Shaw, P. (2002) *Changing Conversations in Organizations.* London: Routledge.

Singh, S., Lipscomb, G., Padmakumar, K., Ramamoorthy, R., Ryan, S., Bates, V., Crompton, S., Dermody, E. and Moriarty, K. (2011) 'Republished: Daily consultant gastroenterologist ward rounds: reduced length of stay and improved inpatient mortality.' *Postgraduate Medical Journal*, 88(1044): 583–87.

Stacey, R. (2003) 'Organisations as complex responsive processes of relating.' *Journal of Innovative Management* 8(2): 25–39.

Turnbull James, K. (2011) *Leadership in Context: Lessons from New Leadership Theory and Current Leadership Development Practice.* Retrieved from www.kingsfund.org.uk/publications/articles/leadership-context-lessons-new-leadership-theory-and-current-leadership (accessed 16 December 2014).

Wojtys, E.M., Schley, L., Overgaard, K.A. and Agbabian, J. (2009) 'Applying lean techniques to improve the patient scheduling process'. *Journal for Healthcare Quality*, 31(3): 10–16.

Womack, J.P. and Jones, D.T. (1996) *Lean Thinking: Banish Waste and Create Wealth in Your Corporation*. New York: Simon & Schuster.

Young, T.P. and McClean, S.I. (2009) 'Some challenges facing Lean thinking in healthcare'. *International Journal for Quality in Healthcare*, 21(5): 309–10.

18 A lean healthcare journey

The Scottish experience

Claire F. Lindsay and Maneesh Kumar

Introduction

For several years now, public sector organisations (PSOs) across the globe have looked to the manufacturing sector for improvement methodologies to combat the growing challenges in tackling demand, capacity, service provision and issues around the reduction of errors and managing variation in processes (Marshall, 2009). Nowhere is this more apparent than in the provision of healthcare, where the lean methodology has gained popularity in its application (Pedersen and Huniche, 2011; Graban, 2009; Fillingham, 2008; Ben-Tovim *et al.*, 2007).

The aim of this chapter is to discuss the development of lean in public sector organisations with particular reference to healthcare. These insights are explored through the drivers for and the process of how lean is implemented in Trust A (a Scottish Health Board and 'early adopter' of lean). It will also be discussed whether this does include a focus on the 'softer' critical areas of cultural change, leadership support and people. The outcomes generated and sustained in their lean projects will be evaluated. The format of this chapter is as follows; initially we will discuss the application of lean in PSOs with a focus on healthcare; next the methodology employed is introduced. Following on, the drivers for, the process of implementation and outcomes, including what has been sustained or further developed from lean are discussed in Trust A. The chapter will conclude by discussing the implications of how lean is being implemented and transferrable insights which may apply for other PSOs.

What is lean?

The original definition of lean thinking is defined by the five principles of; 'precisely specify *value*, by specific product, identify the *value stream* for each product, make value *flow* without interruptions and let customer *pull* value from the producer and pursue *perfection*' (Womack and Jones, 1996: 10). Despite this definition originally being applied to the manufacturing sector, this definition is widely accepted as it is only varied slightly for healthcare. Here boundaries or silos need to be removed so all parties are focused on creating value. In healthcare, lean thinking can be defined as maximising the value of activities and processes for the patient whilst removing waste and improving quality and safety to ensure no harm is caused to the patient in the hospital environment (Jones *et al.*, 2006). Despite this focus on activities and processes, a key facet of lean involves whole cultural change with a focus on people due to 'respect for humanity.' This is a key pillar of the original Toyota Production System (TPS) which emerged from automotive manufacturing (Monden, 1983). The TPS was later best characterised as being lean, as discussed by Womack, Jones and Roos (1990) and Womack and Jones (1996).

Reporting lean successes

Seminal lean texts which brought lean to public consciousness (Womack and Jones, 1996; Womack *et al.*, 1990) focuses more on the process and operational aspects of lean. This has been replicated in the focus on process and operational improvements of lean in healthcare. This is due to the focus on key departments such as the emergency department (ED) and the outcomes these derive (Holden, 2011; Meyer, 2010; Dickson *et al.*, 2009; Ben-Tovim *et al.*, 2007). Multiple case studies are available to demonstrate the applicability of lean in healthcare. Lean is described as being 'mainstream' in Danish PSOs with healthcare providers expected to increase productivity by two per cent per annum (Pedersen and Huniche, 2011). In the UK, the most commonly referred to example is that of Bolton Royal Hospitals Trust who expected to be on a 10–20-year 'lean' journey (Fillingham, 2008). In Australia, it was at Flinders Medical Centre where lean was implemented in patient pathway work after experiencing issues in the ED (Ben-Tovim *et al.*, 2007). In the US, patient safety was the focus at the Virginia Mason Medical Centre in Seattle (Furman and Caplan, 2007), and costs and quality were the drivers of lean at Thedacare in Wisconsin (Toussaint, 2009). Lean was used in increasing service capacity in mental health in Denver (LaGanga, 2011). Many published successes are commonly restricted to projects conducted within hospital sites, with limited work focusing on healthcare provision beyond these boundaries (Grove *et al.*, 2010).

Despite these endorsements and the appearance of popularity, lean has faced sustainability challenges. lean implementations in healthcare are described as being still in their infancy, in comparison to other industries (Radnor, Holweg and Waring, 2012). Many lean implementation examples in literature are predominately provided through examination of the US healthcare system (Graban, 2009). Even exemplary lean US healthcare providers are thin on the ground, as noted by Mark Graban, who asked 'What per cent of US hospitals are using #lean methods' (Twitter, 31 May).

Challenges for lean

Despite this body of knowledge available for quality and service improvement through lean; lean healthcare in the UK is limited in approach and discusses the use of a few key tools. This is also echoed in literature which reviews the implementation of lean in the US and globally (Holden, 2011; Dickson *et al.*, 2009). These tools have been categorised into three activity areas by Radnor *et al.* (2012) as assessment, improvement, and performance monitoring.; but also noted in a similar format in the aforementioned studies Assessment involves reviewing areas of waste, assessing process flow, and process and value stream mapping. Improvement activities involve staff and are commonly conducted through the use of Kaizen or rapid improvement events (RIEs) which bring in the use of problem solving tools or use of 5s (sorting, setting in order, sweeping, standardising and sustaining). Performance monitoring measures the improvements made, usually through the use of visual standards and visual management tools (Radnor *et al.*, 2012). Tools, however, only account for around 20 per cent of effort in lean implementations with 80 per cent of effort required in the management of the social issues of lean (Mann, 2009). It has been noted that there is limited literature on the people aspects of lean (Stone, 2012; Brandão de Souza, 2009; Joosten, Bongers and Janssen, 2009) and literature that focuses on this area highlights areas of conflicts, resistance and attitudes of clinicians (Meyer, 2010; Waring and Bishop, 2010). Recent reviews of lean in healthcare in the UK have shown that lean implementations are often small projects and are disjointed, rather than organisational wide (Radnor and Osborne, 2013; Radnor, 2010).

Sustainability of lean requires a focus on these social aspects of lean at all levels in the organisation (Mann, 2009), as this links to 'respect for people' being a key pillar in the TPS (Monden, 1983). It is not just about a focus on leadership in healthcare improvement, but key stakeholders who include the professional groups (Øvretveit, 2005).

Lean success is associated with adopting 'lean thinking' (Womack and Jones, 1996) and is described as a philosophy involving whole cultural changes (Bhasin and Burcher, 2006). However, cultural change in healthcare is described as complex due to the role of professional groups (Scott *et al.*, 2003). Change, including quality initiatives and improvement, are commonly viewed as the domain of operational managers and clinical staff (Davies, Powell and Rushmer, 2007; McBride and Mustchin, 2013).

Hines, Martins and Beale (2008), Radnor *et al.* (2012) and Radnor and Osborne (2013), all highlight key issues for lean and its modification in PSOs. Radnor and Osborne (2013) argues for the need for linking lean to strategic intent, using 'freed-up' resources and changing patterns of work to meet the needs of service users. Radnor *et al.* (2012) assesses PSOs as being capacity led rather being demand led and how there is a need for effectiveness and equity. Hines *et al.* (2008) identifies the need for a 'critical' focus on the human dimensions of lean (more so in manufacturing), issues over the flow of communication/information, a lack of focus (and perhaps experience) of change, and issues over the identification of the customer.

Organisational readiness

Case studies regarded as 'best practice' highlight organisational readiness for lean. The limitations of these cases are they report projects in their infancy and the long term success of PSOs implementing lean is yet to be viewed. Indeed, Radnor and Osborne (2013) claim lean in the public sector has been 'defective' to date. It is noted that Bolton (Fillingham, 2008), Flinders (Ben-Tovim *et al.*, 2007) and Thedacare (Toussaint, 2009) were described as being at a crisis point when they commenced their lean implementations. Virginia Mason was experiencing problems with patient safety (Furman and Caplan, 2007). All best practice organisations, however, share commonalities of having a focus on patient safety and quality improvement, through adopting a systemic approach to improvement. These organisations also integrated the need to change organisational culture (Radnor and Osborne, 2013; Monden, 1983). Having executive support (Mann, 2009) is also apparent in these cases but also the recognition that there is a need for cross functional teams who include professionals (Øvretveit, 2005). Measuring organisational readiness for lean is therefore in comparison to these aforementioned best practice cases (Bolton, Flinders, Thedacare and Virginia Mason). Limitations resulting from the infancy of the reporting of these cases are noted.

Methodology

The data reported in this chapter is based on content analysis of project documents, observations and interview data with 21 managers and front line staff who have been involved in lean projects in Trust A. In the analysis, the work of Charmaz (2012) was used as both the content analysis of project documents and interview data was coded in the grounded theory method. All methods employed within the case study (see Eisenhardt, 1989 for protocol), focus on four main areas; drivers for the implementation of lean; the process of implementation; outcomes generated and sustained from lean. All project data is taken from the projects conducted in the period of 2006–12.

The NHS in Scotland

The lean methodology has been endorsed for use by the Scottish Government and has been supported for use in NHS Scotland. This support for lean can be viewed in other programmes in use in the NHS in Scotland, such as the Productive Series, Releasing Time to Care (which originated in the NHS Institute for Innovation and Improvement and has been deployed globally) (Scottish Government, 2010). Lean in healthcare is defined by the Scottish Government as supporting service redesign across the patient journey for the improvement of whole processes and improved flow through the reduction of waste and delays (Scottish Government, 2008).

The NHS in Scotland differs from that of the other home nations. Scotland by 2004 had dissolved 23 hospital Trusts, and healthcare was subsequently provided by 15 (now 14) regional health boards and this structure exists today. This reorganisation of the NHS to remove duplication and competition in Scotland was expected to minimise the 'gap between national policy and local practice' (Scottish Executive, 2000: 23). The flatter structure of the NHS in Scotland allowed for decentralisation; with frontline staff acquiring greater influence, chief executives remaining accountable for strategic leadership and governance, and divisional chief executives maintaining control of budgets and performance. This was viewed as 'rebuilding our NHS' as standards of care were prior to re-organisation, variable, with the people of Scotland facing a 'postcode lottery of care' as the focus had moved away from quality and service improvement (*ibid.*). The links with many institutions working with the NHS in England, such as the National Institute for Clinical Excellence (which advises and approves drugs and technologies for use in the NHS), were still maintained.

A Scottish health board, known as Trust A, began implementing lean in 2006. Trust A was chosen as the focus of this chapter, due to being recognised as an 'early adopter' of lean in Scotland and who were supported by NHS Education for Scotland (NES). This support was provided as it was expected learnings could be transferred to other NHS health boards in Scotland. The projects which are reviewed also differ from what has been a common focus in literature (Toussaint, 2009; Fillingham, 2008; Ben-Tovim *et al.*, 2007; Furman and Caplan, 2007). The review focuses on projects which have extended beyond single acute setting boundaries and link into shared services work conducted across the region of Trust A. Trust A is also worthy of focus as it is in the top five of the largest health authorities in the UK through this may be a limitation for sharing learnings across smaller PSOs.

Drivers for Trust A's lean journey

Following the formation of the new health boards, the chief executive (CE) of the newly formed Trust A recognised that there had to be something to 'bind together the constituent parts' of what were formerly four separate organisations. In late 2005, Trust A engaged in conversation with management consultancy organisations so they could begin in 2006, their lean journey. The use of external consultants (ECs) was to bring in expertise from an organisation who 'lived and breathed lean', in order to begin building capacity in Trust A to embed improvement through lean.

Trust A adapted a 'model' for implementing lean in their organisation and this model is described by the CE as being 'based on not just the Kaizen principle but the engineering metrics of how you could actually eliminate waste and steps out of process'.

Trust A and their executives are very proud of their lean successes and are recognised as being early adopters of the lean methodology as 'it was a gutsy thing to do and not in a self-congratulatory way but to have the courage to do it.' Lean is linked to the organisation's strategy for the development of the organisation. This was to be achieved through the development of Trust A staff by promoting quality and patient care. Lean in Trust A is described as a programme, though a systemic approach in line with case studies previously discussed (Fillingham, 2008; Furman and Caplan, 2007). Lean is described as 'the way we do things around here' by the CE. The CE had been a vocal and visual supporter of the lean programme. From the start it has been linked to both the organisation's own strategic objectives and also to those at NHS Scotland and Scottish Government level for the improvement and enhancement of quality in healthcare provision. Strategically, the organisation was also aiming to join 'best in class' global healthcare providers. They were benchmarking with other global healthcare providers through the use of the McKinsey Global Health Tracker.

Lean in Trust A was viewed by the CE and other executive directors as not just focusing on processes but full cultural change as it was recognised that lean would be 'an overall cultural organisational intervention.' The CE emphasises the need for a focus on people and empowerment in healthcare improvement:

> If you work in … an organisation like the NHS, yes, we've got lots of buildings, yes we've got lots of equipment and that sort of stuff but ultimately what makes the difference is our people and so what we are trying to do and what we or lean absolutely successfully did was to empower people to take decisions, to make things better for patients.

Alongside this cultural benefit there was recognition that process improvement would support staff in facing longer term future challenges. By already 'working smarter' the organisation would be prepared for what they were forecasting – future efficiency savings being required under a challenging financial climate.

Developing organisational readiness for lean

From the start, lean was linked to organisational culture and received strong executive support. The CE is viewed as 'bringing lean to Trust A' as lean was designed to support staff in providing patient care. Trust A from the start, formed their own branded 'Lean in Trust A' programme which was supported by five improvement leads (ILs) from within the organisation who were to conduct projects and training with cross function teams.

These five ILs were chosen from the areas of organisational development and modernisation to be fully trained by the ECs who were aiding the lean implementation. All ILs had previous experience of leading and facilitating change programmes. The Trust A ILs would work with the ECs. Each IL was allocated a mentor from the ECs; firstly to complete training courses and then working in three phases. The first phase was for ILs to shadow the ECs on projects. In the second phase, ILs would actively work on a project with their EC mentor, and thirdly, lead their own project with support provided by their EC mentor where required. Training for all staff, regards to lean, was initially delivered from ECs, but training and development of the Trust A ILs was to enhance the organisations' capacity to build lean internally. Trust A ILs took over the provision of training and development for all staff taking on lean projects. By the end of 2011, 355 staff had received full lean training, with 18 per cent of these working out-with the main acute sites, in community health and the local authority. The ILs attempt to maintain contact with all trainees through surveys, which are affected by limited response rates. Not all staff members have followed up this training with leading lean projects (the reasons for which are unknown). There have been projects conducted by staff following training which the ILs report on. This building of internal capacity for lean beyond ILs has seen projects link into wider pathway work and has contributed to the sustainability of lean in these services.

Leadership in lean

Although the CEO has been described as a 'vocal and visual' supporter of lean, other members of the executive support the Trust's branded lean programme. Each project is provided with an executive sponsor who is ultimately in charge of the results generated and maintained from the lean project. The executive sponsor will also attend lean events and the reporting stage. This sends a clear message to staff that there is support for lean at the very top of the organisation. ILs and staff involved in lean projects were also consistent in noting that the CE often attended lean events and for many staff it was their first interaction with him.

At service level, each project is also allocated a process owner who is going to take sole responsibility for the action plan for generating improvement and the sustainability. The process owner directs ILs to service staff so pre-work can be conducted and data can be gathered in the service under review.

The process of implementing lean

Figure 18.1 illustrates how lean projects are implemented in Trust A by ILs. This process was observed by one of the researchers and then verified through interview data and project data to ensure this was the approach undertaken by all ILs working in lean in Trust A. These projects are fed top down by the Executive or requested by the services themselves as a project proposal. The projects are 'a strategic goal the improvement team [IL] has to work with.' Each proposal, if successful, will be given to an IL to work on and from then the IL with contact the service and speak to the process owner (service manager) and further define the project. Recently the team have adopted a project charter for use in their projects due to issues in getting process owners to commit to and take forward lean implementations (sustainability) after the ILs have handed over the project. This project charter cannot be enforced to the point of repercussions. However, it is hoped that by signing, the process owner is demonstrating their commitment to lean by specifying the projects, intended goals, reporting to their executive sponsor and detailing how they will sustain the project in the longer term. Once this has been confirmed with executive and process owner support, the ILs commence pre-work on the lean implementation.

Pre-work or assessment in lean projects

Lean, as has been previously noted by Radnor *et al.* (2012), takes the form of assessment, improvement and performance measurement and this is demonstrated in Trust A as noted in Figure 18.1. Pre-work by ILs involves the assessment period (6–8 weeks of 'pre-work'). The ILs can begin pre-work for the project (see Figure 18.1), by visiting the service, meeting staff and identifying key stakeholders who will be involved in the lean improvement. Pre-work includes meeting process owners and staff, determining the voice of the customer, observing the area/process under study, conducting interviews and gathering data to assess and map process flow and value streams.

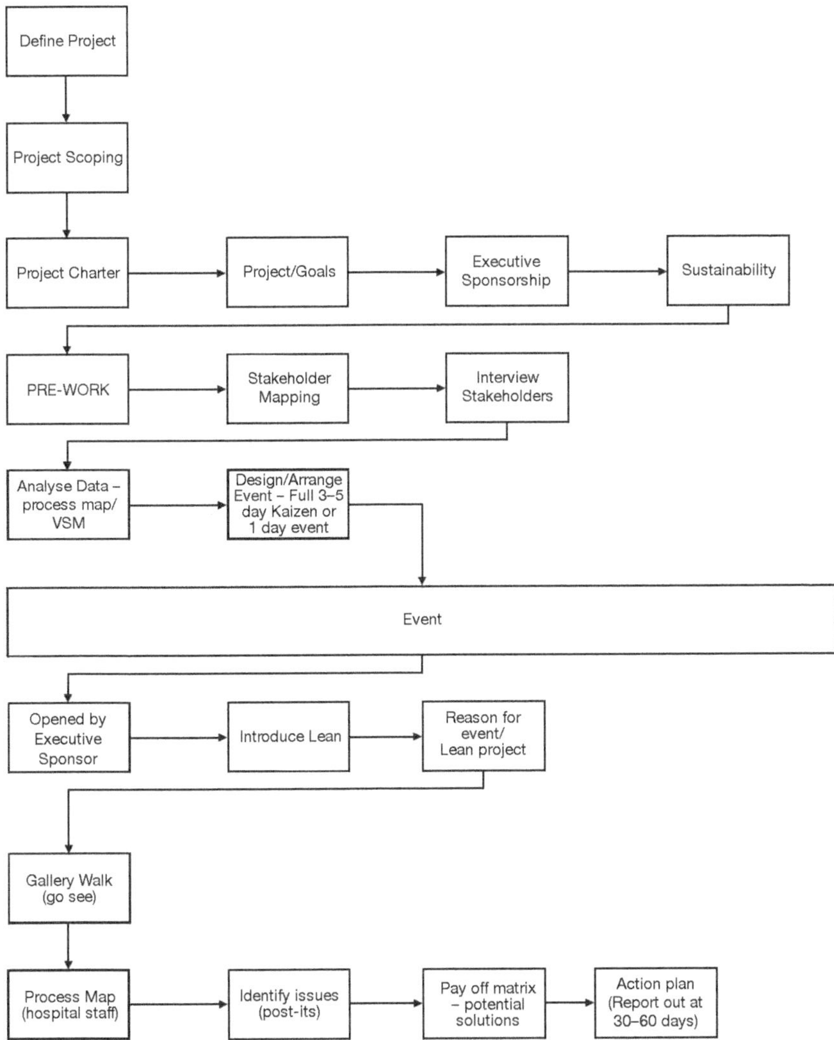

Figure 18.1 Process of implementing lean in Trust A

Respect for people

From the outset, the pre-work stages have included a focus on people through building relationships with staff in services. The multi-disciplinary nature of healthcare and the need for cross functional teams (ILs, physicians, nurses, managers, administrators and partnership (union) representatives to name just a few) show the process of building relationships and communication is key. This is also important in working with shared services where each provider has their own ways of working in how they own their parts of their services. There is cynicism noted by staff due to the nature of change in the NHS and reorganisations. Consequently, this means that engaging staff in lean projects from the earliest stages has been crucial in order to secure future successes. As shown in Figure 18.1, in pre-work stages stakeholder interviews are conducted with staff at all levels within services. These aid the IL in recognising the differing perceptions about, and the implications of the lean project on services. The importance of this is discussed as:

> the stakeholder interviews tell you two things: one, they give you detail about the process, and they also tell you about people which is really, really important. Because lean, although it looks very theoretical and very textbook, I would say in figures, my view is 70 per cent people, if not more. And with the best process in the world if people aren't willing to follow or buy into then you have a problem. So it tells you two things. One is the objective parts but also the other parts, where the tensions are, where there's maybe subjective influences going on which may be having an influence on how their process is performing now, what we might need to address in order for them to get better in the future.
>
> (IL2)

Tensions in lean projects

By the very nature of working with people, tensions are noted by ILs. As lean seeks to improve processes in service, by the very nature of the lean process, people from different backgrounds are involved. Table 18.1 discusses pathway projects and by the very nature of these pathway projects, they include multi-disciplinary and cross functional teams. They also include shared services linkages where health workers share patient pathways with social work and local council employees (delayed discharges) as well as community health and third sector (substance misuse). Full patient pathway projects are noted for their complexity resulting from having shared services stakeholders where some pre-existing relationship tensions may exist. Some of these tensions are those noted previously in PSOs such as those due to issues over communication and information (Hines *et al.*, 2008). These tensions have to be overcome to facilitate success in lean. Full pathway projects are complex, and contained projects are perceived to be easier to get buy-in from staff as 'you can actually get in there, work with the staff, get to know them, it's about hearts and minds' (IL3).

The IL will be involved in the full pathway project, but often staff from each respective part of the service will be involved at the required stages, starting with the initial assessment and improvement work. Breaking down of the processes is viewed to be beneficial; as a physician involved in one full pathway project said, 'I think the good thing about lean is it breaks it down into small manageable chunks and you've got someone overseeing the whole thing.' Some examples of full pathway work are noted in Table 18.1 and discussed below.

Table 18.1 Patient pathway projects in Trust A

Project	*Issues identified*	*Outcomes*	*Measurable benefit*	*Sustainability/Development of Lean*
Delayed Discharges (Medicine for the Elderly – MOE)	Lack of visibility across the board of beds available. Delayed discharges is impacted beyond the hospital and involves multi-agencies. Issues over post-acute care, care packages, patient's progression to nursing home/residential care for transfer or discharge.	3pm notification to MOE central site of beds to be available the following day. Increased utilisation of 'downstream' beds such as GP beds and local hospitals. Use of traffic light system to aid discharge planning and bed management across the health board. Centralised bed management system: patients pulled into the right bed and treatment pathway instead of pushed.	72 Occupational Therapy Assistant slots released per month due to simple changes in ward routines. Estimated 2,500 acute bed days per annum released as patients released/transferred to downstream care. Improved relationships and communication of processes between healthcare sites and agencies means more effective and accurate information available to patients and carers.	Further role out of projects across Trust A in the period of 2006–12. Use of e-booking for patient transport (booked at ward level) generating savings estimated at £60,000 per annum. Projects moving beyond the acute MOE pathway to link into Social Work for managing of further care packages which were identified as impacting on delayed discharges. Standardising acute care and social work paperwork and communications procedures to resolve complexity. Working with local council in partnership to utilise relevant resources, e.g. day centres, crisis care and community resources. Alignment of consultants' job plans to meet service user requirements.

Table 18.1 continued

Project	*Issues identified*	*Outcomes*	*Measurable benefit*	*Sustainability/Development of Lean*
Substance Misuse (South)	Waiting times for new patient appointments. Drugs: Up to 4 months. Alcohol: Up to 6 weeks to see a community psychiatric nurse. Drugs service Did Not Attend (DNA) rate was 40% with some patients receiving multiple appointments. Multi-agency offerings: community healthcare services, social work addictions team and voluntary sector.	Patient-focused booking. Improved standardised appointment schedule and DNA handling. Dedicated appointments booking line. Ability to text message patients with same appointment day reminders New hub to be opened.	Waiting times: Drugs – 4 months to 2 months at longest part. Alcohol – 6 weeks to 4 days at longest wait. Drugs – 28% increase in patients attending. Did not attend (DNA): Alcohol – reduction from 65% to 7%. Drugs: 25% reduction in the first two weeks and then reduced by a further 21%.	Standardised appointment scheduling and patient focused booking system implemented. 534 hours saved in alcohol clinic. 28% increase in drugs patients attending at new appointments. Drugs DNA maintained. Learning from South subsequently applied in West.
Substance Misuse (West)	Drug and alcohol waiting times for appointments. Clients/referrers not all aware of services offered in the area (multi-agency offerings: community healthcare services, social work addictions team and voluntary sector). Lack of standardised assessment.	Inter-agency group formed with monthly sessions to improve working. Website designed with all service information accessible from all providers on one site. Standardised working implemented – single shared assessment protocols were designed and agreed upon across all agencies.	Reduction for drug and alcohol appointments from a maximum of 24 weeks to 3 weeks. Post kaizen waiting list for treatment went from 122 to 40 with longest wait down to 8 weeks. Centralised methadone clinic planned and operational with methadone titration down from 12 weeks to 3 weeks.	Successes maintained in South and West show potential for expansion across the region. Later implemented in South East, and East. HEAT target met and exceeded. Clear pathway established and maintained across referral, care and discharge processes. Safe and effective drug titration maintained and meeting targets.

Table 18.1 continued

Project	*Issues identified*	*Outcomes*	*Measurable benefit*	*Sustainability/Development of Lean*
Dermatology Outpatients	Need to achieve 12 week target for routine referrals and 62 day target for patients who result in a cancer diagnosis. Future challenges also apparent over 18 weeks referral to treatment time guarantee's (Scottish Government target) and 31 days from diagnosis to treatments (cancer patients) target Services impacted by General Practitioner (GP) contract changes so work previously conducted at GP level, now referred to Dermatology speciality.	Improved use of referral form and process meant patient wait for treatment has been cut by 37 days Implemented patient focused booking to include sub specialities which has reduced DNA's. Kaizen work to improve capacity due to additional load from GP's saw changes in consultant job plans. Recognition of increasing demand for specialist services resulted in a review of staff training. Email advice service for GP's now provided by a consultant.\	Work conducted with plastic surgery on cancer treatment has led to the development of parallel clinics reducing the need for secondary appointments and saving days in the patient journey. Changes to job plans for consultants added an extra 228 general appointment slots, 126 phototherapy slots and 462 tumour slots. Traffic light system introduced for triage of referrals – tumour referral within 2-3 weeks and lesions within 4 weeks. Extra training of one nurse for high demand treatment and nurses currently working to establish extra capacity for nurse led treatments. E-triage service being introduced, through subsequent Lean projects being conducted. Improved relations within and across the service post-Kaizen event(s).	Plastics work maintained and feeds into tumour service where urgent melanoma patients are seen within two weeks. Dermatology have subsequently been include in pathology Lean projects and now systems implemented to meet the 62 day targets set. Nurses have continued to work on initiatives to build on further developing capacity for nurse led treatments. GP advice service has been maintained and this has improved management of 'unnecessary' referrals for 'cosmetic' procedures. Further roll out of E-triage was introduced. Patient focused booking is fully centralised, in place and has been extended to cover specialities.

Source: created by the author based on interview and research data

Medicine for the Elderly

The pathway activities encompassed under Medicine for the Elderly (MOE) were a strategic goal the organisation had. This was linked to a need for formulating clear pathways and access points to ensure patients across the Trust A region received equitable and safe quality of treatment. This strategic focus was linked to Scottish Government set 'HEAT' ministerial targets, this acronym representing:

- **H**ealth improvement;
- **E**fficiency and governance improvements;
- **A**ccess to services; and
- **T**reatment appropriate to individuals.

As Table 18.1 shows, Trust A has generated good results in their projects, with support from GPs in the MOE project. Moving beyond the healthcare setting can be a challenge until all actors begin to recognise each part in the process. Even working with different professional groups can be challenging. Staff can fear evaluation of their processes and withhold knowledge, viewing evaluation as criticism. Although sustainability is discussed, there were challenges in engaging staff when rolling out projects across sites. Trust A focus their initial efforts on communication through the pre-work or assessment stage to engage staff, and then common lean tools to aid evaluation and the improvement process are applied.

In work related to the MOE pathway project, an IL discussed problems uncovered and the challenges faced when patients were audited to see how much therapy they were receiving, to determine if this was a factor in delayed discharges:

> You could see there was a mismatch between the therapists' day and the availability of the patient for the therapist which meant there was quite a lot of time where they did not have access to patients, or they were there but it was early morning and it wasn't a reasonable time necessarily to see patients.

Uncovering misalignment such as this has resulted in 72 occupational therapists slots per month being made available through work linking into the MOE pathway project through simple changes to ward routines.

From the sustainability and development of projects discussed in Table 18.1, it is shown that subsequent projects linked in to MOE and delayed discharges. Five ILs have worked across these projects and the original IL discussed opening 'Pandora's Box' as she was first to discover the misalignment of allied health professional therapists' time and patient availability. The others followed in areas across the region. Despite initial challenges of therapists fearing criticism of their work, they were described as being 'movers and shakers' who have continued to support the team in subsequent projects.

Substance misuse projects

The substance misuse project (South), although challenging at first due to the multi-disciplinary, shared services input, overcame initial challenges: 'they ended up working in a very multi-disciplinary way, so with hind sight that was a really successful project' as 'we dropped DNA rates – they actually became leading (in the region) and I think in Scotland to hit targets' (IL1). Government set targets also influenced this project and provided the main drivers of the project. Misuse Services were not meeting current targets and were not expected to meet subsequent targets unless improved processes were embedded in the services. Challenges noted in multi-agency projects like substance misuse were the amount of agencies and sectors involved, all with different systems and protocols. Notable outcomes for managing clients (patients) were around standardisation of process and protocols to improve patients' access, safety of treatment and experience. The success in this project was to see the same IL recruited to help another substance misuse group (West) which led to greater success and better multi-disciplinary and shared services working. Within a three day Kaizen event voluntary, social work and health came together and with support of the executive sponsor, they managed to agree to co-locate to a hub, found premises and were up and running within three months. These projects, although challenging has demonstrated the social attributes of lean such as communication, knowledge sharing and empowerment to lead to lean improvements.

The sustainability and reported success of both South and West has seen the same IL progress to working in South East with the same approach being taken with multi-agency involvement across the regional area. Despite initial suspicions over health and social workers working together and the fear of 'health' telling social work 'what to do', social workers were regarded as 'fantastic' to work with due to their drive in taking the project forward.

Dermatology

Increased demand and unaligned capacity saw dermatology facing huge challenges. Target pressures were apparent and the service was struggling to meet demand without provision of additional out of hour's clinics, further placing strain on service budgets. Changes to GP contracts had resulted in increased demand for minor treatments. Previously these treatments had been conducted at primary care level, but were now being referred to acute services for management. Processes were unaligned, with equity and access to service determined by varying triage procedures across sites, so standardisation was required.

Dermatology was viewed as a successful lean project for Trust A and has since been the focus of additional pathway projects, linking into plastic surgery and pathology. Demand and capacity were better aligned in the service resulting in changes to consultant job plans to meet service users' requirements. This outcome has been limited in lean reporting to date (Radnor and Osborne, 2013). Improved management of referrals was implemented at acute service level. Work was extended into primary care with an advice service for GPs offered in an attempt to minimise inappropriate referrals. Like the previous MOE and substance misuse projects, dermatology outcomes also contributed to the meeting and management of targets. Ongoing initiatives to facilitate demand management are evident in this service.

Sustainability

Although these multi-site projects are recognised as being sustained and have generated further improvement from successive lean projects, this has not been the case in every project generated from Trust A. One IL discussed a 'contained' project in a 'laboratory type' environment which was initially successful. The contained project had won the 'Lean in Trust A' award for best project. Staff supported the project but 'it was picked apart' by a manager and the original state returned. The Improvement Team were dismayed that a change of manager could result in this 'damage' but this only serves to highlight why those viewed as leaders are important in sustaining improvement (Mann, 2009). Other projects have suffered from lack of professional (physician) staff engagement which affected project timescales and outcomes. One lean project linked to the wider MOE project, suffered from a lack of 'professional' (physician) involvement which frustrated one physician as this restricted the ability to make quality improvements through lean. This physician identifies some fellow physician colleagues who regard 'professionalism' as 'being able to do what you want,' rather than engaging in improvement work focusing on patients. This links to the recognition that engagement and involvement of medical professionals is essential in quality improvement initiatives (Øvretveit, 2005).

The focus on people in lean

Although this chapter has reported outcomes from lean projects as conducted by Trust A, it should be noted from Table 18.1 that relationships do feature in discussion over lean. Outcomes in MOE, substance misuse and dermatology have been improved relationships. Especially within MOE and substance misuse, this has included improved shared service relationships. There are still existing tensions in engaging staff and there have been issues with the engagement of physicians, which has impacted projects. Although we have mapped out the implementation process for lean in Trust A, we have noted the processes which are dedicated to focusing on people and the role of multiple stakeholders in the lean projects and the importance of this. This approach reiterates that although it is already noted there has been a large focus on tools and techniques in lean (Radnor *et al.*, 2012) in PSOs, the focus does have to be on people and the management of lean as a change process (Stone, 2012; Mann, 2009; Hines *et al.*, 2008).

Conclusion

We have examined how Trust A, a Scottish Health Board, has implemented lean in the period 2006 to early 2012. It was of particular interest to review the drivers for and the process of implementing lean. Outcomes and the sustainability of lean as viewed through the lens of projects conducted have also been examined. Trust A in the period 2006–12 had conducted 75 projects but we have chosen to focus on those which have included shared services. As this chapter has discussed, this is an organisation that has, by 2014, now been implementing lean for eight years. Trust A share commonalties with other best in class case studies in their focus on changing organisational culture and their readiness to adopt lean for long term improvement (Toussaint, 2009; Fillingham, 2008; Furman and Caplan, 2007).

Trust A is viewed as successfully implementing lean externally and transferrable insights have been shared with other PSOs in Scotland. The restructuring of health provision in Scotland resulted in the desire for a 'cultural intervention' by senior management. This restructuring devolved more power to health boards and openness to improvement was financially supported by NES to share learnings across NHS Scotland. Combined with this was also the recognition of forthcoming financially straightened times with pressures on budgets. This at least highlights the organisation understood lean as involving whole cultural change (Bhasin and Burcher, 2006). Far from being a public sector organisation that had no contingency and lacked linking lean with strategic focus (Radnor and Walley, 2006), the opposite has been shown in Trust A. Trust A focused in aligning lean with strategic intent from the start (Radnor and Osborne, 2013) and focused on building capacity through lean.

This chapter reports the process undertaken by ILs who are implementing lean. This focus does go some way in addressing the lack of focus to date on organisations who are reporting on lean implementations beyond the initial 1–2-year stage. Many public sector organisations have reported using lean, but often this work is a focus on initial projects and quick gains (*ibid.*). From the start, lean in Trust A has been linked to future ambitions and strategy. This is reflected in the process of initiating and implementing lean projects which have been undertaken as part of the lean programme.

The systemic approach is viewed with projects which build upon previous work, linked to strategic objectives, and is supported through building capacity for lean in the organisation. This is facilitated through Trust A's own branded training programme. This builds into the shared services work where lean is being spread and supported by training of external partners.

This support for lean was supported at Executive level with vocal and visible support of leaders which undoubtedly has been a factor in successful projects (Mann, 2009). This can be compared to where projects have failed as senior or influential staff (managers, physicians) have not supported projects despite recognition that this support is essential for success (Øvretveit, 2005).

The projects noted in this chapter do highlight measureable outcomes such as saving in bed days, extra capacity identified and the improved meeting of targets. These projects have also used lean for effectiveness but also for equity for service users in access (dermatology and substance misuse projects) to the service under review (Radnor *et al.*, 2012). Trust A has approached lean in a 'typical manner', with three phases identified, as with previous reporting (*ibid.*). However, these projects do move beyond the traditional reporting of projects conducted in acute (hospital) provisions (Holden, 2011; Fillingham, 2008; Ben Tovim *et al.*, 2007). These projects have moved across the organisation and include cross-regional and shared service provision which has received limited focus to date (Radnor and Osborne, 2013). The projects in the case of dermatology and MOE has also seen demand and capacity aligned for improved service provision by changing of medical consultant job plans which too has not been an outcome noted in project reporting (*ibid.*). Even with these traditional outcomes being reported, the focus on people is reiterated. Improved relationships between staff within and across services is being recognised as a measureable benefit from lean projects. This further contributes to the call for greater focus in this area (Stone, 2012; Brandão de Souza, 2009; Joosten *et al.*, 2009). Despite the target driven nature of lean projects, the successes here demonstrate the applicability of 'manufacturing approaches' such as lean being used in PSOs such as healthcare (Marshall, 2009).

Key contribution

In this chapter we have contributed to the growing body of lean literature in PSOs. We have discussed the importance of multi-agency and cross functional team involvement for improving service provision and relationships in shared services. The multi-agency work undertaken in the projects on substance misuse and MOE pathways addressed some of the resource issues faced by PSOs which were a driver for the projects in Table 18.1. By focusing on people and aligning lean to strategy, this has further sustained lean through building relationships and improving communication for further role out of projects. This, however, leaves scope for further research to be undertaken in this area, and as such the following propositions are provided:

- Proposition 1: A clear alignment between organisational strategic objectives and lean is required for long-term sustainability.
- Proposition 2: A clear process, which including a concentrated focus on people prior to initiation of the lean project, builds consensus for improvement through lean.
- Proposition 3: Cross-disciplinary teams which include the professional groups, are an enabler for lean success and sustainability.
- Proposition 4: Lean implementations focusing on shared services in PSOs can have a far greater impact across the value chain.

References

Ben-Tovim, D.I., Bassham, J.E., Bolch, D., Martin, M.A., Dougherty, M. and Szwarcbord, M. (2007) 'Lean thinking across a hospital: redesigning care at the Flinders Medical Centre'. *Australian Health Review*, 31(1): 10–15.

Bhasin, S. and Burcher, P. (2006) 'Lean viewed as a philosophy'. *Journal of Manufacturing Technology*, 17(1): 56–72.

Brandão De Souza, L. (2009) 'Trends and approaches in lean healthcare'. *Leadership in Health Services*, 22(2): 121–39.

Charmaz, K. (2012) *Constructing Grounded Theory*. London: Sage.

Davies, H.T.O., Powell, A.E. and Rushmer, R.K. (2007) *Healthcare Professionals' Views on Clinician Engagement in Quality Improvement.* Edinburgh: NHS Quality Improvement Scotland.

Dickson, E.W., Angeulov, Z., Vetterick, D., Eller, A. and Singh, S. (2009) 'Use of Lean in the emergency department: a case series of 4 hospitals'. *Annals of Emergency Medicine*, 54(4): 504–10.

Eisenhardt, K.M. (1989) 'Building theories from case study research'. *The Academy of Management Review*, 14(4): 532–50.

Fillingham, D. (2008) *Lean Healthcare - Improving the Patient's Experience.* Chichester: Kingsham.

Furman, C. and Caplan, R. (2007) 'Applying the Toyota production system: using a patient safety alert system to reduce error'. *Joint Commission Journal on Quality and Patient Safety*, 33(7): 376–86.

Graban, M. (2009) *Lean Hospitals: Improving Quality, Patient Safety and Employee Satisfaction.* New York: Productivity Press.

Grove, A.L., Meredith, J.O., MacIntyre, M., Angelis, J. and Neailey, K. (2010) 'UK health visiting: challenges faced during lean implementation'. *Leadership in Health Services*, 23(3): 204–18.

Hines, P., Martins, A.L. and Beale, J. (2008) 'Testing the boundaries of lean thinking: observations from the legal public sector'. *Public Money and Management*, 28(1): 35–40.

Holden, R.J. (2011) 'Lean thinking in emergency departments: a critical review'. *Annals of Emergency Medicine*, 57(3): 265–78.

Jones, D., Mitchell, A., Ben-Tovim, D., Fillingham, D., Makin, C., Silvester, K., Brunt, D. and Glenday, I. (2006) *Lean Thinking for the NHS.* London: NHS Confederation.

Joosten, T., Bongers, I. and Janssen, R. (2009) 'Application of Lean thinking to health care: issues and observations'. *International Journal for Quality in Health Care*, 21(5): 341–47.

LaGanga, L.R. (2011) 'Lean service operations: reflections and new directions for capacity expansion in outpatient clinics'. *Journal of Operations Management*, 29(5): 422–33.

Mann, D. (2009) 'The missing link: lean leadership'. *Frontiers of Health Services Management*, 26(1): 15–26.

Marshall, M. (2009) 'Applying quality improvement approaches to health care'. *BMJ*, 339: 819–20.

McBride, A. and Mustchin, S. (2013) 'Crowded out? The capacity of HR to change healthcare work practices'. *The International Journal of Human Resource Management*, 24(16): 3131–45.

Meyer, H. (2010) 'Life in the "Lean" lane: performance improvement at Denver Health'. *Health Affairs*, 29: 2054–60.

Monden, Y. (1983) *Toyota Production System.* Norcross, GA: Industrial Engineering and Management Press.

Øvretveit, J. (2005) 'Leading improvement'. *Journal of Health Organization and Management*, 19(6): 413–30.

Pedersen, E.R.G and Huniche, M. (2011) 'Determinants of lean success and failure in the Danish public sector: a negotiated order perspective'. *International Journal of Public Sector Management*, 24(5): 403–20.

Pettersen, J. (2009) 'Defining lean production: some conceptual and practical issues'. *The TQM Journal*, 21(2): 127–42.

Radnor, Z.J. (2010) *Review of Business Process Improvement Methodologies in Public Services.* London: Advanced Institute of Management.

Radnor, Z.J. and Osborne, S.P. (2013) 'Lean: a failed theory for public services?' *Public Management Review*, 15(2): 265–87.

Radnor, Z.J. and Walley, P. (2006) 'Lean on me …'. *Public Finance*, 28(1): 13–20.

Radnor, Z.J., Holweg, M. and Waring, J. (2012) 'Lean in healthcare: the unfilled promise?' *Social Science and Medicine*, 74(3): 364–71.

Scott, T., Mannion, R., Davies, H.T.O. and Marshall, M.N. (2003) 'Implementing culture change in health care: theory and practice'. *International Journal for Quality in Health Care*, 15(2): 111–18.

Scottish Executive (2000) *Our National Health: A Plan for Action, a Plan for Change*. Edinburgh: Scottish Executive.

Scottish Government (2008) *Diagnostics Collaborative Programme: Delivering Better Patient Care in Diagnostics*. Edinburgh: Scottish Government.

Scottish Government (2010) *The Healthcare Quality Strategy for NHS Scotland*. Edinburgh: Scottish Government.

Scottish Government (2012) *NHS Scotland: Improvement*. Edinburgh: Scottish Government.

Stone, K.B. (2012) 'Four decades of lean: a systematic literature review'. *International Journal of Lean Six Sigma*, 3(2): 112–32.

Toussaint, J. (2009) 'Writing the new playbook for US health care: lessons from Wisconsin'. *Health Affairs*, 28(5): 1343–50.

Waring, J.J. and Bishop, B. (2010) 'Lean healthcare: rhetoric, ritual and resistance'. *Social Science and Medicine*, 71(7): 1332–40.

Womack, J. and Jones, D. (1996) *Lean Thinking: Banish Waste and Create Wealth in Your Corporation*. New York: Simon & Schuster.

Womack, J.P., Jones, D.T. and Roos, D. (1990) *The Machine that Changed the World*. New York: Macmillan.

19 The English patient experience

Does healthcare service quality matter?

Mel Hudson Smith

Introduction

The development of the performance measurement (PM) field throughout the 1990s, to establish what businesses should measure to improve performance (Neely, 1999; Kaplan and Norton, 1992) coincided with an increased research focus on the need for operational outputs to deliver value to customers, both through the development of the service operations field (Johnston, 1999) and the maturing of the quality movement with initiatives such as TQM and Six Sigma. The results of this research are now considered fundamental to many areas of operations management practice; in that improved quality leads to improved customer satisfaction and that quality can be improved through measuring and monitoring the right things.

Within the public services field, there is a significant area of research focused on service operations in the healthcare sector (Johnston, 2005). However, measuring performance in this sector is recognised as being fraught with difficulties (Gomes *et al.*, 2010). Some of the continuing challenges for PM relate to the measurement of service quality and customer satisfaction, particularly in complex public sector environments where the need for information transparency makes the use of outcome measures more appropriate than process measures (DeGroff *et al.*, 2010).

The majority of research in the healthcare sector is focused on large hospital environments. To date, there is little research looking at general practice (GP), and the issues that arise in this environment, despite the fact that the family doctor is typically the first point of contact for patients and, within the UK at least, is increasingly seen as a 'gatekeeper' for further treatment. As such the performance of the doctor has the potential for a high impact on overall patient care and satisfaction. GP surgeries, therefore, offer an interesting lens through which to examine the impact of PM on satisfaction in a public service environment. Therefore, the aim of this study is to determine whether GP performance, as measured by the standardised PM system adopted by the majority of English GP surgeries, is a predictor of patient satisfaction.

The rest of the chapter is organised as follows: firstly, there is a discussion of the relevant literature, to clarify the relationship between PM and satisfaction in the healthcare context. A summary of the way GP surgeries are organised in the UK follows, including an explanation of the key PM systems used and how they work. The research approach is then presented, along with the data analysis, results and discussion, from which some conclusions and recommendations are drawn.

Background literature

Existing work in the complex areas of customer satisfaction, service quality and PM have addressed the interaction between these three areas in different ways.

Process measures for quality improvement

Best practice in PM highlights the need for balanced measurement systems which encompass not just the areas measured (Kaplan and Norton, 1992), but also the requirement to appraise *how* a job is carried out, rather than simply looking at the outcomes (Melynk *et al.*, 2010). This emphasises the importance of process measures, which are typically described as being lead indicators (i.e. they monitor the processes which lead to the outcomes, and are therefore associated with process improvement; Muchiri *et al.* 2010). For this reason, process measures are also emphasised in the quality movement, whereby the development and use of PM, for example in the Six Sigma methodology, specifically uses process based measurement in achieving quality outcomes (Banuelas *et al.*, 2006).

Despite their popularity, a criticism of process measures is that they still cannot actually identify what improvements should occur – only that the existing process is not yielding the desired results (Meyer, 2004). Further criticism stems from the fact that complexity can blur the link between process measures and their outcomes (DeGroff *et al.*, 2010).

Customer satisfaction as a measure of quality improvements

It has been argued that in services, a process orientation should have a significant and direct impact on customer satisfaction (Nilsson *et al.*, 2001), although, according to Melynk *et al.* (2010), all performance measures should explicitly be linked to the way the organisation delivers value to their customers, while Gomes *et al.* (2011) consider that PM related to customers is an increasingly important area. It is this customer focus which links PM to the quality movement and to customer satisfaction.

Both TQM and 6 Sigma methodologies are focused on customer satisfaction as their prime purpose (Schroeder *et al.*, 2008). Indeed, customer satisfaction has always been a fundamental driver of quality improvements (Deming, 1986). TQM has been found to be correlated with improved customer satisfaction (Mehra and Ranganathan, 2008), although studies have shown that this may be more to do with the 'soft' changes within the organisation, such as internal unity of purpose and the removal of departmental barriers, than more objective, easily quantifiable and measurable improvements (Terziovski, 2006). There is, however, more positive evidence that process improvements which reduce apparent variation in service processes increase customer satisfaction, as do general improvements in service quality (Frei *et al.*, 1999), while there is also evidence that service quality is a predictor of customer satisfaction (Miguel-Davilla *et al.*, 2010). It must be recognised, however, that there is often a lag between process improvements and any corresponding improvement in customer satisfaction (Mitra and Golder, 2006).

Measuring customer satisfaction

There are some obvious benefits for promoting the measurement of customer satisfaction, in terms of providing external feedback on operational performance (Kaplan and Norton, 1992). However, customer satisfaction is a lag indicator and is complicated by its subjective nature and there is an ongoing difficulty in measuring it in an objective, quantitative manner, which means that the quality of such measurement is often of poor (Kim and Kim, 2009). The incentive to find some way to overcome these problems lies in the fact that satisfied customers are more likely to be loyal and spend more (*ibid.*).

Customer satisfaction and service quality are closely linked concepts (Tam, 2004), with service quality considered to be an antecedent of satisfaction (Lee *et al.*, 2000). It appears that while a customer may be satisfied or not with an individual service encounter (Cronin and Taylor, 1992), their satisfaction is made possible by the overall quality of the service, which can be considered a more generalised assessment of service performance over time (Torres, 2014). Given these definitions, it appears that the key difference in the measurement of either construct lies in the scope of measurement, rather than the measure itself.

Service quality has been measured as the gap between customer expectations and perceptions (Parasuraman *et al.*, 1985) across 5 dimensions: empathy, tangibles, reliability, responsiveness and assurance (Parasuraman *et al.* 1991). However, Cronin and Taylor (1992) found that it can be measured effectively using perceptions alone, while Carman (1990) questioned the universal applicability of the 5 dimensions of service quality, arguing that they should be tailored to suit the specific context.

It is reasonable to suggest that customer satisfaction is also based on customer perceptions and, possibly, prior expectations; the difference being that satisfaction is based on an individual encounter, rather than service over time. The difficulty is that both expectations and perceptions are personal constructs, clouded by emotion and prior experience, making satisfaction one of the most challenging measures of performance.

Healthcare quality and patient satisfaction

In healthcare, patients are increasingly referred to as consumers or customers (Sitzia and Wood, 1997) and patient satisfaction is similarly desirable, but difficult, to measure. Patients can certainly be described as a type of customer, albeit a rather specialised type in that they usually only become consumers of healthcare services when something is wrong, or in an effort to prevent things from going wrong.

Patients also differ from typical customers in that, in many areas of the world, patients do not pay directly for healthcare services; they are instead paid for through insurance, or a publicly funded health system, potentially distorting perceptions regarding value. Despite this, there are clearly strong similarities between patients and customers from a conceptual point of view.

Patient satisfaction has been defined as the gap between patients' expectations and actual perceptions (Chow *et al.*, 2009) – the same measure as Parasuraman *et al.* (1985) advocated for measuring service quality. This explicitly recognises the similarities between service quality and satisfaction in this context. It is perhaps understandable, therefore, that unmet expectations have been identified as the root cause of poor patient satisfaction (Jackson *et al.*, 2001). Similarly, if a patient feels that they have received high quality care, they are more likely to be satisfied and this is important because satisfied patients are more likely to comply with suggested medication and treatment, which should lead to better health outcomes (Chow *et al.*, 2009).

However, there are additional factors that feed into patient satisfaction in this context. The important factors for patient satisfaction are understood to be: interpersonal manner; accessibility and convenience; technical quality of care; efficacy and outcomes of care; continuity of care; physical environment and availability of care (Fitzpatrick, 1990; Ware *et al.*, 1983) and it is clear that not all of these directly relate to service quality. The situation is further complicated by factors related to demographics; various studies have shown that old people are more likely to be satisfied than young people and that the more knowledge the patient has, the less satisfied they are (Rundle-Thiele and Russell-Bennett, 2010).

Symptom outcomes have been shown to directly affect patient satisfaction (Jackson *et al.*, 2001) and technical quality of care has been found to be a predictor of patient satisfaction in specific areas such as mental health (Edlund *et al.*, 2003). Similarly, a study of diabetes patients showed that GPs who followed clinical guidelines had better overall patient satisfaction scores (Gross *et al.*, 2003).

Despite the fact that there is evidence that patient satisfaction can be influenced by issues other than overall service quality, instead highlighting the role of health outcomes and technical quality of care, it has been argued that patient satisfaction is not a direct influence in healthcare as it is not a good proxy measure for quality (Cronin *et al.*, 2000). The problem is that although quality healthcare focuses on providing good technical and emotional care (John, 1991), patients overemphasise the emotional care because they do not feel qualified to fully evaluate the technical quality of care (Padma *et al.*, 2010). Perhaps this relates to patient trust and confidence in the healthcare provider – part of the Empathy dimension of service quality according to Parasuraman *et al.* (1991) – which, studies have demonstrated, correlates strongly with satisfaction (Dwyer *et al.*, 2012; Weiss, 1988). The effect of trust and confidence can be seen in one study, which found that in hospitals, where the technical quality of care was assumed to be high, satisfaction was based primarily on behaviour and communication, whereas with GPs, the empathy and emotional care is taken for granted, but often it is the technical quality which is viewed with suspicion (Vuori, 1991).

Despite the obvious complexity in measuring it, it appears that satisfaction is strongest when the patient receives the expected help and when the doctor treats them well (Rahmqvist and Bara, 2010).

Literature summary

To recap then, PM and internal quality improvements are both clearly important in improving customer satisfaction. There are also clear links between customer and patient satisfaction, although patient satisfaction likely also includes aspects of health outcomes and the technical quality of care. While there is a potential issue with patient satisfaction being a poor proxy measure for overall quality of care, this only highlights the service quality aspects, which are easier for patients to assess and are therefore often the key component in patient satisfaction measurement. A compelling reason to measure patient satisfaction, despite the shortcomings of the measure in terms of offering a fully rounded evaluation of overall quality of care, is that satisfied patients are more likely to achieve better health outcomes because they are more likely to comply with treatment regimes.

The UK healthcare context

Healthcare in the UK is primarily delivered through the National Health Service (NHS), using a rather unique model, being controlled through the Government's Department of Health and publicly funded through the tax system to offer medical services that are free at the point of delivery to all residents of the Country (NHS, 2014). Despite some failings that are usually well documented in the British press, the NHS is highly cherished by members of the public and also ranks well among the healthcare systems in other countries; in one recent study of 11 developed nations, it was ranked No 1 on almost all criteria (Davis *et al.*, 2014). The NHS is the biggest provider of healthcare in the world, cost £109bn to run in 2012–13 and is also the world's fourth largest employer, with over 1.7 million employees (NHS, 2014).

Although there are some shared services across country borders, the NHS is generally organised and run slightly differently within each of the 4 countries that make up the UK, with NHS England being by far the largest organisation, accounting for 79 per cent of staff and servicing around 84 per cent of the population of the UK (*ibid.*).

English GP surgeries

Despite the size and scale of the NHS, GP surgeries in England are not usually owned and run through the organisation. Instead, they are effectively run as independent small business suppliers to the NHS. GP Surgeries therefore bid for and are contracted to run local NHS services (BMA, 2010). Prior to 2013, this process happened through Primary Care Organisations, which were strategic bodies set up by the Department of Health, which aimed to identify the local requirements for care and manage this accordingly. However, early in 2013 a significant change was brought in by the Government meaning that now all GPs must now belong to Clinical Commissioning Groups (CCGs), which have replaced Primary Care Organisations (BMA, 2014) in an attempt to hand more power to clinicians to control NHS budgets and be more accountable for the services in their local area.

Under the General Medical Services (GMS) contract introduced in 2004, GP surgeries in England have been funded through several separate income streams, including: a 'per patient' grant called the Global Sum; a performance based payment system called the Quality and Outcomes Framework and payment for services provided in addition to the minimum requirements of the GP contract.

The Quality and Outcomes Framework

The Quality and Outcomes Framework (QOF) was developed to 'reward the provision of quality care' (NHS Employers, 2014) by GPs funded through the NHS GMS contract. The QOF comprises a set of payment-by-performance indicators which are described as being 'useful in patient care' (*ibid.*) and is essentially a standardised PM system through which GP surgeries earn points for achieving both process and outcome targets, being paid by the number of points accrued. It is estimated that for most surgeries, the QOF payments equate to around 15 per cent of GP surgery annual turnover (Leech, 2009). Perhaps unsurprisingly, the vast majority of GP surgeries in England now participate in the QOF despite its voluntary status (NHS Employers, 2014).

Since its inception in 2004, the QOF has undergone many changes in the indicators used and the way that points are allocated, which reflect new clinical evidence and the changing priorities of the NHS. Significant changes were incorporated in 2009, 2011 and 2012, making year-on-year comparisons difficult. However, the underlying structure has remained the same, with 1000 points available across four distinct domains: clinical, organisational, patient experience and additional services (HSCIC, 2014).

The QOF guidance includes an explicit recognition that indicators should only be developed where (among other things) there is good evidence for the health benefits likely to result from improved care (Leech, 2009). Furthermore, the points available for each indicator are determined according to the potential improved outcome for the patient (*ibid.*). Therefore, it is reasonable to assume that high achievement should correlate to high quality patient care and improved patient outcomes, which should lead to increased patient satisfaction.

The GP Patient Survey

While the QOF may be seen as an attempt by the Department of Health to control and improve the quality of care delivered by GP surgeries in key areas, through financial incentives for monitoring and following recommended treatment pathways, it does not directly assess patient satisfaction. The Government therefore commissioned a survey to evaluate patient experiences with their local GP surgery. This survey is known as the GP Patient Survey (GPPS) and is run by Ipsos Mori on behalf of the Department of Health.

Until June 2011, the survey was administered quarterly to a random sample of around 1.4 million adults registered with GP surgeries in England. The survey comprised 11 areas of measurement, covering all aspects of patient experience, including access, interpersonal and technical interactions with the surgery (Campbell *et al.*, 2009) and included a specific question for overall satisfaction with care received at the surgery (GP Patient Survey, 2014).

During 2011 the survey was given a major overhaul, whereby the data collection frequency was reduced to just twice a year and some of the questions were updated and modified. This included the patient satisfaction measure, which was changed to consider the overall experience of the patient with the GP Surgery, rather than specifically focusing on satisfaction (*ibid.*).

Approach

The literature suggests that there is a logical link between PM which drives quality improvement and high service quality, leading to high satisfaction. Within the English GP surgery context, the Government uses PM – through the QOF and GPPS – to drive improvements in the quality of care and to monitor patient experiences. The aim of this study, therefore, is to evaluate the data from these two complementary measurement systems to see if high achievement in the QOF is linked with increased patient satisfaction.

The data from both the QOF and the GPPS are available online (HSCIC, 2014; GP Patient Survey, 2014) and permission was gained to use the data for this study. One year's worth of data was used, which was taken from the same time period in 2009–10 in both cases.

To enable the data from the GPPS to be compared with the QOF data, the study used Surgery level aggregates. Individual patient scores were therefore not required.

The indicators included in the QOF 2009–10 monitored both processes and outcomes and included 134 aspects of GP performance across the four domains, with the 1000 points available, split as follows:

- *Clinical domain; 697 points:* This domain monitored the use of specific prevention, management and treatment pathways for patients with certain target conditions (e.g. cardiovascular disease; depression; heart disease; obesity, cancer, asthma, dementia, diabetes, among others).
- *Organisation domain, 167.5 points:* This domain monitored issues such as patient records, practice management, patient information, education and medicines management.
- *Patient experience domain, 91.5 points:* This domain monitored minimum consultation times and the ability for patients to access their GP in a timely and convenient manner. The data for this came from some specific questions in the GPPS, which covered these areas.

- *Additional services domain, 44 points:* This domain monitored the provision of services such as maternity, child health, cervical screening and contraception.

Hypotheses

The aim of this study was to examine the following hypotheses:

H_1 There will be a positive relationship between the scores achieved in the QOF and the GPPS measure of satisfaction with care received at the surgery.

H_2 The QOF scores will be a key predictor of satisfaction with care received at the surgery.

Data analysis

The study compared practice level results between the QOF and the GPPS. The domain level scores and the total QOF scores for each surgery were loaded into SPSS, along with the surgery level scores from the GPPS showing the percentage of patients who were satisfied with the level of care received from the surgery. To enable meaningful interpretation of the results, the raw QOF scores were converted into percentages before analysis. A total of 8167 GP surgery results were examined; representing every surgery in England which had both QOF and GPPS results for the 2009–10 period.

Initially, correlations were calculated between each QOF domain and patient satisfaction, using Pearson's Correlation Coefficient (Saunders *et al.*, 2009). Table 19.1 shows the results of this basic correlation analysis.

Although the majority of correlations were individually relatively weak, multiple regression was carried out to determine whether it is possible to predict the impact of all the domains together on patient satisfaction.

The regression analysis was conducted in SPSS. A summary of the model developed in SPSS is given in Table 19.2, while Table 19.3 shows the regression coefficients for each model.

Table 19.1 Pearson correlations between Quality and Outcomes Framework domains and selected GP Patient Survey responses

GPPS / *QOF*	*Satisfied with care received at surgery (n = 8167)*	
	R	R^2
Clinical domain	0.193	0.037
Organisation domain	0.134	0.018
Patient experience domain	0.490	0.240
Additional services domain	0.183	0.033

Note: All correlations significant to 0.01 level. Missing values excluded listwise

Table 19.2 Model summary for Quality and Outcomes Framework domain predictors of patient satisfaction

Model	*R*	*R^2*	*Adjusted R^2*	*Std error of estimate*	*Durbin–Watson*
Clinical domain Organisation domain Patient experience domain Additional services domain	0.517	0.267	0.267	0.054130	1.576

Note: All correlations significant to 0.01 level. Missing values excluded listwise

Findings

The results of the analysis show that there are some relatively weak correlations between the QOF scores and patients' satisfaction with care received at the surgery, as monitored by the GP Patient Survey. However, the model developed shows that the QOF scores are only able to explain just over a quarter of the variance in patient satisfaction (R^2 = 26.7 per cent).

The regression model shows that there is some very limited capability to use the QOF scores to predict patient satisfaction scores. In this model, the clinical and patient experience measures have the biggest impact (though still very small overall) on patient satisfaction, with each 1 per cent increase in achievement in these domains contributing around a 0.15 per cent increase in patient satisfaction (the regression coefficient B = 0.159 and 0.146 for these measures, respectively). Due to the difference in the number of points available in each domain, this means that the clinical domain would have to improve by 6.3 per cent (around 44 points) to achieve a 1 per cent increase in patient satisfaction, while the patient experience domain would have to improve by 6.6 per cent (just over 6 points) to achieve this. The organisation and additional services domains made a negligible difference overall to patient satisfaction (B = –0.029 and 0.053 respectively).

Therefore, we can tentatively accept the first hypothesis, which looked for a positive relationship between the QOF scores and the GPPS question, but we tentatively reject the second hypothesis which aimed to identify the QOF scores as key predictors of patient satisfaction with the care received at the surgery. Although

Table 19.3 SPSS multiple regression output for Quality and Outcomes Framework domain predictors of patient satisfaction

Model	*Unstandardised coefficients*		*Standardised coefficients*	*t*	*Sig*
	B	*Std error*	*Beta*		
(Constant)	0.625	0.011		56.844	0.000
Clinical domain	0.159	0.013	0.139	12.106	0.000
Organisation domain	–0.029	0.010	–0.035	–2.817	0.005
Patient experience domain	0.146	0.003	0.476	49.660	0.000
Additional services domain	0.053	0.011	0.067	5.040	0.000

there is some predictive capability, it is clear from both the correlations and the regression model that achievement in the QOF is not a primary predictor of patient satisfaction in GP Surgeries.

In trying to understand these results, it is easy to speculate that perhaps measures in the organisation domain, which are focused on internal efficiency and effectiveness, might not have an obvious significant impact on patient satisfaction. Similarly, as the additional services (such as contraceptive advice or child welfare monitoring) only affect specific areas of the population, it could be suggested that it would be difficult to predict general patient satisfaction from scores in this area. However, it is more difficult to explain the results from the clinical and patient experience domains, which demand a more detailed examination.

Clinical domain

The analysis of the clinical domain shows a weak correlation (0.193) with patient satisfaction, with only 3.7 per cent of the variance in the patient satisfaction scores explained by the clinical domain scores ($R^2 = 0.037$). The multiple regression model showed only a very small predictive capability from this variable ($B = 0.159$). This result is surprising because previous research which looked at technical quality of care suggested that better quality care was associated with better patient satisfaction scores (Edlund *et al.*, 2003). In addition TQM advocates that improving technical quality should drive customer satisfaction (Mehra and Ranganathan, 2008).

The clinical domain has almost two thirds of the QOF points attached to it, which suggests that following clinical guidelines in diagnosis and ongoing care is considered the most important way of improving quality of care overall by the NHS. However, these results suggest that patients do not really take this into account when determining the level of satisfaction with their care.

It could be argued that, for the reasons touched on in the literature (i.e. that patients find it hard to evaluate the technical quality of care, or that patient satisfaction should not be the main objective of quality health care) that the lack of a clear predictive link between clinical quality and patient satisfaction is not an issue. However, if the clinical domain of the QOF is aimed at driving improved clinical outcomes, then patient satisfaction is a critical element, as patients who are satisfied with their care are more likely to comply with medication and treatment which will positively impact on the eventual outcome (Chow *et al.*, 2009).

According to the principles of TQM/Six Sigma, the clinical domain indicators should, in order to drive customer satisfaction, be developed with a focus on the 'voice of the customer'. Quality Function Deployment, a tool commonly advocated by both methodologies, was developed specifically to capture this 'customer voice' by identifying and linking customer requirements directly into the product design process (Schroeder *et al.*, 2008). However it appears that the QOF clinical indicators are developed primarily from the evidence of practitioner studies, which focus on the identification of best practice from a clinical point of view, with little or no direct input from patients. Strengthening the patient input into the development of clinical indicators could be a key way of improving patient outcomes for the future.

Patient experience domain

The strongest correlations (0.49) were identified in the patient experience domain, with 24 per cent of the variance in customer satisfaction explained by the patient experience scores from the QOF ($R^2 = 0.24$). However, despite this, the predictive capability of the patient experience scores on patient satisfaction was still relatively low, at less than 0.15 per cent ($B = 0.146$).

The patient experience indicators aim to ensure that patients have easy access to, and enough time to discuss their situation effectively with, their GP. The limited evidence available in the literature suggests that if these measures can be seen as proxies for patient familiarity with their GP and face-to-face contact time, then together these may improve patient outcomes (Schers *et al.*, 2005) and patient satisfaction (Shipman *et al.*, 2000). It is, therefore, a little surprising that the predictive effect is not more pronounced in this area.

Discussion

The results of this study clearly highlight the dissonance between the two very different 'customer' groups for GPs in England, as there is clearly little overlap between what the NHS is aiming to achieve in terms of service efficiency and effectiveness and what makes patients satisfied. The NHS is the paying customer, specifying the services to be delivered through the GMS contract. Managing this delivery is critical, because although there is a requirement to ensure that patients have access to the resources they need to manage their health, every patient contact has a cost and overachievement cannot be financially rewarded (Tan and Rae, 2009). The patients, on the other hand, are the customers who receive the contracted services and have a right to expect high quality, but do not pay directly for them.

This exposes an issue which is common to the public sector: how to measure value. In private companies, money offers a simple and tangible way of judging value: customers can use price to help evaluate the worth of the product or service. Similarly, most private companies use the wealth they generate as their primary measure of value, thus the rationale for improving customer satisfaction is clear; to generate loyalty and increase revenues (Heskett *et al.* 1994), with increased resources following increased customer spending.

In the public sector, however, the customer does not pay directly for the service and therefore customer value is much more difficult to determine (Fountain, 2001). In addition, public sector firms cannot judge their value in simple financial terms, instead looking to measure *public* value in terms of the collective benefits to society (Cordella and Bonina, 2012).

This raises the question about whether measuring patient satisfaction at all is a bit of a red herring in a situation where GP Surgeries are funded through public taxes, with necessarily constrained resources, through finite budgets, where the key rationale is to reduce costs to taxpayers, while maintaining effective services.

Perhaps this explains the disparity in the results; the QOF measures the things that best practice dictates will deliver the most effective care, based on the resources available, as judged by clinicians, researchers and politicians. In other words, it measures the things that will generate the biggest benefits to society collectively. This may well differ from what patients wish for individually in their dealings with doctors – and which are the things that drive patient satisfaction.

Considering this in more detail, there are two factors that highlight the lack of congruence between patient satisfaction and the measurement of public value, through the QOF. First, the QOF pays GPs for offering standardised best practice in 'priority' areas of clinical care, through the indicators in the clinical domain (NHS Employers, 2009), effectively focusing resources into these areas. Therefore, GPs treating patients who present with problems that are in non-priority areas, where there are no QOF payments available, will have a lack of guidance regarding appropriate treatment pathways as well as fewer resources available for treatment. Thus despite a collective benefit to society in making the best use of constrained resources, these patients individually may well feel that they have been poorly served.

Second, even where a patient does present with a priority disease, then in order to claim the QOF payments, the GP is required to ensure that the relevant administrative boxes are ticked. This would typically include documenting the completion of a series of tests and perhaps referral to a specialist. Although these may be technically correct treatments, it is possible that this makes the process less personal and misses out the 'human dimension' of the service encounter. Looking back at the literature, confidence and trust in the doctor are strongly correlated with satisfaction (Dwyer *et al.*, 2012), but it may be that the QOF encourages GPs to focus on the technical processes, rather than spending time talking to patients, explaining treatments and ensuring that the patient feels that their doctor cares about their personal wellbeing, rather than simply processing them correctly.

According to Osborne *et al.* (2013) many systemic problems are caused in public services due to the influence of manufacturing based product-dominant logic in the design of services. They argue that a service-dominant logic should prevail, as this would more accurately represent the reality of the service delivery by recognising three key distinctions which make services different from traditional, manufacturing-based production. These distinctions are that service processes are intangible in nature; that production and consumption are simultaneous and finally; that users are co-producers of the service. An extension of service-dominant logic, public-service-dominant logic builds on these distinctions, suggesting that public services need to strategically orient their offerings around the needs and expectations of the service users; market public services around relationships and building trust and confidence between the provider and the service user; recognising the intrinsic value of the user in co-producing the process and affecting its outcomes and orienting operations externally, so that they are always focused on effectiveness from the users' perspective (*ibid.*).

It is possible that this may have some relevance to the QOF, which, according to this line of argument, shows the hallmarks of development using a manufacturing-dominant logic; with patients as essentially passive consumers of treatment 'products' in processes which are delivered through GP surgeries. The implications of this are that patients may feel that best practice treatment is something that happens to them, rather than something that they must be actively involved in. Not only could this explain why technically excellent practice does not necessarily result in satisfied patients, but it also suggests that the patients might gain less from the treatment than might be possible if they were more actively engaged.

Using a public-service-dominant approach, the clinical domain of the QOF would need to measure the effectiveness of treatments from the patients' perspective, rather than simply applying and monitoring best practice as determined by the medical profession. In such a scenario, the QOF should probably include indicators that monitor the quality of doctor–patient interactions, in addition to the current set of measures. After all, the placebo effect is real, often confounds medical explanation and appears to be based, at least in part, on the patient–doctor relationship (Kaptchuk *et al.*, 2008). If a placebo treatment can have a positive effect on patients' perceived health outcomes due to the quality of the relationship between the patient and doctor, it suggests that this should be a critical aspect of care.

Conclusion and recommendations

The results of this study show that there is only a limited link between the QOF payment-by-performance measurement system and patient satisfaction in English GP surgeries. The most important predictor of satisfaction is the patient experience domain, which considers ease of access and the amount of time spent with the doctor. However the clinical domain, which accounts for the majority of the indicators (and therefore payments) has only a very small effect on satisfaction.

These results suggest that the QOF is not clearly oriented towards ensuring effectiveness from the perspective of the patient. Retaining the prevailing logic of preserving public value by processing patients through an efficient, standardised, perhaps rather didactic care pathway, based on current best practice, means acknowledging and accepting the quality losses that will occur through lack of patient engagement. An alternative approach is to redesign the QOF around the patient and their perspective of what is effective. This would involve recognising the need for active cooperation with patients, enabling them to participate fully in the process of co-creating their own health outcomes.

To achieve the alternative approach, there is a clear recommendation to include patients in the development of future QOF indicators, while there are also some practical challenges regarding resource allocation. However, perhaps all that is really missing from the QOF is a measure of the empathy of the doctor with the patient during the consultation, which would inspire the confidence and trust required to enable meaningful patient engagement and might well enhance overall health outcomes.

Future research

This study suggests that there are two key areas for further research in the broader field of service operations management. First, there is a need to understand how to effectively measure a number of constructs which have been highlighted by this study, specifically: the measurement of non-monetary value, service effectiveness and user engagement for individual service users, along with how to measure public value in public services. Although there is plenty of research highlighting the need to look beyond monetary value, alternative forms of measurement are less well defined.

Second, considering the concept that service users are co-producers both of value and of the processes that create that value, there is a need for more research into how to effectively operationalise 'co-production' processes. Without a fundamental understanding of how co-production processes differ from traditional production processes at a practical, operational level, it is likely that genuine co-production will remain an attractive, but elusive concept.

Acknowledgements

GP Patient Survey Data used courtesy of the GP Patient Survey Team at the Department of Health. QOF data provided by HSCIC under the Open Government License: Copyright © 2013, Re-used with the permission of the Health and Social Care Information Centre. All rights reserved.

References

Banuelas, R., Tennant, C., Tuersley, I. and Tang, S. (2006) 'Selection of Six Sigma projects in the UK'. *TQM Magazine*, 18: 514–27.

BMA (2010) *General Practitioners: Briefing Paper*. London: BMA. Retrieved from http://bma.org.uk/search?query = general practitioner briefing (accessed July 2014).

BMA (2014) *General Practice in the UK: Background Briefing*. London: BMA. Retrieved from http://bma.org.uk/search?query = general practitioner briefing (accessed July 2014).

Breitbarth, T., Mitchell, R. and Lawson, R. (2010) 'Service performance measurement in a NZ local government organisation'. *Business Horizons*, 53: 397–03.

Buyukozkan, G., Cifci, G. and Guleryuz, S. (2011) 'Strategic analysis of healthcare service quality using fuzzy AHP methodology'. *Expert Systems with Applications*, 38: 9407–24.

Campbell, J., Smith, P., Nissen, S., Bower, P., Elliott, M. and Roland, M. (2009) 'The GP Patient Survey for use in primary care in the NHS in the UK: development and psychometric characteristics'. *BMC Family Practice*, 10, article 57. Retrieved from www.biomedcentral.com/1471-2296/10/57 (accessed 7 April 2015).

Carman, J. (1990) 'Consumer perceptions of service quality: an assessment of the SERVQUAL Dimensions'. *Journal of Retailing*, 66, Spring: 33–55.

Chenhall, R. (1997) 'Reliance on manufacturing performance measures, Total Quality Management and organisational performance'. *Management Accounting Research*, 8: 187–206.

Chow, A., Mayer, E., Darzi, A. and Athanasiou, T. (2009) 'Patient reported outcome measures: the importance of patient satisfaction in surgery'. *Surgery*, 146: 435–43.

Cordella, A. and Bonina, C. (2012) 'A public value perspective for ICT enabled public sector reforms: a theoretical reflection'. *Government Information Quarterly*, 29: 512–20.

Cronin, J. and Taylor, S. (1992) 'Measuring service quality: a re-examination and extension'. *Journal of Marketing*, 56(3): 55–68.

Cronin, J., Brady, M. and Hult, G. (2000) 'Assessing the effects of quality, value and customer satisfaction on consumer behavioural intentions in service environments'. *Journal of Retailing*, 76: 193–218.

Davis, K., Stremikis, K., Squires, D. and Schoen, C. (2014) *Mirror, Mirror on the Wall: How the Performance of the US Health Care System Compares Internationally (2014 Update)*. New York: Commonwealth Fund.

DeGroff, A., Schooley, M., Chapel, T. and Poister, T. (2010) 'Challenges and strategies in applying performance measurement to federal public health programs'. *Evaluation and Program Planning*, 33: 365–72.

Deming, W.E. (1986) *Out of the Crisis*. Cambridge, MA: MIT Press.

Department of Health (2010) *Equity and Excellence: Liberating the NHS*. London: The Stationery Office.

Dwyer, D., Liu, H. and Rizzo, J. (2012) 'Does patient trust promote better care?' *Applied Economics*, 44(18): 2283–95.

Edlund, M., Young, A., Kung, F., Sherbourne, C. and Wells, K. (2003) 'Does satisfaction reflect the technical quality of mental health care?' *Health Services Research*, 38(2): 631–45.

Fitzpatrick, R. (1984) *Satisfaction with Health Care, The Experience of Illness*. R. Fitzpatrick (ed.). pp. 154–75. London: Tavistock.

Fountain, E. (2001) 'Paradoxes of public sector customer service'. *Governance: An International Journal of Policy and Administration*, 14(1): 55–73.

Frei, F., Kalakota, R., Leone, A. and Marx, L. (1999) 'Process variation as a determinant of bank performance: evidence from the retail banking study'. *Management Science*, 45: 1210–20.

Gomes, C.F., Yasin, M.M. and Youssef, Y. (2010), 'Assessing operational effectiveness in healthcare organizations: a systematic approach'. *International Journal of Health Care Quality Assurance*, 23(2): 127–40.

Gomes, C.F., Yasin, M.M. and Lisboa, J. (2011) 'Performance measurement practices in manufacturing firms revisited'. *International Journal of Operations and Production Management*, 31(1): 5–30.

GP Patient Survey (2014) 'Surveys and reports'. Retrieved from http://gp-patient.co.uk/surveys-and-reports (accessed July 2014).

Gross, R., Tabenkin, H., Porath, A., Heymann, A., Greenstein, M., Porter, B. and Matzliach, R. (2003) 'The relationship between primary care physicians' adherence to guidelines for the treatment of diabetes and patient satisfaction: findings from a pilot study'. *Family Practice*, 20(5): 563–69.

Heskett, J., Jones, T., Loveman, G., Sasser, W. and Schlesinger, L. (1994) 'Putting the service profit-chain to work'. *Harvard Business Review*, 72(2): 164–74.

HSCIC (2014) 'Quality and outcomes framework'. Retrieved from www.hscic.gov.uk/qof (accessed July 2014).

Jackson, J., Chamberlin, J. and Kroenke, K. (2001) 'Predictors of patient satisfaction'. *Social Science and Medicine*, 52(4): 609–20.

John, J. (1991) 'Improving quality through patient–provider communication'. *Journal of Health Care Marketing*, 11(4): 51–60.

Johnston, R. (1999), 'Service operations management: return to roots'. *International Journal of Operations and Production Management*, 19(2): 104–24.

Johnston, R. (2005) 'Update: service operations management: from the roots up'. *International Journal of Operations and Production Management*, 25(12): 1298–1308.

Kaplan, D. and Norton, D. (1992) 'The Balanced Scorecard – measures that drive performance'. *Harvard Business Review*, January–February: 71–79.

Kaptchuk, T., Kelley, J., Conboy, L., Davis, R., Kerr, C., Jacobson, E., Kirsch, I., Schyner, R., Nam, B., Nguyen, L., Park, M., Rivers, A., McManus, C., Kokkotou, E., Drossman, D., Goldman, P. and Lembo, A. (2008) 'Components of the placebo effect: a randomized controlled trial in irritable bowel syndrome'. *British Medical Journal*, 336: 998–1003.

Kim, H.-S. and Kim, Y.-G. (2009) 'A CRM performance measurement framework: its development process and application'. *Industrial Marketing Management*, 38: 477–89.

Lee, H. Lee, Y. and Yoo, D. (2000) 'The Determinants of Perceived Service Quality and its Relationship with Satisfaction'. *Journal of Services Marketing*, 14(3): 219–31.

Leech, P. (2009) *QOF Management Guide*, vol. 1. Retrieved from www.pcc.nhs.uk/qof-management-guide (accessed July 2014).

Mehra, S. and Ranganathan, S. (2008) 'Implementing TQM with a focus on enhancing customer satisfaction'. *International Journal of Quality and Reliability Management*, 25(9): 913–27.

Melynk, S., Stewart, D. and Swink, M. (2004) 'Metrics and performance measurement in operations management: dealing with the metrics maze'. *Journal of Operations Management*, 22: 209–17.

Melynk, S., Hanson, J. and Calantone, R. (2010) 'Hitting the target … but missing the point: resolving the paradox of strategic transition'. *Long Range Planning*, 43: 555–74.

Meyer, M. (2004) *Rethinking Performance Measurement*. Cambridge: Cambridge University Press.

Miguel-Davilla, J. Cabeza-Garcia, L. Valdunciel, L. and Florez, M. (2010) 'Operations in banking, the service quality and effects on satisfaction and loyalty'. *Service Industries Journal*, 30(13): 2163–82.

Mitra, D. and Golder, P. (2006) 'How does objective quality affect perceived quality? Short term effects, long term effects and asymmetries'. *Marketing Science*, 25(3): 230–47.

Muchiri, P., Pintelon, L., Martin, H. and De Meyer, A. (2010) 'Empirical analysis of maintenance performance measurement in Belgian industries'. *International Journal of Production Research*, 48(20): 5905–24.

Neely, A. (1999) 'The performance measurement revolution: why now and what next?' *International Journal of Operations and Production Management*, 19(2): 205–28.

NHS (2014) 'The NHS in England'. Retrieved from www.nhs.uk/NHSEngland/thenhs/about/Pages/overview.aspx (accessed July 2014).

NHS Employers (2009) *Quality and Outcomes Framework Guidance for GMS Contract 2009/10*. Retrieved from www.networks.nhs.uk/nhs-networks/london-qof-network/documents/QOF%20Guidance%20The%20Green%20Document%202009-2010_Final.pdf/at_download/file (accessed July 2014).

NHS Employers (2014) 'Quality and outcomes framework'. Retrieved from www.nhs employers.org/your-workforce/primary-care-contacts/general-medical-services/quality-and-outcomes-framework (accessed July 2014).

Nilsson, L., Johnson, M. and Gustafsson, A. (2001) 'The impact of quality practices on customer satisfaction and business results: product versus service organisations'. *Journal of Quality Management*, 6: 5–27.

Osborne, S.P., Radnor, Z.J. and Nasi, G. (2013) 'A new theory for public service management? Toward a (public) service-dominant approach'. *American Review of Public Administration*, 42(2): 135–58.

Padma, P., Rajendran, C. and Lokachari, P.S. (2010) 'Service quality and its impact on customer satisfaction in Indian hospitals: perspectives of patients and their attendants'. *Benchmarking: An International Journal*, 17(6): 807–41.

Parasuraman, A., Zeithaml, V.A. and Berry, L.L. (1985) 'A conceptual model of service quality and its implications for future research'. *Journal of Marketing*, 49: 41–50.

Parasuraman, A., Berry, L.L. and Zeithaml, V. (1991) 'Refinement and reassessment of the SERVQUAL scale'. *Journal of Retailing*, 69(4): 420–60.

Rahmqvist, M. and Bara, A. (2010) 'Patient characteristics and quality dimensions related to patient satisfaction'. *International Journal for Quality in Health Care*, 22(2): 86–92.

Rundle-Thiele, S. and Russell-Bennett, R. (2010) 'Patient influences on patient satisfaction and loyalty for GP services'. *Health Marketing Quarterly*, 27(2): 195–214.

Saunders, M., Lewis, P. and Thornhill, A. (2009) *Research Methods for Business Students* (5th edn). London: FT Prentice Hall.

Schers, H., Hoogen, H., Bor, H., Grol, R. and Bosch, W. (2005) 'Familiarity with a GP and patients' evaluations of care: a cross sectional study'. *Family Practice*, 22: 15–19.

Schroeder, R., Linderman, K., Liedtke, C. and Choo, A. (2008) 'Six Sigma: definition and underlying theory'. *Journal of Operations Management*, 26: 536–54.

Shipman, C., Payne, F., Hooper, R. and Dale, J. (2000) 'Patient satisfaction with out-of-hours services'. *Journal of Public Health Medicine*, 22(2): 149–54.

Sitzia, J. and Wood, N. (1997) 'Patient satisfaction: a review of the issues and concepts'. *Social Science and Medicine*, 45(12): 1829–43.

Tam, J. (2004) 'Customer satisfaction, service quality and perceived value: an integrative model'. *Journal of Marketing Management*, 20(7): 897–917.

Tan, K.H. and Rae, R. (2009) 'Uncovering links between regulation and performance measurement'. *International Journal of Production Economics*, 122: 449–57.

Terziovski, M. (2006) 'Quality management practices and their relationship with customer satisfaction and productivity improvement'. *Management Research News*, 29(7): 414–24.

Vuori, H. (1991) 'Patient satisfaction – does it matter?' *Quality Assurance in Health Care*, 3(3): 183–89.

Ware, J., Snyder, M., Wright, R. and Davies, A. (1983) 'Defining and measuring patient satisfaction with medical care'. *Evaluation and Program Planning*, 6: 247–63.

Weiss, G. (1988) 'Patient satisfaction with primary medical care'. *Medical Care*, 26(4): 383–92.

Part V

Supply chain management

20 Mapping institutional pressures for e-SCM adoption

The case of health care supply chains

Vikram Bhakoo and Amrik S. Sohal

Introduction

Adoption of e-business technologies such as electronic supply chain management (e-SCM) systems has the potential to improve efficiencies, reduces costs, improve competitiveness of organisations and facilitate building relationships with trading partners (Johnson *et al.*, 2007; Silveira and Cagliano 2006; Auramo *et al.*, 2005). However, the e-business adoption debate has been studied largely from a single organisation or a dyadic perspective (Cullen and Taylor, 2009; Sanders, 2007; Power and Simon, 2004). Further, since these decisions are complex and require co-ordination among multiple trading partners in the supply chain to be implemented effectively, it is more likely that taking an holistic view of the supply chain will yield more meaningful insights (Power, 2005). This is important as these technologies play a pivotal role in facilitating integration between complex arrays of trading partners and thereby facilitating collaborative relationships (Bhakoo and Chan, 2011). The literature is also skewed towards understanding the internal drivers of e-business adoption that focus on financial, operational and strategic issues (Bakker *et al.*, 2008), with the result that the traditional theories of the firm that focus on profit maximisation (e.g. transaction cost economics and resource-based view) have dominated the literature (Johnson *et al.*, 2007; Zhu and Kraemer, 2005). Although past studies provide useful insights, these in essence assume a 'static state of play' in terms of the interactions between trading partners. As a result, these studies neglect the dynamic nature of the institutional environment and the role played by institutional forces between trading partners. This is of importance for public hospitals that operate in a complex and dynamic environment, are comprised of trading partners with conflicting objectives and often intersect with supply chains of different industries (Bhakoo and Chan, 2011). Further, the role of commercial trading partners and regulatory bodies (as sources of distinct possible institutional pressures) in e-business adoption becomes crucial for industry sectors such as health care. With the potential for cost savings and efficiencies, there is tremendous pressure from regulatory authorities to accelerate the uptake of these technologies (More and McGrath, 2002).

We propose institutional theory as a useful lens for studying inter-organisational innovation adoption decisions (Rogers *et al.*, 2007; Ketokivi and Schroeder, 2004; Teo *et al.*, 2003). Institutional theory takes into account a set of critical contextual factors and it is increasingly being recognised that technology adoption decisions in the supply chain are influenced by an institutional rationale rather than solely by the potential for technical efficiency (Roberts and Toleman, 2007; Teo *et al.*, 2003). Although institutional theory is advancing the debate on e-SCM adoption, it is still in an embryonic state in terms of its application within a supply chain context. This is essentially because most studies are based on cross-sectional surveys sent to single focal organisations (Khalifa and Davison, 2006; Teo *et al.*, 2003). By capturing the perspective of a specific trading partner in the supply chain, these studies have been narrowly focussed in their endeavour to thoroughly comprehend how different trading partners are influencing e-business adoption.

Against this background, we employ a qualitative research design that seeks to answer the following research question:

> How sensitive are different entities in the health care supply chain to institutional pressures in the adoption of e-SCM systems?

The health care sector provides an ideal platform to evaluate this research question for the following reasons: first, health care supply chains pose unique problems within the operations management (OM) discipline. For example, the decision-making process is complex where individuals such as physicians, surgeons and nurses influence the purchasing and inventory management decisions (Scheller and Smeltzer, 2006). Second, health care supply chains have a specific niche with particular defining characteristics. The nature of the services being provided, the risks and consequences associated with failure, and the subsequent level of regulation typical of this sector provide a unique and challenging service operations context (Shah, 2004). For example, a mandate to implement a specific technology will have the same effect across the retail sector since all the trading partners are profit oriented entities whereas it may result in a differentiated response within the health care supply chain as specific players (e.g. public hospitals) are not typically motivated by profit. Third, at a supply chain level, the relationships between entities is fairly complex due to the specific combinations of services and products provided and the fragmented nature of the industry (Scheller and Smeltzer, 2006). A specific sector of the health care industry of interest in this context is the pharmaceuticals supply chain. Finally, despite constituting an average of 9 per cent of the gross domestic product of OECD countries (OECD, 2008), the health care sector is perceived as a laggard in the effective implementation of supply chain practices (Baltacioglu *et al.*, 2007; McKone-Sweet *et al.*, 2005) and adoption of e-business technologies compared to its manufacturing and retail counterparts (Skinner, 2003; Siau *et al.*, 2002; Becker, 2001; Orr *et al.* 2001). Thus, there is no surprise that scholars have argued for technology adoption issues to be thoroughly investigated within the health care supply chain as doing so would improve the efficiency and service quality of this vital sector (Jarrett, 2006; Chopra *et al.*, 2004).

We define internet enabled supply chain management systems (e-SCM) as information technology solutions that span organisational boundaries and facilitate communication, coordination and collaboration with trading partners (Liu *et al*,

2010). These technologies are a subset of e-business technologies which are defined as 'the use of the Internet or any other digitally enabled inter or intra-organisational information technology to accomplish business processes' (Boone and Ganeshan, 2007: 1195). The other term we would like to clarify is 'entity'. Each of the participants (tiers) in the supply chain such as suppliers, manufacturers, retailers/distributors and customers have been referred to as an 'entity' in this study (Chandra and Grabis, 2007). The term entity relates to each echelon/tier in the supply chain.

Relevant literature

Recent studies assessing the adoption of e-business technologies have highlighted the importance of the context and role of stakeholders in the supply chain as a crucial factor influencing e-business adoption (Bakker *et al.*, 2008; Roberts and Toleman, 2007). This is contrary to studies conducted across different contexts such as small and medium-sized enterprises (SMEs) and third-party logistics providers (3PLs), which have highlighted operational issues, cost savings and organisational competitiveness as key variables influencing e-business adoption (Evangelista and Sweeney, 2006; Levy *et al.*, 2005; Wagner *et al.*, 2003). Review of literature on the drivers or impediments of e-business adoption highlights that studies have largely focused on a specific entity rather than seeking to understand the perspectives from other entities in the supply chain (Liu *et al.*, 2010; Evangelista and Sweeney, 2006; Levy *et al.*, 2005). As highlighted by Craighead *et al.* (2006), it would be interesting to see if the drivers identified by a specific entity in the supply chain differ from their upstream or downstream trading partners. This observation would highlight the conflicts across different entities and also provide guidance to regulatory agencies for developing appropriate policies. Further, studies focusing primarily on surveys tend to be very deterministic as they are primarily aimed at theory testing (Zhu *et al.*, 2006; Levy *et al.*, 2005) and therefore are not able to uncover specific contextual issues influencing e-business adoption behaviour. Inductive, qualitative studies have an advantage in this domain.

Analysing the e-business adoption debate from the health care supply chain perspective reveals that the literature is rather underdeveloped within this domain. Studies have addressed the issue of the drivers and impediments for e-business adoption from the hospital's perspective (Pan and Pokharel, 2007; Ford and Hughes, 2007; Smith and Correa, 2005) and these predominantly focus on the operational drivers such as improving efficiency, reducing inventory and cost containment for technology adoption decisions. To the best of our knowledge, there are limited studies that have discussed the issues dealing with adoption of e-commerce within the health care sector using the supply chain as a unit of analysis (Bakker *et al.*, 2008; Zheng *et al.*, 2006). Papers by Bakke *et al.* (2008) and Zheng *et al.* (2006) are part of a larger UK study that has examined four different supply chains (stents, footwear, blood bottles and IV fluids). The findings advance the debate on e-commerce adoption within health care as they highlight that these strategic decisions are influenced simultaneously by contextual variables and internal organisational characteristics. Although Bakker *et al.* (2008) provide an insight into strategic e-commerce decision-making across four different supply chains what was missing from their discussion was the 'crucial reasons' for e-commerce adoption for each entity in the chain. Further, this study focused on 'e-commerce' which is much narrower in scope compared to the broader application of technologies facilitating e-business (Zheng *et al.*, 2006).

Application of institutional theory in operations management/information systems

Institutional theory focuses on the issue of *social legitimacy* in the eyes of societal stakeholders and the fact that organisations are shaped by the wider social, cultural and institutional environment in which they operate (Grewal and Dharwadkar, 2002; Oliver, 1991; Scott, 1987). In the late 1970s institutional theory went through a renaissance and 'new institutional theory' emerged grounded in the work of DiMaggio and Powell (1983), Oliver (1991) and Zucker (1987) focusing on how actions of organisations are shaped by external influences to acquire social legitimacy. Within the neo institutional school, the work of Meyer and Rowan (1977), along with Zuker (1987) and DiMaggio and Powell (1983), constitutes 'institutional isomorphism'. Meyer and Rowan (1977) argued that since organisations are embedded in socially prescribed structures, they embrace isomorphism in response to their external environment. This argument sowed the seeds for DiMaggio and Powell's (1983) seminal article on institutional isomorphism.

The key tenet of DiMaggio and Powell's article (*ibid.*) was to explain why organisations were acquiring similar forms, structures and practices. This homogeneity across organisations was being dictated by a set of three pressures - coercive, normative and mimetic. They described coercive pressures as formal or informal pressures exerted by an organisation on other organisations upon which they are dependent. These pressures could manifest themselves in the form of a regulatory force (through the government or a dominant supplier), a persuasion or an invitation to join a cartel, subordination to the parent organisation (in the case of a multinational) and conformity to institutional rules to implement a technical system. Normative pressures were described as being associated with professionalisation and these pressures typically manifest themselves in the form of organisations following industry norms such as sourcing their graduates from a particular university or choosing a specific software vendor for their IT needs (*ibid.*). Although normative pressures were not mandatory (as distinct from coercive pressures), non-conformance to these pressures could result in organisations incurring financial losses or a loss of face value among their peers. Mimetic pressures were identified and described as providing a strategy to mitigate uncertainty. This resulted in organisations modelling themselves based on other 'successful' organisations operating within their environment. According to DiMaggio and Powell (*ibid.*), these mimetic pressures primarily provided social legitimacy in their environment rather than improving operational efficiencies.

Although scholars within the information systems (IS) and OM disciplines have delineated coercive, normative and mimetic pressures through cross sectional surveys, they have not explored the sensitivity of these pressures across different trading partners in the supply chain (Teo *et al*, 2003; Son and Benbasat, 2007). With the ensuing health care reform in most OECD counties means that this sector will be subject to institutional pressures in the future and therefore makes it an important sector to study.

Institutional theory has proven its usefulness when discussing the topic of technology adoption (Haughton, 2006; Teo *et al.*, 2003), evaluating supply chain relationships (Koulikoff-Souviron and Harrison, 2008; Barringer and Harrison, 2000) and when multiple stakeholders such as customers, suppliers and regulatory groups are included in the research design (Zsidisin *et al.*, 2005). Damsgaard and Lyytinen (2001) have further illustrated that institutional theory provides a good understanding of the regulatory environment and advocate its use to study complex and networked technologies. All these factors are significant when studying the pharmaceutical hospital supply chain. It is also evident within the Australian context that each player in the health care supply chain is accelerating the uptake of technologies under response from the government and other trading partners (More and McGrath, 2002).

Research methodology

This study is exploratory in nature, asks a 'how' question, uses an inductive methodology and attempts to identify theory in action. As such, a case study approach was adopted which is strongly endorsed by scholars within the general management and OM disciplines (Eistenhardt and Graebner, 2007; Yin, 2003; Stuart *et al.*, 2002). Further, recent studies within the SCM literature employ multiple case studies as their overarching research design in an attempt to take a holistic view of the entire supply chain (Harland and Caldwell, 2007; Zheng *et al.*, 2006; McKone-Sweet *et al.*, 2005). The scope of our supply chain commenced at the manufacturer's end and terminated when the goods reached the pharmacy department in the hospital. Thus the key entities participating in our study were manufacturers, distributors, hospital and third-party logistics providers. We use an embedded case study design where each of the cases was a part of an entity, for example the three manufacturing cases are embedded within the manufacturing entity (Yin, 1994). The fifteen case studies used multiple sources of data such as interviews, analysing organisation's annual reports, plant tours, using their website material and examination of process maps (see Appendix for details).

At the outset, a focus group was held with eight practitioners representing different entities in the supply chain, each having between 10 and 25 years of industry experience. This enabled us to identify potential organisations that had recently adopted an eSCM system and provided guidance on key personnel across each tier in the supply chain to be included in the study.

From the pool of organisations that were identified, the selection of cases was guided by the twin goals of achieving theoretical replication and maximise learning (Eistenhardt and Graebner, 2007; Yin, 2003; Stake, 1995). For example, for the hospital entity which constituted the focal entity in the supply chain only public hospitals were included. The variables used for theoretical replication among the hospital entity included the size of hospitals, number of stock keeping units they handled and their budgets. Based on this criterion, Hospitals A, B and C were selected. However, Hospitals D and E were the specialist and regional hospitals and were selected to take into account any differences. All three 'manufacturing cases' were large pharmaceutical multinational organisations manufacturing branded patented products as well as generics and had a complex and challenging supply chain. Variables such as organisation size and annual turnover were used for replication purposes. Finally, since there are only a handful of wholesalers/distributors operating within the Australian pharmaceutical landscape, the two cases selected in this category were playing a very significant role within this market. Wholesaler/Distributor A is significantly larger but differs from Wholesaler/Distributor B as it supplies not only to hospitals but the retail outlets as well. It also generates a significant amount of its revenue from diagnostic services. The external entities such as technology providers, 3PL and government regulatory agencies were primarily included in the study for triangulation purposes.

All the participating organisations had adopted an eSCM system. The interviewees had, on an average, ten years of experience with some having spent their entire career working within the public health care system. The interview protocol was semi-structured and commenced with general questions followed by several open-ended questions and specific questions relevant to the context of the study. The structure of the interview varied from one informant to the other and was modified in order to take into account the informant's expertise in the specific area (Schutt, 2006). Most interviews lasted between 60 and 90 minutes which was sufficient to flesh out the necessary depth to each of the research questions. This is consistent with expert opinions on interviews (Hermanowicz, 2002). Participants were encouraged to express their views and this was feasible as the informants were assured that their names as well as the names of their organisations will remain anonymous. The questions in the interviews focused on issues such as:

- What do you perceive as the key institutional drivers of e-business adoption in the supply chain?
- What role are different trading partners in the supply chain play to accelerate e-business adoption?
- What kind of pressure (coercive/normative/mimetic) is your organisation experiencing from other entities in the supply chain?
- What is the implication of experiencing coercive/normative/mimetic pressures in the supply chain?
- Do you expect these pressures to remain static or evolve in the future?

Each of these questions received different responses from the interviewees representing different entities in the supply chain. All the 40 interviews conducted were audio-recorded and transcribed. This data was stored and managed using the qualitative analysis software package N-Vivo.

Data analysis

Analysis was conducted at two levels: (i) at the organisational level by conducting a within and cross case analysis of organisations embedded within an entity in the supply chain (e.g. the three cases within the manufacturer category) and (ii) across the four different entities or industry categories of interest (manufacturers, wholesaler/distributor, hospital and 3PL). The strength of conducting the analysis at the entity level facilitated a comparison between the user and provider perspectives and enabled generating fresh theoretical insights (Chivaka, 2005).

In the analysis procedure, the sentences within the text were assigned codes and N-Vivo facilitated these codes to be grouped under a specific theme, modified or removed as required (Schutt, 2006; Boyatzis, 1998). The 'broad' themes were assigned under the driver category and then sub-categories were created and were assigned appropriate names based on the information in the text (Strauss and Corbin, 1998). For example, N-Vivo assisted in coding the data into distinct theoretical categories (coercive, normative and mimetic) according to the responses by each interviewee in the supply chain. In order to accurately reflect the unit of analysis adopted for this study, 'attributes' were assigned to each interview indicating the role of the interviewee (i.e. manufacturer or hospital) within the context of the supply chain. Interviewees also made comments regarding the pressures being experienced by other entities in the supply chain. This was specifically evident in the entities/organisations external to the chain such as the 3PL, government regulatory agencies and technology provider. The comments from these 'external' entities were used for triangulation purposes.

Cognitive maps were used to display some results which proved extremely useful in the process of linking results to the emergent theory (Miles and Huberman, 1994). This helped us to develop a comprehensive understanding of the presence and intensity of the pressures being experienced by different entities in the supply chain. This strategy is highly recommended when the study employs around 5-10 cases to generate patterns which ideally fit the requirements of the current study (*ibid.*).

Reliability and validity was assured by maintaining a case study database, triangulation of data sources, interviewing personnel with similar designations in organisations and using quotes from interviews where appropriate. Finally, draft case study reports were reviewed by key interviewees (Yin, 2003; Anfara *et al.*, 2002; Stuart *et al.*, 2002).

Institutional drivers of adopting e-business technologies

The pressures exerted by each of the entities across the supply chain have been delineated into coercive, normative and mimetic pressures based on the isomorphic lens of institutional theory proposed by DiMaggio and Powell (1983) and further adaptations by Teo *et al.* (2003) and Khalifa and Davison (2006). Table 20.1 provides a breakdown of the proportion of the text in interviews conducted where interviewees discussed each of these institutional pressures. The development of this table was contingent on the coding of the data throughout the transcript as interviewees made comments regarding institutional pressures even when they responded to other questions in the interview protocol. Normative pressures were discussed more broadly by most interviewees across the supply chain. Mimetic pressures were an issue for interviewees from within the hospitals, while manufac-

Table 20.1 Coercive, normative and mimetic pressures within the institutions driver theme

Entity	*Coercive pressures*	*Normative pressures*	*Mimetic pressures*
Manufacturer	53%	40%	–
Wholesaler/distributor	–	95%	–
Hospital	10%	18%	58%
Third party logistics provider	–	90%	–
Technology provider	2%	55%	1%
Government regulatory agency	–	77%	–

Note: Percentage of sentences within the transcripts devoted to discussion on coercive, normative and mimetic pressures within the institutional driver theme

turers were the group most conscious of coercive pressures. Further, each entity had a different story to tell in terms of whether they were the recipients of these pressures or putting pressures on other entities.

The manufacturers predominantly discussed how they were experiencing coercive pressures from the government, their headquarters and normative pressures from the hospitals. They also discussed instances where seeking a specific technology was becoming an industry norm. The wholesaler/distributor predominantly discussed how they were recipients of strong normative pressures from trading partners. Finally, the hospital discussed all three pressures. The coercive pressures they were experiencing stemmed from government mandates to adopt e-SCM systems as they would feed into patient safety outcomes. However, the hospitals provided evidence for how they were exerting normative pressures on the manufacturers and wholesaler/distributor and 18 per cent of the sentences in the transcript were devoted to this specific aspect. The comments made by technology providers, 3PL, and government regulatory agencies have been used for triangulation purposes. For example, 1 per cent of the sentences in the transcripts of the interviews by the technology provider illustrated how the hospitals were mimetic in character as they were looking at replicating practices on inventory management with the adoption of e-SCMS and transferring these learnings from each other.

In order to further examine the nature of these institutional pressures acting on the various entities, the analysis was conducted to identify the sources of each form of institutional pressure (i.e. as identified by each entity).

Evidence and sources of coercive pressures

Table 20.2 illustrates (as perceived by the manufacturers and hospitals) the primary sources of coercive pressure.

All three manufacturers were the recipients of strong coercive pressures by the government as the term 'compliance' continued to surface in the interviews. The pharmaceutical companies had to comply with regulations for packaging and bar-coding as well as adhering to international regulations such as the Sarbanes–Oxley Act of 2002. This act establishes compliance requirements across different

Table 20.2 Coercive pressures

Entity	*Source*
Manufacturer	Manufacturer headquarters (10%) Government regulatory agencies (65%)
Hospital	Government regulatory agencies (25%)

Sources: Percentage of sentences in the transcript devoted to discussion on source of coercive pressures

functions for management and public accounting firms operating in the USA (Borgia and Siegel, 2008). In addition, most of the pharmaceutical manufacturers operating in Australia were subsidiaries of large multinational organisations with headquarters located either in Europe or the USA. In terms of e-business uptake, the Australian subsidiaries were significantly behind their US counterparts (Manufacturers B and C). Thus, these organisations were experiencing strong coercive pressures from senior management to transfer the learning across these regions to Australia.

A 'milder' coercive pressure was also exerted on the hospital pharmacy departments by government regulatory agencies (such as the National e-Health Transition Authority, NeHTA) who were trying to 'entice' them to adopt e-business technologies. This form of enticement becomes clear in the quote below by the Supply Chain Manager of Government Regulatory Agency B:

> because you're looking at the healthcare benefits of having this unique identifier, that you can do barcode dispensing and, you can have a unique identification of the product at the point of ordering. So we're selling it to the pharmacist and the doctors, that here is a standard name for the drug, and here is a standard unique identifier for the drug, which will help them at their business end as well, and will help them with finding better decision support systems. So we're coming top down and we're coming bottom up.

Finally, a within case analysis within pharmacy and the Materials Management Department (MMD) across all five hospitals highlighted that MMD within the public hospitals were subject to coercive pressures from the government as all these departments were migrating onto a similar ERP system (Oracle) throughout the state.

Evidence and sources of normative pressures

Table 20.3 highlights the important role of normative pressures across the pharmaceutical hospital supply chain. Organisations most aware of these normative pressures were the pharmaceutical manufacturers, wholesalers/distributors and 3PL. Manufacturers were experiencing strong pressures from hospitals as explicitly stated in the quote below:

> But, given that it's not until a customer has asked us to get EAN 128 [bar coding standard], that we're doing anything about it, and without customers, demanding that of us, that change is going to take place long-term, rather than short-term. So, my role is to ensure that our manufacturing people, technical operations, understand that there are customers now asking for that level of electronic information, and we need to spend the money to achieve it. If the healthcare provider wasn't asking for it, we wouldn't even be looking at it. Absolutely, the push is 100% driven from the health care provider.
>
> (Supply chain manager, Manufacturer B)

Further, since the manufacturers were supplying not only to hospitals but selling their products over the counter through pharmacies and supermarkets as well, they inevitably became an integral part of the supply chain and this fact was responsible for the significant pressures exerted on them through the retail sector.

The wholesaler/distributor entity was strategically positioned within the supply chain performing the vital function of delivering products to the hospital. This entity experienced normative pressures from the hospitals and the manufacturers as well as from government regulators, the retail sector and their competitors. The following statement sums up the sentiment of the wholesaler/distributor entity: 'The pressure [for e-business adoption] is a lot from the customer side [hospital], the supplier side and the competitor side what they are doing and what we need to do' (customer relationship manager, Wholesaler/Distributor A).

The interviewees within the wholesaler/distributor entity mentioned that recently strong normative pressures were being generated through government initiatives such as NeHTA who approached e-business adoption by specifying specific guidelines. For example, for wholesalers/distributors to be eligible to compete for state government tenders, they had to adhere to certain bar-coding

Table 20.3 Normative pressures

Entity	*Source*
Manufacturer	Technology provider (5%) Hospital (22%) Retail sector (3%) Government regulatory agencies (5%)
Wholesaler/distributor	Retail sector (13%) Hospital and government regulatory agencies (35%)* Manufacturer (5%)
Third party logistics provider	Retail sector (3%)
Government regulatory agencies	Technology providers (4%)
Technology providers	Manufacturers (3%) Government regulatory agencies (2%)

Sources: Percentage of sentences in the transcript devoted to discussion on source of normative pressures

* Comments relating to hospitals and government regulatory agencies have been collapsed under a single category because of references made to both these entities in multiple sentences

standards. These normative pressures on the manufacturers and wholesalers/distributors were making technology providers responsible for administering bar coding standards very powerful entities in the supply chain. Interestingly, the combination of normative and coercive pressures exerted by government regulatory bodies and hospitals meant that technology providers (such as those administering these standards) assumed the status of 'legitimate' organisations for providing e-business solutions (Teo *et al.*, 2003).

The 3PL was the recipient of the normative pressures from the retail sector rather than any entity within the pharmaceutical domain. This is because it was technologically more advanced compared to its partners/members within the supply chain and retailers were its largest customers.

Evidence and sources of mimetic pressures

The third isomorphic pressures evident were mimetic pressures which surfaced in the interviews and document analysis conducted within the hospital pharmacy departments. The hospitals were keen to learn from the more progressive sectors (e.g. retail) that have taken the lead in e-business adoption. Further, interviewees indicated that they were looking for an example of a progressive hospital that had implemented some form of e-business technologies and demonstrated significant savings. The quote below (Monash Project Report) triangulates the evidence in the interviews regarding the source of mimetic pressures across public hospitals. This project was initiated by Hospital A to demonstrate the efficiencies gained by the application of e-business technologies by collaborating with its trading partners.

> The most critical outcome is that this process [e-business adoption] can be duplicated by other hospitals and their suppliers. The key benefit of hospital budgetary and efficiency savings can then be passed on to improve the level of patient care within Australia's hospital and healthcare system, whilst at the same time, improving the profitability of Australia's healthcare industry suppliers.
>
> (Director of pharmacy, Hospital A, Monash Project Phase 2 Industry Report)

In addition, during discussions with hospital pharmacy personnel, frequent references were made to the fact that the retail sector was more progressive in adopting e-business technologies. Hospitals were cognisant of the fact that they could benefit from the experience of the retail sector and use it to accelerate e-business adoption within their organisations.

Thus, institutional pressures by trading partners in the supply chain surfaced as a crucial driver for e-business adoption as the pharmaceutical manufacturers were recipient of coercive and normative pressures, the wholesalers/distributors experiencing normative pressures and the hospital pharmacy departments mimicking the retail sector and more progressive hospitals.

Discussion

Figure 20.1 is a cognitive map that depicts the coercive, normative and mimetic pressures among the various entities across the pharmaceutical hospital supply chain as evidenced by the results. This map was developed by an inductive analysis of the data as reported in the preceding data analysis sections.

In order to explain the different institutional pressures, we adopt an 'isomorphism' lens within institutional theory (DiMaggio and Powell, 1983). The fact that institutional isomorphism resonated in this study is consistent with the findings of a meta-review on the interpretation of institutional theory by management scholars who have reported 'isomorphism' as the central area of concern (Farashahi *et al.*, 2005). According to Farashahi *et al.* (*ibid.*), the primary reason why institutional isomorphism is attracting considerable interest stems from the fact that industry associations and regulatory agencies have exercised considerable influence over establishing standard business norms and practices over the last decade. Two characteristics of the sample used for this study provide an explanatory context for the nature of the relationships outlined in Figure 20.1. First, each entity in the supply chain is at a different stage of e-SCM adoption with the 3PL representing the most progressive entity in the chain while the hospitals and pharmaceutical manufacturers representing the 'laggard' entities. Second, the entities are not immune from external influences as certain entities (3PL, wholesalers/ distributors) intersect with supply chains of different industries (for example retail).

The manufacturers are receiving strong coercive pressures to adopt e-business technologies both from the government and their head-quarters. The fact that large multinational corporations receive coercive pressures from their head-quarters to

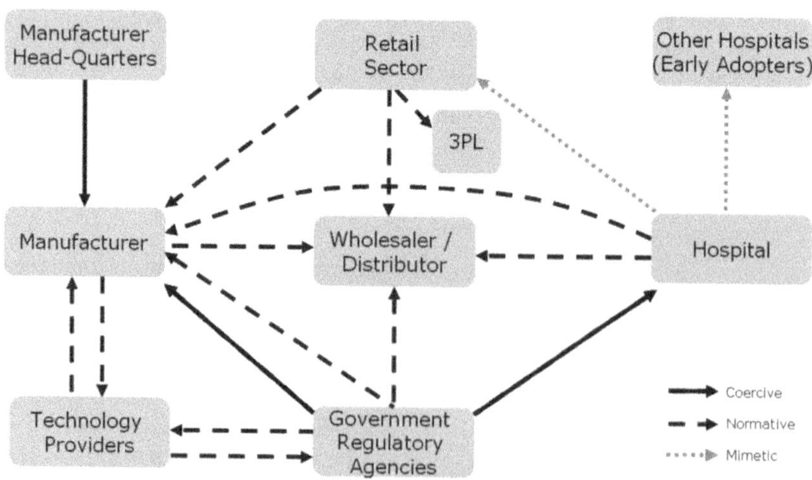

Figure 20.1 Cognitive map of coercive, normative and mimetic pressures among the different entities in the pharmaceutical hospital supply chain

adopt best practices is consistent with the literature (Kostova and Roth, 2002; Ferner and Quintanilla, 1998).

Further, the wholesalers/distributors and manufacturers are on the receiving end of strong normative forces from other trading partners as well as external organisations such as government regulatory agencies and the retail sector. This finding is consistent with some recent studies that have identified government and stakeholder pressures as crucial factors influencing e-business adoption (Roberts and Toleman, 2007; Haughton, 2006; Wymer and Regan, 2005). However, this study goes a step further and distinguishes the influence of the retail sector across the different entities. For example, whereas the wholesalers/distributors and manufacturers are recipients of normative pressures, the hospitals (pharmacy and MMD) are recipients of mimetic pressures from this sector. Another explanation that justifies the presence of normative pressures from the retail sector in this cognitive map stems from the fact that entities such as wholesalers/distributors, manufacturers and 3PLs intersect with the supply chain of the retail sector which is not a part of the pharmaceutical hospital supply chain. The reason why pharmacy and MMD are the only entity in the supply chain subject to mimetic pressures ties in with the discussion in the literature that 'mimicry' resonates with late adopters of an innovation (Tolbert and Zucker, 1983).

The coercive pressures exerted on the manufacturers from government (as shown in Figure 20.1) have the purpose of either seeking compliance with international regulatory requirements or to adhere to specific technology standards (Kumar and Putnam, 2008). Further, studies by Hausman and Stock (2003) and Liu *et al.* (2010) also testify to the fact that coercive pressures encourage adoption of technological innovations. Figure 20.1 also shows that public hospitals are recipients of mimetic pressures from the retail sector and other 'progressive' public hospitals. Since the public hospitals in this study were non-competitive in character, the progressive hospitals (e.g. Hospital A) were sharing their experiences and knowledge acquired by embarking on e-SCM initiatives through press conferences, workshops and in-house seminars with other hospitals. The retail sector is also playing a pivotal role in accelerating the adoption of e-business technologies within the health care sector. Further, the same non-competitive element was visible between industry sectors such as retail and health care.

Figure 20.1 highlights the dominance of normative pressures with the manufacturers and the wholesalers/distributors being the major recipients of these pressures. These pressures were exerted by hospitals and external entities such as technology providers and the government as well as the retail sector. However, the sensitivity of these pressures was experienced with most intensity by the wholesalers/distributors due to the positioning in the supply chain which implied that this entity was the recipients to adhere to industry norms from both upstream and downstream trading partners. However, the intensity of the normative pressures exerted by hospitals was much higher compared to the manufacturers (see Table 20.3), which is indicative of the fact that hospitals possessed significant power in the supply chain. Craighead and Laforge's (2003) study conducted within the manufacturing domain provides evidence that power essentially resides downstream in the chain and our study extends this work to the health care sector by demonstrating that hospitals have significant power in the supply chain. Our findings are also consistent with recent studies identifying government and stakeholder pressures as crucial factors influencing e-business adoption (Roberts and Toleman, 2007; Haughton, 2006; Wymer and Regan, 2005).

Conclusions and implications for operations management theory and practice

In this chapter, we sought to answer the following research question:

> How sensitive are different entities in the health care supply chain to institutional pressures in the adoption of e-SCM systems?

By employing institutional theory to answer this question, we advance the debate on e-SCM adoption and break new ground by building on the isomorphism lens of new institutional theory proposed by DiMaggio and Powell (1983). Our contribution lies in the fact that a cognitive map has been developed that delineates the three isomorphic pressures (coercive, normative and mimetic) for each entity. Scholars have suggested that delineation of these forces is difficult and challenging, though a worthwhile task in the broader study of organisations (DiMaggio and Powell, 1983; Tingling and Parent, 2002). We have also been able to gauge the sensitivity of the different entities towards the different pressures and provide an explanation for their cause.

The value of this contribution is evidenced by Mizruchi and Fein (1999) evaluating how DiMaggio and Powell's (1983) paper on institutional isomorphism has been interpreted by scholars within their studies. Their review of 26 articles found that 75 per cent of the studies had used only one of the three different pressures. Furthermore, only 50 per cent had employed mimetic pressures which has significant implications for organisation theory. It essentially implies that scholars have not grasped the full essence of DiMaggio and Powell's work and their seminal article was being interpreted in a myopic fashion with the result that 'isomorphism' was becoming synonymous with 'mimetic isomorphism.' Mizruchi and Fein (1999: 680) articulate their concerns in the following paragraph:

> The problem (referring to the use of only one pressure) in cases in which authors stipulate only one type of isomorphic process while ignoring equally plausible alternative accounts. When authors assume that only voluntary mimicry accounts for an organisation's behaviour, without considering alternative explanations, including coercion, then one may be providing a limited picture of the phenomenon. If one fails to consider alternative accounts provided by the authors of one source, then one's distortion of that source is not only misrepresenting the theory on which one's analysis is based, but it is providing a limited and biased picture of the processes one is trying to describe.

Our study therefore provides unique insights into the application of neo-institutional theory and therefore responds to calls by scholars to undertake theory building within the SCM domain (Burgress *et al.*, 2006; Wacker, 2008).

Our study is a step forward in addressing the positivist methodological bias within the SCM domain and the broader OM discipline which has been dominated by surveys of focal firms (Spens and Kovács, 2006; Sachan and Datta, 2005). In addition, Harland and Caldwell (2007) comment that it is relatively easier to conduct a survey of senior managers in large organisations that are drawn from a database rather than select organisations that are connected in the chain to gauge the factors responsible for e-business adoption. Further, by collecting data across six entities in the supply chain, including not only members directly in the chain (manufacturer, wholesaler/-distributor, 3PL and hospital) but external entities such as government regulatory agencies and technology providers, this study has responded to the call by scholars in the discipline to conduct empirical field research that takes a 'holistic' view of the entire supply chain (Seuring, 2008; Power, 2005; Svensson, 2003). Although the task of data collection was time consuming and challenging, doing so enabled the researchers to understand and recognise the heterogeneity of organisations embedded in a supply chain and the fact that interview protocols require customisation when personnel from a specific entity are interviewed. Finally, employing an embedded case study design was a departure from studies that have conducted the analysis at the organisational or dyadic level (Giunipero *et al.*, 2008; Halldórsson and Arlborn, 2005).

For the practitioners, our results endorse the fact that wholesalers/distributors need to continue differentiating their service offerings and adopt a more strategic focus in developing and expanding their business models. This recommendation stems from the fact that the wholesaler/distributor entity was centrally located in the supply chain, was completely reliant on distribution margins as a predominant source of revenue and was receiving strong normative pressures from other entities in the chain. Furthermore, since the public hospitals are mimetic in character and have a tight financial budget, they would be in a better position to secure funding from senior management by providing examples of other progressive hospitals which have been able to demonstrate savings by adopting e-business technologies.

Future research should continue to build on institutional theory by exploring the impact of mimetic pressures among competing organisations in the supply chain. Since normative pressures are putting technology providers in a dominant position, it would be worthwhile exploring how this power is actually manifested. Longitudinal research designs would be highly valuable in this endeavour. There are also opportunities for conducting large surveys and the application of innovation diffusion theory (Rogers, 1995) and the resource dependency theory (Pfeffer and Salancik, 2003) in conjunction with institutional theory.

References

Anfara, V.A., Brown, K.M. and Mangione, T.L. (2002) 'Qualitative analysis on stage: making the research process more public'. *Educational Researcher*, 31(7): 28–38.

Auramo, J., Kauremaa, J. and Tanskanen, K. (2005) 'Benefits of IT in supply chain management: an explorative study of progressive companies'. *International Journal of Physical Distribution and Logistics Management*, 35(2): 82–100.

Bakker, E., Zheng, J., Knight, L. and Harland, C. (2008) 'Putting e-commerce adoption in a supply chain context'. *International Journal of Operations and Production Management*, 28(4): 313–30.

Baltacioglu, T., Ada, E., Kaplan, M.D., Yurt, O. and Kaplan, Y.C. (2007) 'A new framework for service supply chains'. *Service Industries Journal*, 27(2): 105–24.

Barringer, B.R. and Harrison, J.S. (2000) 'Walking a tightrope: creating value through interorganizational relationships'. *Journal of Management*, 26(3): 367–403.

Becker, C. (2001) 'Bellying, slowly, up to the barcode'. *Modern Healthcare*, 31(42): 16–18.

Bhakoo, V. and Chan, C. (2011) 'Collaborative implementation of e-business processes within the health care supply chain: the Monash pharmacy project'. *Supply Chain Management: An International Journal*, 16(3): 184–93.

Boone, T. and Ganeshan, R. (2007) 'The frontiers of e-business technology and supply chains'. *Journal of Operations Management*, 25(6): 1195–8.

Borgia, C. and Siegel, P.H. (2008) 'How the Sarbanes–Oxley Act is affecting profitability in the banking industry'. *The CPA Journal*, 78(8): 13–14.

Boyatzis, R.E. (1998) *Transforming Qualitative Information: Thematic Analysis and Code Development*. Thousand Oaks, CA: Sage.

Burgress, K., Singh, P.J. and Koroglu, R. (2006) 'Supply chain management: a structured literature review and implications for future research'. *International Journal of Operations and Production Management*, 26(7): 703–29.

Chandra, C. and Grabis, J. (2007) *Supply Chain Configuration: Concepts, Solutions, and Application*. New York: Springer US.

Chivaka, R. (2005) 'Cost Management along the supply chain – methodological implications'. In Kotzab, H., Seuring, S., Muller, M. and Reiner, G. (eds), *Research Methodologies in Supply Chain Management*. Heidelberg: Physica-Verlag.

Choi, T.Y. and Eboch, K. (1998) 'The TQM paradox: relations among TQM practices, plant performance and customer satisfaction'. *Journal of Operations Management*, 17: 59–75.

Chopra, S., Lovejoy, W. and Yano, C. (2004) 'Five decades of operations management and the prospects ahead'. *Management Science*, 50(1): 8–14.

Craighead, C.W. and Laforge, R.L. (2003) 'Taxonomy of information technology adoption patterns in manufacturing firms'. *International Journal of Production Research*, 41(11): 2431–49.

Craighead, C.W., Patterson, J.W., Roth, P.L. and Segars, A.H. (2006) 'Enabling the benefits of supply chain management systems: an empirical study of electronic data interchange (EDI) in manufacturing'. *International Journal of Production Research*, 44(1): 135–57.

Cullen, A.J. and Taylor, M. (2009) 'Critical success factors for B2B e-commerce use within the UK NHS pharmaceutical supply chain'. *International Journal of Operations and Production Management*, 29(11): 1156–85.

Damsgaard, J. and Lyytinen, K. (2001) 'The role of intermediating institutions in the diffusion of Electronic Data Interchange (EDI): how industry associations intervened in Denmark, Finland and Hong Kong'. *The Information Society*, 17(3): 195–210.

DiMaggio, P.J. and Powell, W.W. (1983) 'The iron cage revisited: Institutional isomorphism and collective rationality in organizational fields'. *American Sociological Review*, 48(2): 147–60.

Donaldson, L. (1995) *American Anti-Management Theories of Organization: A Critique of Paradigm Proliferation*. New York: Cambridge University Press.

Eistenhardt, K.M. and Graebner, M.E. (2007) 'Theory building from cases: opportunities and challenges'. *Academy of Management Journal*, 50(1): 25–32.

Evangelista, P. and Sweeney, E. (2006) 'Technology usage in the supply chain: the case of small 3PLs'. *International Journal of Logistics Management*, 17(1): 55.

Farashahi, M., Hafsi, T. and Molz, R. (2005) 'Institutionalized norms of conducting research and social realities: a research synthesis of empirical works from 1983 to 2002'. *International Journal of Management Reviews*, 7(1): 1–24.

Ferner, A. and Quintanilla, J. (1998) 'Multinationals, national business systems and HRM: the enduring influence of national identity or a process of 'Anglo-Saxonization'. *International Journal of Human Resource Management*, 9(4): 710–31.

Ford, E.W. and Hughes, J.A. (2007) 'A collaborative product commerce approach to value-based health plan purchasing'. *Supply Chain Management: An International Journal*, 12(1): 32–41.

Giunipero, L., Hooker, R.E., Joseph-Mattews, S. and Brudvig, S. (2008) 'A decade of SCM literature: past, present and future implications'. *Journal of Supply Chain Management*, 44(4): 66–86.

Grewal, R. and Dharwadkar, R. (2002) 'The role of the institutional environment in marketing channels'. *Journal of Marketing*, 66(3): 82–97.

Halldórsson, Á. and Arlborn, J.S. (2005) 'Research methodologies in supply chain management – what do we know?' In Kotzab, H., Seuring, S., Muller, M. and Reiner, G. (eds), *Research Methodologies in Supply Chain Management*. Heidelberg: Physica-Verlag.

Harland, C.M. and Caldwell, N.D. (2007) 'Barriers to supply chain information integration: SMEs adrift of eLands'. *Journal of Operations Management*, 25(6): 1234–54.

Haughton, M.A. (2006) 'Information technology projects by international logistics service providers: the case of Canada's small customs brokers'. *Canadian Journal of Administrative Sciences*, 23(1): 17–33.

Hausman, A. and Stock, J.R. (2003) 'Adoption and implementation of technological innovations within long-term relationships'. *Journal of Business Research*, 56(8): 681–6.

Hermanowicz, J.C. (2002) 'The great interview: 25 strategies for studying people in bed'. *Qualitative Sociology*, 25(4): 479–99.

Ho, D.C.K., Au, K.F. and Newton, E. (2002) 'Empirical research on supply chain management: a critical review and recommendations'. *International Journal of Production Research*, 40(17): 4415–30.

Jarrett, P.G. (2006) 'An analysis of international health care logistics: the benefits and implications of implementing just-in-time systems in the health care industry'. *Leadership in Health Services*, 19(1): 1–10.

Johnson, P.F., Klassen, R.D., Leenders, M.R. and Awaysheh, A. (2007) 'Utilizing e-business technologies in supply chains: the impact of firm characteristics and teams'. *Journal of Operations Management*, 25(6): 1255–74.

Kennedy, M.T. and Fiss, P.C. (2009) 'Institutionalization, framing, and diffusion: the logic of TQM adoption and implementation decisions among US hospitals'. *Academy of Management Journal*, 52(5): 897–918.

Ketokivi, M.A. and Schroeder, R.G. (2004) 'Strategic, structural contingency and institutional explanations in the adoption of innovative manufacturing practices'. *Journal of Operations Management*, 22: 63–89.

Khalifa, M. and Davison, M. (2006) 'SME adoption of IT: the case of electronic trading systems'. *Engineering Management, IEEE Transactions*, 53(2): 275–84.

Kostova, T. and Roth, K. (2002) 'Adoption of organizational practice by subsidiaries of multinational corporations: Institutional and relational effects'. *Academy of Management Journal*, 45(1): 215–33.

Koulikoff-Souviron, M. and Harrison, A. (2008) 'Interdependent supply chain relationships as institutions: the role of HR practices'. *International Journal of Operations and Production Management*, 28(5): 412–32.

Kumar, S. and Putnam, V. (2008) 'Cradle to cradle: reverse logistics strategies and opportunities across three industry sectors'. *International Journal of Production Economics*, 115: 305–15.

Lamming, R., Johnsen, T., Zheng, J. and Harland, C. (2000) 'An initial classification of supply networks'. *International Journal of Operations and Production Management*, 20(6): 675–91.

Levy, M., Powell, P. and Worrall, L. (2005) 'Strategic intent and e-business in SMEs: enablers and inhibitors'. *Information Resources Management Journal*, 18(4): 1–20.

Liu, H., Ke, W., Wei, K.K., Gu, J. and Chen, H. (2010) 'The role of institutional pressures and organizational culture in the firm's intention to adopt internet-enabled supply chain management systems'. *Journal of Operations Management*, 28(5): 372–84.

McKone-Sweet, K.E., Hamilton, P. and Willis, S.B. (2005) 'The ailing healthcare supply chain: a prescription for change'. *Journal of Supply Chain Management*, 41(1): 4–17.

Meyer, J.W. and Rowan, B. (1977) 'Institutionalized organizations: formal structure as myth and ceremony'. *American Journal of Sociology*, 83(2): 340–63.

Miemczyk, J. (2008) 'An exploration of institutional constraints on developing end-of-life product recovery capabilities'. *International Journal of Production Economics*, 115: 272–82.

Miles, M.B. and Huberman, M. (1994) *Qualitative Data Analysis* (2nd edn). London: Sage.

Mizruchi, M.S. and Fein, L.C. (1999) 'The social construction of organizational knowledge: a study of the uses of coercive, mimetic and normative isomorphism'. *Administrative Science Quarterly*, 44(4): 653–83.

More, E. and McGrath, M. (2002) 'An Australian case in e-health communication and change'. *Journal of Management Development*, 21(8): 621–32.

OECD (2008) *OECD Annual Report*. Retrieved from www.oecd.org/newsroom/40556222.pdf (accessed 16 December 2014).

Oliver, C. (1991) 'Strategic responses to institutional processes'. *Academy of Management Review*, 16(1): 145–79.

Orr, S., Sohal, A.S., Gray, K., Harbrow, J. and Mennen, A. (2001) 'The impact of information technology on a section of the Australian health care industry'. *Benchmarking*, 8(2): 108–19.

Pan, Z.X. and Pokharel, S. (2007) 'Logistics in hospitals: a case study of some Singapore hospitals'. *Leadership in Health Services*, 20(3): 197–207.

Pfeffer, J. and Salancik, G.R. (2003) *The External Control of Organizations: A Resource Dependence Perspective.* Stanford, CA: Stanford University Press.

Power, D. (2005) 'Supply chain management integration and implementation: a literature review'. *Supply Chain Management: An International Journal*, 10(4): 252–63.

Power, D. and Simon, A. (2004) 'Adoption and diffusion in technology implementation: a supply chain study'. *International Journal of Operations and Production Management*, 24(5/6): 566–87.

Roberts, B. and Toleman, M. (2007) 'One-size e-business adoption model does not fit all'. *Journal of Theoretical and Applied Electronic Commerce Research*, 2(3): 49–61.

Rogers, E. (1995) *Diffusion of Innovations* (4th edn). New York: Free Press.

Rogers, K.W., Purdy, L., Safayeni, F. and Duimering, P.R. (2007) 'A supplier development program: rational process or institutional image construction?' *Journal of Operations Management*, 25(2): 556–72.

Sachan, A. and Datta, S. (2005) 'Review of supply chain management and logistics research'. *International Journal of Physical Distribution and Logistics Management*, 35(9): 664–705.

Sanders, N.R. (2007) 'The benefits of using e-business technology: the supplier perspective'. *Journal of Business Logistics*, 28(2): 177–207.

Scheller, E.S. and Smeltzer, L.R. (2006) *Strategic Management of the Health Care Supply Chain* (1st edn). San Francisco, CA: John Wiley & Sons.

Schutt, R.K. (2006) *Investigating the Social World: The Process and Practice of Research* (5th edn). Thousand Oaks, CA: Sage.

Scott, W.R. (1987) 'The adolescence of institutional theory'. *Administrative Science Quarterly*, 32: 493–511.

Selznick, P. (1996) 'Institutionalism old and new'. *Administrative Science Quarterly*, 41(2): 270–77.

Seuring, S.A. (2008) 'Assessing the rigor of case study research in supply chain management'. *Supply Chain Management: An International Journal*, 13(2): 128–37.

Shah, N. (2004) 'Pharmaceutical supply chains: key issues and strategies for optimisation'. *Computers and Chemical Engineering*, 28(6–7): 929–41.

Siau, K., Southard, P.B. and Hong, S. (2002) 'E-healthcare strategies and implementation'. *International Journal Healthcare Technology and Management*, 4(1–2): 118–31.

Sila, I. (2007) 'Examining the effects of contextual factors on TQM and performance through the lens of organizational theories: an empirical study'. *Journal of Operations Management*, 25: 83–109.

Silveira, G.J.C.d. and Cagliano, R. (2006) 'The relationship between interorganizational information systems and operations performance'. *International Journal of Operations and Production Management*, 26(3): 232–53.

Skinner, R.I. (2003) 'The value of information technology in health care'. *Frontiers of Health Services Management*, 19(3): 3–15.

Smith, A.D. and Correa, J. (2005) 'Value added benefits of technology: e-procurement and e-commerce related to the health care industry'. *International Journal of Healthcare Quality Assurance*, 18(6): 458–73.

Son, J.-Y. and Benbasat, I. (2007) 'Organizational buyers' adoption and use of B2B electronic marketplaces: efficiency- and legitimacy-oriented perspectives'. *Journal of Management Information Systems*, 24 (1): 55–99.

Spens, K.M. and Kovács, G. (2006) 'A content analysis of research approaches in logistics research'. *International Journal of Physical Distribution and Logistics Management*, 36(5): 374–90.

Stake, R.E. (1995) *The Art of Case Study Research*. Thousand Oaks, CA: Sage.

Strauss, A. and Corbin, J. (1998) *Basics of Qualitative Research: Techniques and Procedures for Developing Grounded Theory.* (2nd edn.) Thousand Oaks, CA: Sage.

Stuart, I., McCutcheon, D., Handfield, R., McLachlin, R. and Samson, D. (2002) 'Effective case research in operations management: a process perspective'. *Journal of Operations Management*, 20(5): 419–33.

Svensson, G. (2003) 'Holistic and cross-disciplinary deficiencies in the theory generation of supply chain management'. *Supply Chain Management: An International Journal*, 8(4): 303–16.

Teo, H.H., Wei, K.K. and Benbasat, I. (2003) 'Predicting intention to adopt interorganizational linkages: an institutional perspective'. *MIS Quarterly*, 27(1): 19–49.

Tingling, P. and Parent, M. (2002) 'Mimetic isomorphism and technology adoption: does imitation transcend judgement?' *Journal of the Association of Information Systems*, 3(5): 113–43.

Tolbert, P.S. and Zucker, L.G. (1983) 'Institutional sources of change in the formal structure of organizations: the diffusion of civil service reform, 1880–1935'. *Administrative Science Quarterly*, 28(1): 22–39.

Wacker, J.G. (2008) 'A conceptual understanding of requirements for theory-building research: guidelines for scientific theory building'. *Journal of Supply Chain Management*, 44(3): 5–15.

Wagner, B.A., Fillis, I. and Johansson, U. (2003) 'E-business and e-supply strategy in small and medium sized businesses'. *Supply Chain Management: An International Journal*, 8(4): 343–54.

Wymer, S.A. and Regan, E.A. (2005) 'Factors influencing e-commerce adoption and use by small and medium businesses'. *Electronic Markets*, 15(4): 438–53.

Yeung, A.C.L., Cheng, T.C.E. and Lai, K.-H. (2006) 'An operational and institutional perspective on Total Quality Management'. *Production and Operations Management*, 15(1): 156–70.

Yin, R.K. (1994) *Case Study Research: Design and Methods* (2nd edn). New York: Sage.

Yin, R.K. (2003) *Case Study Research Design and Methods* (3rd edn). Thousand Oaks, CA: Sage.

Zheng, J., Bakker, E., Knight, L., Gilesphy, H., Harland, C. and Walker, H. (2006) 'A strategic case for e-adoption in healthcare supply chains'. *International Journal of Information Management*, 26(4): 290–301.

Zhu, K. and Kraemer, K.L. (2005) 'Post-adoption variations in usage and value of E-Business by organizations: cross country evidence from the retail industry'. *Information Systems Research*, 16(1): 61–84.

Zhu, K., Dong, S., Xu, S.X. and Kraemer, K.L. (2006) 'Innovation diffusion in global contexts: determinants of post-global digital transformation of European companies'. *European Journal of Information Systems*, 15(6): 601–16.

Zsidisin, G.A., Melnyk, S.A. and Ragatz, G.L. (2005) 'An institutional theory perspective of business continuity planning for purchasing and supply management'. *International Journal of Production Research*, 43(16): 3401–20.

Zucker, L.G. (1987) 'Institutional theories of organization'. *Annual Review of Sociology*, 13(1): 443–64.

Appendix

Table 20.4 Organisation profiles and data sources

Organization type	*Headquarters*	*Employees (worldwide)*	*No of stock keeping units*	*Products*	*Annual turnover (worldwide)*	*Supply chain systems*	*Interviewees*	*Data sources*
Manufacturer A	Australia	1600	1200	Oncology	A$687 million	ERP System (SAP)	Supply Chain Manager Operations Manager $n = 2$	Interviews, Plant Tours Website Material
Manufacturer B	USA	44,000	500	Cardio Vascular Neuroscience Oncology	US$20.9 billion	ERP System (Manugistics)	Supply Chain Manager Corporate Affairs Senior Manager IT Manager $n = 3$	Interviews, Plant Tours Website Material, Company Annual Report
Manufacturer C	USA	47,000	9000	Intravenous Solutions IV Fluids	US$9.8 billion	ERP System (JD Edwards)	IT Manager Strategy Manager Operations Manager $n = 3$	Interviews, Plant Tours Website Material Company Annual Strategy Documents
Wholesaler/ Distributor A	Australia	6000	17,000	Pharmacy and Non Pharmacy Products	A$3.4 billion	PC. Net	Customer Relationship Manager Operations Manager $n = 2$	Interviews Website Material
Wholesaler/ Distributor B	Australia	300	17,000	Equipment Medical and Pharmacy Products	A$1.3 billion	SOS	Operations Manager CIO, Sales Manager $n = 3$	Interviews, Website Material, Internal IT Strategy Documents

Table 20.4 continued

Organization type	*Headquarters*	*Employees (worldwide)*	*No of stock keeping units*	*Products*	*Annual turnover (worldwide)*	*Supply chain systems*	*Interviewees*	*Data sources*
Hospital A	Australia	10,000	3000	Pharmacy Products	A$38 million	Merlin	Director Pharmacy Deputy Director Pharmacy Purchasing Manager Ward Staff *n* = 4	Interviews Website Material Hospital Annual Report Examination of 'existing' processes
Hospital B	Australia	7500	4500	Pharmacy Products	A$30 million	Merlin	Director Pharmacy Deputy Director Pharmacy Director Materials Management *n* = 4	Interviews Website Material Hospital Annual Report Examination of 'existing' processes
Hospital C	Australia	4200	3000	Pharmacy Products	A$12 million	ISOP	Director Pharmacy Inventory Manager Purchasing Manager Purchasing Officer Director Materials Management *n* = 4	Interviews Website Material Hospital Annual Report Examination of 'existing' processes
Hospital D	Australia	744	1300	Pharmacy Products	A$1.9 million	Merlin	Director Pharmacy IT Manager Purchasing Manager Director Materials Management *n* = 4	Interviews Website Material Hospital Annual Report Examination of 'existing' processes

Table 20.4 continued

Organization type	*Headquarters*	*Employees (worldwide)*	*No of stock keeping units*	*Products*	*Annual turnover (worldwide)*	*Supply chain systems*	*Interviewees*	*Data sources*
Hospital E	Australia	1020	2500	Pharmacy Products	A$3.9 million	Stocker	Director Pharmacy Director Materials Management $n = 2$	Interviews Website Material Hospital Annual Report Examination of 'existing' processes
Third Party Logistics Provider	Australia	16,000	N/A	N/A	A$2 billion	ERP	Director – Warehousing and Distribution Pharmaceutical Products $n = 1$	Interviews Website Annual Report
Government Regulator A	Australia	12	N/A	Pharmacy and Non Pharmacy Products	A$500 million worth of contracts	N/A	CEO Strategic Procurement Manager $n = 2$	Interviews Website Material Government Documents
Government Regulator B	Australia	30	N/A	N/A	N/A	N/A	Supply Chain Manager Strategic Initiatives Manager $n = 2$	Interviews Website Material Company Presentation
Technology Service Provider A	Belgium	86 (Australia)	N/A	N/A	Not Available	N/A	Business Development Manager Client Services Manager Senior Adviser Industry Services $n = 3$	Interviews Website Material Knowledge Centre Tour
Technology Service Provider B	Australia	10	N/A	Software Vendor for Public Hospital	Not Available	N/A	CEO $n = 1$	Interviews Documentation on Software System

21 Understanding the nature of demand variation of patient arrival for emergency healthcare services

The first challenge

James Aitken, Ann Esain and Sharon J. Williams

Introduction

Public sector operations managers often are presented as using fixed capacity to cope with the challenge of arrival emergency demand. Research in healthcare emergency services predominantly focuses on the emergency department (ED), often referred to as accident and emergency (A&E), which is usually located within a hospital setting. Solely focusing on the ED organisational boundary limits the understanding and visibility of the emergency arrival process. Incoming patient/citizen flows are also part of the emergency arrival process as are the actions of paramedics, ambulance services and a plethora of alternative provision in assessing, diagnosing and stabilising patients prior to arrival at ED. In this chapter we explore this holistic process to understand whether the potential for variations in the process of arrival (prior to ED) can provide insights for managers who are endeavouring to reconcile capacity and emergency demand as a whole. The lens of the theory of 'swift and even flow' is used to analyse literature and challenge operational conventions in emergency healthcare services. From a comprehensive review of the literature, a conceptual model is proposed which includes three discrete stages of arrival demand, which is counter to the well-versed single continuous dimension of demand.

An emergency episode can be triggered at any point from which an accident or emergency occurs to the point at which a diagnosis (and in some cases treatment) is made regardless of organisational boundary. Emergency services imply an 'unexpected combination of circumstances that demands immediate action' (Fitzgerald and Dadich, 2009: 22), are therefore time sensitive (Ahmad *et al.*, 2012), and reside in the context of increasing need. Yet, globally reduced available public funds at a macro level result in a political drive for improved productivity driven by the narrative of new public management (NPM) (Pollitt and Bouckaert, 2004). Combined with these factors emergency public services are commonly believed to contend with an inability to control incoming demand (Sampson, 2000).

It is the potential to understand variation along the emergency arrival process that in turn can inform and possibly shape how responses are managed i.e. communication, co-ordination, control and cognition (Comfort, 2007) and how policy interventions are designed to achieve productive operational flow. Therefore we seek to understand:

- What is the process of arrival for emergency ED services provision?
- What theoretical models can public service managers use to help improve their understanding of the arrival emergency process?
- How will these models help public services managers and policy makers improve the design and performance of emergency services and increase citizen satisfaction?

The chapter is structured as follows; first, the context of public services, particularly regarding NPM and the opportunities theory development present is discussed. The next section provides details of the method used to identify relevant literature to be reviewed. Then a literature review is undertaken examining arrival variation, demand and capacity related to the context of study, from which operations management theories are used to distil themes and gaps in understanding. The discussion section synthesises the findings and finally the conclusion provides an agenda for future research for emergency public healthcare services and operational management.

The macro emergency services context

Public services are free (or at a subsidised cost) to those in need and/or are provided by governments for the public good (Skidelsky, 1989). Public service provision has been reported as going through a global renaissance, generally driven by the theories of NPM at a macro level (Hood, 1991). NPM is intended to stimulate a shift from Webber's model of administration and bureaucracy (Dunleavy and Hood, 1994) to a focus on reform with the underlying objectives of greater efficiency and cost savings (Pollitt and Bouckaert, 2004).

Public services have been described as:

> increasingly exposed to intersectional transfer of generic models of organisation and management. Differences between contemporary private sector firms and public sector healthcare organisations appear to be less pronounced through a process of intersectional blurring, or rather the convergence of public sector organisations onto private sector templates. The greater the convergence, the weaker the argument that models cannot be exported into the public sector because the work undertaken is intrinsically different.
>
> (McNulty and Ferlie, 2002: 50)

NPM contends that public services are becoming more business-like (Hood, 1991) by allowing greater transparency, visibility and review by management and policy makers. NPM strives for more citizen-centred public services within tight performance measurement and management to ensure value for money (a strong theme of this book). The movement equates to the dual objective of increasing citizen satisfaction at the same time as improving quality, safety and productivity. Citizen satisfaction can be defined as 'a closer correspondence between perceptions of actual and desired standards of public services' (Boyne, 2003: 223). Similarly, client-centredness has been described as seeing the system through the patient's eyes and meeting their needs in the ways most valuable to them (Davies, 2012). Understanding value at points of interaction within the public service requires an understanding of the process flow of that service which is integral to person/client centred care.

A weakness of NPM is seen as the ability and willingness of individual managers to understand the system within which they control key processes and their ability to improve the flow of value towards clients. In 'emergency' services, there remains a reliance on highly skilled professionals to ensure operational quality (Tucker and Edmondson, 2003). A general lack of preparedness for commercialism, constrain the real impact of the managerial effort and overestimate vastly the ability of managers to design/improve processes from the former comfortable era of administration (McNulty and Ferlie, 2002). Themes about the impact of the adoption of private sector techniques and the ability to achieve replicable results in the public service context (Boyne, 2002); or the void of underpinning rules in public services for productivity improvement (Radnor *et al.*, 2013) and the transference of NPM across country borders (McLaughlin *et al.*, 2006) means the drive for theory development for public service improvement continues (Ashworth *et al.*, 2010).

One such drive for theory development is founded on networks and alliances (Entwistle, 2010) as a strategy for improvement. Emergency services are managed by a number of different organisations and collaboration provides a potential means of understanding processes, variation within processes and demand along processes. While asserting that collaborations are founded on a spirit of goodwill (Dore, 1983) emergency service settings require the roles and responsibilities of different parties to be clearly understood. In this environment supply chain management, as discussed in operations management literature (Christopher, 2011; Hines, 1997) might be more applicable. The public services dominate logic rejects supply chain management by simply stating supply chains evolved to help organisations advance their own interest, whereas 'inter-organisational collaboratives' are altruistic and 'collaborate to advance public or community goals' (Entwistle, 2010: 163). For emergency services both these drivers can be observed. Public services theory development therefore is also of interest because of the absence of operational management theory (Ashworth *et al.*, 2010); an absence which potentially creates lag in knowledge and understanding where practice is seeking integration (Curry and Ham, 2010).

The micro emergency services context

The first challenge for public service in general and health care organisations in particular is how to manage the incoming demand and the uncertainty around arrival. Emergency services provision in healthcare is facing an increasing global demand for existing provision (Abo-Hamad and Arisha, 2013; Ahmad *et al.*, 2012; Fitzgerald and Dadich, 2009; Burt and McCaig, 2006). In some regions/countries an increasing population (Allon *et al.*, 2013) or aging population (Sinreich and Jabali, 2007) is believed to be driving this rise in demand. In others, it is perceived that capacity constraints are driving the mismatch of capacity with demand and thus developing bottlenecks and constraining flow through the organisational system.

Arrival demand is often described as homogenous assuming that patients 'arrive' at one place with demand for emergency treatment measured at this point. This demand is assumed to occur at the fixed destination of ED. This is often not the case with early treatments at points of first interaction limiting the need to physically move to the ED. Thus the process flow steps prior to arrival at ED may exhibit different demand (variation).

The process of arrival of demand and the variation of arrival patterns have been particularly important to general operations management to inform operational design and practice (Hopp and Spearman, 2008). The same is believed to be true in public healthcare services (Walley *et al.*, 2006; Heskett *et al.*, 1990). This setting has the added dimension of political and social stakeholders (e.g. users of the service, professional bodies, staff, voluntary organisations, fire and police services, etc.). Stakeholders can directly or indirectly influence what constitutes demand. Where demand is not managed at the point of first interaction (law of quality) there is a potential for self-generated duplication of demand (Patrick, 2011; Hansagi *et al.*, 1987), through the communication process and sometimes referred to as failure demand.

It is not only the initial poor quality of interaction that can induce this self-generated arrival demand, public policies can also stimulate arrival demand e.g. legislative changes to 'out of hours' healthcare provision had a marked increase in demand for ED services in the UK (Esain, 2011). Management policies have a similar effect, for example, rewarding performance on speed rather than quality or individual patient (or professional advocate) preference (Cunningham, 2006).

Within the organisational boundary of ED heuristics of communication and co-ordination are in place to prioritise those with more or less urgent needs (Ahmad *et al.*, 2012). Differentiation between unplanned and planned work for hospitals exists (Huh *et al.*, 2013). Experimentation in grouping different levels or types of demand (which may necessitate different strategies specifically from a time and safety dimension) has been initiated drawing on information from the healthcare supply chain but focused on implications for the context of ED (Walley *et al.*, 2001). Such experiments demonstrated improved time outcomes and better citizen satisfaction and thus focusing on the steps related to an emergency episode prior to arriving at the ED provides a further setting for study.

To gain insights for conceptual development a literature review is undertaken to understand the existing knowledge related to emergency services provision, and to consider what constitutes arrival and variation of arrival and demand.

Method

A structured literature review (Levy and Ellis, 2006) provides the foundation for knowledge advancement. Literature reviews are used where research exists and therefore synthesis provides a basis for theory development, uncovering 'areas where research is needed' (*ibid.*: 182). Research into emergency services provision is a growing field of study. Within this context the implications of arrival/demand, variability and the implications for capacity, management and policy decisions are best appraised using a literature review.

Arrival variation related to emergency services provision is reviewed. 171 academic papers (including those in press) and conference papers were identified using the SCOPUS search engine. SCOPUS was used as this draws on 21,915 titles worldwide from 5,000 publishers from 1996 onwards. The search terms *arrival variation* or *demand* and *capacity* and *emergency* were used to identify the broad range of literature in the field. The search was limited to texts in English. All the resulting abstracts were reviewed and those not relevant to the study were excluded (see Table 21.1). The resultant 41 papers were drawn from literature related to business and management, social sciences, medicine, decisions science and healthcare.

A more detailed review of the 41 full papers was undertaken, which resulted in a further 18 papers being excluded for not meeting the objectives of the study; specifically, where the focus was on:

- locations models for EDs (Vidyarthi and Jayaswal, 2014; Yin and Mu, 2012; Chen, 2010; Li *et al.*, 2010; Luo *et al.*, 2010);
- elective versus emergency capacity management (Huh *et al.*, 2013; Adan *et al.*, 2011; Yankovic and Green, 2011); or
- alternative forms of care with upstream management to reduce emergency demand (Patrick, 2011);

or otherwise where full papers were not available. As a consequence of the detailed analysis of the references of the initial papers a number of papers were identified as missing from this review ($n = 8$) through snowballing (Webster and Watson, 2002). The final total of papers for review was 31. Healthcare dominated the literature reviewed. To ensure inclusivity at this point, the search string originally used was widened to add ambulance. This resulted in no additional papers emerging.

Table 21.2 illustrates the global nature of the literature, with a western dominance which may reflect the limitation of reviewing papers written in English. This area of study is emergent and the volume of publications are increasing over time.

Table 21.1 Characteristics of papers rejected at abstract stage

Topics rejected	*No of papers rejected at abstract stage*
Not emergency services and public services	49
Humanitarian logistics/natural disasters	36
Traffic and transport flows/engineering or vehicle routing	21
Not arrival variation/demand and capacity but emergency service	13
Focus of paper inpatient capacity/inpatient Admissions	9
Duplicates	2
Total	129

Table 21.2 Geographical settings of literature (including papers in multiple locations)

Geographical settings of papers reviewed	*Quantity*
USA	14
Canada	4
China	4
UK	4
Australia	3
Netherlands	3
India	2
France	1
Ireland	1
Israel	1
Malaysia	1
Norway	1
Poland	1
Portugal	1
Sweden	1

The literature review findings are subsequently examined through the lens of operations management theory which provides a model that can be used to shape and evaluate the literature to develop themes for future empirical exploration and evaluation.

Literature review

From the synthesis of the 31 papers we inductively identified key themes that emerged when considering the arrival demand of emergency services provision. These naturally grouped into macro influences, methodological approaches and networks.

Macro influences

A macro level analysis of the papers (see Table 21.3) identifies the environmental and political challenges and changes which have impacted on policy and management decisions and in turn have the potential to effect arrival variation.

Changes in demographics, political policy and political constraints are affecting the process of arrival variation through the development of new and revised organisational forms. This is driven by technological advances, the increase in demand at the ED boundary. Hence there are emergency service diagnostics and treatment which take place outside the organisational boundary of ED. This then suggests a much more fuzzy relationship between emergency service demand and the forms of capacity. For example what demand, variation and capacity is required at what step in the arrival process or processes which public sector managers and policy makers have to contend with.

In addition there is a reported global policy challenge with increasing demand on the capacity offered at EDs (Abo-Hamad and Arisha, 2013; Harris and Wood, 2012;

Table 21.3 Macro influences on arrival variation for emergency service provision

Emergency public services policy drivers	*Lead to changes in*	*Effecting arrival variation*	*Authors*
Change in demographics	Clinical care (epistemological and technologies)	New and revised forms of organisation	Almeida and Cima, (2013); Arya *et al.* (2013)
Changes in demographics	Increased need for emergency care (epistemological)		Abo-Hamad and Arisha (2013)
Political policy (no patient to be refused treatment at ED)	Greater pressure on existing resources	New and revised forms of organisation	Ahmad *et al.* (2012)
Political constraints (finance/reduced capacity)	Closure of ED; Resources for clinical care	Overcrowding and Ambulance diversion; New and revised forms of organisation	Almeida and Cima (2013); Abo-Hamad and Arisha (2013); Allon *et al.* (2013); Fitzgerald and Dadich (2009)

Levin *et al.*, 2008) with one study stating in 2003 that approximately a third of ambulances in the USA were being diverted from their original ED destination (Burt and McCaig, 2006). This constitutes failure demand and thus waste and loss of capacity. In contrast, another study indicated that government policy forbids ambulance diversions (Ahmad *et al.*, 2012) forcing ED to receive patients at this point but with no acknowledgements of the implications on the system. This belied a debate about the availability of capacity to meet need at the organisational boundary (ED) where either capacity had remained unchanged, had grown or where it had been reducing over time due to government public service policies (Burt *et al.*, 2006; Siegel, 2004; Melnick *et al.*, 2004).

Methodological approaches

All but three papers of the 31 papers drew upon empirical methods which included queuing theory, discrete event simulation, quality management techniques and visual scenario building. Implicitly historical data are used to predict demand which in turn is assumed to help managers at the micro level of the hospital to manage the capacity available to them. Arrival variation for high volume services has predominantly been handled through the use of predictive techniques to establish regular patterns, such as seasonality (Almeida and Cima, 2013; Cochran and Roche, 2009), regular events (e.g. Christmas, football matches, festivals) and patterns that may emerge from or influence habit, shift working or working routine (Hamrock *et al.*, 2013; Yankovic and Green, 2011; Jelinek *et al.*, 2010; Sinreich and Jabali, 2007). It is also possible to overlay irregular events on the historical data to help predict demand and manage capacity. From this level of data analysis it has been proposed that (with in an accepted tolerance) aggregate levels of the number of patients arriving at an ED by hour (Hamrock *et al.*, 2013; Walley *et al.*, 2001, 2006) but it is not so easy to predict the type of condition with which patients will present (Esain *et al.*, 2006). A systematic literature review of overcrowding in EDs noted themes including non-urgent visits, 'frequent-flyer' patients, and the influenza season as sources of overcrowding which could equally have an impact on arrival variation (Hoot and Aronsky, 2008; Walley *et al.*, 2001).

Systems which manage time pressured services such as emergencies (e.g. fire, police, health) find that matching resources to demand is compounded by the need for a rapid speed of response, knowledge/cognition and skill to make safe and effective decisions. This means that queues (Worthington, 2009), which are often used as the buffer between demand and capacity, are not a satisfactory solution to the conundrum (Allon *et al.*, 2013).

Studies are generally built on the assumption that demand 'arrives' at a single point in time, usually at a physical location such as the ED (e.g. Abo-Hamad and Arisha, 2013; Ahmad *et al.*, 2012). Limited research was available about the process prior to arrival. Although one study of Malaysian origin explained that 'ambulance is part of ED services which is manned by the ED staffs who work as emergency staffs and ambulance crews in parallel' (Ahmad *et al.*, 2012: 10). This study only reviewed the system from the point of arrival at ED but visualised the process of direct admission to ED services (bypassing triage) as part of the segmentation and heuristics determining different classifications of emergency. Al-Shaqsi (2010) described the difference between the Anglo-American and Franco-German models of pre hospital systems, both of which have their main motive to bring the patient to a hospital.

Networks

There were several studies which considered the complexities of networks (Allon *et al.*, 2013; Worthington, 2009). These related largely to the sharing of resources across networks after the patient had arrived at ED but then were unable to treat due to congestion of work and resulted in ambulance diversions (Allon *et al.*, 2013; Capuano *et al.*, 2009). Public services are often part of a larger network of provision (Choi, 2008) with supply chain management (Walley *et al.*, 2001) suggested as an approach for understanding the systems as whole of which ED variation in demand is only one part. Understanding the arrival process and the flows for patients has a potential effect on ED. If emergency services are provided as a series of stage gates (Al-Shaqsi, 2010) with the objective of the patient flowing across services delivered flexibly and through new service forms unrestricted by physical boundaries, the implications for capacity and demand trade off becomes more complex. Multiple decision points will arise with multiple options and it is these decision points where there is a gap in policy and management thinking (Worthington, 2009; Miller and Xiao, 2007).

The global financial crisis has also acted as a cap on available cash flow for emergency services. This has stimulated changes in the shape of provision moving to a more market driven model (Almeida and Cima, 2013; Curry and Ham, 2010) which has resulted in several outcomes such as:

- stimulating the creation of new organisational forms (Utley *et al.*, 2008; Coye, 2008; Siegel, 2004);
- reducing service provision for the citizen to fill the void (Coye, 2008);
- leaving the existing structures to 'cope' thus expecting the system to manage temporary surges in demand i.e. patients on trolleys in ED (Almeida and Cima, 2013; Cochran and Roche, 2009);
- engendering gaming strategies by managers to avoid such strains i.e. matching escalating seriousness with those providing the same service (Almeida and Cima, 2013).

Table 21.4 classifies the literature within the context of the different capacity strategies available to managers (Crandall and Markland, 1996) and reflects the implication of setting emergency services in relation to NPM and context.

The table illustrates that where context stability traditionally exists, supply chains seek control of variation to prevent distortions which in turn reduce overall cost. Yet where volatility exits this strategy is questioned, in particular 'the more variation present in the input parameters, the less effective our control model tends to become' (Christopher and Holweg, 2011: 69).

Crandall and Markland (1996) proposed four capacity strategies which organisations may adopt to achieve stability (Table 21.4). In the context of emergency services these strategies are not fully utilised, a situation confirmed by Walley (2013). It is possible therefore that these strategies may not have the full exploratory powers originally suggested. This can only be amplified where professional management must deal with fuzzy organisational boundaries.

This section of the chapter has provided an analysis of the existing relevant literature within three key themes: macro influences, methodological approaches and networks. The next section now considers the results of this review within the context of supply chain management (SCM) and operations management.

Analysing literature findings using operations and supply chain management theories

Operations and SCM researchers have developed approaches and techniques that drive improvement in productivity alongside increasing volume of activity and the proliferation of product and service offerings (Christopher, 2011). The modification and movement of manufacturing SCM best practice to the service sector has gained pace over the last decade (Goldhar and Berg, 2010; Sengupta *et al.*, 2006). One of the major contributors to the development of SCM in manufacturing and more recently service has been the understanding of the gains that can be achieved through collaborative and relational based exchanges. Cooperation between organisations in supply chains and their wider networks has increased the flow and quality of information leading to a reduction in uncertainty and improved decision making

Table 21.4 Limited application of influence on demand as a strategy in emergency services

Traditional capacity strategies (Crandall and Markland, 1996)	*Doctrinal components of new public management (Hood, 1991)*	*Context turbulence (Christopher and Holweg, 2011)*	*Focus of emergency public services literature (from review)*
Match: capacity equals demand	Stress on greater discipline and parsimony in resource use	Political: change in structure due to regulation	Almeida and Cima (2013), measurement of cost of excess capacity Allon *et al.* (2013), through shared capacity of hospital networks Hamrock *et al.* (2013), through prediction of demand Ahmad *et al.* (2012), through political directive
Provide: have sufficient capacity to be able to serve maximum demand	'Hands-on professional management' in the public sector Stress on private sector styles of management practice Stress on greater discipline and parsimony in resource use	Technology: shifts in dominant designs and disruptive innovations	Harris and Wood (2012), mini triage as an innovation Brailsford and Vissers (2011), balancing capacity and demand Fitzgerald and Dadich (2009) Cochran and Roche (2009)
Control: control demand to load smooth	'Hands-on professional management' in the public sector	Demand side strategy – shift in consumer demand Political: change in structure due to regulation	Patrick (2011), managing upstream demand and streaming LTC – to an alternative level of care Ullman *et al.* (1978), using primary care to elevate ED admissions Jayawarna *et al.* (2010), use of acute medicine units
Influence: reduce peaks and troughs of demand and try to match capacity to this adjusted profile	'Hands-on professional management' in the public sector Shift to desegregation of units in the public sector Shift to greater competition in the public sector	Regulation: shift in consumer perception	Abo-Hamad and Arisha (2013), through redesign

(Christopher, 2011). With increased turbulence as consumers drive shorter lead-times, customised services and lower prices and in turn developing networks which can be agile and flexible enough to respond to variable and uncertain demand is becoming critical to organisations (Christopher and Holweg, 2011).

Operations management theories support decision making under uncertainty and variability (Filippini, 1997). One of the dominant theories of operations management which is used to investigate processes and their performance is systems dynamics (SD). Providing a lens and structure, characterised by feedback loops, accumulation processes and revealing delays from cause and effect (Grobler *et al.*, 2008). Through a SCM perspective, instead of a localised and sometimes dis-aggregated approach, SD can support an understanding of flow in a holistic system. The uncertainty circle model derived by Mason-Jones and Towill (1998) reflects the typical structure offered by SD models with the supply (client input of information and self), added value (delivery of service), quality control (managing service delivery) and demand (client service needs) processes being portrayed as a system with a goal that should execute 'smooth and seamless material (or service) flow' based on minimising variability and uncertainty within a coordinated and cooperative supply chain (Towill, 1997). SD has also been recommended as the next area of study in understanding the process of arrival for emergency services (Ahmad *et al.*, 2012).

Smooth and seamless is analogous to the theory of swift, even flow (TSEF), which states that 'the more swift and even the flow of materials [service] through a process, the more productive a process is' (Schmenner and Swink, 1998: 102). TSEF offers the opportunity to examine arrival variation as it provides a mechanism for understanding how variation in service provision impacts on flow of value to clients (Devaraj *et al.*, 2013). TSEF is based on the premise that throughput time is the relevant measure and is indicative of variance in a process. Increases in the process variation associated with information or customer flow will have an impact on throughput (Schmenner, 2004). Variation relates to non-conformities in the delivery of a service not the range of services provided (which is known as variety or variety mix for bundles of services or practices). By examining the flow of patients and information through the lens of TSEF it is possible for managers to develop an understanding of how emergency services process arrival variation will affect throughput hence productivity and citizen satisfaction (Fredendall *et al.*, 2009). This is an important area for research in operations and SCM (Hopp and Spearman, 2008).

For emergency services provision throughput time would equate to fault-free quality with timely and consistent patient flow (Devaraj *et al.*, 2013). The TSEF approach moves the discussion away from a focus on utilisation of resources and labour efficiency to throughput as the traditional measures of performance are not highly correlated to productivity (Schmenner, 2012; Devaraj *et al.*, 2013). TSEF provides the opportunity for managers to analyse and develop controls for the key processes in their systems. TSEF builds upon a set of five supporting laws of operation management that help explain productivity differences across organisations (Table 21.5).

Table 21.5 Supporting laws of operational management

Law	*Example*
Law of quality	Improve service outcomes through strenuous waste removal and reduction of non-value added activities (Harris and Wood, 2012)
Law of bottlenecks	Within health care unevenness in flow can develop bottlenecks if the focus is on speeding up the operation without given consideration to the capacity of activities (Deveraji *et al.*, 2013)
Law of factory focus	Focusing operations on a limited number of activities is not pertinent to the ED area due to the complexity and variety of health care
Law of scientific management	An empirical, Industrial engineering, approach to understanding the flow of patients through health care processes highlighting bottlenecks and variances (Fredendall *et al.*, 2009)
Law of variability	Increasing levels of variability will lengthen throughput and lead-times (Schmenner, 2012)

Conceptual model

Understanding the flow of incoming patients can lead to improved performance at ED and support managers in focusing their efforts (Devaraj *et al.*, 2013). Developing greater insights into arrivals requires a detailed analysis of the constituent parts of the process (Al-Shaqsi, 2010). Grobler *et al.* (2008) describe one of the 'blind spots' of a SD based approach to understanding variation as the lack of recognition of 'discrete events'. The authors of this chapter recognise this issue in the challenges of researching arrival variability and its impact on the flow of patients. As Schmenner (2012: 274) remarks 'the greater the variability of either the demand striking the process or the process itself ... the longer is the throughput time'. An important observation, as the emergency services are often free at the point of use which hinders the use of demand management techniques (Walley, 2013). Additionally the trigger for emergency services is also unclear providing difficulty for managing demand and variability.

In our proposed model the flow of service begins at the point the emergency services arrive and interact with the patient. This excludes issues around the time when the patient makes initial contact and the services arrive (we note this is a stage that needs to be investigated in future studies as it moves the supply chain discussion forward into networks). We propose that there are three discrete stages of arrival demand which is counter to the perceived wisdom of a single continuous dimension of demand (Figure 21.1). With each stage having a supply, value-add, demand and control element that together enable the flow of value to clients.

Stage 1: pre-arrival

On arrival at the incident the emergency team assess the condition of the patient to ascertain the severity of the situation and determine the appropriate action. Service

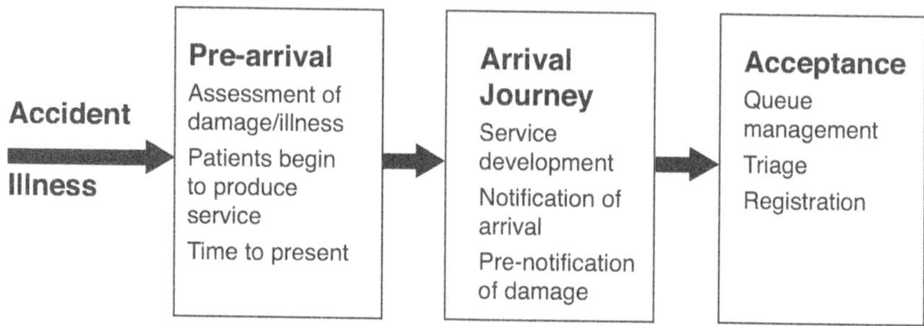

Figure 21.1 Three stages of arrival variation

provision begins with the citizen (patient and/or carer) and where possible supplies inputs to the service supply chain. The team begins to assess the patient and provides value-added medical treatment on site, or commences the transfer process to the ED depending upon the patient's health demands (Ahmad *et al.*, 2012). About half of all patients transported to ED by ambulance are released without referral or any significant treatment (Al-Shaqsi, 2010). The flow of patients to ED and the substantial release figures, suggests that there are issues related to the initial assessment process. It is hypothesised this may be inherited from historical heuristics of patient safety and treatment.

Understanding the reasons for variation in process controls and patient flow in the pre-arrival stage is important to develop a more productive process. Researching the issues using the TSEF lens can highlight multiple factors that affect the flow of value through healthcare processes (Fredendall *et al.*, 2009). Investigating quality in terms of conformance to specifications, as required by the patient and healthcare sector protocols (standards), and variability of assessment could throw light on the performance of the pre-arrival stage. Providing the opportunity for service organisations to re-focus their efforts from finding ways to maximise the utilisation of resources to delivering value (and meeting the increased demand by the public to reduce loss) by addressing the complex relationship issues between quality and system utilisation (Walley, 2013).

Stage 2: arrival journey

The next stage of the process is the journey from patient pick-up to ED. During this stage the service can be developed passively or interactively as the patient engages and supplies inputs to the treatment process to meet their needs. At this point in the process the patient is analogous to work-in-progress (WIP) within a manufacturing environment. WIP travels through the value-adding process moving at various speeds and passing through different routes depending upon the final product destination. During this stage it can enter rework and experience delays that absorb the capacity from the process and interrupts flow (Schmenner, 2012). For example transmission of incorrect information (poor communication, coordination and control) to the ED can lead to delays in the acceptance of the patient and waste any preparative work. Bottlenecks can occur in the ED as a result of patients arriving with conditions that were unreported or arrive quicker than had been notified (Ahmad *et al.*, 2012). Diverting ambulances can result as bottlenecks appear in ED due to pre-notification errors that force the network (supply chain) to find alternative hospitals (Allon *et al.*, 2013). Understanding variances that occur as the service is developed during transit to ED can improve the flow of value for both patient and healthcare provider.

Stage 3: acceptance

On arrival at the ED the ambulance crew and the patient may have to join a queue for registration at the hospital reducing throughput and slowing flow. Queues at ED have been widely researched with many solutions, models and optimisation strategies being suggested. Through the provision of capacity (Table 21.3) that either equals the expected maximum demand or controlling the demand to smooth the load researchers have suggested alternatives approaches to reducing or removing bottlenecks caused by surges in demand (Abo-Hamad and Arsiha, 2013; Harris and Wood, 2012; Patrick, 2011; Crandall and Markland, 1996). Matching capacity and demand at ED will provide an even flow of patients into the service process. Understanding the reasons for variation and their impact on the flow of information and patients can reduce the queues and bottlenecks within the process without lowering quality and increasing costs (Devaraj *et al.*, 2013). TSEF suggests that reducing the throughput time of the system can diminish the impacts of variation whether it is externally (demand) or internally (process controls or managerial policy (Wacker, 1987) derived.

Once accepted into the ED process patients are put into triage (or mini triage) to assess their needs and the type of services, resources and speed at which further diagnosis or a course of treatment is required (Harris and Wood, 2012). This is not the start as treatment action may have commenced at pre or arrival stages (Figure 21.1) which may have sufficiently stabilised the situation (as is demonstrated by the number of patients who get released after further observation). Through understanding process variation in terms of conformance to standards, bottlenecks derived from increasing process speed and unevenness in flow EDs have the opportunity to increase throughput and citizen satisfaction without raising costs (Schmenner, 2012).

Conclusion

The findings of the literature review point to a lack of clarity in the understanding of the process of arrival of emergency services provision. The literature focuses on a single point of entry and occasionally to the network of public services required for accidents and emergencies. There is little explanation of the types and effects of coordination at different points along the process and how arrival should be defined. This chapter has sought to propose an alternative and better explanation through the lens of operations management and SCM. It calls into question what might be termed the simplistic of ED as the point of 'arrival'. We propose there are multiple points of entry and exit which need to be better understood and defined to order to help:

- *Public sector managers* in their quest for improved performance and citizen satisfaction;
- *Policy makers* in their quest for productivity and improved service levels; and
- *Society* in its desire to reduce loss as a consequence of accidents and emergencies.

At the start of the chapter we set three questions. First was the need to understand the process of arrival of emergency services provision. From the literature we found within EDs arrival demand has historically been viewed as homogenous in nature with segmentation being left to triage once the patient has been accepted into the hospital system (Almeida and Cima, 2013; Harris and Wood, 2012). This is an overly simplistic approach to understanding and managing arrival demand. Constraining the arrival process to one organisational boundary (e.g. ED) limits the visibility and understanding of the patient flow, process and system.

The second and third questions focused on the theoretical models that can be employed by public service managers to help improve decision making for improved performance and citizen satisfaction. Extending the arrival process enables the arrival data and the variation and interaction at the multiple points of demand to be modelled across the service network, providing both capacity and demand based solutions for the arrival process. Specifically theoretical models drawn from SD are argued to be best placed to deal with both the complexities associated with uncertainty and the SCM challenges related to communication, coordination, control and cognition. SD presents a means by which whole systems (processes) can be evaluated, enabling multiple outcomes to be achieved.

Through the lens of the TSEF hospital managers have the opportunity to analyse and understand the stages of demand arrival by investigating the flow of patients. This operations management based theory has been successfully deployed in a number of service sectors including healthcare. TSEF has been able to identify and reduce variation in patient flow for processes such as Perioperative surgery. Managing arrival variation, demand and capacity challenges within the ED environment can be supported by understanding the enabling and inhibiting factors of the flow of value through the system, therefore increasing throughput and citizen satisfaction. Operations management concepts such as TSEF provide the opportunity for managers to redress their approach to making decisions and the manner in which they deploy the instruments available to them. Decision support tools which are used at a single point in time without questioning if demand can be managed (i.e. assuming that capacity is the only management tool for addressing work in emergency public services) can often lead to sub-optimisation of the system. With the blurring of boundaries between services and operations in both a theoretical and practical sense, occurring at the same time as private and public sectors intersect, there is the opportunity for models, derived from the private sector, to be developed and deployed by the healthcare sector.

Private service organisations attempt to manage queues (inventory of clients) in a number of ways, such as the development of complementary services; the portioning of demand; offering price incentives; promoting off-peak demand and by delaying the arrival time–for example by maintaining service lead-times and utilising an appointment system (Fitzsimmons and Fitzsimmons, 2004). These demand management approaches are difficult to utilise in an emergency services environment where time-sensitive support can mean life or death. Although studies are emerging in the portioning of work (Harris and Wood, 2012; Walley *et al.*, 2006), attempting to control external demand without having the internal processes free of variation will not remove bottlenecks or increase the flow of value. Reducing internal variation that impacts on flow and throughput times will assist organisations in managing external demand fluctuations (Patrick, 2011; Fitzgerald and Dadich, 2009).

This chapter has focused on the provision of emergency services within healthcare. This became a necessity due to the limited research into arrival variation for emergency services. In terms of future research it is important that arrival variation, in combination with the ambulance, fire and police service, is sought. These services should enable a whole systems approach to emergency services policy and provision to achieve better levels of citizen satisfaction and improvement in system performance.

The important dimension of flow is fundamental to future research particularly as discussions move from a linear supply chain perspective into networks of emergency authorities each with their different and often misaligned processes, professional perspectives and public service policy drivers. Reducing variation that occurs in delivery of service is paramount to improving process performance and flow. Developing controls to manage variability requires research of TSEF in the context of system dynamics which has control systems at the centre of value-adding process.

The dissonance between public services theory (collaborations and alliances) and operational management theory (SCM) surfaces the need for reflection on espoused concepts of organisational altruism (Dore, 1983) and organisational selfishness (Entwistle, 2010) as separate motivational traits for improvement. This is particularly timely with the NPM policy shift towards third sector organisations emerging as part of healthcare and public service delivery networks. It is proposed that such concepts should be tested and may define the extremes in a range of organisational drivers of motivation or indeed identify whether other logics are more appropriate.

We recognise that our model commences at the point when the emergency services arrive and begin to interact with the patient therefore excluding issues involving the period between the patient initial contact and services arrival – a critical area in terms of response time. Additionally the information flows for public services emergency provision have presumed that information is timely, accurate and correct. This assumption needs to be the subject of further research given that information can impact on the amplification of variation if 'over communication' occurs and has the possibility to cause risks if co-ordinating activities are using inaccurate data.

References

Abo-Hamad, W. and Arisha, A. (2013) 'Simulation-based framework to improve patient experience in an emergency department'. *European Journal of Operational Research*, 224(1): 154–66.

Adan, I., Bekkers, J., Dellaert, N., Jeunet, J. and Vissers, J. (2011) 'Improving operational effectiveness of tactical master plans for emergency and elective patients under stochastic demand and capacitated resources'. *European Journal of Operational Research*, 213(1): 290–308.

Ahmad, N., Ghani, N.A., Kamil, A.A., Tahar, R.M. and Teo, A.H. (2012) 'Evaluating emergency department resource capacity using simulation'. *Modern Applied Science*, 6 (11): 9–19.

Allon, G, Sarang, D. and Lin, W. (2013) 'The impact of size and occupancy of hospital in the extent of ambulance diversion: theory and evidence'. *Operations Research*, 61 (3): 544–62.

Almeida, A.S. and Cima, J.F. (2013) 'Demand uncertainty and hospital costs: an application to Portuguese public hospitals'. *European Journal of Health Economics*, December: 1–11.

Al-Shaqsi, S. (2010) 'Models of international emergency medical service (EMS) systems'. *Oman Medical Journal*, 5(4): 320–23.

Arya, R., Wei, G., McCoy, J.V., Crane, J., Ohman-Strickland, P. and Eisenstein, R.M. (2013) 'Decreasing length of stay in the emergency department with a split emergency severity index 3 patient flow model'. *Academic Emergency Medicine*, 20(11): 1171–79.

Ashworth, R., Boyne, G. and Entwistle, T. (2010) *Public Service Improvement: Theories and Evidence*. Oxford University Press, Oxford.

Boyne, G. (2002) 'Public and private management: what is the difference?' *Journal of Management Studies*, 39(1): 97–122.

Boyne, G. (2003) 'What is public service improvement?' *Public Administration*, 81(2): 211–27.

Brailsford, S. and Vissers, J. (2011) 'OR in healthcare: a European perspective'. *European Journal of Operational Research*, 212: 223–34.

Burt, C. and McCaig, L. (2006) *Staffing, Capacity, and Ambulance Diversion in Emergency Departments: United States, 2003–04, United States, 2003–04*. Hyattsville, MD: National Center for Health Statistics.

Burt, C., McCaig, L. and Valerde, R. (2006) 'Analysis of ambulance transports and diversions among US emergency departments'. *Annals of Emergency Medicine*, 47(4): 317–636.

Capuano, T., MacKenzie, R., Pintar, K., Halkins, D. and Nester, B. (2009) 'Complex adaptive strategy to produce capacity-driven financial improvement'. *Journal of Healthcare Management*, 54(5): 307–18.

Chen, D. (2010) 'Resource allocation model with transportation capacity constrain in emergency logistics'. In *ICLEM 2010: Logistics for Sustained Economic Development – Infrastructure, Information, Integration – Proceedings of the 2010 International Conference of Logistics*, 385: 2650–65. Chengdu, China: American Society of Civil Engineers.

Choi, S.O. (2008) 'Emergency management: implications from a strategic management perspective'. *Journal of Homeland Security and Emergency Management*, 5(1): 1.

Christopher, M. (2011) *Logistics and Supply Chain Management* (4th edn). London: FT Prentice Hall.

Christopher, M. and Holweg, M. (2011) 'Supply Chain 2.0: managing supply chains in the era of turbulence'. *International Journal of Physical Distribution and Logistics Management*, 41(1): 63–82.

Chopra, S. and Lariviere, M. (2005) 'Managing service inventory to improve performance'. *MIT Sloan Management Review*, Fall, 47(1): 56–63.

Cochran J.K. and Roche, K.T. (2009) 'A multi-class queuing network analysis methodology for improving hospital emergency department performance'. *Computers and Operations Research*, 36(5): 1497–1512.

Comfort, L. (2007) 'Crisis management in hindsight: cognition, communication, co-ordination and control'. *Public Administration Review*, 67: 189–97.

Coye, M.J. (2008) 'Health care financing: outside the box'. *Hospitals and Health Networks*, 82(5): 10.

Crandall, R.E. and Markland, R.E. (1996) 'Demand management – today's challenge for service industries'. *Production and Operations Management*, 5(1): 106–20.

Cunningham, P.J. (2006) 'What accounts for differences in the use of hospital emergency departments across U.S. communities? Reducing ED use defies simple solutions such as expanding insurance coverage or restricting access for noncitizens'. *Health Affairs*, 25(5): w324–36.

Curry, N. and Ham, C. (2010) *Clinical and Service Integration: The Route to Improved Outcomes*. King's Fund. Retrieved from www.kingsfund.org.uk/publications/clinical-and-service-integration (accessed 26 March 2015).

Davies, J. (2012) *Person Driven Care*. Cardiff: 1000 Lives Plus.

De Bruin, A.M., Van Rossum, A.C., Visser, M.C. and Koole, G.M. (2007) 'Modeling the emergency cardiac in-patient flow: an application of queuing theory'. *Health Care Management Science*, 10(2): 125–37.

Devaraj, S., Ow, T. and Kohli, R. (2013) 'Examining the impact of information technology and patient flow: a theory of swift even flow (TSEF) perspective'. *Journal of Operations Management*, 31: 181–92.

Di Mascio, R. (2007) 'A method to evaluate service delivery process quality'. *International Journal of Service Industry Management*, 18(4): 418–42.

Dore, R. (1983) 'Goodwill and the spirit of market capitalism'. *British Journal of Sociology*, 34(4): 459–842.

Dunleavy, H. and Hood, C. (1994) 'From old public organization to new public management'. *Public Money and Management*, July-September: 9–16.

Entwistle, T. (2010) 'Collaboration'. In Ashworth, R., Boyne, G. and Entwistle, T. (eds), *Public Service Improvement: Theories and Evidence*, pp. 162–83. Oxford: Oxford University Press.

Esain, A. (2011) *A Socio-technical Systems Perspective of the Operational Delivery of Secondary Care in the NHS*. Cardiff: Cardiff University.

Esain, A., Angel, L. and Robertson, K. (2006) *Solutions for Problems: The NHS, Lean Thinking and Six Sigma*. Working Paper Series, L2006/24. Cardiff: Cardiff Business School.

Filippini, R. (1997) 'Operations management research: some reflections on evolution, models and empirical studies in OM'. *International Journal of Operations Production Management*, 17(7): 655–70.

Fitzgerald, J.A. and Dadich, A. (2009) 'Using visual analytics to improve hospital scheduling and patient flow'. *Journal of Theoretical and Applied Electronic Commerce Research*, 4(2): 20–30.

Fitzsimmons, J. and Fitzsimmons, M. (2004) *Service Management* (4th edn). New York: McGraw Hill.

Fredendall, L., Craig, J., Fowler, P. and Damat, U. (2009) 'Barriers to swift, even flow in the internal supply chain of preoperative surgical services department: a case study'. *Decision Science*, 40(2): 327–48.

Goldhar, J. and Berg, D. (2010) 'Blurring the boundary: convergence of factory and service processes'. *Journal of Manufacturing Technology Management*, 21,(3): 341–54.

Grobler, A., Thun, J.-H. and Milling, P. (2008) 'Systems dynamics as a structural theory in operations management'. *Production and Operations Management*, 17(3): 373–84.

Hamrock, E., Paige, K., Parks, J., Scheulen, J. and Levin, S. (2013) 'Discrete event simulation for healthcare organizations: a tool for decision making'. *Journal of Healthcare Management*, 58(2): 110–24.

Hansagi, H., Carlsson, B., Olsson, M. and Edhag, O. (1987) 'Trial of a method of reducing inappropriate demands on a hospital emergency department'. *Public Health*, 101(2): 99–105.

Harris, M. and Wood, J. (2012) 'Resuscitate ED metrics with split-flow design'. *Healthcare financial management : journal of the Healthcare Financial Management Association*, 66(12): 76–9.

Heskett, J. A., Sasser, W.E. and Hart, C.W. (1990) *Service Breakthroughs*. New York: Free Press.

Hines, P. (1997) 'A comparative typology of intercompany networking'. In Cox, A. and Hines, P. (eds), *Advanced Supply Management*. Stratford-upon-Avon: Earlsgate Press.

Hood, C. (1991) 'A public management for all seasons'. *Public Administration*, 69(1): 3–19.

Hoot, N. and Aronsky, D. (2008) 'Systematic review of emergency department crowding: causes, effects, and solutions'. *Annals of Emergency Medicine*, 52(2): 126–36.

Hopp, W. and Spearman, M. (2008) *Factory Physics* (3rd edn). New York: McGraw-Hill.

Huh, W.T., Liu, N. and Truong, V.A. (2013) 'Multi resource allocation scheduling in dynamic environments'. *Manufacturing and Service Operations Management*, 15(2): 280–91.

Jayawarna, C., Atkinson, D., Ahmed S.V. and Leong, K. (2010) 'Acute medicine units: the current state of affairs in the north-west of England'. *Journal of the Royal College of Physicians of Edinburgh*, 40(30): 201–4.

Jelinek, G.A., Weiland, T.J. and MacKinlay, C. (2010) 'Supervision and feedback for junior medical staff in Australian emergency departments: findings from the emergency medicine capacity assessment study'. *BMC Medical Education*, 10(1): 74.

Kannan, V. and Tan, K. (2005) 'Just in time, total quality management, and supply chain management'. *OMEGA, The International Journal of Management Science*, 33: 153–62.

Leveson, N. (2004) 'A new accident model for engineering safer systems'. *Safety Science*, 42: 1–8.

Levin, S., Han, J., Aronsky, D., Zhou, C., Hoot, N., Kelly, L. and France, D. (2008) 'Stranded on emergency isle: Modelling competition for cardiac services using survival analysis'. In *IEEM 2007: 2007 IEEE International Conference on Industrial Engineering and Engineering Management*, pp. 1772–6. Singapore: Industrial Engineering and Engineering Management.

Levy, Y. and Ellis, T.J. (2006). 'A systems approach to conduct an effective literature review in support of information systems research'. *Informing Science Journal*, 9: 181–212.

Li, G., Zhang, J. and Liu S. (2010) 'Mixed-integer programming model of urban emergency logistics facilities location under unconventional emergency'. In *ICLEM 2010: Logistics for Sustained Economic Development – Infrastructure, Information, Integration: Proceedings of the 2010 International Conference of Logistics*. Chengdu, China: American Society of Civil Engineers.

Luo, J. Y., Wang, J.Y. and Yu, H. (2010). *A Dynamic Vehicle Routing Problem for Responding to Large-Scale Emergencies: Proceedings of the International Conference on E-Business and E-Government, ICEE*. Guangzhou, China: IEEE.

Mason-Jones, R. and Towill, D.R. (1998) 'Shrinking the supply chain uncertainty circle'. *The Institute of Operations Management Control Journal*, 24(7): 17–22.

McLaughlin, K., Osborne, S.P. and Ferlie, E. (eds) (2006) *New Public Management: Current Trends and Future Prospects*. New York: Routledge.

McNulty, T. and Ferlie, E. (2002) *Reengineering Health Care*. Oxford: Oxford University Press.

Melnick, G.A., Nawathe, A.C., Bamezai, A. and Green, L. (2004) 'Emergency department capacity and access in California, 1990–2001: an economic analysis'. *Health Affairs (Millwood)*, January–June: 136–42.

Miller, A. and Xiao, Y. (2007) 'Multi-level strategies to achieve resilience for an organisation operating at capacity: A case study at a trauma centre'. *Cognition, Technology and Work*, 9(2): 51–66.

Niranjan, T. and Weaver, M. (2011), 'A unifying theory of goods and services supply chain management'. *Service Industries Journal*, 31(14): 2391–2410.

Niranjan, T., Wagner, S. and Aggarwal, V. (2011) 'Measuring information distortion in real-world supply chains'. *International Journal of Production Research*, 49(11): 3343–62.

Oliva, R. and Sterman, J. (2001) 'Cutting corners and working overtime: quality erosion in the service industry'. *Management Science*, 47(7): 894–914.

Osborne, S.P. (2010) 'Delivering public services: time for a new theory?' *Public Management Review*, 12(1): 1–10.

Patrick, J. (2011) 'Access to long-term care: the true cause of hospital congestion?' *Production and Operations Management*, 20(3): 942–55.

Pollitt, C. and Bouckaert, G. (2004) *Public Management Reform: A Comparative Analysis* (2nd edn). Oxford: Oxford University Press.

Radnor, Z.J., Holweg, M. and Waring, J. 2012. 'Lean in healthcare: the unfulfilled promise?' *Social Science and Medicine*, 74: 364–71.

Sampson, E. (2000) 'Customer-supplier duality and bidirectional supply chains in service organisations'. *International Journal of Service Industry Management*, 11(4): 348–64.

Schmenner, R.W. (2004) 'Service business and productivity'. *Decision Sciences*, 35(2): 333–47.

Schmenner, R.W. (2012) *Getting and Staying Productive*. Cambridge: Cambridge University Press

Schmenner, R.W. and Swink, M.L. (1998) 'On theory in operations management'. *Journal of Operations Management*, (17): 97–113.

Sengupta, K., Heiser, D. and Cook, L. (2006) 'Manufacturing and service supply chain performance: a competitive analysis'. *Journal of Supply Chain Management*, 42(4): 4–15.

Siegel, B. (2004) 'The emergency department: rethinking the safety net for the safety net'. *Health Affairs (Millwood)*, January–June: 146–8.

Sinreich, D. and Jabali, O. (2007) 'Staggered work shifts: a way to downsize and restructure an emergency department workforce yet maintain current operational performance'. *Health Care Management Science*, 10(3): 293–308.

Skidelsky, R. (1989) 'Keynes and the state'. In Helm, D. (ed.), *The Economic Boarders of the State*. Oxford: Oxford University Press.

Spring, M. and Araujo, L. (2009) 'Service, services and products: rethinking operations strategy'. *International Journal of Operations and Production Management*, 29(5): 444–67.

Staats, B. and Upton, D.M. (2011) 'Lean knowledge work'. *Harvard Business Review*, 89(10): 100–110.

Seddon, J. (2005) *Systems Thinking in the Public Sector*. Axminster: Triarchy Press.

Taylor, A. and Taylor, M. (2009) 'Operations management research: contemporary themes, trends and potential future directions'. *International Journal of Operations and Production Management*, 29(12): 1316–40.

Towill, D.R. (1997) 'FORRIDGE – principles of good practice in material flow'. *Production Planning and Control*, 8(1): 622–32.

Tucker, A. and Edmondson, A. (2003) 'Why hospitals don't learn from failures: organisational and psychological dynamics that inhibit systems change'. *California Management Review*, 45(2): 55–71.

Utley, M., Jit, M. and Gallivan, S. (2008) 'Restructuring routine elective services to reduce overall capacity requirements within a local health economy'. *Health Care Management Science*, 11(3): 240–47.

Ullman, R., Block, J.A., Boatright, N.C. and Stratmann, W.C. (1978) 'Impact of a primary care group practice on emergency room utilization at a community hospital'. *Medical Care*, 16(9), pp 723–9.

Vidyarthi, N. and Jayaswal, S. (2014) 'Efficient solution of a class of location-allocation problems with stochastic demand and congestion'. *Computers and Operations Research*, 48: 20–30.

Wacker, J. (1987) 'The complementary nature of manufacturing goals by their relationship to throughput time: A theory of internal variability of production systems'. *Journal of Operations Management*, 7(1): 91–105.

Walley, P. (2013) 'Does the public sector need a more demand-driven approach to capacity planning?' *Production Planning and Control*, 24(10–11): 877–90.

Walley, P., Watt, A., Davies, C., Huang, A. and Ma, K. (2001) *A Study of Demand for Emergency Access Health Services in Two UK Health and Social Care Communities*. December. Warwick: Warwick Business School.

Walley, P., Silvester, K and Styne, R. (2006) 'Managing variation in demand: lessons from the UK National Health Service'. *Journal of Healthcare Management*, 51(5): 309–20.

Webster, J. and Watson, R.T. (2002) 'Analyzing the past to prepare for the future: writing a literature review'. *MIS Quarterly*. 26(2): xiii–xxiii.

Worthington, D. (2009) 'Reflections on queue modelling from the last 50 years'. *Journal of the Operational Research Society*, 60(S1): s83–92.

Yankovic, N. and Green, L. (2011) 'Identifying good nursing levels: a queuing approach'. *Operations Research*, 59(4): 942–55.

Yin, P. and Mu, L. (2011) 'Modular capacitated maximal covering location problem for the optimal siting of emergency vehicles'. *Applied Geography*, 34(2): 247–54.

22 Applying supply chain logic to criminal law enforcement

The case of The Netherlands

Carolien de Blok, Dirk Pieter van Donk, Aline Seepma and Inge Roukema

Introduction

The criminal justice chain is often perceived as being inefficient, among others due to barriers and disconnections between the organisations involved in this chain. It thus seems suitable to apply a supply chain perspective in order to improve the efficiency and effectiveness in this chain. This chapter sets out to explore contingencies effecting the improvement of criminal justice chain performance by means of a case study in The Netherlands. The findings provide insight into how factors that are central to operations and supply chain management (the management of customers, processes, and professionals and organisations) challenge the applicability of supply chain logic in the context of the criminal justice system.

In many developed countries, public services are seemingly under attack. There are numerous complaints about inadequate systems, poor delivery and often the public is concerned about the quality, timeliness and adequacy of the government as a service provider. Public systems performance is also of interest to governments themselves, as they are aiming to reduce expenses. Overall, many governments have been criticised for years of spending on structure and infrastructure of their systems that has not led to long-term gains in either productivity or effectiveness (Osborne, Radnor, Vidal and Kinder, 2014; Karwan and Markland, 2006).

Within the public services, some specific service types such as the legal system are getting extra attention because - perceived - mistakes are seen as a sign of injustice and inadequacy. Thus, improving both effectiveness and efficiency of these services is a clear objective for governments (Carmona and Grönlund, 2003). Improvement initiatives have been started in legal services in, among others, England and Wales (Iannacci, 2014; Radnor and Bucci, 2010), Portugal (Martins and Carvalho, 2013), Finland (Pekkanen and Niemi, 2013; Pekkanen, 2011), the US and Italy (Steelman and Fabri, 2008). These initiatives largely centred around the application of lean within one organisation active in the legal system (mainly courts), aiming to eliminate waste. Despite these initiatives, most governments still struggle to achieve sustainable, long-lasting improvements in the legal system as a whole.

Legal services, among which criminal law enforcement, are produced in a chain of public service providers. To enforce criminal law, the police, public prosecution, the court system and execution services (prisons, community service organisations, etc.) are working together in a more or less sequential manner, thus forming a chain of interdependent organisations. Together, they have the aim to come to a fair and impartial judgment for each suspected offender of the law. In The Netherlands, as in some other European countries, other overall improvement aims of the chain are to process more cases successfully, bring suspects to court more quickly and punish delinquents more effectively (Dutch Ministry of Security and Justice, 2013). This requires the parties in the chain to work more closely together and tune their respective activities and information requirements. Given the aims of the criminal justice chain concerning quality, speed and costs, supply chain management (SCM) practices could be of great use. The field of SCM is focused on bringing about an evenly distributed and controlled stream of activities that transforms 'raw materials' into the final 'product' that meets the needs of the customer in terms of quality, costs and timeliness. However, most parties in this public service chain are not used to think along the lines of SCM.

Karwan and Markland (2006) argued that, in general, public performance improvements are unlikely to be realised without a clear understanding of how public processes work, how they are affected by both internal and external as well as organisational and sectorial developments, and what other operational considerations are at stake. That implies that just transferring insights from product based supply chains (SCs) to the criminal justice chain might not help. This is in line with the contextual dependencies as introduced by Sousa and Voss (2008): when aiming for quality improvement in SCs the organisational context as well as the differences between different types of organisations need to be taken into account. We thus need to know what elements and factors are unique to the criminal justice chain in order to improve supply chain performance.

While there is a managerial and public interest in improving the criminal justice chain there is also reason to believe that this is an interesting avenue for research due to the specific, sometimes conflicting aims of the criminal justice supply chain. In criminal law enforcement, streamlining the supply chain might collide with aims that are perceived as being important, such as doing justice, thoroughness of investigations, and independence and autonomy of professionals and institutions involved. Attributes of criminal justice services and resulting operational and performance considerations at stake have been studied *within* organisations involved. These studies resulted in insights concerning the optimisation of individual parts of the criminal justice chain, primarily the improvement of performance in courts (Martins and Carvalho, 2013; Pekkanen and Niemi, 2013; Pekkanen, 2011; Hines, Martins and Beale, 2008). However, to the best of our knowledge no such research has been conducted in supply chains involving multiple public organisations. So, no attention has been given to the criminal justice *chain*. As a consequence we lack knowledge about what characterises the criminal justice chain from a SCM perspective as well as about the implications of these characteristics for the application of SC principles, and their possible effects on performance. Therefore our main research question is:

> Which context factors define the criminal justice supply chain and to what extent do these factors collide or align with principles that aim to improve supply chain performance?

The empirical base of our study is a case study performed in the Dutch criminal justice chain, which consists of autonomous organisations and professionals taking care of various interconnected activities (investigation, prosecution, trial). We look into the chain of police, public prosecution and court, other parties that may be involved such as organisations involved in the execution of penalties or the defence of the suspect are out of the scope of this study. A first objective of this chapter is to identify the key elements defining the criminal justice chain. Second, we aim to find out to what extend supply chain principles can be applied for improvement and how they need to be adapted to match specific criminal justice characteristics.

Theoretical background

The following section first presents literature on SCM in services and in professional services. Thereafter, insights on SCM in a specific public service setting, being the criminal justice chain, will be presented.

Supply chain management in services

Over the past decade, attention has been paid to the design, management and optimisation of SCs in service sectors (Ellram *et al.*, 2004; Baltacioglu *et al.*, 2007; Giannakis, 2011). Service supply chain management has been defined as: 'the management of information, processes, capacity, service performance and funds from the earliest supplier to the ultimate customer' (Ellram *et al.*, 2004: 25). Ellram *et al* (*ibid.*) argue that the underlying aims for the management of product based and service supply chains are the same. As such, integration and cooperation are important to ensure that different parties in a service supply chain do not act as individual silos but rather as a unified whole. As in product-based supply chains (Van der Vaart and Van Donk, 2008), this can probably be achieved through SC practices (activities and technologies used in collaboration), SC patterns (communication and interaction patterns), and SC attitudes (relations and trust). The majority of studies on SC integration (and cooperation) and performance have found a positive relationship between these two (*ibid.*), however these studies have mainly focused on product-based supply chains.

Despite similar underlying aims, the service context introduces some particularities that influence the management of service supply chains (Ellram *et al.*, 2004). This is in line with contingency theory stating that the environment or context wherein an organisation operates shapes its structures and processes. This suggests that organisations should match their structures and processes to their context in order to maximise performance (Lawrence and Lorsch, 1967). The organisational context encompasses, among others, national context and culture, firm size and strategic context (Sousa and Voss, 2008), but also the sector the organisation is active in, including its particularities, laws, and regulations. In line with contingency theory, services have been identified as being not only different from physical goods but also different among themselves. As such, different service types can be distinguished that in turn require different organisational structures and production processes (Cook *et al.*, 1999) and supply chains (Stavrulaki and Davis, 2014) in order to meet required performance.

Supply chain management in professional services

One type of services that has been identified is professional services. Professional services have been defined as having high levels of customer contact, service customisation and fluid/flexible processes with low capital/high labour intensity (Schmenner, 2004; Silvestro *et al.*, 1992; Wemmerlöv, 1990). Furthermore, research has emphasised the key role of the professional service employees who are seen as 'guiding, nudging, and persuading' (Malhotra *et al.*, 2006: 175) activities and operations rather than, for example, standard operating procedures (Kellogg and Nie, 1995: 329). Professional services cover both private and public services; examples range from private services as accountancy, investment banking, and consultancy to public services as law enforcement, education, and health care (Von Nordenflycht, 2010). Lewis and Brown (2012) recently showed that professional services encompass specific challenges and trade-offs when compared to other service types. These authors identified that three service context dimensions of professional services, being the management of customers, of processes, and of professionals and organisations, influence the way in which professional service operations (i.e. within organisations) are managed. As we will argue next, these three dimensions might also influence the management of supply chains of professional services as well.

Managing customers

Customers are a primary supplier of inputs to the service supply chain (Maull et *al.*, 2012; Sampson, 2000). Customers can be an input themselves (e.g. surgery) or they can provide the specifications for a service needed (e.g. consultancy). Both forms of input can differ in the degree of homogeneity required and will thus introduce a certain degree of input variability into the service supply chain. High variability impedes control and reduces opportunities for process standardisation and automation of practices (Lewis and Brown, 2012). At the same time, in many professional services, information asymmetry between professional and customer reduces the customer's ability to provide inputs or an exact specification of the service required, thus diminishing the degree of customer influence (Kellogg and Nie, 1995). In service supply chains, the degree and homogeneity of customer inputs will influence the flexibility required. SC partners need to deploy the right practices in order to balance customisation and efficiency as well as to communicate customer requirements up the supply chain.

Managing processes

Due to little input variability, mass services are suitable for standardisation and automation of processes. Professional services however, require flexible, highly variable delivery processes in which individual judgement has a central role in service delivery (Lewis and Brown, 2012). In service supply chains, this might imply the need for different practices to pace the work between departments and organisations as well as different controls (measure outputs versus measuring time-inputs to a service project). Also, whereas for some service types it might be possible to streamline the workflow between organisations, for professional services this might be hard due to complex assignments that take place over an extended timeframe with uncertain and highly variable completion time (Sasser *et al.*, 1978).

Managing professionals and organisations

The degree of autonomy of professional service employees and the knowledge intensiveness of their jobs will influence internal operations (Lewis and Brown, 2012). In professional service organisations, professionals autonomously provide their services based on a particular knowledge system. This system is often externally controlled and regulated in its content and application (e.g. in order to be an accountant, medical doctor or lawyer you need to 'gain entry' through exams). Furthermore, professionals adhere to explicit codes of ethics and implicit norms that guide appropriate behaviour (Lewis and Brown, 2012; Mintzberg, 1979) and control operations. For partners in a service supply chain, this would imply that they have to be able to understand, connect to and deal with each other's knowledge base, and external and internal codes and norms. As a consequence, integration might not only be required on an organisational level, but on a professional level as well. Soft mechanisms such as trust and power might play a large role in this.

Supply chain management in the criminal justice chain

Public services, such as criminal law enforcement, differ from private services in their goal and required performance for the greater public. Public service organisations have to strive for equity, which means to equally provide services to all citizens (e.g. public transport, garbage collection), ensure equal access to those who require the specific services provided (e.g. health care, justice system) (Karwan and Markland, 2006; Berman, 1998), or apply rules to all citizens similarly (justice, tax). Besides, while public services are non-profit driven, there is a politically driven urge to 'introduce more market and to get public enterprises to align to the operating modes of private enterprises in order to be more efficient' (Arlbjørn *et al.*, 2011: 285). In the next paragraphs, we will use the three dimensions of Lewis and Brown (2012) to explore the management of service supply chains in the public sector, in particular in the criminal justice supply chain.

Managing customers

As for private sector services, homogeneity of needs might be high for some public services (e.g. fire protection), whereas for others citizen needs are largely heterogeneous (e.g. education) (Roth and Bozinoff, 1989). This will influence the variety that the public service supply chain needs to deliver. In the criminal justice chain it is not so much customer needs that differ but the homogeneity of the content of each case. As a result, 'the "manufactured item" is crafted by highly skilled, independently working professionals' (Pekkanen and Niemi, 2013: 605). Furthermore, the time required to complete each process phase strongly varies, as does the time needed to complete a case (*ibid.*). This likely holds true for each partner in the criminal justice chain. In addition, since public services serve both society and individuals different goals have to be adhered to by the public service chain depending on the perspective one takes on who is being served (society versus individual) (Martins and Carvalho, 2013). Juridical services contribute to a society's/national (feelings of) safety and security. At the same time, these services are provided to individual citizens (suspects and victims), who are aiming for being released from/being charged for a particular crime. To provide quality, the parties in this chain should have a double reference: the fulfilment of requirements expected by the individual citizen-client, and the fulfilment of requirements of the community (Miguel-Dávila and Suarez-Barraza, 2014). According to Pekkanen and Niemi (2013), who focused their research specifically on courts, it is difficult to completely avoid tension between the needs and wishes of the two groups of customers. This likely will hold true as well for the criminal justice chain as a whole.

Managing processes

Public services differ from each other in the frequency and directness of the customer taking part in the public service process (Roth and Bozinoff, 1989). Frequency refers to the amount of times a citizen has experienced a particular public service, and determines the volume that the public service chain has to be able to handle. For individual citizens frequency of use of the criminal justice chains will be rather low, and demand will not rise because people want to make use of the services offered by the chain or because of a prior good experience with the chain. However, on a national level demand can still be high. In the Netherlands (almost 17 million inhabitants) 200,000 criminal cases were processed in one of the country's 11 courts in 2013. Because many cases are either discharged or terminated before they come to court the inflow, and thus the required processing volume, at the beginning of the chain is much higher.

Directness refers to the degree of individual citizen contact with the service (e.g. direct for education and indirect for road maintenance). It influences the extent to which individual citizens will actively take part in the public service supply chain and thus the degree of input variability introduced in the public service supply chain. As discussed under the heading 'Managing customers', variability in the criminal justice chain is not so much introduced by citizens, but by the heterogeneous contents and advancement of criminal cases. In a court hearing, for example, it is always possible that a case needs to be adjourned or that a witness does not turn up and as such it is impossible to determine beforehand which case will go through on the day of a trial (Pekkanen and Niemi, 2013). This might introduce a rather high degree of uncertainty in the chain's processes that the organisations involved have to deal with together.

Managing organisation and professionals

From an organisational perspective, many public services are provided as monopoly services, resulting in a low number of suppliers (e.g. one public prosecution office or court per region). Furthermore, many public services and especially the criminal justice chain are subject to laws, rules and regulations that are determined on a national or regional level (Miguel-Dávila and Suarez-Barraza, 2014). Both characteristics influence the degree to which citizens can actively influence the criminal justice service process. Since this influence is limited due to laws, regulations, the citizen is more an input to the criminal justice chain itself, rather than an active party in service delivery. Furthermore, both characteristics also influence the degree to which organisations in the criminal justice chain, and their respective professionals are entitled to work together and can be integrated with each other to a certain degree. A final observation concerning the management of professionals in courts was clearly stated by Pekkanen and Niemi (2013: 606):

> perhaps the most distinctive characteristic is the even greater emphasis on the autonomy and self-management of the employees than in other professional services. … The fear of losing objectivity and autonomy can manifest in the form of a negative attitude towards process improvement … the fixed role and duties of the different participants create silo-thinking and restrict the possibilities to utilize cooperation more in the production process.

This indicates that criminal justice chains are dealing with a very particular group of service employees who have strong influence on the supply chain process as well as on possibilities for improvement.

In the previous sections, theoretical insights on contextual characteristics of professional services, and more specifically the criminal justice chain that might influence supply chain principles have been identified. The characteristics are categorised as being related to customer, processes and professional/organisation and have been summarised in Figure 22.1. The existence and influence of these characteristics will now be further empirically explored by means of a case study in one particular public service supply chain, being the Dutch criminal justice supply chain.

Research framework

Based on the presented theoretical background, the characteristics of the criminal justice chain that either stem from literature concerning services or public and legal services can be summarised as in Figure 22.1. The existence of these characteristics, that can range from high (H) to low (L), and their possible influence on supply chain principles will now be further empirically explored by means of one illustrative case, being the criminal justice chain in the Netherlands.

Illustrative case: methods

Criminal justice is extremely interesting as in order to safeguard, for example, justness and privacy, the law provides numerous procedural rules and checks that make it specific in terms of the chain.

To shed light on the context characteristics in the Dutch criminal justice chain that would influence the application of SC management principles, interviews were held throughout this chain. We carefully selected interviewees for their ability to reflect on the chain from various perspectives, both with respect to the parties active in this chain and with respect to the organisational and legal context of this chain (see Table 22.1). Interviews were recorded and transcribed. In order to verify the contents, the interviews were sent back to the interviewees and if required, changes were made. Relevant documentation – reports, presentation, opinion articles, (evaluation) research, letters – from the three main parties in the SC, and from the Dutch Ministry of Security and Justice were collected via the interviewees and via the internet. Based on the data collected, the organisation of the chain was described in detail, taking the flow of information through this chain as a starting point. The description of and information flow in the chain were verified by means of discussions with a group of experts. Furthermore, building upon the work of Lewis and Brown (2012), the criminal justice chain was analysed. To this end, interviews and relevant documentation were coded based on the research framework presented; codes reflected the perspectives of customer, process, and professional/organisation management in order to get insight into the context factors at stake.

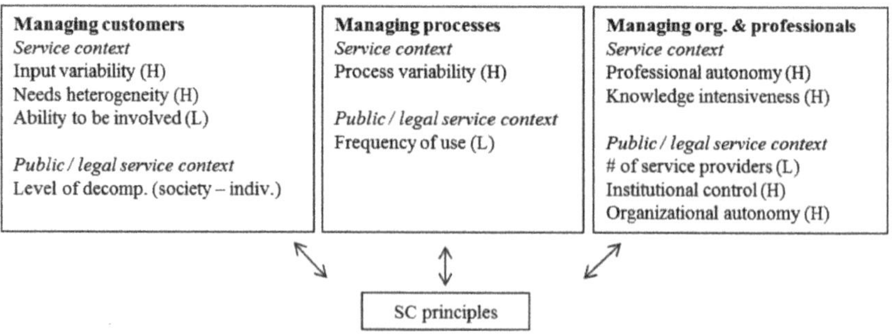

Figure 22.1 Factors influencing the criminal justice chain

Source: based on Lewis and Brown (2012)

Table 22.1 Number of people interviewed and their perspectives

Police	*No.*	*Public prosecution service*	*#*	*Court*	*No.*
Organisational		Organisational	1	Organisational	1
Legal	1	Legal	1	Legal	1
Criminal justice chain-wide organizations/institutions					
Policy level (ministry): legal					2
Policy level (ministry): organizational					5
Organisations/bodies for chain improvement and innovation					5
Total number of interviews					*17*

Illustrative case: preliminary results

Description of the Dutch criminal justice chain

The Dutch criminal justice chain consists of organisations that together take care of criminal law enforcement: from investigation, via prosecution and trial up to the execution of punishments and penalties. The Netherlands has one national police force and ten regional forces. There are 10 public prosecution offices and 11 courts spread around the country. 85 judicial facilities (e.g. jails, forensic psychiatric facilities, youth facilities, etc.) take care of the final phase in the chain, together with a judicial fines agency and probation services. This final phase, however, is outside the scope of this research. The Dutch Ministry of Security and Justice is in the end responsible for maintaining the rule of the law, and thus the criminal justice chain, in The Netherlands. However this research focuses on the three primary organisations that are active in the day-to-day activities in the criminal justice chain (i.e. police, prosecution and court).

The ultimate goal of the chain is to come to a verdict (and its execution). Each party involved provides value to the chain by working towards this verdict. The main vehicle for this is the case file. In the Dutch situation, the case file is filled with information throughout the SC. The case file is ultimately seen as containing all the evidence and is therefore used to come to a verdict in court. This is different from the use of the case file in for example England, Wales and Denmark, where documents in the case file are in principle not seen as direct evidence. Instead, all (documented) evidence must be presented in court to be perceived as evidence by the judge and based on this, the judge comes to a decision. In the Netherlands, the judge has a leading role in court, chairing the trial, and bases his or her decision on the contents of the case file. The Dutch criminal justice system does not acknowledge guilty pleas, instead, a verdict has to be based on a minimal amount of legally obtained and irrefutable evidence from sources other than the accused.

Case setting: working together in the chain

When the police are notified of a crime, they start an investigation to gather evidence (individually or with help of other organisations/bodies) against a known or unknown suspect. This evidence is gathered in an official report in the police IT system. Some cases are shelved by the police, others are offered for public prosecution. For the latter, the police print the official report, sign it and send it to the prosecutor where it is scanned into the prosecutor system. The presence and completeness of all required documentation is checked. If incomplete the prosecutor requests additional information either from the police or other parties. Thereafter the prosecutor decides whether or not to bring a case to court, thereby offering the case file to the judge either digitally or on paper (in which case it is posted and scanned again). The judge(s) study the information (presented in the case file and during trial), and come to a verdict, to which a suspect can appeal. The parties involved in the chain (together with the Dutch Ministry of Security and Justice) aim to improve the chain's performance, primarily with respect to lead times, prevention of outflow, and execution of sentences while maintaining or even improving quality provided by the SC. Various improvement projects have started in which key elements are better cooperation between chain partners, and digitalisation and automation of information and activities. At the time of data collection, one major aim for the parties involved was to work towards a digital criminal case file; as of 2016 information should be exchanged electronically.

Managing customers in the criminal justice chain

The criminal justice chain aims to contribute to a national feeling of safety, security and justice, and, simultaneously aims to come to a fair verdict for each case that is brought to court. As such, society as a whole can be seen as a customer, as well as the victim(s) and the suspect(s) (although neither are 'voluntary customers') and their representatives. The two levels of decomposition interact as perceived outcomes at an individual citizen level (e.g. serious offender released from charges) can influence perceived outcomes at societal level (e.g. perceived speed of the process or perceived justice of the outcome). However, according to interviewees, it is not the heterogeneous needs or perceived outcomes of customers that influence the activities executed for each case or the time it takes to complete a case. Rather it is the law that should be independently and rightly applied by judges to each case.

Between cases but also within a single case, needs are heterogeneous. Individual citizens play a role as providers of input to the criminal justice chain. Suspects, victims and witnesses involved in a particular case all provide information that is relevant to the case. As each of these input providers might have different aims (on the one extreme the suspect who in general wants to be acquitted and on the other extreme the victim who wants a suspect to be convicted) this introduces variability in the SC, that, in the end, is to be objectified by the application of law by an independent professional being the judge. Even though suspects and victims cannot be seen as customers of the SC in the traditional way, parties in the chain are obliged to take good care of them in terms of privacy, safety protection, etc. In addition, care should be taken that the law is equally applied to everyone.

In sum, interviewees claim that it is not the needs and wants of individuals or society that demands for heterogeneity in working processes but the equal application of the law to each criminal case. At the same time, individuals do provide heterogeneous inputs into the criminal justice chain, which are then used to come to a fair judgement.

Managing processes in the criminal justice chain

The information stream is central to the criminal justice chain. Processes between partners in the criminal justice chain serve to transfer information that is gathered/produced at one party to the next. All relevant information related to a particular case should ultimately be bundled in the case file in order to be able to come to a verdict at the end of the chain. Whereas in many goods or service SCs information is supportive to the stream of goods or people, in the criminal justice SC information is key to the service that is delivered. In many cases, this information is supported by a stream of visual and physical evidence (photographs, video, hair, clothes, weapons) or people such as witnesses. Still, a smooth flow of information and information completeness are seen by the interviewees as key to managing the process that the criminal case file goes through.

Interviewees estimated that about 80 per cent of the cases are standard, the rest of the cases are complex. However, the actual complexity of a case can in general only be determined in hindsight, for example by looking back at how much capacity was involved in bringing it to court. Therefore, although in general terms inputs, activities and outputs are known (being a reported offence, activities to gather information, and a complete case file), the exact contents cannot be planned in advance but are determined when executing the process. In this, the process is dependent upon the complexity and circumstances of the case itself. Even if a case seems rather simple, its context can make it unique still. In addition, the process is dependent upon the police officer/public prosecutor who can decide him or herself on what legal activities to undertake to fill the case file. As such, flexible, highly variable processes are required in which individual professional judgement plays a major role. Advance planning is hardly possible.

Despite the high degree of flexibility and openness in processes, the information that is gathered in and the result of these processes has to meet strict juridical requirements. In order to ensure that the case file on which the final decision will be based contains the truth with respect to the case under investigation, information always has to meet up to the requirements stated in Table 22.2. Controls such as (wet/hand written) autographs, certificates and watermarks play an important role in ensuring the requirements. The requirements to information output influence how this information comes into existence and how it is transferred in the SC, and thus the design and execution of processes in the criminal justice chain.

In sum, inputs to the criminal justice chains as well as processes in this chain are highly variable. The information that is produced in and is the outcome of this chain has to be specific to a case while at the same time it has to obey strict and prescribed conditions that apply to all cases. As a result processes are highly variable, however they seem to be so within law and regulatory-set boundaries.

Table 22.2 (Legal) requirements to information in criminal justice chain

Requirement	*Meaning*
Authenticity	The information provided is original
Integrity	No information has been added or adapted after the information has been 'sealed' and the information is coming from the person it is said to be coming from
Completeness	All documents are present in the case file, and the content of all documents is complete
Chain of custody	Establish that the alleged evidence is in fact related to the alleged crime a chronological and logical procedure or trail, showing the seizure, custody, control, transfer, analysis, and disposition of physical or electronic evidence
Accessibility (of information)	Only those who are working on a case have to have access to the information, no access to those who are not involved

Managing professionals and organisations in the criminal justice chain

Organisations in the Dutch criminal justice chain work largely independent from each other. This organisational independence is at least partly caused by the nature of the system. As in many democratic countries separation of powers and decision-making (*trias politica*) has been important in The Netherlands for over two centuries to prevent one entity in the system from misusing its power over the others. Even though on a system level this power separation is vital for any democracy to work, on an operational level it has led to strictly separated organisations, each with its own working processes, information streams, governance systems, information and communication systems, etc. Thereby, separation on a system level, has led to administrative separation as well as a tendency not to think in terms of chains. However, as one of the interviewees asked, 'does independent organisational position also imply that you have to have an independent administrative position as well?'

Because of the organisational silos, all parties involved in the chain (and their sub-organisations in various regions) independently developed their processes, information and communication structures, and took initiatives in ICT implementation. Over the years, each organisation invested in its own IT system(s) that were designed and built from their own point of view, working towards their own national or regional norms, strategies and targets, and started to implement these at their own pace. As each party also resides within different management, budget, and decision making structures, change processes mostly are directed to separate partners and hardly ever at the chain as a whole.

In all parties active in the criminal justice SC, highly educated professionals are contributing to the chain. Their jobs require a high knowledge component, that especially for prosecutors and judges is quite specialised. Professionals are used to work autonomously and, being led by the law they take pride in their decisions having an impact for society as a whole. Professionals strongly identify with their peers, and professionals from each party in the SC have their own implicit values and work habits that are hard to change. One interviewee explained that, having worked with paper for centuries, judges, 'trust paper blindly and have an enormous mistrust in information that is digitally exchanged' – thus influencing the work process design as well as (future) improvement initiatives taken.

In sum, a chain perspective seems to be lacking on both a system and administrative level. Over the years, each party has independently developed its working processes and structures. Professionals in the organisations involved have strong values and habits that are hard to change and align.

Discussion and conclusions

The main idea of this chapter is that the context of a service SC will influence the application of SC principles and activities. More specifically, building upon Lewis and Brown (2012), we argue that in the context of the criminal justice chain, factors concerning customer, process and professional/organisation might collide or align with practices that aim to manage these SCs. Empirical exploration of the criminal justice SC allows us to determine whether and the degree to which various context factors such as heterogeneity of needs and inputs, a double reference for outputs, process variability, professional autonomy, and institutional control are indeed present and how they influence SC management. Furthermore, the criminal justice chain provides insight into new variables in the categories managing customers, processes and professionals/organisations as well as system-wide context factors that influence each of the three categories. Based on these findings we are able to adapt our initial research framework and specify it for the characteristics and context factors that define and influence the criminal justice supply chain (see Figure 22.2).

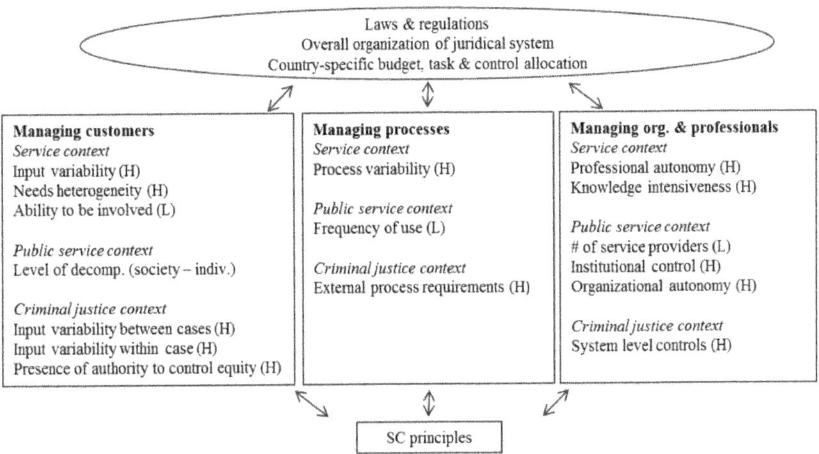

Figure 22.2 Factors defining and influencing criminal justice supply chain

Note: Abbreviations: H, high; L, low

Taking an SCM perspective to the criminal justice chain provides insight into hindering factors as well as interesting dilemma's when aiming to apply SCM principles to improve performance of the chain. First, the criminal justice system aims for equal treatment of all citizens, victims and suspects alike. All cases in the system should be treated justly and fairly through right application of the law. In the perception of professionals involved, the aim of equity hinders the SCM strive for streamlining processes and creating flow. Doing justice and a fair application of the law is often accompanied by a lengthy period to study complex assignments, apply professional knowledge and judgment at each supply chain party in order to come to a just verdict at the end of the chain. The high degree of adaptation of the work process to each case and application of knowledge in this process, make automation and standardisation of process steps difficult and inhibit the application of advance planning and workflow control. This offers an interesting dilemma: criminal justice is very much process oriented in the sense that the law and subsequent procedures must be followed and obeyed to, but that same orientation is part of the barrier to the application of process logic and streamlining from SCM when it comes to information sharing, joint planning, workflow management, and shared information systems.

Second, the organisation underlying the criminal justice system is based on power division and autonomous decision making. Over the years, however, this system-induced autonomy resulted in processes that are largely disconnected. Moreover, each SC partner has been developing and improving processes at its own pace. Silos and organisational inertia have thus been created as an unintended result of the *trias politica* principle. The criminal justice organisations' strive for independency creates a dilemma with the SCM strive and need for integration. In order to work towards increased integration and cooperation in the management of the SC itself, the process and administrative autonomy have to be diminished first, while preserving independence in power and decision making. Again the dilemma is on the intersection of principles of organisational redesign to enhance a smooth flow of information, and the juridical principles that are required to safeguard integrity and independence.

Finally, the law provides strict prerequisites to inputs and outputs of the criminal justice supply chain. Especially external information requirements have to be obeyed. This creates a specific form of output standardisation that generates a dilemma with the high process variability and flexibility required by professionals to deal with the specifics of every criminal case. Whereas the boundaries to and standards for information and evidence require strict output controls as well as strictly controlled practices, IT systems and forms of communication, professional behaviour needs to be guided by soft input controls, norms and ethics in order to enable them to practice customisation required for each case. Here a final dilemma is visible between professional behaviour and judgment and a smooth flow of the inputs to be able to arrive at and make such judgments. This dilemma is not restricted to criminal law, as also physicians and other professionals such as academics might experience this.

Performance measures in SCM are mainly efficiency-related, supplemented with flexibility, quality, and speed. In criminal justice chains, these are all overruled or replaced by justice as the final and only counting performance measure, despite public or political stress on speed and cost reductions. For many judges, doing justice and independent decision making are synonyms. So, what does it imply for SCM and are there options for improving the chain as a whole, while maintaining justice for society and the individual? Our case findings do offer some insights into the three dimensions of supply chain integration: attitudes, patterns and practices. Attitudes and culture fuelled by the organisational and system arrangement, form a major barrier. Moreover, different centrally orchestrated attempts to streamline information flow or make information electronically available, have not been not very successful, adding to mistrust in this type of solutions. SC practices (activities and technology) and patterns (communication and interaction) are currently dominated and limited by – the interpretation – of laws and by habits. In an attempt to break organisational silos, we observed an interesting re-arrangement of persons for simple cases in one region in the Netherlands. In this initiative, people from different chain partners were physically located together, without clear instructions for how to organise the workflow, while maintaining to required procedures. Here, different technologies were used for keeping track of workflow, for example, and different types of interaction and communication were instrumental to process criminal cases from different areas simultaneously. Such arrangements could be an exemplar for more complex cases with larger and more unpredictable throughput times and workloads.

This chapter provided a first exploration into the specifics of one type of public service supply chain that influence the application of SCM principles. The criminal justice supply chain provided us with interesting insights and dilemma's to be resolved. All of its characteristics, including the organisational silo mentality, the high commitment to doing justice, professional integrity and professionalism, make up a SC that has been rationally designed to safeguard justice, but runs into irrationalities that are counterproductive given an almost unmanageable workload that needs a fresh look from a SC perspective. However, finding the balance between juridical and SC principles is still our final problem and probably offers the ultimate dilemma. This then also provides a first lead for future research. Furthermore, it would be interesting to broaden the scope of this research, that focused only on the criminal justice chain in the Netherlands. Research in other countries with different criminal justice systems as well as in other juridical supply chains is needed to shed further light on the particularities of these chains as well as on the integration practices used to make various parties work together. As a large number of countries aim to improve the performance of their criminal justice supply chains, among others by applying various forms of information and communication technology, it would be interesting to see how these chain-wide initiatives affect the management of customers, processes and professionals.

References

Arlbjørn, J.S., Freytag, P.V. and De Haas, H. (2011) 'Service supply chain management – a survey of lean application in the municipal sector'. *International Journal of Physical Distribution and Logistics Management*, 41(3): 277–95.

Baltacioglu, T., Ada, E., Kaplan, M.D., Yurt, O. and Kaplan, Y.C. (2007) 'A new framework for service supply chain'. *Service Industries Journal*, 27(2): 105–24.

Berman, E.M. (1998) *Productivity in Public and Non-Profit Organizations*. Thousand Oaks, CA: Sage Publications.

Carmona, S. and Grönlund, A. (2003) 'Measures vs. actions: the balanced scorecard in Swedish law enforcement'. *International Journal of Operations and Production Management*, 23(12): 1475–96.

Cook, L.S., Bowen, D.E., Chase, R.B., Dasu, S., Stewart, D.M. and Tansik, D.A. (2002) 'Human issues in service design'. *Journal of Operations Management*, 20(2): 159–74.

Dutch Ministry of Security and Justice (2013) *Letter of the Minister of Security and Justice*, 14 November. Kamerstukken 2013–2014, No. 29279-177. Retrieved from https://zoek.officielebekendmakingen.nl/kst-29279-177.html (accessed 7 April 2015).

Ellram, L., Tate, W. and Billington, C. (2004) 'Understanding and managing the services supply chain'. *Journal of Supply Chain Management*, 40(4): 17–32.

Giannakis, M. (2011) 'Conceptualizing and managing service supply chains'. *Service Industries Journal*, 31(11): 1809–23.

Hines, P., Martins, A.L. and Beale, J. (2008) 'Testing the boundaries of lean thinking: observations from the legal public sector'. *Public Money and Management*, 28(1): 35–40.

Iannacci, F. (2014) 'Routines, artefacts and technological change: investigating the transformation of criminal justice in England and Wales'. *Journal of Information Technology*, 29(4): 294–311.

Karwan, K.R. and Markland, R.E. (2006) 'Integrating service design principles and information technology to improve delivery and productivity in public sector operations: the case of the South Carolina DMV'. *Journal of Operations Management*, 24(4): 347–62.

Kellogg, D.L. and Nie, W. (1995) 'A framework for strategic service management'. *Journal of Operations Management*, 13(4): 323–37.

Lawrence, P.R. and Lorsch, J.W. (1967) 'Differentiation and integration in complex organizations'. *Administrative Science Quarterly*, 12(1): 1–47.

Lewis, M.A. and Brown, A.D. (2012) 'How different is professional service operations management?' *Journal of Operations Management*, 30(1–2): 1–11.

Malhotra, N., Morris, T. and Hinings, C.B. (2006) 'Variation in organizational form among professional service organizations'. *Research in the Sociology of Organizations*, 24: 171–202.

Martins, A.L. and de Carvalho, J.C. (2013) 'Slimming lead times in courts of law–a case study'. *International Journal of Industrial Engineering and Management*, 4(3): 123–30.

Maull, R., Geraldi, J. and Johnston, R. (2012) 'Service supply chains: a customer perspective'. *Journal of Supply Chain Management*, 48(4): 72–86.

Miguel-Dávila, J.Á. and Suárez-Barraza, M.F. (2014) 'Assessing the design, management and improvement of Kaizen projects in local governments'. *Business Process Management Journal*, 20(3): 392–411.

Mintzberg, H. (1979) *The Structuring of Organizations*. Englewood Cliffs, NJ: Prentice Hall.

Osborne, S.P., Radnor, Z.J., Vidal, I. and Kinder, T. (2014) 'A sustainable business model for public service organizations?' *Public Management Review*, 16(2): 165–72.

Pekkanen, P. (2011) 'Delay reduction in courts of justice – possibilities and challenges of process improvement in professional public organizations'. Doctoral thesis, Lappeenranta University of Technology.

Pekkanen, P. and Niemi, P. (2013) 'Process performance improvement in justice organizations – Pitfalls of performance measurement'. *International Journal of Production Economics*, 143: 605–11.

Radnor, Z.J. and Bucci, G. (2010) *Evaluation of the Lean Programme in HMCS*. Kenilworth: AtoZ Business Consultancy.

Roth, V.J. and Bozinoff, L. (1989) 'Consumer satisfaction with government services'. *Service Industries Journal*, 9(4): 29–43.

Sampson, S.E. (2000) 'Customer–supplier duality and bidirectional supply chains in service organizations'. *International Journal of Service Industry Management*, 11(4): 348–64.

Sasser, W.E., Olsen, R.P. and Wyckoff, D.D. (1978) *Management of Service Operations*. Boston, MA: Allyn and Bacon.

Schmenner, R.W. (2004) 'Service businesses and productivity'. *Decision Sciences*, 35(3): 333–47.

Silvestro, R., Fitzgerald, L., Johnston, R. and Voss, C. (1992) 'Towards a classification of service processes' *International Journal of Service Industry Management*, 3(3): 62–75.

Sousa, R. and Voss, C.A. (2008) 'Contingency research in operations management practices'. *Journal of Operations Management*, 26(6): 697–713.

Stavrulaki, E. and Davis, M.M. (2014) 'A typology for service supply chains and its implications for strategic decisions' *Service Science*, 6(1): 34–46.

Steelman, D.C. and Fabri, M. (2008) 'Can an Italian court use the American approach to delay reduction?' *Justice System Journal*, 29(1): 1–23.

Van der Vaart, J.T. and van Donk, D.P. (2008) 'A critical review of survey-based research in supply chain integration'. *International Journal of Production Economics*, 111(1): 42–55.

Von Nordenflycht, A. (2010) 'What is a professional service firm? Toward a theory and taxonomy of knowledge-intensive firms'. *Academy of Management Review*, 35(1): 155–74.

Wemmerlöv, U. (1990) 'A taxonomy for service processes and its implications for system design'. *International Journal of Service Industry Management*, 1(3): 20–40.

23 Final reflections

The future research agenda on public service operations management

Ann Esain, Maneesh Kumar and Sharon J. Williams

Reflections

This book has discussed a wide variety of opportunities and challenges relating to public services operations management. While not anticipated to be a complete evaluation of the field these chapters represent a foundation upon which this important and contemporary area can cultivate future contributions. Therefore this book has presented a collection of critical assessments both of mid-range theory (as defined by Soltani *et al.*, 2014) and empirically driven instruments used to unpack meanings and implications for public services operations management researchers and practitioners.

From inception this book has evolved from the belief that public services operations management holds with the grand theory of 'input, process, and output' (Radnor and Bateman, Chapter 1). Central to this theory is product logic (Smith *et al.*, 2014) for organisational systems (Kast and Rosenzweig, 1985; Katz and Kahn, 1969). More recently this theory has evolved with the inclusion of service dominant logic. In tandem traditional public management theories have been challenged for suitability to service orientated contexts particularly for operations management (Radnor and Osborne, 2013). Research in public services has predominantly been related to the political regulation (Martin, 2010), organisational governance versus organisational ambiguity (Rainey and Steinbauer, 1999; Rainey, 1993) and implications of different collaborative institutional logics rather than how public services operate. The attention on improvement of current public service organisational and supply based arrangements in this book is a reflection of the gap in public services theory.

This final chapter has two main aims. First, to assimilate the key themes which have been raised in this book as well as identifying the contemporary gaps for knowledge which are critically absent. By evaluating these themes, opportunities are identified to extend existing theories and operational approaches in order to develop public services operations managers and this area of management.

Second, this chapter reflects on the current knowledge of public services operation management and outlines a future agenda for public services operations management scholars. Tackling this subject domain provides a range of routes to set a research agenda that evaluates the specific underpinnings of public services operations management. The contributions herein also help to feed forward thinking from various public services contexts. Particularly the book chapters provide a means for learning from public services who seek to tackle the extremes of operations management, to those commercial organisations also facing similar issues (e.g. volatile demand, quick response and limited resources, dealing with cultural and ethical differences).

It is observed that public services draw upon organisations which have a layer of social and environmental motivation (Doherty *et al.*, 2014), which can be quite different from the private sector (see Table 23.1). These different types of organisations regularly work together or contract with each other, to exploit opportunities for service integration or build networks of service provision for specific populations (Al-Tabbaa, Leach and March, Chapter 3). This final chapter presents insights on operational features and supply chain/networks management from both wholly public organisations (in the idealised form) and a range of variants of third sector organisations.

Specifically, this chapter does not elaborate on context specific future research that contributors raise in individual chapters, or constrain commentary through the books organisational structure but rather focuses on more general operations management themes which have emerged. These have been organised to first focus on operational strategy. Second, consideration is given to the implications on and for senior and middle managers within public services operations management. This group has been selected as they traditionally have the span of control to design operational systems, processes within the organisational boundary. Thirdly, focus is centred on tactical aspects of operations management which form part of the day-to-day management of the organisation. Finally supply and network based practices are considered, which may provide the requisite variety (Ashby, 1958) to satisfy the complex and challenging market segments that have remained or emerged as unfulfilled through existing channels/segmentation of public services organisations. Supply chain and network management has the potential to provide a responsive, comprehensive and innovative mix of public services provision. To evaluate and influence these changes, there has also been the emergence of regulatory agencies (Boyne *et al.*, 2010): in the USA, the Office of Social Innovation and Civic Participation (White House, 2014); in Europe, the Social Business Initiative (European Commission, 2014); in the UK, the Office for Civil Society (Cabinet Office, 2014) has been running since 2010 (Alcock, 2010).

Future research agenda

To advance this fledgling body of knowledge, testing of predictions that logically flow from theoretical assumptions is necessary. Areas of validation covered in this book are:

- the transferability between and across private and public service contexts of existing operations management theory, which on the one hand is disputed (Radnor and Bateman, Chapter 1) and on the other is presumed (Adderley and Kirkbright, Chapter 10).

Table 23.1 Comparison of governance characteristics and operational features of different sectors

Organisation idealised forms	*Governance characteristics*	*Unique operational features*
Private sector	• Guided by market forces to maximise financial return • Owned by shareholders or partners • Governed according to size of share ownership • Resourced by revenue from sales and fees	• History of professional management • Able to design operational systems to satisfy segmented demand that will make profit • Variability in financial plan to actual expected • Drive towards flexibility • Greater readiness to learn from experiences external to the organisation
Public sector	• Guided by the principles of public benefit and collective choice • Owned by the state • Governed by the state • Resourced through taxation	• History of public administration • Mostly mechanistic organisational structure • Little influence over the design of operational systems or ability to segment demand (often activities which are necessary but not profit making) • Variability in financial plan to actual not accepted • Slow in changing operational practices by learning from experiences external to the organisation
Third sector (non-profit-sector organisations/ voluntary and community organisations)	• Guided by social and environmental goals • Owned by members • Governed by private election of representatives • Resourced by revenue from membership fees, donations and legacies	• Staffed by a combination of employees and volunteers (Doherty *et al.*, 2014) • May have existing operational systems but can segment demand • Organic organisational structure (Taylor and Taylor, this volume, ch. 11) • Limited knowledge on pre-existing promising operational practices (Leseure *et al.*, 2004) for adaption/adoption
Third sector (for profit social enterprises)	• Guided by the belief the business can bring about social and environmental change • Ownership varies (no single unified regulatory body) • Governed to be autonomous of the state (Social Enterprise Coalition, 2014) • Resourced through trade relationships, to make profit and reinvest the majority of that profit	• Competing with the other idealised forms • May have existing operational systems but can segment demand • Presumed more of an organic organisational structure • The boundaries of what is legitimate work in these organisations is less well understood • Limited knowledge on pre-existing promising operational practices (Leseure *et al.*, 2004) for adaption/adoption

Source: based on Doherty *et al.* (2014)

- the validation of operations management theory related to combinations of multiple types of organisations to deliver social value (Al-Tabbaa, Leach and March, Chapter 3; Aitken, Esain and Williams, Chapter 21; Pettit, Beresford, Knight and Sohn, Chapter 5; and Adderley and Kirkbright, Chapter 10).

Implications for operational strategy

Satisfying customers to maximise equity is the undisputed objective of the private sector (see Table 23.1). It is generally believed that private sector organisational and supply chain strategy aims to achieve operational excellence through the optimisation of operational design which in turn most effectively delivers customer needs and wants (Bowersox *et al.*, 2000). Some commentators see this wholly in the context of economic efficiency, yet others challenge this single lens. For public service, customer satisfaction and social value is less well understood in the context of operations management (see Adderley and Kirkbright's argument for service dominant logic in Chapter 10, Hudson Smith's examination of a standardised PM system as a predictor of patient satisfaction in Chapter 19, and Moxham's horizontal comparison of measurement systems in Chapter 13). While the notion of social value is under investigated (Doherty *et al.*, 2014), the consequences for systems operational design are twofold:

- Balancing the external social and environmental aspirations with the internal arrangements for physical flows to meet social and environmental parameters (the technical systems).
- Organisation and flexibility of human resource capacity where organisation, team and individual installed value may differ (Al-Tabbaa, Leach and March, Chapter 3; Taylor and Taylor, Chapter 11; Burgess, Radnor and Furnival, Chapter 17; Bateman, Maher and Randall, Chapter 8) as do their contractual relationships (the social systems). For example, the professions in public sector organisations such as doctors (Burgess, Radnor and Furnival, Chapter 17; Hudson Smith, Chapter 19) who are perceived to hold technical power over organisational operating systems. This picture of the social system (in healthcare) where professions dominate the ability to enable change and improvement in operational design is not always correct, as can be seen in Chapter 18 by Lindsay and Kumar. This theme is further explored by de Blok, van Donk, Seepma and Roukema (Chapter 22), but within the Netherlands criminal justice system.

The technical system (as discussed above) requires active interaction of citizens to gain the value of insights of consumers of the services. When insights are purposefully collected, collated and interpreted, these in turn provide public service organisations with a potential greater understanding of citizen's needs and wants. The role of external citizens has broadened (Adderley and Kirkbright, Chapter 10) to include active input into operational design (co-design) and delivery (co-mobilisation) mandated through an espoused political change of focus away from top down policy (as noted for example by the White House, 2014). In the UK this has been driven partially through the role of Big Society, although the approach is not new (Adderley and Kirkbright, Chapter 10). This movement is immature, is contested and has been less easy to deploy and operationalise to create strategic visions (Ransome, 2011). Al-Tabbaa, Leach and March, (Chapter 3) offer some insights into such current challenges.

Western governments have also diverted regulatory bodies (discussed above) with the objective of divesting responsibility to users of public services, although this may have added a further layer of personal concern in the strategic direction and operational design for public services through the lever of purchasing/commissioning (see Moxham, Chapter 13). Hudson Smith (Chapter 19) also questions whether focusing on the needs of the wider society is at odds in delivering individual levels of satisfaction.

As for the social system, it presupposes that the internal operations management arrangements are potentially more complex and more motivational to those working within well-articulated and strategically aligned value based arrangements. This positive view enables co-mobilisation and assumes capacity and capability to bring about efficient and effective delivery of such systems (Al-Tabbaa, Leach and March, Chapter 3). Anything other than this represent challenges for operational managers, for both the professionally capable and the enthusiastic optimist.

Having skilful and trained human resources may address some of the issues of effective service delivery as reported in public sector organisations. Meehan, Drake, Vogel and Parkhouse (Chapter 9) emphasise the realisation that operations management skills in particular are lacking in many public services. Here, the further and higher education sector could play a key role in curriculum design potentially helping to develop graduates with entrepreneurial skill sets that can contribute to effective functioning of public sector organisations and society (Adderley and Kirkbright, Chapter 10). This also has implications for operations management as discussed within this book.

Pettit, Beresford, Knight and Sohn (Chapter 5) and Aitken, Esain and Williams (Chapter 21) further highlight the difficulty of understanding social and environmental value where there is no direct means to gather value input or co-design processes (e.g. humanitarian aid; emergency services, where the recipient may not be conscious). In these cases, the trade-off between speed and goal alignment is also highlighted. Where a multi-cultural dimension exists in time starved operations, the need for more work in the area of 'respect for and sensitivity to' culture, religion and climate is also highlighted. This area of research could inform the topical ethical and sustainability debate in supply chain management more generally.

The interaction of social and environmental value is contextualised through societal change and the impact this may have on operational effectiveness – for example Bateman, Maher and Randall (Chapter 8) examine the changes that are happening within the UK fire service, Barton and Matthews (Chapter 15) the UK police force, Lindsay and Kumar (Chapter 18) in Scottish health care, and Taylor and Taylor (Chapter 11) look more broadly at the emergence of social enterprises. In making societal change a reality, another emergent area is sports operations enabling promotion of sports to directly improve public health and connecting with strategic community cohesion objectives (Bamford, Moxham, Kauppi and Dehe, Chapter 2).

In brief, the implications of what may, in principle, seem like a simplification of relationships and flows of action need to be addressed by operational design for public sector organisations, actually represents something more complex. Recent work on hybrid organisations (Doherty *et al.*, 2014) infers convergence with a movement towards less difference between public and private enterprises and instead a broader range of strategies. An example is the adoption of e-SCM principles to improve the integration of hospital supply chains (Bhakoo and Sohal, Chapter 20) illustrating the wide range of operational combinations to achieve operational effectiveness. It is important to reinforcing the need for operational managers to be clear about the antecedents of operations strategies deployed and their alignment with the context, technical and social systems within which these are to be enacted (see Barton and Matthews, Chapter 15)

Implication for public sector managers

The implications of the preceding discussion suggest operations managers need to consider the arrangements for whole systems and their operational ability for flexibility and change. Where operations represent brown field facilities, the challenge is to address and sustain improvement in a politically sensitive environment. The chapters in this book touch upon this book from various perspectives (see Burgess, Radnor and Furnival, Chapter 17; Bhakoo and Sohal, Chapter 20; Hudson Smith, Chapter 19; Bateman, Maher and Randall, Chapter 8; Ritchie and Walley, Chapter 7; Matthias and Buckle, Chapter 4; and Barton and Matthews, Chapter 15).

The need for operational effectiveness and the use of scarce resources (such as time and money) has the potential to lead to more intensely scrutinised organisations from the perspective of external co-design, internal co-mobilisation of resources and political regulation. It is therefore unsurprising that a significant portion of this book is devoted to the implications of measurement. For example, voluntary organisations are considered to squander resources (Moxham, Chapter 13). To avoid this, the introduction of measurement systems required by commissioners and/ or regulators (Ramesh and Sheikh, Chapter 12) and the implications to public sector operations management is highlighted. Specifically, measurement is presented as a means to achieving organisational goals, regulatory standards (Boyne *et al.*, 2010) or a mixture of both systems (Moxham, Chapter 13; Bhakoo and Sohal, Chapter 20). Measurement is also presented as an enabler to improvement (White House, 2014), assuming it is possible to measure what matters. In all cases the objective of measurement is to achieve a better use of the scarce resources available. Drawing on theories such as the resource-based view of the firm and dynamic capabilities will help to generate further insights.

The chapters of this book reveal a range of problems with measurement. For example, Meehan, Drake, Vogel and Parkhouse (Chapter 9) reiterate the call for public service organisations to be outwardly focused on external effectiveness for service users as opposed to focused on internal measures of success (Osborne *et al.*,

2014). This inward-facing view is also linked to the lack of strategic thinking which often results in functionally-driven operations (Matthias and Buckle, Chapter 4). Another issue raised is the need to access these organisations from various perspectives. Moxham (Chapter 13) explores the public services organisation perspective and reveals the inconsistencies across multiple agencies in their demands. This requirement for differing reporting systems imposed inefficiencies, diverts from the core purpose of public service organisations and represents opportunities for quality failure and staff demotivation. Research into public service commissioning (or funding) particularly related to good procurement practice and supply chain development is necessary, particularly with the emergence of the new regulatory structures and shift in the societal context. While Adderley and Kirkbright (Chapter 10) suggests the need for entrepreneurial skills development and provision for public services, there is an assumption that commissioning services (often within governments) can commission entrepreneurially. Public services operations management research should provide theoretical mid-range theories to help solve the objective of making it easier for public services to work with government (Cabinet Office, 2014).

Another avenue of research has been the Balanced Scorecard (BSC) but it is not tested in the third sector (Taylor and Taylor, Chapter 11) and could require further development for these settings; for example, the Public Sector Scorecard (Moullin, Chapter 14):

> There has been very little empirical research carried out to study BSC implementation in non-profit organisations apart from a few descriptive single case studies … In comparative investigation, BSC implementation was seen to focus on measurement instead of strategy, and to place greater emphasis on financial indicators than non-financial and longer-term perspectives (i.e. it has been found to be largely unsatisfactory).
>
> (Taylor and Taylor, Chapter 11)

BSC measurement systems (Moullin, Chapter 14) are claimed to arise from lean movement (Witcher and Chau, 2007). The operational practices from lean focus on high/medium volume demand versus low/medium variety service range, or arrangements that enable not only economies of scale, but economies of scope (Esain and Rich, 2005). This measurement approach is assumed to be appropriate for uniform application to public services settings regardless of purpose. It is suggested there is a place for a different type of measurement system. One possible area is measurement systems that assist operations managers in the low volume almost bespoke bundles of services (which may exhibit high variety and low volume) in uncertain environments.

This leads to the contentions of the editors that public services are often at the end of the distribution of mainstream services provision (Pettit, Beresford, Knight and Sohn, Chapter 5, and Aitken, Esain and Williams, Chapter 21 are examples). Such as the erratic issues of time/demand and/or the high cost of spare capacity (making private firms less attracted to the risk versus return proposition). Notionally these aspects of public service operations management services do not sit well with for profit organisations and a potential juxtaposition with a drive for financial efficiency (replicated from private organisations). In the context of social value ,there needs to be a greater understanding of how the scarce resources of charitable funding, philanthropy, etc. can achieve more if enabled to challenge preconceived notions of financial efficiency and replace with notions of 'readiness'. It is suggested that the need for cross-sectorial studies which look at the extremes of operations management to build towards common themes could drive towards counterintuitive theory development.There may be learning from humanitarian aid (Pettit, Beresford, Knight and Sohn, Chapter 5) and the healthcare supply chain (Aitken, Esain and Williams, Chapter 21) for private firms (e.g. the theory of swift and even flow is appropriate for some form of organisational types and a new theory is required for systems of extreme demand and fast response). Agile has been put forward (Pettit, Beresford, Knight and Sohn, Chapter 5) but is still not satisfactory.Visualising these contextual issues through other perspectives such as systems thinking and supply network theory may elevate functional thinking (e.g. understanding the e-SCM implementation in the supply network of a hospital; Bhakoo and Sohal, Chapter 20). Potentially there is a place for multiple operations management designs which can be used in a modular way to mix that which exhibits complex operational problems and those which exhibit in part or in some space of time simplicity.

Tactical and operational effectiveness

Enabling innovative public services operations management provision through the use of emergent technology is an important theme to help organisations move beyond current operational trade-offs. While public services deploying an e-portal for addressing citizen complaints is not so new, the key challenges and benefits of doing so in an emerging country context is (Ramesh and Sheikh, Chapter 12). Similarly, opportunities exist for scholars to further develop operations management in public services by drawing on theories, such as organisational learning, absorptive capacity, social exchange theory, which are often associated with innovation (Narasimhan, 2014).

The re-emergence of the technique service blueprinting (Radnor and Osborne, Chapter 16) is also a means of engaging with service users. More research is needed in this area to understand not only the operational process but also the different parties engaged in the co-mobilisation of public services (Sinha and Pastellas, Chapter 6) and the interfaces therein. This is illustrated by the assertions that commissioners create waste in systems by asking for (and expecting) different types of measurement and reporting systems. This in turn means public service organisations may have to deal with multiple requirements (which they may not have the knowledge or capacity to satisfy; see Taylor and Taylor, Chapter 11 and Moxham, Chapter 13).

Fundamentals of operations management such as managing capacity and demand are critical to understanding and controlling the system. Research needs to continue in this area to provide a deeper understanding of whether and how extra capacity might generate additional demand in other service settings (Ritchie and Walley, Chapter 7). In addition, understanding types of demand rather than volume of demand will help in better process design and capacity management in public sector organisations (Sinha and Pastellas, Chapter 6; Seddon, 2008). Adjustments to operations management language may also be needed to fit with socially oriented organisations. Terms such as efficiencies and waste minimisation are commonly understood in the operations management community but for some public services (e.g. social housing) these terms are emotive issues as they can infer cuts to services and reductions in quality (Meehan, Drake, Vogel and Parkhouse, Chapter 9).

Integrated services and network capability

The presumption that the degree of integration (Aitken, Esain and Williams, Chapter 21; Moxham, Chapter 13; Pettit, Beresford, Knight and Sohn, Chapter 5) or 'degree of inter-agency co-operation and collaboration' (Taylor and Taylor, Chapter 11) is a factor in high performing organisations requires empirical validation. A hypothesis that 'the closer groups work the better' belies the expectation that developed relationships will remain consistent and fixed. Whereas the nature of public service provision often requires dynamic reshaping of customer delivery and care in quick time. Moullin (Chapter 14) opens the discussion on measuring cross organisational boundaries and proposes the Public Services Scorecard as a means of control. The example from Sinha and Pastellas (Chapter 6), addressing how new service design involving the concept of value co-creation can be effective in service delivery provides an alternative means to gain cohesion. The delivery of integrated services is a prospect that many organisations (both private and public) are striving towards. The service redesign and collaborative partnerships required to support this notion are still very much in their infancy among many public service providers. Several of the contributors to the book emphasise the need for organisations to move from local optimisation to whole systems thinking in terms of performance and design (Ritchie and Walley, Chapter 7; Burgess, Radnor and Furnival, Chapter 17; Bhakoo and Sohal, Chapter 20). Systems thinking and supply network theory play a critical role in integrating the entire value chain in delivery of efficient and effective public services and sustain those benefits over time. Management in public services should have a systems view of the organisation with managers and staff being hands-on and concerned about flow and the focus on the end customer, rather than just the part they play individually in their silos (McQuade, 2008). Narasimhan (2014) provides an interesting and novel proposal when observing organisational linkages and transactions and suggests that researchers might want to develop a theory based on 'observables'.

Conclusion

The aims of this chapter were to assimilate the key themes presented by the contributors and present a research agenda in which to advance public services operations management. Future qualitative and quantitative empirical studies are needed to develop and test existing theory. There is also a need for theory development; a consequence of the under-investigation of this sector.

An area of theory development could focus on new configurations of social enterprises, arising from complexity in the context of operational management. With the elaboration of new organisational arrangements and structures comes the need for governance capability to manage integrated operations and networks. This book and related research contend that the boundaries between idealised organisational forms outlined in Table 23.1, are becoming increasingly blurred. There is a need to understand how dual or multiple goals affect internal processes, supply and commissioning arrangements. The shift of Western government philosophy to engage with and promote entrepreneurial solutions to social and environmental problems requires inward reflection; for example, do public sector organisations have the capability, mandate (governance) and capacity to commission entrepreneurial solutions? It is proposed that some of the human skills and operational capability required in this new world will be novel and some will not fit as well with current institutional logics.

The overarching desire that delivery of public services (which operate in the context of societal changes) are considered and enacted upon from a citizen perspective, is presented as an ambition for commissioners. This is a more difficult task than it might seem at first glance. The concept of what constitutes value to and for citizens, needs further evaluation, particularly where monetary exchange is indirect or absent. While much research is available related to value and economic exchange, different theoretical lenses may well offer further insights which in turn could impact on citizen satisfaction. Operations management concepts applied to the public services environment are still in their infancy. The focus has been more on meeting the targets and efficiency gain – as in healthcare (Lindsay and Kumar, Chapter 18) or municipalities (Ramesh and Sheikh, Chapter 12) – in an era where public resources are constrained or depleting which in turn burdens further the funding available to public services organisations. The perceptions, knowledge and views of employees are paramount to providing innovative approaches to and better service delivery. Both internal customers (employees) and external customers (citizens) should be involved in the design and co-creation of service processes (Sinha and Pastellas, Chapter 6; Bateman, Maher and Randall, Chapter 8; Adderley and Kinkbright, Chapter 10) to meet the expectations of both parties.

The preceding chapters have shown a support towards transferability of private sector methodologies in public and third sector. Care should be taken to adapt, rather than adopt (see Barton and Matthews, Chapter 15), with time and education being necessary to embed change. Operations management for public services at the extreme (e.g. low volume, high variety, rapid response) represent another potential fruitful line of enquiry. This area of study can draw upon exiting theory (as has been the case in the chapters presented in this book) and potentially link to research which enables a better understanding of citizen value. In turn research could inform new ways to address the dilemma of capacity and demand for public services operations managers. Operations at the extreme also provide the opportunity for theory building through the rich data provided by qualitative case studies. Extremes of operational need and any underlying assumptions for new theory should include measurement of performance.

The application and consideration of supply chain management theory to collaborative working is a theme for enlargement. Of particular interest is the implication of strategic supply chain alignment across organisations (or other alternatives) and implications for effective and flexible performance (within organisations or across partnering groups). Respect for and sensitivity to culture, religion and climate have implications for public services organisations, specifically research into these factors and development of appropriate design and delivery of new supply chain/network based arrangements is also an important avenue of investigation.

Austere environments, technology advancements and ageing population are examples of variables which public services are contingent upon and will affect the way operations managers are able to deliver their services. Such variables can be viewed from many perspectives and through many different interested groups. It is proposed that through a better understanding of the overlaps and gaps in different viewpoints of stakeholders (e.g. citizens, governments, society, third sector organisations, etc.) will offer the potential to create new theories for public services operations management.

As with other studies in this area, the contributions in this book are largely Western (Doherty *et al.*, 2014); while a limitation, the contribution from Ramesh and Sheikh (Chapter 12) observing public services in India) offers some insights. For example, the potential to explore technology alongside other innovative concepts which, in themselves, can feed backwards into the Western arena, and have significance as these insights are unconstrained by Western culture.

This chapter has developed an exciting and challenging agenda for future research within public services operations management. The delivery on some or all of the challenges highlighted will provide a greater insight into the operational effectiveness required of public services.

References

Alcock, P. (2010) 'Building the Big Society: a new policy environment for the third sector in England'. *Voluntary Sector Review*, 1: 379–89.

Ashby, W.R. (1958) 'Requisite variety and its implications for the control of complex systems'. *Cybernetica*, 1(2): 83–99.

Bowersox, D.J., Closs, D.J. and Stank, T.P. (2000) 'Ten mega-trends that will revolutionize supply chain logistics'. *Journal of Business Logistics*, 21(2): 1–15.

Boyne, G., Entwistle, T. and Ashworth, R. (2010) 'Theories of public sector improvement' In Ashworth, R., Boyne, G. and Entwistle, T. (eds), *Public Service Improvement; Theories and Evidence*: 1–14. Oxford: Oxford University Press.

Cabinet Office (2014) 'Office for Civil Society'. Retrieved from www.civilsociety.co.uk/directory/home/company/2765/office_for_civil_society/tab/content#/directory/home/company/2765/office_for_civil_society/tab/1 (accessed 25 October 2014).

Doherty, B., Haugh, H. and Lyon, F. (2014) 'Social enterprises as hybrid organizations: a review and research agenda'. *International Journal of Management Review*, 16: 417–36.

Esain, A. and Rich, N. (2005) 'Exploring patient pathways: a grounded approach to managing complexity'. In Tavakoli, M. and Davies, H. (eds), *Reforming Health Systems: Analysis and*

Evidence, Strategic Issues in Health Care Management, pp. 83–97. St Andrews: University of St Andrews.

European Commission (2014) 'Social entrepreneurship'. Retrieved from http://ec.europa.eu/internal_market/social_business/index_en.htm (accessed 26 October 2014).

Gadrey, J. (2000) 'The characterization of goods and services: an alternative approach'. *Review of Income and Wealth*, 46(3): 369–87.

Kast, F.E. and Rosenzweig J.E. (1985) *Organisation and Management*. New York: McGraw-Hill.

Katz, D. and Kahn R.L (1969) 'Common characteristics of open systems'. In Emery, F. E. (ed.), *Systems Thinking*, pp. 86–104. Harmondsworth: Penguin.

Leseure, M., Birdi, K., Bauer, J., Denyer, D. and Neely, A. (2004). *Adoption of Promising Practice, A Systematic Literature Review*. London: Advanced Institute of Management Research.

Martin, S. (2010) 'Regulation'. In Ashworth, R., Boyne, G. and Entwistle, T. (eds), *Public Service Improvement: Theories and Evidence*, pp.36–59. Oxford: Oxford University Press.

McQuade, D. (2008) 'New development: leading lean action to transform housing services'. *Public Money and Management*, 28: 57–60.

Narasimhan, R. (2014) 'Theory development in operations management: extending the frontiers of a mature discipline via qualitative research'. *Decision Sciences*, 45(2): 209–27.

Osborne, S.P., Radnor, Z.J., Vidal, I. and Kinder, T. (2014) 'A sustainable business model for public service organizations?' *Public Management Review*, 16(2): 165–72.

Ostrom, A.L., Bitner, M.J., Brown, S.W., Burkhard, K.A., Goul, M., Smith-Daniels, V., Demirkan, H. and Rabinovich, E. (2010) 'Moving forward and making a difference: research priorities for the science of service'. *Journal of Service Research*, 13(1): 4–36.

Radnor, Z.J. and Osborne, S.P. (2013) 'Lean: a failed theory for public services?' *Public Management Review*, 15(2): 265–87.

Rainey, H.G (1993) 'A theory of goal ambiguity in public organisations'. In Perry, J.L. (ed.), *Research in Public Administration*, volume 2, pp. 121–66. Greenwich, CT: JAI Press.

Rainey, H.G. and Steinbauer, P. (1999) 'Galloping elephants: developing elements of a theory of effective government organisations'. *Journal of Public Administration Research and Theory*, 9(1): 1–32.

Ransome, P. (2011) 'The Big Society: fact or fiction? A sociological critique'. *Sociological Research*, 16(2). Retrieved from www.socresonline.org.uk/16/2/18.html (accessed 12 November 2014).

Sampson, S. and Froehle, C. (2006) 'Foundations and implications of a proposed unified services theory'. *Production and Operations Management*, 15: 329–43.

Seddon, J. (2008) *Systems Thinking in the Public Sector*. Axminster: Triarchy Press.

Smith, A.D. and Synowka, D.P. (2014) 'Lean operations and SCM practices in manufacturing firms: multi-firm case studies in HRM and visual-based metrics'. *International Journal of Procurement Management*, 7(2): 183–200.

Soltani, E., Ahmed, P., Liao, Y. and Anosike, P. (2014) 'Qualitative middle-range research in operations management: the need for theory-driven empirical inquiry'. *International Journal of Operations and Production Management*, 34(8): 1003–27.

White House (2014) 'About SICP – the community solutions agenda'. Retrieved from www.whitehouse.gov/administration/eop/sicp/about (accessed 26 October 2014).

Witcher, B.J. and Chau, V.S. (2007) 'Balanced scorecard and Hoshin Kanri: dynamic capabilities for managing strategic fit'. *Management Decision*, 45(3): 518–38.

Index